THOSE SO-CALLED ERRORS:

Debunking the Liberal, New Evangelical, and
Fundamentalist Myth that You Should Not Hear,
Receive, and Believe All the Numbers of Scripture

by

Dr. Chester W. Kulus

Copyright ©2003 & 2009 by Chester W. Kulus
All rights reserved
Printed in the United States of America
First Printing: 573 copies

Library of Congress Control Number: 2009924248
REL006410: Religion: Biblical Reference – Language Study
REL006210: Religion: Biblical Studies – Old Testament

ISBN 978-0-9820608-9-6

Address all inquiries to:
THE OLD PATHS PUBLICATIONS, Inc.
142 Gold Flume Way
Cleveland, Georgia, U.S.A.

Web: www.theoldpathspublications.com
E-mail: TOP@theoldpathspublications.com

Emmanuel Baptist Theological Press
296 New Britain Avenue
Newington, Connecticut 06111

2.0

FOREWORD

As Dean of *Emmanuel Baptist Theological Seminary*, I am pleased to see the publication of this significant and timely work entitled *Those So-Called Errors* by Dr. Chester W. Kulus. This volume under the current title was originally Dr. Kulus' doctoral dissertation for the D. Min. Degree from *Emmanuel Baptist Theological Seminary* entitled "I Heard the Number of Them: General Principles for Handling Apparent Biblical Contradictions with Specific Application of the Principles to the Alleged Numeric Contradictions in I Samuel to II Chronicles."

Dr. Kulus starts with the presupposition that the Masoretic Hebrew text is the faithful rendering of the preserved original Hebrew text. Then he attempts to give possible Biblical solutions to the alleged numeric problem passages, never succumbing to the "scribal error" tendency common among many New-Evangelical and Fundamental Bible critics. Not only does he engage himself with the current positions and interpretations of Bible critics, but also he offers valuable exegesis from the Hebrew text for the serious scholar and edifying words to the pastor and church member alike. His chapter on the reasons the Lord would allow apparent contradictions is sufficient reason to buy this work. Dr. Kulus brings his years of research and ministry into succinct focus as he defends the preserved Scriptures of the Hebrew Old Testament. He has clearly and carefully debunked the myth of "scribal errors" in the Old Testament with the Scriptures.

I am thankful to the Lord Jesus Christ for allowing Dr. Kulus' book to be printed for a generation of Baptist churches that need to hear and receive the Lord's preserved Words (I Thessalonians 2:13).

Thomas M. Strouse, M. Div., Ph. D., Th. D.
Dean Emeritus,
Emmanuel Baptist Theological Seminary

TO THE READER

I thank you for purchasing this book. It is my desire that it will aid in your understanding of God's Words. If you should find any typographical errors, I would appreciate it if you would bring them to my attention.

This book sets forth the complete reliability and trustworthiness of the Words of God. The Bible is so trustworthy that you can trust your soul's destiny to what the Scriptures teach. Dear Reader, have you trusted what the Bible teaches about salvation? Would you please consider the following points from the Word of God?

>The Bible says, "For all have sinned, and come short of the glory of God" (Romans 3:23). According to the Word of God, you have sinned.

>The Bible says, "For the wages of sin *is* death" (Romans 6:23a). Your sin results in death: physical death, spiritual death, and the second death. Concerning the second death, the Bible says, "And death and hell were cast into the lake of fire. This is the second death. And whosoever was not found written in the book of life was cast into the lake of fire" (Revelation 20:14,15). Your sin will ultimately take you to the lake of fire.

>The Bible says, "But God commendeth his love toward us, in that, while we were yet sinners, Christ died for us" (Romans 5:8). Jesus died for your sins. As He died on the cross, Jesus shed His blood. He was then buried. And on the third day, He rose again. He is the only One ever to have done this; therefore, He is the only One Who can save you. The Bible says of Jesus, "Neither is there salvation in any other: for there is none other name under heaven given among men, whereby we must be saved" (Acts 4:12).

>The Bible says, "For by grace are ye saved through faith; and that not of yourselves: *it is* the gift of God: not of works, lest any man

should boast" (Ephesians 2:8,9). You cannot possibly save yourself. No amount of good works, sacraments, or prayers to Mary will save your lost soul from hell and the second death. Only Jesus can save you. You must put all of your faith and trust in Him.

The Bible says, "Repent ye therefore, and be converted, that your sins may be blotted out" (Acts 3:19a). Would you repent and receive Christ as your Saviour? The Bible says, "For whosoever shall call upon the name of the Lord shall be saved" (Romans 10:13). Pray to Him and ask Him to save you.

If you have received Christ as your Saviour or would like to find out more about this all-important decision, please contact me.

Chester W. Kulus
873 NH Rt 4A
Enfield, NH 03748
March, 2009

PREFACE

This second edition of *Those So-Called Errors* contains a number of new features. Among the new features are (1) an expanding of the Table of Contents thereby giving a far more comprehensive overview of the work and by its use making it easier to find certain topics in the work; (2) a correcting of a number of typographical errors; (3) an adding of new material on the subject of *tittle* in Matthew 5:18 showing that it refers to the smallest of the Hebrew vowels; (4) a repositioning of material that was in the first edition's introduction to the end of the book, thus allowing the reader to delve right into the main argument of the book; (5) a rewriting of certain portions to make them clearer; (6) an updating of the Greek words to include the accents; (7) an including of information on the *English Standard Version* giving examples of where it departs from the Traditional Hebrew Text; (8) a printing in paperback so as to reduce the cost of production and make it more affordable; (9) an expanding of the last chapter to include a summary of the material; (10) an adding of 48 footnotes to the main section of the book; (11) a transliterating of most Hebrew words; (12) an adding of material discussing in more detail the context and pronouns of Psalm 12:7; (13) an adding of a chart showing the transmission of the Old Testament; and (14) an including of an appendix on II Samuel 21:19.

I am very thankful to many of you who told me of the blessing that you received from the first edition. I trust that the second edition will be a blessing, encouraging people to have a greater confidence in the Words of God.

The Author

ACKNOWLEDGEMENTS

I thank various ones who assisted in this project. First, I thank the Lord Jesus Christ for (1) saving me; (2) giving me the Bible, a wonderful book which captivates my mind; and (3) giving me good health over the bulk of this work. "Blessing, and glory, and wisdom, and thanksgiving, and honour, and power, and might, *be* unto our God for ever and ever. Amen" (Revelation 7:12).

I especially thank both Pastor Richard Anderson and Dr. Thomas Strouse for encouraging me to pursue a doctoral degree. Both of these men also thoroughly proofread this dissertation and provided valuable insights on its content. Also, I especially thank Calvary Independent Baptist Church in Lebanon, NH for their financial and spiritual support during this endeavor.

And I thank various others: (1) David Bohn for his financial support in helping to underwrite the project; (2) Dr. H. D. Williams for his assistance in getting the book to print; (3) my wife, Nancy, for her prayers and support; (4) my son, Chester Haddon Kulus for his work on the cover; (5) Pastor Ken Brooks, Robert Brobst, and Susan Klefstad for their suggestions on writing style; (6) Mike Rucker for proofreading, as well as assisting on computer matters; (7) Tom Kennedy for the use of some of his books as well for gathering information from the internet; (8) Dr. Donald Waite for taking time out of his busy schedule to consult with me on several matters; (9) Marjorie Carr of the Enfield Public Library for obtaining books through inter-library loan and for allowing me to access the library's on-line database; and (10) those past and present who have defended or are defending the Traditional Texts for their insights into various alleged contradictions in these texts.

TABLE OF CONTENTS

FOREWORD iii

TO THE READER v

PREFACE vii

ACKNOWLEDGEMENTS ix

CHAPTER ONE: I HEARD THE NUMBER OF THEM 1

   SOME WILL NOT HEAR THE NUMBERS 3
      Some Claim Samuel, Kings, and Chronicles Have Numerical Errors 3
         Introduction 3
         McClintock and Strong 3
         Zondervan Pictorial Encyclopedia 3
         Hastings' Bible Dictionary 4
         Unger 4
         Conclusion 4
      Some Claim Specific Verses Have Numerical Errors 4
         Bob Jones University on I Samuel 6:19 5
         Bob Jones University and Others on II Chronicles 22:2 5
         Central Baptist Theological Seminary on Various Verses 6
         Calvary Baptist Theological Seminary on I Samuel 6:19 and 13:5 7
         The Defender's Study Bible on Various Verses 8
         The Scofield Study Bible on Various Verses 8
      Conclusion 9
   JOHN HEARD THE NUMBER 10
      Two Hundred Thousand Thousand 10
      Two Hundred Thousand Thousand Is a Literal Quantity 10
      John Heard This Number 12
   CONCLUSION 14

CHAPTER TWO: JESUS RECEIVED THE OLD TESTAMENT 15

- The Credentials of Jesus 16
- The Old Testament Text of Jesus 18
  - The Autograhpa 18
  - The Copies 21
    - It Is Written 21
    - Still Stood Written 25
  - Jesus' Copy 26
- JESUS REPEATEDLY SAYS IT IS WRITTEN OF THE OLD TESTAMENT 27
  - The Significance of the Perfect Tense 27
  - The Verses of the Perfect Tense 30
    - A List 30
    - Luke 18:31 & 24:44 31
    - Luke 21:22 32
  - Conclusion 33
- JESUS REPEATEDLY REFERS TO OLD TESTAMENT PASSAGES 33
  - Jesus' Use of Old Testament Verses 33
  - Jesus' Authentication of Old Testament Events 36
  - Jesus' Confidence in Old Testament Wording 38
  - Jesus' Revelation of Old Testament Preservation 39
- JESUS REPEATEDLY REFERS TO OLD TESTAMENT NUMERICAL PASSAGES 40
  - List of Numbers 40
  - Reception of Numbers 41
    - Jesus 41
    - Ninevites 42
    - Abraham 42
  - Rejection of Numbers 42
    - Hananiah and the King's Servant 42
    - Moses and Peter 43
  - Observations About Numbers 44
    - Jesus Never Questioned Old Testament Numbers 44
    - Jesus Received Old Testament Numbers 44
    - Jesus Received All Types of Old Testament Numbers 45
  - Diminution of Numbers 46
    - Fuller 46
    - Glenny 47
- JESUS REPEATEDLY VALIDATES THE OLD TESTAMENT 48
  - Matthew 5:17-18 48
    - Fulfil the Law and the Prophets 48
    - Not to Destroy 49
    - For Verily I Say Unto You 50
    - Till Heaven and Earth Pass 51
    - One Jot or One Tittle 51
    - Shall in No Wise Pass 57
    - From the Law 58
    - Till All Be Fulfilled 66
    - Conclusion 66

 Matthew 24:35; Mark 13:31; & Luke 21:33 67
 Luke 16:17 69
 Luke 24:25 70
 John 10:35 72
  Scripture 72
  Cannot Be Broken 73
  Gods 75
 John 17:17 76
JESUS NEVER ONCE CRITICIZES THE OLD TESTAMENT 78
 Jesus Does Not Correct the Text 78
 Jesus Corrects Misinterpretations 80
 Conclusion 81
CONCLUSIONS 85
TRANSMISSION OF OLD TESTAMENT 90

CHAPTER THREE: RECEIVE THE OLD TESTAMENT NUMBERS 91

ALPHABET ALLEDGEDLY USED FOR NUMBERS 91
 DeHoff 92
 Haley 93
 Keil 94
 The Pulpit Commentary 94
 Unger 94
 Conclusion 95
ALPHABET NOT USED FOR NUMBERS 95
OTHER SYSTEMS ALLEGEDLY USED FOR NUMBERS 97
 Kaiser, Jr., Davids, Bruce, and Brauch 97
 Wolf 98
 Davis 99
OTHER SYSTEMS NOT USED FOR NUMBERS 99
CONCLUSION 100

CHAPTER FOUR: REASONS FOR APPARENT CONTRADICTIONS 101

MAKING AN IMPRESSION 102
PROMOTING STUDY 103
 General Statements 103
 Specific Verses 104
  II Timothy 2:15 104
  I Peter 1:10-11 105
   Introduction 105
   Enquired 105
   Searched Diligently 105
   Searching 106
   Conclusion 106
CHEWING MEAT 106
HUMBLING THE STUDENT 108
PRAYING TO GOD 109

SHOWING GOD'S MIND	110
CONCEALING GOD'S MIND	112
SEPARATING FROM THE EVENTS	112
SUBSTANTIATING INSPIRATION	113
DEFINING DOCTRINE	114
COMPLEMENTING ACCOUNTS	115
TESTING FAITH	117
Fundamentalists and Jehovah's Witnesses	118
Moses and Quail	118
King's Servant and Food Prices	119
Conclusion	119
REMOVING CHAFF	120
CONFOUNDING UNBELIEVERS	122
CONTRADICTING OF SINNERS	122
CONCLUSION	124

CHAPTER FIVE: HANDLING APPARENT CONTRADICTIONS 125

MUST HAVE SALVATION OF CHRIST	125
MUST HAVE OBEDIENCE TO THE LORD	125
MUST ACCEPT INSPIRATION OF THE BIBLE	126
MUST ACCEPT PRESERVATION OF THE BIBLE	126
Preservation and Jesus' Example	126
No Criticism of the Old Testament	127
An Infallible Copy of the Old Testament	127
It Is Written	128
Confidence in the Wording of the Old Testament	131
Preservation and Inspiration	132
Matthew 4:4	132
John 10:35	133
I Peter 1:23-25	133
Psalm 12:6-7	135
The Words of the Lord Are Purified Words	135
The Words of the Lord Are Preserved Words	136
The Preservation of the Poor?	136
The Context	137
The Pronouns	138
Psalm 119:152	141
Psalm 100:5 & 119:160	142
Isaiah 30:8	143
Isaiah 40:8	144
Conclusion	144
Preservation and Doctrinal Content	146
Conclusion	148
MUST NOT CORRECT THE WORDS OF GOD	148
MUST BELIEVE THE WORDS OF GOD	150
MUST EXERCISE HUMILITY BEFORE GOD	152

MUST EXERCISE PRAYER TO GOD	153
MUST EXERCISE PATIENCE IN GOD	154
MUST UTILIZE STUDY OF THE BIBLE	156
Read the Bible	157
Examine the Context	158
Look for Differences	159
Compare Scripture with Scripture	161
Use Study Tools	162
MUST UNDERSTAND LANGUAGE OF THE BIBLE	164
MIGHT ASK A MAN OF GOD	165
MUST ACCEPT WORD CHANGE BY THE SPIRIT	165
New Testament Writers Were Spirit-Guided	166
In Their Application of the Old Testament	166
In Their Quotation of the Old Testament	167
New Testament Writers Were Not LXX-Users	167
Conclusion	170
CONCLUSION	170

CHAPTER SIX: RAMIFICATIONS OF SAYING PRESERVED TEXT HAS NUMERICAL ERRORS 171

QUESTIONING CHRIST	172
The Liberal View of Accommodation	172
The Fundamentalist View of Limitation	174
Introduction	174
Glenny	174
The Committee	175
Combs	177
Conclusion	177
QUESTIONING VERSES	177
RELINQUISHING THE BATTLE FOR THE BIBLE	179
OPENING THE DOOR TO CRITICISM	181
A Hypothetical Case	182
Actual Cases	183
Fundamentalists	184
E. J. Young	184
Robert Mounce	185
Conclusion	185
TREATING BIBLE LIKE ANY OTHER ANCIENT DOCUMENT	186
DESTROYING THE FOUNDATION	188
DESTROYING FAITH	190
DESTROYING AUTHORITY	194
Archer's Comments	194
Minnick's Comments	195
Spurgeon's Comments	195
Paisley's Comments	196
Hills' Comments	197

EXALTING HUMAN REASONING, SUPPOSITION, AND TEXTUAL CRITICISM 198
COMING CLOSE TO ADDING TO OR SUBSTRACTING FROM THE BIBLE 201
MAKING IT IMPOSSIBLE FOR MAN TO LIVE BY EVERY WORD OF GOD 201
GETTING CLOSER TO NEW EVANGELICALISM, LIBERALISM, AND CATHOLICISM .202
    Discrediting Chronicles 202
    Acting as if The Bible Has Moot Points 204
    Holding to Conceptual Preservation 205
    Placing Faith in Text Critics 207
    Engaging in Double-Talk 209
    Appealing to History 211
    Criticizing Numbers 213
CONCLUSION 214

CHAPTER SEVEN: APPARENT NUMERICAL CONTRADICTIONS IN I SAMUEL 217

I SAMUEL 6:19 217
    The Passage 217
    The Apparent Problem 217
    Some Solutions 219
        Receive the Number 219
        Receive the Syntax 219
        Understand the Population 221
        Allow for Two Possible Groups 222
I SAMUEL 13:1 222
    The Passage 222
    The Apparent Problem 222
    Some Solutions 224
        Receive the Number 224
        Understand the Syntax 224
        Do Not Correct the Verse 225
I SAMUEL 13:5 226
    The Passage 226
    The Apparent Problem 227
    Some Solutions 228
        Receive the Number 228
        Receive the Size of the Army 230
        Allow for Possible Metonymy 230
I SAMUEL 16:10-11 AND I CHRONICLES 2:13-15 231
    The Passages 231
    The Apparent Problem 231
    A Solution 231
I SAMUEL 18:27 AND II SAMUEL 3:14 232
    The Passages 232
    The Apparent Problem 232
    A Solution 233

CHAPTER EIGHT: APPARENT NUMERICAL CONTRADICTIONS IN II SAMUEL 235

II SAMUEL 2:8 AND I CHRONICLES 10:6 235
The Passages 235
The Apparent Problem 235
A Solution 235
II SAMUEL 3:14 237
II SAMUEL 6:23 AND II SAMUEL 21:8 237
The Passages 237
The Apparent Problem 237
Some Solutions 238
Michal, a Previous Wife of Adriel 238
Michal, a Surrogate Mother for Merab 238
An Objection 239
An Answer to the Objection 239
II SAMUEL 8:4 AND I CHRONICLES 18:4 241
The Passages 241
The Apparent Problem 241
A Solution 242
II SAMUEL 8:13; I CHRONICLES 18:12; AND PSALM 60 (TITLE) 242
The Passages 242
The Apparent Problems 243
Some Solutions 243
Different Accounts 243
Samuel and Chronicles, the Same Account 243
Differences in Names 243
Differences in Slain 244
All Three Are the Same Account 244
Differences in Names and Numbers 245
Differences in Slain 246
II SAMUEL 10:18 AND I CHRONICLES 19:18 246
The Passages 246
The Apparent Problem 247
A Solution 247
II SAMUEL 14:27 AND II SAMUEL 18:18 247
The Passages 247
The Apparent Problem 248
Some Solutions 248
II SAMUEL 15:7 AND I KINGS 2:11 248
The Passages 248
The Apparent Problem 249
A Solution 250
II SAMUEL 18:18 251
II SAMUEL 21:8 251
II SAMUEL 21:19 251

II Samuel 23:8 and I Chronicles 11:11 251
   The Passages..251
   The Apparent Problems 252
   Some Solutions 252
      Two Different Men 252
      The Same Man 253
         Differences in Names...253
         Differences in Numbers 254
II Samuel 23:39 254
   The Passage 254
   The Apparent Problem..254
   Some Solutions 255
II Samuel 24:9 and I Chronicles 21:5 255
   The Passages..255
   The Apparent Problems 255
      Numbers 256
      Largeness 256
   Some Solutions 256
      Numbers 257
      Largeness 257
II Samuel 24:13 and I Chronicles 21:11-12..........................258
   The Passages..258
   The Apparent Problem..258
   Some Solutions 259
      Reduction of Seven-Year Famine 259
      Famine "in thy land" 260
      Rejection of LXX 261
II Samuel 24:24 and I Chronicles 21:25 262
   The Passages..262
   The Apparent Problems 262
   Some Solutions 263
      Differences in Numbers 263
      Differences in Names..264

CHAPTER NINE: APPARENT NUMERICAL CONTRADICTIONS IN I KINGS..265

Chronological Factors..265
   Calendar...265
   Accession Versus Non-Accession 267
   Tabulation of Years 267
   Conclusion...270
I Kings 2:11...270
I Kings 4:26 and II Chronicles 9:25 270
   The Passages..270
   The Apparent Problem..271
   A Solution..272

I Kings 5:11 and II Chronicles 2:10 273
   The Passages..273
   The Apparent Problem..273
   A Solution..274
I Kings 5:15-16 and II Chronicles 2:2, 17-18...274
   The Passages..274
   The Apparent Problem..274
   Some Solutions..275
I Kings 6:1 and Acts 13:18-20 275
   The Passages..275
   The Apparent Problem..276
   Some Solutions..278
      The Period of the Judges 278
         Judges from Moses to Samuel 278
            Judges 278
            After That 280
                Other Than Chronological?...280
                Biblical?...281
         Judges from Othniel to Eli 284
         Redemption Time 287
      The Period before the Judges 288
I Kings 6:2, 17..290
   The Passages..290
   The Apparent Problem..290
   A Solution..291
I Kings 7:15 and II Chronicles 3:15 291
   The Passages..291
   The Apparent Problem..291
   A Solution..292
I Kings 7:16 and II Kings 25:17 293
   The Passages..293
   The Apparent Problem..293
   Some Solutions..293
I Kings 7:20, 42; II Chronicles 4:13; and Jeremiah 52:23 294
   The Passages..294
   The Apparent Problem..294
   A Solution..295
I Kings 7:23..296
   The Passage 296
   The Apparent Problem..296
   A Solution..297
I Kings 7:26 and II Chronicles 4:5 297
   The Passages..297
   The Apparent Problem..297
   Some Solutions..298
I Kings 7:42..300

I KINGS 9:23 AND II CHRONICLES 8:10 300
    The Passages..300
    The Apparent Problem..300
    Some Solutions..300
I KINGS 9:28 AND II CHRONICLES 8:18 301
    The Passages..301
    The Apparent Problem..301
    Some Solutions..302
I KINGS 15:33; 16:6-8; AND II CHRONICLES 16:1..302
    The Passages..302
    The Apparent Problem..303
    A Solution..304
I KINGS 16:8-10 306
    The Passage 306
    The Apparent Problem..306
    A Solution..307
I KINGS 16:15, 16, 23, 29 307
    The Passages..307
    The Apparent Problems 307
    A Solution..308
I KINGS 16:29; 22:41, 51 308
    The Passages..308
    The Apparent Problem..309
    A Solution..309
I KINGS 20:30 311
    The Passage 311
    The Apparent Problem..311
    A Solution..312
I KINGS 22:41, 51 312
I KINGS 22:51 AND II KINGS 3:1 312
    The Passages..312
    The Apparent Problem..313
    A Solution..313

CHAPTER TEN: APPARENT NUMERICAL CONTRADICTIONS IN
II KINGS **315**

    II KINGS 1:17; 8:16 315
        The Passages..315
        The Apparent Problem..315
        A Solution..316
    II KINGS 3:1 317
    II KINGS 8:16 317
    II KINGS 8:25; 9:29 318
        The Passages..318
        The Apparent Problem..318
        A Solution..318

II KINGS 8:26 AND II CHRONICLES 22:2 319
   The Passages 319
   The Apparent Problem 319
   Some Solutions 320
      Omri's Dynasty Age 320
         Using Six Years for Omri's Reign 322
         Using Twelve Years for Omri's Reign 323
      Ahaziah's Physical Age 326
      Athaliah's Physical Age 328
      Conclusion 329
II KINGS 9:29 329
II KINGS 10:36; 12:1; 13:1 329
   The Passages 329
   The Apparent Problem 329
   A Solution 330
II KINGS 12:1 332
II KINGS 13:1 332
II KINGS 13:10; 14:1; AND II CHRONICLES 24:1 332
   The Passages 332
   The Apparent Problem 333
   A Solution 333
II KINGS 14:1 335
II KINGS 14:23; 15:1, 8; AND II CHRONICLES 25:1 336
   The Passage 336
   The Apparent Problems 336
      Apparent Problem One 336
      Apparent Problem Two 337
   Some Solutions 337
      Some Solutions to Apparent Problem One 337
      Some Solutions to Apparent Problem Two 339
II KINGS 15:1, 8 341
II KINGS 15:2, 27, 32 341
   The Passages 341
   The Apparent Problems 342
      Apparent Problem One 342
      Apparent Problem Two 342
   Some Solutions 343
      Solution to Apparent Problem One 343
      Solution to Apparent Problem Two 343
II KINGS 15:8 344
II KINGS 15:27 344
II KINGS 15:30, 33 344
   The Passages 344
   The Apparent Problem 344
   A Solution 345

II Kings 15:30; 17:1 347
   The Passages 347
   The Apparent Problem 347
   A Solution 348
II Kings 15:32 350
II Kings 15:33 350
II Kings 16:2; 18:2 350
   The Passages 350
   The Apparent Problem 350
   The Solution 351
II Kings 17:1 351
II Kings 18:2 351
II Kings 18:13 351
   The Passage 351
   The Apparent Problem 352
   A Solution 354
      Preliminary Issues 354
      Solution 357
      Conclusion 359
II Kings 22:3-4 and II Chronicles 34:3-4 359
   The Passages 359
   The Apparent Problem 359
   A Solution 360
II Kings 24:8 and II Chronicles 36:9 360
   The Passages 360
   The Apparent Problems 360
   Some Solutions 361
      Some Solutions to the First Apparent Problem 361
      Solution to the Second Apparent Problem 363
II Kings 24:12 and Jeremiah 52:28 364
   The Passages 364
   The Apparent Problem 364
   A Solution 364
II Kings 24:14 and Jeremiah 52:28-30 364
   The Passages 364
   The Apparent Problem 365
   A Solution 365
II Kings 25:8-9 and Jeremiah 52:12-13 365
   The Passages 365
   The Apparent Problem 366
   Some Solutions 366
II Kings 25:17 367
II Kings 25:19 and Jeremiah 52:25 367
   The Passages 367
   The Apparent Problem 367
   Some Solutions 368

II KINGS 25:27 AND JEREMIAH 52:31 368
    The Passages 368
    The Apparent Problem 369
    A Solution 369

CHAPTER ELEVEN: APPARENT NUMERICAL CONTRADICTIONS IN I CHRONICLES 371

I CHRONICLES 2:13-15 371
I CHRONICLES 2:22-23; JOSHUA 13:30; AND JUDGES 10:3-4 371
    The Passages 371
    The Apparent Problem 372
    A Solution 372
I CHRONICLES 3:10-13 AND MATTHEW 1:7-9 372
    The Passages 372
    The Apparent Problem 372
    A Solution 373
I CHRONICLES 3:22 373
    The Passage 373
    The Apparent Problem 373
    Some Solutions 373
I CHRONICLES 10:6 374
I CHRONICLES 11:11 374
I CHRONICLES 18:4 374
I CHRONICLES 18:12 374
I CHRONICLES 19:18 374
I CHRONICLES 21:5 374
I CHRONICLES 21:11-12 374
I CHRONICLES 21:25 374
I CHRONICLES 22:14; 29:3-4 375
    The Passages 375
    The Apparent Problem 375
    A Solution 375

CHAPTER TWELVE: APPARENT NUMERICAL CONTRADICTIONS IN II CHRONICLES 377

II CHRONICLES 2:2 377
II CHRONICLES 2:10 377
II CHRONICLES 2:17-18 377
II CHRONICLES 3:4 377
    The Passage 377
    The Apparent Problem 378
    The Solution 378
II CHRONICLES 3:15 378
II CHRONICLES 4:2 378
II CHRONICLES 4:5 378
II CHRONICLES 4:13 379

II CHRONICLES 8:10 379
II CHRONICLES 8:18 379
II CHRONICLES 9:25 379
II CHRONICLES 16:1 379
II CHRONICLES 22:2 379
II CHRONICLES 24:1 379
II CHRONICLES 25:1 379
II CHRONICLES 34:3-4 379
II CHRONICLES 36:9 380

CHAPTER THIRTEEN: SUMMARY AND CONCLUSION **381**

SUMMARY 381
CONCLUSION 385

APPENDIX A: PRELIMINARIES **391**

METHODOLOGY BEHIND THE WORK 391
DELIMITATIONS OF THE WORK 393
DEFINITION OF TERMS IN THE WORK 394

APPENDIX B: PREVIOUS STUDIES **397**

WORKS TREATING BIBLE DIFFICULTIES 397
  Haley 397
  Dehoff 398
  Archer 398
  Ruckman 399
  Cloud 400
  Other Older Works 401
  Other Newer Works 401
COMMENTARIES 402
  Commentaries on the Whole Bible 402
    Henry 403
    Poole 403
    Gill 404
    Conclusion 405
  Commentaries on Individual Books 405
    Eisemann 406
    Slotki 406
WORKS REFERRING TO DIFFICULTIES IN PASSING 407
  General Works 407
  Chronological Works 408
CONCLUSION 409

APPENDIX C: II SAMUEL 21:19 ....**411**

INTRODUCTION 411
  The Questioning of II Samuel 21:19 412
  The Questioning of Samuel 413

    The Preserving of Samuel and II Samuel 21:19 414
TYPICAL VIEW 415
    Presentation of the Typical View 415
    Weaknesses of the Typical View 417
        Geographical Weakness 417
        Scriptural Weakness 418
PREPOSITIONAL VIEW 419
    Particle Use 419
        Nominative Use 420
        Accusative Use 420
    Prepositional Use 421
ELLIPTICAL VIEW 422
    General Use of Ellipsis in Scripture 422
        Moncrieff 422
        Gill 423
        Poole 423
        Genesis 423
    Specific Use of Ellipsis in II Samuel 21:19 425
        Eisemann 425
        Poole 425
PREPOSITIONAL-ELLIPTICAL VIEW 427
    II Samuel 21:19 427
    Other Verses 428
        Joshua 17:12 428
        Judges 1:19 429
        Judges 1:27 429
    CONCLUSION 429

BIBLIOGRAPHY 431
    BOOKS 431
    ARTICLES, SERMONS, AND VIDEOS 457

SCRIPTURE INDEX 469

BIOGRAPHICAL SKETCH 487

CHAPTER ONE:
I HEARD THE NUMBER OF THEM

What is in a number? Are numbers important? Numbers certainly are important when it comes to balancing your check-book, or when keeping the score of a game, or when seeing the grade on your test; but what about the numbers in the Bible? Are they important? Consider the fact that God defines Himself by numbers when He states: "For there are three that bear record in heaven, the Father, the Word, and the Holy Ghost: and these three are one" (I John 5:7). In this verse are two numbers, *three* and *one*, and these numbers are very important to the doctrine of God. Consider that the Bible reveals that the antichrist has associated with him the number *six hundred threescore and six* (Revelation 13:18), which will be an important identifying mark of the antichrist. Consider further that all the numbers of Scripture are part of the Words of God. Are numbers in the Bible important? Surely, they are. However, so-called Bible believers question certain numbers of Scripture.

But just what is a Bible believer? Certainly any definition must include the idea that a Bible believer is one who believes that whatever the Bible says is so; however, many self-proclaimed Bible believers are questioning the Bible, instead of believing the Bible. This questioning of the Bible by so-called Bible believers is especially evident when it comes to the numbers in the Old Testament books of Samuel, Kings, and Chronicles. Instead of doing as the Apostle John did in Revelation 9:16 when he said, "I heard the number of them" concerning the largest of all numbers in the Bible (200,000,000), some Fundamentalists are not hearing, that is, not receiving and not believing, some of the numbers of the Old Testament.

Indeed, trusted commentators as well as the faculty of trusted colleges, universities, and seminaries question the numbers of the Hebrew Old Testament. Such activity ministers "questions, rather than godly edifying which is in faith" (I Timothy 1:4) thereby undermining the trustworthiness of Scripture and leading students to think that the Bible that they have believed and obeyed is now a book with errors. One might expect Liberals to question the Bible, but what is alarming is that Fundamentalists question the Bible in the very same way. Especially do Fundamentalists question numbers in Samuel, Kings, and Chronicles. Despite what some Fundamentalists and others may claim about some of the numbers of the Bible, it is this work's contention that no real contradictions of any type are in the Bible, only apparent ones. Indeed, the alleged numerical contradictions of Samuel, Kings, and Chronicles are not contradictions at all, for every word of the Traditional Text of the Bible is pure and preserved (Psalm 12:6-7).

Chapter One documents the erroneous claim of many that one should not hear all the numbers of Scripture. Such an attitude, however, is contrary to what the Apostle John did when he heard, that is, received and believed the largest number in all of the Bible, *two hundred thousand thousand* (Revelation 9:16). Also, rejecting some of the numbers of the Bible is contrary to the teaching and example of Jesus, Who received all of the Old Testament. Chapter Two gives a detailed treatment of Jesus' view of the Old Testament. Every Bible believer should adopt Christ's position. Some, however, claim that scribes used an abbreviation system for numbers, which then introduced errors into the text. Chapter Three demonstrates that an-abbreviated-system-for-numbers explanation for the numerical difficulties of the Old Testament is completely without merit. Chapters Four, Five, and Six address the matters of why would God allow apparent contradictions, how to study apparent contradictions, and the ramifications of claiming that the preserved Hebrew Text has numerical errors. Chapters Seven through Twelve apply the principles developed in Chapters One through Six to the alleged numerical discrepancies in I Samuel through II Chronicles. The entire work points to the fact that one can hear, receive, and believe all that the Bible says. The Apostle John demonstrated that attitude and so should every Bible believer. Jesus said, "Thy word is truth" (John 17:17).

SOME WILL NOT HEAR THE NUMBERS

Some Claim Samuel, Kings, and Chronicles Have Numerical Errors

Introduction

Bible commentators and Bible teachers make much concerning the numerical difficulties in the books of I Samuel, II Samuel, I Kings, II Kings, I Chronicles, and II Chronicles.

McClintock and Strong

An article in McClintock and Strong's *Cyclopedia* states:

> It is well known, although the cause has not fully hitherto been ascertained, that the text of the books of Samuel, Kings, and Chronicles is in a worse condition than that of the other inspired writings. . . . But the principal contradictions relate to numbers.[1]

This author disagrees with the statement that the text of Samuel, Kings and Chronicles is in a worse condition than that of the other inspired books. But the above quote illustrates the recognition of apparent numerical difficulties in these books.

Zondervan Pictorial Encyclopedia

Schultz in *The Zondervan Pictorial Encyclopedia of the Bible* writes, "The transmission of numerals in the Heb[rew] text of Chronicles accounts for a number of difficulties."[2] Schultz correctly recognizes that apparent numerical difficulties are in the books of I and II Chronicles, but the author rejects his assertion that the transmission of the numbers is somehow faulty.

---

[1] "Chronicles" in *Cyclopedia of Biblical, Theological, and Ecclesiastical Literature*, ed. John McClintock and James Strong (New York: Harper & Brothers, 1891), 2:291.

[2] S. J. Schultz, "Chronicles, Books of" in *The Zondervan Pictorial Encyclopedia of the Bible*, ed. Merrill C. Tenney (Grand Rapids: Zondervan, 1976), 1:813.

Chapter 1   *I Heard the Number of Them*

Hastings' Bible Dictionary

Brown in *Hastings' Bible Dictionary* says, "One peculiarity of Ch[ronicles], which involves some discrepancies with the earlier books is a fondness for large numbers."[3] Brown correctly recognizes that apparent numerical difficulties are in some of the numbers of the Chronicles; however, he incorrectly refers to them as discrepancies and implying that they are somehow in error.

Unger

Merrill Unger asserts that when comparing the text of Chronicles to the texts of Samuel and Kings, "divergencies" become obvious. These "must be handled with extreme caution and fairness" because some "disagreements may be only apparent," whereas "other difficulties are due to the state of the transmitted text."[4] Herein Unger allows for the possibility of error in the current Hebrew text.

Conclusion

The author rejects the conclusions of McClintock, Strong, Schultz, Brown, and Unger. However, the above citations illustrate the recognition of apparent difficulties in the books of Samuel, Kings, and Chronicles. Furthermore, the citations reveal a need for an answer to these difficulties, especially an answer that does not claim that the difficulties are the result of scribal errors.

Some Claim Specific Verses Have Numerical Errors

While some question the general character of the books of I Samuel to II Chronicles, others question specific verses in these Biblical books. One might expect Liberals to question the Bible, but it is alarming when Fundamentalists claim that the Bible is in error.

---

[3] Francis Brown, "Chronicles, I. and II." in *A Dictionary of the Bible Dealing with Its Language, Literature, and Contents*, ed. James Hastings (New York: Charles Scribner's Sons, 1898), 1:394.

[4] Merrill F. Unger, *Introductory Guide to the Old Testament* (Grand Rapids: Zondervan, 1979), 409. On page 296 of this book, Unger says "that the Hebrew text of Samuel is in a poorer state of preservation than any other part of the Old Testament" and, therefore, concludes that II Samuel 21:19 "has suffered corruption in the course of transmission."

Chapter 1 *I Heard the Number of Them*

Bob Jones University on I Samuel 6:19

I Samuel 6:19 speaks of the Lord smiting fifty thousand and threescore and ten (50,070) men. The author never realized that I Samuel 6:19 was a problem until he was in his second year of Bible college at Bob Jones University (1977 – 1978). Terry Rude, the professor of the Old Testament Survey course, informed the class that the 50,070 could not be correct, that it probably should be 70.[5] Did a Fundamentalist Bible teacher in a Fundamentalist Bible college teach his students that the Bible has an error? Indeed, he did. When one attends a Fundamentalist Bible college, he should expect his teachers to strengthen his faith and confidence in the Bible, but more, and more Fundamentalist Bible teachers are teaching their students to ask, "Yea, hath God said?" (Genesis 3:1), instead of teaching them that all of God's precepts concerning all things are right and that they should hate every false way (Psalm 119:128).

Bob Jones University and Others on II Chronicles 22:2

II Chronicles 22:2 says, "Forty and two years old was Ahaziah when he began to reign," whereas II Kings 8:26 says, "Two and twenty years old was Ahaziah when he began to reign." Some Fundamentalists claim that the *forty and two years* in II Chronicles 22:2 is incorrect. One such Fundamentalist is Randy Jaeggli of Bob Jones University. David Doran of Detroit Baptist Theological Seminary asked Jaeggli in a panel discussion about the text of Scripture, "Is it accurate to say or act like textual criticism is unnecessary in the Old Testament text?" Jaeggli responded,

> Absolutely not, as a matter of fact, in the Old Testament, anyone who has ever studied the Old Testament in any depth realizes that from time to time he runs across apparent discrepancies from one passage to another. . . . For instance, in II Kings 8:26 the Masoretic text . . . says that Ahaziah was 22 years old when he ascended to the throne. In II Chronicles 22:2 the text says he was 42. Now obviously he couldn't be 22 and 42, one or the other of those numbers is correct and the other is in error. . . . II Kings 8:26 preserves the correct number there. . . . Now, if we don't make any provision for scribal error in transmission, we have a real problem there because what we would have in that case is a mistake in the Bible and that would bomb our entire doctrine of inerrancy. So we must have room for these scribal errors in transmission of the text and textual criticism takes

---

[5] The author bases this statement on his recollection, as well as upon undated class notes.

Chapter 1 *I Heard the Number of Them*

into account the existence of these scribal errors and answers the question, "Okay, of the available readings which one is correct?"[6]

Jaeggli made the above statement in the presence of Robert Delnay from Clearwater Christian College, Sam Horn from Northland Baptist Bible College, Larry Oats from Maranatha Baptist Bible College, William Combs from Detroit Baptist Theological Seminary, Dave Burgraff from Calvary Baptist Theological Seminary, Thurman Wisdom from Bob Jones University, and Kevin Bauder from Central Baptist Theological Seminary with their apparent approval. Do these men think that the *forty and two* in II Chronicles 22:2 is wrong and that the Bible, therefore, is in error and that Bible readers should not receive, believe, and hear this verse? It seems so. Instead of believing that both readings in the preserved Hebrew Masoretic Old Testament are correct and seeking an answer for this apparent discrepancy, these Fundamentalists question the Bible itself.

Central Baptist Theological Seminary on Various Verses

A book written by the faculty of Central Baptist Theological Seminary, a Fundamentalist school, states:

> The problems in the Old Testament text are easy to demonstrate in the KJV. In I Samuel 13:1 the KJV, following the MT [Masoretic Text], reads, 'Saul reigned one year; and when he had reigned two years over Israel.' Apparently at least one of the numbers in this verse has been lost; it makes no sense as it reads.[7]

The faculty of Central Baptist Theological Seminary have gone on record saying they will not receive, believe, and hear the numbers in 1 Samuel 13:1. Such an approach is contrary to the approach of John who heard, received, and believed the number God gave to him in Revelation 9:16. Should not the faculty of a Fundamentalist seminary follow the example of John with the numbers God has preserved in the Bible? Sadly, the numbers in I Samuel 13:1 are not the only numbers that the faculty of Central Baptist question. In addition to the numbers in I Samuel 13:1, the faculty questions *seven hundred* in II Samuel 8:4, *forty and two* in

---

[6] *Fundamentalism and the Word of God* (Allen Park, MI: Coalition for the Defense of the Scriptures, 1998), videocassette.

[7] W. Edward Glenny, "The Preservation of Scripture" in *The Bible Version Debate: The Perspective of Central Baptist Theological Seminary*, ed. Michael A. Grisanti (Plymouth, MN: Central Baptist Theological Seminary, 1997), 84-85.

Chapter 1 *I Heard the Number of Them*

II Chronicles 22:2, and *eight* in II Chronicles 36:9.[8] According to the faculty of Central Baptist Theological Seminary, Bible believers should not hear these numbers. In other words, Bible believers should not believe these verses in their Bible!

Concerning the overall books of Samuel, the Central Baptist book asserts in an endnote that "most notorious in the Masoretic tradition for its poorer quality is the book of Samuel."[9] Should such statements be coming from a Fundamentalist institution? Or, rather, should not a Fundamentalist seminary be instilling in its students faith and confidence in the Words of God? The above statements well illustrate the problem that many a student faces where his professor will teach him not to take the Traditional Hebrew Masoretic Text simply for what it says. Is it not a sad day in Fundamentalism when Fundamentalist teachers teach their students to question the Bible, instead of to receive the Bible?

Calvary Baptist Theological Seminary on
I Samuel 6:19 and 13:5

Central Baptist Theological Seminary is not the only Fundamentalist seminary that questions some of the numbers of the Old Testament. The author was present in a 1983 course at Calvary Baptist Theological Seminary on the United Monarchy taught by Jeffrey Tuttle. In the syllabus for that class a comment on I Samuel 6:19 states, "It is doubtful that the number of '50,070' is correct."[10] In other words, the student should not receive this number in his Bible.

In this same course, Tuttle informed the class that the number for 30,000 chariots in I Samuel 13:5 could not be correct; it was probably far fewer than that, perhaps 3,000. The author never realized a problem existed with this number until, not a Liberal, but a Fundamentalist Bible teacher brought attention to it. Professor Tuttle taught his seminary students that the preserved Hebrew Old Testament is incorrect and, therefore, not to hear, believe, and receive this number of 30,000. Should not a Fundamentalist seminary teach its students to hear, believe, and receive

---

[8] Ibid., 85.

[9] Roy E. Beacham, "The Old Testament Text and English Versions" in *The Bible Version Debate*, 37.

[10] Jeffrey Tuttle, "United Monarchy #623." (Lansdale, PA: Calvary Baptist Theological Seminary, 1982), 12.

Chapter 1 *I Heard the Number of Them*

all that the Bible says and thereby edify in godliness, rather than minister questions (I Timothy 1:4)?

The Defender's Study Bible on Various Verses

In addition to Fundamentalist schools that question some of the numbers in I Samuel to II Chronicles, some editions of the *Authorized Version* of the Bible also question various numbers. *The Defender's Study Bible*, a study Bible that some Fundamentalists use, has annotations prepared by Henry Morris. This study Bible claims that the "annotations seek to explain the Bible's difficult passages, resolve its alleged contradictions, point out the evidence of its divine origin, confirm its historical accuracy."[11] However, these very same annotations question several numbers in I Samuel to II Chronicles. Morris' annotations question I Samuel 6:19; 13:1, 5; II Samuel 8:4; 10:18; 15:7; I Kings 4:26; I Chronicles 11:11; 22:14; II Chronicles 3:4, 15; 4:5; and 22:2.[12] Furthermore, a note introducing the book of II Chronicles states:

> There are a number of apparent contradictions between the histories of Chronicles and those of Samuel and Kings. Most of these are only superficial and can be easily resolved on closer study. However, a significant number have to do with numerical quantities, which are in clear conflict. These can usually best be explained in terms of copyists' errors.[13]

Should not a Bible entitled *The Defender's Study Bible* teach a person to defend the entire Bible, rather than to teach him to question some of the Bible? But if one believes the notes of *The Defender's Study Bible*, he would think quite a few numbers in I Samuel to II Chronicles are indefensible because they are supposedly in error!

The Scofield Study Bible on Various Verses

The Scofield Study Bible, another study Bible that Fundamentalists use, states:

> Some discrepant statements concerning numbers are, however, found in the existing manuscripts of the Hebrew Scriptures. These are most natu-

---

[11] *The Defender's Study Bible*, ed. Henry Morris (Iowa Falls: World Publishing, 1995), v.

[12] Ibid., 325, 331, 363, 475, 365, 371, 391, 382, 485, 489, 394, 490, 507.

[13] Ibid., 487.

Chapter 1   *I Heard the Number of Them*

rally ascribed to the fact that the Hebrews used letters in place of numerals. . . . Errors in transcription of Hebrew numbers thus becomes easy, preservation of numerical accuracy difficult.[14]

Such a statement opens the door to charge "scribal error" for almost any numerical discrepancy in the Old Testament. Perhaps it was a statement such as this that led to *The New Scofield Reference Bible* alleging scribal errors in I Samuel 6:19; 13:1; II Samuel 8:4; 10:18; I Kings 20:30;[15] I Chronicles 11:11;[16] and II Chronicles 3:4.[17] In *The Scofield Study Bible*, which is older, the author could only find one note suggesting the possibility of scribal errors. In contrast, *The New Scofield Reference Bible*, as indicated above, has seven such notes in the books from I Samuel to II Chronicles alone. The increase in such notes reveals the progressive danger of suggesting the existence of errors in the Bible. Whereas *The Scofield Study Bible* opens the door with its one note, *The New Scofield Reference Bible* has jumped through the door with both feet! Truly, "a little leaven leaveneth the whole lump" (I Corinthians 5:6). By following the notes of *The New Scofield Reference Bible*, a Bible reader would not hear, believe, and receive a good quantity of numbers in I Samuel to II Chronicles.

Conclusion

A major problem exists in Fundamentalism concerning the numbers in Samuel, Kings, and Chronicles. That Liberals or New Evangelicals would question such things comes as no surprise, but when Fundamentalists engage in the attack, it is sad indeed. Are these Fundamentalists saying that God's people are not to hear, believe, and receive certain numbers? It seems so, but such an attitude is so contrary to the Apostle John's attitude toward the largest of all numbers in the Bible, an attitude wherein John "heard the number of them" (Revelation 9:16).

---

[14]*The Scofield Study Bible*, ed. C. I. Scofield (New York: Oxford University Press, 1945), 1220. This explanation of the Hebrew numerals while popular is erroneous (see Chapter Three for further discussion).

[15] *The New Scofield Reference Bible*, ed. C. I. Scofield (New York: Oxford University Press, 1967), 328, 334, 366, 368, 419.

[16] Ibid., 472. The note on this page questions several other verses including I Chronicles 21:5; II Chronicles 2:2, 17-18; 8:18; 22:2; 36:9.

[17] Ibid., 396.

JOHN HEARD THE NUMBER

Two Hundred Thousand Thousand

In Revelation 9:13-15 the Apostle John hears the sixth angel sound his trumpet and then watches as the angel looses the four angels who are bound in the Euphrates River. These four angels commandeer an army that will slay one-third of mankind (Revelation 9:15-18). In verse sixteen John writes, "And the number of the army of the horsemen were two hundred thousand thousand: and I heard the number of them." *Two hundred thousand thousand* is 200,000,000 and is the largest definite number in the Bible. In the Greek this number is δύο μυριάδες μυριάδων,[18] that is, two ten thousands of ten thousands, or two hundred thousand thousand. The word μυριάδες is a nominative feminine plural noun and μυριάδων is a genitive feminine plural noun. Both words are from μυριάς, the basis for the English word *myriad*.[19] Thayer lists meanings for μυριάς: (1) ten thousand, or (2) an innumerable multitude.[20]

Two Hundred Thousand Thousand Is a Literal Quantity

Some understand *two hundred thousand thousand* simply as a large quantity instead of understanding "that an exact number is intended."[21] Walvoord comments on Revelation 9:16:

---

[18] The Hebrew and Greek fonts that the author uses in this work are BWHEBB, BWHEBL [Hebrew]; BWGRKL, BWGRKN, and BWGRKI [Greek] Postscript® Type 1 and TrueTypeT fonts Copyright © 1994-2005 BibleWorks, LLC. All rights reserved. These Biblical Greek and Hebrew fonts are used with permission from BibleWorks, software for Biblical exegesis and research.

[19] William Morrris, ed., *The American Heritage Dictionary of the English Language* (Boston: Houghton Mifflin, 1982), 867.

[20] Joseph H. Thayer, *A Greek-English Lexicon of the New Testament* (Grand Rapids: Baker, 1977), 419. While Thayer puts Revelation 9:16 under the meaning of an innumerable multitude, he fails to take into account that a numerical adjective precedes μυριάδες μυριάδων, which makes it a definite quantity (see discussion that follows).

[21] G. K. Beale, *The Book of Revelation* in *The New International Greek Testament Commentary*, ed. I. Howard Marshall and Donald A. Hagner (Grand Rapids: Eerdmans, 1999), 509. Beale argues that "a figurative meaning is demanded by a literal translation of the number, since its plural forms leave it too indefinitely stated to be calculated precisely" (Ibid.). However, one can calculate it precisely as $2 \times 10,000 \times 10,000 = 200,000,000$.

Because the number 'ten thousand times ten thousand' is often used of an innumerable company (cf. 5:11) some have held that this [that is, the number in Revelation 9:16] should not be understood as a literal number. Scott does not believe that the army of 200 million should be taken literally.[22]

There is, however, an important distinction between Revelation 9:16 and 5:11 — a numerical adjective precedes the quantity in Revelation 9:16, whereas this is not the case in Revelation 5:11. Beale observes:

> When μυριάς ("ten thousand") designates a countable number, it is in the plural and prefixed by limiting numerical adjectives (e.g., 1 Macc. 11:45: δώδεκα μυριάδας [120,000]; cf. the plural of μύριοι ["ten thousand"] with a numerical adjective: δισμυρίων ["20,000"] in 2 Macc. 8:9 and τριδ μυρίων [30,000] in Esth. 1:7 LXX). On the other hand, without exception, μυριάς ("ten thousand") designates an incalculable immensity whenever it is used without any numerical adjective.[23]

Therefore, Revelation 5:11, not having a numerical adjective, presents an indefinite number.[24] On the other hand, Revelation 9:16, having a limiting numerical adjective, δύο (*two*), preceding the plurals μυριάδες and μυριάδων,[25] presents a definite quantity.

---

[22] John F. Walvoord, *The Revelation of Jesus Christ* (Chicago: Moody, 1977), 166. Walvoord quotes Scott: "A literal army consisting of 200 million of cavalry need not be thought of. The main idea in the passage is a vast and overwhelming army, one beyond human computations, and exceeding by far any before witnessed" (Ibid., quoting Walter Scott, *Expostion of the Revelation of Jesus Christ* (London: Pickering and Inglis Ltd., n.d.), 211). But if this were a "vast and overwhelming army," "and exceeding by far any before witnessed," then why could not it be 200,000,000? An army of 200,000,000 would indeed be a "vast and overwhelming army" "and exceeding by far any before witnessed."

[23] Beale, 509. In every instance in the LXX where a numerical adjective precedes the plural a definite quantity is in view (Exodus 38:26; Ezra 2:64; Nehemiah 7:66, 71, 72; Jonah 4:11).

[24] Walvoord may be thinking also of Luke 12:1; Acts 21:20; Hebrews 12:22 and Jude 14 where μυριάς is correctly translated indefinitely as "an innumerable multitude," "thousands," "an innumerable company," and "ten thousands" respectively. In none of these verses, however, does a numerical adjective precede μυριάς and, therefore, one should regard them as indefinite quantities.

[25] Though the Critical Text reads δισμυριάδες μυριάδων where δισ- is prefixed to the plural, it is, nonetheless, a definite quantity as Beale points out above in 2 Macc. 8:9. However, Beale, who follows the CT, rather inconsistently avoids this conclusion by saying, "The prefix δισ- ('twice') intensifies the figurative aspect of innumerality" (Beale, 509). But if a figurative sense is present here, then why not simply use μυριάδες μυριάδων

Chapter 1 *I Heard the Number of Them*

Walvoord quotes H. B. Swete: " 'These vast numbers forbid us to seek a literal fulfillment, and the description that follows supports this conclusion.' "[26] On the contrary, it is the description that follows that solidifies the belief that the 200,000,000 is a literal number, for the description of the horsemen indicates that "these armies are demonic, not human, so the largeness of the number is no obstacle."[27] But even if one does not believe the army to be demonic, nothing in the context demands that the 200,000,000 is figurative. In fact, "the number of the horsemen forming the vast invading force was stated to be 200 million and John added that he heard the number, thereby indicating that the exact number was intended and not merely a large number."[28]

John Heard This Number

Unlike several commentators, John, unquestionably, heard, that is, received and believed, the number of 200,000,000. This number along with all the rest of the book of Revelation was accurately conveyed from God the Father to Jesus Who "signified it by His angel unto His servant John" (Revelation 1:1). *Signified* is an aorist active indicative from σημαίνω and

---

as in Revelation 5:11? Beale says that διο - intensifies the figurative aspect, but how can a figure be more intensely figurative? And what would be the purpose in making a figure more intensely figurative? Beale seems inconsistent. The *Textus Receptus* uses δύο, which clearly distinguishes the quantity in Revelation 9:16 as a definite quantity.

[26] Walvoord, 166, quoting Henry B. Swete, *The Apocalypse of St. John* (Grand Rapids: Wm. B. Eerdmans Publishing Co., n.d.), 122.

[27] Robert L. Thomas, *Revelation 8-22: An Exegetical Commentary*, ed. Kenneth Barker (Chicago: Moody, 1995), 46. Evidence that these horsemen are demonic rather than human is: (1) their being under the control of previously bound angels (Revelation 9:14-15) indicating that the angels are fallen angels or devils (II Peter 2:4; Jude 6; the Bible never says that good angels are bound); (2) "the fact that the horses rather than the riders are the destructive agents and that they and their riders wear brightly colored breastplates matching the destructive forces proceeding from their mouths suggests that the combination of horse and rider is of superhuman origin" (Thomas, 46); and (3) the fact that the description of the horses "differs so greatly from any ordinary horse" indicates "that these horses must be of another order" (Thomas, 46). Thomas particularly notes in the description of Revelation 9:17 that there are "breastplates of fire, jacinth, and brimstone," not "as of fire and brimstone." In other words, the breastplates are literally fire, jacinth, and brimstone.

[28] Frederick A. Tatford, *The Revelation* (Minneapolis: Klock & Klock, 1985), 327.

means "make known, declare."[29] Acts 11:28 uses the exact same word: "And there stood up one of them named Agabus, and signified by the Spirit that there should be great dearth throughout all the world: which came to pass in the days of Claudius Caesar." Just as the Spirit of God made known to Agabus the coming dearth so the angel of Christ made known to John "things which must shortly come to pass" (Revelation 1:1).

What did John do with that which the angel made known to him? Revelation 1:2 states that he "bare record of the word of God." In other words, God the Father gave the revelation to Christ, Christ's angel then sent and made it known to John, and it was still the Word of God by the time it got to John. Nothing was lost in the transmission of the Words of God. Everything was accurately conveyed and relayed from God the Father to John who then wrote it down.

Two hundred thousand thousand is a number that probably went beyond anything John had ever encountered in his whole life. How did he respond to this quantity? Did he claim that it was too large and should be reduced by a factor of ten, as some[30] do with *thirty thousand chariots* in I Samuel 13:5? No, he received it. Did he claim that it was too large and should be reduced by a factor of one hundred, as some others[31] do with *thirty thousand chariots* in I Samuel 13:5? No, he believed it. Did he claim that something was lost or added in the transmission of the number to him, as some[32] do with numbers in I Samuel 13:1 and other verses? No, he heard it. John received *two hundred thousand thousand* without question. He had to receive it by faith, and he did. History knows nothing of an army this big, yet John received the number. John heard the number of them, believed it, received it, and recorded it as the Word of God.

---

[29] Spiros Zodhiates, *Wordstudy NT Dictionary* in *The Complete Word Study Bible & Reference CD* [CD-ROM] (Chattanooga, TN: AMG Publishers, 1997), 4591.

[30] See discussion earlier in this chapter in the subsection "Calvary Baptist Theological Seminary on I Samuel 6:19 and 13:5," and see discussion on I Samuel 13:5 in Chapter Seven.

[31] See discussion on I Samuel 13:5 in Chapter Seven.

[32] See discussion earlier in this chapter in the subsection "Central Baptist Theological Seminary on Various Verses," and see discussion on I Samuel 13:1 in Chapter Seven. Also, discussions on other verses in Chapters Seven through Twelve point out instances where commentators allege something was lost in transmission.

Chapter 1 *I Heard the Number of Them*

CONCLUSION

John's attitude towards the biggest of all numbers in Scripture ought to be the attitude of every Bible student toward all the numbers in Holy Scripture. Sadly, many are not following the example of John and hence the need for this book to address this issue. But where did John get the idea that he should receive and believe the numbers of Scripture and, in fact, all the words of the Bible? The Lord Jesus Christ instilled such an attitude into John by His teaching and testimony. The next chapter presents the teaching and testimony of the Lord Jesus Christ concerning the Words of God.

CHAPTER TWO:
JESUS RECEIVED THE OLD TESTAMENT

Jesus used the Old Testament on many occasions and since this work is dealing with a portion of the Old Testament, it is wise to study His use of the Old Testament. Before getting into exactly how Jesus approached the Old Testament, let the reader consider a few introductory matters namely: (1) the credentials of Jesus; and (2) the Old Testament of Jesus. Jesus has unique credentials and, therefore, one should believe Him on the text issue over all others. Also, Old Testament of Jesus is a text in which the saints of old had the very words of the *autographa*, even though it was composed of copies of copies of the *autographa*. Building on the introduction, the main body of the chapter details Jesus' assessment of this Old Testament text, showing that (1) He repeatedly says "it is written" of His Old Testament, indicating that the actual words of the Old Testament writers wrote were still in existence and would continue; (2) He repeatedly refers to Old Testament passages thereby demonstrating that the Old Testament is fully accurate and reliable; (3) He repeatedly refers to Old Testament numerical passages showing that the numbers are accurate and authoritative; (4) He repeatedly validates the Old Testament text, which He does in Matthew 5:18; 24:35; Mark 13:31; Luke 16:17; 21:33; 24:25; and John 10:35; 17:17; and (5) He never once criticizes the Old Testament text. In looking fairly at this evidence, Chapter Two concludes that the Traditional Hebrew Old Testament is trustworthy. The last page of the chapter presents a chart showing the transmission of the Hebrew Old Testament. The chart demonstrates that God's Words have been accurately and fully transmitted to this present day. No one can legitimately say that the preserved Hebrew Old Testament has error(s) without impugning the Person and character of the Lord Jesus Christ.

Chapter 2 *Jesus Received the Old Testament*

The Credentials of Jesus

Jesus is the Cornerstone (Psalm 118:22; cf. Matthew 21:42); the Counselor (Isaiah 9:6); wise, understanding, and knowledgeable (Isaiah 11:2[33]); eternal (Micah 5:2); the Beloved Son (Matthew 12:18); great (Luke 11:31); "the Word" (John 1:1); "the true Light" (John 1:9); omniscient (John 2:24); the authority (John 5:27); "the light of the world" (John 8:12); the "I am" (John 8:58); "the door" (John 10:7); "the good shepherd" (John 10:11); "the way, the truth, and the life" (John 14:6); a "witness unto the truth" (John 18:37); "the Holy One and the Just" (Acts 3:14); the head of the church (Ephesians 1:22); the preeminent One (Colossians 1:18); God manifest in the flesh (I Timothy 3:16); sinless (Hebrews 7:26); "the author and finisher of our faith" (Hebrews 12:2); "the chief Shepherd" (I Peter 5:4); "Alpha and Omega, the beginning and the ending" (Revelation 1:8); "the faithful and true witness" (Revelation 3:14); and "KING OF KINGS AND LORD OF LORDS" (Revelation 19:16). Jesus is all of this and more. Who, then, is better qualified to speak on the text issue than Jesus? Should the Bible student appeal to textual critics, instead of to Jesus? Should he refer to the pages of history more than to Jesus? Should he look upon human scholars, no matter how conservative or knowledgeable, as more authoritative than Jesus? The answer to each of these questions is no, yet many who write about the Bible or the text issue, instead of starting with the Bible or with Jesus, start with history or man's theories.[34]

Who has better credentials than Jesus? Jesus is the Word of God (John 1:1), and the Spirit of Christ spoke through the prophets of old (I Peter 1:11); therefore, Jesus has perfect understanding and knowledge of the Old Testament. On several occasions He confounded the supposed Old Testament experts of His day as He rightly divided the Word of Truth (Matthew 22:23-32; Mark 12:35-37; Luke 2:46-47). If anyone is an ex-

---

[33] Colossians 2:3 says of Christ, "In whom are hid all the treasures of wisdom and knowledge."

[34] For instance, the book *One Bible Only?* waits until chapter 4 and over 100 pages before getting into a serious discussion of the verses that deal with the text issue, and then when it does get to these verses, it explains away most of them. Another example is from the video tape *Fundamentalism and the Word of God* (Allen Park, MI: Coalition for the Defense of the Scriptures, 1998) wherein only one speaker out of nine coalition members alluded to one verse on inspiration and that was toward the end of the tape. One member alluded to one verse on inspiration, no members mentioned any verses on preservation, but they had much to say about history and textual criticism.

Chapter 2 *Jesus Received the Old Testament*

pert concerning the Old Testament, it is Jesus. One cannot do better than to take the same view of the Old Testament that Jesus took. Gleason Archer makes a wonderful statement in this regard:

> Whatever Jesus Christ believed about the trustworthiness of Scripture must be accepted as true and binding on the conscience of every believer. If Christ believed in the complete accuracy of the Hebrew Bible in all matters of scientific or historical fact, we must acknowledge His view in these matters to be correct and trustworthy in every respect. Moreover, in view of the impossibility of God's being guilty of error, we must recognize that even matters of history and science, though not per se theological, assume the importance of basic doctrine. Why is this so? Because Christ is God, and God cannot be mistaken. That is a theological proposition that is absolutely essential to Christian doctrine. A careful examination of Christ's references to the Old Testament makes it unmistakably evident that He fully accepted as factual even the most controversial statements in the Hebrew Bible pertaining to history and science.[35]

At this point Archer refers to Jesus' mentioning Jonah (Matthew 12:40); Noah and the flood (Matthew 24:38-39); the feeding of the Israelites with manna (John 6:49); God's speaking to Moses from the burning bush (Matthew 22:32; cf. Exodus 3:6); and Adam and Eve (Matthew 19:5; cf. Gen 2:24).[36] W. H. Griffith Thomas says, "We naturally inquire what our Master thought of the Old Testament, for if it comes to us with His authority, and we can discover His view of it, we ought to be satisfied."[37] Indeed, the true child of God should gladly view anything in the same way as Jesus. "It is enough for the disciple that he be as his master, and the servant as his lord" (Matthew 10:25). But before examining how Jesus viewed the Old Testament, it is necessary to ask this question: what Old Testament did Jesus have?

---

[35] Gleason L. Archer, Jr., *Encyclopedia of Bible Difficulties* (Grand Rapids: Zondervan, 1982), 20-21. While this is an excellent statement on the part of Archer, it is regrettable that he does not follow his own words. Archer correctly states that Jesus "believed in the complete accuracy of the Hebrew Bible in all matters." Yet Archer, later in his book, questions the accuracy of some of the numbers of the Old Testament, though those numbers are firmly based in the Hebrew Bible. Examples of Archer's questioning some of the numbers of the Old Testament especially in the books of I Samuel to II Chronicles are on pages 169, 171, 172, 184, 206, 211, 214, 221, 222, 223, and 226 of his book.

[36] Ibid., 21-22.

[37] W. H. Griffith Thomas, "Old Testament Criticism and New Testament Christianity" in *The Fundamentals – A Testimony to the Truth*, ed. R. A. Torrey, A. C. Dixon, et al. in *The Master Christian Library*, version 8 [CD-ROM] (Rio, WI: Ages Software, 2000), 1:115.

Chapter 2 *Jesus Received the Old Testament*

The Old Testament Text of Jesus

In examining the Old Testament text that Jesus used, it is necessary to trace the transmission of the Old Testament text from the *autographa*, to the copies, then to Jesus.

The Autograhpa

The Bible states that "Moses wrote all the words of the LORD" (Exodus 24:4). Moses wrote (Deuteronomy 31:9, 24) at the command of the Lord (Exodus 34:1, 27; Numbers 33:2). God commanded that the completed writings of Moses, that is, the book of the law, be "put in the side of the ark of the covenant of the LORD" (Deuteronomy 31:25-26). Later, Joshua added words to the book of the law (Joshua 24:26). Samuel wrote words in a book "and laid it up before the LORD" (I Samuel 10:25), that is, placed the newly written book "by the side of the ark of the covenant with the copy of the Law."[38] A conclusion based on these verses is that the *autographa* were placed with the ark of the Lord.

During the reign of Josiah (about 640 B.C., over 800 years after Moses), II Chronicles 34:14 states, "Hilkiah the priest found a book of the law of the LORD given by Moses." The exact expression "given by Moses," based on the Hebrew בְּיַד־מֹשֶׁה (*beyad Moseh*), literally is "by the hand of Moses" and indicates that the book that Hilkiah found was the actual autograph of Moses as written by his own hand.[39] Was it the only copy of the law in Israel?

---

[38] J. M.. Fuller, ed., "I Samuel" in *I Samuel – Esther* in vol. 2 of *Barnes' Notes on the Bible*, Heritage Edition (London: Blackie & Son, 1847, reprinted Grand Rapids: Baker Book House, 2005), 26.

[39] *A Hebrew and English Lexicon of the Old Testament* bears out that *given by Moses* refers to the autograph of Moses by listing II Chronicles 34:14 under the meaning of "by the agency or instrumentality of" in their discussion of the word יָד (*yad*) when used with the preposition בְּ (*be*) (Francis Brown, S. R. Driver, and C. A. Briggs, *A Hebrew and English Lexicon of the Old Testament With an Appendix Containing the Biblical Aramaic: Based on the Lexicon of William Gesenius as Translated by Edward Robinson* (Oxford: Clarendon Press, 1980), 391). Furthermore, Ackroyd asserts that בְּיַד (*beyad*) is "used frequently to designate the agent through whom a particular action is performed" (R. Ackroyd, "יָד" in *Theological Dictionary of the Old Testament: the Authorized and Unabridged Translation of Theologisches Wörtenbuch Zum Alten Testament*, trans. David Green, ed. G. Johannes Botterweck and Helmer Ringgren (Grand Rapids: Eerdmans, 1986), 5:410). Also, that this book written by the hand of Moses would have lasted for

Chapter 2   *Jesus Received the Old Testament*

There are some who think that it was the only copy of the law at that time. For instance, Glenny writes,

> The Old Testament text was not even preserved publicly throughout Israel's history. King Manasseh must have tried to destroy the Book of the Law, but it was found again in the house of the Lord during the reign of Josiah. . . . Thus, for many years (long enough for it to be forgotten), the only extant copy of God's Word was hidden in the Temple and inaccessible to God's people.[40]

Mincy states,

> The indication here is that the written Word of God had been lost for some time, probably during the reign of wicked Manasseh. God's promises for the preservation of His words do not apparently necessitate the availability of that written Word at every moment of history. It is therefore possible for a portion of His words to be unavailable at a point in time, only to be found later.[41]

---

800 years should not be considered out of the question, especially when some Greek manuscripts of the New Testament are over 1500 years old and the Dead Sea Scrolls are about 2000 years old.

[40] W. Edward Glenny, "The Preservation of Scripture and the Version Debate" in *One Bible Only?*, ed. Roy E. Beacham and Kevin T. Bauder (Grand Rapids: Kregel, 2001), 114. Wallace makes a similar point in his article entitled "Inspiration, Preservation, and New Testament Textual Criticism," *Grace Theological Journal*, 12 (Spring, 1991), 33-34.

[41] John Mincy, "Preservation of the Copies" in *God's Word in Our Hands The Bible Preserved for Us*, ed. James B. Williams (Greenville, S.C.: Ambassador Emerald International, 2003), 124. After making the above statement, Mincy refers to the restorations of the Ten Commandments in Exodus 34:1 and the scroll of Jeremiah in Jeremiah 36:27-28 as examples of how God "replaced 'lost' words."

Concerning the Ten Commandments, these were not lost words. Exodus 24:4 states that Moses wrote all the Words of the Lord and since God gave the Ten Commandments in Exodus 20, then what Moses wrote at that time included the Ten Commandments. Therefore, when Moses broke the tables of the Ten Commandments (Exodus 32:19) that was not the only extant copy of the Ten Commandments. The conclusion is that even though Moses broke the tables, no words were ever lost.

Concerning the case of Jeremiah's scroll in Jeremiah 36, when King Jehoiakim burned Jeremiah's scroll (Jeremiah 36:23), these were not lost words. Jeremiah had a personal copy of the Words that God gave to him, for in Jeremiah 30:2 God had commanded Jeremiah to "write thee all the words that I have spoken unto thee in a book." *Write thee* is כְּתָב־לְךָ (*ketob-leka*), which literally is *write thou for thee*, and indicates that Jeremiah was to write the words for himself, that is, he was to keep his own record of all the words that God gave to him. McKane observes, "The one was inscribed with a view to public proclamation (chapter 36) and the other in order to create a permanent rec-

But to conclude that the copy of the law that Hilkiah found was the only copy of the law fails to take into account several factors: (1) the Bible does not state that the it was the only extant book of the law of the Lord at this time: all it says is that Hilkiah found a book of the law of the Lord given by Moses; (2) Psalm 12:6-7 promises that the Lord will preserve His Words from that generation forever, that is, that the Words of the Lord would be available; and (3) history, even God's inspired history, does not present all the details of history, therefore, one may not know for certain how many people had the Words of God and in what towns the Words of God were available, but one should have confidence in the promise of God that they were available according to Psalm 12:6-7.

The fact is that the copy that Hilkiah found was not the only extant copy of the law, for Deuteronomy 17:18 commanded that the king "shall write him a copy of this law in a book out of that which is before the priests the Levites." Perhaps not every king obeyed Deuteronomy 17:18, but surely at least some of the good kings did and, therefore, had their own copy of Scripture. Scribes could assure the accuracy of the copies by comparing them with the existing *autographa*. Reference to one of the copies is in II Kings 11:12 and II Chronicles 23:11 where Jehoiada the priest gave to Joash at his coronation "the testimony," that is, "the book of

---

ord" (William McKane, *A Critical and Exegetical Commentary on Jeremiah* in *The International Critical Commentary on the Holy Scriptures of the Old and New Testaments*, ed. J. A. Emerton, C. E. B. Cranfield, and G. N. Stanton (Edinburgh: T & T Clark, 1996),749,750). The conclusion is that though Jehoiakim burned the scroll of Jeremiah 36, no words were ever lost.

A note about Jeremiah 30:2 is in order. Many commentators are undecided as to whether the words God wanted Jeremiah to write were the entire book of Jeremiah, or just a portion of Jeremiah, namely chapters 30 and 31. Most commentators lean toward Jeremiah's writing only chapters 30 and 31. However, inasmuch as God promised the preservation of His Words (Psalm 12:6-7) and inasmuch as Jesus stated that Scripture cannot be broken (John 10:35), it is impossible that when Jehoiakim burned the scroll of Jeremiah that he was removing from the face of the earth the only extant copy of Jeremiah. It is, therefore, the conclusion of the author that the command of Jeremiah 30:2 refers to the entire book of Jeremiah, not just a portion.

Thank God that He has promised to preserve His Words "from this generation for ever" (Psalm 12:7) and that "the scripture cannot be broken" (John 10:35). Though men may destroy a copy or a portion of the Words of God, they are not able to remove totally those words.

the law, as the rule of his life and action as king, according to the precept in Deut. 17:18, 19."[42]

God commanded Isaiah to "go, write it before them in a table, and note it in a book, that it may be for the time to come for ever and ever" (Isaiah 30:8). Herein God promises that the Words of God written by Isaiah will be preserved "for the time to come for ever and ever." As God's people assembled the various books of the Old Testament, they referred to these books as "the book of the LORD" (Isaiah 34:16). Fausset, commenting on "the book of the LORD," says it is "the volume in which the various prophecies and other parts of Scripture began henceforward to be collected together."[43]

The Copies

Priests (Deuteronomy 17:18; II Kings 11:9-12; II Chronicles 23:9-11) and scribes (Ezra 7:6,11; Jeremiah 8:8; 36:1-4, 32; 45:1)[44] copied the books of the Old Testament. The people (Deuteronomy 6:6-9; 11:20; 31:1-19); the elders (Deuteronomy 27:1-3, 8); Joshua (Joshua 8:30-32); and the men of Hezekiah (Proverbs 25:1) also copied portions of Scripture.

It Is Written

The work of the priests in copying the Scriptures (Deuteronomy 17:18-19) was so accurate that David when referring to his copy said to Solomon, "Keep the charge of the LORD thy God, to walk in His ways, to keep His statutes, and His commandments, and His judgments, and His

---

[42] C. F. Keil, *1 and 2 KINGS 1 and 2 CHRONICLES* in vol. 3 of *Commentary on the Old Testament* (Edinburgh: T & T Clark, 1866-91, reprinted, Peabody, MA: Hendrickson Publishers, Inc., 2001), 257.

[43] A. R. Fausset, *Isaiah* in part 1, vol. 2 of *A Commentary Critical, Experimental, and Practical on the Old and New Testaments* (Grand Rapids: Eerdmans, 1984), 669. E. J. Young makes a similar observation (E. J. Young, *The Book of Isaiah* (Grand Rapids: Eerdmans, 1978), 2:442).

[44] I Chronicles 2:55 mentions the existence of "the families of the scribes." Whether these were religious or secular scribes, the Bible does not indicate. But if they were religious scribes, then there was an organized group of scribes whose job it was to copy the books of the Old Testament.

testimonies, as it is written in the law of Moses" (I Kings 2:3).⁴⁵ *As it is written*, כַּכָּתוּב (*kakkathuv*), is a Qal passive participle from כָּתַב (*kathav*) with the prefix כְּ (*ka*) pointed for the definite article, meaning *the like*, therefore giving the idea of *the like written*.

> Now King Solomon would only have had access to a copy, such as is mentioned in Deuteronomy 17:18, 19; but observe how this copy is described as what is "written in the law of Moses." Such painstaking care had taken over the copying that the resultant manuscript retained the authority of the original. It was the Word of God and it could be cited as such.⁴⁶

The Qal is the only stem with a passive participle. "The passive participle describes the action in a given state" functioning "in the sentence as a predicate adjective,"⁴⁷ which means that it complements or modifies the subject.⁴⁸ David's use of the passive participle in I Kings 2:3 indicates that the laws, statutes, and judgments of the law of Moses were in the state of having been written; that is, what Moses wrote in the past still stood written in David's day. Other verses teach that the God-inspired Words that Moses wrote in the past still stood written in Daniel's day (Daniel 9:13), in Ezra and Nehemiah's day (Nehemiah 8:14-15), in Jesus' day (Matthew 4:4) and in Paul's day (Romans 4:17).⁴⁹ The fact that the

---

⁴⁵ Psalm 1:2 and 119:97-99 may establish that David had his own personal copy of the law as these verses speak of meditating in the Word and the Word being ever with the Psalmist. Concerning Psalm 1, Gill says, "This psalm, though without a title, may reasonably be thought to be a psalm of David; since the next psalm, which is also without a title, is ascribed to him, Ac 4:25; and since both are joined together as one psalm by the Jews" (John Gill, *An Exposition of The Old & New Testaments* (London: Mathews and Leigh, 1810, reprinted Paris, Arkansas: The Baptist Standard Bearer, Inc., 1989), III:524). And concerning Psalm 119, Gill states, "This psalm is generally thought to be written by David" (Ibid., IV:209). Indeed, it would be fitting that David, who was "the sweet psalmist of Israel" (II Samuel 23:1), would be its human author. Furthermore, Psalm 119 alludes to events that parallel David's life (for example, compare Psalm 119:19 with I Samuel 26:9; compare Psalm 119:23 with I Samuel 20:31 and 22:7-13; and compare Psalm 119:87 with I Samuel 20:3 and 23:26-27).

⁴⁶ Malcolm H. Watts, "The Lord Gave the Word: A Study in the History of the Biblical Text" [article on-line] (London: Trinitarian Bible Society, 1998); available from http://www.trinitarianbiblesociety.org; Internet.

⁴⁷ Warren Vanhetloo, "Hebrew Syntax 202." (Lansdale, PA: Calvary Baptist School of Theology, 1980), 13.

⁴⁸ John C. Hodges and Mary E. Whitten, *Harbrace College Handbook 7ᵗʰ Edition* (New York: Harcourt Brace Jovanovich, Inc., 1972), 469, 472, 486.

⁴⁹ For more information on these verses, see further.

Chapter 2   *Jesus Received the Old Testament*

God-inspired Words that Moses wrote in about 1491 B.C. stood written in the days of David (1015 B.C.), Daniel (538 B.C.), Ezra (454 B.C.), Christ (26 A.D.),[50] and Paul (57 A.D.)[51] indicates that the *it-is-written* words stand written and would remain written for the ages to come. Two points substantiate the fact that the *it-is-written* words stand written and would remain written for the ages to come: (1) the syntax of the expression *it-is-written* (see further); and (2) the promises of the Lord Jesus Christ. Jesus promises that God's inspired Words that Moses wrote in the past will still stand written into this modern day and beyond (Matthew 5:18; Luke 16:17; John 10:35).[52] Thank God for such promises! The believer can be assured that he has the actual inspired Words that God gave to Moses. There is no need to go about trying to recover or restore the text, the text is already here. All one need do is to receive it, just as the disciples did (John 17:8).

Theological Dictionary of the Old Testament says כַּכָּתוּב (*kakkathuv, as it is written*) is an "absolute expression . . . which lies behind the NT idiom *hōs/hōper/kathōs/kathaper gégraptai*, conceives of the Torah as a single normative entity (2 Ch. 30:5, 18; Ezr. 3:4; Neh. 8:15)."[53] *Gegraptai* (*it is written*) is a Greek perfect tense word, which the author will discuss in more detail in the next section. But for now, it is sufficient to say that the Greek word *gegraptai* means that what was written in the past still stands written in the present, indicating that what was written in the past is preserved to this day. The comment from *Theological Dictionary of the Old Testament* links the Old Testament word כַּכָּתוּב (*kakkathuv, as it is written*) with the New Testament word *gegraptai* (*it is written*). In other words, according to *Theological Dictionary of the Old Testament* the Old Testament word כַּכָּתוּב (*kakkathuv, as it is written*) and the New Testament word *gegraptai* (*it is written*) have the same meaning. Such a conclusion is valid when one considers that the Bible uses both words of the law of Moses (Joshua 8:31; 23:6; I Kings 2:3; II Kings 14:6; II Chronicles 23:18; Ezra 3:2; Daniel 9:11, 13; I Corinthians 9:9). The fact that the Bi-

---

[50] The dates for Moses to Christ are from Floyd Nolen Jones, "Chart 6: Creation to Creator" in *Chronology of the Old Testament: A Return to Basics* (The Woodlands, TX: Kings Word Press, 1999).

[51] The date for Paul comes from the date in which he wrote Romans. In Romans Paul used *it is written* of quotations from Moses.

[52] For more information on these verses, see further.

[53] H. Haag, "כָּתַב" in *Theological Dictionary of the Old Testament*, 7:379.

ble uses both words of the law of Moses establishes a continuity of the text of Scripture from Old Testament days into New Testament days.

Also, *the* Bible not only uses *gegraptai* (*it is written*) and כַּכָּתוּב (*kakkathuv, as it is written*) of Scripture but also of the names written in the book of life in Daniel 12:1 (כָּתוּב *kathuv, written*) and in Revelation 13:8; 17:8 (γέγραπται, *written*). This further substantiates that *gegraptai* (*it is written*) and כַּכָּתוּב (*kakkathuv, as it is written*) have the same meaning. The use of these words in connection with the book of life indicates that the names of those who would be saved were written in the book of life from the foundation of the world and will have stood written in the book of life throughout the ages. The same is true of the Words of God: they were written in the past and stand written throughout the ages. The grammar, then, behind the Qal passive participle argues strongly for the preservation of the words of the law of Moses.[54] The Old Testament uses this same construction with the Qal passive participle in Joshua 8:31; II Kings 14:6; II Chronicles 25:4; 30:5, 18; 31:3; 35:26; Ezra 3:2, 4; Nehemiah 8:15; and 10:34-36. The Scriptures use the Qal passive participle without the prefix כְּ (*ka, the like*) in Joshua 1:8 (with article); 8:34 (with article); 23:6 (with article); I Chronicles 16:40 (with article); 29:29 (plural); II Chronicles 23:18 (with article); 32:32 (plural); 33:19 (plural); Nehemiah 8:14; 12:23 (plural); 13:1; Ecclesiastes 12:10 (with ו, *w*); Jeremiah 51:60 (plural with article); and Daniel 9:11 (feminine ending), 13. These

---

[54]II Kings 14:6 and II Chronicles 25:4 both appeal to what is written in the book of the law of Moses (Deuteronomy 24:16) and use the exact same Qal passive participle in so doing. As far as the author knows, this is the only place in the Old Testament where *it is written* is used of a direct quote from the law of Moses. Yet, if one were to carefully compare II Kings 14:6 with Deuteronomy 24:16 and do the same with II Chronicles 25:4, he would find slight differences in each. The differences would indicate that either the Spirit of God directed the writers of II Kings and II Chronicles to give an inspired commentary upon Deuteronomy 24:16, however so slight, or that the writers were not quoting directly from Moses. The fact remains, though, that the words of Moses, which had been written in the past, still stood written in the present and were available. Chapter Five gives more information about differences in quotes.

Some may suppose that such differences indicate that God did not preserve the exact Words; however, Jesus asserts that the Words are preserved right down to the last jot and tittle (Matthew 5:18, see discussion later in this chapter). Furthermore, Psalm 12:6,7 states that the Lord keeps and preserves His Words (see further discussion in Chapter Five). Therefore, the author's explanation that the differences in the quotes of Deuteronomy 24:16 reflect the Holy Spirit's inspired commentary is valid and consistent with teaching elsewhere in Scripture.

other verses are also very instructive and this book devotes more attention to them shortly.

Still Stood Written

When the Babylonians destroyed Jerusalem in 586 B.C., they not only destroyed the city, but also burned the Temple (II Chronicles 36:17-19). Since the *autographa* were laid up beside the ark (Deuteronomy 31:25-26; I Samuel 10:25), perhaps the *autograhpa* were also destroyed at that time. However, copies of the Words of God still existed, which the saints of old regarded as fully authoritative and accurate. For example, Daniel in Babylon had the words of the law of Moses (Daniel 9:13). Daniel uses the Qal passive participle כָּתוּב (*kathuv, written*) indicating that the law of Moses still stood written and was not lost or destroyed. Not only did Daniel have an accurate and preserved copy of the law of Moses, but he also had the book of Jeremiah (Daniel 9:2). Daniel regarded Jeremiah as fully authoritative even in the matter of the numerical quantity of the seventy years to be accomplished "in the desolations of Jerusalem." Herein Daniel is not at all like his modern-day brethren who question the numbers of the Old Testament. Instead, Daniel received, believed, and heard this number as fully preserved and, therefore, accurate and authoritative, although it did not directly concern itself with matters of faith.

Later, when the Jews returned from the captivity in about 536 B.C., "then stood up Jeshua the son of Jozadak, and his brethren the priests, and Zerubbabel the son of Shealtiel, and his brethren, and builded the altar of the God of Israel, to offer burnt offerings thereon, as it is written in the law of Moses" (Ezra 3:2, see also Ezra 3:4). In these verses, *as it is written* is another use of the Qal passive participle and indicates that what Moses originally wrote still stood written. The Ezra passage, no doubt, refers to a copy.

In about 454 B.C., those with Nehemiah and Ezra "found written in the law which the LORD had commanded by Moses" the command concerning the feast of tabernacles (Nehemiah 8:14-15). In this passage, the Bible uses the Qal passive participle indicating that what Moses had written over 1,000 years ago still stood written. They had the preserved Words of God in that day. Nehemiah 10:34-36 and 13:1 teach the same thing. Nehemiah 12:23 refers to something written in Chronicles (cf. I Chronicles 9:14), indicating that Chronicles also stood written. The Old Testament saints regarded these copies of the law of Moses and of

Chronicles as fully authoritative. Should not Bible believers today have the same attitude toward the *it-is-written* copies of the Old Testament?

Other uses of the Qal passive participle כָּתוּב (*kathuv*) are equally instructive. Joshua 1:8; 8:31, 34; and 23:6 use כָּתוּב (*kathuv*) to refer to what is written in the law. I Chronicles 29:29 uses כָּתוּב (*kathuv*) of the books of Samuel. II Chronicles 32:32 uses the same Qal passive participle of a portion of Isaiah dealing with King Hezekiah (Isaiah 36-39). II Chronicles 33:19 uses כָּתוּב (*kathuv*) of what is written in "the sayings of the seers," that is, the prophets. Ecclesiastes 12:10 uses it of "what was written in this book [Ecclesiastes], or in any other part of Scripture,"[55] which refers to any of the books that had been written up to the time of Ecclesiastes (Genesis – Samuel, Job, some of the Psalms, some of the Proverbs, and the Song of Solomon). Also, Jeremiah 51:60 uses the Qal passive participle of what had been written in his book about Babylon. The above survey demonstrates that *it is written* refers to all three sections of the Old Testament (the law, the prophets, and the writings), indicating that all of the Old Testament stands written and is preserved.

Jesus' Copy

Ezra, Nehemiah, Daniel, David, Joshua, and others regarded their *it-is-written* copies of the law as the preserved Words of God. Each of these *it-is-written* copies had text identical to the *autographa*. The Old Testament saint could have confidence that God preserved His Words (Psalm 12:6-7).

Now, upon the stage of history, the Author of the Old Testament is made flesh and dwells among men, and what does He say about His copy of the Old Testament? Why, He emphatically teaches that the Old Testament of His day is fully authoritative, accurate, inerrant, and infallible. Several considerations demonstrate the truth of this statement: (1) Jesus repeatedly uses *it is written* of the Old Testament text of His day; (2) Jesus repeatedly quotes or refers to Old Testament passages; (3) Jesus repeatedly quotes or refers to Old Testament numerical passages; (4) Jesus repeatedly makes statements supporting the Old Testament text of His day; and (5) Jesus never once criticizes the Old Testament text of His day.

---

[55] John Gill, *An Exposition of The Old & New Testaments* (London: Mathews and Leigh, 1810, reprinted Paris, Arkansas: The Baptist Standard Bearer, Inc., 1989), IV:628-629.

Chapter 2 *Jesus Received the Old Testament*

JESUS REPEATEDLY SAYS IT IS WRITTEN OF THE OLD TESTAMENT

The Significance of the Perfect Tense

Jesus recognized the full authority of the Old Testament text of His day by repeatedly quoting the Old Testament text and saying before the quotations, "It is written," or "that are written," or similar words. Jesus uses *it is written* (γέγραπται, the perfect passive indicative third masculine singular from γράφω) to refer to the Old Testament nineteen times. In addition, Jesus also uses *that are written* {from γεγραμμένα (Luke 18:31; 21:22; 24:44), γεγραμμένον (Luke 4:17; 20:17; 22:37; John 6:31, 45; 10:34; 12:14), or γεγραμμένος (John 15:25), all perfect passive participles} eleven times in referring to the Old Testament. Since these words are in the perfect tense, they indicate that something done in the past has its results continue into the present.

Blass and Debrunner say of the perfect tense that it "combines in itself, so to speak, the present and the aorist in that it denotes the continuance of completed action."[56] Dana and Mantey state that the perfect's "basal significance is the progress of an act or state to a point of culmination and the existence of its finished results."[57] Wallace states, "The perfect may be viewed as combining the aspects of both the aorist and present tenses. It speaks of completed action (aorist) with existing results (present)."[58] Wallace, commenting on *as it is written* in Romans 3:10 (καθὼς γέγραπται), says, "This common introductory formula to OT quotations seems to be used to emphasize that the written word still exists. It implies a present and binding authority."[59] Robertson writes concerning

---

[56] F. Blass and A. Debrunner, *A Greek Grammar of the New Testament and Other Early Christian Literature: A Translation and Revision of the ninth-tenth German Edition incorporating supplementary notes of A. Debrunner, by Robert W. Funk* (Chicago: The University of Chicago Press, 1961), 175.

[57] H. E. Dana and Julius Mantey, *A Manual Grammar of the Greek New Testament* (New York: Macmillan, 1957), 200.

[58] Daniel B. Wallace, *The Basics of New Testament Syntax* (Grand Rapids: Zondervan, 2000), 247.

[59] Ibid., 248. While Wallace makes this statement, which argues for the preservation of the Old Testament text, yet he writes elsewhere: "It is demonstrable that the OT text does not meet the criteria of preservation by majority rule—nor, in fact, of preservation at all in some places. A number of readings that only occur in versions or are found only in

Chapter 2 *Jesus Received the Old Testament*

γέγραπται in Matthew 4:7: " 'It was written (punctiliar) and still is on record' (durative)."[60]

Wuest, commenting on the word γέγραπται (*it is written*) in Mark 1:2, states:

> The perfect tense, speaking of an act completed in past time having present results, is used here to emphasize the fact that the Old Testament records were not only carefully preserved and handed down from generation to generation to the first century, but that they are a permanent record of what God said. They are, in the language of the Psalmist, "forever settled in heaven." One can translate, "It has been written, with the present result that it is on record," or, "it stands written."[61]

Lenski states of Jesus' use of γέγραπται (*it is written*) in Matthew 4:4: " 'It has been written' [is in] the perfect tense with the implication: 'and once written, now stands forever.' "[62] Wenham states: "Jesus understood 'It is written' to be equivalent to 'God says.' There is a grand and solid objectivity about the perfect tense γέγραπται, 'it stands written': 'here is the permanent, unchangeable witness of the Eternal God, committed to writing for our instruction.' "[63] Waite, also commenting on Matthew 4:4, says, " 'It is written' is in the perfect tense, meaning it has been written in the past and stands written now, preserved until the present time. So the Lord Jesus Christ AUTHORIZED the Old Testament He had in His

---

one or two early Qumran MSS have indisputable claim to authenticity over against the errant majority. Moreover in many places all the extant witnesses are so corrupt that conjectural emendation has to be employed. Significantly, many (but not all) such conjectures have been vindicated by the discovery of the Dead Sea scrolls. Hence because of the necessity of conjectural emendation the doctrine of preservation is inapplicable for the OT" (Wallace, "The Majority Text Theory: History, Methods and Critique," *Journal of the Evangelical Theological Society*, 37 (June, 1994), 203, 204). How can "the doctrine of preservation" be "inapplicable for the OT" when the New Testament repeatedly states, "It is written" of the Old Testament Scriptures demonstrating "that the written word still exists"? One ought to have his faith in the statements of Scripture that indeed the Old Testament Scriptures are written instead of relying on the statements of the textual critics.

[60] A. T. Robertson, *A Grammar of the Greek New Testament in the Light of Historical Research* (Nashville: Broadman Press, 1934), 895.

[61] Kenneth S. Wuest, "Mark in the Greek New Testament" in *Wuest's Word Studies from the Greek New Testament* (Grand Rapids: Eerdmans, 1975), 1:12.

[62] R. C. H. Lenski, *The Interpretation of St. Matthew's Gospel* (Minneapolis: Augsburg Publishing House, 1963), 144.

[63] John W. Wenham, *Christ and the Bible* (London: Tyndale Press, 1972), 22.

Chapter 2 — *Jesus Received the Old Testament*

hand."[64] In other words, Jesus made it clear that the Traditional Hebrew Old Testament Text is the Word of God. The use of the perfect tense by Christ with the verb *it is written* or with the participle *that are written* indicates that the exact words written in the past by the writers of the Old Testament still existed and stood written in Christ's day and that these very words would be preserved for the ages to come. Such a fact means that the Bible student does not have to venture on a quest to recover or restore the Words of God, but, rather, he simply has to receive them.

A great example of the perfect tense is when Jesus said, "It is finished" (John 19:30). *It is finished* is the perfect passive indicative τετέλεσται and indicates that Jesus' payment for sin was complete and that the payment would stand for the ages to come (see Hebrews 10:10-14). Lenski commenting on John 19:30 states: "Our great Substitute has paid the great price of ransom, paid it to the uttermost farthing . . . the redemptive shedding of his blood, done once for all, is finished and stands as finished forever."[65] Mounce also commenting on John 19:30 says, "The perfect describes an action that was fully completed and has present-day consequences. . . . the ongoing effects are that you and I are offered the free gift of salvation so that we can be with him forever. Praise the Lord. Τετέλεσται."[66] In light of the fact that it is finished, Jesus does not have to go to the cross again: the effects of His finished work on Calvary stand forever. But just as some will not receive by faith that *it is finished* and, therefore, seek to add things to Christ or to adjust the doctrine of Christ, Who is the living Word; so some will not receive by faith *it is written* and, therefore, seek to add to or adjust the written words. This is not to say that all who dispute the impact of *it is written* are unsaved, though some may be, but it illustrates the need for faith to receive *it is written* just as one must exercise faith to receive *it is finished*.[67]

---

[64] D. A. Waite, *Defending the King James Bible* (Collingswood, NJ: Bible for Today, 1992), 33.

[65] R. C. H. Lenski, *The Interpretation of St. John's Gospel* (Minneapolis: Augsburg Publishing House, 1961), 1309.

[66] William D. Mounce, *Basics of Biblical Greek Grammar* (Grand Rapids: Zondervan, 1993), 218.

[67] Just as the Catholics refuse to accept the implication of the perfect indicative of *it is finished* and, therefore, add to the sacrifice of Christ and try to finish the work of salvation on their own; so some refuse to accept the implication of the perfect indicative of *it is written* and, therefore, seek to complete the Words of God on their own through the use of

Chapter 2   *Jesus Received the Old Testament*

The Verses of the Perfect Tense

A List

It is instructive to list the twenty-nine places where Jesus used the perfect passive indicative, γέγραπται (*it is written*), and the perfect passive participles, γεγραμμένον, γεγραμμένα, or γεγραμμένος (*that are written, that is written, which are written, which were written*), as He referred to Old Testament verses. The list denotes by the abbreviation *part.* those verses using the perfect passive participle.

1. Matthew 4:4 refers to Deuteronomy 8:3

2. Matthew 4:7 refers to Deuteronomy 6:16

3. Matthew 4:10 refers to Deuteronomy 6:13

4. Matthew 11:10 refers to Malachi 3:1 or Isaiah 40:3

5. Matthew 21:13 refers to Isaiah 56:7

6. Matthew 26:24 refers to various verses including Psalm 41:9; Isaiah 53:4-9; and Daniel 9:26-27

7. Matthew 26:31 refers to Zechariah 13:7

8. Mark 7:6 refers to Isaiah 29:13

9. Mark 9:12 refers to various verses including Psalm 41:9; Isaiah 53:4-9; and Daniel 9:26-27

10. Mark 11:17 refers to Isaiah 56:7

11. Mark 14:21 refers to various verses including Psalm 41:9; Isaiah 53:4-9; and Daniel 9:26-27

12. Mark 14:27 refers to Zechariah 13:7

13. Luke 4:4 refers to Deuteronomy 8:3

14. Luke 4:8 refers to Deuteronomy 6:13

15. Luke 4:17-19 (part.) is from Isaiah 61:1, 2

16. Luke 7:27 is referring to Malachi 3:1 or Isaiah 40:3

17. Luke 10:26 referring to the law of Moses

18. Luke 18:31 (part.) speaking of "all things that are written by the proph-

---

the Catholic manuscripts Sinaiticus and Vaticanus as well as with the help of Catholic theologians such as Carlos Martini, one of the editors of the Critical Text.

ets concerning the Son of man" refers to a multitude of Old Testament verses

18. Luke 19:46 refers to Isaiah 56:7
19. Luke 20:17 (part.) refers to Psalm 118:22
20. Luke 21:22 (part.) is referring to various verses about the tribulation and the Millennial kingdom
21. Luke 22:37 (part.) is from Isaiah 53:12
22. Luke 24:44 (part.) wherein Christ speaks of the things "which were written in the law of Moses, and in the prophets, and in the psalms, concerning" Himself and is referring to a multitude of Old Testament verses
23. Luke 24:46 speaks of Christ's suffering and rising from the dead and refers to a multitude of Old Testament verses
24. John 6:31 (part.) is from Psalm 78:24-25
25. John 6:45 (part.) is from Isaiah 54:13 and may also refer to Micah 4:1-4 and Jeremiah 31:34
26. John 8:17 is from Deuteronomy 17:6 and 19:15
27. John 10:34 (part.) is from Psalm 82:6
28. John 12:14 (part.) refers to Zechariah 9:9
29. John 15:25 (part.) is from Psalm 35:19 and 69:4

Luke 18:31 & 24:44

Jesus refers to all three divisions of the Old Testament: the law, the prophets, and the writings. Of particular note are Luke 18:31 and 24:44 where Jesus refers to passages written in the law of Moses, the prophets, and the psalms that speak of Him. The Old Testament is full of verses about Christ. In fact, Jesus says of the Scriptures, "They are they which testify of Me" (John 5:39) meaning that the Old Testament is full of testimony to Christ. After Christ arose, He walked with two disciples to Emmaus, "and beginning at Moses and all the prophets, He expounded unto them in all the scriptures the things concerning Himself" (Luke 24:27). Christ's exposition involved a multitude of Old Testament verses. A. T. Pierson "affirmed that there are over 300 prophecies" in the Old Testa-

Chapter 2   *Jesus Received the Old Testament*

ment concerning Christ.[68] Indeed, Acts 10:43 teaches that all the prophets give witness to Jesus.

The things concerning himself in Luke 24:27 is not limited to Old Testament Messianic prophetic verses. For instance, many verses speak of the Angel of the Lord Who was a pre-incarnate appearance of Christ.[69] The Bible also teaches that the ceremonial law of the Old Testament points to Christ (Colossians 2:16-17 and Hebrews 10:1), which involves a large percentage of the books of Exodus, Leviticus, Numbers, Deuteronomy, and even more since the prophets also spoke of the law. Furthermore, Christ is of the seed of Abraham (Hebrews 2:16) and of the root and offspring of David (Revelation 22:16) and since the Old Testament repeatedly mentions Abraham and David, then this leads to another multitude of Old Testament verses that concern Christ.[70]

Luke 21:22

In addition to the Christological verses, Jesus states that all prophetic verses stand written. In Luke 21:22 Jesus says, "All things which are written may be fulfilled" referring to all of the prophetic verses of the Old Testament, not just Messianic prophecy. Jesus says that all of the verses about Him as well as all prophetic verses stand written; that is, Jesus teaches that all of these things that were written in the past still stood written in His day as they had been originally written. Jesus' statement in Luke 21:22 encompasses verses from every part of the Old Testament: the law (e.g., Genesis 49:10); the prophets (e.g., Jeremiah 23:5-6); and the writings (e.g., Psalm 22). These verses include prophetic passages (e.g., Isaiah 53), historic passages (e.g., Joshua 5:13-15), and poetic passages (e.g., Psalm 2). These verses are in the oldest book of the Old Testament,

---

[68] Herbert Lockyer, *All the Messianic Prophecies of the Bible* (Grand Rapids: Zondervan, 1973), 17, 21.

[69] See Thomas M. Strouse, *But God Meant It Unto Good: An Exegetical Commentary on Genesis* (Virginia Beach: Tabernacle Baptist Theological Press, 1999), 98.

[70] Edward Glenny, who argues that God only preserved doctrinal content as opposed to all the words, states that Jesus "is the One to Whom all the OT points (Luke 24:25-27, 44-46)" (Glenny, 87). While his assessment of Jesus and the Old Testament is correct, he fails to connect these verses with the fact that Jesus said that these things are written. Therefore, it is not merely the doctrinal content that is preserved, but the actual Words that were written in the past and, therefore, still stand written today. It is evident that Glenny teaches that not all the words are preserved when he states about I Samuel 13:1: "At least one of the numbers in this verse has been lost" (Ibid., 85).

Chapter 2 *Jesus Received the Old Testament*

Job (Job 19:25), as well as in the most recently completed book of the Old Testament, Malachi (Malachi 3:1). These verses are in the first book of the Old Testament, Genesis (Genesis 3:15), and in the last book of the Old Testament, Chronicles (I Chronicles 17:11-12). These verses are in the shortest book of the Old Testament, Obadiah (Obadiah 15), and in the longest book of the Old Testament, Psalms (Psalm 68:18).

Conclusion

Jesus says, "It is written," or "that are written" concerning many verses and passages of the Old Testament. Can there be any doubt from this one consideration alone that Jesus believed that the Old Testament of His day had the very original words that God first gave? If Jesus looks at the Old Testament in this way, should Bible students treat it in any other way?

JESUS REPEATEDLY REFERS TO OLD TESTAMENT PASSAGES

Jesus' Use of Old Testament Verses

Besides the verses of which Jesus says, "It is written," Jesus frequently refers to other passages from the Old Testament. In referring to these other passages, He displays again that the Old Testament is fully accurate and reliable. It is instructive to put together a list of these verses so that one may comprehend "what is the breadth, and length, and depth, and height" of Jesus' trust in the Old Testament of His day.

1. In Matthew 6:29 Jesus refers to I Kings 10 and II Chronicles 9

2. In Matthew 8:4 Jesus refers to Leviticus 14

3. In Matthew 9:13 Jesus refers to Hosea 6:6

4. In Matthew 11:23 Jesus teaches Sodom was a real place which had been destroyed, just as Genesis 19 teaches

5. In Matthew 12:3-4 Jesus refers to David eating the shewbread as found in I Samuel 21:1-7

6. In Matthew 12:5 Jesus speaks about the priests working on the Sabbath as related in Numbers 28:9

7. In Matthew 12:7 Jesus refers to Hosea 6:6

Chapter 2 *Jesus Received the Old Testament*

8. In Matthew 12:40 Jesus refers to Jonah 1:17
9. In Matthew 12:41 Jesus refers to Jonah 3:5-10
10. In Matthew 12:42 Jesus refers to I Kings 10:1-13 and II Chron. 9:1-12
11. In Matthew 13:14-15 Jesus refers to Isaiah 6:9,10
12. In Matthew 15:4 Jesus refers to Exodus 20:12; 21:17; Leviticus 20:9; and Deuteronomy 5:16
13. In Matthew 15:8, 9 Jesus refers to Isaiah 29:13
14. In Matthew 17:11 Jesus refers to Malachi 4:5, 6
15. In Matthew 19:4 Jesus refers to Genesis 1:27
16. In Matthew 19:5 Jesus refers to Genesis 2:24
17. In Matthew 19:8 Jesus refers to Deuteronomy 24:1
18. In Matthew 19:18, 19 Jesus refers to Exodus 20:12-16; Leviticus 19:18; and Deuteronomy 5:16-20
19. In Matthew 21:16 Jesus refers to Psalm 8:2
20. In Matthew 21:42 Jesus refers to Psalm 118:22
21. In Matthew 22:32 Jesus refers to Exodus 3:6
22. In Matthew 22:37 Jesus refers to Deuteronomy 6:5 and 10:12
23. In Matthew 22:39 Jesus refers to Leviticus 19:18
24. In Matthew 22:44 Jesus refers to Psalm 110:1
25. In Matthew 23:35 Jesus refers to Genesis 4:8, 9 and II Chron. 24:20, 21
26. In Matthew 24:15 Jesus refers to Daniel 9:27 and 12:11
27. In Matthew 24:37-39 Jesus refers to Genesis 6-9
28. In Mark 1:44 Jesus refers to Leviticus 14
29. In Mark 2:25-26 Jesus refers to David eating the shewbread in I Samuel 21:1-7
30. In Mark 7:6-7 Jesus refers to Isaiah 29:13
31. In Mark 7:10 Jesus refers to Exodus 20:12; 21:17; Leviticus 20:9; and Deuteronomy 5:16
32. In Mark 9:12 Jesus refers to Malachi 4:5,6
33. In Mark 10:3-5 Jesus refers to Deuteronomy 24:1
34. In Mark 10:6 Jesus refers to Genesis 1:27
35. In Mark 10:7-8 Jesus refers to Genesis 2:24

Chapter 2 — *Jesus Received the Old Testament*

36. In Mark 10:19 Jesus refers to Exodus 20:12-16; Leviticus 19:18; and Deuteronomy 5:16-20
37. In Mark 12:10-11 Jesus refers to Psalm 118:22
38. In Mark 12:26 Jesus refers to Exodus 3:6
39. In Mark 12:29 Jesus refers to Deuteronomy 6:4
40. In Mark 12:30 Jesus refers to Deuteronomy 6:5 and 10:12
41. In Mark 12:31 Jesus refers to Leviticus 19:18
42. In Mark 12:36 Jesus refers to Psalm 110:1
43. In Mark 13:14 Jesus refers to Daniel 9:27 and 12:11
44. In Luke 4:17-19 Jesus refers to Isaiah 61:1,2
45. In Luke 4:25-26 Jesus refers to I Kings 17:8-24 and 18:1, 45
46. In Luke 4:27 Jesus refers to II Kings 5
47. In Luke 5:14 Jesus refers to Leviticus 14
48. In Luke 6:3-4 Jesus refers to David eating the shewbread as found in I Samuel 21:1-7
49. In Luke 10:12 Jesus teaches that Sodom had been destroyed just as Genesis 19 teaches
50. In Luke 10:26-27 Jesus refers to Deuteronomy 6:5; 10:12; and Leviticus 19:18
51. In Luke 11:29,30 Jesus refers to Jonah 1:17
52. In Luke 11:31 Jesus refers to I Kings 10:1-13 and II Chronicles 9:1-12
53. In Luke 11:32 Jesus refers to Jonah 3:5-10
54. In Luke 11:49 Jesus could be referring to II Chronicles 36:15, 16
55. In Luke 11:51 Jesus refers to Genesis 4:8-9 and II Chronicles 24:20-21
56. In Luke 12:27 Jesus referred to I Kings 10 and II Chronicles 9
57. In Luke 17:26-27 Jesus refers to Genesis 6-9
58. In Luke 17:28-29 Jesus refers to Genesis 19
59. In Luke 17:32 Jesus refers to Genesis 19:26
60. In Luke 18:20 Jesus refers to Exodus 20:12-16; Leviticus 19:18; and Deuteronomy 5:16-20
61. In Luke 20:37-38 Jesus refers to Exodus 3:6
62. In Luke 20:42-43 Jesus refers to Psalm 110:1

Chapter 2 — Jesus Received the Old Testament

63. In John 3:14 Jesus refers to Numbers 21:8-9
64. In John 6:32 Jesus refers to Exodus 16
65. In John 7:22 Jesus refers to Leviticus 12:3
66. In John 19:28 Jesus refers to Psalm 69:21

Jesus refers directly to Genesis, Exodus, Leviticus, Numbers, Deuteronomy, I Samuel, I Kings, II Kings, I Chronicles, II Chronicles, Psalms, Isaiah, Daniel, Hosea, Jonah, and Malachi. This list of books covers the first (Genesis) and last books (Chronicles) of the Hebrew Old Testament. This list is also from all three parts of the Old Testament: the law (Genesis to Deuteronomy); the prophets (I Samuel, I Kings, II Kings, Isaiah, Hosea, Jonah, and Malachi); and the writings (Psalms, Daniel, I Chronicles, and II Chronicles). In fact, in one verse Jesus refers to both the first and last books of the Old Testament at one time (Matthew 23:35 and Luke 11:51 where He refers to Genesis 4:8-9 and II Chronicles 24:20-21). Jesus regards every part of the Old Testament as authoritative.

Jesus' Authentication of Old Testament Events

Jesus also authenticates some of the most disputed events of the Old Testament. Although the critics often treat these events as myths, Jesus treats them as factual. These events include:

1. Creation (Matthew 19:4 referring to Genesis 1:27);
2. Adam and Eve (Matthew 19:4-5 referring to Genesis 1:27 and 2:24);
3. The slaying of Abel (Matthew 23:35 referring to Genesis 4:8-9);
4. The flood in Noah's day (Matthew 24:37-39 and Luke 17:26-27 referring to Genesis 6-9);
5. The existence and destruction of Sodom (Matthew 11:23 and Luke 17:28-29 referring to Genesis 19);
6. The turning of Lot's wife into a pillar of salt (Luke 17:32 referring to Genesis 19:26);
7. The burning bush (Mark 12:26 referring to Exodus 3:6);
8. The miracle of the manna (John 6:32 referring to Exodus 16);
9. The healing wrought by those who looked at the brazen serpent (John 3:14 referring to Numbers 21:8-9);
10. Moses as the human author of Genesis (Mark 10:2-9 referring to Genesis 1:27; 2:24);

11. The greatness of Solomon (Matthew 6:29 referring to I Kings 10 and II Chronicles 9);

12. The historicity of the Queen of Sheba (Matthew 12:42 referring to I Kings 10:1-13 and II Chronicles 9:1-12);

13. The miraculous supply of meal and oil for the feeding of Elijah by the widow of Sarepta (Luke 4:25-26 referring to I Kings 17:8-24);

14. The healing of Naaman the leper (Luke 4:27 referring to II Kings 5);

15. Isaiah as the human author of Isaiah (Matthew 13:14-15; Mark 7:6; John 12:38-41 referring to Isaiah 6:9-10; 29:13; 53:1);

16. The historicity of the account of Jonah and the whale (Matthew 12:40 referring to Jonah 1:17);

17. The repenting of the men of Nineveh (Matthew 12:41 referring to Jonah 3:5-10);

18. Daniel as the human author of the last chapters of Daniel (Matthew 24:15 referring to Daniel 9:27 and 12:11).

Jesus believes the Old Testament even when it speaks on controversial matters as well as when it speaks of things that go contrary to human reasoning. Jesus does not dispute these things or claim that they are the result of a scribal error, but He receives them, believes them, and hears them. The people of God should follow the example of Jesus. Gleason Archer wrote:

> Nothing could be clearer than that our divine Saviour believed in the literal truthfulness of the entire Old Testament record, whether those accounts dealt with doctrinal matters, matters of science, or history. He who refuses to go along with the Lord in this judgment stands guilty of asserting that God can err (since Jesus is God as well as Man) and that the sovereign Creator (John 1:1-3) stands in need of instruction and correction by the finite wisdom of man.[71]

May the reader note: Jesus placed His complete confidence in an Old Testament that was the product of years of copying. As one looks at the preserved copy that has come down to this day, he, too, should have complete confidence in all that it teaches, no matter if it be in matters of doctrine, history, or science. May the reader further note: Jesus has complete trust in matters of Old Testament history and science even though they

---

[71] Archer, 25. Again, Archer makes another excellent statement, but he fails to follow his own counsel, for later in his book, as an earlier footnote shows, he alleges scribal errors are in the Old Testament.

Chapter 2 *Jesus Received the Old Testament*

might fall into the category of what some claim is not essential to salvation. One should believe all these things.

Jesus' Confidence in Old Testament Wording

Furthermore, Jesus in Matthew 22:32 demonstrates His complete confidence in the Hebrew Old Testament. In Matthew 22, the Sadducees confront Jesus about the resurrection. In answer to their question, He bases the teaching of the resurrection upon Exodus 3:6 where the Hebrew implies the present-tense nature of the relationship between God and Abraham, Isaac, and Jacob.[72]

A literal translation of Exodus 3:6 might be: "And He said, I the God of thy father, the God of Abraham, the God of Isaac, and the God of Jacob. And Moses hid his face because he was afraid because of looking upon God." In the Hebrew, it is necessary to supply a form of the verb *to be* between *I* and *the God*. The need to supply a *to be* verb is not unusual in Hebrew or Greek and the context would determine if the form should be past, present, or future.[73] Since Abraham, Isaac, and Jacob had died some time ago, then the only two possibilities for the supplied form of *to be* are the present tense *am* or the past tense *was*. The context of Exodus 3 demands the use of the present tense because (1) Exodus 3:14 states that God is the I AM and is, therefore, ever present; (2) Exodus 3:15 states that "the God of Abraham, the God of Isaac, and the God of Jacob, hath sent" Moses to the Israelites and, therefore, God was still the God of Abraham, Isaac, and Jacob when He appeared to Moses even though Abraham, Isaac, and Jacob had been dead for some years; and (3) Exodus 3:16 states that "the God of Abraham, the God of Isaac, and the God of Jacob, appeared unto" Moses therefore teaching again that He was still the God of Abraham, Isaac, and Jacob at the time that He appeared to Moses.

---

[72] It is interesting that Jesus did not refer to one of the clear passages in the Old Testament about the resurrection (Job 19:25-26; Isaiah 26:19; Daniel 12:2). Rather, Jesus uses a verse from Moses, which in the absence of Jesus' teaching, few would use to teach the resurrection. Jesus use of Exodus 3:6 to teach the resurrection shows the marvelous depth of Scripture.

[73] Kelly states: "Sentences that employ independent personal pronouns as subjects [which is the case with Exodus 3:6] will often be verbless sentences (with the verb "to be" understood)" (Page H. Kelly, *Biblical Hebrew An Introductory Grammar* (Grand Rapids: Eerdmans, 1992), 52).

Chapter 2 *Jesus Received the Old Testament*

Furthermore, Jesus uses the present tense in Matthew 22:32 (εἰμι, *am*, a present indicative verb). That is, Jesus does not leave the verb unsupplied, but directly uses the present indicative form of *to be*. Jesus has such confidence in the preserved Hebrew Old Testament text of His day that He bases the important doctrine of the resurrection on the fact that the Hebrew text implied the use of the present tense form of *to be*. Archer points out: "From the present tense implied by the Hebrew verbless clause, our Lord drew the deduction that God would not have described Himself as the God of mere lifeless corpses moldering in the grave but only of living, enduring personalities enjoying fellowship with Him in glory."[74]

Jesus was not concerned that somewhere in the copying process the verb for *was* had originally been in the text, but had been lost, which if the verb had been *was*, it would have destroyed His argument about the resurrection. The Sadducees did not argue about the use of the present tense by Jesus, thereby indicating that they too held to the present tense being the correct understanding based on the preserved Hebrew Old Testament. God is, present tense, the God of Abraham, Isaac, and Jacob and, therefore, is not the God of the dead, but the God of the living. Van Oosterzee says, "Would not God be ashamed to name Himself centuries after their decease a God of wasting corpses? Impossible! Then He would at all events have had to say, 'I *have been* the God of Abraham, Isaac, and Jacob.' "[75]

Jesus' Revelation of Old Testament Preservation

But what is even more astounding about Matthew 22:32 is that in the previous verse Jesus says, "But as touching the resurrection of the dead, have ye not read that which was spoken unto you by God, saying" (Matthew 22:31). Matthew 22:31 teaches that the words of Exodus 3:6, though spoken by God to Moses over 1500 years earlier, not only had a message for Moses, but were also intended for the Sadducees of Christ's day! Woudstra, in commenting on Matthew 22:31, observes: "Through the medium of Scripture the words of God originally spoken to Moses under the solemn circumstances of the burning bush are also spoken to the

---

[74] Archer, 22.

[75] J. J. Van Oosterzee, *The Gospel According to Luke in Commentary on the Holy Scriptures: Critical, Doctrinal, and Homiletical, with Special Reference to Ministers and Students*, ed. John Peter Lange, trans. Philip Schaff (Grand Rapids: Zondervan, n.d.), 310.

Sadducees."[76] Since the inspired words God gave to Moses had to speak to the Sadducees of Christ's day, then God insured the preservation of those words. Herein is an illustration that inspiration demands preservation.

By the same reasoning, since "whatsoever things were written aforetime were written for our learning, that we through patience and comfort of the scriptures might have hope" (Romans 15:4), then all of the inspired words of the Old Testament must be preserved for the people of God in this day and age (see also Romans 4:23-24; I Corinthians 9:9-10; 10:6, 11; and II Timothy 3:16-17). These verses demonstrate that one of God's purposes in giving the inspired words of the Old Testament is that these words would survive for the people of God. In other words, inspiration demands preservation. Today's Bible students can have full confidence that God has preserved His Words to this very day. Later, this book will delve more fully into the subject of inspiration demanding preservation.

For now, the point of this section is that Jesus repeatedly refers to Old Testament passages and He did so in such a way as to demonstrate His complete confidence in the Old Testament. But not only did Jesus repeatedly refer to Old Testament passages, but He also repeatedly referred to Old Testament numbers.

JESUS REPEATEDLY REFERS TO OLD TESTAMENT NUMERICAL PASSAGES

List of Numbers

Jesus reveals that "the very hairs of your head are all numbered" (Luke 12:7). Would such a God, Who has all of one's hairs numbered, allow the numbers of the Old Testament to be lost? Would the God, Who has magnified His Word above all His name (Psalm 138:2), take greater care of the numbers of one's hairs than He takes for the numbers in His Own Word? It cannot be. In fact, from the manner in which Jesus refers to the numbers of the Old Testament, it is obvious that Jesus regards these numbers as accurate and fully authoritative. It is instructive to examine a

---

[76] Marten H. Woudstra, "The Inspiration of the Old Testament" in *The Bible – The Living Word of Revelation*, ed. Merrill C. Tenney (Grand Rapids: Zondervan, 1968), 137.

Chapter 2 — *Jesus Received the Old Testament*

list of the Old Testament numbers in which Jesus expresses the fullest confidence.

1. One

> In Mark 12:29 Jesus refers to Deuteronomy 6:4 about one Lord.
>
> In Matthew 19:5-6 and Mark 10:8 Jesus refers to Genesis 2:24 about one flesh.

2. Two

> In Matthew 18:16 and John 8:17 Jesus refers to Deuteronomy 17:6; 19:15 and other verses about testimony being established in the mouth of two or three witnesses.
>
> In Matthew 19:5-6 and Mark 10:8 Jesus refers to Genesis 2:24 about the twain shall be one flesh.

3. Three

> In Matthew 12:40 Jesus refers to Jonah 1:17 about Jonah being three days and three nights in the belly of the whale.
>
> In Matthew 18:16 Jesus refers to Deuteronomy 17:6 and other verses about testimony being established in the mouth of two or three witnesses.
>
> In Luke 4:25 Jesus refers to I Kings 18:1, 45 about heaven being shut up for three years and six months.

4. Twelve

> In Matthew 19:28 and Luke 22:30 Jesus refers to Genesis 49:28; Exodus 24:4; 28:21; 39:14; Joshua 3:12; 4:8; I Kings 18:31; Ezra 6:17; and Ezekiel 47:13 about the 12 tribes of Israel.

Reception of Numbers

Jesus

Jesus never corrects a number from the Old Testament. Jesus' lack of criticism is in direct contrast to many a Bible teacher and commentator of this day. Men would be far wiser to follow the example of Jesus in not questioning the numbers of the Bible.

Chapter 2 — *Jesus Received the Old Testament*

Ninevites

The people of Nineveh were very wise not to question the number God gave to Jonah when Jonah told them, "Yet forty days, and Nineveh shall be overthrown" (Jonah 3:4). Humanly speaking, Jonah's statement must have seemed incredible because

> the city was about sixty miles in circumference. . . . It was much larger than Babylon. The walls of Nineveh were one hundred feet high; they were broad enough to allow three chariots to ride abreast. It had 1,500 lofty towers. Since there were more than 120,000 children in the city (4:11), it has been estimated that the city boasted a million inhabitants.[77]

Not only this, but Jonah also says that Nineveh would be overthrown wherein he uses the same word that God used of the overthrow of Sodom (Genesis 19:21, 25, 29), possibly indicating a supernatural destruction of the city. The wording seems to indicate that no visual threat to the city existed at that time, such as an army waiting to invade. The overthrowing of Nineveh in "yet forty days" did not seem humanly possible, but the people received, believed, and heard this number. Therefore, they repented and God saved them. Men are wise not to question the numbers of the Bible.

Abraham

When God told Abraham that his seed would be as the number of the stars of heaven (Genesis 15:5), it did not seem possible because at that time Abraham had no children (Genesis 16:1). Abraham did not rely on his faulty human understanding but, instead, believed God and it was counted unto him for righteousness (Genesis 15:6). Are not men wise simply to hear, that is, to receive and to believe, the numbers of the Bible?

Rejection of Numbers

Hananiah and the King's Servant

On the other hand, those who questioned the numbers of the Bible were never wise. When the false prophet Hananiah indirectly disputed

---

[77] Charles Feinberg, *The Minor Prophets* (Chicago: Moody, 1982), 143.

Jeremiah's prophecy of the seventy year Babylonian captivity, he died shortly thereafter (Jeremiah 25:11; 28:1-4, 10-17). Likewise, when a servant of the king questioned a number that Elisha gave as the Word of the Lord, he, too, died shortly thereafter (II Kings 7:1-2, 17-20). In some cases, questioning a number can be deadly.

Moses and Peter

In other cases, questioning a number resulted in God strongly rebuking the questioner. For instance, when God told Moses that the children of Israel would eat quail for a whole month, Moses was incredulous. Therefore, the Lord rebuked him (Numbers 11:19-23). It was not wise for Moses to question God. Although Moses had shown great faith in the past (e.g., Exodus 14:13), here he shows a lack of faith.

At this point it is very important to pause and to emphasize that the numbers that Hananiah, the king's servant, and Moses questioned, were not directly connected with doctrinal content or a fundamental of the faith. But in questioning the numbers, they were assaulting the veracity of God as well as His ability to perform as promised, which are very serious matters and explain why Hananiah and the King's servant died and why God rebuked Moses. When Bible believers so lightly treat the numbers of the Bible claiming that some are the result of scribal errors and that no doctrine of the Bible is affected thereby, they had better think again. Since the number they question is not the result of a scribal error, but really is from God, then they too are guilty of questioning the veracity and ability of God. Indeed, doctrine is affected if the numbers are incorrect.

Now back to Moses – though he had great faith on one occasion, yet he demonstrated a lack of faith on another occasion. Another one who did likewise is Peter. Peter expressed great faith in identifying Jesus as the Son of the Living God (Matthew 16:16-17). However, when Jesus spoke of His upcoming crucifixion and resurrection on the third day, Peter would not receive, believe, and hear it (Matthew 16:21-22); therefore, the Lord strongly rebuked him (Matthew 16:23). Some might suppose that Peter was disputing only the statement of Christ's violent death. The fact is, however, that he was also disputing Christ's resurrection on the third day, since Christ's statement mentions this as well.

The cases of Moses and Peter demonstrate how good men can be valiant for the truth at one time and then show unbelief at another time. Men of this day and age display the same tendency. For example, in one passage, a writer makes a great statement about the inspiration and the

Chapter 2 *Jesus Received the Old Testament*

authority of the Bible, but in another passage, he claims that the Bible has a numerical error.[78] As the Lord rebuked Moses and Peter for questioning God's Words in relation to numerical quantities, would He not also rebuke men today for the same thing? As Moses and Peter both ultimately repented of their unbelief, hopefully, many who question God's Words will likewise repent of their unbelief.

Observations About Numbers

May the reader seriously consider several observations about Jesus' use of Old Testament numbers.

Jesus Never Questioned Old Testament Numbers

One observation about Jesus' use of Old Testament numbers is that, unlike Moses, Peter, Hananiah, the king's servant, and some men today, He never questioned a number in the Old Testament. May believers follow Jesus' example.

Jesus Received Old Testament Numbers

Another observation about Jesus' use of Old Testament numbers is that He simply received, believed, and heard them as correct. When Jesus referred to heaven being shut in the days of Elijah for three years and six months (Luke 4:25), He was receiving, believing, and hearing as correct a

---

[78] Gleason Archer is another one who, after making a great statement about the inspiration of the Bible, will claim that it has an error (see earlier in this chapter). E. J. Young does likewise. Young wrote: "On whatever subject the Scripture speaks, it speaks the truth, and one may believe its utterances. . . . If the Bible is the Word of God, then it would follow that all which God has spoken is in accord with truth and fact." But shortly after these wonderful statements, Young suggests changing a date concerning Hezekiah: "Instead of reading 'fourteenth' in the two passages adduced [II Kings 18:13 and Isaiah 36:1], one may simply read 'twenty-fourth.' . . . At the same time one must note that there is no manuscript evidence in its favor" (E. J. Young, "Are the Scriptures Inerrant?" in *The Bible – The Living Word of Revelation*, 104, 112, 113). Why would Young make such wonderful statements on page 104 only to contradict himself on pages 112 and 113? There is no logical explanation, but only to say that both Moses and Peter did similar things when questioning the Words of God, and that it is a sin. Men are sinners who at one time may show great faith, while at another time they may show great unbelief. Archer and Young are not the only ones manifesting this dichotomy. But the fact that many are involved in this dichotomy does not make it right. Indeed, such people should repent.

Chapter 2   *Jesus Received the Old Testament*

chronological statement in the Old Testament where I Kings 18:1, 45 teaches that the drought ended in the third year.[79]

Not only this, but Jesus also received, believed, and heard another chronological statement from the Old Testament, namely the account of Jonah being three days and three nights in the belly of the whale (Jonah 1:17; Matthew 12:40). Many have refused to take the account of Jonah and the whale literally. For example, Baldwin states: "The possibility arises that 'three days and three nights' is an idiom, not to be interpreted literally." After further discussion, she concludes: "A symbolic rather than a literal meaning is uppermost."[80] However, in contrast to Baldwin, Jesus received, believed, and heard the full accuracy of the chronological detail of three days and three nights without question. Whom should one believe, Jesus or Baldwin? When skeptics, or historians, or others question the chronological details of the Old Testament, the Bible student ought to believe Jesus and follow His example in receiving, believing, and hearing the numbers in the preserved text, instead of questioning them.

Jesus Received All Types of Old Testament Numbers

A third observation about Jesus' use of Old Testament numbers is that He did not make a distinction between numbers relating to faith and numbers that are historical. Of the numbers to which Jesus refers, He received, believed, and heard all of them with equal authority. For example, in one passage, Jesus refers to one Lord (Mark 12:29), which certainly has great theological importance concerning the doctrine of God. But then in another passage, Jesus refers to the twain being one flesh (Mark 10:8), which, perhaps in the opinion of some, would merely be an historical detail and, therefore, not as important as the Lord being one Lord. But Jesus does not treat the number relating to one flesh as any less authoritative than the number for one Lord.[81] Jesus treats the Old Testament as a uni-

---

[79] As Jones points out, the chronology of Elijah's drought is based on a non-inclusive reckoning: "The drought which produced a great famine in the days of Elijah was said to have lasted three years and six months, but the same period is also referred to as having been three years, not four as would be demanded by inclusive reckoning (I Ki. 17:1; 18:1, c Luk. 4:25; Jam. 5:17)" (Floyd Nolen Jones, *Chronology of the Old Testament: A Return to Basics* (The Woodlands, TX: KingsWord Press, 1999), 125).

[80] Joyce Baldwin, *Jonah* in *The Minor Prophets*, vol. 2, ed. Thomas Edward McComiskey (Grand Rapids: Baker, 2000), 566.

[81] In fact, the Gospels give two accounts of Jesus referring to the one flesh (Matthew 19:5 and Mark 10:8), whereas only once do they give the account of Jesus mentioning one

form whole, with all parts equal, which is exactly what the Bible teaches about itself, for "all scripture is given by inspiration of God" (II Timothy 3:16). The theological parts of the Bible are not somehow more inspired than the historical or scientific parts of the Bible: all parts are equally inspired and, therefore, equally authoritative. The rest of II Timothy 3:16 states: "And is profitable for doctrine, for reproof, for correction, for instruction in righteousness."

Diminution of Numbers

In spite of the teaching concerning the inspiration of the Bible, some regard the historical passages of the Bible as less reliable than the theological passages. The historical passages often contain numbers; therefore, in regarding the historical passages as less reliable than the theological passages, a diminution of the numbers in those historical passages occurs.

Fuller

Harold Lindsell in summarizing Daniel Fuller's position concerning the Bible says,

> The "slight corrective" Fuller proposed to Warfield's view "is to understand that verbal plenary inspiration involves accommodation to the thinking of the original readers in non-revelational matters" [e.g., historical details]. In other words, nonrevelational Scripture has errors in it; revelational Scripture [that is, when Scripture presents matters of faith] can be fully trusted.[82]

One might expect someone from Fuller Theological Seminary to hold such a position, but what is disturbing is that some Fundamentalists are coming very close to the very same position.

Lord (Mark 12:29). If one were to go only by the numbers, sort to speak, he might reason that the Gospels present Jesus as giving more credence to the historical number as opposed to the theological number. Of course, the author does not subscribe to this, but merely mentions it to show the ridiculous nature of those who try to make a distinction between matters of history and science as opposed to matters of faith.

[82] Harold Lindsell, *The Battle for the Bible* (Grand Rapids: Zondervan, 1977), 113.

Chapter 2   *Jesus Received the Old Testament*

Glenny

For example, W. Edward Glenny of Central Baptist Theological Seminary while arguing against the preservation of the actual words of the *autographa* says, "God has providentially preserved the text of Scripture through history so that none of its doctrinal content is lost or affected adversely."[83] As Chapter One of this book demonstrates, Glenny questions several chronological passages in the Old Testament. While admitting that God has not preserved these chronological passages, Glenny argues for the preservation of the doctrinal content. In other words, some parts of the Bible are somehow less important than other parts, and these supposed lessor parts of the Bible need not be preserved. Such an attitude toward the Words of God is not substantiated by II Timothy 3:16, which teaches the profitability of all Scripture. Nor is Glenny's attitude substantiated by the Words of Jesus Who says, "Man shall not live by bread alone, but by every word that proceedeth out of the mouth of God" (Matthew 4:4). Jesus teaches that man needs every word, not just the doctrinal content. In light of Jesus' statement in Matthew 4:4 and in light of how Jesus treats the Old Testament, regarding both historical and theological passages as equally authoritative, one should believe that every Word of God is available to men today.

But herein is a question for those who claim that doctrinal content has been preserved, whereas chronological content has not been: if God can providentially preserve the doctrinal content of Scripture, then why could He not also providentially preserve the chronological content? The one is no harder than the other. But to believe that God has also preserved the chronological content of Scripture may involve more faith, especially in the face of unbelieving archaeology with its "finds" that contradict the Bible. Herein may be the real crux of the problem: a lack of faith. It is high time that those who call themselves Bible believers to walk by faith and not by sight (II Corinthians 5:7).

Sadly, some unbelievers demonstrate a greater reception of the preserved text than do some of the saved. For example, Moshe Eisemann, a rabbi and, therefore, perhaps not saved, has written commentaries on I and II Chronicles[84] wherein he does not question a single letter of the Tradi-

---

[83] Glenny, 95.

[84] Eisemann, Moshe. *I Chronicles / A New Translation with a Commentary Anthologized from Talmudic, Midrashic and Rabbinic Sources*. Brooklyn, NY: Mesorah Publications, ltd., 1987; and *II Chronicles / A New Translation with a Commentary An-*

Chapter 2 *Jesus Received the Old Testament*

tional Hebrew Text. How can it be that an apparent unbeliever will receive all the letters of the preserved text of I and II Chronicles, whereas declared Bible believers will not? This ought not to be. Dunnet observes: "For the rabbis Scripture was homogeneous; it contained no contradictions, and differences were only apparent."[85] This is how Bible believers should approach the Bible as well. In fact, if anyone should defend every letter of the preserved text, it ought to be the Fundamentalists.

JESUS REPEATEDLY VALIDATES THE OLD TESTAMENT

Through usage of the phrase *it is written*, quotations of various Old Testament verses, and references to numerical passages from the Old Testament; Jesus gives clear testimony to the authority and accuracy of the Old Testament. But Jesus' testimony to the accuracy of the Old Testament does not stop here, for He gives "heaps upon heaps" of testimony sufficient to slay a thousand critics (Judges 15:16). In addition to all the times where Jesus refers directly to the Old Testament, He also makes general statements about the Old Testament that testify greatly to its authority and accuracy, thereby validating the Old Testament. Some of the verses wherein Jesus validates the Old Testament are Matthew 5:17-18; 24:35; Mark 13:31; Luke 16:17; 21:33; 24:25; John 10:35 and 17:17.

Matthew 5:17-18

Fulfil the Law and the Prophets

In Matthew 5:17 Jesus says, "Think not that I am come to destroy the law, or the prophets: I am not come to destroy, but to fulfil." Jesus came to fulfil the law and the prophets. The prophets gave inspired commentary upon the law, and hence the connection between the law and the

---

thologized from Talmudic, Midrashic and Rabbinic Sources. Brooklyn, NY: Mesorah Publications, ltd., 1992.

[85] Walter M. Dunnett, *The Interpretation of Holy Scripture* (Nashville: Thomas Nelson, 1984), 43.

Chapter 2 *Jesus Received the Old Testament*

prophets. *The law and the prophets*[86] encompasses the entire Old Testament (Matthew 7:12; 11:13; 22:40; and Luke 16:16). Jesus, therefore, is the fulfillment of the Old Testament. He is the One of Whom the Old Testament Scriptures testify (John 5:39).

The word for *fulfil*, πληρῶσαι from πληρόω, is an aorist active infinitive and means " 'to fulfil a demand or claim.' "[87] Jesus came to fulfil the demands and claims of the law and the prophets. Because Jesus is perfect, He fulfills the demands of the law. Because Jesus is the Messiah, He fulfills the prophecies of the Old Testament. Also, because Jesus is the Lamb of God, He fulfills the types in the law (Colossians 2:16-17; Hebrews 10:1). Jesus came to fulfil the law and the prophets.

Not to Destroy

Furthermore, Jesus did not come to destroy the law or the prophets. The word for *destroy*, καταλῦσαι, is an aorist active infinite from καταλύω and means "to dissolve, demolish, destroy, or throw down."[88] Jesus did not come to dissolve, or to destroy, or to throw down any part of the Old Testament of His day. Simply put: Jesus did not come as a textual critic.[89]

---

[86] While Matthew 5:17 does not specifically mention the writings (cf. Luke 24:44), yet the writings that included Daniel and Psalms both of which have a good amount of prophecy in them and, therefore, could possibly be included in the term *prophets*.

[87] Gerhard Delling, "πληρόω" in *Theological Dictionary of the New Testament*, ed. Gerhard Friedrich (Grand Rapids: Eerdmans, 1993), 6:292.

[88] Zodhiates, 2647.

[89] According to Wenham, "There are four main examples of our Lord's teaching that have been used to illustrate the thesis that He criticized, and so by implication repudiated, parts of the Old Testament" (Wenham, *Christ and the Bible*, 30). If such is the case, then the words of Matthew 5:17 cannot be true and Jesus is a liar and, therefore, unworthy of any trust. The four examples to which Wenham refers are where: (1) Jesus said He was Lord of the Sabbath (Matthew 12:8; Mark 2:28; and Luke 6:5) and, therefore, did not keep the tradition of the elders relating to the Sabbath--but this refers to Jesus' refusal to follow the tradition of the elders and not to Scriptural commands; (2) Jesus cited Hosea 6:6 in Matthew 9:13 and 12:7, "I will have mercy, and not sacrifice" --but inasmuch as this is a quote of the Old Testament how can it be tearing down the Old Testament?; (3) Jesus taught that what goes into a man does not defile him because it passes through into the draught (Mark 7:18-19), which some understand (see *New International Version*) to mean that Jesus is declaring all food clean contrary to the dietary restrictions of Leviticus, which were still in force at this time--but this is not a problem if one follows the Received Text wherein *purging* (καθαρίζον an accusative masculine singular present active participle) refers grammatically to *draught* (ἀφεδρῶνα an accusative masculine singular noun) and, therefore, to the passing of the food through the body, whereas the Critical Text has

Chapter 2 *Jesus Received the Old Testament*

Jesus' attitude toward Scripture is very important and should establish the way in which one approaches the Old Testament today. If the all-knowing, perfect Son of God did not destroy even one verse, or even one word, or even one letter, or even one part of a letter, or even one vowel point of the Old Testament; but let all the parts of the letters and all the vowel points and all the letters and all the words and all the verses stand as accurate and authoritative, then should not Bible students of this day do likewise? Are they truly followers of Christ, or are they not? Let it be the motto of the present-day Bible teacher that he is not come to destroy the law or the prophets.

In the next verse Jesus substantiates that He upholds even the smallest parts of the words of the Old Testament where He says, "For verily I say unto you, Till heaven and earth pass, one jot or one tittle shall in no wise pass from the law, till all be fulfilled" (Matthew 5:18). Jesus' statement in Matthew 5:18 is highly instructive and should be the cornerstone of one's approach to the Old Testament.

For Verily I Say Unto You

Matthew 5:18 starts with *for*, which connects it with the previous verse, giving a reason why Jesus came not to destroy, but, instead, to fulfil. Jesus then gives words of strong affirmation, "Verily I say unto you." For Jesus to make a statement should be enough, but when He precedes that statement by *verily*, it heightens the importance of the statement and should indicate to everyone that Jesus' statement is serious. The word for *verily*, ἀμὴν, is the basis for the English *amen*[90] and means "to be firm, steady, truthworthy" and in Matthew 5:18 "indicates affirmation."[91] Of

---

καθαρίζων a nominative masculine singular present active participle and would function as a nominative absolute referring back to the subject of *He saith* and would mean that Jesus pronounced all meats clean; and (4) Jesus said in the Sermon on the Mount, "But I say unto you" (Matthew 5:22, 28, 32, 34, 39, 44)--but in these cases Jesus was not negating "any of the Old Testament commands but" was showing "their full scope and" stripping "off current misinterpretations of them" (Wenham, 32). An examination of these supposed evidences of Jesus' criticizing the Old Testament reveals them to be a desperate and an unconvincing attempt to overthrow the authority of the Old Testament and the veracity of the Lord Jesus Christ.

[90] William Morris, ed., *The American Heritage Dictionary* (Boston: Houghton Mifflin Company, 1982), 41.

[91] Zodhiates, 281.

course, Jesus knew the Old Testament text would come under attack and, perhaps, because of this, He says, "Verily."

Furthermore, Jesus is the One Who is making this affirmation as He says, "I say." The speaker is not one of the disciples who might be speaking with unguarded zeal to try to win a point. But the Lord Jesus Christ makes this affirmation; therefore, it carries all the authority of the God of the Universe. And the affirmation is "unto you." Who is the *you*? The *you*, according to Matthew 5:1, is the disciples and the multitudes (see Matthew 7:28-29). The teaching of Matthew 5:18 is for the disciples, and disciples today must receive, believe, and hear it. If a man says he is a follower of Jesus, then Jesus' affirmation in Matthew 5:18 ought to settle his view on the Old Testament text. Of course, Jesus knew that some of His very Own disciples would question the accuracy of the Old Testament text and because of this may have deliberately said, "I say unto you."

Till Heaven and Earth Pass

Jesus then states, "Till heaven and earth pass." These words give the extent of the promise. The promise is valid for as long as heaven and earth are in existence. This is a long time and is perhaps one reason why men struggle with believing that the text of the Old Testament can remain intact for all that time. It is rather sad that evolutionists believe that "all things continue as they were from the beginning of the creation" (II Peter 3:4[92]), but that Bible believers will not believe that the Old Testament text has continued. The evolutionist believes a lie while, in this case, some Bible believers refuse to believe the truth!

One Jot or One Tittle

Jesus then speaks of one jot or one tittle. A *jot* refers to the smallest consonant of the Hebrew alphabet, the *yodh* (׳). The word for *jot*, ἰῶτα, is the basis for the English *iota*.[93] *Tittle* (κεραία) many understand to refer to "the little lines, or projections, by which the Hebr[ew] letters in other

---

[92] That II Peter 3:3-7 includes evolutionists amongst the scoffers is evident in that these scoffers reject the evidence for a worldwide flood while arguing for uniformitarianism, both of which are true of evolutionists.

[93] William Morris, 690.

Chapter 2 *Jesus Received the Old Testament*

respects similar differ from each other,"[94] that is, the smallest differences between the consonants. These differences could be a square edge as contrasted to a rounded edge, an overhang as contrasted with no overhang, or a small opening as contrasted with no opening. One can see examples of slight differences by comparing ה (*He*) with ח (*Kheth*); ג (*Gimel*) with נ (*Nun*); ו (*Vav*) with ז (*Zayin*); ב (*Beth*) with כ (*Kaph*); and ד (*Daleth*) with ר (*Resh*). However, the author believes that *tittle* refers to the smallest Hebrew vowel point, *chirek*, which is a single dot; rather than to the small differences between the consonants. The writer bases his reasoning on several considerations.

The first reason is that κεραία can mean *point*. Thayer states that κεραία means "*a little horn; extremity, apex, point*; used by the Grk. Grammarians of the accents and diacritical points."[95] One of Thayer's meanings is that of *point*, which certainly is descriptive of the smallest of the Hebrew vowel points, the *chirek*, which is simply a dot, that is, a point. Thayer also states that Greek grammarians use κεραία of diacritical marks. One of the Greek diacritical marks is a diæresis (¨), which writers place over two vowels to show that one should pronounce the vowels as two separate sounds.[96] An example of a diæresis is in Revelation 19:1 with the word Ἀλληλουϊα. Clearly, according to Thayer, κεραία can refer to a point. Despite this observation, Thayer states that in Matthew 5:18 and Luke 16:17, the Bible uses κεραία "of the little lines, or projections, by which the Hebr. Letters in other respects similar differ from each other, as ח and ה, ד and ר, ב and כ."[97]

Perschbacher states that κεραία means "*a horn-like projection, a point, extremity*; in N.T. *an apex, or fine point*; as of letters, used for *the minutest part, a tittle*, Matt. 5:18; Luke 16:17."[98] It is interesting to note that Perschbacher, a modern-day lexicographer, uses the English word *tittle* to define κεραία. *Webster's* gives as the primary modern-day meaning for

---

[94] Joseph H. Thayer, *A Greek-English Lexicon of the New Testament* (Grand Rapids: Baker, 1977), 344.

[95] Thayer, 344.

[96] William D. Mounce, *Basis of Biblical Greek Grammar* (Grand Rapids: Zondervan, 1993), 11.

[97] Thayer, 344.

[98] Wesley J. Perschbacher, *The New Analytical Greek Lexicon* (Peabody, MA: Hendrickson Publishers, 1990), 236.

the English word *tittle* as "1. A point or small sign used as a diacritical, punctuation, or similar mark, in writing or printing; variously: a. *Obs.* A cedilla b. a tilde c. the dot over *I* or *j* d. a vowel point or accent, as in Hebrew or Arabic."[99] In addition to giving to tittle the primary meaning of *point, Webster's* connects, among other things, the English word *tittle* with a Hebrew vowel point or accent. In light of the fact that Matthew 5:18 refers to the law, that is, to something written in Hebrew, Webster's definition is most significant. Furthermore, *The Oxford English Dictionary* lists as a meaning for the English word *tittle*, "The dot over the letter *i*; a punctuation mark; a diacritic point over a letter; any one of the Hebrew and Arabic vowel-points and accents; also, a pip on dice."[100] Oxford's definition, also, is most significant in light of Matthew 5:18's reference to the Hebrew Old Testament. Lexically, *tittle* can refer to a vowel-point.

A second reason for understanding *tittle* to mean a vowel-point is a contextual one. While is it true that lexically, *tittle* can refer to part of a consonant, therefore, having a consonantal meaning; it can also have a non-consonantal meaning, referring to a vowel point. An examination of the context of Matthew 5:18 decides the case for *tittle* having a non-consonantal meaning, specifically that it refers to a vowel point. Several aspects of the context lead to the conclusion that *tittle* refers to a vowel-point. One factor is that since the least consonant of the Hebrew alphabet, the *yodh* (י), shall not perish from the Law, then neither will any of the greater consonants (see Luke 16:10). Therefore, no *beths* (ב) or *caphs* (כ), though similar, shall perish from the Law. No *daleths* (ד) or *reshes* (ר), though similar, shall perish from the Law. No *waws* (ו), *zayins* (ז), *gimels* (ג), or *nuns* (נ), though all similar, shall perish from the Law. No *hehs* (ה) or *cheths* (ח), though similar, shall perish from the Law. No *mems* (מ) or *samechs* (ס), though similar, shall perish from the Law. No *seens* (שׂ) or *sheens* (שׁ), though similar, shall perish from the Law.[101]

---

[99] William Allan Neilson, ed., *Webster's New International Dictionary of the English Language*, 2nd ed. (Springfield, MA: G & C Merriam Company, Publishers, 1961), 2656.

[100] "Tittle" in *The Oxford English Dictionary*, 2nd ed., prepared by J. A. Simpson and E. S. C. Weiner (Oxford: Clarendon Press, 1989), XVIII: 159.

[101] Gray observes: "The elder Lightfoot, the Hebraist and rabbinical scholar of the Westminster Assembly time, has called attention to an interesting story of a certain letter yod found in the text of Deuteronomy 32:18. It is in the word *teshi*, to forsake, translated in the *King James* as 'unmindful.' Originally it seems to have been written smaller even

Chapter 2 *Jesus Received the Old Testament*

Since the promise that the least consonant shall not perish guarantees that all the other consonants are safe, then there is no need for Jesus to refer to consonants again with the word *tittle*. This observation bolsters the conclusion that *tittle* is not referring to consonants, but to something else, namely, the vowels.

A second contextual factor showing that *tittle* means a vowel-point comes from the phrase *one jot or one tittle*. This phrase uses the disjunctive conjunction[102] (ἢ *or*), which "denotes an opposition of the ideas expressed by the words or clauses it connects."[103] Therefore, *jot* and *tittle* are different things. Since *jot* refers to a consonant, then *tittle* must refer to something else. In particular *tittle* is not referring to consonants, and if it is not referring to consonants, then in this context it must have a non-consonantal meaning, that is, a *vowel point, accent,* or *diacritical mark*. Strouse observes, Christ's use of "the disjunctive particle ἢ ('or'), indicates that He differentiated between the consonant jot and the vowel tittle. Redundancy would have been meaningless."[104] The previous paragraph

---

than usual, i.e., undersized, and yet notwithstanding the almost infinite number of times in which copies have been made, that little yod stands there today just as it ever did. Lightfoot spoke of it in the middle of the seventeenth century and although two more centuries and a half have passed since then with all their additional copies of the book, yet it still retains its place in the sacred text" (James M. Gray, "The Inspiration of the Bible – Definition, Extent and Proof" in *The Fundamentals – A Testimony to the Truth*, ed. R. A. Torrey, A. C. Dixon, and others [CD-ROM] (Rio, WI: Ages Software, 2000), II:26).

[102] Randolph O. Yeager, *Matthew 1-7* in *The Renaissance New Testament* (Gretna, LA: Pelican Publishing Co., 1986), 370. This work gives a grammatical identification for every word of every verse in the New Testament. Another work that gives a grammatical identification for every word of the Greek New Testament is *Analytical Greek New Testament* by Timothy and Barbara Friberg. The Fribergs' work identifies ἢ in Matthew 5:18 as a coordinating conjunction. May the reader note that *disjunctive conjunction* is a subcategory under the broader category of *coordinating conjunction*. In other words, the Fribergs give a more general classification, whereas Yeager gives a more specific classification.

[103] Neilson, ed., *Webster's New International Dictionary*, 641.

[104] Strouse, "Luke 16:17 – One Tittle," 10. Some may think that the *or* in the phrase *one jot or one tittle* necessitates that *jot* and *tittle* be completely synonymous, but such is not the case, for *or* is a disjunctive particle. Later in Matthew 5:36, Jesus uses the same word when He said, "Thou canst not make one hair white or black." *White* and *black* are not at all synonymous, yet they are connected by the word *or*.

Bishop writes, "The words of Christ, 'jot,' 'tittle' (see Matt. v:18), are no repetition of some common and exaggerated proverb, and they are no tautology" (Bishop, 3). If anyone dare claim that Jesus was using a common exaggerated proverb, then he would, in

demonstrates that "redundancy would have been meaningless." Since one jot will not pass, then neither will any of the other consonants pass; therefore there is no need for Jesus to refer to consonants twice, which would be the case if *tittle* had a consonantal meaning. The disjunctive conjunction means that *tittle* is not synonymous with *jot*; therefore, *tittle* does not have a consonantal meaning. Consequently, when Jesus stated that *one jot or one tittle shall in no wise pass from the law*, He was stating a truth about both the consonants and the non-consonants of the Hebrew Old Testament.

A third contextual factor showing that *tittle* means a vowel-point comes from the expression *till all be fulfilled*, which refers to the fulfillment of prophecy, the exact fulfillment of which depends on the vowels. For instance in Genesis 49:10 is it, "Until Shiloh come," or is it, "Until tribute comes to him," as some would like to read it by changing the vowels? The repointing would remove the Messianic reference in the verse. A Bible version that suggests this change to Genesis 49:10 is *The Holy Bible, English Standard Version*. In I Kings 17:4, a prophecy concerning the feeding of Elijah, is it, "Ravens," or is it, "Arabians," as some would like to read it by changing the vowels? To change the word *ravens* to *Arabians*, would remove the miracle of Elijah's feeding. One commentator who suggests the change to *Arabians* is Frederick W. Farrar.[105]

A fourth contextual factor showing that *tittle* means a vowel-point comes from the expression *one of these least commandments* in the next verse, Matthew 5:19. The least of the commandments depends on the vowels. For example, in Exodus 23:19, is the prohibition against seething a kid in his mother's milk. Some might classify this command as one the least of the commandments. Since one could repoint the word *milk* (חֲלֵב, *chalēb*) to get *fat* (חֵלֶב, *chēleb*), then without the vowel pointing one, thinking that the word was *fat* instead of *milk*, could easily break this commandment and teach others also to break it. If one is not going to break one of the least of the commandments, he must have the vowel

---

essence, be claiming that Jesus "stretched the truth," that is, that He lied. It is best to believe Jesus, instead of claiming that He lied.

[105] Frederick W. Farrar, *The First Book of Kings*, in vol. 2 of *The Expositor's Bible*, ed. W. Robertson Nicoll (Grand Rapids: Eerdmans, 1947), 303. Other verses where repointing would affect the exact fulfillment of prophecy are Job 24:12; 37:23; Psalm 2:9; Proverbs 12:19; 29:14; Isaiah 19:10; 21:13; Jeremiah 8:13; 15:19; 25:24; 48:4; 50:38; Daniel 9:27; Hosea 13:7; Micah 6:9; Zephaniah 3:8; and Malachi 2:3. These verses are all prophecies that some would like to repoint, but repointing would affect the fulfillment, making it impossible to know if they are fulfilled.

Chapter 2 *Jesus Received the Old Testament*

points so that he clearly knows the demands of the commandment. Some might claim that the context could decide what word it should be, but in the case of Exodus 23:19, the context is not decisive for one word or the other. In other words, the only way to know for sure what is the proper command is to have the vowels.

A third reason for understanding *tittle* to mean a vowel-point is a Scriptural reason. God spoke words involving the use of both vowels and consonants (Genesis 22:16; Exodus 4:22; 24:4; Jeremiah 30:2; 36:1-4; Matthew 4:4). These words God's prophets wrote necessitating their having used vowels (Exodus 34:27; Matthew 22:31; Luke 24:25; John 1:23; 12:38; Acts 3:22; 7:48-49; 8:32-34; 28:25; Romans 9:29; 12:19; 14:11; I Corinthians 9:10; Hebrews 3:7; II Peter 3:2). Since Jesus guaranteed the perfect preservation of God's Words, then the vowels must be part of the preserved text (Matthew 24:35; John 10:35; 17:17); therefore, both vowels and consonants are preserved.

The above Scriptural considerations, along with the fact that God's Words are sure (Psalm 93:5; 111:7; II Peter 1:19) and are the sole authority for faith and practice (II Timothy 3:16-17) demand the presence of vowels. If the Hebrew vowels are not inspired, then many words in the Old Testament become uncertain causing the Old Testament to lose its authority.[106] Scripture, then, demands and teaches the inspiration and preservation of the vowels of the Old Testament, which teaching is in exact agreement with understanding *tittle* in Matthew 5:18 to be a vowel point.

A fourth reason for understanding *tittle* to mean a vowel-point is an etymological reason. Gill states: "As the least letter in the *Hebrew* alphabet *Yod* is referred to, the least of the points in use, *Chirek*, is also; between which and the *Greek* word κεραια, used by the Evangelist, is great nearness of sound, and seems to be no other than that point made *Greek*."[107] In other words, Gill indicates that κεραία is a transliteration into Greek of the Hebrew חִירֶק (*chirek*). The author accepts Gill's con-

---

[106] For proof of this statement, see the author's *One Tittle Shall in No Wise Pass: Destroying the Scholarly Myth that God Did Not Inspire the Vowels of the Old Testament* (Newington, CT: Emmanuel Baptist Theological Press, 2009), 187-244.

[107] Gill, *A Dissertation Concerning the Antiquity of the Hebrew Language, Letters, Vowel-Points, and Accents* (London: G. Keith, 1767), 223.

tention as valid.¹⁰⁸ For lexical, contextual, Scriptural, and etymological reasons, the author believes that *tittle* refers to a vowel-point.

It is a common belief that the Masoretes invented vowel points and added them to a consonantal Hebrew text. However, inasmuch as Moses and others wrote the Words of the Lord (Exodus 24:4; Deuteronomy 31:24) and inasmuch as words presuppose vowels and consonants, then vowels were present in the *autographa*. Jesus guarantees that the vowels of the *autographa* were present in His day and will be preserved for future generations.

Jesus does not say, "One concept," or "one idea," or "one thought shall in no wise pass," but in no uncertain terms speaks of the very tiniest parts of the Hebrew words.¹⁰⁹ In spite of the fact that Hebrew words, letters, and vowel points have such small differences, which a person could easily confuse, Jesus reassures one and all that each of these little differences are fully and accurately preserved. One's faith about these things does not have to be in the copyists, but in the God Who guarantees preservation and Who will bring it to pass. One may not have all the answers why differences are in various manuscripts. However, one should have faith in this clear statement of Jesus and trust that God is able to get the Words of God to him and by faith receive, believe, and hear those Words (John 17:8).

Shall in No Wise Pass

After speaking of one jot or one tittle, Jesus says, "Shall in no wise pass." The verb here for *pass*, παρέλθῃ, is the very same verb used earlier in the phrase, "Till heaven and earth pass." Παρέλθῃ is an aorist active subjunctive third person singular from παρέρχομαι. Here it is used "metaphorically" meaning "to pass away" or to "perish." Applying this definition to the second occurrence of παρέλθῃ in Matthew 5:18, it means that

---

[108] For a further discussion on *tittle* etymologically being the *chirek* see the author's *One Tittle Shall in No Wise Pass*, 310-346.

[109] From the language that Jesus uses in Matthew 5:18, it is clear that He is speaking of the actual words. But despite this some say, "This passage is not speaking about the preservation of the exact words found in the *autographa*; it is declaring that all the prophecies in the OT which pointed to Christ will be fulfilled down to the smallest detail" (Glenny, 87). But are not the smallest details of the prophecies of the Old Testament conveyed with words? And if all the words of the *autographa* are not preserved, then how can one determine when the prophecies are "fulfilled down to the smallest detail"?

" 'not even the smallest part shall pass away from the law,' *i.e.* so as no longer to belong to it."[110] Not even one of the smallest letters, or one of the smallest differences between the letters, or one of the smallest vowel points shall perish from or cease to belong to the law.

Perhaps because men would find it difficult to believe that the smallest parts of the Hebrew Old Testament words are preserved, Jesus uses a double negative in the Greek, οὐ μὴ, *no wise*. Zodhiates says of οὐ μὴ: "A double neg[ative] strengthening the denial, meaning not at all, no never. . . . When these two neg[atives] are coupled together they refer to emphatic negations as to the fut[ure], meaning not at all, by no means, construed particularly with the fut[ure] indic[ative] or more commonly with the aor[ist] subjunctive,"[111] which is exactly the tense Matthew 5:18 uses. The double negative with the aorist subjuntive is the exact same construction that Jesus uses concerning the preservation of His Words in Matthew 24:35; Mark 13:31; and Luke 21:33.

Jesus also uses the double negative with the aorist subjunctive in John 6:37 where He promises, "All that the Father giveth Me shall come to Me; and him that cometh to Me I will in no wise cast out." Just as Jesus emphasizes the eternal security of the believer by using the double negative with the aorist subjunctive, so by use of the same syntax, He emphasizes the verbal preservation of the words of the Old Testament. Just as some men have a hard time believing in the eternal security of the soul of the believer, so some men have a hard time believing in the verbal preservation of all the words of the Old Testament. However, Jesus deliberately emphasizes the certainty of these things. Oh, that men would simply believe the Lord, for this would greatly encourage and strengthen their faith.

From the Law

"One jot or one tittle shall in no wise pass from the law." *Law* can have various meanings. That the meaning of *law* must have something to do with the Old Testament is clear, for Jesus speaks of the fulfillment of the law. *Fulfillment* points back to prophecies or statements that need fulfillment: the only statements or prophecies requiring fulfillment from Jesus' historical perspective were in the Old Testament. The question then becomes this: does *law* mean the Mosaic law (i.e., the Pentateuch),

---

[110] Thayer, 382-383.

[111] Zodhiates, 3364.

precepts from the Mosaic law, the entire Old Testament, or some other portion of the Old Testament?

That *law* can refer to the Mosaic law or to precepts in the Mosaic law is clear from Matthew 12:5; 22:36; Luke 2:22, 23, 24, 27, 39; John 1:17, 45; 7:23; 8:5, 17; Acts 6:13; 7:53; 13:39; 15:5; 18:13; 21:20; 23:3; 28:23; Romans 2:12, 13, 15, 18, 20, 23, 25, 26, 27; 3:19, 20; 4:15; 7:1, 5, 14; 8:3; I Corinthians 9:8, 9; 15:56; Galatians 2:19; 3:13, 17, 21, 23, 24; 4:4, 21; Ephesians 2:15; I Timothy 1:8, 9; and Hebrews 7:5, 12, 19, 28; 9:22; 10:1.

However, *law* can also refer to more than just the Mosaic law or parts of it. In John 10:34 Jesus uses *law* to refer to a verse from Psalm 82:6. Likewise the people use *law* in John 12:34 to refer to Psalm 110:4 and, or Daniel 2:44. Comparing John 15:25 with Psalm 35:19 and 69:4; and I Corinthians 14:21 with Isaiah 28:11-12 produce other examples where *law* refers to more than the Mosaic law.

Can one determine from the context of Matthew 5:18 whether *law* only refers to the Mosaic law or to the entire Old Testament? In the verses before Matthew 5:18, Jesus makes some wonderful promises that He bases upon Old Testament verses, none of which are from the law of Moses. In Matthew 5:18 Jesus could be reiterating promises made elsewhere in the Old Testament, none of which are in the law of Moses. Also, in the verses after Matthew 5:18, Jesus refers to passages from both the Mosaic law and other parts of the Old Testament. The list below presents this information with the verse from Matthew 5 in bold followed by verses from the Old Testament that relate to it.

> Vs. 3 **Blessed *are* the poor in spirit: for theirs is the kingdom of heaven**.
>
>> Isaiah 57:15: "For thus saith the high and lofty One that inhabiteth eternity, whose name *is* Holy; I dwell in the high and holy *place*, with him also *that is* of a contrite and humble spirit, to revive the spirit of the humble, and to revive the heart of the contrite ones."
>>
>> Isaiah 66:2: "For all those *things* hath mine hand made, and all those *things* have been, saith the LORD: but to this *man* will I look, *even* to *him that is* poor and of a contrite spirit, and trembleth at my word."
>
> Vs. 4 **Blessed *are* they that mourn: for they shall be comforted**.

Chapter 2 *Jesus Received the Old Testament*

> Isaiah 61:2-3: "To proclaim the acceptable year of the LORD, and the day of vengeance of our God; to comfort all that mourn; to appoint unto them that mourn in Zion, to give unto them beauty for ashes, the oil of joy for mourning, the garment of praise for the spirit of heaviness; that they might be called trees of righteousness, the planting of the LORD, that he might be glorified."

Vs. 5 Blessed *are* the meek: for they shall inherit the earth.

> Psalm 37:11: "But the meek shall inherit the earth; and shall delight themselves in the abundance of peace."

Vs. 6 Blessed *are* they which do hunger and thirst after righteousness: for they shall be filled.

> Psalm 17:15: "As for me, I will behold thy face in righteousness: I shall be satisfied, when I awake, with thy likeness."

> Isaiah 65:13: "Therefore thus saith the Lord GOD, Behold, my servants shall eat, but ye shall be hungry: behold, my servants shall drink, but ye shall be thirsty: behold, my servants shall rejoice, but ye shall be ashamed."

Vs. 7 Blessed *are* the merciful: for they shall obtain mercy.

> II Samuel 22:26-27: "With the merciful thou wilt shew thyself merciful, *and* with the upright man thou wilt shew thyself upright. With the pure thou wilt shew thyself pure; and with the froward thou wilt shew thyself unsavoury."

> Psalm 18:25-26: "With the merciful thou wilt shew thyself merciful; with an upright man thou wilt shew thyself upright; with the pure thou wilt shew thyself pure; and with the froward thou wilt shew thyself froward."

Vs. 8 Blessed *are* the pure in heart:[112] for they shall see God.

---

[112] Wenham points out: "In the Sermon on the Mount, the phrase 'the pure in heart' and the sentence 'the meek shall inherit the earth' are not original to Jesus, but come from the Old Testament (Pss. 73:1; 37:11)" (Wenham, 29).

Chapter 2   *Jesus Received the Old Testament*

> Psalm 24:3-4: "Who shall ascend into the hill of the LORD? or who shall stand in his holy place? He that hath clean hands, and a pure heart; who hath not lifted up his soul unto vanity, nor sworn deceitfully."

Vs. 9 Blessed *are* the peacemakers: for they shall be called the children of God.

> Psalm 34:12-16: "What man *is he that* desireth life, *and* loveth *many* days, that he may see good? Keep thy tongue from evil, and thy lips from speaking guile. Depart from evil, and do good; seek peace, and pursue it. The eyes of the LORD *are* upon the righteous, and his ears *are open* unto their cry. The face of the LORD *is* against them that do evil, to cut off the remembrance of them from the earth."

Vss. 10 – 12 Blessed *are* they which are persecuted for righteousness' sake: for theirs is the kingdom of heaven. Blessed are ye, when *men* shall revile you, and persecute *you*, and shall say all manner of evil against you falsely, for my sake. Rejoice, and be exceeding glad: for great *is* your reward in heaven: for so persecuted they the prophets which were before you.

> Isaiah 66:5: "Hear the word of the LORD, ye that tremble at his word; Your brethren that hated you, that cast you out for my name's sake, said, Let the LORD be glorified: but he shall appear to your joy, and they shall be ashamed."

Vs. 18 For verily I say unto you, Till heaven and earth pass, one jot or one tittle shall in no wise pass from the law, till all be fulfilled.

> Psalm 12:6-7: "The words of the LORD *are* pure words: *as* silver tried in a furnace of earth, purified seven times. Thou shalt keep them, O LORD, thou shalt preserve them from this generation for ever."

> Psalm 119:89: "For ever, O LORD, thy word is settled in heaven."

> Psalm 119:152: "Concerning thy testimonies, I have known of

old that thou hast founded them for ever."

Isaiah 40:8: "The grass withereth, the flower fadeth: but the word of our God shall stand for ever."

Vs. 19 Whosoever therefore shall break one of these least commandments, and shall teach men so, he shall be called the least in the kingdom of heaven: but whosoever shall do and teach *them*, the same shall be called great in the kingdom of heaven.

Psalm 119:4-6: "Thou hast commanded *us* to keep thy precepts diligently. O that my ways were directed to keep thy statutes! Then shall I not be ashamed, when I have respect unto all thy commandments."

Vs. 21 Ye have heard that it was said by them of old time, Thou shalt not kill; and whosoever shall kill shall be in danger of the judgment.

Exodus 20:13: "Thou shalt not kill."

Deuteronomy 5:17: "Thou shalt not kill."

Vs. 27 Ye have heard that it was said by them of old time, Thou shalt not commit adultery.

Exodus 20:14: "Thou shalt not commit adultery."

Deuteronomy 5:18: "Neither shalt thou commit adultery."

Vs. 31 It hath been said, Whosoever shall put away his wife, let him give her a writing of divorcement.

Deuteronomy 24:1: "When a man hath taken a wife, and married her, and it come to pass that she find no favour in his eyes, because he hath found some uncleanness in her: then let him write her a bill of divorcement, and give *it* in her hand, and send her out of his house."

Vs. 33 Again, ye have heard that it hath been said by them of old time, Thou shalt not forswear thyself, but shalt perform unto the Lord thine oaths.

Leviticus 19:12: "And ye shall not swear by my name falsely,

Chapter 2   *Jesus Received the Old Testament*

> neither shalt thou profane the name of thy God: I *am* the LORD."

> Deuteronomy 23:23: "That which is gone out of thy lips thou shalt keep and perform; *even* a freewill offering, according as thou hast vowed unto the LORD thy God, which thou hast promised with thy mouth."

> Psalm 76:11: "Vow, and pay unto the LORD your God: let all that be round about him bring presents unto him that ought to be feared."

> Ecclesiastes 5:4: "When thou vowest a vow unto God, defer not to pay it; for *he hath* no pleasure in fools: pay that which thou hast vowed."

Vs. 34-35 But I say unto you, Swear not at all; neither by heaven; for it is God's throne: nor by the earth; for it is his footstool: neither by Jerusalem; for it is the city of the great King.

> Isaiah 66:1: "Thus saith the LORD, The heaven *is* my throne, and the earth *is* my footstool: where *is* the house that ye build unto me? and where *is* the place of my rest?"

Vs. 38 Ye have heard that it hath been said, An eye for an eye, and a tooth for a tooth.

> Exodus 21:24: "Eye for eye, tooth for tooth, hand for hand, foot for foot."

> Leviticus 24:20: "Breach for breach, eye for eye, tooth for tooth: as he hath caused a blemish in a man, so shall it be done to him *again*."

> Deuteronomy 19:21: "And thine eye shall not pity; *but* life *shall go* for life, eye for eye, tooth for tooth, hand for hand, foot for foot."

Vs. 43 Ye have heard that it hath been said, Thou shalt love thy neighbour, and hate thine enemy.

> Leviticus 19:18: "Thou shalt not avenge, nor bear any grudge against the children of thy people, but thou shalt love thy neighbour as thyself: I *am* the LORD."

> Vs. 45 **That ye may be the children of your Father which is in heaven: for he maketh his sun to rise on the evil and on the good, and sendeth rain on the just and on the unjust.**
>
> Job 25:3: "Is there any number of his armies? and upon whom doth not his light arise?"
>
> Vs. 48 **Be ye therefore perfect, even as your Father which is in heaven is perfect.**
>
> Leviticus 19:2: "Speak unto all the congregation of the children of Israel, and say unto them, Ye shall be holy: for I the LORD your God *am* holy."
>
> Leviticus 20:26: "And ye shall be holy unto me: for I the LORD *am* holy, and have severed you from *other* people, that ye should be mine."
>
> Deuteronomy 18:13: " Thou shalt be perfect with the LORD thy God."

Surely, in the verses before Matthew 5:18, Jesus alludes to verses in the Old Testament that are not in the Pentateuch. In Matthew 5:18 Jesus may refer to verses which are not in the Pentateuch, and in these verses (Psalm 12:6-7; 119:89, 152; Isaiah 40:8) God promises that all of His Words will be preserved, not just the Pentateuch. In the verses following Matthew 5:18, Jesus refers to a mix of verses from both the Pentateuch and other parts of the Old Testament.

Of particular interest is Matthew 5:19, which is very similar in tone to Psalm 119:4-6. Some might believe that since Matthew 5:19 speaks of *the least of these commandments*, it refers to the commandments of the Pentateuch and, therefore, limits Matthew 5:18 to the Pentateuch. However, the use of *therefore*, οὖν, in Matthew 5:19 indicates "that something follows from another necessarily" and "hence it is used in drawing a conclusion."[113] Matthew 5:19, therefore, derives a specific application from the teaching in Matthew 5:18; that is, since one jot or tittle shall in no wise pass from the law, then the least of the commandments is important. In light of this, *commandments* in Matthew 5:19 does not govern the meaning of *law* in Matthew 5:18. Indeed, since Jesus refers to verses

---

[113] Thayer, 463.

Chapter 2   *Jesus Received the Old Testament*

from the Pentateuch, the Prophets, and the Writings before, during, and after Matthew 5:18; then the word *law* in Matthew 5:18 refers to the entire Old Testament.

In addition to the above contextual study establishing that the word *law* refers to the entire Old Testament, a summarization of Matthew 5:17-19 also points to the same conclusion. In Matthew 5:17 Jesus speaks of fulfilling *the law or the prophets*, a reference to the entire Old Testament (see above at beginning of this section on Matthew 5:17,18). Matthew 5:18 starts with *for*, which gives the basis or reason for Matthew 5:17; that is, one jot or one tittle shall in no wise pass from the law till all be fulfilled. If *law* in Matthew 5:18 is referring only to the Pentateuch, then how would Matthew 5:18 serve as the basis or reason for Jesus fulfilling the prophets? Indeed, if *law* is referring only to the Pentateuch, then Matthew 5:18 would be a reason or basis for Jesus only fulfilling the Pentateuch and not the Prophets. In order for Matthew 5:18 to serve as a reason or basis for Matthew 5:17, then *law* must refer to the entire Old Testament.

Lenski makes this observation:

> "The Law" refers to the Torah in the broader sense, namely, the entire Old Testament, for which the fuller term, "the Law and the Prophets," was used in v. 17. It is unwarranted to regard "the Law" as referring only to the legal requirements of the Old Testament, to something found in the Old Testament, a part of it. Every part of that old written Word shall stand, prophecy as well as command.[114]

Matthew 5:19 subsequently draws a conclusion from Matthew 5:18, stating that the least of the commandments is important. In other words, since all of the jots and tittles of the Old Testament will not pass, then even the least of the commandments is important.

The studied conclusion of the author is that *law* in Matthew 5:18 refers to the entire Old Testament, not just merely to the Pentateuch. Jesus, therefore, is speaking of the preservation of every jot and tittle of the entire Old Testament. Jesus promises that every jot and tittle of the Hebrew Old Testament text would be kept from perishing, which very definitely argues for the preservation of the actual words of Jesus' Hebrew Old Testament. The preservation of the words of that Hebrew Old Testament will last till heaven and earth pass, therefore, every jot and tittle that was

---

[114] R. C. H. Lenski, *The Interpretation of St. Matthew's Gospel* (Minneapolis: Augsburg Publishing House, 1963), 208-209.

Chapter 2 *Jesus Received the Old Testament*

in Jesus' Old Testament is still in existence today. How many really believe this? How many, instead of believing this, claim that words are missing from the Old Testament, and, therefore, contradict Jesus' teaching in Matthew 5:18?

Till All Be Fulfilled

The last phrase of Matthew 5:18 is, "Till all be fulfilled." Since parts of the Old Testament speak of the Millennial Kingdom (Isaiah 11), and since some parts speak of the new heaven and the new earth (Isaiah 65:17; 66:22), and since these things await fulfillment; then this assures the preservation of the Old Testament well into the future and that, therefore, the Old Testament text is preserved in this day. Some[115] understand *till all be fulfilled* to mean that all the Old Testament prophecies will be fulfilled down to the smallest detail. However, Matthew 5:18 is not merely arguing for the fulfillment of all the Old Testament prophecies down to the smallest detail. Matthew 5:18 is teaching that every single jot and tittle, which make up the words of the entire text of the Hebrew Old Testament, will endure—not just the jots and tittles in prophetic passages. Jesus received the Traditional Old Testament text of His day, and He promised that not a single jot or tittle would pass from that Old Testament. Therefore, one should receive the Traditional Old Testament text of this day and believe by faith in Matthew 5:18 that every single jot and tittle are preserved therein, that these jots and tittles are the very same jots and tittles of Jesus' Old Testament, and are the very same jots and tittles of the *autographa*. Such a position is based upon receiving, believing, and hearing the promise of Jesus that "till heaven and earth pass, one jot or one tittle shall in no wise pass from the law, till all be fulfilled."

Conclusion

D. Martyn Lloyd-Jones says of Matthew 5:17-18:

> Our Lord Jesus Christ in these two verses confirms the whole Old Testament. He puts His seal of authority, His *imprimatur*, upon the whole of

---

[115] For example, see Glenny, 87. Chapter Six, in the section "Questioning Christ," presents further information about Glenny's contention. James Borland of Liberty University writes: "The emphasis is . . . that not even the least aspect of God's promises would ever fail to be fulfilled by the Almighty God who created and now sustains this magnificent universe" (James A. Borland, "The Preservation of the New Testament Text: A Common Sense Approach," Master's *Seminary Journal* 10 (Spring 1999): 41-42).

the Old Testament canon, the whole of the law and the prophets. Read these four Gospels, and watch His quotations from the Old Testament. You can come to one conclusion only, namely, that He believed it all and not only certain parts of it! He quoted almost every part of it. To the Lord Jesus Christ the Old Testament was the Word of God; it was Scripture; it was something absolutely unique and apart; it had authority which nothing else has ever possessed nor can possess. Here, then, is a vital statement with regard to this whole matter of the authority of the Old Testament.[116]

Jesus had complete confidence that, in spite of copying, nothing was missing in the Words of God. Even though Jesus had a copy of a copy of a copy of the *autographa*, He believed it to be fully authoritative! How many Bible teachers today have this same confidence? If their faith is in Jesus, they ought to have this same confidence. But if their faith is in the shifting-sand opinions of textual critics, then they will be woefully lacking.

Matthew 24:35; Mark 13:31; & Luke 21:33

In Matthew 24:35, Mark 13:31, and Luke 21:33, Jesus says, "Heaven and earth shall pass away, but My words shall not pass away." While this promise of Jesus certainly applies to the preservation of Jesus' New Testament canonical words;[117] this promise also applies to the preservation of Old Testament words, for Jesus spoke in the Old Testament. Jesus, as the Angel of the Lord, spoke on several occasions in the Old Testament. Furthermore, the Bible teaches that the Spirit of Christ worked in the Old Testament prophets. I Peter 1:10-11 says, "Of which salvation the prophets have enquired and searched diligently, who prophesied of the grace that should come unto you: searching what, or what manner of time the Spirit of Christ which was in them did signify, when it testified beforehand the sufferings of Christ, and the glory that should follow." The Spirit of Christ was in the Old Testament prophets testifying to them about the sufferings and glory of Christ. The testimony of the Spirit of Christ to the Old Testament prophets is the Word of Christ and, therefore, is included in the promise of Christ that His Words shall not pass away. Waite states:

---

[116] D. Martyn Lloyd-Jones, "Christ and the Old Testament" in *Studies in the Sermon on the Mount* (Grand Rapids: Eerdmans, 1989), 1:187.

[117] Thomas M. Strouse, "The Translation Model Predicted By Scripture" (Newington, CT: Emmanuel Baptist Theological Seminary, 2000), 9-10.

The Lord is talking of His *Words*, the New Testament. Not the Masoretic Hebrew Old Testament only, but His Words will not pass away. That means the promise extends to the New Testament. I believe, personally that the Lord Jesus was the Source and Author of every Hebrew Old Testament text. He was the Revelator. He is the Word of God. In a very real sense, therefore, His *Words* include the entire Old Testament.[118]

Shall not pass away uses the double negative, οὐ μὴ, as in Matthew 5:18. *Pass away*, παρέλθωσι, is an aorist active subjunctive third person plural from παρέρχομαι, which Matthew 24:35 uses "metaphorically" meaning "to pass away" or to "perish."[119] Παρέλθωσι is from the same root as παρέλθῃ in Matthew 5:18. Matthew 24:35, then, parallels the teaching of Matthew 5:18 and clearly teaches the preservation of the actual Words of God, not merely thoughts, content, or ideas.

Combs understands Matthew 24:35 to be "hyperbolic language," which has "reference to the authority of Jesus' oral words."[120] However, nothing in the context suggests it is figurative or hyperbolic language. Just as heaven and earth will pass away literally (spoken of in the first part of Matthew 24:35), so Christ's Words literally shall not pass away. Indeed, to say that it is hyperbolic language is tantamount to saying that Christ lied. Do "scholars" even realize that in making such a suggestion they are impugning the holy and spotless character of Jesus? Why do "scholars" have such a hard time just simply believing Jesus? Better, it were for them to reject their scholarship and to believe Jesus.

Moreover, if, according to Combs, Matthew 24:35 refers only to the authority of Jesus' oral words, then what authority do Jesus' oral words really have since the oral words have long since passed away? The fact that Jesus speaks of His Words not passing away refers to those words being preserved, and the Words of Jesus that have been preserved are those words that are written in the Bible. Matthew 24:35, therefore, is not speaking of Jesus' oral words, but of His written words, that is, His canonical words. Strouse further notes:

> The words to which He was referring must be His canonical words since they will be the basis for judging mankind. After all, the Lord said, "*He that rejecteth me, and receiveth not my words, hath one that judgeth him:*

---

[118] Waite, 11.

[119] Zodhiates, 3928.

[120] William W. Combs, "The Preservation of Scripture," *Detroit Baptist Seminary Journal* 5 (Fall 2000): 24-25.

the word that I have spoken, the same shall judge him in the last day" (Jn. 12:48). His preserved words are the standard for Christian living in every generation and will be the basis for His righteous judgment in the future.[121]

Luke 16:17

In Luke 16:17 Jesus states, "And it is easier for heaven and earth to pass, than one tittle of the law to fail." This is very similar to Matthew 5:18 and parallels its teaching. Both verses speak of the law, that is, the entire Old Testament, being preserved. Jesus, then, repeats here His teaching of Matthew 5:18. Perhaps He wants to make sure that Bible students notice this teaching. As much as some would like to ignore such instruction, Jesus emphasizes it.

The first part of Luke 16:17 states, "It is easier for heaven and earth to pass." Lenski states that this refers to heaven and earth passing "away in one sweep (παρελθεῖν, aorist)."[122] Only the power of God Almighty will bring about the passing away of heaven and earth in one sweep (Isaiah 65:17). No one else is able to do such a thing. Now since it is easier for heaven and earth to pass, than for one tittle of the law to fail; and since only the power of God can make heaven and earth pass away; and since no one else has such power; then no man, no fallen angel, or even Satan himself can cause a single tittle of the Old Testament to fail. Some believe that, through scribal errors, some things have been lost from the Old Testament, but not according to Jesus. The complete Old Testament will continue to stand in spite of all attacks or mishandling from created beings!

The middle part of Luke 16:17 speaks of the tittle, which refers to the vowel points.[123] The tittle is the smallest little bit of the Hebrew Old

---

[121] Strouse, 9. Elsewhere Strouse writes: "It is utter foolishness to interpret this verse as meaning that the Lord promised to preserve all of His oral words, because He has not done that. He has preserved His canonical words and these words (i.e., the words of written Scripture) will be the standard to which all men should live (at least from the time of the inscripturation of the book of Revelation and on) and by which all men will be judged (Jn. 12:48)!" (Thomas M. Strouse, "Article Review: A review of Combs, William W. 'The Preservation of Scripture' " (Newington, CT: Emmanuel Baptist Theological Seminary, 2001), 7).

[122] R. C. H. Lenski, *The Interpretation of St. Luke's Gospel* (Minneapolis: Augsburg Publishing House, 1963), 841.

[123] For further information, see discussion earlier on Matthew 5:18.

Testament. Jesus is teaching that no human or demonic power is able to cause even the smallest bit of the Hebrew Old Testament to fail. If all anti-God power were concentrated on one small vowel point, it would be impossible for that power to cause one small vowel point to fail! What a promise is this!

The last part of Luke 16:17 uses the word *fail*. *Fail*, πεσεῖν, is a second aorist active infinitive from πίπτω. The verse uses it metaphorically, "meaning to fall to the ground, to fail, become void."[124] Jesus promises that not a single tittle of the Old Testament will fall to the ground and be lost. Again, what a wonderful promise is this! Oh, that men would just receive, believe, and hear these precious promises instead of questioning them. Sadly, through their skepticism, many miss out on the blessings that could be theirs.

Luke 24:25

In Luke 24:25 the risen Christ says to the two disciples on the road to Emmaus, "O fools, and slow of heart to believe all that the prophets have spoken." Jesus rebukes these two disciples for not believing all that the prophets spoke. God has preserved the very words of the Old Testament prophets, and the disciples should have believed all of this written record. Luke 24:25 reveals a couple of things.

First, disciples of the past have sometimes found it hard to believe the Bible (Numbers 11:20-23; Matthew 16:21-23). Likewise, some of the brethren today find it hard to believe certain parts of the Bible. The word for *believe*, πιστεύειν a present active infinitive from πιστεύω, means "to be firmly persuaded as to something."[125] Since the verb is a present infinitive it "can be assumed to be durative,"[126] that is, continuous; therefore, the Lord desires that His disciples continuously believe all that was spoken. The two disciples were having difficulty reconciling the Lord's death with the seemingly contradictory prophecies of His glory (Luke 24:20-21). But in spite of the apparent contradiction, the Lord wanted them to believe. They were continuously to believe, even in the face of apparent contradictions. They were continuously to believe, even in the

---

[124] Zodhiates, 4098.

[125] Zodhiates, 4100.

[126] Robertson, 890.

Chapter 2 *Jesus Received the Old Testament*

face of skepticism. They were continuously to be firmly persuaded of all, all the time. If the Lord wanted that of His disciples in that day, would He expect any less of His disciples in this day? Disciples today face the contradictory sayings of archaeologists, historians, textual critics, commentators, and even Fundamentalist Bible teachers; but in the face of all these contradictory sayings, the Lord expects His disciples to believe all that the prophets have spoken.

Second, just as God rebuked Moses (Numbers 11:21-23), and just as Jesus rebuked Peter (Matthew 16:21-23), so the risen Lord rebukes these disciples for not believing the Bible. When disciples do not believe the Bible, they deserve a rebuke. In fact, Jesus strongly rebukes them by calling them fools. Lenski notes that, with the use of the word *fools*, Jesus "reproves their intellect and intelligence." Lenski further comments: "Unbelief often lays claim to great intellectual powers and penetration; it is in reality the most pitiful and painful ignorance."[127] Unbelieving believers suppose themselves to be so smart, but Jesus calls them fools.

Third, Jesus clearly teaches that His disciples must believe all that the prophets have spoken. Where are the words that the prophets spoke? The *autographa* are non-existent, so where are the disciples of Jesus to find all that the prophets spoke? They are to find the spoken words of the Old Testament prophets in the traditional Hebrew Old Testament, which is based on copies of copies going back to the *autographa*. Although the traditional Hebrew text is not the *autographa*, Christ's disciples should trust this text, for it is an accurate copy of the *autographa*. The word *all* in *all that the prophets have spoken* includes more than just the prophecies about Jesus: it means everything, including statements of chronology, science, and numbers. The true disciples of Jesus must believe everything in the prophets as well as everything else in the Bible. What books make up the prophets? In the Hebrew Bible the prophets are Joshua, Judges, I and II Samuel, I and II Kings, Isaiah, Jeremiah, Ezekiel, and the twelve minor prophets. It is interesting that I and II Samuel and I and II Kings are included in *the prophets*, for these books have some things that some of the brethren have a hard time believing. As the Lord rebuked these two disciples for their unbelief, would He not likewise rebuke those who have expressed unbelief concerning all that the prophets have spoken? It is unpleasing to the Lord of Glory not to believe all that the prophets have spoken.

---

[127] Lenski, 1187.

Chapter 2   *Jesus Received the Old Testament*

John 10:35

In John 10 Jesus disputes with the Pharisees, and in the midst of it, He summons a verse from the Old Testament (John 10:34 quoted from Psalm 82:6) to substantiate His point.[128] After referring to Psalm 82:6, Jesus says in John 10:35, "The scripture cannot be broken." When Jesus said that the Scripture cannot be broken, He was referring to the Traditional Hebrew Text of His day, not the *autographa*, for the *autographa* had long since disappeared. Jesus regarded His copy of the Old Testament as Scripture.

Scripture

The word *scripture*, γραφή, is a singular noun. Generally, the Bible uses γραφή in the singular to refer to a single passage, as opposed to the entire Old Testament (Mark 12:10; 15:28; Luke 4:21; John 13:18; 19:24, 28, 36, 37; Acts 1:16; 8:35; Romans 4:3; 9:17; 10:11; 11:2; Galatians 3:8; 4:30; I Timothy 5:18; James 2:8, 23; 4:5). However, the singular sometimes refers to more than just one passage or phrase of the Old Testament. John 2:22; 7:38, 42; 17:12; and 20:9 all use γραφή to refer to more than one Old Testament verse. In Acts 8:32, γραφή speaks of the overall Scripture from which the eunuch read. Galatians 3:22 says, "The scripture hath concluded all under sin" wherein *scripture* is not referring to one particular verse but to the teaching of the Old Testament in general. I Peter 2:6 uses γραφή to teach that one verse, Isaiah 28:16, is in Scripture. The Bible further uses γραφή in II Timothy 3:16 and I Peter 1:20 to refer to the entirety of Scripture.

---

[128] Concerning John 10:34, Ryle states: "Our Lord's defence of His own language against the charge of blasphemy is very remarkable. It is an argument from a lessor to a greater. If princes, who are merely men are called gods, He who was the eternal Son of the Father could surely not be justly chargeable with blasphemy for calling Himself the 'Son of God' " (J. C. Ryle, *Expository Thoughts on John* (Carlisle, PA: Banner of Truth Trust, 1986), 2:249). Ryle further states: "The expression, 'I said ye are gods,' is drawn from the 82nd Psalm, in which Asaph is speaking of princes and rulers, and their position and duties. Their elevation above other men was so great, and their consequent responsibility for the state of nations so great, that compared to other men, it might be said, 'You are as gods.' A King is called 'the Lord's anointed.' (2 Sam. i. 14.) So 'Ye judge not for man, but for the Lord.' (2 Chron. xix. 6.) Princes and magistrates are ordained of God, derive their power from God, act for God, and stand between the people and God. Hence, in a sense, they are called 'gods' " (Ibid., 250). Also, compare Exodus 7:1 where "the LORD said unto Moses, See, I have made thee a god to Pharaoh: and Aaron thy brother shall be thy prophet."

Chapter 2   *Jesus Received the Old Testament*

Is *scripture* in John 10:35 referring only to the one phrase from Psalm 82:6, or is it referring to the entire Old Testament? Morris, commenting on John 10:35, says, "The singular is usually held to refer to a definite passage from the Old Testament and to Scripture as a whole. Even so, what was true of this passage [Psalm 82:6] could be true only because it was part of the inspired Scriptures and showed the characteristics of the whole."[129] In other words, Morris understands *scripture* to apply to the whole Old Testament. Thayer,[130] Arndt and Gingrich,[131] and *The Theological Dictionary of the New Testament*[132] all understand γραφή in John 10:35 to refer to the entire Old Testament, and it is in this sense that the author understands it. Therefore, Jesus, after quoting a portion of Psalm 82:6 in John 10:34, bases His conclusion about Psalm 82:6 on the general principle in John 10:35 that the Scripture cannot be broken.[133]

Cannot Be Broken

In the Greek, *cannot be broken* is οὐ δύναται λυθῆναι. *Can be* is the translation of δύναται, which is a present middle indicative from δύναμαι, and means "to be able, have power."[134] An aorist passive infinitive (λυθῆναι *broken*) follows δύναται, and in such cases δύναται is "implying

---

[129] Leon Morris, *The Gospel According to John*, revised edition, in *The New International Commentary on the New Testament*, ed. Ned B. Stonehouse, F. F. Bruce, and Gordon D. Fee (Grand Rapids: Eerdmans, 1995), 468.

[130] Thayer, 121.

[131] Ardnt and Gingrich, 166.

[132] Gottlob Schrenk, "γραφή" in *Theological Dictionary of the New Testament*, 1:754,755.

[133] Concerning the word *Scripture*, Wenham makes an interesting observation: "We find cases where 'scripture' is used when one would expect 'God,' and 'God' is used when one would expect 'scripture.' " For evidence of this he points to Romans 9:17, "For the Scripture saith unto Pharaoh, Even for this same purpose have I raised thee up." Wenham comments, "This means simply, 'In the scripture narrative, God says to Pharaoh . . .', but 'scripture' has been personalized to replace 'God.' " Other examples Wenham gives are Galatians 3:8 and Matthew 19:4-5 of which Wenham says, "So truly is God regarded as the author of scriptural statements that in certain contexts 'God' and 'scripture' have become interchangeable" (Wenham, 27, 28). This is an interesting observation and it is substantiated by how attributes of God are attributed to Scripture such as truth (Daniel 10:21); immutability (John 10:35); and holiness (Romans 1:2). Those who attack Scripture are attacking God Who has magnified His Word above all His name (Psalm 138:2).

[134] Zodhiates, "1410. δύναμαι."

Chapter 2 *Jesus Received the Old Testament*

transient or momentary action, either past or pres[ent]."[135] Also, since the negative particle (οὐ) accompanies δύναται, then it is denying that Scripture is able to be momentarily broken,[136] let alone permanently broken. The fact that Scripture cannot be broken speaks of the continuing and abiding quality of the Words of God, which is something that Peter also addresses in I Peter 1:23: "Being born again, not of corruptible seed, but of incorruptible, by the word of God, which liveth and abideth for ever." It is impossible to stamp out any part of the Word of God even momentarily. *The Scripture cannot be broken* is a strong statement for the preservation of the Scripture. The word *broken*, λυθῆναι, an aorist infinitive, means "to loose, loosen what is fast, bound, meaning to unbind, untie," and "by implication, to destroy . . . figuratively of a law or institution, to loosen its obligation, i.e., either to make void, to do away."[137] It is impossible to do away with Scripture – it is indestructible. Note: Jesus said this of the text of His day, by implication, then, the traditional texts in both the Old and New Testaments cannot be broken.[138]

These traditional texts have the words of the *autographa*. Robert Lightner, commenting on John 10:35, states:

> The word "cannot" expresses a Divine and moral impossibility. The point is, Scripture cannot be annulled, dissolved, abrogated, or rendered void because it declares the will and purpose of God. Of equal importance in Christ's statement is the word "broken." By this expression He empha-

---

[135] Ibid.

[136] Some may think that when Moses broke the tables of the Ten Commandments (Exodus 32:19) and when Jehoiakim burned Jeremiah's scroll (Jeremiah 36:23) that Scripture was destroyed, albeit, only for a short time. However, before Moses broke the tables he had already written God's Words, which words included the Ten Commandments (Exodus 24:4). Therefore, when Moses broke the tables, Scripture was not momentarily lost. In the case of Jeremiah's scroll in Jeremiah 36, when King Jehoiakim burned the scroll, he was not destroying the only extant copy of the book of Jeremiah, for, according to Jeremiah 30:2, Jeremiah had written a personal copy of all the words that God had given to him. Therefore, when Jehoiakim burned the scroll, Scripture was not momentarily lost. For more information see toward the beginning of this chapter and the section entitled "The Old Testament Text of Jesus." Especially take care to read the footnotes in that section.

[137] Ibid., 3089.

[138] While it is true that wicked men seek to destroy copies of the Words of God (Jeremiah 36:23) and to corrupt the Words of God (II Corinthians 2:17; 4:2; II Thessalonians 2:1-2; II Peter 3:15-16); yet the true Words of God still continue. The true Words of God were propagated by the Jews (Acts 7:38; Romans 3:2) and local churches (I Timothy 3:15).

sizes not only the Divine authority but also the unity and solidarity of Scripture. What cannot happen to one minute part cannot happen to the whole.[139]

Oliver B. Greene states:

> It was an acknowledged principle among the Jews that the Word of God could not be broken, annulled, or destroyed, and Jesus reminded them of this fact. Everything in the Word should receive reverence, not one jot or tittle should be refused or disregarded. The Jews believed this; they believed that everything in their Scriptures was to be given full weight, not one word was insignificant, not one word should be removed, passed over, or evaded because every word was the Word of Jehovah God.[140]

E. J. Young states:

> Our Lord said, "The scripture cannot be broken." If there be errors in the Scripture, then the Scripture is broken. . . . The assertion that there are errors in Scripture is a contradiction of Christ, for He held the view of the Bible which is today called orthodox; namely, that Scripture is the infallible, inerrant Word of the living God. If Scripture is not inerrant, then Jesus Christ was mistaken. . . . Our souls may then rest upon the truth of that holy Word of God, the Scriptures of the Old and New Testaments, which can never be broken.[141]

Gods

Scripture does not have any errors in it. In fact, Jesus held to this so strongly that, in quoting a part of Psalm 82:6 and in emphasizing one particular word from that part, *gods*, He demonstrates that, even in "what we might perhaps call without disrespect a rather run-of-the-mill passage,"[142]

---

[139] Robert Lightner, *The Saviour and the Scriptures* (Philadelphia: Presbyterian and Reformed Publishing Co., 1978), 102.

[140] Oliver B. Greene, *The Gospel According to John* (Greenville: The Gospel Hour, 1976), 2:154,155.

[141] E. J. Young, "Are the Scriptures Inerrant?" in *The Bible: The Living Word of Revelation*, ed. Merrill C. Tenney (Grand Rapids: Zondervan, 1968), 118-119. While Young makes this wonderful statement in commenting on Jesus' statement referring to the text of His day, Young is inconsistent in not believing the Traditional Hebrew Old Testament text of this day is without error when he alleges a mistake in the chronology of Isaiah 36:1 and II Kings 18:13 (Young, 112).

[142] Leon Morris, 468. Lightner observes: "Frequently the weight of His entire argument rested upon one or two words which He quoted from the Old Testament. If that word or those words did not have the authority which He claimed for them His arguments would

every word of every part of every verse of every chapter of every book of the entire Old Testament is solid and sure, authoritative and accurate, inerrant and infallible. Concerning Christ's use of Psalm 82:6 in John 10:34, Lightner observes that Christ's argument

> is founded entirely for its validity upon the single word "gods." More than that, the very plural number of the word is essential to His argument.
>
> Christ argues from the infallibility of the word "gods" to the infallibility of the phrase in which it occurs . . ., to the infallibility of the record in which that phrase occurs. That record He ascribes as law though it appears in the Psalms and in a particular Psalm which from every human viewpoint might be considered incidental.[143]

Lightner later writes about this same passage:

> He [Christ] hangs the validity of His entire argument upon one word of that verse. That word is "gods." This one word which He calls written law and Scripture is that which cannot be annulled. Upon this one word He defends His claim to be the Son of God. The conclusion is obvious that if one single word cannot be annulled then certainly the whole of Scripture possesses the same divine authority.[144]

How wonderful it is that God has given to the sons of men such a Book! What a foundation is the Bible!

John 17:17

In John 17:17 Jesus makes another statement about the Old Testament when, as He was praying to the Father, He said, "Thy word is truth." *Thy word is truth* in Greek is ὁ λόγος ὁ σὸς ἀλήθειά ἐστι, which literally is: "the word the Thy truth is." The fact that Jesus uses the definite article

---

have been fruitless and would certainly have been recognized as such by His critics who knew the Scriptures so well" (Lightner, 63). Another example where Jesus bases a teaching on a single word is in Mathew 22:43-44, "He saith unto them, How then doth David in spirit call him Lord, saying, The LORD said unto my Lord, Sit thou on my right hand, till I make thine enemies thy footstool?" This is a quote from Psalm 110:1 from which Christ is "sustaining His view of the doctrine of the deity of the Messiah on a single word," that is, *Lord*. (Lightner, 65).

[143] Lightner, 66.

[144] Ibid., 101.

Chapter 2 *Jesus Received the Old Testament*

both before λόγος (*word*) and σὸς (*Thy*) "lends emphasis: ὁ λόγος ὁ σὸς not merely ὁ λόγος σὸς. This is the only Word that is wholly truth."[145]

Lenski points out that *thy word* "signifies all of it, the word of the Old Testament on which Jesus placed His approval again and again, plus the revelation that Jesus added in person with the promise of its perfect preservation through the Paraclete ([John] 14:26; 16:13)."[146] In Mark 7:13 and John 10:35 Jesus specifically says that His quotes from the Old Testament are the Words of God. *Thy word*, therefore, includes the written Words of God; that is, this statement of Jesus is not limited to merely God's spoken words. It is interesting that Lenski speaks of the "perfect preservation" of God's Words because when Jesus says that verses from the Old Testament are the Word of God, He is quoting not from the *autographa*, but from the Traditional Hebrew Old Testament text of His day. Additionally, Jesus uses the present tense verb *is*, ἐστι a present active indicative from εἰμι, instead of *was* or *had been*. Therefore, one can use the phrase *the Word of God* of the preserved text.

Truth, ἀλήθειά, "is a representation of things as they are"[147] and refers to "what is true in any matter under consideration (opp[osed] to what is feigned, fictitious, [or] false)."[148] Therefore, Old Testament chronology, history, numbers, and all other things are as they are: they are the way it really is. One, then, should not elevate Assyrian, Babylonian, or any other records above the Old Testament Scriptures. Where a conflict exists, it is the Old Testament that is true, and the other records are false. How many take this approach to Old Testament studies? Yet, this approach honors the Lord Jesus Christ Who guarantees that the Old Testament is truth.

Truth "certifies the inerrancy and infallibility of the Word excepting no portion of it. The holy garment of the Word is seamless; it has no rents of errors—or call them mistakes—which hands today must sew up."[149] Furthermore, the word *truth*, which is the predicate in this statement, Je-

---

[145] R. C. H. Lenski, *The Interpretation of St. John's Gospel* (Minneapolis: Augsburg Publishing House, 1963), 1148.

[146] Ibid., 1149.

[147] Albert Barnes, "John" in *The Gospels* in vol. 9 of *Barnes' Notes on the Bible*, Heritage Edition (London: Blackie & Son, 1847, reprinted Grand Rapids: Baker Book House, 2005), 357.

[148] Thayer, 26.

[149] Lenski, 1149.

Chapter 2 *Jesus Received the Old Testament*

sus connects to *Thy word*, the subject, with *is*, ἐστι a present active indicative from εἰμι. *Is*, ἐστι, "connects the subject with the predicate, where the sentence shows who or what a person or thing is as respects character, nature, disposition, race, power, dignity, greatness, age, etc."[150] John 1:1 uses this same grammatical construction when it states, "And the Word was God." The grammatical construction in John 1:1 shows that the Word has the very essence, attributes, and characteristics of God. Likewise, *Thy word* has the very attribute, characteristic, and essence of truth. What a powerful testimony John 17:17 is to the preservation of the Words of God and to the perfect nature of the Traditional Hebrew Old Testament! It is not necessary to have textual critics paste and cut, all one need do is to believe Jesus. In making this statement, Jesus repeats the testimony of the Psalmist who said, "Thy word is true from the beginning: and every one of Thy righteous judgments endureth forever" (Psalm 119:160).

JESUS NEVER ONCE CRITICIZES THE OLD TESTAMENT

Jesus, by His use of the Old Testament and by His statements about the Old Testament, demonstrates His view that the Old Testament Hebrew text of His day is preserved, authoritative, inerrant, and infallible. One more aspect of Jesus' treatment of the Old Testament is that He never offers or gives any criticism of the Old Testament Hebrew text. Unlike many a Fundamentalist seminary or college professor, Jesus never once corrects the Old Testament Hebrew text. Jesus' example is one that more men ought to follow, especially those who say that they are Christians, that is, followers of Christ. It behooves Christians to be more Christ-like in their treatment of the Old Testament.

Jesus Does Not Correct the Text

Jesus offers no criticism of the Old Testament text. He, Who knows all things, certainly would know if there were errors; and if there were errors, what an opportunity He had to correct the text to set it straight. Especially one would think that He would correct errors because of the very importance He places on every single Word of God when He says,

---

[150] Thayer, 176.

Chapter 2   *Jesus Received the Old Testament*

"Man shall not live by bread alone, but by every word that proceedeth out of the mouth of God" (Matthew 4:4). It would be the height of inconsistency for Jesus, after expressing the importance of every word, not to correct errors in the Old Testament, if, indeed, those errors were present. John Owen asks, "Now, can it be once imagined that there should be at that time such notorious varieties in the copies of the Scripture, through the negligence of that church, and yet afterward neither our Savior nor his apostles take the least notice of it?"[151]

The fact that Jesus offers no criticism or correction of the Old Testament indicates that the Old Testament is correct. Furthermore, Jesus directly teaches in John 10:35 and John 17:17, as well as in other verses, that the Old Testament of His day needed no correction. Archer states: "It is safe to say that in no recorded utterance of Jesus Himself, or any of His inspired apostles, is there the slightest suggestion that inaccuracy in matters of history or science ever occurs in the Old Testament."[152] Waite observes: "The Lord Jesus Christ never refuted any text, any word, or any letter in the Hebrew Old Testament. He didn't say, 'Now Moses was misquoted here, it should have been this.' He offered no textual criticism whatever."[153]

In an extended passage, Sidney Collett makes this excellent statement about the testimony of Christ in relation to the Old Testament:

> Is it not very remarkable that the Lord Jesus spent the whole of His public earthly ministry in expounding the Old Testament Scriptures, and never once—even by the slightest hint—warned any one about the existence of these supposed errors? Is it not very unlike our Lord, when we remember in what scathing language He showed up and denounced the errors of His day (Matt. xxiii.), and how quick He was to detect and correct errors or faults in His own people (Luke ix. 55), that He should have known—as He must have known—of these errors, and yet that He should have remained absolutely silent about them? Had any such errors really existed, would

---

[151] John Owen, "Of the Integrity and Purity of the Hebrew and Greek Text of the Scripture" in vol. 16 of *The Works of John Owen*, ed. William H. Goold (Edinburgh: Johnstone & Hunter, 1850-53, reprinted, Edinburgh: The Banner of Truth Trust, 1968), 408. In the above quote, it appears that Owen is using *church* incorrectly to refer to Old Testament Israel.

[152] Archer, 21,22. Another good statement by Archer, however, as previous footnotes state, he does not seem to follow through on his excellent statements because in several places he says that the Old Testament text is in error.

[153] Waite, 35.

Chapter 2 *Jesus Received the Old Testament*

He not as "the faithful and true witness" (Rev. iii. 14), have sounded a warning note, making it clear that certain passages had somehow got into the Old Testament Scriptures which were not inspired by His Spirit, and were therefore not trustworthy; knowing—as none else could know—how many myriads of souls would be staking their eternal well-being upon some of the very words of Scripture?

But instead of this, what do we find? Why, we find His unfailing testimony to be exactly the opposite. Whenever our Lord referred to the Scriptures, He invariably did so in terms calculated to inspire the most absolute confidence in every word. And the whole of His life fails to furnish one single exception to this rule.[154]

Jesus Corrects Misinterpretations

Jesus repeatedly corrects the Pharisees and others for their false interpretations of the Old Testament (Matthew 5:21-48; 12:1-13; 15:1-9; 22:23-33; Luke 11:38-42; 16:19-31; 18:9-14; and John 7:19-23[155]), but He never once corrects the Hebrew text of His day. Herein is the methodology that every true Bible teacher should emulate: correct false interpretations, but never correct the text. John Owen states: "The security we have that no mistakes were voluntarily or negligently brought into the text before the coming of our Savior, who was to *declare* all things, is that he not once reproves the Jews on that account, when yet for their false glosses on the word he spares them not."[156] Owen later says, "Now, whatever was done about the Scripture in the Judaical church before the times of our Savior is manifest to have been done by divine authority, in that it is no-

---

[154] Sidney Collett, *All About the Bible: Its Origin—Its Language—Its Tradition—Its Canon—Its Symbols—Its Inspiration—Its Alleged Errors and Contradictions—Its Plan—Its Science—Its Rivals* (Westwood, NJ: Fleming H. Revell Company, 1964), 96. Lightner observes that Christ "never uttered a word to indicate that He supposed their Scriptures were not true. We must account for this silence. There is a threefold alternative: first, there are no errors in Scripture, second, Scripture contains errors but the Saviour did not know it, third, He knew about the errors but chose not to tell them. If Christ was what He claimed to be and what the New Testament writers made Him out to be, only the first alternative can be accepted" (Lightner, 75).

[155] If one does not understand how some of these passages refute the false interpretations of the Pharisees and others, he should consult a good commentary.

[156] Owen, 358.

where by him reproved, but rather the integrity of every word is by him confirmed."[157]

William Caven, concerning Jesus and His interactions with the Jews of His day, writes:

> He never charges them with adding to or taking from the Scriptures, or in any way tampering with the text. Had they been guilty of so great a sin it is hardly possible that among the charges brought against them, this matter should not even be alluded to. The Lord reproaches His countrymen with ignorance of the Scriptures, and with making the law void through their traditions, but He never hints that they have foisted any book into the canon, or rejected any which deserved a place in it.[158]

Jesus questioned the misinterpretation of the Jews but did not charge them with mistransmission of the text. It was the Jews to whom God committed the oracles of God (Romans 3:2) to convey to succeeding generations (Acts 7:38). By the time, those oracles, that is, the Words of the Living God, arrived in the first century; Jesus asserts that they were complete, entire, and inerrant, although the *autographa* had long ago passed off the scene.

Conclusion

Since Jesus fully received the text of His day, then the Bible student does not need to concern himself with "several recensions that emerged in the post-exilic era,"[159] the theory that numbers were originally abbreviated and then later fully written out in words,[160] the numerous ways copyists made errors,[161] statements that "no two manuscripts contain exactly the

---

[157] Owen, 393. "The Judaical church" of which Owen speaks was not a church at all, but rather he is referring to the Jews of Israel who lived during Old Testament times.

[158] William Caven, "The Testimony of Christ to the Old Testament" in *The Fundamentals*, 1:168.

[159] Bruce K. Waltke and O'Connor, M., *An Introduction to Biblical Hebrew Syntax* (Winona Lake, IN: Eisenbraus, 1990), 22. The several recensions need not concern the Bible student since Jesus followed the Traditional Hebrew text.

[160] This is a charge that several writers allege as they try "to explain" apparent contradictions in the Old Testament, but such a charge does not hold up under scrutiny. See Chapter Three for more information.

[161] Archer gives a list of ways copyists might have made errors and then tries to show that such errors crept into the Masoretic Hebrew text (Archer, 32-42). But in light of how Jesus regarded the Traditional Hebrew text of His day, then one should believe that

Chapter 2 *Jesus Received the Old Testament*

same words,"[162] statements that scribes "felt free to revise the script" of the Old Testament,[163] the LXX, the Syriac Peshitta, the Leningrad Codex,[164] Dead Sea Scrolls,[165] or any other of these kind of matters. Jesus has decided for the Bible student that the Traditional Hebrew Old Testament text is the text of choice. Some may accuse the author of being an obscurantist or of being a non-intellectual, but they may as well accuse Jesus of this as well, for He just simply received the preserved text of His day.

---

such copyist's errors were not present in the Hebrew text of Jesus' day. And since Jesus promised that the text He possessed would be preserved to the end (Matthew 5:18), then one can have faith that God has provided a text free from copyist's errors.

[162] Kevin T. Bauder, "An Appeal to Scripture" in *One Bible Only? Examining Exclusive Claims for the King James Bible*, ed. Roy E. Beacham and Kevin T. Bauder (Grand Rapids: Kregel, 2001), 155. See also pages 163, 164, and 173. But how do the authors of this book know that no two manuscripts contain the same words? Have they examined every manuscript? On page 171, Bauder admits that concerning New Testament manuscripts, he does not "know of anyone who has ever done that, and" doubts "that anyone ever could." While the author will readily admit that not all the manuscripts agree, yet to say that no two agree is quite a different statement, but even if it were true, it did not concern Jesus for He received the preserved text as His authority. Likewise, the believer can content himself in knowing that God has promised to preserve His Words (Psalm 12:6-7) and that these Words are available to him today.

[163] Waltke and O'Connor, 17. For one to suggest that these alleged revisions have caused the loss of some words is to contradict what Jesus promised in Matthew 5:18. A person is wise to believe Christ's promise over a statement like that of Waltke's and O'Connor's. Concerning the parallel passages (II Samuel 22 and Psalm 18; II Kings 18:13-20:19 and Isaiah 36-39; II Kings 24:18-25:30 and Jeremiah 52; Isaiah 2:2-4 and Micah 4:1-3; Psalm 14 and Psalm 53; Psalm 40:14-18 and Psalm 70; Psalm 57:8-12 and Psalm 108:2-6; Psalm 60:7-14 and Psalm 108:7-14; Psalm 96 and I Chronicles 16:23-33; Psalm 106:1, 47, 48 and I Chronicles 16:34-36), which Waltke and O'Connor point to as evidence of their contention, it is best to believe they are somewhat like the synoptic passages in the Gospels wherein each Gospel writer is not revising the script, but is providing supplementary details that the other writer(s) left unmentioned. In other words, the differences in these parallel passages are not the result of later revision, but are the result of original inspiration.

[164] For more information on the Leningrad Codex, see footnotes following.

[165] Many appeal to the Dead Sea Scrolls, however, they are a relatively recent discovery and do fit God's promise of the availability of His preserved Words (Matthew 4:4). Furthermore, because the Dead Sea Scrolls were not available to local churches, they were not received by local churches, who are God-appointed guardians of the Bible (I Timothy 3:15). Therefore, the Dead Sea Scrolls should never be the basis for overthrowing the *Textus Receptus* of the Old Testament, the Ben Chayyim Masoretic Text (see further).

The Old Testament of Jesus' day was a text that was in the keeping of the Jews, since God had committed to them His oracles[166] (Romans 3:2). In other words, the Jews had a responsibility to preserve God's Words and Jesus by His assertions that the text of His day was fully accurate, authoritative, and without error; therefore, indicates that the Hebrew Old Testament Text of His day had been fully preserved. That Jesus used the Hebrew Text is clear by His reference to jot and tittle in Matthew 5:18 and to tittle in Luke 16:17, which refer to Hebrew and Aramaic words. It is clear, therefore, that He did not use the Greek LXX. For more information on the LXX see Chapter Five and the subsection entitled "New Testament Writers Were Not LXX-Users." Furthermore, it is obvious that Jesus used the Traditional Hebrew Text of His day from the fact that as He dealt with foes, not a single individual ever questioned the text He was using. Christ's Jewish enemies often accused and questioned Christ about various things, but they never accused Him of departing from the text that God had committed to their keeping (Romans 3:2). Indeed, when He disputed with the Sadducees about the resurrection from the dead, Jesus' appeal to the Hebrew Old Testament put them to silence (Matthew 22:34).

While the Jews were at one time the custodians of the Old Testament Scriptures (Romans 3:2); with the Great Commission, God committed the keeping of the Scriptures, both Old and New Testaments, to local churches (Matthew 28:19-20; I Timothy 3:15; Jude 3; Revelation 3:8, 10). Local churches received the Masoretic Text, and made it the *Textus Receptus* of the Old Testament. Burnett indicates that Jacob ben Chayyim's Hebrew Text[167] of 1525 "became accepted (at least among Christians) as

---

[166] *Oracles* (λόγια an accusative neuter plural noun from λόγιον) refers to "the declarations of God" (Zodhiates, "3051. λόγιον").

[167] A competing Hebrew Text is that of Ben Asher, which is in agreement with the Leningrad Codex. The Leningrad text appears in the 1937 edition of the *Biblia Hebraica* by Kittel, and subsequent editions by Kittel. The Ben Asher text "was not the traditional Masoretic Text that was used for 400 years" (Waite, 27). In other words, the Ben Asher Text is not the *Textus Receptus* of the Old Testament and was not promoted by local churches. The Leningrad Codex is the basis for the 1937 edition of the Kittel Hebrew Old Testament, which "has about fifteen to twenty suggested changes in the Hebrew text placed in the footnotes on each page. If you multiply this by the 1424 pages in the Kittel Bible, it comes out to between 20,000 and 30,000 changes in the Old Testament. They could be major changes, or they could be minor changes. Does that sound like a 'preserved' Bible to you?" (Waite, 21). Of course, this does not sound like Bible preservation at all, but rather it sounds like Bible demolition. The Leningrad Codex in its printing by Hendrickson Publishers also removes Joshua 21:36-37 and Nehemiah 7:68 from the Bible. Such a scenario does not fit the promise of preservation that Jesus gave in Matthew 5:18.

the 'received text'."[168] Ginsburg also states of this text that it "came to be recognized as the true masoretic text."[169] Chayyim's Hebrew text was published by Daniel Bomberg in 1524-25 and became "in time the 'textus receptus' of the Old Testament" and "was the basis for the Old Testament for many Reformation-era translations such as the English Authorised Version."[170] The local church is the pillar and ground of the truth (I Timothy 3:15) and local churches through the years have passed along God's Words for the Old Testament as they are in the Ben Chayyim Masoretic Text. Rather than trying to recover or restore words, one should receive the Traditional Hebrew Old Testament. Jesus received the Traditional Hebrew Text as passed down to Him from the Jews, who were the caretakers of the oracles of God (Romans 3:2). Likewise in this day, one should receive the Hebrew Text passed down to him from the caretakers of that text, local churches. Please see the chart at the end of this chapter to see the transmission of the Hebrew Old Testament.

W. H. Griffith Thomas states:

> No one can go through the Gospels without being impressed with the deep reverence of our Lord for the Old Testament, and with His constant use of it in all matters of religious thought and life. His question, "Have ye never read?" His assertion, "It is written," . . . are plainly indicative of His view of the Divine authority of the Old Testament as we have it. He sets His seal to its historicity and its revelation of God. He supplements, but never supplants it. He amplifies and modifies, but never nullifies it. He fulfills, i.e. fills full, but never makes void.[171]

Jesus never criticizes the Old Testament text of His day.

---

[168] Stephen G. Burnett, *From Christian Hebraism to Jewish Studies: Johannes Buxtorf (1564-1629) and Hebrew Learning in the Seventeenth Century* (NY: E. J. Brill, 1996), 170.

[169] Christian D. Ginsburg, "Prolegomenon" in *Jacob Ben Chajim Inn Adonijah's Introduction to the Rabbinic Bible, Hebrew and English; with Explanatory Notes*, 2nd edition, in *The Library of Biblical Studies*, ed. Harry M. Orlinsky (NY: KATV Publishing House, Inc., 1968), XI.

[170] "Preface to the Bomberg / Ginsburg Hebrew Old Testament" in *Hebrew Old Testament* (London: Trinitarian Bible Society, 1998), i.

[171] W. H. Griffith Thomas, 117.

Chapter 2 *Jesus Received the Old Testament*

CONCLUSIONS

Several conclusions are apparent from Jesus' teaching about the Old Testament. First, from Jesus' use of *it is written* and the general statements that Jesus makes concerning the Bible (Matthew 5:18; Luke 16:17; John 10:35; 17:17), one should conclude that Jesus held to the perfect preservation[172] not only of all the words, but of all the letters and of all the vowel points of the Hebrew Old Testament.

Second, *it is written* in Nehemiah's day, in David's day, and in the days of other Old Testament saints means that their copies of the Words of God had the words of the *autographa*. *It is written* in Jesus' day means that His copy also had the words of the *autographa*. Since there is only one *autographa*, then the *it-is-written* copies of Old Testament saints were the same as the *it-is-written* copy of Jesus: they all had the same words. The use of *it is written* directly connects the Old Testament of Jesus with the Old Testament of the saints of old, with each having the words of the *autographa*.[173]

---

[172] Many dispute this because they are walking by sight. If they walked by faith, they would see that the plain teaching of Christ is that God indeed has perfectly preserved His Words.

[173] Some might point to the quotes of the New Testament not being exactly the same as what is written in the Old Testament. Such an occurrence takes place when one compares Deuteronomy 8:3 with Matthew 4:4 and Luke 4:4. Chapter Five deals with this more fully, however, Strouse states: "The Lord's citation of Dt. 8:3 is not a direct quote, but is His inspired commentary on the Scripture. Luke's slightly different rendering of the Lord's Words indicates that the Lord restated Dt. 8:3 in several ways, two of which were accurately recorded by Matthew and Luke" (Thomas M. Strouse, *"But My Words Shall Not Pass Away": The Biblical Defense of the Doctrine of the Preservation of Scripture* (Newington, CT: Emmanuel Baptist Theological Press, 2001), 12). In a comment on Matthew 5:18 *The Pulpit Commentary* says, "We may, perhaps, see in our Lord's reference to *yod* and a 'tittle' an indication that even already scrupulous care was taken of the text. The objection to this, derived from the non-literal quotations in the New Testament is due to a misunderstanding of Jewish methods of quotation" (A. Lukyn Williams, *Matthew*, vol. 1, in vol. 15 of *The Pulpit Commentary*, ed. H. D. M. Spence and Joseph S. Exell (Peabody, MA: Hendrickson Publishers, n.d.), 156). And Wenham states: "We have a right to expect that quotations should be sufficiently accurate not to misrepresent the passage quoted; but, unless the speaker makes it clear that his quotation is meant to be verbatim, we have no right to demand that it should be so. In the nature of the case, the modern scholarly practice of meticulously accurate citation, with the verification of all references, was out of the question. There were no printed books, no chapter and verse divisions, no marginal references, no concordances. There were probably not even bound codices. The verification of references required the laborious scrutiny of a lengthy parchment roll, which itself would not necessarily be ready to hand. Thus quotations were nor-

Third, since Jesus possessed an *it-is-written* copy of the Old Testament, and since Jesus' *it-is-written* copy had the words of the *autographa*, and since these words are the Words of God, and since the Word of God is truth (John 17:17); then Jesus possessed in His hands an infallible copy of the Hebrew Old Testament.[174]

Fourth, from the fact that Jesus speaks of *jot* and *tittle* in Matthew 5:18 and *tittle* in Luke 16:17, which terms refer to the smallest Hebrew consonant and to the smallest Hebrew vowel point, then Jesus limited His teaching of perfect preservation and infallibility to the Hebrew and Aramaic of the Traditional Old Testament. His promises in these verses do not extend to any other text. Albeit, if a translation of this perfectly preserved and infallible Hebrew Old Testament is accurate, then one can look upon it as the Words of God in that language, which is exactly what one has in the *King James Version* since it is an accurate translation of the Traditional Hebrew Old Testament into English.

Fifth, if one follows the example of Jesus, then deciding which Old Testament text to use is a relatively easy matter. However, Paul's words apply here: "But I fear, lest by any means, as the serpent beguiled Eve

---

mally from memory and the writers did not pretend that they were anything else" (Wenham, 92-93). Lightner states: "It cannot always be determined when a direct quotation is intended" (Lightner, 8). These statements may explain some of the differences between the Old Testament text and citations of that text in the New Testament, but these statements do not explain all the reasons for such differences. As the author will present later, sometimes the Holy Ghost deliberately altered the phrasing of Old Testament verses to bring forth additional truth and revelation (see "Must Accept Word Change by the Spirit" in Chapter Five).

[174] Believers throughout church history have believed in the existence of an infallible copy of the Bible. Before giving the following quotes, the author cautions the reader not to make church history the rule for faith and practice. The existence of an infallible copy is firmly based upon the teaching of the Bible, and if no one else ever in church history held to this position, it would not make such a position null. Nonetheless, others throughout history saw the same teaching as this work presents. John Owen stated, "But yet we affirm, that the whole Word of God, in every letter and tittle, as given from him by inspiration, is preserved without corruption" (Owen, 16:388). The Westminster Confession of Faith and The New Hampshire Confession teach the same thing. The Helvetic Consensus Formula says, " 'God saw to it that His word . . . was entrusted to writing not only through Moses, the prophets and apostles but also He has stood guard and watched over it with a fatherly concern to the present time that it not be destroyed by the cunning of Satan or by any other human deceit' " (Donald L. Brake, "The Preservation of the Scriptures" in *Counterfeit or Genuine*, ed. David Otis Fuller (Grand Rapids: Grand Rapids International Publications, 1975), 181, giving his personal translation of "Formula Consensus Ecclesiarum Helveticarum Reformatarum," *Collectio Confessionum in Ecclesiis Reformatis Publicaarum*, ed. H. A. Niemeyer (Lipsiae: Sumptibus Iulii Klinkhardti, 1840), 730).

through his subtilty, so your minds should be corrupted from the simplicity that is in Christ" (II Corinthians 11:3). Many have corrupted minds when it comes to the text issue and make the issue far more complicated than it should be. The disciples never attempted to restore or recover the text, but simply received the text, just as Jesus did (John 17:8; Acts 2:41; 7:38; 8:14; 11:1; 17:11; I Thessalonians 1:6; 2:13; James 1:21).[175] The text that Jesus received was the Traditional Hebrew Old Testament passed down to Him by the Jews (Romans 3:2) and this is the text that believers today should receive as well – a text passed down to them by local churches (I Timothy 3:15), who made it the *Textus Receptus* of the Old Testament.

Sixth, since Jesus demonstrates such a high regard for the Hebrew Old Testament, and since He rebuked His disciples for not believing it (Luke 24:25), and since He Himself promises that all of it would be preserved down to the smallest details (Matthew 5:18; Luke 16:17); then disputing the Traditional Masoretic Hebrew Old Testament is questioning the truthfulness and ability of Jesus.[176] Sadly, many Fundamentalists are unknowingly doing just this. May they repent.

Seventh, Jesus never once criticizes the Old Testament, for He came not "to destroy the law, or the prophets" (Matthew 5:17). The Bible teacher should have this as his motto.

Eighth, from the fact that Jesus has impeccable credentials and since He received every word, letter, and vowel point of the Hebrew Old Testament; then those who question the Old Testament act as if they know more than Jesus! The Bible says, "Knowledge puffeth up" (I Corinthians 8:1). If one's knowledge puffs him up so much that He thinks that he

---

[175] For a treatment of most of these verses, see Strouse, *"But My Words Shall Not Pass Away"*, 19-24.

[176] "We conclude that our Lord's positive statements on the subject of the Old Testament are not to be rejected without charging Him with error. If, on these points, on which we can test and verify Him, we find that He is not reliable, what real comfort can we have in accepting His higher teaching, where verification is impossible? We believe we are on absolutely safe ground when we say that what the Old Testament was to our Lord, it must be and shall be to us" (W. H. Griffith Thomas, 119). Also Lightner quotes Packer: " 'The question, 'What think ye of the Old Testament?' resolves into the question, 'What think ye of Christ?' and our answer to the first proclaims our answer to the second. . . . To undercut Christ's teaching about the authority of the Old Testament is to strike at His own authority at the most fundamental point' " (Lightner, 89, quoting J. I. Packer, *"Fundamentalism" and the Word of God* (Grand Rapids: Wm. B. Eerdmans Publishing Co., 1960), 59-61).

knows more than Jesus, then he has the wrong kind of knowledge. Let him abandon such knowledge, and let him be instructed by Jesus to simply receive the preserved Words of God.

Ninth, "It must be said, however, that the question of our attitude to the Old Testament inevitably raises the question of our attitude towards the Lord Jesus Christ."[177] "The moment you begin to question the authority of the Old Testament, you are of necessity questioning the authority of the Son of God Himself, and you will find yourself in endless trouble and difficulty."[178]

Tenth, from the fact that Jesus rebuked His Own disciples for being slow of heart to believe all that the prophets spoke (Luke 24:25), then those "believers" who do not believe deserve a rebuke.

> Christ made no distinction between facts of history, geography, science or theology. He referred to them all—to that which was directly revealed by God and to that which was not so revealed—always endorsing the Scriptures with the divine authority which they possessed and investing them with His own divine authority (Matt. 5:17, 18; Luke 24:44; John 10:34, 35).[179]

In light of this, here are some good questions: "If God may not be trusted in the things He has revealed which do not relate to faith and life, how may He be trusted at all? How is one to decide what is a matter of faith and life and what is not?"[180] Jesus left no instruction on how to make such a distinction, for He teaches that one should hear, that is, receive and believe all of the Bible.

Eleventh, just as a person is saved by faith by putting his trust in the Lord Jesus Christ, so the believer should walk by faith and trust Christ on the text issue.

Twelfth, a Christian should follow Jesus' example. When a Fundamentalist says that an Old Testament passage has an error, he is not following the example of Jesus, but, rather, is following the example of Satan who says, "Yeah, hath God said?" (Genesis 3:1). This is very danger-

---

[177] Lloyd-Jones, 1:187.

[178] Ibid., 1:188.

[179] Robert Lightner, *Neoevangelicalism Today* (Schaumburg, IL: Regular Baptist Press, 1979), 86.

[180] Ibid., 85.

ous. The devil, in questioning God's Words, influenced Eve also to question God's Words, thereby bringing her down to the place where she no longer believed God. This was tragic for her. Likewise, Fundamentalists, who question the preserved text, persuade others also to question the Bible, thereby bringing them down to the place where they do not believe God, Who promises that He will preserve His Words.[181] This, too, will be tragic for them.

> The evidence is clear:
>
> To Christ the Old Testament was true, authoritative, inspired.
>
> To Him the God of the Old Testament was the living God, and the teaching of
>
> > the Old Testament was the teaching of the living God.
>
> To Him, what Scripture said, God said.[182]

This, then, establishes the basis for a study of the Old Testament. Just as one receives the Living Word by faith for salvation, so he must receive the written words by faith for sanctification (John 17:17). And just as one must believe the promises of God for an assured salvation, free from doubts (I John 5:13); so one must believe the promises of God for a sure foundation, free from conjectures. What a joy it is for one to know for sure that he is saved, and what a joy it is for one to know for sure that he has the very Words of God. The Psalmist said long ago in Psalm 19:7-11:

> The law of the LORD *is* perfect, converting the soul: the testimony of the LORD *is* sure, making wise the simple. The statutes of the LORD *are* right, rejoicing the heart: the commandment of the LORD *is* pure, enlightening the eyes. The fear of the LORD *is* clean, enduring for ever: the judgments of the LORD *are* true *and* righteous altogether. More to be desired *are they* than gold, yea, than much fine gold: sweeter also than honey and the honeycomb. Moreover by them is thy servant warned: *and* in keeping of them *there is* great reward.

---

[181] "The attitude of Christ to the Old Testament Scriptures must determine ours. He is God. He is truth. His is the final voice. He is the Supreme Judge. There is no appeal from that court. Christ Jesus the Lord believed and affirmed the historic veracity of the whole of the Old Testament writings implicitly (Luke 24:44)" (Dyson Hague, "The History of the Higher Criticism" in *The Fundamentals*, 1:26).

[182] Wenham, 37.

Chapter 2   *Jesus Received the Old Testament*

TRANSMISSION OF OLD TESTAMENT

Inspiration   **God Spoke**
Exodus 3:4
⇩

Inscripturation   **Moses Wrote**[183]
Exodus 24:4 (1491 B.C.)
⇩

P   **God Commits Oracles to Jews and They Copy Them**
Dt 6:6-9; 11:20; 17:18; 27:1-3, 8; 31:1-19; Josh 8:30-32; II Ki 11:9-12; II Chr 23:9-11;
R   Ezra 7:6, 11; Pro 25:1; Jer 8:8; 36:1-4, 32; 45:1; Acts 7:38; Rom 3:2
(***God guarantees perfect preservation*** Ps 12:7; 100:5; 119:152, 160; Isa 40:8)
E   ⇩   ⇩   ⇩   ⇩   ⇩
     It is written   ⇩   ⇩   ⇩   ⇩
S   David's day   *It is written*   ⇩   ⇩   ⇩
     I Kings 2:3   Daniel's day   *It is written*   ⇩   ⇩
E   (1015 B.C.)   Daniel 9:13   Ezra's day   *It is written*   ⇩
     ⇩   (538 B.C.)   Neh 8:14-15   Jesus' day   *It is written*
R   ⇩   ⇩   (454 B.C.)   Mt 4:4   Paul's day
     ⇩   ⇩   ⇩   (26 A.D.)   Rom 4:17
V   ⇩   ⇩   ⇩   ⇩   (57 A.D.)
     ⇩   ⇩   ⇩   ⇩   ⇩

A   **Local Churches Receive the *It-Is-Written* Words**
Jn 17:8; Acts 2:41; 8:14; 11:1; 17:11; Rom 4:23-24; 15:4;
T   I Cor 9:9-10; 10:6, 11; I Thes 1:6; 2:13; II Tim 3:16-17; James 1:21
⇩

I   **Local Churches Are to Guard and Preserve God's Words**
Mt 28:20; II Cor 2:17; 4:2; I Tim 3:15; Jude 3; Rev 3:8, 10
O   (***Jesus guarantees perfect preservation*** Mt 5:18; 24:35; Lk 16:17; Jn 10:35)
⇩

N   **Local Churches Recognize Ben Chayyim Masoretic Text as the**
       It-is-written **Text Making It the *Textus Receptus* of the OT**
I Timothy 3:15
⇩

Translation   **King James Version**
Being a faithful translation of OT *Textus Receptus* is Word of God in English
Neh 8:1-8; Acts 2:11

---

[183] One could produce similar charts using the other writers of the Old Testament.

CHAPTER THREE:
RECEIVE THE OLD TESTAMENT NUMBERS

Believers should hear, that is, receive and believe, all of the numbers of the Traditional Hebrew Old Testament. If Bible students would simply follow the example of the Lord Jesus Christ, Who received all the words of the Old Testament, including the numerical words, then there would be no need for this chapter. Indeed, Jesus never questioned anything in the Old Testament, for He came not to destroy (Matthew 5:17). As Chapter One demonstrates, the Apostle John followed the example of Christ by his receiving the largest of all numbers in the entire Bible (Revelation 9:16). But the sad reality is that many do not follow the example of the Lord Jesus Christ. While calling Him, "Lord, Lord," they do not the things that He says (Luke 6:46; see also Luke 24:25); therefore, they do not receive all the Old Testament numbers. Hence, the need of this chapter, which is to answer the objections and arguments of those who will not follow Jesus and receive all the words of the Old Testament, in particular, all the numerical words. Such people argue that many Old Testament numbers are in error and that the Bible student should not receive them.

ALPHABET ALLEDGEDLY USED FOR NUMBERS

Many commentators and teachers claim that errors are in the numbers of the Old Testament. They reason that at some point, Old Testament scribes used a form of shorthand notation for numbers such that subsequent scribes could easily confuse the shorthand for one number with the shorthand for another. Some of these commentators and teachers allege that each letter of the Hebrew alphabet represented a number as the following chart demonstrates.

Chapter 3   *Receive Old Testament Numbers*

א = 1	ל = 30
ב = 2	מ = 40
ג = 3	נ = 50
ד = 4	ס = 60
ה = 5	ע = 70
ו = 6	פ = 80
ז = 7	צ = 90
ח = 8	ק = 100
ט = 9	ר = 200
י = 10	ש = 300
כ = 20	ת = 400[184]

    It is easy to see that if scribes used such a system, and if it were strictly left up to man, then scribes could easily confuse certain numbers, such as the symbol for 6 and 7, and the symbol for 50 and 3, as well as the symbol for 2 and 20, and the symbol for 4 and 200. Those who do not hold to the preservation of the Old Testament seize upon this potential for confusion and then conjecture how scribes could have incorporated errors into the Traditional Text.

DeHoff

For example, George DeHoff writes:

> In the ancient Hebrew, letters were, in all probability, used for numerals. Rawlinson observes, "Nothing in ancient manuscripts is so liable to corruption from mistakes of copyists as the numbers; the original mode of writing them appears in all countries of which we have any knowledge to have been by signs, not very different from one another; the absence of any context determining in favor of one number rather than another, where

---

[184] Georges Ifrah, *The Universal History of Numbers* (New York: John Wiley & Sons, Inc., 2000), 241. See also, John J. Davis, *Biblical Numerology: A Basic Study of the Use of Numbers in the Bible* (Grand Rapids: Baker, 1983), 39.

the copy is blotted or faded, increases the chances of error, and thus it happens that in almost all ancient works the numbers are found to be deserving of very little reliance."

The invention of printing has done much to eliminate errors of this kind. Some of the discrepancies concerning numbers, kings, genealogies, etc. are so obscure as to have little interest for thinking people anyway. Fortunately the length of time a certain king ruled can have nothing to do with our salvation anyway.[185]

The above quote comes from *Alleged Bible Contradictions Explained*, which might better be titled *Alleged Bible Contradictions Left Unexplained*. Sadly, the above quote reflects the belief of not a few who, while holding to errors in the Traditional Hebrew Text, fail to hear, that is, to receive and to believe, the promises of Jesus concerning the Old Testament. Furthermore, for Dehoff to assert that these numbers "have nothing to do with our salvation" shows a lack of understanding of Jesus' promises about the Old Testament. The Lord Jesus Christ asserts that all is well with the Traditional Hebrew Old Testament Text (Matthew 5:18; 24:35; Luke 16:17; John 10:35; 17:17). But if all is not well, as DeHoff and others assert, then Jesus is a liar. And if Jesus is a liar, then He is a sinner and powerless to save. Do Bible teachers understand this? How can Jesus be right, if the Old Testament is in error? If the Old Testament numbers are in error; then Jesus is in error, and there is no salvation!

Haley

Haley, based upon the assumption that scribes used a shorthand notation for numbers, suggests numerous scribal errors in the transmission of the numbers. For instance, concerning the apparent discrepancy in the age of Jehoiachin wherein II Kings 24:8 states that he was eight years old and II Chronicles 36:9 states that he was eighteen years old, Haley writes: "Bahr thinks that י, 10, has dropped out of the latter text."[186] In another example, where I Kings 9:28 speaks of four hundred twenty talents, but II

---

[185] George DeHoff, *Alleged Bible Contradictions Explained* (Grand Rapids: Baker, 1951), 38-39.

[186] John W. Haley, *Alleged Discrepancies of the Bible* (Springdale, PA: Whitaker House, n.d.), 400. Haley alleges a jot, that is, a י has dropped out of the text, but this is directly contrary to Jesus' promise: "One jot or one tittle shall in no wise pass from the law, till all be fulfilled" (Matthew 5:18).

Chapter 3   *Receive Old Testament Numbers*

Chronicles 8:18 speaks of four hundred fifty talents, Haley suggests that "כ, 20, [has been] confounded with נ, 50."[187]

Keil

Keil, commenting on the difference between I Kings 9:28 and II Chronicles 8:18, states: "The difference between 420 and 450 may be accounted for from the substitution of the numeral letter n (50) for k (20)."[188]

The Pulpit Commentary

The Pulpit Commentary states:

> There is one particular, however, in which our text [the Traditional Hebrew Text], as it now stands, is open to some suspicion, and that is the matter of *dates*. Some of these, it would appear, have been accidentally altered in the course of transcription — a result which need cause us no surprise, if we remember that anciently numbers were represented by letters, and that the Assyrian, or square characters, in which the Scriptures of the Old Testament have been handed down to us, are extremely liable to be confounded. The reader will see at a glance that the difference between ב and כ (which represent respectively *two* and *twenty*), between ד and ר *(four* and *two hundred)*, between ח and ת *(eight* and *four hundred)*, is extremely slight.[189]

Unger

Unger, quoted by Davis, states (emphasis mine):

> But, though, on the one hand it is **<u>certain</u>** that in all existing manuscripts of the Hebrew text of the Old Testament the numerical expressions are written at length, yet, on the other, the variations between themselves and from the Hebrew text, added to the evident inconsistencies in numerical statements, between certain passages of that text itself, **<u>seem</u>** to prove that

---

[187] Ibid., 383.

[188] Keil, *1 and 2 KINGS 1 and 2 CHRONICLES*, 104.

[189] J. Hammond, "Introduction to the Books of the Kings" in *I Kings* in vol. 5 of *The Pulpit Commentary*, ed. H. D. M. Spence and Joseph Exell (Peabody, MA: Hendrickson Publishers, n.d.), xiv-xv.

some shorter mode of writing was originally in vogue, liable to be misunderstood by copyists and translators. These variations **_appear_** to have proceeded from the alphabetic method of writing numbers.[190]

As the emphasis indicates, Unger goes from certainty at the beginning of his statement to uncertainty later in the quote when he uses the words *seem* and *appear*. In Unger's mind, "inconsistencies" exist that are unexplainable, except by saying a scribe made an error. By faith he should hear, that is, receive and believe, the text as it is, just as Jesus did, and leave behind the conjectures. Instead, he walks by sight down the highway of conjecture, rather that walking by faith in the pathway of certainty.[191]

Conclusion

The above quotes demonstrate the pervasive thinking that the scribes of the Old Testament used an abbreviation or shorthand system to represent numbers with the result that later scribes easily confused these symbols, thereby introducing errors into the Hebrew Old Testament. But where is the proof for this? Is there any? Or, is this merely a fabrication to give cover to men who want to question the Scriptures and not submit to its authority?

ALPHABET NOT USED FOR NUMBERS

Davis, in commenting on a proposed solution for the numerical difficulties in the lists of Nehemiah 7 and Ezra 2 states: "There is some doubt as to the antiquity of the alphabetic method of numerical notation and therefore this solution is rather tenuous."[192] Davis quotes Gunner: " 'The idea of using letters of the alphabet for numerals originated from Greek

---

[190] John J. Davis, *Biblical Numerology* (Grand Rapids: Baker, 1983), 35, quoting Merrill F. Unger, ed., *Unger's Bible Dictionary* (Chicago: Moody Press, 1957), 799.

[191] Simply receiving the Words of God produces certainty. When the disciples received the Words of God from Jesus they knew surely that Jesus came from the Father (John 17:8). Receiving the words by faith produces certainty, whereas conjecturing about the words produces uncertainty. For instance, when the Thessalonians forgot God's Words through Paul (II Thessalonians 2:5) and received a false epistle (II Thessalonians 2:2), they were troubled. When people receive teachings contrary to God's Words, they become troubled and shaken in mind.

[192] Davis, 35.

influence, and, as far as is known, first appeared on Maccabean coins' "[193] in about 140 B.C.[194] 140 B.C. is over three hundred years after Malachi wrote the last book of the Old Testament in 442 B.C.[195] Davis states: "There is no epigraphical evidence of the use of the Hebrew alphabet for numerals before the second century B.C."[196] In other words, evidence for a system of using the Hebrew alphabet for numerals does not go back far enough for the human authors of the Old Testament to have used it. Therefore, those who use scribal confusion of numerical symbols as a "solution" to the apparent numerical discrepancies in the Old Testament are being rather tenuous. But even if scholars were to unearth earlier evidence, it should not concern the follower of Christ who should simply believe that he has the words of the *autographa* in the *it-is-written* preserved text (Matthew 5:18).

Another problem with suggesting that the original writers and, or scribes used the alphabet for Old Testament numerals is that all the numbers in the Hebrew Old Testament are fully written out with words. For example, instead of using 450, the text of the Bible has "four hundred and fifty" (Numbers 2:16). John Davis makes the following observations: "The numbers found in the Hebrew text of the Old Testament are always written out," "in the Hebrew Old Testament, numbers are spelled out," and "the existing manuscripts of the Old Testament do not evidence knowledge of such notation," that is, a shorthand notation for numbers. "The Aramaic numbers found in the Bible are, like the Hebrew numbers, written out in word form."[197] Since these written-out numbers are in the

---

[193] Ibid., 39, quoting R. A. H. Gunner, "Number," *The New Bible Dictionary*, ed. J. D. Douglas (Grand Rapids: William B. Eerdmans Publishing Co., 1963), 895. Ifrah refers also to "a clay seal in the Jerusalem Archaeological Museum" which "bears an inscription in palaeo-Hebraic characters which can be translated as: 'Jonathan, High Priest, Jerusalem, M.' The letter *mem* at the end is still a puzzle, but it could be a numeral, with a value (= 40) referring to the reign of Simon Maccabeus, recognised by Demetrius II in 142 BCE as the 'High Priest, leader and ruler of the Jews.' If this were so, then the seal would date from 103 BCE (the 'fortieth year' of Simon Maccabeus) and thus constitute the oldest known document showing the use of Hebrew alphabetic numerals" (Georges Ifrah, *The Universal History of Numbers*, 234). A distinction between Ifrah's quote and Davis' is that Ifrah refers to "the oldest known document" whereas Davis refers to a coin.

[194] E. Kautzsch, ed., *Gesenius' Hebrew Grammar*, 2d ed, revised in accordance with the 29th ed. by A. E. Cowley (Oxford: Clarendon Press, 1982), 10, 30.

[195] Jones, "Chart #6: Creation to Creator" in *Chronology of the Old Testament*.

[196] Davis, 45.

[197] Ibid., 26, 28, 31, 35.

Chapter 3 *Receive Old Testament Numbers*

it-is-written preserved text of the Hebrew Old Testament, then these written-out numbers were in the *autographa* (see Chapter Two, and the section "Jesus Repeatedly Uses It Is Written of the Old Testament").

The writers of Scripture did not use an alphabet abbreviation for the numbers of the Old Testament. First, such a system was not in place when the original writers wrote. Second, all the numbers in the Hebrew Old Testament are fully written out, never abbreviated.

OTHER SYSTEMS ALLEGEDLY USED FOR NUMBERS

An alphabetic system was not used for Old Testament numbers, but this does not stop some scholars from speculating. While the numbers in the Hebrew Old Testament are always fully written, "this was not always the case in other contemporary literature."[198] Because other contemporary literature did not always fully write out numbers, commentators suppose that the Old Testament scribes must have used some sort of shorthand system as well. In other words, some treat the Bible just like any other ancient literature!

Kaiser, Jr., Davids, Bruce, and Brauch

Hard Sayings of the Bible states:

> In the Old Testament documents now available to us, all the numbers are spelled out phonetically. This is not to say, however, that a more direct numeral system or cipher notation was not also in use originally for at least some of these numbers. While no Biblical texts with such a system have been found, mason's marks and examples of what may well be simple tallies have been attested in excavations in Israel.[199]

Why do so many have such an unquenchable desire to impose upon the Old Testament writers some sort of cipher, abbreviated, or shorthand system of numerical notation, especially when, by their own admission, evidence is totally lacking in any Old Testament manuscript that such occurred? Could it be that some scholars are so enamored with textual criticism and the desire to correct the text and have a corresponding refusal to

---

[198] Ibid., 28.

[199] Walter C. Kaiser, Jr., Peter H. Davids, F. F. Bruce, and Manfred T, Brauch, *Hard Sayings of the Bible* (Downers Grove, IL: InterVarsity Press, 1996), 51.

walk by faith in God's promises of preservation that they see the suggestion of a cipher system as a way to introduce their textual criticism into the Old Testament?

The suggestion that Biblical scribes used a cipher system would allow scholars to emend not only the Traditional Hebrew Masoretic Text, but also to emend when there is no manuscript evidence contrary to the Traditional Hebrew Masoretic Text. In other words, after creating the phantom that the Biblical writers used a cipher system for numbers, these scholars then suppose that they can correct the text of the preserved Hebrew Masoretic Text. Scholars even suppose that they can correct the Hebrew Text in places where there is not a shred of manuscript evidence to the contrary (see the very next section on Wolf for evidence). The author is not somehow suggesting that it is acceptable to correct the Masoretic Text when there is other manuscript evidence to the contrary, but is simply illustrating the extent to which these scholars will go.

Wolf

By suggesting that scribes used a cipher system, commentators are able to throw the door wide open to adjust any number simply on their own personal whim or fancy. For example, concerning the matter of the fourteenth year of Hezekiah in II Kings 18:13 and Isaiah 36:1 Wolf writes (emphasis mine):

> A better theory involves a textual correction of "fourteenth" to "twenty-fourth" as the original reading in [Isaiah] 36:1. . . . Although **_there is no manuscript evidence to support a different reading_**, the ancient method of writing numbers made scribal errors of this sort all too easy.[200]

It would be bad enough for him to correct the preserved Hebrew text if there were evidence to the contrary, but to do so when "there is no manuscript evidence to support a different reading," takes it a step further and demonstrates, at least in the author's opinion, to what extent some scholars are willing to exalt their own ideas over the clear declarations of the Words of God. Such scholars seem more enthralled with their own intellect, than with the pure Words of the Living God. Instead of submitting to

---

[200] Herbert M. Wolf, *Interpreting Isaiah* (Grand Rapids: Zondervan, 1985), 22. See also John S. Oswalt, *The Book of Isaiah Chapters 1-39* in *The New International Commentary on the Old Testament*, ed. R. K. Harrison and Robert L. Hubbard, Jr. (Grand Rapids: Eerdmans, 1986), 631. For further discussion on the fourteenth year of Hezekiah see discussion on II Kings 18:13 in Chapter Ten.

the Words of God, they want to make the Words of God submit to their ideas! How contrary such an attitude is to the Spirit and statements of the Lord Jesus Christ Who never once questioned the Old Testament text.

Davis

Davis, after making statement after statement that the Hebrew Old Testament does not use a shorthand system (see above), nonetheless says, "To what extent Biblical writers employed such a system can only be conjectured."[201] Davis, despite his repeated observation that numbers in the Old Testament are fully written, nonetheless, ignores this testimony to open the door to conjecture. Why not simply take the state of the Old Testament text as definitive testimony that scribes did not use a cipher system and go from there to receive, believe, and hear the numbers written therein? But no, conjecture continues.

OTHER SYSTEMS NOT USED FOR NUMBERS

If one should argue that the original writers or the scribes of the Old Testament abbreviated numbers by a system other than an alphabetic system,[202] then where is the evidence? Again, none is forthcoming. Why does no evidence show that the original writers of the Old Testament or that the scribes of the preserved text ever used a cipher system? Could the answer simply be that they did not use a cipher system? Could it be that simple? Why not listen to Jesus Who repeatedly stated, "It is written" meaning that the preserved text of His day was an accurate representation of what had been written in the *autographa* and that the words of the *autographa* will continue to stand written throughout the ages in the preserved text? Indeed, what believers possess today in the preserved text

---

[201] Davis, 35.

[202] Ifrah points out: "The Samarian *ostraca* consist of bills and receipts for payments in kind to the stewards of the King of Israel, and reveal that the Jews wrote out their numbers as words and also used a real system of numerals" (Ifrah, 236). "From the tenth to the sixth century BCE (the era of the Kingdom of Israel), the Hebrews used Egyptian hieratic numerals; from the fifth to the second century BCE, they used Aramaic numerals; and from around the start of the common era, many Jews used Greek alphabetical numerals" (Ifrah, 239). Evidence then exists for a system of numerals in use by the Jews during from about 1000 B.C. to the time of Christ, but there is no evidence that the original writers of Scripture ever used such a system in the *autographa*.

are the very words that had been written in the *autographa* (see chart on last page of Chapter Two), and since there are no abbreviated numbers in the preserved text, then there were no abbreviated numbers in the *autographa*.

CONCLUSION

Since the numbers of the Hebrew Old Testament are fully written, then the authors of the Hebrew Old Testament did not use an alphabet system or any other system to represent the numbers of Scripture. Sadly, however, many have more trust in the words of the critics instead of in the Words of Christ. They have it all backwards, for they are receiving the words of men as if the words of men are the final word, whereas they treat the final word from the lips of Jesus as the words of a mere man (cf. I Thessalonians 2:13).[203] It is time that the critics return to the Bible for a correct view of Bibliology. When they do, they will simply receive, believe, and hear all the numbers in the Bible.

---

[203] Those who trust the words of the critics do not have a received-text mindset as the Thessalonians had, or as the first disciples had (John 17:8). Instead of relying on the conjectural statements of the scholars, one should rely on the concrete statements of the Saviour.

CHAPTER FOUR:
REASONS FOR APPARENT CONTRADICTIONS

God not only inspired His Words (II Timothy 3:16), but He also preserved those inspired words (Psalm 12:6-7)[204] in the Traditional Hebrew Masoretic Text of the Old Testament (Matthew 5:18) and in the Received Text of the New Testament (John 17:8; I Peter 1:23-25). When these inspired, preserved words from these texts are accurately translated, they are the Words of God in that particular language. For English reading people the translation that meets these criteria is the *Authorized Version*; therefore, the *Authorized Version* is the Word of God in English. However, as one works with the Traditional Masoretic Hebrew Text, the Received Text, and the *Authorized Version* apparent contradictions may surface.[205]

Believing that the Ben Chayyim Masoretic Text of the Old Testament and the Received Text of the New Testament accurately convey the words of the inspired *autographa* and that the *Authorized Version* accurately translates these words, then the question might arise, why would God allow apparent contradictions in the Bible, or why are apparent contradictions in the Bible? Several reasons or explanations are possible for why God might allow apparent contradictions in the Bible.

---

[204] While God promises that He Himself will keep and preserve His Words, He nonetheless used the Jews to transmit the Old Testament (Acts 7:38; Romans 3:2) and local churches to keep all of His Words (I Timothy 3:15). See chart on the last page of Chapter Two.

[205] Andrew Fuller states: "Admitting the Divine authority of the Holy Scriptures, their harmony ought not to be called in question; yet it must be allowed by every considerate reader that there are *apparent* difficulties" (Andrew Fuller, "Passages Apparently Contradictory" in *The Complete Works of Andrew Fuller* (Harrisonburg, VA: Sprinkle Publications, 1988), 1:667).

Chapter 4   *Reasons for Apparent Contradictions*

MAKING AN IMPRESSION

Sometimes apparent contradictions attract attention, arouse interest, and make a lasting impression. Concerning apparent contradictions Bishop Whately, quoted by Walter Kaiser, writes: " 'Instructions thus conveyed are evidently more striking and more likely to arouse attention; and thus, from the very circumstance that they call for careful reflection, more likely to make a lasting impression.' "[206] Charles Spurgeon while preaching on Isaiah 43:26 which appears to be in contradiction with the verse before it, Isaiah 43:25, says,

> This looks like a contradiction; but, as a wise teacher will win attention by dark sayings, so doth the word of God abound in expressions by which thought is excited, and the lesson is more deeply impressed upon the mind. Many are the paradoxes of the prophets, and of the Lord and leader of all the prophets. Who can read without attention two such sentences as these in succession?[207]

Some of the teachings of Jesus make an impression through apparently contradictory statements. For example, in the Sermon on the Mount Jesus says, "Blessed are the poor in spirit" (Matthew 5:3a) and "blessed are they that mourn" (Matthew 5:4a). How can the poor in spirit or mourners be blessed? It seems impossible until one reads the last part of these verses: "Blessed are the poor in spirit: for theirs is the kingdom of heaven," and "blessed are they that mourn: for they shall be comforted." The poor in spirit are blessed because they will possess heaven, and the mourners are blessed because they will be comforted. The first parts of these verses attract attention and arouse interest so that the Bible makes a lasting impression. Jesus uses another apparently contradictory statement to arouse interest when He says, "He that findeth his life shall lose it: and he that loseth his life for my sake shall find it" (Matthew 10:39). This seems impossible. But because of this seeming impossibility, interest is aroused, and one wonders, "How can this be?" The answer lies in the fact that *life* is used in two different senses, that is, he who wants to save his earthly life, will lose eternal life.

---

[206] Walter Kaiser, Jr.; Davids, Peter H.; Bruce, F. F.; and Brauch, Manfred T, *Hard Sayings of the Bible* (Downers Grove, IL: InterVarsity Press, 1996), 16, quoting *On Difficulties in the Writings of St. Paul*, Essay VII, sec. 4.

[207] Charles Spurgeon, "A Loving Entreaty" in *Metropolitan Tabernacle Pulpit* (Pasedena, TX: Pilgrim Publications, 1973), 29:541.

Chapter 4 *Reasons for Apparent Contradictions*

Apparent contradictory statements that arouse interest are also in passages that use numerals. For example, Jesus says, "But many that are first shall be last; and the last shall be first" (Matthew 19:30).[208] Those who, because of their relationship to Jesus, are last in this world shall be first in the world to come (Matthew 5:3-5). Jesus' wording has made a lasting impression so that even the unsaved use the expression, "The last shall be first." Another example of an apparently contradictory numeric statement is in I John 5:7, which says, "For there are three that bear record in heaven, the Father, the Word, and the Holy Ghost: and these three are one."[209] How can three be one? It is possible because of the nature of the triune God. *These three are one* makes a lasting impression about the teaching of the Trinity. Sometimes the Bible uses apparent contradictions to make a lasting impression.

PROMOTING STUDY

As one encounters these apparent contradictions, they can motivate and encourage him to study the Words of God to attempt a solution.

General Statements

Geisler and Howe state:

> The Christian scholar approaches the Bible with the same presumption that what is thus far unexplained is not therefore unexplainable. He or she does not assume that discrepancies are contradictions. And, when he encounters something for which he has no explanation, he simply continues to do research, believing that one will eventually be found.[210]

---

[208] The Gospels repeat this in various ways (Matthew 20:16; Mark 9:35; 10:31; and Luke 13:30).

[209] The Critical Text leaves out the words, "in heaven, the Father, the Word, and the Holy Ghost: and these three are one" from I John 5:7 and the words, "and there are three that bear witness in earth" from I John 5:8. Just as many a Fundamentalist has accepted the removal of *these three are one* by adopting the critical text, so they have accepted an attack upon other numerical passages of the Bible.

[210] Norman Geisler and Thomas Howe, *When Critics Ask: A Popular Handbook on Bible Difficulties* (Wheaton: Victor Books, 1992), 15. While Geisler and Howe make an excellent statement, it is deplorable that for some of the apparent contradictions, they claim that "a scribal or transcription" (Ibid., 156) error has probably occurred. Compare

Derickson writes:

> The word is complete and trustworthy. When a seeming contradiction comes up in your study, you may have confidence that it isn't a mistake. You may have a confidence that you will find an answer to the problem if you are diligent and seek after an answer.[211]

George DeHoff states:

> The alleged discrepancies have stimulated the human intellect. . . . they have called forth a multitude of defenders of the faith. They have prompted men to search the scriptures asking: "How are these difficulties to be solved?" Things "hard to be understood" present a special attraction to the inquiring mind.[212]

In a statement that particularly applies to the topic of this book, Haley writes:

> The rabbis have a saying that "the book of Chronicles was given for argument," that is, to incite men to investigation and discussion. The history of sacred criticism demonstrates that the book has answered this purpose remarkably well; its discrepancies being salient points which attract attention.[213]

Apparent contradictions promote a study of the Words of God, and study of the Words of God is exactly what God desires from His people.

Specific Verses

II Timothy 2:15

II Timothy 2:15 declares, "Study to shew thyself approved unto God, a workman that needeth not to be ashamed, rightly dividing the word of truth." The word for *study*, σπούδασον from σπουδάζω, is an aorist active imperative denoting a command and has the meaning "to make every ef-

---

also pp. 159, 160, 171, 181, 194, 197, 199, and 209. It would have been far better had they continued researching, rather than question the text that God has preserved.

[211] Stanley L. Derickson, *Derickson's Notes on Theology* in *The Master Christian Library*, version 8 [CD-ROM] (Albany, OR: Ages Software, 1997), 45.

[212] George W. Dehoff, *Alleged Bible Contradictions Explained* (Grand Rapids: Baker, 1951), 42.

[213] Haley, 32.

fort to do one's best, to be eager."²¹⁴ God desires His people to approach His Words with an excellent and eager effort, and the apparent contradictions promote this kind of diligent study.

I Peter 1:10-11

Introduction

The prophets did the diligent study that II Timothy 2:15 demands when they confronted the apparent contradiction between the prophesied glory of Christ and the prophesied sufferings of Christ. I Peter 1:10-11 says,

> Of which salvation the prophets have enquired and searched diligently, who prophesied of the grace that should come unto you: searching what, or what manner of time the Spirit of Christ which was in them did signify, when it testified beforehand the sufferings of Christ, and the glory that should follow.

Several words here speak of the prophets' study of this apparent contradiction.

Enquired

First, the prophets enquired. *Enquired*, ἐξεζήτησαν from ἐκζητέω, is a compound of two Greek words, ἐκ meaning out and ζητέω meaning to seek diligently, or to seek out diligently. "In the NT [it is] used metaphorically, to seek in order to . . . know."²¹⁵

Searched Diligently

Also, the prophets searched diligently. In the Greek *searched diligently* is ἐξηρεύνησαν, which is from ἐξεραυνάω, and is another compound

---

[214] Zodhiates, 4704.

[215] Zodhiates, 1567. Zodhiates points out that this same usage of ἐξεζήτησαν is illustrated in the LXX in Ps. 44:21, "Shall not God search this out?" God will seek it out to make known the secrets of the heart.

Chapter 4 *Reasons for Apparent Contradictions*

from ἐκ meaning out and ἐρευνάω meaning to search. The word, then, means "to search out, explore, to search very diligently or carefully."[216]

Searching

Thirdly, the prophets were searching what, or what manner of time. *Searching* is from the Greek word ἐρευνάω and differs only from the word for *searched diligently* in that it does not have the prefix ἐκ. It is a present active participle indicating that the prophets engaged themselves in an ongoing process.

> The general meaning of ἐρευνάω is to "search after," both literally and figur[atively]. It is first used . . . of animals in the sense of "to sniff out" with the nose. . . . It is then used . . . of men in the sense of "to search." . . . It then came to mean . . . "to investigate a matter," esp[ecially] in the legal sense, though also in the more general sense of enquiry. . . . This gives us the further sense of "to test" or "fully to examine" a statement, more particularly from the academic standpoint.[217]

Conclusion

Enquiring, searching diligently, and *searching* well illustrate the approach a student should take in the study of the Words of God, especially in the apparent contradictory places of the Words of God. Note that these actions by the prophets involved chronology as they were investigating "what manner of time the Spirit of Christ which was in them did signify." Therefore, in grappling with the apparent contradiction concerning the sufferings and the glory of Christ, the prophets very likely studied passages involving numbers. One such passage might have been the seventy weeks of Daniel (Daniel 9:24-27).

CHEWING MEAT

Another reason why apparent contradictions are in the Bible is that the Bible contains strong meat. Hebrews 5:12-14 states:

---

[216] Zodhiates, 1830.

[217] Delling, "ἐρευνάω, ἐξερευνάω" in *Theological Dictionary of the New Testament*, ed. Gerhard Kittel, trans. and ed. Geoffrey Bromiley (Grand Rapids: Eerdmans, 1993), 2:656.

For when for the time ye ought to be teachers, ye have need that one teach you again which *be* the first principles of the oracles of God; and are become such as have need of milk, and not of strong meat. For every one that useth milk *is* unskilful in the word of righteousness: for he is a babe. But strong meat belongeth to them that are of full age, *even* those who by reason of use have their senses exercised to discern both good and evil.

Strong meat is in contrast to milk. *Milk* refers to the first principles or *ABC's*[218] of the Words of God, whereas *strong meat* refers to the more difficult teachings in the Bible. The word for *strong* is στερεᾶς, which is from στερεός, and is an adjective meaning "solid, hard, [or] rigid."[219] Since some apparent contradictory passages of the Bible are indeed hard knots,[220] then *strong meat* could include such passages.

Only those, "who by reason of use have their senses exercised to discern both good and evil," can handle strong meat. *Exercised* is from γεγυμνασμένα and is a perfect passive participle from γυμνάζω, indicates that those who can handle strong meat have been exercised in the past. Because they have been exercised, they are able to handle the strong meat in the present by means of discerning both good and evil. English bases *gymnasium* upon γυμνάζω,[221] which means "to exercise vigorously, in any way, either the body or the mind."[222]

The senses of such believers have been exercised by reason of use. *Reason of use* means "that by long use and habit they had arrived to that state."[223] John Owen commenting on the word γεγυμνασμένα states:

---

[218] According to Zodhiates, the word for *principles*, στοιχεῖα from στοιχεῖον, means "the basic parts, rudiments, elements, or components of something. Among the ancient Greek philosophers, it designated the four basic and essential elements of which the universe consisted, namely, earth, water, air, and fire" (Zodhiates, 4747).

[219] *Online Bible Greek Lexicon* in *Online Bible Millennium Edition* [CD-ROM], 4731.

[220] Augustine in dealing with the apparent contradiction between Matthew 5:32 and I Corinthians 7:10 says, "Holy Scripture causes a hard knot in this matter" (Augustine, *The Good of Marriage*, trans. C. L. Cornish in *The Nicene and Post-Nicene Fathers First Series*, ed. Philip Schaff (Peabody, MA: Hendrikson Publishers, Inc., 1994), 3:402).

[221] William Morris, 588.

[222] Thayer, p.122. I Timothy 4:7 uses the present active imperative form of γυμνάζω to command exercising oneself in godliness.

[223] Albert Barnes, *Hebrews* in vol. 13 of *Barnes' Notes*, Heritage Edition (London: Blackie & Son, 1847, reprinted Grand Rapids: Baker Books, 2005), 118.

Chapter 4 *Reasons for Apparent Contradictions*

> The word doth not denote an actual exercise, but that readiness, ability, and fitness for any thing, which is attained by an assiduous exercise; as a soldier who is trained is ready for his duty, or a wrestler for prizes (whence the allusion is taken) unto his strivings. Wherefore, to have our senses exercised in the way intended, is to have our understandings and minds, through constant, sedulous study, meditation, prayer, hearing of the word, and the like means of the increase of grace and knowledge, to become ready, fit, and able to receive spiritual truths, and to turn them into nourishment for our souls.[224]

The above comment agrees with what God said in II Timothy 2:15 about study and is similar to what the prophets did (I Peter 1:10-11). The whole purpose of exercising the senses is to discern both good and evil. The word for *discern*, διάκρισιν from διάκρισις, "is an exact judgment, putting a difference between things proposed to us; a determination upon a right discerning of the different natures of things."[225] Discerning is exactly the kind of skill that one needs in order to handle apparent contradictions.

HUMBLING THE STUDENT

As the student encounters hard passages, some of these passages should humble him as he comes to realize that he is not a know-it-all and that he must do further study. David Cloud, commenting on II Samuel 24:13 and I Chronicles 21:11-12, where one speaks of seven years of famine and the other three years, humbly admits:

> As is the case with many Biblical difficulties, no one knows for absolute certain why there is a difference between these passages, but the Hebrew text is properly translated in the KJV in both passages and we can be certain that the problem is in our understanding.[226]

The Pulpit Commentary points out: "Those Divine contradictions save us from self-dependence and spiritual pride."[227] While apparent contradictions can have an humbling affect on many of God's servants, sadly,

---

[224] John Owen, *An Exposition of the Epistle to the Hebrews*, vol. 20 of *The Works of John Owen*, ed. William H. Goold (Edinburgh: Johnstone & Hunter, 1854-55, reprinted Edinburgh: The Banner of Truth Trust, 1991), 598,599.

[225] Ibid.

[226] David W. Cloud, *Things Hard To Be Understood: A Handbook of Bible Difficulties* (Port Huron, MI: Way of Life Literature, 2001), 60.

[227] P. C. Barker, *I Chronicles* in vol. 6 of *The Pulpit Commentary*, 276.

Chapter 4 *Reasons for Apparent Contradictions*

some, in pride and arrogance, charge the preserved texts of the Scriptures with error. In so doing, they exhibit the attitude of Satan who says, "Yea, hath God said?" (Genesis 3:1). Such a devilish attitude is very dangerous and can only lead ultimately to ruin. For example, when the false prophet Hananiah indirectly disputed Jeremiah's prophecy of the seventy year Babylonian captivity, he died shortly thereafter (Jeremiah 25:11; 28:1-4, 10-17).[228] Surely, not all who question something in the Bible die shortly thereafter, but all who question the Words of God are engaging in risky business. Is belief in the seventy-year captivity necessary for salvation? Most would say no, but God took the life of a man who did not believe it. Certainly, it is important to believe all of the Words of God, even those parts that may not directly bear on salvation and even those parts where numbers are incredible to the human mind. It is better for a person to submit humbly to the Words of God than to question them.

PRAYING TO GOD

When the apparent contradictions of the Words of God humble the student, he should *pray* to God for wisdom (James 1:5). Daniel is an example of one who prayed for wisdom. As Daniel was studying the book of Jeremiah he found that seventy years would be accomplished "in the desolations of Jerusalem" (Daniel 9:2). Unlike the false prophet Hananiah (Jeremiah 25:11; 28:1-4, 10-17), Daniel heard, that is, received and believed this number as fully accurate and authoritative, which is how all of God's people should respond to the numbers of the Bible. But Daniel did not understand something about the seventy year number, leading him to pray. In response to his prayer, the angel Gabriel came to give him "skill and understanding" (Daniel 9:22). *Understanding,* בִּינָה (*binah*), is a noun which means insight.[229] In the etymology of the root for this word, בִּין (*bin*), the original meaning is to distinguish, to separate, to be clear,

---

[228] In questioning the seventy year captivity, Hananiah made the people to trust in a lie (Jeremiah 28:15) and taught rebellion against the Lord (Jeremiah 28:16). These are serious matters and should cause anyone to think twice before disputing a number in the preserved texts.

[229] Willem A. VanGemeren, ed., *New International Dictionary of Old Testament Theology and Exegesis,* version 2.8 [CD-ROM] (Grand Rapids: Zondervan Reference Software, 2001), H1069 בִּינָה.

Chapter 4   *Reasons for Apparent Contradictions*

and to be understandable;[230] therefore, the root word includes the idea of being able to discern. Gabriel came to give Daniel more skill in understanding, insight, or discernment. Gabriel's giving to Daniel additional understanding prompted Walvoord to observe that "although Daniel's prayer was not directed to his own need of understanding God's dealings with the people of Israel, this is the underlying assumption of his entire prayer."[231] In other words, Daniel prayed about something in the Words of God that he did not fully understand. Praying is something that all students of the Words of God ought to do when not understanding a portion of Scripture.

SHOWING GOD'S MIND

The Words of God reveal the mind of God and in revealing the mind of God, it is evident that the mind of God is above the mind of man and, therefore, at times hard to comprehend. The Lord says, "For my thoughts are not your thoughts, neither are your ways my ways, saith the LORD. For as the heavens are higher than the earth, so are my ways higher than your ways, and my thoughts than your thoughts" (Isaiah 55:8-9). The Words of God reveal some things that some have difficulty understanding. For example, how can three be one (I John 5:7)? How can Jesus be both fully man and fully God (I Timothy 3:16)? How can a virgin give birth (Matthew 1:20-23)? Concerning the inspired writings of Paul II Peter 3:15-16 states:

> And account that the longsuffering of our Lord is salvation; even as our beloved brother Paul also according to the wisdom given unto him hath written unto you; as also in all his epistles, speaking in them of these things; in which are some things hard to be understood, which they that are unlearned and unstable wrest, as they do also the other scriptures, unto their own destruction.

Hard to be understood is an adjective from δυσνόητος and occurs only here in the New Testament. It "indicates something difficult for the mind to grasp, either because the statement is ambiguous or because it is capa-

---

[230] Helmer Ringgren, "בין" in *Theological Dictionary of the Old Testament*, ed. G. Johannes Botterweck and Helmer Ringgren, trans. John T. Willis (Grand Rapids: Eerdmans, 2000), 2:99.

[231] John F. Walvoord, *Daniel the Key to Prophetic Revelation* (Chicago: Moody, 1977), 215.

Chapter 4 *Reasons for Apparent Contradictions*

ble of misinterpretation."[232] This meaning could include the matter of apparent contradictions and certainly demonstrates that not everything is easy in the Word of God. George DeHoff states: "The nature of God Himself presents some difficulties. How could an infinite God be completely comprehended and understood by our finite intelligence?"[233]

R. A. Torrey states:

> Some people are surprised and staggered because there are difficulties in the Bible. For my part, I would be more surprised and staggered if there were not. What is the Bible? It is a revelation of the mind and will and character and being of an infinitely great, perfectly wise and absolutely holy God. God Himself is the Author of this revelation. But to whom is the revelation made? To men, to finite beings, to men who are imperfect in intellectual development and consequently in knowledge, and who are also imperfect in character and consequently in spiritual discernment. The wisest man measured on the scale of eternity is only a babe, and the holiest man compared with God is only an infant in moral development. There must, then, from the very necessities of the case, be difficulties in such a revelation from such a source made to such persons. When the finite tries to understand the infinite, there is bound to be difficulty. When the ignorant contemplate the utterances of one perfect in knowledge, there must be many things hard to be understood, and some things which to their immature and inaccurate minds appear absurd. When beings whose moral judgments as to the hatefulness of sin and as to the awfulness of the penalty that it demands are blunted by their own sinfulness listen to the demands of an absolutely holy Being, they are bound to be staggered at some of His demands, and when they consider His dealings, they are bound to be staggered at some of His dealings. These dealings will appear too severe, too stern, too harsh, too terrific.[234]

The Apostle Paul writes: "Oh the depth of the riches of the knowledge of God!" (Romans 11:33). The mind of God is so very deep that one cannot expect to understand everything easily. Charles Haddon Spurgeon writes: "I believe that all the contradictions in Scripture are only apparent ones. I cannot expect to understand the mysteries of God, neither do I

---

[232] D. Edmond Hiebert, *Second Peter and Jude: An Expositional Commentary* (Greenville: Unusual Publications, 1989), 173.

[233] DeHoff, 28.

[234] R. A. Torrey, *Difficulties and Alleged Errors and Contradictions in the Bible* (Chicago: Moody Press, 1907), 9, 10.

wish to do so. If I understood God, he could not be the true God."[235] Because the Words of God reveal the mind of God, one must expect to come across things that are hard to be understood.

CONCEALING GOD'S MIND

But the Words of God, while revealing the mind of God, do not reveal the entire mind of God. God conceals some of His mind. It is the concealing of God's mind that can lead to further apparent contradictions. Deuteronomy 29:29 declares: "The secret things belong unto the LORD our God: but those things which are revealed belong unto us and to our children for ever, that we may do all the words of this law."[236] God has not chosen to reveal all things: some things are secret. The word for *secret* is a Niphal participle from סָתַר (*sathar*) and means "to be hidden, be concealed."[237] No doubt, these secret things contributed to the Old Testament prophets' inability to understand the sufferings of Christ and the glory that should follow (I Peter 1:10-11).

SEPARATING FROM THE EVENTS

Something akin to the concealing of the mind of God, but distinct from it, is that modern-day students of the Bible are removed by thousands of years from the time when Biblical events took place. People of this day may have no understanding of some of the things that earlier generations took for granted. In recognition of a possible lack of understanding, I Samuel 9:9 informs the reader that "beforetime in Israel, when a man went to enquire of God, thus he spake, Come, and let us go to the seer: for he that is now called a Prophet was beforetime called a Seer." In this case, Scripture informs a later generation about a matter, which an earlier generation took for granted. Could it be that in other places in the Bible, the Word of God does not explain certain customs and that this lack of explanation produces some of the apparent contradictions? David

---

[235] Charles H. Spurgeon, "The Hairs of Your Head Numbered" in *The Metropolitan Tabernacle Pulpit* (Pasedena, TX: Pilgrim Publications, 1974), 34:54.

[236] In addition to Deuteronomy 29:29, see also Proverbs 25:2; John 21:25; Acts 1:7; and Romans 11:33-34.

[237] *Online Bible Hebrew Lexicon* in *Online Bible Millennium Edition* [CD-ROM], 05641.

Chapter 4 *Reasons for Apparent Contradictions*

Cloud writes: "We are separated from the Bible events by thousands of years and vast cultural and linguistic differences. It is not reasonable to expect there will [be] no problems in understanding these things."[238]

SUBSTANTIATING INSPIRATION

The apparent contradictions of the Bible prove the inspiration of the Bible, which is a point that several writers make. For instance, DeHoff states:

> The alleged discrepancies are strong proof that there was no collusion between the various writers. Their differences go far to establish, in this way, the credibility of these authors. Had the Biblical writers agreed in all particulars, even the minutest details, had there been no 'discrepancies' in their writings, we would have heard the cry of 'Collusion, Collusion! Frameup!' all along the line from Celsus and Porphyry to Colenso and Renan.[239]

Concerning the difficulties in harmonizing the Gospels, Fausset states:

> The very variations disprove collusion. Reconcilable diversity is a confirmation of the truth, as alleged by mutually independent witnesses. Entire sameness in all four would make all but the first mere copies. Contradictions would prove one or other inaccurate. Substantial unity, with circumstantial diversity, partial and reconcilable, is the highest kind of internal evidence. As in architecture a front and a side view, a ground plan and an elevation, are different, yet harmonize in viewing the connected whole, so the four, though not facsimiles, have an inner harmony when one first looks to the purpose and the individual spiritual character of each, and then to the mutually connected whole in its fourfold aspect.[240]

---

[238] Cloud, 11.

[239] DeHoff, 45. Kaiser, Davids, Bruce, and Brauch make essentially the same point in *Hard Sayings of the Bible*, 16. Also, Haley mentions the Howland will case in which the issue was whether the signature on the second page of the will was Howland's or a forgery. Haley points out that investigators determined that the signature was a forgery because the signature on the second page agreed too well with that of the signature on the first page (Haley, 36).

[240] A. R. Fausset, "Gospels" in *Fausset's Bible Dictionary* in *The Master Christian Library*, version 8 [CD-ROM] (Albany, OR: Ages Software, 1997), 2:110. Albert Barnes makes a similar observation concerning the cursing of the fig tree by Christ as recorded in Mark 11:12-13 (Albert Barnes, *Barnes' Notes on the Bible*, 12:421).

Chapter 4 *Reasons for Apparent Contradictions*

Concerning the differences in the inscription on the cross of Christ (Matthew 27:37; Mark 15:26; Luke 23:38; John 19:19), Sir Robert Anderson says, "Such differences only prove that the Gospels are not, as the critics would tell us, copied from one another, or from a common source, but that they are wholly independent narratives."[241]

Not only did different writers write different parts of the Bible, but also they wrote at different times. "Moses wrote all the words of the LORD" (Exodus 24:4). Paul, who lived over 1500 years later, also wrote inscripturated words (Philemon 19). Furthermore, different writers wrote from different locations. For example, Daniel wrote from Babylon, Moses wrote from Egypt and then from the wilderness, and Jeremiah wrote from Judah. In addition to these differences, some of the writers of Scripture were kings such as David and Solomon, others were prophets, and some "were unlearned and ignorant men" (Acts 4:13). With all of the variety in the people whom God used to write Scripture, certainly there would be differences in expression. The differences in expression may lead to apparent contradictions, albeit not real contradictions, and these apparent contradictions substantiate the teaching of Scripture that God did use various people in various times and in various places to write His Words.

DEFINING DOCTRINE

Apparent contradictions in the Bible also help to define and to limit doctrine. The discussion of Paul and James concerning the place of works is a classic case. Paul makes it clear that salvation is "not of works" (Ephesians 2:9), but this does not mean that works are unimportant, for James speaks of showing one's faith by his works (James 2:18). While works do not secure salvation in the least little bit, yet a proper faith is a faith that works. These two passages, then, define and limit the doctrine about works.

The doctrine of the Godhead also illustrates a defining and limiting of doctrine by apparent contradictions. For instance, Scripture teaches there is one God (Deuteronomy 6:4; Isaiah 45:6, 21), while at the same time teaching the Father is God (I Chronicles 29:10), Jesus is God (I Timothy

---

[241] Sir Robert Anderson, *The Bible and Modern Criticism: A Free and Popular Presentation of the Results of an Independent Study of the New Criticism as Set Forth in Representative Works* (London: Pickering & Inglis, n.d.), 231.

Chapter 4   *Reasons for Apparent Contradictions*

3:16), and the Holy Spirit is God (Acts 5:3-4). How can all of these statements be true? The fact is that all of the statements are true because they are all in the Bible. The statements about the Godhead help define and limit the doctrine of the Trinity that the "three are one" (I John 5:7). There is not more than one God, but there is one God made up of three persons, and these three are one.

In another example of an apparent contradiction defining and limiting doctrine, Spurgeon in a message entitled "Mongrel Religion" based on II Kings 17:41 says,

> It had a look in the right direction, and consequently the Scripture says that they feared God; but yet this fear of God was so hollow that, if you turn to the thirty-fourth verse, you will read, "They fear not the Lord." Sometimes a verbal contradiction most accurately states the truth. They feared the Lord only in a certain sense; but, inasmuch as they also served other gods, it came to this when summed up, that they did not fear God at all.[242]

George DeHoff quotes Whatley:

> The seeming contradictions in scripture are too numerous not to be the result of design; and doubtless were designed, not as mere difficulties to try our faith and patience, but as furnishing the most suitable mode of instruction that could have been devised, by mutually explaining and modifying or limiting or extending one another's meaning.[243]

COMPLEMENTING ACCOUNTS

Closely akin to defining and limiting doctrine is another possible reason for apparent contradictions, which is a complementing of various accounts in the Bible in order to provide a fuller and more complete picture of what occurred. For instance, some have supposed that the accounts of Judas' death are contradictory. On the surface of it, the accounts do appear to contradict, but the accounts complement rather than contradict one another, thereby providing a fuller understanding of what took place at Judas' death.

---

[242] Spurgeon, "Mongrel Religion" in *The Metropolitan Tabernacle Pulpit*, 27:722.

[243] DeHoff, 42, quoting Whatley, *On Difficulties in Writings of St. Paul*, Essay 7, Sec. 4.

Chapter 4 *Reasons for Apparent Contradictions*

Matthew 27:5 states that after Judas cast down the thirty pieces of silver into the temple that he then "went and hanged himself." Matthew goes on to say that the chief priests took Judas' money and bought the potter's field, which also became known as the field of blood (Matthew 27:7-8). Acts 1:18 says that Judas "purchased a field with the reward of iniquity; and falling headlong, he burst asunder in the midst, and all his bowels gushed out." Acts does not contradict Matthew, but rather complements Matthew. In putting the two accounts together, one understands that Judas hung himself and then fell headlong and burst asunder so that the field wherein this happened became known as "the field of blood" (Acts 1:19).

Barnes' writes:

> There has been supposed to be some difficulty in reconciling these two accounts, but there is really no necessary difference. Both accounts are true. Matthew records the *mode* in which Judas *attempted* his death by hanging. Peter speaks of the result. Judas probably passed out of the temple in great haste and perturbation of mind. He sought a place where he might perpetrate this crime. He would not, probably, be very careful about the fitness of the means he used. In his anguish, his haste, his desire to die, he seized upon a rope and suspended himself; and it is not at all remarkable, or indeed unusual, that the rope might prove too weak, and break. Falling headlong—that is, on his, face—he burst asunder, and in awful horrors died—a double death, with double pains and double horrors—the reward of his aggravated guilt.[244]

The chief priests took Judas' money and bought the very field wherein Judas' gruesome death occurred. Since the chief purchased the field with Judas' money, then the Bible states that Judas himself purchased it. Gill writes:

> It is somewhat difficult, that Judas should be said to purchase it, when Matthew says the chief priests bought it, Mt 27:7. Both are true; Judas having received his money of the chief priests two days ago, might not only intend to purchase, but might really strike a bargain with the potter for his field; but repenting of his sin, instead of carrying the money to make good the agreement, went and threw it to the chief priests, and then hanged himself; when they, by a secret providence, might be directed to make a purchase of the same field with his money; or he may be said to purchase it, because it was purchased with his money.[245]

---

[244] Barnes, *Matthew-John* in *Barnes' Notes on the Bible*, 556.

[245] Gill, *An Exposition of The Old & New Testaments*, 8:144.

Chapter 4 *Reasons for Apparent Contradictions*

Both accounts are true with both accounts complementing one another and providing a fuller picture of what actually happened at Judas' death.

The writers of Scripture did not write the Bible in the style of a systematic theology with, for instance, one chapter on Bibliology, another chapter on Theology, and yet other chapters on other topics. Rather, the Bible often gives a bit of information on a topic in one place and then more information about the same topic in another place. Not only is such a thing true with Judas' death, but is also true with almost every topic in the Bible. The giving of bits of information here and there with the result that various accounts complement one another is especially so with the alleged numerical discrepancies of I Samuel to II Chronicles, where in one passage one writer uses one number, and in another passage, another writer uses a different number. Chapters Seven through Twelve have many examples where the numbers, rather than contradict one another, complement one another and thereby provide a more complete picture of conditions at that time.

TESTING FAITH

While apparent contradictions can strengthen faith, since they can define and limit doctrine, substantiate inspiration, and motivate study of the Bible; yet they can also serve as a test of faith. If the preserved text has an apparent contradiction, the responsibility of the student is to receive the preserved Words of God (John 17:8) by faith and to believe that they are without error (John 17:17). For instance, the Bible says in one place that "Jehoiachin was eighteen years old when he began to reign" (II Kings 24:8) and in another place that "Jehoiachin was eight years old when he began to reign" (II Chronicles 36:9). Perhaps one cannot explain this apparent contradiction, but since both statements are in the Bible, they are both correct. Such passages will test the student's faith, but he is better off to receive the Words of God by faith and thereby please God (Hebrews 11:6).

Apparent contradictions test faith. Will the student pass the test of faith, or will he flunk? When it comes to apparent contradictions, will a person just simply believe the Bible? Will he continue to believe the Bible, though he does not have an answer for an apparent contradiction? Despite his faith being tested, will he trust that the preserved Words of God are "pure words" (Psalm 12:6) and, therefore, inerrant? Will he show complete trust in God and in His promises? Or, will he question the apparent contradictory words? Will he charge that the words are error-

Chapter 4 *Reasons for Apparent Contradictions*

ridden? Will he claim that since a particular number does not make sense to him, it should not be in the Bible?

Fundamentalists and Jehovah's Witnesses

Some Fundamentalists claim that some numbers are erroneous because they do not seem to make sense (see Chapter One and Chapters Seven through Twelve for evidence). Rather than exercise faith in the Words of God, believing that the Words of God are correct in all matters, these Fundamentalists claim that the Bible is in error. When their faith is tested by some of the apparent contradictions, they flunk the test.

But what is the difference between the attitude of questioning a number, because it does not seem to make sense, and the attitude of the Jehovah's Witness who questions Biblically sound doctrine about the Trinity and hell because it does not make sense to him?[246] The Jehovah's Witness flunks the test of faith. But what is disturbing is that Fundamentalists, who question the preserved text just because it does not make sense, are exhibiting the same ungodly spirit!

Moses and Quail

The Bible has two interesting illustrations concerning the rejection of numbers by men who thought certain numbers were incredible. In the first of the illustrations, God told Moses that the congregation would eat quail for a whole month, which seemed incredible to Moses, and he said,

> The people, among whom I am, are six hundred thousand footmen; and thou hast said, I will give them flesh, that they may eat a whole month. Shall the flocks and the herds be slain for them, to suffice them? or shall all the fish of the sea be gathered together for them, to suffice them? (Numbers 11:21-22).

Moses had difficulty believing that God could provide quail for 600,000 men, let alone the whole congregation of Israel. The number of quail needed seemed incredible to him and he let the Lord know exactly what

---

[246] See *Let God Be True* (Brooklyn, NY: Watchtower Bible and Tract Society, 1946), 99-100. Page 99 states: "The doctrine of a burning hell where the wicked are tortured eternally after death cannot be true, mainly for four reasons: . . . (2) it is unreasonable." In reference to the doctrine of the Trinity, page 100 states: "Such a doctrine with its attempted explanation, is very confusing."

he thought; therefore, the Lord said, "Is the LORD'S hand waxed short? thou shalt see now whether my word shall come to pass unto thee or not" (Numbers 11:23). Of course, the Lord's Words are true, God provided the quail in such a large quantity, Moses flunked the test of faith, and God rebuked him for not believing His Words. Just as God rebuked Moses for his unbelief in this matter, so those today who question some of the so-called incredible numbers in the Bible deserve a rebuke.

King's Servant and Food Prices

In the days of Elisha, a king's servant questioned a seemingly incredible quantity. II Kings 7 relates a Syrian siege of Samaria wherein food prices skyrocketed. It was at this time that "Elisha said, Hear ye the word of the LORD; Thus saith the LORD, To morrow about this time shall a measure of fine flour be sold for a shekel, and two measures of barley for a shekel, in the gate of Samaria" (II Kings 7:1). A measure of fine flour is two gallons of dry measure and would sell "for a shekel - 64¢."[247] Compared to what the prices had been, namely eighty shekels or "$51.20 for an ass's head"[248] (II Kings 6:25), one of the king's servants thought it was incredible that prices could come down so dramatically and expressed his unbelief (II Kings 7:2). To this servant, the numbers, in light of the present circumstances, seemed like a contradiction. The servant, therefore, flunked the test of faith. In flunking the test of faith, the servant was actually questioning the Words of God and, consequently, lost his life (II Kings 7:17). Was it wise of the servant to question these numbers? No, he should have had faith in the Words of God and in particular that the numbers of the Words of the Lord are accurate. Not to receive, believe, and hear these numbers is to question the accuracy of the Words of God and what true Bible-believer would want to be in that position?

Conclusion

Surely, some of the apparent contradictions of the Bible serve as a testing of faith. Will a man believe God above all else? Concerning apparent contradictions and the testing of faith, Spurgeon says,

---

[247] Finis Jennings Dake, *Dake's Annotated Reference Bible* (Lawrenceville, GA: Dake Publishing, Inc., 2001), 675.

[248] Ibid.

Chapter 4 *Reasons for Apparent Contradictions*

Again, if we knew a man who could not lie, we should believe him in the teeth of fifty witnesses the other way. Why, we should say, 'They may say what they will, but they can lie.' You might have good evidence that they were honest men usually, but you would say, 'They can lie; they have the power of lying; but here is a man who stands alone, and cannot lie; then his word must be true.' This shows us, beloved, that we ought to believe God in the teeth of every contradiction.[249]

Regardless of the difficulty that the Bible may cause men, they ought to believe God. As the Bible says, "Let God be true, but every man a liar" (Romans 3:4). If it comes down to whether one should believe man or God, God should win every time, irrespective of how intelligent or educated a particular man might be. Spurgeon continued his above comments: "Why, if God cannot lie, let us give him what we would give to a man if he were of the same character—our full confidence even in the teeth of contradiction—for he is 'God, that cannot lie'."[250] Spurgeon states this well and, oh, that such a spirit would reign among Bible students today.

REMOVING CHAFF

While the apparent contradictions of the Bible will test the faith of some, they will also reveal the lack of faith in others and will be the partial means by which God removes the chaff of unbelievers from the assembly of believers. Christ's discourse in John 6 is an example where the Lord uses an apparent contradiction to remove chaff. In John 6 Jesus says, "I am the living bread which came down from heaven: if any man eat of this bread, he shall live for ever: and the bread that I will give is my flesh, which I will give for the life of the world" (John 6:51). To this, the Jews responded, "How can this man give us his flesh to eat?" (John 6:52). The Jews saw Jesus' statement as a contradiction.

But Jesus continues:

> Verily, verily, I say unto you, Except ye eat the flesh of the Son of man, and drink his blood, ye have no life in you. Whoso eateth my flesh, and drinketh my blood, hath eternal life; and I will raise him up at the last day. For my flesh is meat indeed, and my blood is drink indeed. He that eateth

---

[249] Spurgeon, "What God Cannot Do!" in *The Metropolitan Tabernacle Pulpit*, 10:325.

[250] Ibid., 326.

my flesh, and drinketh my blood, dwelleth in me, and I in him. As the living Father hath sent me, and I live by the Father: so he that eateth me, even he shall live by me. This is that bread which came down from heaven: not as your fathers did eat manna, and are dead: he that eateth of this bread shall live for ever (John 6:53-58).

Many of Jesus' disciples, after hearing this, said, "This is an hard saying: who can hear it?" (John 6:60), that is, who will believe it and receive it? As a result, "many of His disciples went back, and walked no more with Him" (John 6:66). In this case, the apparent contradiction of how they could eat His flesh and drink His blood drove away much of the chaff.

Concerning the passage in John 6, the writers of *Hard Sayings of the Bible* say, "Indeed, the apparent harshness and obscurity of some of our Lord's sayings rid him of followers who were unwilling to be taught or were halfhearted in their search."[251]

George DeHoff, also alluding to the John 6 passage, says,

> These Bible 'difficulties' serve as a test of moral character. Those who have no depth of conviction[252] will be tested by problems such as these. Men's characters and motives will be revealed. The chaff will be sifted from among the wheat. The indolent and superficial, the proud and fastidious were discouraged and repelled by the teaching which Jesus gave (John 6:53). . . . When the scriptures are approached with a reverent mind, the study of the 'contradictions' tends to establish us in the faith but when they are dealt with in an unfair manner they may well become the 'strong delusion' and instrument of our punishment.[253]

The apparent contradictions of the Words of God have the effect of removing the chaff from the wheat.

---

[251] Kaiser, Jr., 16-17.

[252] The phrase *no depth of conviction* reminds the author of the parable of the seed and the sower wherein the seed into stony places depicts the one who did not have "root in himself, but dureth for a while: for when tribulation or persecution ariseth because of the word, by and by he is offended" (Matthew 13:21). Because of his offense to the Word, he leaves.

[253] DeHoff, 46.

Chapter 4 *Reasons for Apparent Contradictions*

CONFOUNDING UNBELIEVERS

In addition to removing the chaff, the apparent contradictions also perform another action upon some unbelievers and that is to confound them. Jesus' parables have such an effect upon some unbelievers. When the disciples asked Jesus why He spoke to the people in parables, He responded, "Therefore speak I to them in parables: because they seeing see not; and hearing they hear not, neither do they understand" (Matthew 13:13). The parables served as a means of hiding the truth from unbelieving skeptics as well as confounding them, and just as the parables served this purpose so do the apparent contradictions of the Bible.

Matthew Henry writes: "The seeming contradictions that are in the word of God are great stumbling-blocks to men of corrupt minds."[254] James Orr says that the Word of God to the saved

> is a lamp to the feet and a light to the path (Psalm 119:105). But to the proud, the unbelieving, and the presumptuous, it is only darkness. These can see nothing in it but difficulties, incredibilities, contradictions, moral monstrosities. It is full of stumbling-blocks. The more they read it, the more are they blinded by it.[255]

Why would God confound the unbeliever? Confounding of unbelievers could be God's way of not casting His pearls before swine (Matthew 7:6). Also, since a man reaps what he has sown, if a man sows rejection to the light of God's Words, it becomes darkness to him. For the light of God's Words to shine upon a man's life, he must open his eyes to it. Jesus says, "If any man will do His will, he shall know the doctrine" (John 7:17).

CONTRADICTING OF SINNERS

Speaking about unbelievers raises yet another reason for apparent contradictions and that is the contradicting of sinners. God, in His longsuffering (II Peter 3:9), allows sinners a certain amount of time on earth. Unsaved sinners have a decided disadvantage in understanding the Scriptures, for the Bible says, "The natural man receiveth not the things of the

---

[254] Matthew Henry, *Matthew to John* in vol. 5 of *Matthew Henry's Commentary* (Peabody, MA: Hendrickson Publishers, Inc., 1991), 217.

[255] James Orr, "Light to the friend, darkness to the foe" in *Exodus*, vol. 1, in vol. 1 of *The Pulpit Commentary*, 342.

Chapter 4 *Reasons for Apparent Contradictions*

Spirit of God: for they are foolishness unto him: neither can he know them, because they are spiritually discerned" (I Corinthians 2:14). This verse presents a number of truths.

First, *the natural man* refers to man in his natural unsaved condition, under the control of his fleshly passions and desires.[256]

Second, since the Spirit of God had a part in giving the Words of God (II Samuel 23:2; Mark 12:36; Acts 1:16; 28:25; I Peter 1:11; II Peter 1:20-21), then "the things of the Spirit of God" include the Scriptures.

Third, the things of the Spirit of God are foolishness to the natural man. *Foolishness*, μωρία, is a noun that comes from μωρός, and is the basis for the English *moron*,[257] and means "folly, foolishness, absurdity."[258] "When, therefore, it is said that the things of the Spirit are foolishness to the natural man, it means that they are to him absurd, insipid and distasteful."[259] To the natural man, then, the Scriptures are absurd. Consequently, when the natural man approaches the Scriptures, he does not see perfection in them (Psalm 19:7), but rather he sees absurdities, contradictions, myths, as well as other supposed errors.

The unsaved man's seeing problems with Scripture is compounded by a fourth truth in I Corinthians 2:14, namely: "neither can he know them, because they are spiritually discerned." The natural man is incapable of knowing the things of the Spirit of God. The word for *know*, γνῶναι a second aorist active infinitive from γινώσκω, means "to discern the nature of any thing, whether as true, or good, or beautiful."[260] The lost man does not discern Scriptures' nature because the things of the Spirit of God are spiritually discerned, which means that "they are discerned through the Spirit."[261] Since the natural man does not have the Spirit of God (John 3:6; Romans 8:9), then he cannot truly understand the Scriptures. Since the natural man cannot truly understand the Bible, then it is easy for him to imagine and concoct all kinds of supposed contradictions in the Bible.

---

[256] Barnes, 14:81-82.

[257] William Morrris, 854.

[258] Zodhiates, 3472.

[259] Charles Hodge, *A Commentary on 1 & 2 Corinthians* (Carlisle, PA: The Banner of Truth Trust, 1974), 43.

[260] Ibid.

[261] Ibid., 44.

Indeed, as a saved Bible student reads the writings of natural men about so-called contradictions in the Bible, he will discover that many are not contradictions at all, but rather imaginations of the unsaved man's mind.

CONCLUSION

God could have given the Bible with no apparent contradictions at all, and God could have limited the activity of sinners to point out so-called contradictions in the Bible, but He has not so chosen. The above fifteen reasons for why God might allow apparent contradictions manifest God's wisdom. Apparent contradictions aid the saved to grow in the Lord by means of humility, prayer, study, and faith, as well as in other areas. On the other hand, apparent contradictions cause several difficulties for the unsaved who are unwilling to believe the Bible. Indeed, the manner in which the Bible is written is, as it were, the savour of death unto death and the savour of life unto life (II Corinthians 2:16). For those who rightly divide the Word of Truth, the Bible is a precious fountain of life unto life.

Sir Robert Anderson, after dealing with several Scriptural difficulties, says, "I have selected examples of various classes of difficulties, and have shown how some that may seem to be insoluble can not only be explained, but so explained as to become helps to faith."[262] Apparent contradictions are helps to faith only for those who rightly divide the Word of Truth. For those who refuse to take the Bible as it is in truth the Word of God and not the word of men (I Thessalonians 2:13), the Bible is a giant stumblingblock that will one day crush their unbelief. Hosea 14:9 says, "Who *is* wise, and he shall understand these *things*? prudent, and he shall know them? for the ways of the LORD *are* right, and the just shall walk in them: but the transgressors shall fall therein." The wise will seek to understand the Bible and walk therein, rather than question it; whereas the transgressors will fall because of their lack of understanding the Bible.

---

[262] Sir Robert Anderson, *The Bible and Modern Criticism*, 259.

CHAPTER FIVE:
HANDLING APPARENT CONTRADICTIONS

The Bible has apparent contradictions. But now the question is this: how should one handle these apparent contradictions? As with any problem, it is good to have a plan or strategy in tackling a problem. Just what should the plan of attack be for tackling the apparent contradictions of the Bible? Such a plan should include several items.

MUST HAVE SALVATION OF CHRIST

Everything in the Christian life starts with salvation, including the ability to understand the Bible properly. I Corinthians 2:14 states: "But the natural man receiveth not the things of the Spirit of God: for they are foolishness unto him: neither can he know *them*, because they are spiritually discerned." If, to the natural man, the things of the Spirit of God are foolishness, then how can he ever hope to understand them? By receiving Christ as his personal Saviour a man is born of the Spirit (John 1:12; 3:6), at which point he has the Spirit (Romans 8:9), and consequently the ability to discern the things of the Spirit of God. Without the salvation of the Lord Jesus Christ, a man could never hope to understand the Bible correctly.

MUST HAVE OBEDIENCE TO THE LORD

After salvation comes obedience. Obedience is vital. Without obedience, the Lord will not hear a man's prayer (Psalm 66:18). But one of the reasons God allows apparent contradictions is to lead a man to pray; therefore, a man must be right with the Lord.

Chapter 5 *Handling Apparent Contradictions*

Furthermore, obedience is necessary to grow in the Lord, especially to grow in grace and knowledge according to the command of II Peter 3:18, which says, "But grow in grace, and in the knowledge of our Lord and Saviour Jesus Christ." Those who are carnal will not be able to understand the Bible as they ought. Paul says, "And I, brethren, could not speak unto you as unto spiritual, but as unto carnal, *even* as unto babes in Christ. I have fed you with milk, and not with meat: for hitherto ye were not able *to bear it*, neither yet now are ye able" (I Corinthians 3:1-2). Because of the Corinthians' carnality, Paul was limited to giving them milk. Jesus says that "if any man will do His will, he shall know of the doctrine" (John 7:17). A man must do the will of God in order to grow in knowledge. On the other hand, the disobedient stumble at the Word (I Peter 2:8). Obedience, then, is necessary for understanding the Bible.

MUST ACCEPT INSPIRATION OF THE BIBLE

If a person is walking in obedience, then he will receive, believe, and hear all that the Bible says, which includes what the Bible says about its own inspiration. The Bible states, "All Scripture is given by inspiration of God, and is profitable for doctrine, for reproof, for correction, for instruction in righteousness" (II Timothy 3:16). This verse states that all Scripture is given by inspiration of God, not just doctrinal or moral portions of the Scriptures, but all, including numbers, history, and science: all of it is inspired of God.

MUST ACCEPT PRESERVATION OF THE BIBLE

In addition to accepting the inspiration of the Bible, one must also accept the preservation of the inspired words. To arrive at a solution other than scribal error for alleged contradictions, a person must believe that he has the correct words. In other words, he must believe that the words that God inspired have been preserved.

Preservation and Jesus' Example

Jesus believed that He had an infallible (John 17:17) and authoritative (John 10:35) copy of the Old Testament with no omissions (Luke 16:17) and that it will remain that way till heaven and earth pass (Matthew 5:18). The Old Testament text of Jesus was a text that came to Him from the

Jews, who were the caretakers of the oracles of God (Romans 3:2). The caretakers of the Words of God in the New Testament era are local churches (I Timothy 3:15), who have also made the Traditional Hebrew Text the *Textus Receptus* of the Old Testament.[263] Since Jesus received the Traditional Hebrew Text of His day, evidencing faith in God's promises and plan of preservation, then this ought to be the position of His followers as well (see Luke 24:25).

No Criticism of the Old Testament

The position of Jesus toward the Bible is the position that the book of Acts, the epistles, and Revelation espouse. Just as no one can point to even a single instance where Jesus ever questions the Old Testament or even hints at a problem with the Traditional Hebrew Text, so no one can point to a single example of such a thing in any of the books of the New Testament.[264] With today's emphasis upon textual criticism, one wonders how the apostles missed this "all-important field of study." Paul, in addressing Timothy, does not give even a single rule for textual criticism. Paul says nothing to Timothy about recovering or restoring the text. Paul says nothing about the axioms that the shortest reading is the best, the oldest reading is the preferred, or the more difficult reading is most likely genuine. Paul says nothing about intrinsic probability, transcriptional probability, or conjectural emendation.

An Infallible Copy of the Old Testament

Was Timothy's ministerial training, therefore, lacking?[265] Not at all, in fact, Paul furthered Timothy's training by instilling into him a belief in

---

[263] For more information on the Traditional Hebrew Text being the *Textus Receptus* of the Old Testament, see the conclusion to the subsection entitled "Jesus Never Once Criticizes the Old Testament" in Chapter Two. Also, see chart on last page of the chapter.

[264] Some might point to the way in which the New Testament writers quoted the Old Testament as evidence. The author deals with this later in this chapter.

[265] Daniel Wallace states: "Of the more than five thousand manuscript copies of the Greek New Testament no two of them agree completely. It is essential, therefore, that anyone who expounds the Word of God be acquainted to some degree with the science of textual criticism, if he or she is to expound that Word faithfully" (Wallace, "Inspiration, Preservation, and New Testament Textual Criticism," *Grace Theological Journal*, 12 (Spring, 1991), 17). Wallace expresses the sentiment of many today, but Paul does not hint of the need for textual criticism in his inspired admonition to Timothy. Rather, God's people must receive the text (John 17:8; I Thessalonians 2:13), not restore it and not re-

the inspiration of the *autographa* and in the preservation of the words of the *autographa*. Paul taught Timothy that "all Scripture is given by inspiration of God" (II Timothy 3:16a). But then in the remainder of II Timothy 3:16 and in the next verse the Bible says, "And is profitable for doctrine, for reproof, for correction, for instruction in righteousness: that the man of God may be perfect, throughly furnished unto all good works" (II Timothy 3:16b,17). Paul teaches that all Scripture is given by inspiration of God and that this very same Scripture has practical benefits for today's man of God. The benefits are not merely for those who are acquainted with the *autographa*, but also for those who have copies, as Timothy did (II Timothy 3:15). Therefore, Paul argues for an infallible copy of the *autographa*, which is available and able to benefit the man of God in Timothy's day, and also is available and beneficial to the man of God in this day. In other words, the passage in II Timothy presents a connection between the inspiration of the Scripture and the preservation of that very same Scripture.

It Is Written

Another comparison between the writers of the New Testament books and Jesus involves the use of *it is written*. *It is written* conveys the idea that what was written in the past still continues or stands written. Therefore, the Words that God originally inspired in the *autographa* are still in existence. Just as Jesus repeatedly uses *it is written* concerning His references to the Old Testament, so the writers of the New Testament books do the same. Their use of *it is written* shows that their Bibliology is the same as Jesus' Bibliology. If one is to handle the apparent contradictions of the Bible properly, he better have the same Bibliology as Christ's Bibliology. The writers of the New Testament repeatedly use *it is written* both as a perfect passive indicative verb and as a perfect passive participle (part.). The following list presents these verses.

1. Matthew 27:37 (part.) — Matthew refers to the inscription on the cross of Jesus. The inscription stands written, for it is recorded in the Gospels.

2. Mark 1:2 — Mark refers to the prophets, in particular, Isaiah 40:3 and Malachi 3:1.

---

cover it. God's Words are not in need of restoration but in need of reception, especially by those who claim to believe it. Sadly, many who claim to believe the Bible are spending a lot of time criticizing the Bible.

Chapter 5 — *Handling Apparent Contradictions*

3. Luke 2:23 — Luke refers to Exodus 13:2.

4. Luke 3:4 — Luke refers to Isaiah 40:3.

5. Luke 4:17 (part.) — Luke refers to Isaiah 61:1-2.

6. Luke 23:38 (part.) — Luke refers to the superscription on the cross.

7. John 2:17 (part.) — John refers to Psalm 69:9.

8. John 12:14 (part.) — John refers to Zechariah 9:9.

9. John 12:16 (part.) — John refers to some things written in his Gospel.

10. John 15:25 (part.) — John refers to Psalm 35:19 and 69:4.

11. John 19:19-20 (part.) — John refers to the title on the cross.

12. John 20:31 — John uses γέγραπται of his Gospel, indicating that his Gospel was written and would stand written.

13. Acts 1:20 — Peter refers to Psalm 69:26.

14. Acts 7:42 — Stephen refers to Amos 5:25-26.

15. Acts 13:29 (part.) — Paul refers to the things that Christ had to fulfill by His sufferings, which would include many Old Testament verses.

16. Acts 13:33 — Paul refers to Psalm 2:7.

17. Acts 15:15 — James refers to Amos 9:11-12.

18. Acts 23:5 — Paul refers to Exodus 22:28.

19. Acts 24:14 (part.) — Paul expresses his belief in "all things which are written in the law and in the prophets," that is, the entire Old Testament. Herein Paul expresses his belief in a copy of the Old Testament that had all the words of the Old Testament *autographa*.

20. Romans 1:17 — Paul refers to Habakkuk 2:4.

21. Romans 2:24 — Paul refers to Isaiah 52:5 and Ezek 36:20, 23.

22. Romans 3:4 — Paul refers to Psalm 51:4.

23. Romans 3:10 — Paul refers to Psalm 14:1-3 and 51:1-3.

24. Romans 4:17 — Paul refers to Genesis 17:5.

25. Romans 8:36 — Paul refers to Psalm 44:22.

26. Romans 9:13 — Paul refers to Malachi 3:1-2.

27. Romans 9:33 — Paul refers to Isaiah 8:14 and 28:16.

28. Romans 10:15 — Paul refers to Isaiah 52:7.

29. Romans 11:8 — Paul refers to Deuteronomy 29:4 and Isaiah 29:10.

Chapter 5 — *Handling Apparent Contradictions*

30. Romans 11:26 — Paul refers to Isaiah 59:20.

31. Romans 12:19 — Paul refers to Deuteronomy 32:35.

32. Romans 14:11 — Paul refers to Isaiah 45:23.

33. Romans 15:3 — Paul refers to Psalm 69:9.

34. Romans 15:9 — Paul refers to Psalm 18:49.

35. Romans 15:21 — Paul refers to Isaiah 52:15.

36. I Corinthians 1:19 — Paul refers to Isaiah 29:14.

37. I Corinthians 1:31 — Paul refers to Jeremiah 9:23-24.

38. I Corinthians 2:9 — Paul refers to Isaiah 44:4.

39. I Corinthians 3:19 — Paul refers to Job 5:13.

40. I Corinthians 4:6 — Paul refers to all of Scripture, showing his belief that all of it is preserved.

41. I Corinthians 9:9 — Paul refers to Deuteronomy 25:4.

42. I Corinthians 10:7 — Paul refers to Exodus 32:6.

43. I Corinthians 14:21 — Paul refers to Isaiah 28:11-12.

44. I Corinthians 15:45 — Paul refers to Genesis 2:7.

45. I Corinthians 15:54 (part.) — Paul refers to Isaiah 25:8.

46. II Corinthians 4:13 (part.) — Paul refers to Psalm 116:10.

47. II Corinthians 8:15 — Paul refers to Exodus 16:18.

48. II Corinthians 9:9 — Paul refers to Psalm 112:9.

49. Galatians 3:10 — Paul refers to Deuteronomy 27:26.

50. Galatians 3:10 — Paul, quoting Deuteronomy 27:26, says, "Cursed is every one that continueth not in all things which are written in the book of the law to do them" wherein the quote itself uses the participle to refer to all that is written in the Pentateuch and to declare that it still stands written.

51. Galatians 3:13 — Paul refers to Deuteronomy 21:23.

52. Galatians 4:22 — Paul refers to Genesis 16 and 21.

53. Galatians 4:27 — Paul refers to Isaiah 44:1.

54. Hebrews 10:7 — quotes Christ as saying, "Lo, I come (in the volume of the book it is written of Me) to do Thy will, O God," which is a quote from Psalm 40:7, wherein the volume of the book refers to the then canonical books of the Old Testament.

55. I Peter 1:16 — Peter refers to Leviticus 11:44.

56. Revelation 1:3 (part.) — John refers to the words of the prophecy of the book of Revelation.

57. Revelation 22:18 (part.) — John refers to the words that are written in the book of Revelation.

58. Revelation 22:19 (part.) — John again refers to the words that are written in the book of Revelation.

The above list clearly demonstrates that the writers of the New Testament, and others, use *it is written* to refer to all parts of the Old Testament as well as to the entire Old Testament (Acts 24:14; I Corinthians 4:6). Is not this in concert with Jesus' use of *it is written* in regard to the Old Testament? Indeed it is and shows that these men had the same Bibliology as that of Jesus in that they believed that the words of the *autographa* were present in their day. Not only did they have this attitude toward the Old Testament Scriptures, but also toward the New Testament Scriptures (Matthew 27:37; Luke 23:38; John 19:19-20; 20:31; and Revelation 1:3; 22:18-19).

Confidence in the Wording of the Old Testament

The teaching of the above verses demonstrates that Paul very clearly accepted the preservation of the Old Testament, so much so that he bases an entire argument on the difference between the plural and the singular. In Galatians 3:16 Paul says, "Now to Abraham and his seed were the promises made. He saith not, And to seeds, as of many; but as of one, And to thy seed, which is Christ." Galatians 3:16 is referring to Genesis 22:18, where the Hebrew word for *to thy seed* is בְזַרְעֶךָ (*bezaraka*), whereas the Hebrew word for *to thy seeds* would be בְזַרְעֶיךָ (*bezareka*). The two words differ by a jot (י) to the left of ע and a vowel underneath ע (in the first word and   in the second). By making such an argument, Paul demonstrates faith that one jot or one tittle has in no wise passed from the law (Matthew 5:18). The insertion of just one jot and one tittle would have changed his whole point. Does Paul argue from the *autographa*? No, he argues from a copy, and so confident is he that the copy was accurate that he bases his whole argument on a jot and a tittle. What confidence he shows in the preservation of the Words of God!

In contrast to Paul's example, many Fundamentalists are following Pache, who writes of the need " 'to reconstruct from all the witnesses available to us the text essentially preserved in all, but perfectly preserved in none'."[266] Though Pache mentions preservation, he actually expresses reservation – reservation about knowing for sure what are the actual Words of God. Paul and Jesus had no reservations about the Words of God, for they believed they possessed the *it-is-written* words of the very *autographa* (see chart on last page of Chapter Two). Fundamentalists need to cancel their reservation and follow the example of Jesus.

Preservation and Inspiration

A number of verses also present evidence that inspiration demands preservation and that, therefore, the student of Scripture should believe that he has the correct words.

Matthew 4:4

In Matthew 4:4 Jesus says, "It is written, Man shall not live by bread alone, but by every word that proceedeth out of the mouth of God." Jesus speaks of "every word that proceedeth out of the mouth of God," which points to the inspiration of those words. At least 802 Old Testament verses state, "Saith the Lord," indicating that the inspired words that men of God spoke proceeded from the mouth of God. The fact that man needs these inspired words from the mouth of God in order to live demands the preservation and availability of those very words. Since the purpose of the words that proceed from the mouth of God is that man can live by them, then the words must be preserved for the very preservation of man himself. If God merely inspired the words and then did not preserve them, then only those men who had the *autographa* would be able to live and no one else. But Jesus teaches that those words are still available so that men can live in this day. Inspiration demands preservation.

Hills agrees with this discussion of Matthew 4:4 when he says,

> If the doctrine of the *divine inspiration* of the Old and New Testament Scriptures is a true doctrine, the doctrine of the *providential preservation* of the Scriptures must also be a true doctrine. It must be that down through the centuries God has exercised a special, providential control over the copying of the Scriptures and the preservation and use of the copies, so that trustworthy representatives of the original text have been available to God's people in every age. God must have done this, for if

---

[266] Keith Gephart, "Are Copies Reliable?" in *God's Word in our Hands*, 182, quoting Rene Pache, *The Inspiration and Authority of Scripture* (Chicago: Moody, 1969), 197.

He gave the Scriptures to His Church by inspiration as the perfect and final revelation of His will, then it is obvious that He would not allow this revelation to disappear or undergo any alteration of its fundamental character.[267]

John 10:35

In John 10:35,[268] Jesus says, "The scripture cannot be broken." *Scripture* is the very same word which II Timothy 3:16 uses: γραφή. Since "all scripture is given by inspiration of God," then the word *Scripture* speaks of inspiration. That Scripture cannot be broken speaks of preservation. It will stand throughout time. None of it will be lost, for it cannot be broken. Jesus' argument, as He quotes from Psalm 82:6, is that the Scripture, simply because it is Scripture, will be preserved. It is the very nature of Scripture that, once given, it must endure. It cannot be extinguished.

I Peter 1:23-25

In I Peter 1:23-25, Peter speaks of the Word of God: "Being born again, not of corruptible seed, but of incorruptible, by the word of God, which liveth and abideth for ever. For all flesh *is* as grass, and all the glory of man as the flower of grass. The grass withereth, and the flower thereof falleth away: but the word of the Lord endureth for ever. And this is the word which by the gospel is preached unto you." *The word of God* and *the word of the Lord* both speak of inspiration. It is God Who spoke in the Old Testament as well as in the New Testament, for "all Scripture is given by inspiration of God" (II Timothy 3:16).

Combs expresses the idea that Peter's emphasis in this passage is on "the gospel message as proclaimed to his readers, not on God's written revelation."[269] However, Peter emphasizes that the word that was preached to his hearers, "liveth and abideth forever" and "endureth for

---

[267] Edward F. Hills, *The King James Version Defended: A Space-Age Defense of the Historic Christian Faith*, 3d ed. (Des Moines: The Christian Research Press, 1973), 2. Hills capitalizes *church*, perhaps referring to a universal church. However, God gave His Words to local churches, which are the pillar and the ground of the truth (I Timothy 3:15).

[268] For a more detailed treatment of John 10:35, see Chapter Two.

[269] Combs, "The Preservation of Scripture," 26. Daniel Wallace argues similarly in "Inspiration, Preservation, and New Testament Textual Criticism," *Grace Theological Journal* 12 (1991): 42.

ever." In what way would a merely oral communication live, abide, and endure forever? Would not a merely oral communication have passed off the scene? Peter argues for the preservation of the Words of God and that these very words are living, abiding, and enduring today, all of which speaks of the words having been written. Indeed, the preaching of the Gospel by Peter is written in the book of Acts (Acts 2:14-36; 3:12-26; 4:8-12; 10:34-43; 15:7-11). Peter bases his preaching on the Old Testament written Words of God (Acts 2:16-21, 25-28, 34-35; 3:18, 21-24; 4:11; 10:43). Peter says that the Gospel was preached unto them (I Peter 1:25). True preaching is based on the written Words of God. The Bible commands, "Preach the word" (II Timothy 4:2), which, according to the context, is the preaching of God's inscripturated words (II Timothy 3:16-17), which words are able to make a person "wise unto salvation" (II Timothy 3:15). Furthermore, the basis of the Gospel is (1) recorded in the four gospels; (2) defined in I Corinthians 15; and (3) elaborated upon in the epistles. Peter, then, is very definitely arguing for the preservation of God's written words. Strouse aptly points out that Combs' "argument that the expression 'the word(s) of God (Lord)' does not ultimately refer to the final inscripturation of God's canonical revelation has the ring of neo-orthodoxy and should be shunned by Fundamentalists."[270]

Donald Brake quotes Alfred Martin quoting an unidentified source:

> Why should God have worked a stupendous miracle in order to preserve the writers of the Biblical books from error and make the autographs of their books completely true, if He intended then to leave the books thus produced to the mere chance of transmission from generation to generation by very human and often careless copyists?[271]

This is a good question and the answer is that God did not leave His Words up to the whim and vicissitudes of men, for He states that His Word endureth forever. Brake himself says,

> It is incredible to think that a God Who Divinely inspired the writings of the autographs so that every word was without error, would then leave His Holy Word in the hands of sinful and imperfect men who could miscopy and perhaps lose some of His words so that in a matter of a few years the

---

[270] Thomas M. Strouse, "Article Review," 6. On the same page Strouse states: "The whole direction of the Bible teaching of divine revelation moves from God's revelation, albeit in various forms including oral communication, to the final inscripturation of the inspired and canonical words of God (cf. II Tim. 3:16-17; Rev. 22:18-19 *et al*)."

[271] Brake, 178, quoting Alfred Martin, "The Word of the Lord Endureth Forever," *Founders Week Messages 1966* (Chicago: Moody Bible Institute, 1966), 284.

Scriptures would no longer be inerrant. The statement that the words of God "will endure forever" shows that it is quite safe to maintain that the Scriptures recording these words will be preserved from their inception to their consummation—forever.[272]

Peter, therefore, connects inspiration and preservation. Furthermore, since Peter states that the very Words of God were preached unto them, then the Words of God were available to them. The Words of God were not buried somewhere in a multitude of manuscripts.

Psalm 12:6-7

The Old Testament also teaches that inspiration demands preservation. Psalm 12:6-7 is a classic passage: "The words of the LORD *are* pure words: *as* silver tried in a furnace of earth, purified seven times. Thou shalt keep them, O LORD, thou shalt preserve them from this generation for ever."

The Words of the Lord Are Purified Words

The words of the LORD in verse 6 speaks of inspiration. Verse 6 also says that these words are pure. The fact that the Words of the Lord are pure words testifies to the inerrancy of the inspired words. Spurgeon says of these pure words,

> What a contrast between the vain words of man, and the pure words of Jehovah. Man's words are yea and nay, but the Lord's promises are yea and amen. For truth, certainty, holiness, faithfulness, the words of the Lord are pure as well refined silver. In the original there is an allusion to the most severely purifying process known to the ancients, through which silver was passed when the greatest possible purity was desired; the dross was all consumed, and only the bright and precious metal remained; so clear and free from all alloy of error or unfaithfulness is the book of the words of the Lord.[273]

---

[272] Ibid., 188. The fact "that the Scriptures recording these words will be preserved from their inception to their consummation" does not mean that all copies of the Scriptures agree with themselves or that no corruptions occurred, for the Bible speaks of many who corrupt the Word of God (II Corinthians 2:17); rather the preservation of the Scriptures recording the Words of God means that God will insure that His Words remain intact. It cannot be that any of His Words will perish (Matthew 5:18).

[273] Charles H. Spurgeon, *The Treasury of David*, Part 1 of Vol. 1 (Peabody, MA: Hendrikson Publishers, n.d.), 143.

Chapter 5　　　　　　　　　　　*Handling Apparent Contradictions*

The Words of the Lord Are Preserved Words

Verse 7, then, speaks of the preservation of these pure words. The Lord Himself will keep and preserve these words for ever, not just for as long as the *autographa* last, but forever. *Thou shalt keep them* is a Qal imperfect second masculine singular with a third masculine plural suffix from שָׁמַר (*shamar*). "The underlying root meaning is 'to pay careful attention to,' "[274] and " 'to exercise great care over'."[275] Exodus 21:29 and 36 use this same word preceded by the negative of a man not keeping his harmful ox in a pen but, instead, letting the ox go loose. In contrast to the man of Exodus 21, the LORD will not let His Words be loosed from the Bible. He will keep them. The LORD promises to exercise great care over and to pay careful attention to His Words. *LORD* emphasizes that God is well able to keep His Words because *LORD* comes from the word *Jehovah* teaching that God is the self-sufficient, self-sustaining, eternal One (Exodus 3:14).

Not only will the LORD keep His Words, but the Bible also says, "Thou shalt preserve them," which is a Qal imperfect second masculine singular with a third masculine singular suffix from נָצַר (*natzar*). In this context it has "the concept of 'guarding with fidelity'."[276] The LORD will faithfully guard His Words. This is a wonderful promise for the preservation of God's Words.[277]

The Preservation of the Poor?

Some, however, claim that Psalm 12:7 is not a promise for the preservation of the Words of the Lord, but is a promise for the preservation of the poor and needy mentioned in verse 5. Proponents for having verse 7

---

[274] Keith N. Schoville, "שָׁמַר" in *New International Dictionary of Old Testament Theology and Exegesis CD.*

[275] John E. Hartley, "2412 שָׁמַר" in *Theological Wordbook of the Old Testament*, ed. R. Laird Harris (Chicago: Moody Press, 1981), 2:939.

[276] Walter C. Kaiser, "1407 נָצַר" in *Theological Wordbook of the Old Testament*, 2:595.

[277] While the Lord promises to keep and to preserve His Words, He used the Jews to assist (Acts 7:38; Romans 3:2) and local churches (Matthew 28:20; Jude 3; Revelation 3:8, 10).

Chapter 5   *Handling Apparent Contradictions*

refer to the preservation of the poor put forth two reasons for their view: (1) the overall context of the Psalm; and (2) the pronouns in verse 7.

The Context

Glenny argues from the context that Psalm 12:7 refers to the preservation of the poor. He states:

> The psalm is an expression of David's confidence in the pure words of God. In verses 1-4, he prays for deliverance from the proud flatterers all around him who cannot be trusted (v. 2b). Verse 5 gives the source of David's confidence; he is assured that the Lord will deliver him from those who are maligning him. In verses 6-8, David declares that his confidence is in God's Word. In this context, David's expression of confidence in verse 6 refers to his confidence in God's affirmation that He will deliver the afflicted (v. 5). Then in verse 7, on the basis of his confidence in God's Word (vv. 5-6), David declares his assurance that God will preserve forever the righteous, who are being afflicted by the wicked of "this generation."[278]

In order to bolster his argument from the context, Glenny then goes on to make a point about the pronouns in verse 7 (see below).

Contrary to Glenny, Strouse, who argues that Psalm 12:7 speaks of the preservation of God's Words, states:

> Psalm 12 is a psalm of contrasts. It contrasts the godly with the ungodly, and the Words of the Lord with the words of men. The latter contrast gives the backdrop to one of the clearest promises in the OT for the preservation of God's Words.[279]

Strouse also speaks of the structure of the Psalm and states:

> The structure of the psalm is asymmetric. The psalmist moved from the recognition of the need for help to the threat of the wicked, finally focusing on the promises' of God. He then gave the antidote to man's words, which in turn are the Words of God. He concluded with the recognition of the need for divine Help. This structure causes the focus to be on God's Promises.[280]

---

[278] Glenny, "The Preservation of Scripture and the Version Debate" in *One Bible Only?*, 119.

[279] Thomas M. Strouse, *An Exegesis of Psalms 1-41* (Newington, CT: Emmanuel Baptist Theological Press, 2006), 95.

[280] Ibid.

Chapter 5 *Handling Apparent Contradictions*

Strouse concludes his discussion of Psalm 12 saying:

> David recognized that the proud words of the wicked flatterers would always be around, but so would the perfect Words of God to counter man's lies. Jeremiah expresses succinctly this tension between God's Words and man's words, stating *"all the remnant of Judah . . . shall know whose words shall stand, mine, or theirs"* (Jer. 44:28).
>
> The structure, context, and exegesis of the Masoretic Hebrew text of Psalm 12 all argue forcefully and irrefragably for the promise of the everlasting preservation of the perfect Words of the Lord. This is one of several clear passages in which the Lord promised to preserve His canonical Words for every generation. Man's ever-present words are lies, God's ever-present Words are Truth. This is the tangible help from the Lord that the righteous man has in every generation.[281]

Glenny argues from the context that Psalm 12:7 refers to the preservation of the poor, whereas Strouse argues from the context that Psalm 12:7 refers to the preservation of God's Words. Which of these views is correct? In order to determine the correct view, one must examine the pronouns of verse 7. It is from an examination of the pronouns that it becomes clear, as Strouse maintains, that verse 7 is referring to the preservation of God's Words.

The Pronouns

Glenny, in arguing for understanding Psalm 12:7 to refer to the preservation of the poor, appeals to the pronouns. He states:

> Hebrew grammar requires that it be the righteous whom God is keeping and preserving in verse 7. In Hebrew, nouns and pronouns have gender and number, and the gender and number of each pronoun normally should be the same as that of its antecedent. The pronoun *them* (v. 7a) is a masculine suffix whereas the noun *words* (v. 6a) is feminine. Furthermore, in the Hebrew text verse 7b reads, "You will preserve him from this generation for ever." Delitzsch says that the *him* refers "to the man who yearns for deliverance mentioned in the divine utterance" (v. 5 in Eng.). This connection is clear in the Hebrew because the pronoun on the verb preserve (v. 7b) is third person, masculine, and singular.[282]

Another proponent for understanding Psalm 12:7 to refer to the preservation of the poor states:

---

[281] Ibid., 100, 101.

[282] Glenny, 120.

Chapter 5 *Handling Apparent Contradictions*

> The fact that "words" in verse six is feminine indicates that this pronoun cannot have "words" as its antecedent. That which is preserved must also be masculine. The grammar of the passage indicates that the references to "keeping" and "preserving" are to God's promise to guard and protect the righteous (masculine gender) so the wicked will not ultimately prevail.[283]

Such argumentation may sound convincing to one who has not studied Hebrew grammar. The fact is, however, that Hebrew grammar does not require that "it be the righteous whom God is keeping and preserving in verse 7." While it is true that "the gender and number of each pronoun normally should be the same as that of its antecedent," it is not always the case. Several sources prove that the masculine plural *them* of *thou shalt keep them* of verse 7 can refer to the feminine plural *words* of verse 6. Thomas Strouse states:

> The antecedent of "them" (v. 7) in "shalt keep them" (*tishermerem*) must be "words" (*'imeroth*) in verse 6 because of the Hebrew rule of proximity. Even though "words" is feminine plural and "shalt keep them" is masculine plural [the verb itself is masculine singular, but it has a masculine plural suffix], this gender discordance is not uncommon, especially with reference to the writer's apparent effort to "masculinize" this extension of the patriarchal God – His words (cf. Psm. 119:111, 129, 152, 167).[284]

Since the Bible refers to the LORD in masculine terms, then the words that come from Him can be thought of as masculine, and, therefore, the Psalmist refers to these words with the masculine pronoun.

In another work Strouse illustrates the tendency for Hebrew masculine pronouns to refer to feminine antecedents that speak of Scripture. Below is a list of some of Strouse's examples. In the following list "f.s." means feminine singular; "m.s." means masculine singular; "f.p." means feminine plural; and "m.p." means masculine plural.

> *That thou mayest observe to do according to all the **law** (torah--f.s.)...turn not from **it** (mimmennu--m.s.),* (Joshua 1:7).

---

[283] James B. Williams, ed., *God's Word in Our Hands*, 88.

[284] Strouse, *"But My Words Shall Not Pass Away"*, 10. The verses that Strouse cites are very instructive. In Psalm 119:111 the masculine plural pronoun *they* refers back to *testimonies*, a feminine plural noun. In Psalm 119:129 the masculine plural pronoun *them* attached as a suffix to the verb *keep* refers back to *testimonies*, a feminine plural noun. In Psalm 119:152 the masculine plural suffix pronoun *them* attached to the verb *founded* refers to *testimonies*, a feminine plural noun. In Psalm 119:167 the masculine plural pronoun *them* attached as a suffix to the verb *love* refers to *testimonies*, a feminine plural noun.

Chapter 5 *Handling Apparent Contradictions*

> *For he established a **testimony** (`eduth--f.s.) in Jacob, and appointed a **law** (torah f.s.) in Israel, which he commanded our fathers, that they should make **them** (am--m.p.) known to their children* (Psalm 78:5).
>
> *Therefore shall ye keep my **commandments** (mitzwoth--f.p.), and do **them** ('otham--m.p.): I am the LORD* (Leviticus 22:31).
>
> *If ye walk in my **statutes** (chuqqoth--f.p.), and keep my **commandments** (mitzwoth--f.p.), and do **them** ('otham--m.p.)* (Leviticus 26:3).
>
> *And remember all the **commandments** (mitzwoth--f.p.) of the LORD, and do **them** ('otham--m.p.)* (Numbers 15:39).
>
> *If thou wilt walk in my **statutes** (chuqqoth--f.p.), and execute my **judgments** (mishpat--m.p.), and keep all my **commandments** (mitzwoth--f.p.) to walk in **them** (hem--m.p.)* (I Kings 6:12).
>
> *And you shall keep my **statutes** (chuqqoth--f.p.), and do **them** ('otham--m.p.)* (Leviticus 20:8).
>
> *For they have refused my **judgments** (mishpat--m.p.) and my **statutes** (chuqqoth--f.p.), they have not walked in **them** (hem--m.p.)* (Ezekiel 5:6).
>
> *And hath kept all my **statutes** (chuqqoth--f.p.), and hath done **them** ('otham--m.p.)* (Ezekiel 18:19).
>
> *They shall also walk in my **judgments** (mishpat--m.p.); and observe my **statutes** (chuqqoth--f.p.), and do **them** ('otham--m.p.)* (Ezekiel 37:24).[285]

An Introduction to Biblical Hebrew Syntax states: "Grammarians speak of the masculine gender as '*the prior gender*' because its form sometimes refers to female beings."[286] The book then goes on to list four examples from Genesis 1:27; 32:1; Leviticus 13:29; and Exodus 20:10; as well as examples where the Bible uses a feminine plural noun with a masculine plural verb such as Judges 21:21 and Leviticus 26:33.[287]

Gesenius' Hebrew Grammar says, "Through a weakening in the distinction of gender . . . *masculine* suffixes (especially in the plural) are not infrequently used to refer to *feminine* substantives."[288] It is plain, then,

---

[285] Strouse, "Strouse's Law of the Tendency for Hebrew Pronouns to Masculinize their corresponding Feminine Antecedents" (Newington, CT: Emmanuel Baptist Theological Seminary, 2006), 1-2.

[286] Bruce K. Waltke and M. O'Connor, *An Introduction to Biblical Hebrew Syntax* (Winona Lake, In: Eisenbrauns, 1990), 108.

[287] Ibid., 110.

[288] E. Kautzsch, ed., *Gesenius' Hebrew Grammar*, 440.

that Hebrew grammar does not require that *them* in Psalm 12:7 refer back to *the poor* in verse 5.

Furthermore, the *them* of *thou shalt preserve them* in verse 7 being a third person masculine singular pronoun suffixed to the verb can also refer to the feminine plural *words* of verse 6. *Gesenius' Hebrew Grammar* after pointing out "the plural of persons . . . is sometimes construed with the singular of the predicate, when . . . each severally is to be represented as affected by the statement," then states that "analogous to the examples above mentioned [showing that the singular can refer to the plural] is the somewhat frequent use of suffixes in the singular (distributively) referring to plurals."[289] In other words, the singular suffix attached to *thou shalt preserve them* of verse 7 can refer to the plural *words* of verse 6 with the meaning that God preserves every one of the words.

Therefore, the teaching of Psalm 12:7 is: (1) God collectively keeps all the inspired inerrant words, and (2) God preserves each single word. Herein is the foundational verse for the plenary, verbal preservation of the inspired, inerrant Words of the Lord.

Psalm 119:152

Psalm 119:152 says, "Concerning thy testimonies, I have known of old that thou hast founded them for ever." *Concerning Thy testimonies*, מֵעֵדֹתֶיךָ (*me'edoteyka*), is from עֵדָה (*'edah*). Deuteronomy 6:17 and 20 use *'edah* to refer to the very testimonies that God had commanded for the children of Israel and, therefore, these testimonies were inspired of God. Of these testimonies, the Psalmist says, "I have known of old that Thou hast founded them for ever." God has founded forever His inspired testimonies. *Thou hast founded them* is a Qal perfect second masculine singular verb with a third masculine plural suffix referring back to *testimonies*[290] from יָסַד (*yāsad*). "The primary meaning of *yāsad* is 'to found, to fix firmly,' from which the major nominal meaning derives, i.e., 'founda-

---

[289] Ibid., 464.

[290] The masculine plural suffix pronoun, *them*, refers to *testimonies*, a feminine plural noun. This same type of construction occurs in Psalm 12:6-7 where the verb, *thou shalt keep them*, also has the masculine plural suffix pronoun, and just as in Psalm 119:152 where the masculine pronoun refers to a feminine noun, so in Psalm 12:7 the masculine pronoun refers to the feminine noun *words* in verse 6.

tion' especially of a building."²⁹¹ "There are overtones of solidity and permanence in many passages where the qal or niphal of *ysd* appears; this is almost always true in connection with the creation of the earth (cf. Ps. 24:2 and figuratively 119:152)."²⁹²

Thou hast founded them is, then, speaking of the permanence and preservation of God's testimonies. The fact that God gave His testimonies speaks of inspiration and that He founded them forever speaks of preservation. Here again the Bible connects inspiration and preservation. Not only that, but the Psalmist also says, "I have known of old"; that is, it was well known. How is it that so many of this day have missed this teaching? Could it be that they are not willing to believe God's Words, which of old have taught the preservation of His inspired Words?

Psalm 100:5 & 119:160

Psalm 119:160 says, "Thy word is true from the beginning; and every one of Thy righteous judgments *endureth* for ever." *Thy word* speaks of God's inspired Words. *Is true from the beginning* speaks of the inerrancy of God's Words indicating that from the moment God gave them, they are true. *True*, אֱמֶת (*'emeth*), "carries [the] underlying sense of certainty, dependability . . . it is frequently applied to God as a characteristic of His nature . . . [and] it is a term fittingly applied to God's Words (Ps 119:142, 151, 160; Dan 10:21)."²⁹³ "The meaning 'to be true' has arisen from the original meaning 'to be constant, permanent, faithful.' Truth is that which is constant and unchangeable."²⁹⁴

> As creator, God "keeps *'emeth*," and man can rely on Him "for ever" (Ps. 146:6). . . . He is great in *chesedh* and *'emeth* (Ex. 34:6; Ps. 86:15). Thus, *'emeth* belongs to God. This applies to the word of God in particular. The word of man may be often deceitful, but God's speech is *'emeth*! . . . It is characteristic of Yahweh's deity that a person can rely on His words. . . . Frequently the poet of Ps. 119 emphasizes the reliability of the divine

---

²⁹¹ Paul R. Gilchrist, "875 יָסַד," in *Theological Wordbook of the Old Testament*, 1:384.

²⁹² R. Mosis, "יָסַד," in *Theological Dictionary of the Old Testament*, 6:116.

²⁹³ Jack B. Scott, "116 אָמַן" in *Theological Wordbook of the Old Testament*, 1:52.

²⁹⁴ Alfred Jepsen, "אָמַן" in *Theological Dictionary of the Old Testament*, 1:310.

Chapter 5 *Handling Apparent Contradictions*

word (vv. 43, 160), divine instruction (v. 142), and divine commandments (v. 151; cf. Ps. 19:10[9]; Neh. 9:13).[295]

God's Words being true means that they are not only faithful, but they are also permanent; that is, they are preserved.

The second half of the verse also teaches the preservation of these true words when it states, "Every one of Thy righteous judgments *endureth* forever." The translators supplied the word *endureth*, which is certainly warranted by the use of *true* in the first part of the verse and by the words *for ever* at the end of the verse. *Endureth for ever* applies to every one of God's righteous judgments. Certainly, inspiration demands preservation. What God inspired is true and, therefore, constant and permanent. Spurgeon says,

> That which thou hast decided remains irreversible in every case. Against the decisions of the Lord no writ of error can be demanded, neither will there ever be a repealing of any of the acts of his sovereignty. There is not one single mistake either in the word of God or in the providential dealings of God. Neither in the book of revelation nor of providence will there be any need to put a single note of errata. The Lord has nothing to regret or to retract, nothing to amend or to reverse. All God's judgments, decrees, commands, and purposes are righteous, and as righteous things are lasting things, every one of them will outlive the stars. "Till heaven and earth pass, one jot or one tittle shall in no wise pass from the law, till all be fulfilled."[296]

Psalm 100:5 makes a similar point: "For the LORD *is* good: his mercy is everlasting; and his truth [from אֱמֶת (*'emeth*, see above)] *endureth* to all generations." What a Book is the Bible!

Isaiah 30:8

Isaiah 30:8 states, "Now go, write it before them in a table, and note it in a book, that it may be for the time to come for ever and ever." God commanded Isaiah to write in a book. Isaiah wrote the inspired Words of God in the following verses (Isaiah 30:9ff). Why would God have Isaiah write these words in a book? God had Isaiah write these words so that they "may be for the time to come for ever and ever," in other words, that

---

[295] Ibid., 313.

[296] Spurgeon, *The Treasury of David*, Part 1 of Vol. 3, 416.

Chapter 5   *Handling Apparent Contradictions*

these inspired words would be preserved. Inspiration demands preservation. Matthew Henry states:

> The prophet must not only preach this, but he must write it (*v.* 8), *write it in a table*, to be hung up and exposed to public view; he must carefully *note it*, not in loose papers which might be lost or torn, but *in a book*, to be preserved for posterity, *in perpetuam rei memoriam—for a standing testimony* against this wicked generation; let it remain not only to the next succeeding ages, but for ever and ever, while the world stands; and so it shall, for the book of the scriptures no doubt, shall continue, and be read, to the end of time.[297]

Isaiah 40:8

Isaiah 40:8 states, "The grass withereth, the flower fadeth: but the word of our God shall stand for ever." E. J. Young, commenting on this verse, says,

> To God's word there is a permanent character. Unlike the flesh of man, which withers and fades, it stands forever. It rises up, stands, and endures. In contrast to all flesh with its perishable nature, the word of God is imperishable and endures forever. The thought is similar to that of our Lord's, "The Scripture cannot be broken." When God speaks, His word expresses the truth; and that truth cannot be annulled or changed.[298]

I Peter 1:25 quotes Isaiah 40:8 and comments from that verse apply here. It is interesting that the Bible repeats some of the verses on preservation (cf., for example, Matthew 5:18 and Luke 16:17; Matthew 24:35, Mark 13:31, and Luke 21:33). Is this by accident? Not at all, for the Lord emphasizes the doctrine of preservation, while some are trying their best to ignore or minimize it.

Conclusion

That inspiration demands preservation is a point that the author emphasizes because it is a teaching that has come under attack by those who say they love the Bible. Kevin Bauder of Central Baptist Theological Seminary declares, "The Bible nowhere explicitly links the doctrines of inspiration and inerrancy with a concomitant promise of perfect preserva-

---

[297] Matthew Henry, *Isaiah to Malachi* in vol. 4 of *Matthew Henry's Commentary*, 131.

[298] E. J. Young, *The Book of Isaiah* (Grand Rapids: Eerdmans, 1978), 3:35.

tion."²⁹⁹ In the same book, W. Edward Glenny says, "The perfect preservation of God's Word is not a necessary corollary of the inspiration of God's Word."³⁰⁰ Later, in the same book, Bauder continues: "The King James-Only advocates insist that belief in the preciseness of verbal inspiration (which we all affirm) is useless unless it is followed by exactness in verbal preservation (which the authors of this book do not affirm)."³⁰¹ Such statements fly in the face of Psalm 12:6-7; 100:5; 119:152, 160; Isaiah 30:8; 40:8; Matthew 5:18; 24:35; Mark 13:31; Luke 16:17; John 10:35; 17:17; and I Peter 1:23-25. In addition, the statements of Glenny and Bauder neglect the significance of *it is written*, wherein the Words of God that were written in the past still stand written to this day.

The Bibliology that rejects the perfect preservation of God's inspired words, to which many Fundamentalists adhere, is not the Bibliology of Jesus, Paul, Peter, or the Prophets. Until these Fundamentalists accept the Bibliology of Jesus, they will not produce good solutions to the apparent contradictions of the Bible. Indeed, Fundamentalists, instead of accepting the Bibliology of Jesus, are trying to explain it away or questioning it. The fact that Fundamentalists reject the Bibliology of Jesus has resulted in these same Fundamentalists questioning the Bible itself. To reject the teaching of the Incarnate Word, often leads to a rejection of the written words. Glenny writes, "Has God perfectly preserved His Word so that no words have been lost? The evidence from the OT text suggests that such is not the case. We might have lost a few words through negligence."³⁰² Is not Glenny's assertion in direct contradiction to the teaching of Jesus? If Glenny is right, then one would have to conclude that Jesus did not know whereof He spoke when He gave the promise of Matthew 5:18. Whom is one to believe, Glenny or Jesus? The author, for one, is going to believe the statements of Jesus rather than the statements of fallible men. The position espoused by these men is most dangerous.

---

²⁹⁹ Kevin T. Bauder, "The Issues at Hand" in *One Bible Only?*, 24. It seems that the operative word in Bauder's statement, as one continues to read, is the word *perfect*. While he speaks of a preservation of the text, he does not believe that God has preserved all the words. But define his terms as he will, the Bible does teach that God has preserved all the words.

³⁰⁰ Glenny, 115. Another one who criticizes the view that inspiration demands preservation is Daniel B. Wallace. See Wallace, "Inspiration, Preservation, and New Testament Textual Criticism," *Grace Theological Journal*, 12 (Spring, 1991), 45.

³⁰¹ Bauder, "An Appeal to Scripture" in *One Bible Only?*, 158.

³⁰² Glenny, 121.

Chapter 5 *Handling Apparent Contradictions*

Preservation and Doctrinal Content

What Bauder and Glenny argue for, then, is not the preservation of the exact words of the *autographa* but for the preservation of the ideas or doctrinal content of the *autographa*. Glenny writes, "God has providentially preserved the text of Scripture in multiple manuscripts throughout history so that none of its doctrinal content is lost or affected adversely."[303]

The above statement by Glenny is illogical. What does it mean that God has preserved the text with the result that none of its doctrinal content is lost? Especially what does this mean when Glenny has already stated that not all of the words are preserved?[304] Does not *text* refer to words? And is not doctrine based on the exact words of Scripture (Galatians 3:16; II Timothy 3:16)? But how does Glenny know that "none of its doctrinal content is lost or affected adversely"? If God has not preserved the words themselves, then how does Glenny know that there is no loss of doctrinal content? Furthermore, if none of the Bible's "doctrinal content is lost or affected adversely" meaning that it has stood the test of time and is still in our possession, that is, preserved; then why is just the doctrinal content preserved?[305] Why are not other parts preserved such as the historical sections of I Samuel to II Chronicles some of which Glenny questions, as this book presents in Chapter One? Is it harder to preserve historical pas-

---

[303] Glenny, 122.

[304] Mark Minnick of Bob Jones University comes close to this same position, if not, actually espousing it, when he says, "In the cases where we may not be sure which variant most accurately repeats the original wording, not one doctrine is affected. Not one truth is compromised. Every doctrine and truth of God's Word is taught in so many other places, in synonymous or verbatim wording, that no variant obscures it" (Mark Minnick, "Let's Meet the Manuscripts" in *From the Mind of God to the Mind of Man: A Layman's Guide to How We Got Out Bible*, 3d ed., ed. James B. Williams (Greenville, SC: Ambassador-Emerald International, 1999), 96). But how does Mark Minnick know that not one truth is compromised? If one is not assured that he has all the words, then he cannot be sure that not one doctrine is affected. The position of Mark Minnick is illogical. Also, Donald Brake observes, "Many theologians such as Young and Skilton believe that the doctrine of preservation guarantees only that no point of doctrine has been affected" (Brake, 188).

[305] Another important question to ask is: who decides what is doctrinal content? What if one were to believe that the entire Bible is doctrinal, that is, essential for faith and practice? Did not Jesus believe this way? See Matthew 4:4. Or is doctrinal content to be determined by some panel or by majority vote? Who determines what doctrinal content is? Is it going to be the textual critics, or is it going to be Biblicist Baptist preachers? Who has the final say on what is doctrinal content?

Chapter 5 *Handling Apparent Contradictions*

sages than doctrinal content? To say that one section of the Bible is preserved and another is not preserved is very illogical. Besides, who is the final arbiter to decide which parts are preserved and which are not? Who becomes the Textual Pontiff?

The contention that God only preserved doctrinal content is not only illogical, but also more importantly, it is unscriptural. If God did not preserve the historical content, then how can one be convinced that He preserved the doctrinal content? No doubt, those who argue for a doctrinal-content preservation would say that the doctrinal content is of greater importance than the historical content. But Jesus taught, "He that is faithful in that which is least is faithful also in much: and he that is unjust in the least is unjust also in much" (Luke 16:10). If the preservation of the Bible is not faithful in that which is least (historical content), then how can one trust preservation in that which is much (doctrinal content)? Interestingly, just a few verses after Luke 16:10, Jesus said, "And it is easier for heaven and earth to pass, than one tittle of the law to fail" (Luke 16:17). It is as if Jesus is giving assurance that God has preserved His Words in that which is least (one tittle) and, therefore, one can trust God's Words in much. Furthermore, Jesus said to Nicodemus, "If I have told you earthly things, and ye believe not, how shall ye believe, if I tell you of heavenly things?" (John 3:12). Those who believe in a doctrinal-content preservation have a real problem here. If one cannot trust the present text of Scripture when it speaks of earthly things such as history, science, and chronology; then how can one trust it in heavenly things? If it is flawed in the one area, then it is also flawed in the other area.[306] The position of doctrinal-content preservation suffers from serious scriptural deficiencies in this regard.

Additionally, if God did not preserve historical content, then doctrine is affected. Jesus said, "One jot or one tittle shall in no wise pass from the law" (Matthew 5:18). If God allowed the loss of historical content from the Scriptures, then Jesus is a liar and, therefore, not God and, therefore, also unable to save. This is serious indeed. Furthermore, if the Lord did not preserve historical content, then what about all the promises concerning preservation? If God did not preserve historical content, then the

---

[306] Consider this: if the preserved text of the Bible is flawed in matters of history, then there are books that are more accurate than the Bible text, and these books stand in judgment upon the Biblical text, instead of the text of the Bible judging these other books. Something is seriously wrong with a position that makes other books more accurate than the Scriptures. Jesus said, "Thy word is truth" (John 17:17). What can be truer than truth?

doctrine of the preservation of the Bible is affected. Furthermore, if God did not preserve historical content, then man does not have every word that proceedeth out of the mouth of God and, therefore, cannot live (Matthew 4:4). In espousing a doctrinal-content preservation, Glenny and others introduce real doctrinal problems.

Conclusion

Inspiration demands the preservation, not only of the doctrinal content, but also of all the inspired words. John Owen states:

> That as the Scriptures of the Old and New Testament were immediately and entirely given out by God himself, his mind being in them represented unto us without the least interveniency of such mediums and ways as were capable of giving change or alteration to the least iota or syllable; so, by his good and merciful providential dispensation, in his love to his word and church, his whole word, as first given out by him, is preserved unto us entire in the original languages; where, shining in its own beauty and lustre (as also in all translations, so far as they faithfully represent the originals), it manifests and evidences unto the consciences of men, without other foreign help or assistance, its divine original and authority. . . . But what, I pray, will it advantage us that God did so once deliver his word, if we are not assured also that that word so delivered hath been, by his special care and providence, preserved entire and uncorrupt unto us?[307]

Crucial to the proper handling of apparent Biblical contradictions is this: one must believe that inspiration demands preservation and that, therefore, God has preserved the Scriptures entirely, inerrantly, and infallibly. The failure to understand that the Traditional Hebrew and Greek Texts accurately convey the *autographa* leads men to propagate unacceptable solutions to the apparent contradictions such as scribal error, lost words, lost letters, and more.

MUST NOT CORRECT THE WORDS OF GOD

God inspired inerrant words, and He has fully preserved those inerrant words. Jesus referred to the Traditional Hebrew Text of His day as truth (John 17:17); therefore, the inerrant, inspired, and God-preserved words are in the Traditional texts. Bible students should receive these Tradi-

---

[307] John Owen, "Of the Integrity and Purity of the Hebrew and Greek Test of the Scripture" in *The Works of John Owen*, 16:450.

Chapter 5 *Handling Apparent Contradictions*

tional texts as the infallible record of the inspired, inerrant words. This being the case, one should not correct the Scriptures. On the contrary, the Bible corrects the man of God (II Timothy 3:16), not the man of God, the Bible. Is not something horribly wrong when the man of God thinks he can judge God's Words? He is not acting very godly at all, for he has usurped God's authority and needs to repent and humbly submit himself to the authority of the Words of God.

When a man fully submits himself to the authority of God's Words, then he will not say that the preserved text has errors, additions, or omissions. Whenever modern science or archaeology questions the Bible, such a man will reject the science so-called and believe what is written in the Bible. Paul said to Timothy, "O Timothy, keep that which is committed to thy trust, avoiding profane *and* vain babblings, and oppositions of science falsely so called" (I Timothy 6:20). Geisler and Howe say,

> And even though God's Word is perfect (Ps. 19:7), as long as imperfect human beings exist, there will be misinterpretations of God's Word and false views about His world. In view of this, one should not be hasty in assuming that a currently dominant view in science is the final word on the topic. Prevailing views of science in the past are considered errors by scientists in the present. So, contradictions between popular opinions in science and widely accepted interpretations of the Bible can be expected.[308]

It is best not to correct the Bible, but to believe the Bible over all else. Waite says,

> There may be some places in the text of the Daniel Bomberg Hebrew edition of the Masoretic text where there are seeming contradictions. For instance, the king may be eighteen years old or eight years old. Even if there are seeming contradictions, I feel it is imperative to go by what the traditional Masoretic text has as its reading and let the Lord figure out what may seem contradictions to us. Keep what God has given and preserved through the ages and let the Lord figure out why.[309]

If one cannot answer a seeming contradiction, then, instead of correcting the Bible, he should leave with it the Lord. This may not satisfy the pride

---

[308] Geisler and Howe, 17.

[309] Waite, 31-32. The instance Waite refers to concerns King Jehoiachin where II Chronicles 36:9 says he was eight years old when he began to reign, but then II Kings 24:8 says he was eighteen. See discussion on II Kings 24:8 in Chapter Ten for more information.

of some, but it is the best course of action, and if a man were to do so, he would show himself extremely wise. The Psalmist says, "I have more understanding than all my teachers: for thy testimonies are my meditation. I understand more than the ancients, because I keep thy precepts" (Psalm 119:99-100).

MUST BELIEVE THE WORDS OF GOD

If one should not correct the Bible, then he should believe the Bible over all else. He should believe the Bible over what scholars, commentators, his own senses, scientists, historians, and theologians say. Over all else to the contrary, he should believe the Bible.

Spurgeon makes some wonderful statements about this. In one such statement, Spurgeon says,

> Sometimes you will meet with an undoubted teaching of God's word which you do not understand. You know that the doctrine is taught in the word, but you cannot make it coincide with some other truth, and you cannot quite see, perhaps, how it glorifies God. Then, dear brother, dear sister, glorify God by believing it. To believe a doctrine which you see to be true by mere reason is nothing very wonderful. There is no very great glory to God in believing what is as clear as the sun in the heavens; but to believe a truth when it staggers you—oh, gracious faith! oh, blessed faith! You will perhaps remember an illustration taken from Mr. Gough, where the little boy says, "If mother says it is so, it is so if it is not so." That is the kind of believing for a child towards its mother, and that is the sort of believing we ought to exercise towards God. I do not see the fact, and I cannot quite apprehend it, but God says it is so, and I believe him. If all the philosophers in the world should contradict the Scriptures, so much the worse for the philosophers; their contradiction makes no difference to our faith. Half a grain of God's word weighs more with us than a thousand tons of words or thoughts of all the modern theologians, philosophers, and scientists that exist on the face of the earth; for God knows more about his own works than they do. They do but think, but the Lord knows. With regard to truths which philosophers ought not to meddle with, because they have not specially turned their thoughts that way, they are not more qualified to judge than the poorest man in the church of God, nay, nor one-half so much. Inasmuch as the most learned unregenerate men are dead in sin, what do they know about the living things of the children of God? Instead of setting them to judge we will sooner trust our boys and girls that are just converted, for they do know something of divine things, but carnal philosophers know nothing of them. Do not be staggered, brothers and sisters, but honor God, glorify God, and magnify him by be-

Chapter 5   *Handling Apparent Contradictions*

lieving great things and unsearchable-past your finding out—which you know to be true because he declares them to be so. Let the *ipse dixit* of God stand to you in the place of all reason, being indeed the highest and purest reason, for God, the Infallible, speaks what must be true.[310]

In another place Spurgeon writes:

> If my heavenly Father makes a promise, or reveals a truth, am I not to believe him till I have asked the philosophers about it? Is God's word only true when finite reason approves of it? After all, is man's judgment the ultimatum, and is God's word only to be taken when we can see for ourselves, and therefore have no need of revelation at all? Far from us be this spirit. Let God be true, and every man a liar. We are not staggered when the wise men mock at us, but we fall back upon "thus saith the Lord." One word from God outweighs for us a library of human lore. To the Christian, God's *ipse dixit* stands in the stead of all reason. Our logic is, "God has said it," and this is our rhetoric too. If God declares that the dead shall be raised, it is not a thing incredible to us. Difficulty is not in the dictionary of the Godhead. Is anything too hard for the Lord? Heap up the difficulties, if you like, make the doctrine more and more hard for reason to compass, so long as it contains no self-evident contradiction and inconsistency, we rejoice in the opportunity to believe great things concerning a Great God.[311]

To these statements by Spurgeon, the author says, "Amen." One does not need to wait to see what the philosophers say before he can believe his Bible. Believe the Bible over all else. This is very important. Harold Lindsell writes:

> If we cannot trust what Scripture says about itself, there is no reason to trust Scripture at all. If Scripture claims to be inerrant and we find that there are places that call this claim into question, then we must choose between those Scriptures that claim inerrancy and those that purportedly are in error. If we opt for error, then we must conclude that the claim of Scripture to inerrancy is in error too. But if we opt for the claim of Scripture to inerrancy, then we must conclude that the problem areas are not erroneous and that when all the facts are in, adequate solutions will be found for them.[312]

---

[310] Charles H. Spurgeon, "The Key-Note of a Choice Sonnet" in *The Metropolitan Tabernacle Pulpit*, 26:45-46.

[311] Spurgeon, "The Resurrection Credible" in *The Metropolitan Tabernacle Pulpit*, 18:597.

[312] Lindsell, 182-183.

Chapter 5 — *Handling Apparent Contradictions*

Those who claim the Scriptures have errors are destroying the Biblical claim that those very same Scriptures are inerrant. Would any Fundamentalist want to be in that position? Alas, some are in that position by questioning certain statements in the Bible. When the author was preaching on the apparent contradiction in the age of Jehoiachin (II Chronicles 36:9 saying that he was eight; whereas II Kings 24:8 says that he was eighteen), he put forth the question, "Which one is right?" The answer that he gave was, "Both are right." Could not the Fundamentalists do the same? Ask one of them to explain fully the Trinity and not a one will be able to do so, but yet they still believe it, and they believe it by faith. But when they cannot understand two numbers, why do they say one is in error, instead of using the same approach that they use with the Trinity?

It is easy to believe the Bible over all else, when a person regards the Bible as the highest authority. Writing about this very subject, Edward Mack says,

> Surely the time has come, when all fair-minded men should recognize that a clear and straightforward declaration of the Sacred Scriptures is not to be summarily rejected because of its apparent contradiction by some unknown and irresponsible person, who could stamp clay or chisel stone. It has been all too common that archaeological and critical adventurers have doubted and required accurate proof of every Bible statement, but have been ready enough to give credence to any statement from ancient pagan sources. We assume, as we have every reason to do, the trustworthiness of the Bible records, which have been corroborated in countless instances; and we shall follow their guidance in preference to any other. The help of contemporaneous history and the witness of archaeology can be used to advantage, but should not be substituted for the plain facts of the Scriptures, which are full worthy of our trust and regard.[313]

MUST EXERCISE HUMILITY BEFORE GOD

Exercising humility agrees with the above statements. Thomas Adams writes:

> Pride is a barricade against all graces, therefore against knowledge; it makes the heart incapable of goodness, as cold iron cannot be wrought to

---

[313] Edward Mack, "Chronology of the Old Testament" in *International Standard Bible Encyclopedia*, ed. James Orr (Grand Rapids, MI: Wm. B. Eerdmans Publishing Co., 1939), 1:636.

Chapter 5 *Handling Apparent Contradictions*

any fashion. A heart full of pride, is but a vessel full of air; this self-opinion must be blown out of us, before saving knowledge be poured into us. Humility is the knees of the soul, and to that posture the Lamb will open the book; but pride stands upon tiptoes, as if she would snatch the book out of Christ's hand, and unclasp it herself. The first lesson of a Christian is humility; and he that hath not learned the first lesson, is not fit to take out a new. Humble eyes are most capable of high mysteries.[314]

"God resisteth the proud, and giveth grace to the humble" (I Peter 5:5). Those who approach the Bible with such pride as to think that they are going to set the Scripture straight will not be able to unlock the treasures contained therein. Psalm 25:14 says, "The secret of the LORD *is* with them that fear him; and he will shew them his covenant."

MUST EXERCISE PRAYER TO GOD

If one approaches the Bible with humility, then he will also see his need for prayer. A person's lack of prayer is often the root cause for a lack of understanding the Bible. One can pray to the Author of the Book, and He can open the Bible to him. The Psalmist asked the Lord, "Open thou mine eyes, that I may behold wondrous things out of thy law" (Psalm 119:18). Throughout Psalm 119, the Psalmist asks the Lord to teach him (Psalm 119:12, 27, 33, 66), and as he does this he approaches the Bible with the utmost reverence (Psalm 119:152, 160). David Cloud quotes William Arndt:

> What will a pious, obedient, loving child do when he hears the father make a remark which on the surface appears objectionable? Instead of criticizing him and condemning his utterances as wrong, the child will ask him for an explanation. If we find stumbling blocks in the Holy Scriptures, let us take the attitude of such a loving child.[315]

Thomas Adams writes about prayer,

> When all fails, this will do it. Why did God write His mind to us in so mystical a dialect? We answer, the obscurity is not in His dialect, but in our intellect. . . . St. Augustine was so bold as to beg of God, that Moses might come, and tell him what he meant by some places in Genesis. We

---

[314] Thomas Adams, *A Commentary on the Second Epistle General of St. Peter*, revised and corrected by James Sherman (Ligonier, PA: Soli Deo Gloria Publications, 1990), 784.

[315] Cloud, 13. Cluod does not give a citation for the quote.

Chapter 5 *Handling Apparent Contradictions*

dare not do so; but yet we may beg of the Spirit of God, Who opens dark things, settles us in the truth, and keeps the key of Scripture, to inform our hearts what Paul meant by some passages of his writings. . . . Prayer is the remedy, the cure of all obscurity; especially being accompanied with fervour and frequency. Though we have fished all night and caught nothing, yet let us cast out the net again; pray still.[316]

When a person is trying to understand the apparent contradictions of the Bible, he ought to pray for wisdom. The Bible says, "If any of you lack wisdom, let him ask of God, that giveth to all men liberally, and upbraideth not; and it shall be given him" (James 1:5).

MUST EXERCISE PATIENCE IN GOD

As a person prays, he learns to wait patiently on the Lord, for the Lord sometimes does not answer his prayer right away. Those who have waited patiently on the Lord have been blest (Psalm 27:14; 37:34; Proverbs 20:22). Likewise, those who have waited on the Lord concerning the apparent contradictions have also been blest because with time, solutions have come. For instance,

> The historicity of the kings mentioned in Genesis 14 was once seriously questioned by criticism, but this is impossible today, for their historical character has been proved beyond all question, and, in particular, it is now known that the Amraphel of that chapter is the Hammurabi of the Monuments and a contemporary with Abraham. The puzzling story of Sarah and Hagar is also now seen to be in exact agreement with Babylonian custom. Then again, the Egypt of Joseph and Moses is true to the smallest details of the life of the Egypt of that day and is altogether different from the very different Egypt of later ages. Sargon, who for centuries was only known from the one reference to him in Isaiah 20:1, is now seen to have been one of the most important kings of Assyria. And the Aramaic language of Daniel and Ezra, which has so often been accused of lateness, is proved to be in exact accord with the Aramaic of that age, as shown by the Papyri discovered at Elephantine in Egypt.[317]

Instead of charging the Scripture with error, one is wise to wait and to exercise patience in God. Waiting is hard; therefore, men are quick to conclude that Scripture must be wrong. It is regrettable that they will not

---

[316] Adams, 784-785.

[317] W. H. Griffith Thomas, 114-115.

Chapter 5   *Handling Apparent Contradictions*

wait and give, as it were, God the benefit of the doubt. Sir Robert Anderson gives yet another example where waiting yielded a solution:

> Belshazzar's case is specially interesting. Scripture plainly states that he was King of Babylon at its conquest by the Medo-Persians, and that he was slain the night Darius entered the city. On the other hand, not only does no ancient historian mention Belshazzar, but all agree that the last king of Babylon was Nabonidus, who was absent from the city when the Persians captured it, and who afterwards submitted to the conquerors at Borsippa. Thus the contradiction between history and Scripture appeared to be absolute. Skeptics appealed to history to discredit the book of Daniel; and commentators solved or shirked the difficulty by rejecting history. The cuneiform inscriptions, however, have now settled the controversy in a manner as satisfactory as it was unexpected. On clay cylinders discovered by Sir H. Rawlinson at Mughier and other Chaldean sites, Belshazzar (Belsaruzur) is named by Nabonidus as his eldest son. The inference is obvious, that during the latter years of his father's reign, Belshazzar was King-Regent in Babylon. According to Ptolemy's canon Nabonidus reigned seventeen years (from B.C. 555 to B.C. 538), and Ussher gives these years to Belshazzar.[318]

The authors of *When Critics Ask* say,

> Many difficulties for which scholars once had no answer have yielded to the relentless pursuit of truth through history, archaeology, linguistics, and other disciplines. For example, critics once proposed that Moses could not have written the first five books of the Bible because there was no writing in Moses' day. Now we know that writing was in existence . . . before Moses. Likewise, critics once believed that the Bible was wrong in speaking of the Hittite people, since they were totally unknown to historians. Now, all historians know of their existence by way of their library that was found in Turkey. This gives us confidence to believe that the Biblical difficulties that have not yet been explained have an explanation and that we need not assume there is a mistake in the Bible.[319]

The above examples well illustrate that if a solution is not readily available, it is best to wait. If one has to wait until he gets to heaven, he is better off to do so, than to charge the Bible with error. Although this may take a degree of faith, will not the Lord say to such a one, "Well done, thou good and faithful servant: thou hast been faithful over a few things, I

---

[318] Sir Robert Anderson, *The Coming Prince* in *The Master Christian Library*, version 8 [CD-ROM] (Albany, OR: Ages Software), 126.

[319] Geisler and Howe, 16.

Chapter 5   *Handling Apparent Contradictions*

will make thee ruler over many things: enter thou into the joy of thy lord" (Matthew 25:21)?

MUST UTILIZE STUDY OF THE BIBLE

After reading of the need to pray and to wait on the Lord, one might think that all he need do is to sit back and let the answers to the apparent contradictions of the Bible come to his door, but this is not the case. While the Bible student should pray and wait on the Lord, at the same time he should study. "Much study is a weariness of the flesh" (Ecclesiastes 12:12), but sometimes much study is necessary in order to understand the Bible. The Bible commands: "Study to shew thyself approved unto God, a workman that needeth not to be ashamed, rightly dividing the word of truth" (II Timothy 2:15). The word for *study*, σπούδασον from σπουδάζω, is an aorist active imperative, therefore a command, and has the meaning "to exert one's self, endeavor, give diligence."[320] In what way is one to exert himself? He is to exert himself in "rightly dividing the word of truth." The phrase *rightly dividing*, ὀρθοτομοῦντα from ὀρθοτομέω, is a present active participle, therefore, indicating continuous action. Kent, Jr., in speaking of this word, says that the workman

> is to "cut straight" (*orthotomounta*). The metaphor has been understood of apportioning food, plowing, quarrying, or laying out a road. Since the context does not provide any light as to what type of workman was in Paul's mind, the interpreter dare not dogmatize. Perhaps he was thinking of his own craft, tentmaking, and pictures the artisan trimming the hides precisely so that they will fit together. In some such manner, God's workman must treat with discernment the Word of God. Simpson says it "enjoins on every teacher of the Word straightforward exegesis."[321]

The student must exert himself to properly exegete the Word of Truth. It is the Word of Truth. Sadly, many Fundamentalists approach the Word of Truth as if it were the word of error and, therefore, go about to correct it repeatedly. How can a person obtain God's approval by questioning His Words? Remember that Jesus rebuked Peter when he questioned the Word (Matthew 16:21-23), and God rebuked Moses when he questioned the Words of the Lord (Numbers 11:18-23). God did not approve these

---

[320] Thayer, 585.

[321] Homer A. Kent, Jr., *The Pastoral Epistles: Studies in I & II Timothy & Titus* (Chicago: Moody Press, 1979), 274.

men when they questioned the Words of Truth. Homer Kent says of the word *approved*, "The laborer for God must give diligence to the kind and quality of his work, so that when he meets God's inspection, he will stand the test and be approved (*dokimon*), having no need for shame because of faulty workmanship (*anepaischunton*)."[322] Will those who question God's Words stand the test?

The words for *truth* and *word* are the same words Jesus used in John 17:17: "Thy word is truth." *Truth* "certifies the inerrancy and infallibility of the Word excepting no portion of it. The holy garment of the Word is seamless; it has no rents of errors—or call them mistakes—which hands must sew up."[323]

At the time Paul gave this admonition to Timothy the Old Testament *autographa* were not in existence. For the Old Testament, Timothy had to rely on copies, yet Paul refers to it as *the word of truth*; therefore, Paul regarded Timothy's copy of the Old Testament as infallible. To divide rightly the Word of Truth, one must approach the Word of Truth as truth, that is, receive, believe, and hear all of its statements as accurate and as truly relating what was said or done. Besides these general statements that one is to receive fully all that the Bible says, and to approach the Bible prayerfully and humbly, how is one to study the Bible?

Read the Bible

First, one should start with the Bible itself, letting the Bible speak for itself, instead of starting with what others have said about the Bible. Paul instructed Timothy to give attendance to reading (I Timothy 4:13), which includes reading the Bible. The book of the covenant was read in the audience of the people (Exodus 24:7; cf. Deuteronomy 31:11; Joshua 8:34-35; II Kings 23:2; II Chronicles 34:30; Nehemiah 8:3, 18; 9:3; Jeremiah 36:6). God commanded the king to have a copy of the law and to read it "all the days of his life" (Deuteronomy 17:19). The Lord commanded Joshua not to let the book of the law depart out of his mouth, but to meditate therein day and night (Joshua 1:8). The blessed man is one whose "delight is in the law of the LORD; and in His law doth he meditate day and night" (Psalm 1:2). The writer of Psalm 119 repeatedly mentions how he delighted in the Words of God (cf. Psalm 119:97-104). Isaiah

---

[322] Kent, Jr., 274.

[323] Thayer, 176.

Chapter 5 *Handling Apparent Contradictions*

34:16 says, "Seek ye out of the book of the LORD, and read." Jesus commanded that the Pharisees "search the scriptures" (John 5:39). The Bereans "received the word with all readiness of mind, and searched the scriptures daily" (Acts 17:11). Paul commanded that I Thessalonians "be read" (I Thessalonians 5:27). Clearly, the Bible commands a careful reading of the Scriptures.

A careful reading of the Scriptures is very important to understanding the Bible. The Sadducees did not understand the resurrection because they did not carefully read the account of Moses at the burning bush (Matthew 22:31; Mark 12:26). Jesus repeatedly says, "Have ye not read" (Matthew 12:3, 5; 19:4; 21:16, 42; Mark 2:25; 12:10; Luke 6:3) to those who, if they had read carefully, would have understood the Scriptures. God commands a careful, deliberate reading of His Words and such a reading will go a long way to understanding the Scriptures. When one reads the Bible he needs to take into account the context, words used, person(s) speaking, people being addressed, time in which the passage occurs, dispensation, pronouns used, and much more. Sometimes the reading of a passage several times will assist in its proper understanding. Studying the Bible should start with reading the Bible. As one elderly woman put it, "Reading the Bible sure sheds a lot of light upon the commentaries."

Examine the Context

When studying the Bible, one should consider the verses before and after a passage and sometimes even the entire book. Some years ago, the author happened upon a Mormon who directed his attention to Ezekiel 37:16-17. The Mormon claimed that this passage speaks about the *Book of Mormon* and the *King James Bible* and that when both are put together they form one complete revelation from God. However, upon reading the following verses, the author soon discovered that Ezekiel was not at all talking about books being joined together, but about God joining Judah and Ephraim into one nation (Ezekiel 37:18-22). One can easily pull verses out of context to teach anything or to make them look as if they contradict other parts of the Bible. McClintock and Strong's *Cyclopedia* gives an example of this very thing:

> Another instance of the alleged discrepancies is that, according to one account, Moses' reception from his brethren was very discouraging (Exodus 6:9), whereas the other narrative describes it as quite the reverse (Exodus 4:31). De Wette calls this a striking contradiction, but it is only such when the intermediate section (Exodus 5:19-23), which shows the change

Chapter 5 *Handling Apparent Contradictions*

that in the interval had occurred in the prospects of the Israelites, is violently ejected from the narrative — a process fitted to produce contradictions in any composition.[324]

Look for Differences

When studying two or more passages, one should look for differences in the passages. Sometimes two authors are looking at the same event but giving different details about that same event as is the case with the superscription on the cross of Christ (Matthew 27:37; Mark 15:26; Luke 23:38; John 19:19). Concerning the superscription on the cross, Gray writes:

> Another class of differences, however, is where the same event is sometimes given differently by different writers. Take that most frequently used by the objectors, the inscription on the Cross, recorded by all the evangelists and yet differently by each. How can such records be inspired, it is asked. It is to be remembered in reply, that the inscription was written in three languages calling for a different arrangement of the words in each case, and that one evangelist may have translated the Hebrew, and another the Latin, while a third recorded the Greek. It is not said that any one gave the full inscription, nor can we affirm that there was any obligation upon them to do so. Moreover, no one contradicts any other, and no one says what is untrue. Recalling what was said about our having to deal not with different human authors but with one Divine Author, may not the Holy Spirit here have chosen to emphasize some one particular fact, or phase of a fact of the inscription for a specific and important end? Examine the records to determine what this fact may have been. Observe that whatever else is omitted, all the narratives record the momentous circumstances that the Sufferer on the cross was THE KING OF THE JEWS. Could there have been a cause for this? What was the charge preferred against Jesus by His accusers? Was He not rejected and crucified because He said He was the King of the Jews? Was not this the central idea Pilate was providentially guided to express in the inscription? And if so, was it not that to which the evangelists should bear witness? And should not that witness have been borne in a way to dispel the thought of collusion in the premises? And did not this involve a variety of narrative which should at the same time be in harmony with truth and fact? And do we not have this very thing in the four gospels? These accounts supplement, but do not

---

[324] "Exodus" in *Cyclopedia of Biblical, Theological, and Ecclesiastical Literature*, ed. John McClintock and James Strong (New York: Harper & Brothers, 1891), 3:413.

Chapter 5 *Handling Apparent Contradictions*

contradict each other. We place them before the eye in the order in which they are recorded.[325]

Albert Barnes writes:

> One thing should always be borne in mind by all who read the Gospels, namely, that the sacred narrative of an event is what it is declared to be by ALL the evangelists. That a thing is omitted by one does not prove that another is false because he has recorded it, for the very object of the different Gospels was to give the testimony of independent witnesses to the great facts of the life and death of Jesus. Nor does it prove that there is a contradiction because one relates facts in a different order from another, for neither of them professes to relate facts in the precise order in which they occurred. The object was to relate the facts themselves.[326]

Sometimes, by examining the differences, one sees that the passages are speaking of two different, but similar events, as is the case when Jesus fed the 5,000 (Matthew 14:21) and then fed the 4,000 (Matthew 15:38).

Differences sometimes demonstrate that the Bible is speaking of different times such as in Genesis 1:31 when God saw that everything was very good immediately after the creation as compared to 1500 years later in Genesis 6:6 when God saw the wickedness of man just before the flood. DeHoff points out, "These statements (Gen. 1:31 and Gen. 6:6) are used by skeptics to show that the Bible contradicts itself."[327] But there is no contradiction when one understands the chronological differences in the passages.

Now and then, differences are the result of different methods of computation (examples of such a thing are in Chapters Seven through Twelve).

Differences sometimes result from a person having more than one name. For example, "one of the twelve apostles is called by the following

---

[325] James M. Gray, "The Inspiration of the Bible – Definition, Extent and Proof" in *The Fundamentals*, 2:28-29.

[326] Albert Barnes, *Matthew – John* in *Barnes' Notes on the Bible*, 12. Later, on page 585, Barnes says, "John mentions only Mary Magdalene. He does this, probably, because his object was to give a particular account of her interview with the risen Saviour. There is NO contradiction among the evangelists; for while one mentions only the names of a part of those who were there, he does not deny that 'others' were present also. It is an old maxim, that 'he who mentions a few does not deny that there are more.' "

[327] DeHoff, 30.

Chapter 5 *Handling Apparent Contradictions*

names: Simon, Simeon, Peter, Cephas, Simon Peter, Simon Bar-Jona and Simon Son of Jonas."[328]

At times, differences result when one writer arranges a subject topically, whereas another arranges the same subject chronologically.

Occasionally, differences are the result of different ways of computing chronology. Haley states:

> Many ancient and several modern nations have two kinds of year in use, the civil and the sacred. The Jews employed both reckonings. . . . Even among us, the academic and the fiscal do not begin and end with the civil year. . . . It follows, therefore, that when two ancient writers fail to agree as to the month and day of a given event, we must inquire whether or not they employ the same chronological reckoning. . . . It was one peculiarity of the Jewish reckoning that fractional years were counted for whole ones.[329]

Compare Scripture with Scripture

In studying the Bible, one should compare Scripture with Scripture. The Bible is it's own best interpreter (I Corinthians 2:12-13). In order to see the whole Scriptural picture upon a subject, one should assemble together verses dealing with the same subject. R. A. Torrey states:

> If you find a difficulty in one part of the Bible, look for other Scripture to throw light upon it and dissolve it. Nothing explains Scripture like Scripture. Time and again people have come to me with some difficulty in the Bible that had greatly staggered them, and asked for a solution, and I have been able to give a solution by simply asking them to read some other chapter and verse, and the simple reading of that chapter and verse has thrown such a light upon the passage in question that all the mists have disappeared and the truth has shown as clear as day.[330]

But one needs to exercise caution here as Haley points out when he states:

> A favorite exegetical principle adopted by some of these critics appears to be, that *similar events are necessarily identical.* Hence, when they read that Abraham twice equivocated concerning his wife [Genesis 12:19; 20:2]; that Isaac imitated his example [Genesis 26:7]; that David was

---

[328] Ibid., 36.

[329] Haley, 11-12.

[330] Torrey, 28.

Chapter 5 *Handling Apparent Contradictions*

twice in peril in a certain wilderness [I Samuel 23:19; 26:1], and twice spared Saul's life in a cave [I Samuel 24:6; 26:9], they instantly assume that in each case these double narratives are irreconcilable accounts of one and the same event. The absurdity of such a canon of criticism is obvious from the fact that *history is full of events which more or less closely resemble one another.*[331]

Further, in comparing Scripture with Scripture, the student should remember that

> the Scriptures should be accepted as a unit of revelation, and one part should be interpreted in harmony with every other part. The liberal critic would most emphatically dissent from this rule, but in doing so he rejects the unique character of the Bible as contained in distinctive revelation from God. We could not conceive of God giving a message to man which was not self-consistent, without revising the standard Christian conception of God.[332]

As one compares Scripture with Scripture, all the while seeking for a harmonious interpretation, he will understand that the Bible is consistent with itself. No true contradictions are in the Bible, only what might seem to be contradictions. The solution to the apparent contradictions will be in harmonizing the various passages.

Use Study Tools

A student of the Bible will find study tools helpful. Paul writes, "The cloke that I left at Troas with Carpus, when thou comest, bring with thee, and the books, but especially the parchments" (II Timothy 4:13). What were these books and parchments? Although one cannot be dogmatic, they possibly included study tools. At any rate, a student of the Words of God should have books. For instance, a very useful tool in comparing Scripture with Scripture is *The Treasury of Scripture Knowledge*, which lists hundreds of thousands of cross-references, thereby enabling the student to use Scripture to interpret Scripture. Another good useful study tool is a computerized Bible, especially the *Online Bible*, which, along with other study aids, includes *The Treasury of Scripture Knowledge* enabling students to look up verses rapidly. Original language texts, a concordance, lexicons, theological dictionaries, and grammatical works are

---

[331] Ibid., 26.

[332] Richard V. Clearwaters, "The Bible Its Own Interpreter" in *The Great Conservative Baptist Compromise* (Minneapolis: Central Seminary Press, n.d.), 103.

all very useful. In the opinion of the author, only after one has compared Scripture with Scripture, examined the original language text, looked up word meanings of key words; then, and not until then, do commentaries truly become useful. Spurgeon writes:

> In order to be able to expound the Scriptures, and as an aid to your pulpit studies, you will need to be familiar with the commentators: a glorious army, let me tell you, whose acquaintance will be your delight and profit. Of course, you are not such wiseacres as to think or say that you can expound Scriptures without the assistance from the works of divines and learned men who have laboured before you in the field of exposition. If you are of that opinion, pray remain so, for you are not worth the trouble of conversion, and like a little coterie who think with you, would resent the attempt as an insult to your infallibility. It seems odd, that certain men who talk so much of what the Holy Spirit reveals to themselves, should think so little of what He has revealed to others.[333]

A student of Scripture should work on developing a good library of good books. Perhaps the student should set aside a monthly allowance for books. However, not only must a student develop a good library, but also he must use it. David Cloud points out, "It is one thing to own concordances and commentaries; it is quite another to USE them!"[334]

In addition to being self-taught through the reading of books, one should also think about getting formal training from faithful men. Paul told Timothy, "And the things that thou hast heard of me among many witnesses, the same commit thou to faithful men, who shall be able to teach others also" (II Timothy 2:2). One should find such faithful men who are true to the Bible and receive further instruction from them. The main thing is to find faithful men: the facilities are not as important as the faculty. Remember, Jesus had no buildings, yet trained men who then turned the world upside down (Acts 17:6). Instruction should include Greek, Hebrew, Aramaic, exegesis, hermeneutics, and theology, as well as other things. This list of subjects may sound intimidating; however, it is best to get the best training for the Lord's service. Instruction from others must include faithful attendance in a Biblicist Baptist Church (Acts 2:41-42; Hebrews 10:25), wherein faithful pastors and teachers will teach and preach the Words of God (Ephesians 4:11-14; II Timothy 4:1-4).

---

[333] Charles H. Spurgeon, "A Chat about Commentaries" in *Commenting & Commentaries: A Reference Guide to Book Buying for Pastors, Students, and Christian Workers* (Grand Rapids: Baker, 1981), 1.

[334] Cloud, 12.

Chapter 5 *Handling Apparent Contradictions*

MUST UNDERSTAND LANGUAGE OF THE BIBLE

While one is studying the Bible, he must understand certain things about the language of the Bible. The Bible records, for instance, the lies of Satan (Genesis 3:4), Abraham (Genesis 12:13; 20:1-13), and Rahab (Joshua 2:4); but does not approve of them. Therefore, such things are not contradictions in the Bible, but the Bible is simply recording the facts of what actually occurred, even though what occurred was wrong.

Furthermore, the Bible uses figures of speech. Geisler and Howe state:

> The Bible reveals a number of literary devices. Several whole books are written in the *poetic* style (e.g., Job, Psalms, Proverbs). The synoptic Gospels are filled with *parables*. In Galatians 4, Paul utilizes an *allegory*. The NT abounds with *metaphors* (e.g., 2 Cor. 3:2-3; James 3:6) and *similes* (cf. Matt. 20:1; James 1:6).[335]

Of course, when the Bible uses a figure of speech, the student must understand it as a figure of speech. A literal interpretation of the Bible demands that the student take figures of speech as figures of speech.

Also, the Bible uses everyday, non-technical language. James Orr observes:

> When science is said to contradict the Bible, I should like to ask first, What is meant by contradiction here? The Bible was never given us in order to anticipate or forestall the discoveries of modern twentieth century science. The Bible, as every sensible interpreter of Scripture has always held, takes the world as it is, not as it is seen through the eyes of twentieth century specialists, but as it lies spread out before the eyes of original men, and uses the popular every-day language appropriate to this standpoint. As Calvin in his commentary on Genesis 1 says, "Moses wrote in the popular style, which, without instruction, all ordinary persons endowed with common sense are able to understand. . . . He does not call us up to heaven; he only proposes things that lie open before our eyes." It does not follow that because the Bible does not teach modern science, we are justified in saying that it contradicts it.[336]

Henry Morris writes:

---

[335] Geisler and Howe, 23.

[336] James Orr, "The Early Narratives of Genesis" in *The Fundamentals*, 1:197.

Chapter 5 *Handling Apparent Contradictions*

It is obvious, of course, that the Bible is not a scientific textbook in the sense of giving detailed technical descriptions and mathematical formulations of natural phenomena. If it were merely that kind of a textbook, it would quickly become outdated, like other science textbooks. Nevertheless, it does deal extensively with a broad variety of natural phenomena, as well as with numerous and varied events in history. It especially deals with the basic principles of science and the key events in history, and many of its revelations in spiritual and moral matters are keyed to its revelations on scientific and historical matters. . . . Whenever a Biblical passage deals either with a broad scientific principle or with some particular item of scientific data, it will inevitably be found on careful study to be fully accurate in its scientific insights. Often it will be found even to have anticipated scientific discoveries. The Bible is indeed a book of science, as well as a book of history, literature, psychology, economics, law, education, and every other field. It does not use the technical jargon of particular disciplines, of course, but speaks in the universal language of human experience.[337]

MIGHT ASK A MAN OF GOD

Yet, another technique one can use in handling apparent Biblical contradictions is to ask a man of God, which is what the Ethiopian eunuch did when a passage from Isaiah confounded him (Acts 8:26-35). God gave to the local church "pastors and teachers; for the perfecting of the saints, for the work of the ministry, for the edifying of the body of Christ" (Ephesians 4:11-12). Faithful men of God in addition to being "apt to teach" (I Timothy 3:2) are "to teach others" (II Timothy 2:2). David Cloud states that "God has given gifted men to the churches for the edification of the saints, and it is crucial that Christians benefit from this wisdom."[338]

MUST ACCEPT WORD CHANGE BY THE SPIRIT

As one studies the apparent contradictions of the Bible, he may come across a situation where a New Testament writer does not exactly quote an Old Testament verse, or even where an Old Testament writer does not exactly quote an earlier Old Testament verse. Since the Spirit of God

---

[337] Henry M. Morris, *The Biblical Basis for Modern Science* (Grand Rapids: Baker, 1987), 19-20.

[338] Cloud, 14.

moved in holy men of old (II Peter 1:21), then one must accept the fact that in these cases the Spirit of God changed the wording when referring to an earlier passage.

New Testament Writers Were Spirit-Guided

Jesus told the apostles that when the Spirit of truth came, He would guide them into all truth (John 16:13). The Spirit's guiding New Testament writers into all truth affected the application as well as the quotation of Old Testament verses.

In Their Application of the Old Testament

Holy Spirit guidance is evident by looking at how New Testament writers applied Old Testament verses. For instance, Matthew 2:15 uses the last part of Hosea 11:1 to refer to Lord Jesus Christ. Hosea 11:1 says, "When Israel was a child, then I loved him, and called my son out of Egypt." Without the New Testament revelation, would one understand the last part of Hosea 11:1 as referring to Jesus coming out of Egypt? It is doubtful, but through His teaching ministry, the Spirit makes the truth of Hosea 11:1 clear.

John, in speaking of the soldier piercing the side of Jesus and not breaking His leg bones, says, "For these things were done, that the scripture should be fulfilled, A bone of him shall not be broken. And again another scripture saith, They shall look on him whom they pierced" (John 19:36-37). "A bone of him shall not be broken" is a reference to Psalm 34:20. But if one reads Psalm 34, he might not realize that Psalm 34:20 is referring to the Messiah, but the Holy Spirit again makes the truth clear. Also, "They shall look on him whom they pierced" is a quote from Zechariah 12:10. But if one reads Zechariah 12:10, without knowing about John 19:36-37, he would think that "they shall look upon me whom they have pierced" is referring to when the Jews will see Jesus descending from heaven at the end of the tribulation. But the Holy Spirit, guiding John into all truth, teaches that this refers to the time of Christ's crucifixion. Would one arrive at this teaching simply by reading Zechariah 12:10? Probably not, but with the Holy Spirit's teaching in the New Testament, He makes this clear.

Chapter 5   *Handling Apparent Contradictions*

In Their Quotation of the Old Testament

In a similar fashion, could not the Holy Spirit guide the New Testament writers when referring to Old Testament verses to use a different word so as to clarify the exact nuance and meaning of Old Testament verses? For instance, Psalm 40:6 says, "Sacrifice and offering thou didst not desire; mine ears hast thou opened: burnt offering and sin offering hast thou not required." The New Testament quote of Psalm 40:6 in Hebrews 10:5-6 says, "Wherefore when he cometh into the world, he saith, Sacrifice and offering thou wouldest not, but a body hast thou prepared me: in burnt offerings and *sacrifices* for sin thou hast had no pleasure." Psalms says, "Mine ears hast thou opened," whereas Hebrews says, "A body hast thou prepared me." Some claim that in this case, the writer of Hebrews used the LXX,[339] or that a contradiction is here.[340] But would not a better explanation be that the Spirit of God was guiding the writer of Hebrews into all truth by giving him the exact nuance of "mine ears hast thou opened"? With this additional revelation, the Spirit reveals that *mine ears hast thou opened* concerns the preparation of a body for the Lord Jesus Christ; that is, *ears* presuppose a body. Therefore, the Spirit of God teaches that Psalm 40:6 refers to God's preparing a body for Christ. Both passages, then, are correct with no contradiction between them. Would one have ever come to the teaching that God the Father would prepare a body for Jesus just by reading Psalm 40? Probably not, but with the New Testament teaching ministry of the Holy Spirit, such teaching is evident.

New Testament Writers Were Not LXX-Users

Did Jesus and the writers of the New Testament use the LXX for their quotes from the Old Testament? The evidence suggests that they did not.

---

[339] For example, Lenski, *The Interpretation of the Epistle to the Hebrews and the Epistle of James* (Minneapolis: Augsburg Publishing House, 1966), 328. However, it is not certain the entire LXX was available to the New Testament writers. If the entire LXX was completed after the New Testament, is it not possible that the agreement between the LXX and the New Testament quotations reflects the LXX interpolating the New Testament verse back into the Old Testament? For example, in the case of Hebrews 10:5-6, if the LXX portion of Psalms was completed after the writing of Hebrews, then could not the writers of the LXX have examined how Hebrews 10:5-6 referred to Psalm 40:6 and then wrote the words from Hebrews 10:5-6 into their rendering of Psalm 40:6?

[340] For example, Clarke discusses how Kennicott supposes that the Hebrew in Psalm 40:6 is corrupt (Adam Clarke, *Hebrews* in vol. 8 of *Clarke's Commentary* in *Master Christian Library* CD-ROM (Albany, OR: AGES Software, 1997), 525.

Chapter 5 *Handling Apparent Contradictions*

First, scholars have not fully established that a complete copy of the LXX was in existence at the time of the writing of the New Testament.[341]

Second, Jesus obviously used the Hebrew Old Testament and not the LXX. Jesus referred to jots and tittles, which refer to Hebrew letters (Matthew 5:18; Luke 16:17) as opposed to the Greek letters of the LXX. Furthermore, in Luke 11:51 Jesus spoke of the blood of Abel (mentioned in the first book of the Hebrew Old Testament in Genesis 4:8) and the blood of Zacharias (mentioned in the last book of the Hebrew Old Testament in II Chronicles 24:20) being required of that generation. By referring to the first and last books of the Hebrew Old Testament, Jesus indicates that He was using the Hebrew and not the LXX. Also, in Luke 24:44 Jesus showed the disciples the things concerning Himself from the law, the prophets, and the psalms. Luke 24:44 refers to the three-fold division of the Hebrew Old Testament, that is, (1) the law; (2) the prophets; and (3) the writings, psalms being in the writings (also see Matthew 7:12; 11:13; 22:40). The LXX has an Old Testament book order very similar to modern Bibles, wherein Psalms is in the middle of the Old Testament, as opposed to being toward the end. If Jesus were using the LXX, then Luke 24:44 should read: "And he said unto them, These *are* the words which I spake unto you, while I was yet with you, that all things must be fulfilled, which were written in the law of Moses, and *in* the psalms, and *in* the prophets, concerning me." But this is not how it reads. The fact that Jesus mentions Psalms last indicates a Hebrew order to the books of the Old Testament as opposed to a LXX order of the books and points to His use of the Hebrew Old Testament.

Third, even if a complete LXX were available, Christ and the apostles had no need to resort to a Greek translation of the Old Testament since

---

[341] Douglas K. Kutilek in a chapter entitled "The Background and Origin of the Version Debate" in *One Bible Only?* on page 51 says, "Both Philo and Josephus, *not later than the first century a.d.*, are aware of and do not dispute the account of the origin of a Greek translation of the Law as related in the Letter of Aristeas." If these accounts are accurate, then they establish the existence of a Septuagint Pentateuch by the end of the first century, but not of the rest of the Old Testament. That Kutilek is using *Law* to refer to only the Pentateuch is evident from an earlier statement by him on page 32, wherein he says that Iranaeus "asserts that the LXX is the whole Hebrew Old Testament, not just the Law as Aristeas says." Here Kutilek does not use *Law* in its broad sense of the entire Old Testament, but in its narrow sense of the books of Moses. On the same page, Kutilek states that Irenaeus "in the second half of the second century A.D." spoke in defense of "the accuracy of the Septuagint translation of Isaiah 7:14." This would argue for the existence of the entire Septuagint at some point between 150 – 200 A.D., but would not establish that it was available to Jesus and the apostles from about 25 – 95 A.D.

Chapter 5 *Handling Apparent Contradictions*

they knew Hebrew (Luke 23:38; John 5:2; 19:13, 17; Acts 21:40; 22:2; 26:14; Revelation 9:11; 16:16).

And fourth, in writing the New Testament, the writers were under the guidance of the Holy Spirit (John 16:13) Who could have them alter the quotes from the Old Testament as earlier statements above explain. Waite writes:

> Does a mere similarity in wording in the Greek N.T. to that of the Greek O.T. Septuagint [LXX] necessarily mean that these were direct "quotations"? Is not God the Holy Spirit, Who inspired the very words of the O.T. and the N.T., able to pick and choose what set of words He wishes to employ to reveal God's truth in the N.T.? Is He bound to His Own words exactly on every occasion in the O.T. Hebrew text, or does He not have liberty to alter at will or re-interpret, or to add to or subtract to that which He Himself wrote in the Old Testament?[342]

Collett states:

> It should ever be borne in mind that none but the Holy Ghost knows the exact and full meaning of His own words, as recorded in the Old Testament, and only He can infallibly reproduce His message in other words. And surely He has a perfect right to do this, without our finding fault or charging Him with carelessness. But, further, may not there be a special design in these very differences—viz. that, by giving us an old truth in new words, we might be able to see some new and deeper teaching, which really lay hidden in the old, but which we never should have see had it not been given us in a different form?[343]

Robert Lightner states: "All of the words of the end product are inspired whether it is a complete and perfect quotation or not. . . . the Spirit of God must be allowed total freedom to modify and select expressions which He inspired in the Old Testament."[344] James Gray makes a similar point:

---

[342] Donald A. Waite, *Dr. Stewart Custer Answered on the T.R. & K.J.V* (Collingswood: The Bible for Today, 1985), 104

[343] Collett, 143-144.

[344] Robert Lightner, *The Saviour and the Scriptures*, 9. Lightner goes on to speak of the words *that it might be fulfilled*, "A study of the contexts in which this formula occurs reveals that Christ did not always intend by its use to make a direct quotation. Sometimes the quotations are paraphrased, sometimes the passage is only alluded to, and on other occasions there is a direct quotation. Whatever the case may be, the Spirit of God must be allowed freedom to modify or alter the expressions He inspired in the Old Testament" (Lightner, 19).

Chapter 5 *Handling Apparent Contradictions*

There are the differences in the narratives themselves. In the first place, the New Testament writers sometimes change important words in quoting from the Old Testament, which it is assumed could not be the case if in both instances the writers were inspired. But it is forgotten that in the scriptures we are dealing not so much with different human authors as with one Divine Author. It is a principle in ordinary literature that an author may quote himself as he pleases, and give a different turn to an expression here and there as a changed condition of affairs renders it necessary or desirable. Shall we deny this privilege to the Holy Spirit? May we not find, indeed, that some of these supposed misquotations show such progress of truth, such evident application of the teaching of an earlier dispensation to the circumstances of a later one, as to afford a confirmation of their divine origin rather than an argument against it?[345]

Conclusion

Based on the above considerations, the New Testament writers did not use the LXX. Furthermore, where differences exist between an Old Testament passage and a New Testament reference to that passage, the Spirit of God altered the wording for His Own purposes and such alterations are not contradictions, but further revelation.

CONCLUSION

For a student to properly handle the alleged contradictions of the Bible, he (1) must have salvation of Christ; (2) must have obedience to the Lord; (3) must accept the inspiration of the Bible; (4) must accept preservation of the Bible; (5) must not correct the Words of God; (6) must believe the Words of God; (7) must exercise humility before God; (8) must exercise prayer to God; (9) must exercise patience in God; (10) must utilize study of the Bible; (11) must understand the language of the Bible; (12) might ask a man of God; and (13) must accept word change by the Spirit of God. If one will accept and operate according to these principles, then he will have complete confidence in what the Bible says, even in those instances where he cannot answer all the questions raised by skeptics.

---

[345] James M. Gray, "The Inspiration of the Bible – Definition, Extent and Proof" in *The Fundamentals*, 2:28.

CHAPTER SIX:
RAMIFICATIONS OF SAYING PRESERVED TEXT HAS NUMERICAL ERRORS

Many claim that some of the apparent numerical contradictions in the Bible are the result of a scribal error. In making such a claim, they will reassure their readers or students that these supposed errors affect no vital point of doctrine. Haley, in a section entitled "Concerning Numbers," suggests there are "mistakes in numbers" and that "these mistakes which we find in considerable numbers, touch no vital point of scripture. No precept, promise, or doctrine is in the least degree impaired by them; nor do they militate against any well-balanced theory of inspiration."[346] The author does not believe that this is the case.

Some of the numerical passages commentators question are right next to doctrinal passages. One such example is Isaiah 36:1 where the Bible speaks of the fourteenth year of Hezekiah, which is a quantity that commentators often question.[347] However, Isaiah 36:1 immediately follows Isaiah 35:10, which says, "And the ransomed of the LORD shall return, and come to Zion with songs and everlasting joy upon their heads: they shall obtain joy and gladness, and sorrow and sighing shall flee away." Sir Robert Anderson points out the inconsistency of implicitly believing the prophet in 35:10 but not believing him in 36:1.[348] In other words, if 36:1 is in error, then how can one be sure that 35:10 is not also in error? To admit an error in 36:1 is to allow the possibility of error elsewhere,

---

[346] Haley, 380.

[347] For example, see Herbert M. Wolf, *Interpreting Isaiah* (Grand Rapids: Zondervan, 1985), 172. And see discussion on II Kings 18:13 in Chapter Ten.

[348] Sir Robert Anderson, *The Bible and Modern Criticism*, 90.

even in doctrinal passages. As one might gather, quite a bit is at stake if errors are in the preserved text. What are some of the ramifications of saying that numerical errors are in the preserved text?

QUESTIONING CHRIST

When a person questions a number in the Old Testament, he is at the same time questioning Christ Who promised that not one jot or one tittle shall pass from the law (Matthew 5:18; Luke 16:17). Now, whom is one to believe, Jesus or Haley, Jesus or *The Pulpit Commentary*, Jesus or the Fundamentalist Bible teacher? Has God preserved all the jots and tittles, or has He not? Did Jesus tell the truth, or did He exaggerate and, therefore, lie? If scribal errors really are in the preserved text, and Jesus did not realize it; then how can He be God? Archer claims that in some instances, "it is quite possible that the original message has been irrecoverably altered."[349] How can one believe such a statement and at the same time believe what Jesus says about the Old Testament text? Liberals and Fundamentalists have come up with various answers; however, the "answers" result in questioning Christ.

The Liberal View of Accommodation

Some will claim that Jesus knew of errors in the Old Testament, but that He spoke with the language of accommodation. This means that He merely went along with the commonly held belief that the Jews' copy of the Hebrew Old Testament was infallible and inerrant (John 10:35; 17:17), when all the time it really was not infallible and inerrant. However, such a view poses real problems.

Hague, speaking of accommodation, says,

> What they mean is practically that Jesus did know perfectly well that Moses did not write the Pentateuch, but allowed His disciples to believe that Moses did, and taught His disciples that Moses did, simply because He did not want to upset their simple faith in the whole of the Old Testament as the actual and authoritative and Divinely revealed Word of God. . . . Or else, that Jesus imagined, like any other Jew of His day, that Moses wrote the books that bear his name, and believed, with the childlike Jewish belief of His day, the literal inspiration, Divine authority and historic

---

[349] Archer, 29.

veracity of the Old Testament, and yet was completely mistaken, ignorant of the simplest facts, and wholly in error. In other words, He could not tell a forgery from an original, or a pious fiction from a genuine document. (The analogy of Jesus speaking of the sun rising as an instance of the theory of accommodation is a very different thing). This, then, is their position: Christ knew the views He taught were false, and yet taught them as truth. Or else, Christ didn't know they were false and believed them to be true when they were not true. In either case the Blessed One is dethroned as True God and True Man. If He did not know the books to be spurious when they were spurious and the fables and myths to be mythical and fabulous; if He accepted legendary tales as trustworthy facts, then He was not and is not omniscient. He was not only intellectually fallible, He was morally fallible; for He was not true enough "to miss the ring of truth" in Deuteronomy and Daniel. And further, if Jesus did know certain of the books to be lacking in genuineness, if not spurious and pseudonymous; if He did know the stories of the Fall and Lot and Abraham and Jonah and Daniel to be allegorical and imaginary, if not unverifiable and mythical, then He was neither trustworthy nor good. "If it were not so, I would have told you." We feel, those of us who love and trust Him, that if these stories were not true, if these books were a mass of historical unveracities, if Abraham was an eponymous hero, if Joseph was an astral myth, that He would have told us so. It is a matter that concerned His honor as a Teacher as well as His knowledge as our God.[350]

In other words, the Liberal view of accommodation questions both the teaching and person of Christ. According to the accommodation view, the Bible's teaching was incorrect, and Christ either lied or was ignorant about it. Any of these conclusions is fatal to the veracity and deity of the Lord Jesus Christ. One can apply the above comments from Hague to the numbers of the Old Testament and, in fact, to all the jots and tittles of the Old Testament, since Jesus promised that not a single tittle would be lost (Luke 16:17). For a person to question any one of the numbers in the preserved text of the Old Testament is for him to either knowingly or unknowingly join the Liberal attack against the veracity and ultimately the deity of the Lord Jesus Christ!

---

[350] Dyson Hague, "The History of the Higher Criticism" in *The Fundamentals*, 1:26-27.

Chapter 6

The Fundamentalist View of Limitation

Introduction

Some Fundamentalists seemingly understand that if Matthew 5:18 speaks of the preservation of every jot and tittle of the Old Testament and that if they claim that errors are in the Old Testament, then they would be contradicting Jesus. No Fundamentalist would want to be guilty of contradicting Jesus. At the same time, no Fundamentalist would want to be guilty of disbelieving the Bible. Therefore, for these Fundamentalists to simultaneously maintain their belief in Jesus and their claim of errors in the preserved Old Testament Hebrew Text, they must try to explain away or limit Christ's teaching about preservation in Matthew 5:18, which states: "For verily I say unto you, Till heaven and earth pass, one jot or one tittle shall in no wise pass from the law, till all be fulfilled."

Glenny

One such attempt at explaining away and limiting Matthew 5:18 comes from Glenny who says that Matthew 5:18

> is not speaking about the continual preservation, through written copies, of the exact words found in the *autographa*; it is declaring that all of the prophecies in the OT that pointed to Christ will be fulfilled down to the smallest detail.[351]

Glenny alleges that Christ's teaching in Matthew 5:18 is not speaking of "the continual preservation, through written copies, of the exact words." Glenny's explanation suffers from a couple of problems. First, Jesus is speaking of something continual for He says, "Till heaven and earth pass"; therefore, He is speaking of something that will continue from His day until the passing of heaven and earth. Second, Jesus is speaking of preservation for He asserts that "one jot or one tittle shall in no wise pass from the law." Every jot and tittle of the Old Testament will be preserved. Third, Jesus is speaking of written copies because the *autographa*, no doubt, had been destroyed hundreds of years before Christ. If the *autographa* had been destroyed, then where are the jots and tittles that shall in no wise pass? The jots and tittles are in the copies. Therefore, Jesus is speaking about the continual preservation, through written copies, of the exact words found in the *autographa*.

---

[351] Glenny, 116.

Glenny further alleges that Matthew 5:18 "is declaring that all of the prophecies in the OT that pointed to Christ will be fulfilled down to the smallest detail." This also suffers from several problems. First, Matthew 5:18 speaks of all the law being fulfilled, not just the prophecies that point to Christ. Second, how is one to know that the prophecies have been fulfilled down to the smallest detail, if the details are missing, that is, if God did not preserve all of the jots and tittles? God gave the prophecies with words; but if some of the words are missing or in error, then how could one ever know that the prophecies are being fulfilled down to the smallest detail? But third, and most importantly, Glenny's explanation is somewhat ignoring the middle Matthew 5:18 and is almost treating the verse as if it said, "For verily, I say unto you, Till heaven and earth pass, all will be fulfilled." The fact is that the middle of the verse states, "One jot or one tittle shall in no wise pass from the law," which speaks of the preservation of all the jots and tittles of the Old Testament text, not just those jots and tittles of prophecy. Glenny and others like him seek to limit the teaching of the preservation of all the jots and tittles of the Old Testament text. But one cannot legitimately avoid the teaching that God promises the preservation of all the jots and tittles, for the Bible is clear: "One jot or one tittle shall in no wise pass from the law."

The Committee

J. Drew Conley, Paul W. Downey, John K. Hutcheson, Sr., Mark Minnick, Randolph Shaylor, and James B. Williams form The Committee on the Bible's Text and Translation. They wrote "The Changing King James Version" in *From the Mind of God to the Mind of Man*. In their writing, they seek to limit and explain away Christ's teaching in Matthew 5:18.

The Committee asks, "What does Matthew 5:18 really mean? Doesn't God's Word say that not even one English letter, the cross of a *t* or the dot of an *i* would pass away?"[352] Of course, the question is a straw man, which The Committee knocks down, for the *jot* and *tittle* in Matthew 5:18 are not referring to English letters but to Hebrew letters.[353] The Committee then proceeds to say, "When the Lord gave that Bible truth, his reference point was with the Hebrew and Greek Scriptures or the

---

[352] The Committee on the Bible's Text and Translation, "The Changing King James Version" in *From the Mind of God to the Mind of Man*, 164.

[353] For further discussion, see Chapter Two's material on Matthew 5:18.

original manuscripts."[354] This is inaccurate for Jesus is only referring to the Hebrew Old Testament in Matthew 5:18 and not to the Greek. And further if by *original manuscripts* the committee refers to the *autographa*, then they propagate another inaccuracy. When Jesus spoke the words of Matthew 5:18, the *autographa* of the Old Testament had long since passed away; therefore, Jesus was referring to the preserved copy of the *autographa* and not to the *autographa* itself.

The Committee continues: "By one estimate there are over 200,000 jots and tittles in the Old Testament Scriptures alone and be sure that not a single one of them will pass away without the Lord's fulfillment."[355] While it is true all will be fulfilled, Matthew 5:18 clearly teaches that "one jot or one tittle shall in no wise pass from the law, till all be fulfilled." That is, Matthew 5:18 is not merely speaking about fulfillment but is also speaking of the preservation of every jot and tittle of the Old Testament. Those who do not hold to verbal, plenary preservation must somehow limit Matthew 5:18 to teach only the fulfillment of the Old Testament, but these attempts fail in the light of the clear teaching of the verse itself.

Glenny's and the Committee's "explanations" are nothing more than an attempt to limit and explain away the clear teaching of Matthew 5:18. But if one wants to hold to rationalistic, naturalistic, and humanistic textual criticism and at the same time profess belief in the Lord Jesus Christ, then he is somewhat forced into contrived "explanations" of verses like Matthew 5:18. But make no mistake about it, such "explanations" are not explanations at all. They are, rather, a limiting and an explaining away of what Jesus teaches, and thereby manifest unbelief in the Words of the Lord Jesus Christ and, furthermore, are a questioning of Christ's teaching.[356]

---

[354] Ibid., 165.

[355] Ibid.

[356] Some may think these to be harsh words, but they are far less severe compared to the words Jesus used of Peter when Peter would not believe Jesus' Words (Matthew 16:21-23). Let it be clear that while the author takes serious exception with those who put forth such "explanations," he is not saying that all who put forth these "explanations" are unbelievers in the sense of being lost, though some may very well be lost, but others are, no doubt, like Peter, who, though saved, nonetheless doubted Jesus' Words.

Chapter 6 — *Ramifications*

Combs

In fact, sometimes unbelief in the Words of Jesus comes very close to calling Jesus a liar. Consider Combs' attempt at limiting Christ's teaching in Matthew 5:18, when he says that "Matthew 5:18 is first of all an example of hyperbole."[357] However, nothing in the context of Matthew 5:18 suggests that Jesus is using figurative or hyperbolic language. Just as heaven and earth will literally pass away (spoken of in the first part of Matthew 5:18), so one jot or one tittle shall literally in no wise pass from the law. Just as all will be literally fulfilled (spoken of in the last part of the verse), so, again, one jot or one tittle shall literally in no wise pass from the law. *One jot or one tittle shall in no wise pass from the law* is surrounded by literal statements, establishing that it, too, is literal. Therefore, to say that Matthew 5:18 is hyperbolic is tantamount to saying that Christ lied. How far will Fundamentalists go in questioning Christ?

Conclusion

Has God preserved all the jots and tittles, or has He not? Did Jesus tell the truth, or did He exaggerate? It seems that both Liberals and some Fundamentalists could answer these questions with the same answers. This is very sad. May the Fundamentalists repent and simply receive Christ's Words, instead of questioning Him.

QUESTIONING VERSES

When commentators, teachers, and others claim that scribal errors are in the Traditional Hebrew Text, they are questioning a number of Old Testament verses. As Chapter One presents, Fundamentalists question I Samuel 6:19; 13:1, 5; II Samuel 8:4; 10:18; 15:7; 23:39; I Kings 4:26; 20:30; I Chronicles 11:11; 22:14; and II Chronicles 3:4, 15; 22:2; 36:9; which is fifteen verses in six Old Testament books. Are these the only verses that Fundamentalists would question? Probably not, for perhaps some Fundamentalists would agree with Haley in questioning far more than fifteen Old Testament verses. On pages 382 and 383 of Haley's book, *Alleged Discrepancies*, Haley lists at least forty-one verses of which

---

[357] William W. Combs, "The Preservation of Scripture," *Detroit Baptist Seminary Journal* 5 (Fall 2000): 22. On pages 24 and 25 Combs makes similar remarks about Matthew 24:35. His remarks on Matthew 24:35 are discussed earlier in Chapter Two.

he states, "In all these cases the hypothesis of copyist's errors affords a very facile and reasonable explanation."[358] As the author perused Haley's entire book, he counted more than 115 verses in which Haley gave the "explanation" of scribal error.

Would some Fundamentalists agree with Haley's conclusions? Some Fundamentalists have already rejected Mark 16:9-20; John 5:4; 7:52-8:12; Acts 8:37; I John 5:7; as well as phrases, words, and letters in the New Testament by adopting the Critical Text and English translations based upon the Critical Text. Therefore, it would seemingly be easy for them to agree with Haley and reject 115 verses from the Old Testament. Indeed, these Fundamentalists already have, what the author calls, a rejected-texts mindset; therefore, what would it be for them to reject some more verses from the Old Testament? Where will this rejected-texts mindset stop? It seems that the Fundamentalists are all too willing to reject pieces of the Bible.

How can Fundamentalists reject so much of the Bible when Jesus says, "Man shall not live by bread alone, but by every word that proceedeth out of the mouth of God" (Matthew 4:4)? Should not Fundamentalists be contending for every word? The Bible commands that the saints should "earnestly contend for the faith which was once delivered unto" them (Jude 3). *The faith which was once delivered unto the saints* is based on the very Words of God (Romans 10:8; I Timothy 4:6); therefore, the saints should be fighting for every single word of the Bible. Sad to say, however, many are all too eager to reject the once-delivered words, phrases, and verses.

The rejected-texts mindset comes from the devil who said, "Yea, hath God said" (Genesis 3:1), whereas the true Bible believer should have a received-text mindset (John 8:47; 17:8; Acts 2:41; 8:14; 11:1; 17:11; I Thessalonians 1:6; 2:13; James 1:21). John 8:47 states: "He that is of God heareth God's Words: ye therefore hear them not, because ye are not of God." Jesus says that the Pharisees continually refused to hear (ἀκούετε, a present active indicative) God's Words, which was a definite sign of their lost estate (cf. John 10:27). Those who persist in a rejected-texts mindset are acting like the lost and place themselves in a very dangerous position because Jesus also says, "He that rejecteth Me, and receiveth not My words, hath one that judgeth him: the word that I have spoken, the same shall judge him in the last day" (John 12:48).

---

[358] Haley, 383.

Lenski says of John 12:48, "Jesus is rejected, cast aside as worthless, when His sayings are not received or appropriated with all that they convey."[359] Where does John 12:48 place the Fundamentalist who follows a rejected-texts mindset and, therefore, rejects parts of the preserved Old Testament text, especially when Jesus states that all the jots and tittles of the *autographa* are in that preserved text (Matthew 5:17-18; Luke 16:17)? Also, where does John 12:48 place the Fundamentalist who attempts to explain away Jesus' statements on the perfect preservation of the Old Testament (Matthew 5:17-18; Luke 16:17; John 10:35; 17:17)? *Rejecteth* and *receiveth* in John 12:48 are both present active participles, therefore, indicating a continuous action. When a person does not continually receive Christ's Words, at what point does the Lord consider that person to have rejected Jesus continually? The author cannot tell, but it seems to him that these Fundamentalists are going down a wrong road, and no one should follow them down that road. It is never wise to question any verse of the preserved texts.

RELINQUISHING THE BATTLE FOR THE BIBLE

When a Fundamentalist says errors are in the preserved text, then he is practically giving up the battle for the Bible. Reeve writes:

> Many try to be critics and conservative at the same time. They would "run with the hare and hunt with the hounds," professing to be in full sympathy with evangelical Christianity while abiding their opportunity to inculcate their own views, which, as we have seen, is really to forsake the Christian standpoint.[360]

A Fundamentalist may profess to be in full sympathy with evangelical Christianity, but if he claims that the preserved text is in error, on whose side is he? To be a critic "is really to forsake the Christian standpoint," for neither Jesus nor the apostles criticize the preserved Hebrew text of the Old Testament. The Christian standpoint is to receive the words (John 17:8), not to criticize them. But in criticizing the words, Fundamentalists are relinquishing the battle for the Bible. Sorenson, writing of the New Testament, says,

---

[359] Lenski, *The Interpretation of St. John's Gospel*, 896.

[360] J. J. Reeve, "My Personal Experience with the Higher Criticism" in *The Fundamentals*, 1:299.

Chapter 6 *Ramifications*

> New-Evangelical church historian, George Marsden has made this assessment: "What chiefly distinguished Fundamentalism from earlier evangelicalism was its militancy toward modernist theology and cultural change." Sadly, many Fundamentalists have no militancy toward the modernist textual editors who have produced the critical text.[361]

What Sorenson says of the New Testament equally applies to the Old Testament, for Fundamentalists have accepted the notion of the textual critics that the Masoretic Text has words missing, in addition to other errors. One might expect Liberals and Modernists to take such a position, and, indeed, they do as evidenced by their commentaries, but when Fundamentalists take such a position, they cease to contend earnestly for the faith (see Jude 3). George Dollar observes:

> It was in the midst of a widespread turning away from the faith of our fathers that a valiant few arose to defend the complete trustworthiness of the Scriptures; without regard for personal costs they alerted their disciples to the perils of the times and sounded bugle calls to join the battle to preserve the faith once and for all delivered to the saints.[362]

In the past, some defended the complete trustworthiness of the Scriptures, but, sadly, many Fundamentalists today are not defending the complete trustworthiness of the Scriptures. Instead, they are claiming the existence of errors as well as the loss of words in the Hebrew Old Testament text. In so doing, they have given up the fight and gone over to the camp of the enemy. But should not those who love the Bible "go forth . . . unto Him without the camp, bearing His reproach" (Hebrews 13:13)?

Why would a Fundamentalist state that words are missing and errors are present in the Masoretic Text? Could he be trying through humanistic, naturalistic, and rationalistic means to remove verses to which skeptics easily object in the name of science or history? For example, when an unbeliever reads that Ahaziah was twenty-two in II Kings 8:26 but in II Chronicles 22:2 he reads that Ahaziah at the same time was forty-two, he will think that the Bible clearly is in error. The Fundamentalist, either knowingly or unknowingly, accommodates this kind of thinking by saying that indeed the verse in Chronicles is in error (see Chapter One). This is a very dangerous thing for a Fundamentalist to do. Machen states:

---

[361] David H. Sorenson, *Touch Not the Unclean Thing: The Text Issue and Separation* (Duluth, MN: Northstar Baptist Ministries, 2001), 160.

[362] George W. Dollar, *A History of Fundamentalism in America* (Greenville: Bob Jones University Press, 1973), 2.

Chapter 6　　　　　　　　　　　　　　　　　　　　　　　*Ramifications*

> In trying to remove from Christianity everything that could possibly be objected to in the name of science, in trying to bribe off the enemy by those concessions which the enemy most desires, the apologist has really abandoned what he started out to defend. Here as in many other departments of life it appears that the things that are sometimes thought to be hardest to defend are also the things that are most worth defending.[363]

In other words, when a Fundamentalist agrees with a skeptic that a verse is in error, he then ceases to defend an inerrant Bible. In saying errors are in the preserved texts, Fundamentalists are travelling down the pathway of accommodation with unbelief, and is a most dangerous path to travel, and in so doing they have relinquished the battle for the Bible. It is best to defend the entire Bible, even the parts that some believe are the hardest to defend.

OPENING THE DOOR TO CRITICISM

Once Fundamentalists accept the criticism of numbers in the preserved text where does it stop? Once Fundamentalists have opened the door to criticism when does the door get shut, if ever it gets shut? "A little leaven leaveneth the whole lump" (I Corinthians 5:6). Once a Fundamentalist questions one verse, will he question another and another and another? Chapter One documents the case where the *Scofield Study Bible* went from questioning one verse to questioning many verses. If a Fundamentalist agrees that one number in the preserved text is incorrect, then could he come to the conclusion that other numbers are also incorrect? If one allows for the questioning of a number, then why not also allow for the questioning of other words? If God did not preserve numbers from error, then did He really preserve non-numerical words from error? If one can adjust numbers, then why could he not adjust other parts of Scripture? If one allows changes in numbers, then why not allow other changes? Where does it stop and who determines where it stops? If one allows for an error in a number simply because it does not make immediate sense to him, then where does he stop?

---

[363] J. Gresham Machen, *Christianity & Liberalism* (Grand Rapids: Eerdmans, 1987), 7-8.

Chapter 6 — Ramifications

A Hypothetical Case

Consider the creation account in Genesis. Why not change some words in Genesis to make it agree with evolution? For example, if one did not believe that God created in six actual days but that each day represented a period of time, then he could suppose that the original word in Genesis 1 was *yomim*, that is, *days*, instead of *yom*, that is, *day*, and conjecture that a later scribe contracted the original word. It would not matter that the traditional Hebrew text of the Old Testament has *yom* because conjecture need not deal much with facts. It might be further objected that *yom* being contracted from *yomim* would involve six changes (Genesis 1:5, 8, 13, 19, 23, 31) in twenty-seven verses. But is not this similar to what the Fundamentalists suggest in I Samuel 13:1, 5? In that passage, they suggest three changes in just five verses (I Samuel 13:1 involving two changes concerning the age of Saul and I Samuel 13:5 involving the 30,000 chariots). How about II Kings 18:1-10 wherein Thiele suggests three changes in ten verses (II Kings 18:1, 9, 10)?[364] If one objects that other verses such as Exodus 20:8-11 show that the days of Genesis 1 were actual days, someone could conjecture that something has been left out or adopt a symbolic interpretation. The above example demonstrates that once one opens the door to conjecture, then he can prove anything. The Scriptures are no longer authoritative. Do Fundamentalists want to go in such a direction? If not, then let them reject even taking the first step in that direction.

John Owen writes:

> If these hundreds of words were the critical conjectures and amendments of the Jews, what security have we of the mind of God as truly represented unto us, seeing that it is supposed also that some of the words in the margin were sometimes in the line? And if it be supposed, as it is, that there are innumerable other places of the like nature standing in need of such amendments, what a door would be opened to curious, pragmatical wits to overturn all the certainty of the truth of the Scripture every one may see. Give once this liberty to the audacious curiosity of men priding themselves in their critical abilities, and we shall quickly find out what

---

[364] Edwin R. Thiele, *The Mysterious Numbers of the Hebrew Kings* (Grand Rapids: Kregel, 1994), 199, 204.

wo[e]ful state and condition the truth of the Scripture will be brought unto.[365]

Conjecture is very subjective.[366] If one allows for conjecture, then would he only have a Bible if it meets the approval of certain scholars, schools, or textual critics? What happened to God giving the words and His people simply receiving the words by faith? Some may think that such an approach is rather simple, but should not the just live by faith (Hebrews 10:38)? Just as one receives by faith that God created (Hebrews 11:3), even though he may not have all the answers concerning the creation, so one should receive by faith that the inerrant text of the Old Testament survives to this day (Matthew 5:18).

Actual Cases

Opening the door to criticism is very dangerous, for it can ultimately lead to a denial of inerrancy and into further error. Lindsell warns:

> The weight of history and all the evidence it supplies leads me to no other conclusion than that even if these friends are able to stop at this point [that is, a certain point of criticism], those who follow after them will not stop where they have stopped. The second generation will follow through on the implications contained in the abandonment of inerrancy and will make concessions on the questions that pertain to matters of faith and practice as well as to matters of history, science, and chronology. When inerrancy goes, it opens a small hole in the dike, and if that hole is not closed, the levee will collapse and the whole land will be overrun with the waters of unbelief not unlike that exhibited by Bultmann and theological liberalism.[367]

---

[365] John Owen, "Of the Integrity and Purity of the Hebrew and Greek Text of the Scripture" in *The Works of John Owen*, 16:517.

[366] Young says, "If the Bible has once proved itself to be false, is there any guarantee that it will not err more than once? This poses another question. If there actually are errors in the Scripture, what is the standard by which one is to judge what these errors are? . . . If one concedes that the statements of the Bible may be erroneous, the door has been opened to a host of difficulties and the authority of the Word of God has been undermined. If Scripture has faltered at one step, how does one know that it has not faltered at more than one step?" (E. J. Young, "Are the Scriptures Inerrant?" in *The Bible: The Loving Word of Revelation*, 105). Sadly, Young is not consistent as he questions the fourteenth year of Hezekiah on pages 112-113.

[367] Lindsell, 159-160.

Chapter 6 — *Ramifications*

Fundamentalists

As far as the author knows, no Fundamentalist has gone on record denying the inerrancy of the *autographa*, but are not some dangerously close to doing just that? When a Fundamentalist says a number in the preserved text is erroneous, even though Jesus says the preserved text perfectly preserves the *autographa* (Matthew 5:18; John 10:35; 17:17); then would not a logical conclusion be that the error in the preserved text was part of the *autographa*, and, therefore, the *autographa* were not really inerrant? Instead of coming to this conclusion, and repenting of their faulty reasoning, some Fundamentalists attack the clear teaching of Matthew 5:18 (see previous section in this chapter on questioning Christ), and, therefore, come very close to denying inerrancy. To put it another way: once one says a numerical quantity is in error, how can he be certain that the erroneous number was not in the *autographa*? If his answer is that he receives by faith that God inspired the *autographa* and, therefore, the *autographa* were without error; then why cannot he receive by faith that God preserved those inspired words as the Bible teaches that He did?

E. J. Young

Consider the case of E. J. Young. Young had difficulty believing that in the fourteenth year of King Hezekiah, Sennacherib came up against Judah (Isaiah 36:1). To him, the chronology just did not seem to work, so he conjectured that the true reading should be *twenty-fourth* and suggested that the change came about through a scribal error during copying. However, he admits, "There is no manuscript evidence in its favor."[368] Now if there is no manuscript evidence in favor of *twenty-fourth*, and if a commentator states that *fourteenth* is in error, then could not one come to the conclusion that the *autographa* had *fourteenth* and, therefore, are in error, and that the *autographa* are not inerrant? Young never arrived at such a conclusion, but it seems to the author that Young's position of scribal error with no manuscript evidence is only one little step away from an errant *autographa*. Likewise, by speculating that scribal errors occurred even

---

[368] Young, "Are the Scriptures Inerrant?" in *The Bible: The Living Word of Revelation*, 113.

when there is no manuscript evidence to support their claim,[369] some Fundamentalists are only one little step away from an errant *autographa*.

Robert Mounce

Mounce believes in a limited inerrancy, that is, that the Bible is inerrant in matters of faith, but not necessarily in matters of history. To substantiate his claim, Mounce points to a numerical discrepancy where in Numbers 25:9 the Bible says that 24,000 died, whereas in I Corinthians 10:8 the Bible says that only 23,000 died. The answer to this apparent contradiction is that I Corinthians gives the number who died in one day, whereas Numbers gives the total number who died. Mounce rejects this explanation. While admitting that the numbers were indeed in the *autographa*, Mounce claims that they are in error. Consequently, Mounce believes that the *autographa* have an error.[370] Now some Fundamentalists also reject the explanations for some of the apparent numerical discrepancies holding that the numbers are in error. Although the Fundamentalist would say that the error occurred during the copying of the text, a person like Mounce, however, may say that the error was in the *autographa*. Therefore, when the Fundamentalist says certain numbers are in error, is he not providing ammunition for people like Mounce to say the *autographa* are errant? Is not the Fundamentalist just a short step away from doing the same thing? It is the contention of the author that when the Fundamentalist says the Bible has numerical errors, he is opening the door to criticism and that will ultimately lead to more destructive criticism (see I Corinthians 5:6).

Conclusion

John Owen writes:

> It is readily acknowledged that there are many difficult places in the Scripture, especially in the historical books of the Old Testament. . . . The industry of learned men of old, and of late Jews and Christians, has been

---

[369] The author is not suggesting that if one can find manuscript evidence contrary to the preserved text that it is okay to question the preserved text. One should follow the preserved text no matter what other evidence exists. But the author makes the above statement to show how some have absolutely no basis, not even a faulty basis, for suggesting a change in the preserved text. In the absence of any true basis, would not one logically conclude that the critic is either wrong or the *autographa* were errant?

[370] Lindsell, 163, 167.

well exercised in the interpretation and reconciliation of them: by one or other a fair and probable account is given of them all. Where we cannot reach the utmost depth of truth, it hath been thought meet that poor worms should captivate their understandings to the truth and authority of God in his word. If there be this liberty once given, that they may be looked on as corruptions, and amended at the pleasure of men, how we shall be able to stay before we come to the bottom of questioning the whole Scripture I know not.[371]

The author concurs with Owen. Once men start to correct the Bible according to their own fancies, how long will it be before they do away with the whole Bible?

TREATING BIBLE LIKE ANY OTHER ANCIENT DOCUMENT

In suggesting that the Bible contains scribal errors, Fundamentalists essentially are treating the Bible just like any other ancient document. In their treatment of I Samuel 13:1 and I Kings 4:26, some Fundamentalists regard the Bible as no more reliable than ancient Assyrian or Babylonian literature (see discussions on these verses in Chapters Seven and Nine). Ernest Pickering states that in modern religious unbelief "the Bible was viewed as a merely human book and was treated as any other piece of literature. The critics did not appreciate its uniqueness and, as a result, popularized the idea that it was full of errors, both scientific and otherwise."[372] In light of Pickering's statement, when a Fundamentalist claims that a verse is in error is he not helping to substantiate the position of modern religious unbelief that the Bible is full of errors and is merely a human book? Chapter One relates an account where a professor from Calvary Baptist Theological Seminary questioned I Samuel 13:5. News of the professor's questioning got to a church member who took the questioning of I Samuel 13:5 to mean that the seminary was teaching that the Bible has errors. Very clearly, the questioning of I Samuel 13:5 led the church member rightfully to conclude that the seminary was not paying due respect to the Bible.

---

[371] Owen, "Of the Integrity and Purity of the Hebrew and Greek Text of the Scripture" in *The Works of John Owen*, 16:533.

[372] Ernest Pickering, "The Rise and Impact of Modern Religious Unbelief" in *Biblical Separation: The Struggle for a Pure Church* (Schaumburg, IL: Regular Baptist Press, 1979), 78.

Chapter 6 — *Ramifications*

Claiming the Bible has errors puts one in the same camp with modern religious unbelief. But, further, when one claims "the same fate attended the Scripture in its transcription as hath done other books," he is bordering "on atheism. Surely the promise of God for the preservation of his word, with his love and care of his church, of whose faith and obedience that word of his is the only rule, requires other thoughts at our hands."[373] Would a Fundamentalist want to be bordering on atheism? Surely not, and, if not, then let him repent of his criticism of the Old Testament text.

William Caven writes:

> The Christian Church has followed its Master in regarding the Old Testament as the Word of God, as the Bible of the ages before the Advent, and as still part of the Bible for the Christian Church. Not until the days of developed rationalism was this position called in question. . . . But it is obvious that the style of criticism which, in our own time, is frequently applied to the Old Testament (not to say anything about the New), touching its histories, its laws, its morality, is quite inconsistent with the recognition of any special divine characteristics or authority as belonging to it. The very maxim so often repeated, that criticism must deal with these writings precisely as it deals with other writings is a refusal to Scripture. . . . If a special divine authority can be vindicated for these books, or for any of them, this fact, it is clear, ought to be taken into account by the linguistic and historical critic. Logically, we should begin our study of them by investigating their title to such authority, and, should their claim prove well founded, it should never be forgotten in the subsequent critical processes. The establishment of this high claim will imply in these writings moral characteristics (not to mention others) which should exempt them from a certain suspicion which the critic may not unwarrantably allow to be present when he begins to examine documents of an ordinary kind.[374]

---

[373] Owen, "Of the Integrity and Purity of the Hebrew and Greek Text of the Scripture" in *The Works of John Owen*, 16:458.

[374] William Caven, "The Testimony of Christ to the Old Testament" in *The Fundamentals*, 1:175. Sir Robert Anderson points out: "The Jews insisted that the Lord should be judged like any other human being, just as the critics maintain that the Bible must be treated like any human book. And the inevitable result in the one case was the crucifixion of Calvary: in the other, it is the apostasy of the *Encyclopedia Biblica*. That 'a book written by human pens, and handed down by human methods,' should be the Word of God, does not seem so wild a suggestion as that 'the carpenter, the son of Mary,' should be the Son of God" (Anderson, *The Bible and Modern Criticism*, 61-62). Anderson makes the point that to treat the Bible as any human book leads to apostasy. Is it possible that some who name the name of Christ are headed down the road to apostasy?

The inspiration and preservation of the Bible set the Bible apart from any other book. If anyone approaches the Bible not believing in both inspiration and preservation, then to some extent he is regarding the Bible like any other literature. By denying inspiration, he regards the Bible as a merely human production. By denying preservation, he treats the Bible as being transmitted solely by human means. Either way, or in both ways, to one extent, or to the other extent, he is regarding the Bible just like any other ancient literature when he should be as the Thessalonians who, when they "received the word of God, . . . received it not as the word of men, but as it is in truth, the word of God" (I Thessalonians 2:13). One should receive, believe, and hear all of the Words of God as they are in truth. They are the Words of God whether they involve numbers, science, history, chronology, or theology: all of them are truly the Words of God.

When Peter refused to receive the Words of God from the lips of Jesus concerning Jesus' dying and rising again (Matthew 16:21-22), one of the things that Jesus said to him was, "Thou savourest not the things that be of God, but those that be of men" (Matthew 16:23). Could not Jesus make this charge against those who question the Bible today? Today's Fundamentalist certainly did not learn how to question the Bible from the God-man, the Lord Jesus Christ. Instead, he learned it from men, namely textual critics who treat the Bible as if it were just like any other piece of ancient literature. Peter repented of his savouring of the things of men, and so should these Fundamentalists.

DESTROYING THE FOUNDATION

When a Fundamentalist questions a number in the preserved text, he is helping to destroy a number of things. One thing he is helping to undermine is the foundation upon which the Christian faith rests: the Words of God. Archer states:

> In any court of law, whether in a civil or criminal case, the trustworthiness of a witness on a stand is necessarily an important point at issue if his testimony is to be received. Therefore, the attorney for the opposing side will make every effort in his cross-examination of the witness to demonstrate that he is not a consistently truthful person. If the attorney can trap the opposing witness into statements that contradict what he has said previously or furnish evidence that in his own community the man has a reputation for untruthfulness, then the jury may be led to doubt the accuracy of the witness's testimony that bears directly on the case itself. This is true even though such untruthfulness relates to other matters having no relationship to the present litigation. While the witness on the stand may

indeed be giving a true report on this particular case, the judge and jury have no way of being sure. Therefore, they are logically compelled to discount this man's testimony. The same is true of Holy Scripture. If the statements it contains concerning matters of history and science can be proven by extrabiblical records . . . to be contrary to the truth, then there is grave doubt as to its trustworthiness in matters of religion.[375]

When a Fundamentalist claims there are errors in matters of history, is he not, then, undermining the trustworthiness of the Bible in matters of religion? Indeed, it is so, for Jesus said to Nicodemus, "If I have told you earthly things, and ye believe not, how shall ye believe, if I tell you of heavenly things?" (John 3:12). In order to believe the heavenly things, it is necessary to believe the earthly things. But if one doubts the earthly things in the Bible such as history or chronology, then will he not be open also to doubt the heavenly things? Surely, someone who calls himself a Fundamentalist would not want to lead people away from confidence in the Bible, but this is exactly what he is doing when he claims the preserved text has errors.

George Dollar relates the fight that John Roach Straton waged "against Modernism in all its forms." Dollar states: "The lesson was clear to Straton, for he concluded that when we do anything to discount the Bible, we are cutting from beneath our feet the only ground on which we have to stand; we are destroying the very breath of our lives."[376]

John Owen gives four ways men criticize and mend the Old Testament. First, the critic replaces כ (k) with ב (b) or vice versa and "if by this means any new sense that is tolerable and pleaseth the critic doth emerge," then the critic claims "the scribe was mistaken in the likeness of the letters or in the affinity of the sound" even though all the copies agree to the contrary. Second, he transposes letters and derives words of contrary senses. Third, the critic changes the vowel points which the "three letters דבר . . . as it may be pointed, it will afford eight several senses." And, fourth, the critic examines the LXX or other old translations, and if he finds any word that suits him, then he considers "what Hebrew word answers unto it." Even if "the word is as far different from what is read in

---

[375] Archer, 23. While Archer makes an excellent statement, yet he thinks errors are in the preserved text as it relates to history. Little does he realize that he is one of those who is undermining the trustworthiness of the Bible in matters of religion.

[376] Dollar, 139-140.

the Bible as can be imagined," yet if it gives a better sense to the critic, then a new reading "is found out." Owen concludes:

> And these are the chief heads and springs of the criticisms on the Old Testament, which, with so great a reputation of learning, men have boldly obtruded on us of late days. It is not imaginable what prejudice the sacred truth of the Scripture, preserved by the infinite love and care of God, hath already suffered hereby; and what it may further suffer, for my part I cannot but tremble to think. Lay but these two principles together — namely, that the points are a late invention of some Judaical Rabbins (on which account there is no reason in the world that we should be bound unto them), and that it is lawful to gather various lections by the help of translations, where there are no diversities in our present copies . . . and for my part I must needs cry out . . ., not seeing any means of being delivered from utter uncertainty in and about all sacred truth.[377]

According to John Owen, and the author concurs, when men criticize and mend the Old Testament, they are going down a path wherein uncertainty about all sacred truth will abound. It is a fairy tale for Fundamentalists to think that they can criticize the Old Testament in its numbers and not affect more than just the numbers. Indeed, by criticizing the numbers of the preserved text, they are putting a crack in the foundation of the faith.

DESTROYING FAITH

Once men have attacked the foundation of the faith (the Words of God), then it will not be too long before an accompanying destroying of faith occurs, for "faith cometh by hearing, and hearing by the word of God" (Romans 10:17). Dyson Hague sarcastically states:

> Men used to think that inaccuracy would affect reliability and that proven inconsistencies would imperil credibility. But now it appears that there may not only be mistakes and errors on the part of copyists, but forgeries, intentional omissions, and misinterpretations on the part of authors, and yet, marvelous to say, faith is not to be destroyed, but to be placed on a firmer foundation.[378]

The author is one who still thinks that inaccuracy imperils credibility and, therefore, destroys faith.

---

[377] Owen, "Of The Divine Original, Authority, Self-Evidencing Light, and Power of the Scriptures" in *The Works of Owen*, 16:375-376.

[378] Hague, "The History of the Higher Criticism" in *The Fundamentals*, 1:23.

Chapter 6 *Ramifications*

Throughout the ages, believers have had a mindset of expecting "to receive God's preserved Words"[379] (John 17:8; Acts 2:41; 8:14; 11:1; 17:11; I Thessalonians 1:6; 2:13; James 1:21). *The Westminster Confession of Faith* (1643-48) demonstrates the mindset that believers had in regard to receiving God's Words when it states: " 'The Old Testament in Hebrew . . . and the New Testament in Greek . . . being immediately inspired by God, and, by His singular care and providence, kept pure in all ages, are therefore authentical.' "[380] Strouse points out: "Since other confessions such as the *Articles of Faith of the Baptist Bible Union of America* (1923) and *The Baptist Faith and Message* (1925) of the Southern Baptist Convention affirm the doctrine of the Providential Preservation of Scripture as well, the argument is established that Christians have held to this doctrine historically."[381] Christians of the past believed they had God's preserved words. Van Pelt states:

> In the generation following the Reformation, the strictest and most literal theory of inspiration and inerrancy found general acceptance. Over against such a body of presuppositions, criticism, some generations later, began to allege certain errors and discrepancies in the Bible. Of course the orthodox sought to repel all these claims; for they felt that the Bible, whatever the appearances might seem to indicate, must be free from error, else it could not be the word of God.[382]

The attitude of God's people has been that the Bible must be free from error, not merely the *autographa*, but the preserved text of the Hebrew, Aramaic, and Greek. When a Fundamentalist claims that errors are in the preserved text, he is contradicting the Biblically based belief of many Bible believers that the Bible must be free from error. By so doing, he could cause some to wonder if the Scriptures are really the Words of God. Is this what a Fundamentalist should be doing? Shame on these Fundamentalists: when they should be instilling faith, instead, they are destroying faith.

Sir Robert Anderson in writing about two Bible dictionaries, the one more conservative, the other more liberal, gives an apt illustration:

---

[379] Strouse, *But My Words Shall Not Pass Away*, 20.

[380] Ibid., 27, quoting *The Westminster Confession of Faith* (Philadelphia: Great Commission Publications, n.d.), 4.

[381] Ibid., 28.

[382] J. R. Van Pelt, "Discrepancies, Biblical" in *International Standard Bible Encyclopedia*, 3:255.

Chapter 6 *Ramifications*

The one set of writers hand me a purse of coins, with an assurance that most of them are genuine.[383] The other set of writers hand me a purse of coins, with a warning that most of them are counterfeit. But as I am unable to distinguish between the base coins and the gold, honesty forbids my trading with any of them, and therefore all my seeming wealth is practically useless. In either case the Bible is like a lottery bag, from which blanks and prizes must be drawn at random. If the one section of critics may be trusted, the prizes abound; if the other section be right, the blanks predominate. But in either case, I repeat, faith is impossible, and therefore Christianity is destroyed.[384]

Fundamentalists may think they are reassuring believers by saying that most or supposedly 99.9% or 99.8% of the text is trustworthy,[385] but

---

[383] Does not this sound like some Fundamentalists? For example, Minnick, speaking of the New Testament, says, "And in the cases where we may not be sure which variant most accurately repeats the original wording, not one doctrine is affected" (Minnick, 96). In other words, most of it is genuine. Smallman makes a similar comment (William H. Smallman, "Printed Greek Texts" in *From the Mind of God to the Mind of Man*, 183).

[384] Anderson, *The Bible and Modern Criticism*, 14-15.

[385] Randolph Shaylor espouses 99.9% (Randolph Shaylor, "Our Final Authority" in *From the Mind of God to the Mind of Man*, 24) as does Mark Minnick (Minnick, 85,86). William H. Smallman espouses 99.8% (Smallman, 183). The author uses the word *supposedly* because the 99.9% figure comes from Hort's calculations (*From the Mind of God to the Mind of Man*, 84) and is suspect. Not only that, but the 99.8% figure is also suspect. "The *Textus Receptus* has 140,521 Greek words, but the *Textus Criticus* [which is based on Westcott and Hort's work] changes (primarily by adding or subtracting) 9,970 Greek words. This results in a 7% difference between the *CT* and the *TR*" (Strouse, *But My Words Shall Not Pass Away*, 25,26). Those Fundamentalists who favor Westcott and Hort as espoused in *From the Mind of God to the Mind of Man*, in all honestly, should be saying 93%, instead of 99.9% or 99.8%. This is one problem with these figures. A second problem with these figures arises from a statement by Shaylor wherein he states, "It is because we have such a large number of manuscripts and because of the 'sameness' between them that we can be confident that we have the inspired Bible" (Shaylor, *From the Mind of God to the Mind of Man*, 24). But should not one's confidence be in the promise of the Lord? The Lord promised to keep His pure Words and to preserve them (Psalm 12:6,7), which results in a 100% trustworthy text as opposed to 99.9% as claimed by some, or, in reality, 93%. Who is claiming 99.9% certainty? A man is. But Who certifies 100% certainty? God does. Where should one have his faith, in man or in God? A statement such as Shaylor's moves a person's trust away from God and to the shifting-sand opinions of men. This is most dangerous, for it erodes away the faith one should implicitly have in the Words of God. A third problem with these figures is in a statement by Smallman wherein he states, "We are fully assured that the full range of testimonies to the text in the witness stand today include every 'jot and tittle' of the original autographs, only slightly clouded by some extra material" (Smallman, *From the Mind of God to the Mind of Man*, 183). The problem here is this: whose job is it to determine what the "extra material" is? If it were

Chapter 6 — *Ramifications*

in reality, as Anderson points out, faith is destroyed. Sorenson writes about the New Testament, which comments can equally apply to the Old Testament:

> The very essence of modern text criticism—transcriptional probabilities, conjectural emendations, editorial recensions—begins with the premise of doubt. "Did God really say this?" The endless minutia of the modern critical apparatus begs the question of textual authority. In reading the writings of proponents of the critical text and their discussions over textual variants, the net result is question and doubt and never certainty.[386]

Pink, in a section entitled "It Is A Sure Foundation For Our Faith," writes of the Bible:

> Man craves for certainty. Speculations and hypotheses are insufficient where eternal issues are at stake. When I come to lay my head upon my dying pillow, I want something surer than a "perhaps" to rest it upon. And thank God I have it. Where? In the Holy Scriptures. I know that my Redeemer liveth. I know that I have passed from death unto life. I know that I shall be made like Christ and dwell with Him in glory throughout the endless ages of eternity. How do I know? Because God's Word says so, and I want nothing more. The Bible gives forth no uncertain sound. It speaks with absolute assurance, dogmatism, and finality. Its promises are certain for they are promises of Him who cannot lie. Its testimony is reliable for it is the inerrant Word of the Living God. Its teachings are trustworthy for they are a communication [from] the Omniscient. The believer then has a sure foundation on which to rest, an impregnable rock on which to build his hopes. For his present peace and for his future prospects he has a, "Thus saith the Lord," and that is sufficient.[387]

Amen to that and thank God that He has given to believers a sure foundation. "How firm a foundation, ye saints of the Lord, is laid for your faith in His excellent Word!"

---

the job of textual critics, then again man's faith is in the shifting sand of man's opinion, instead of the solid promise of God.

[386] Sorenson, 146-147.

[387] Pink, *The Divine Inspiration of the Bible*, 65.

Chapter 6 — Ramifications

DESTROYING AUTHORITY

When a Fundamentalist claims scribal errors are in the Bible, not only is he destroying the foundation and faith, but also he is destroying authority.

Archer's Comments

Archer observes: "It is a matter of basic self-contradiction for a partial-inerrantist to hold that in matters of history and science the Bible may err and yet for him to expound any text from the Scripture as having authority in its own right."[388] If Archer's statement is true for the partial inerrantist, then is it not equally true for those who claim that scribal errors are in the text? If an error is in one place, could not an error be in another place? Such a possibility leads to a destroying of authority. Archer continues:

> It is morally indefensible to put down the Bible—which presents itself as the uniquely authoritative Word of God—as the object of man's critical judgment so that one may decide (at least for himself personally) which parts of Scripture he may accept as binding on him and which parts he may safely disregard. To treat the Bible in this way is to trifle with God, and it can only result in a process of progressive stultification and a steady loss of theological certainty and moral conviction. Indeed, it can be reasonably argued that the plea to shy away from the defense of the accuracy and trustworthiness of Scripture whenever it is attacked on factual matters is hardly to be distinguished in principle from a policy of defending and adhering to the moral standards laid down in Scripture only when they do not conflict with modern standards of morality or when in one's personal life they do not conflict with what the professing Christian *wants* to do (whether or not it is the will of God).[389]

---

[388] Archer, 26.

[389] Ibid., 26-27. This is another good statement by Archer; however, it is regrettable that he fails to follow his own words in that he allows for scribal errors in the preserved text. Apparently, he must believe that he can hold to the absolute trustworthiness of Scripture even in historical matters and at the same time claim that scribal errors have entered into the text and in his own mind this may be consistent by saying that the *autographa* are inerrant, but that errors entered during the transmission process. However, if one must defend "the accuracy and trustworthiness of Scripture whenever it is attacked on factual matters," he must defend the Scripture that he has, that is, the preserved text, for it is the preserved text that is coming under attack. Therefore, in the author's estimation, Archer's overall position is inconsistent.

Chapter 6 *Ramifications*

In short, if one attacks the Bible on factual matters, then the Bible loses authority in moral matters. In the end, the critic's word becomes the final authority, and not God's Words. The Bible then only has authority if the critic says it has authority. Man's faith has then been shifted away from simply believing the Bible to trusting the pronouncements of the critic.

Minnick's Comments

Mark Minnick makes a revealing statement when he admits that "as a preacher of God's Word" he "must rely upon the findings of textual critics."[390] If such is the case, then does not the ultimate authority become the textual critic? Minnick, no doubt, would dispute that the ultimate authority becomes the textual critic, but for all practical purposes is it not so? When a man receives Christ as his Saviour, he does not need the word of a man, no matter how good the man may be, for him to know he has Christ and, therefore, is saved. He can just simply take God at His word that if he received Christ as Saviour, he is saved (John 1:12). If he must rely on a man to know that he is saved, then is not his trust ultimately in that man, instead of God? Likewise, one does not need the word of a man, no matter how good, for him to know that he has the written Words of God. He can simply take God at His Word that He inspired His Words and preserved those inspired Words so that all he has to do is to receive them. He does not need to wait upon some official pronouncement that he has God's Words, or else his trust is ultimately in man's pronouncement rather than in God's promises. If he is trusting in the pronouncement of man to assure him that he has the Words of God, then the opinion of man is exalted and the authority of the Words of God are diminished. Indeed, one may as well put himself back under the pronouncements, pontifications, and predicaments of priestcraft and popery as to rely on the textual critics to tell him that he has the Words of God.

Spurgeon's Comments

Spurgeon wrote at the end of his life:

---

[390] Minnick, 85. In the same book, John Ashbrook, speaking of his car, says, "When it comes to diagnosis, tune-ups, and the onboard computer, I have to turn to men with special training. The same is true in the realm of the text" (John E. Ashbrook, "The History of the Textus Receptus" in *From the Mind of God to the Mind of Man*, 108).

Are these correctors of Scripture infallible? Is it certain that our Bibles are not right, but that the critics must be so? The old silver is to be depreciated; but the German silver, which is put in its place, is to be taken at the value of gold. . . . Are we now to believe that infallibility is with learned men? Now, Farmer Smith, when you have read your Bible, and have enjoyed its precious promises, you will have, to-morrow morning, to go down the street to ask the scholarly man at the parsonage whether this portion of the Scripture belongs to the inspired part of the Word, or whether it is of dubious authority. It will be well for you to know whether it was written by the Isaiah, or whether it was by the second of the "two Obadiahs." All possibility of certainty is transferred from the spiritual man to a class of persons whose scholarship is pretentious, but who do not even pretend to spirituality. We shall gradually be so bedoubted and becriticized, that only a few of the most profound will know what is Bible, and what is not, and they will dictate to all the rest of us. I have no more faith in their mercy than in their accuracy: they will rob us of all that we hold most dear, and glory in the cruel deed. This same reign of terror we shall not endure, for we still believe that God revealeth himself rather to babes than to the wise and prudent, and we are fully assured that our own old English version of the Scriptures is sufficient for plain men for all purposes of life, salvation, and godliness. We do not despise learning, but we will never say of culture or criticism, "These be thy gods, O Israel!"[391]

Paisley's Comments

Must one rely on the scholars to tell him what are the Words of God? Paisley writes:

> The Bible is not the production of man but the product of God. It is the Word of God. It was not delivered unto the scholars—Greek, Hebrew, or otherwise, but to the saints. *"The faith which was once delivered to the saints"* Jude 3.
>
> God has delivered His Book to the custody, not of the scholars, the universities, colleges or seats of learning, but only to His saints.
>
> Can any ordinary saint who has no knowledge whatever of the original languages know what is a proper version of God's Word or which is absolutely reliable? The answer is "yes" or else Jude verse 3 is error. Jude verse 3 is not error but divinely revealed truth.

---

[391] Charles H. Spurgeon, *The Greatest Fight in the World* in *The Charles H. Spurgeon Library*, version 2 [CD-ROM] (Albany, OR: Ages Software, 1998), 17-19.

Chapter 6 _Ramifications_

> The attempt to bamboozle the ordinary saints of God with irrelevant controversy must be demonstrated. The ploy to take from the saints their divinely appointed role of custody of the Book and place it in the hands of scholars must be exposed for what it is, a device of the devil himself.
>
> Thank God for the simplicity which is in Christ which devastates the duplicity which is in Satan.
>
> But how can the saint know?
>
> The answer is as plain as the midday sun—The saint knows the Author of the Book and has received what no amount of learning can impart—the divinely imparted gift of spiritual discernment.
>
> "But the natural man receiveth not the things of the Spirit of God: for they are foolishness unto him: neither can he know them, because they are spiritually discerned" (I Corinthians 2:14).[392]

Hills' Comments

Hills writes:

> The Bible version which you must use is not a matter for you to decide according to your whims and prejudices. It has already been decided for you by the workings of God's special providence. If you ignore this providence and choose to adopt one of the modern versions, you will be taking the first step in the logic of unbelief. For the arguments which you must use to justify your choice are the same arguments which unbelievers use to justify theirs, the same method. If you adopt one of these modern versions, **you must adopt the naturalistic New Testament textual criticism upon which it rests** [emphasis mine]. This naturalistic criticism requires us to study the New Testament text in the same way in which we study the texts of secular books which have *not* been preserved by God's special providence. In other words, naturalistic textual criticism regards the special, providential preservation of the Scriptures as of no importance for the study of the New Testament text. But if we concede this, then it follows that the infallible inspiration of the Scriptures is likewise unimportant. For why is it important that God should infallibly inspire the Scriptures, if it is not important that He should preserve them by His special providence?
>
> Where, oh where, dear brother or sister, did you ever get the idea that it is up to you to decide which Bible version you will receive as God's holy Word. As long as you harbor this false notion, you are little better than an

---

[392] Ian Paisley, *My Plea for the Old Sword* (Belfast: Ambassador Publications, 1997), 75-76.

unbeliever. As long as you cherish this erroneous opinion, you are entirely on your own. ***For you the Bible has no real authority, only that which your rebellious reason deigns to give it*** [emphasis mine]. For you there is no comfort, no assurance of faith. Cast off, therefore, this carnal mind that leads to death! Put on the spiritual mind that leads to life and peace! Receive by faith the True Text of God's holy Word, which has been preserved down through the ages by His special providence and now is found in the Masoretic Hebrew text, the Greek Textus Receptus, and the King James Version and other faithful translations![393]

Although Hills is speaking primarily of deciding which Bible version to use, what he says applies just as well to those who seek to decide which Hebrew or Greek readings or texts to use. Once one makes himself the final arbiter in determining what the text should say, as one does when he claims errors are in the text, then the text has no real authority: authority is destroyed.

EXALTING HUMAN REASONING, SUPPOSITION, AND TEXTUAL CRITICISM

When one claims that errors are in the preserved text, he is exalting textual criticism, human reasoning, and supposition. First consider this: if the preserved text has errors, then there is something truer than the preserved text. What is truer? Can this other thing lay claim to God's promise of preservation? No, it cannot. Therefore, when one asserts that the preserved text has an error, he is exalting something else over the preserved text whether that be his own intellect, science, secular history, Assyrian chronology, opinions of men, or something else. At this point a non-preserved source takes precedence over the preserved text, and then how is one to decide what is truth?

J. J. Reeve, writing about his personal experience with higher criticism, states:

> Supremely satisfied with its self-constituted authority, the mind thinks itself competent to criticize the Bible, the thinking of all the centuries, and even Jesus Christ Himself. The followers of this cult have their full share of the frailties of human nature. Rarely, if ever, can a thoroughgoing critic be an evangelist, or even evangelistic; he is educational. How is it possible for a preacher to be a power for God, whose source of authority is his

---

[393] Edward F. Hills, *The King James Version Defended*, 243.

own reason and convictions? The Bible can scarcely contain more than good advice for such a man.[394]

When a man thinks he can judge the Bible, in the end, he exalts his mind over the Bible. This is a dangerous trap into which many a man has fallen, for "there is a way that seemeth right unto a man, but the end thereof *are* the ways of death" (Proverbs 16:25). Ashbrook states:

> We need to remember that it was in the schools of Germany that the great truths of the Protestant Reformation were first compromised and then surrendered to the rationalists and higher critics. Martin Luther's words of warning were prophetic indeed when he warned: "When we first meet the Devil in the Bible he is camped unto the tree of knowledge and he has been camped there ever since."[395]

But the Bible teaches that faith should not be in the wisdom of men but in the power of God (I Corinthians 2:5). Furthermore, teaching should not be in the words that man's wisdom teaches, but in words that the Holy Ghost teaches (I Corinthians 2:12-13). Bettex says,

> We will not attempt to improve the Scriptures and adapt them to our liking, but we will believe them. We will not criticize them, but we will ourselves be directed by them. We will not exercise authority over them, but we will obey them. We will trust Him who is the way, the truth, and the life. His word shall make us free.[396]

When one supposes that the preserved text has errors, he has entered the land of supposition, for how does he know that the preserved text has an error? He does not have the *autographa* whereby to ascertain that the preserved text is in error, so he only can suppose that it is in error, he cannot know for certain. He will suppose that his suppositions are better than what is preserved in the text. He will suppose that others should follow his suppositions over what is written, which leads to "a jumble of mere hypotheses, imaginings and assertions, brought forward often without even the shadow of proof, and with no real certainty."[397] The Bible instructs the believer to walk by faith (II Corinthians 5:7). The believer, however, who questions the Bible, is not walking by faith, but by sight.

---

[394] J. J. Reeve, "My Personal Experience with the Higher Criticism" in *The Fundamentals*, 1:298.

[395] William E. Ashbrook, *Evangelicalism: The New Neutralism* (Columbus, OH: Calvary Bible Church, n.d.), 22.

[396] F. Bettex, "The Bible and Modern Criticism" in *The Fundamentals*, 1:75.

[397] Ibid., 71.

Chapter 6 *Ramifications*

Such sight is not very clear, for it is the clouded sight of the critic. So clouded is this "sight" that when Jesus asked the Pharisees about the baptism of John, they said, after reasoning among themselves, that they could not tell if John's baptism was from heaven or from men. Therefore, Jesus would not give them any further instruction (Matthew 21:25-27). By exalting their own human reasoning and prejudice, the Pharisees had no certainty; therefore, they were not able to see such a clear matter that John's baptism was from heaven. Likewise, those who follow their own human reasoning are not able to see the clearly revealed statements of the Bible, but rather suppose them to be in doubt or in error.

When one questions the preserved texts, not only is he exalting human reasoning and supposition, but he is also exalting textual criticism. Concerning the logic, which the Critical Text position uses, Sorenson writes that in this position:

> (1) the original documents . . . may or may not have been inspired and inerrant; (2) moreover, the *autographa* has been lost; (3) what exists today are conflicting copies (apographs) of those manuscripts, all of which have some degree of errors included therein; (4) therefore, through textual criticism, the original text hopefully can be reconstructed by scientific means.[398]

Sorenson then concludes:

> Modern textual criticism accordingly has become the supreme court determining what is the Word of God and what is not. . . . The committees of modern textual critics issue their verdicts whether a given word, verse, or portions of a chapter should be a part of the Bible. Truly the collective judgments of the critics have determined the composition of the critical text of the New Testament. Modern text critics are the supreme court justices and none are Fundamental Baptists. Moreover, those of this position clearly teach that we must rely upon the findings of these text critics.[399]

Sorenson speaks of the New Testament text, but the same is true of the Old Testament text. As pointed out in Chapter One, when David Doran of Detroit Baptist Theological Seminary asked Jaeggli, "Is it accurate to say or act like textual criticism is unnecessary in the Old Testament text?" Jaeggli responded, "Absolutely not."[400] Jaeggli then gave exam-

---

[398] Sorenson, 60.

[399] Ibid., 60.

[400] *Fundamentalism and the Word of God* (Allen Park, MI: Coalition for the Defense of the Scriptures), videocassette.

Chapter 6 — *Ramifications*

ples where he thinks textual criticism must be used in the Old Testament text. Is one left to the conjectures of the textual critics concerning the words of the Bible? Once one relinquishes control of the Bible to the textual critics is he not putting his faith in them, instead of in the promises of God to keep His Words? Putting faith in man is a very dangerous place to be. "Thus saith the LORD; Cursed be the man that trusteth in man, and maketh flesh his arm, and whose heart departeth from the LORD" (Jeremiah 17:5).

COMING DANGEROUSLY CLOSE TO ADDING TO OR SUBSTRACTING FROM THE BIBLE

If the Traditional Text is the preserved Word of God; then when a person tampers with it, he is tampering with the very Words of God. The Bible warns against taking away or adding to His Words (Revelation 22:18-19). The Bible also speaks of the false prophets presuming to speak for God, when He had not spoken (Ezekiel 13:7). Is this not close to what some Fundamentalists do, when they correct the Bible? The Bible critics presume to speak for God by correcting the Bible, when they do not even know what God actually has said. Fundamentalists, who seek to correct the text, are pitching their tent toward taking away or adding to the Bible and toward the activity of false prophets. Instead of leaning in such a direction, should they not be showing faith in the promises of God to preserve His Words?

MAKING IT IMPOSSIBLE FOR MAN TO LIVE BY EVERY WORD OF GOD

Jesus said that man needs every Word of God in order to live (Matthew 4:4). Fundamentalists, however, state that man does not have every Word of God. For example, Fundamentalists claim that, in the case of I Samuel 13:1, "at least one of the numbers in this verse has been lost."[401] Therefore, it appears that not all the words are available to man today. But if man needs every Word of God in order to live and if he does not have every word, then how is he to live? Waite says of Matthew 4:4,

---

[401] Glenny, 114.

Chapter 6 *Ramifications*

How can a man or woman live by every Word of God that proceeds out of the mouth of God unless God has preserved this Word to listen to? It is impossible. . . . What the Lord Jesus Christ was telling Satan was that the Old Testament has been preserved. He's quoting from Deuteronomy. The Old Testament had been preserved right down until His day and man should live by that very Word. That is a number of years, about 1500 years from Moses until Jesus' day. He kept, guarded, and preserved "EVERY WORD."[402]

Paisley states: "To say that God has preserved most of the Original Scriptures but not them all, robs us of every Word of God. Therefore we cannot live."[403] But thank God that this is not the case, for the very same Lord Jesus Christ Who states that man needs every word, promises the preservation of every word (Matthew 5:18).

GETTING CLOSER TO NEW EVANGELICALISM, LIBERALISM, AND CATHOLICISM

As Fundamentalists question some of the numbers of the Old Testament, they are getting closer to a New Evangelical, Liberal, and even Catholic position.

Discrediting Chronicles

When Fundamentalists question some of the numbers of Chronicles, they are aiding the Liberals in discrediting Chronicles. J. J. Reeve points out that the higher critic goes after Chronicles because it "records many facts about the temple and its services which do not fit in with the critics' hypothesis, and therefore something must be done to discredit the Chronicler and get rid of his testimony."[404] But Chronicles is not all that is in the sight of the Liberals, for "the discrediting of Chronicles is part of a theory which denies the historical trustworthiness of practically all parts of the Old Testament and New Testament."[405] Questioning Chronicles leads to

---

[402] D. A. Waite, *Defending the King James Bible*, 9.

[403] Paisley, 103.

[404] J. J. Reeve, "My Personal Experience with the Higher Criticism" in *The Fundamentals*, 1:297.

[405] Willis J. Beecher, "Chronicles, Books of" in *International Standard Bible Encyclopedia*, 2:943.

Chapter 6 *Ramifications*

questioning other parts of the Bible. One cannot tamper with one part of the Bible, no matter how insignificant he may think that part, without affecting other parts of the Bible. One way commentators discredit Chronicles is to claim that "the large numerals in Chronicles" are "extravagant and incredible."[406] Some Fundamentalists have claimed that *fifty thousand and threescore and ten* in I Samuel 6:19 and *thirty thousand* in I Samuel 13:5 are incredible, thereby discrediting Samuel. Specifically, concerning Chronicles, some of these Fundamentalists also question:

1. 300 in I Chronicles 11:11 (see discussion in Chapter Eight on II Samuel 23:8);

2. 100,000 talents of gold in I Chronicles 22:14 (see discussion in Chapter Eleven on I Chronicles 22:14);

3. 1,000,000 (thousand thousand) talents of silver in I Chronicles 22:14 (see discussion in Chapter Eleven on I Chronicles 22:14);

4. 120 in II Chronicles 3:4 (see discussion in Chapter Twelve on II Chronicles 3:4);

5. 35 in II Chronicles 3:15 (see discussion in Chapter Nine on I Kings 7:15);

6. 3000 in II Chronicles 4:5 (see discussion in Chapter Nine on I Kings 7:26);

7. 42 in II Chronicles 22:2 (see discussion in Chapter Ten on II Kings 8:26); and

8. 8 in II Chronicles 36:9 (see discussion in Chapter Ten on II Kings 24:8).

While not all of these numbers are large, yet in questioning them, Fundamentalists are in harmony with the Liberal agenda. It is instructive at this juncture to repeat an earlier quote from *The Defender's Study Bible* for II Chronicles:

> There are a number of apparent contradictions between the histories of Chronicles and those of Samuel and Kings. Most of these are only superficial and can be easily resolved on closer study. However, a significant number have to do with numerical quantities, which are in clear conflict. These can usually best be explained in terms of copyists' errors.[407]

The above note from *The Defender's Study Bible*, no doubt, is expressive of the views of many who call themselves Fundamentalists. While

---

[406] Ibid.

[407] Henry M. Morris, *The Defender's Study Bible*, 487.

Henry Morris, who prepared the annotations for *The Defender's Study Bible*, may not be as blatant as some of the higher critics in his statements, yet he questions numbers with the result that Chronicles as well as other books are discredited and the Liberal agenda is furthered. Additionally, the fact that these Fundamentalists question some of the large numbers in Samuel, and the fact that they question some numbers in Chronicles, and the fact "that a little leaven leaveneth the whole lump" (I Corinthians 5:6); it may not be long before they actually start questioning more numbers in Chronicles. It is a curious thing indeed that some Fundamentalists find themselves in league with the higher critics in opposing the Bible.[408] The Bible, however, commands: "Have no fellowship with the unfruitful works of darkness, but rather reprove them" (Ephesians 5:11). Instead of speaking for the cause of Liberals, Fundamentalists need to separate from and to reprove the Liberals' unfruitful works of darkness.

Acting as if The Bible Has Moot Points

Why would Fundamentalists question numbers in the Bible? Could these Fundamentalists believe that the numbers are not important? It seems that this is the case. A quote presented earlier in Chapter Three is applicable here. George DeHoff writes:

> Some of the discrepancies concerning numbers, kings, genealogies, etc. are so obscure as to have little interest for thinking people anyway. Fortunately the length of time a certain king ruled can have nothing to do with our salvation anyway.[409]

DeHoff and other Fundamentalists like him do not believe that such numbers are important. Could these men be in agreement with the New Evangelical position that the Bible has moot points? It seems so. The word *moot* means "subject to debate; arguable; unresolved."[410] The New Evangelical believes that the Bible has debatable or arguable points. John Ashbrook quotes Harold Ockenga, one of the founding fathers of New Evangelicalism: "The evangelical believes that Christianity is intellectu-

---

[408] Chapters Seven through Twelve give numerous examples of where Fundamentalists are in agreement with Liberals in discrediting the Masoretic Text. Some of those examples are I Samuel 6:19; 13:1; II Samuel 8:4; 10:18; 15:7; 24:13; I Kings 4:26; II Kings 8:26; 18:13; 24:8; and II Chronicles 3:4.

[409] George DeHoff, *Alleged Bible Contradictions Explained* (Grand Rapids: Baker, 1951), 38-39. For further discussion of DeHoff's faulty position, see Chapter Three.

[410] William Morris, 852.

Chapter 6 *Ramifications*

ally defensible, but the Christian cannot be obscurantist in scientific questions pertaining to the creation, the age of man, the universality of the flood and other moot Biblical questions."[411] While Ockenga may have considered some of these things to be debatable, Jesus, however, regarded the creation and the flood as facts (Matthew 19:4-6; 24:37-39). These are not moot points. In fact, as one looks at Jesus' approach to the Old Testament, Jesus considers nothing about the Old Testament moot. Jesus received, believed, and heard all the Old Testament without question. There is not a single moot point about any of the Old Testament: to Jesus every jot and tittle was and is settled (Matthew 5:18). But the New Evangelical believes there are moot points. When the Fundamentalist says certain numbers are in error, is he not also admitting there are moot points? Is he not, then, partaking of this same New Evangelical spirit?

Holding to Conceptual Preservation

Akin to the idea of moot points in the Bible is the idea of conceptual preservation, that is, that only doctrinal content or content about faith and conduct is preserved but that content about other matters may not be preserved. The fact that some Fundamentalists hold a conceptual-preservation position is something that this book documented earlier. For example, W. Edward Glenny of Central Baptist Theological Seminary while arguing against the actual words of the originals being preserved says, "God has providentially preserved the text of Scripture in multiple manuscripts throughout history so that none of its doctrinal content is lost or affected adversely."[412] Such a position is New Evangelical and, or Liberal. Strouse writes:

> The Liberals and Modernists held to the Dynamic (Conceptual) Inspiration view, maintaining that God inspired His thoughts but not His Words. This led to their view of Dynamic Preservation, that God preserved His thoughts, and these Divine thoughts are manifested in the *CT* [Critical Text], and in the modern versions utilizing Dynamic Equivalence. Fundamentalists, including conservatives and evangelicals, battled with the Modernists over the liberal Dynamic Inspiration View. Fundamentalists maintained that God not only inspired the very Words of Scripture (Verbal, Plenary Inspiration), but that He preserved all of them perfectly (Ver-

---

[411] John E. Ashbrook, *New Neutralism II* (Mentor, OH: Here I Stand Books, 1992), 8, quoting a December 8, 1957 news release from Harold Ockenga.

[412] Glenny, 122.

bal, Plenary Preservation), as manifested in the *TR* [Textus Receptus], and these Historic Fundamentalists have used the *AV* translated upon Formal Equivalence principles.

In the last half of the 20th century a new group has emerged, which is in transition from Fundamentalism to modernism, and is called New Evangelicalism. This "*in-flux*" or transitory group holds to Verbal, Plenary Inspiration, Dynamic Preservation, the *CT*, and the resultant modern versions based on Dynamic Equivalence. . . . *Regrettably, some within the Fundamentalist camp are now promoting this middle and shifting position. These New Fundamentalists argue that God has preserved His Word, not His Words, and their presuppositions, arguments, tenor and fruit, parallel the liberals!* [Emphasis mine].[413]

Ernest Pickering quotes William Lasor, a professor at Fuller Theological Seminary, a leading New Evangelical institution:

> There is in my mind a clear difference between saying that the Bible is entirely without error in all that it teaches, and in saying that the Bible is without error in all matters (such as geology, astronomy, genealogy, figures, etc.) when these matters are not essential to the teaching of the context.[414]

In other words, Lasor argued that the Bible is inerrant when it teaches on faith but may have error in other matters. Lasor may also be arguing against the inerrancy of the *autographa*. But whether one argues for errant *autographa*, as many New Evangelicals, or for an errant Traditional Text of the *autographa*, as many Fundamentalists, the end result is the same: the Bible which believers now possess is errant, but more than this, the original language texts are also errant. While starting from different starting points, both Fundamentalists and New Evangelicals come to the same conclusion that the current original language texts and the Bibles translated from them have errors. Sadly, Fundamentalists and New Evangelicals are in agreement in an area in which they should not be in agreement. Shame on the Fundamentalists!

---

[413] Strouse, "But My Words Shall Not Pass Away", 39-40.

[414] Ernest Pickering, *Biblical Separation: The Struggle for a Pure Church* (Schaumburg, IL: Regular Baptist Press, 1979), 132, quoting William LaSor, "Life Under Tension" in *The Authority of Scripture at Fuller* (Pasadena: Fuller Theological Seminary, n.d.), 27.

Chapter 6 *Ramifications*

Placing Faith in Text Critics

If the original language texts are errant, then how can one determine the correct reading? This is where the textual critic comes to the "rescue." If one does not have faith that the Lord has preserved His Words, then where is his faith? Many put their faith in the textual critics to restore the text. This is another New Evangelical and Liberal position. Strouse in reviewing the book *From the Mind of God to the Mind of Man* says,

> The goal of modern Textual Criticism is to restore or reconstruct the Biblical text (p. 106) that God apparently chose not to preserve. The liberals' humanistic approach seems obvious, but why do some Fundamentalists fail to see that the Lord does not need man's help? It is strange indeed for Fundamentalists to countenance liberal views, either deliberately or by default.[415]

Strouse mentions that modern textual criticism is a humanistic approach. Indeed, it is because modern textual criticism fails to believe that God has fully preserved His Words and that, therefore, man must restore the words of the Bible through his own efforts. This, Strouse maintains, is a Liberal position. However, some Fundamentalists take this same Liberal position. As pointed out earlier, Minnick makes a revealing statement when he admits that "as a preacher of God's Word" he "must rely upon the findings of textual critics."[416] Therein Minnick finds himself in the same position as the Liberals placing his faith in the textual critics.

What Minnick states about relying on the findings of the textual critics is also very similar to what New Evangelicals say. Walter Dunnet, a professor of Biblical Studies at Northwestern College in Roseville, MN and a man who received several degrees from Wheaton College and, therefore, is probably in the New Evangelical camp, makes similar comments about textual criticism as does Fundamentalist Minnick. Dunnet states:

> Before interpreting a text, one must be assured of the accuracy of the text. Is this what the author originally wrote? While most readers may not have a knowledge of Hebrew and/or Greek to be able to read the Bible in its original languages, they can be assured that the science of textual criticism has provided readers with a highly accurate reproduction of the original text. Despite many variants in the original language texts, scholars assure

---

[415] Thomas M. Strouse, "Review 1" in *Reviews of the Book From the Mind of God to the Mind of Man* (Pensacola: Pensacola Theological Seminary, 2001), 4-5.

[416] Minnick, 85.

us that our present editions of the Bible, along with several good English translations, give a sound basis for proceeding to interpretation of the text.[417]

Gephart is another Fundamentalist who relies on textual criticism. He states: "Christian scholars must strive to recover 'the exact form of the words and phrases used in the original'."[418] Earlier, he makes it clear that the method for recovery is through the use of textual criticism when he quotes Green as saying that the function of textual criticism is " 'to restore the text to its pristine purity as it came from the hands of the original writers'."[419] It is very instructive for the reader to note that it was in 1899 when Green made his statement about restoring the text. Gephart quotes Green in 2003, indicating that the attempt to recover the text is still an ongoing process. In other words, for over 100 years the textual critics have been trying to restore the text and have not yet completed the task! In contrast, Jesus did not have to wait over 100 years to get an authoritative, *it-is-written* Old Testament, nor did the apostles. They all simply believed that they God had gotten His Words to them and that they possessed all of His Words right there and then. They did not have to go about recovering and restoring. Indeed, to say that one needs to recover and restore the text is to say that the current text is flawed and faulty, which is to contradict Jesus directly, Who believed that His text of the Old Testament has nothing missing (Matthew 5:18), has the Words of the *autographa* (Matthew 4:4), and is true (John 17:17). To claim that the Bible must be restored and recovered is to reject God's promises of perfect preservation. How much better it is to follow Jesus and receive the Words of God, instead of going on a futile mission of recovery and restoration. Rather than trying to restore the Words of God, Fundamentalists should work at restoring their faith and confidence in God's promises of perfect preservation.

Brooks makes an excellent observation when he writes:

> What good is a Bible God inspired if His people do not have it? Without preservation, inspiration is moot. Yet the same Fundamentalists who hold

---

[417] Walter M. Dunnett, *The Interpretation of Holy Scripture* (Nashville: Thomas Nelson Publishers, 1984), 91-92.

[418] Keith Gephart, "Are Copies Reliable?" in *God's Word in Our Hands*, 166, quoting from William Henry Green, *General Introduction to the Old Testament-the Text* (New York: Charles Scribner's Sons, 1899), 168.

[419] Ibid., quoting Green, 162.

to verbal-plenary inspiration of the Bible, because that is what the Bible teaches of itself, reject the preservation of the Bible.[420]

Many Fundamentalists reject the Biblical teaching of the perfect preservation of God's Words. Indeed, as much as the restoration-of-the-text Fundamentalist may speak of preservation,[421] in reality by claiming that he must restore the text, he is rejecting preservation. Brooks continues:

> In rejecting divine preservation, "scholars, teachers, denominational leaders, and educators within" Fundamentalism have now adopted many of the same tenets of rationalistic textual criticism that brought Modernism to our shores over a century ago, provoking the start of the Fundamentalist movement in the first place. In a very real sense, Fundamentalism has become what is set out to oppose.[422]

Fundamentalism is getting closer to Liberalism. How sad!

Fundamentalists who think that the textual critics are the arbiters of the text are again in agreement with Liberals and New Evangelicals. Instead, they should be in agreement with Jesus Who said, "One jot or one tittle shall in no wise pass from the law" (Matthew 5:18).

Engaging in Double-Talk

In *The Battle for the Bible*, Harold Lindsell mentions that Daniel Fuller did not hold to inerrancy and that after becoming president of Fuller Seminary, he changed the doctrinal statement to read: " 'All the books of the Old and New Testaments, given by divine inspiration, are the written Word of God, the only infallible rule of faith and practice'." such a statement may sound good, but Lindsell points out that

> the key to an understanding of the new viewpoint is to be found in the words that the books of the Old and New Testaments "are the written Word of God, the only infallible rule of faith and practice." It is where the

---

[420] Kenneth T. Brooks, *Why Cumbereth It The Ground? An examination of the origins and impact of American Christian Fundamentalism* (West Redding, CT: Danbury Baptist Press, 2008), 85.

[421] In the previous paragraph the author has a couple of quotes from Gephart who advocates a restoration of the text. It is interesting that the sub-title of the book in which Gephart makes his statement is *The Bible Preserved For Us*. As much as Gephart and others may claim that the Bible is preserved for us, they contradict themselves by claiming that they must still find the Words of Scripture.

[422] Brooks, 86.

word *infallible* is placed that makes the difference. Had the statement said that the Books of the Old and New Testaments "are the infallible Word of God, the only rule of faith and practice," it would have in different words what the first statement of faith had said. But what the new statement does is this: it limits infallibility to matters of faith and practice. And this is the view espoused by Daniel Fuller in his address on Warfield. Scripture that does not involve matters of faith and practice is not infallible.[423]

The Bible teaches that all of the Bible is infallible, not just the parts that speak of faith and practice (John 17:17). In the case of the doctrinal statement of Fuller Seminary, a person, on the one hand, could deny the infallibility of the Scriptures in non-doctrinal matters and, on the other hand, say that he held to the infallibility of the Scriptures! This is nothing more than New Evangelical double-talk. True Bible believers should not use double-talk. The Bible says, "Let your yea be yea; and your nay, nay" (James 5:12). II Corinthians 4:2 says, "But have renounced the hidden things of dishonesty, not walking in craftiness, nor handling the word of God deceitfully; but by manifestation of the truth commending ourselves to every man's conscience in the sight of God." What is disturbing is that some Fundamentalists, through a clever use of words, sound orthodox when they are not at all orthodox. These Fundamentalists are engaging in the same New Evangelical double-talk that went on at Fuller Seminary.

An example of double-talk is from Glenny who writes:

> The Scriptures do not teach that God has perfectly preserved every word of the original autographs in one manuscript or text type. A proper understanding of the doctrine of preservation is a belief that God has providentially preserved His Word in and through all of the extant manuscripts, versions, and other copies of Scripture. . . . Obviously, God has preserved His Word through the ages for and through His people. Has God perfectly preserved His Word so that no words have been lost? The evidence from the OT text suggests that such is not the case. We might have lost a few words through negligence, but the amount that has been lost is so minimal that it has no effect on overall doctrine and little, if any, on historical or other details. God has wonderfully and providentially preserved His Word in the multiplicity of extant manuscripts.[424]

While Glenny says, "God has providentially preserved His Word," it is clear from the above quote that he does not mean the preservation of every single word. While speaking of the preservation of the word, he

---

[423] Lindsell, 116.

[424] Glenny, 121-122.

does not mean the preservation of every single word. Glenny's statement parallels that of Daniel Fuller wherein Fuller said that he believed in infallibility, but it is not an infallibility of every part of the Bible. Glenny is using the same double-talk tactic as the New Evangelicals from Fuller Seminary. The unwary of the past were fooled by Fuller Seminary into thinking that the seminary still held to infallibility, when in reality it did not. Likewise, the unwary of the present might also be fooled by Glenny's words into thinking that he and others like him hold to preservation, when in reality they do not.

Appealing to History

Dell Johnson shows that those who will not let the Bible speak for itself on the matter of its own preservation try to resolve this theological issue by appealing to historical sources. This, Johnson declares, is an essentially Liberal technique known as traditionalism.[425] Are not some Fundamentalists appealing primarily to history to support their position as opposed to letting the Bible speak for itself? In the book *One Bible Only?* are some statements that reveal a reliance on history to settle the preservation issue. For instance, Kevin Bauder says, "As this book has shown, the Bible contains no promise whatsoever that includes the preservation of all the words of the *autographa* (without addition or deletion) in a single, publicly accessible source."[426] Such a statement fails to take into account a proper understanding of Matthew 5:18; John 10:35; II Timothy 3:15-17; and other verses. However, in believing that Scripture does not settle the issue, this book appeals to history to decide the matter of preservation.

W. Edward Glenny in the same book writes:

> The Scriptures do not teach that God has perfectly preserved every word of the original autographs in one manuscript or text type. A proper understanding of the doctrine of preservation is a belief that God has providentially preserved His Word in and through all of the extant manuscripts, versions, and other copies of Scripture. *This conviction is based on the evidence of history* [emphasis mine]. . . . No passage of Scripture states

---

[425] Dell Johnson, *Preservation of the Bible: A Bible Foundational Doctrine* (Pensacola: Pensacola Christian College, 3/7/02), cassette.

[426] Bauder, 158.

that God has used multiple manuscripts to preserve His Word, but *the evidence of history leaves no doubt that such is the case* [emphasis mine].[427]

Glenny holds to preservation not because it is Scriptural, but because it is based on the evidence of history.

Glenny further writes:

> Obvious from *the evidence of history* [emphasis mine] is the fact that God has providentially preserved His Word for the present generation. However, also obvious from *the evidence of history* [emphasis mine] is the fact that God has not miraculously and perfectly preserved every word of the Biblical text in any one manuscript or group of manuscripts, or in all of the manuscripts.[428]

Why do not these Fundamentalists get their Bibliology from the Bible? They make constant appeals to history. Of course, from history one can prove just about anything, no wonder it is a Liberal tactic. But why would Fundamentalists adopt such a tactic? A proper exegesis of various verses points to the preservation of all the words of the *autographa*. Could it be that since, for whatever reason, these Fundamentalists do not want to hold to this Scriptural position, they are relegated, then, to rely on history? It seems that this is the case.

In the message by Johnson he refers to a paper entitled, "Trusted Voices on Translation" published in 2001 which appeals to historical leaders of the Fundamentalist movement showing their belief that an English reading person can use other translations besides the *King James Version*. Johnson observes that apparently without any help from the Bible, one can settle the text issue! Is not this typical Liberalism where what the Bible says does not matter? Johnson concludes his remarks with a rebuke based on Mark 7:9: "Full well ye reject the commandment of God, that ye may keep your own tradition."[429]

But there is more. The Evangelicals and Catholics Together coalition released a "statement titled 'Your Word Is Truth' which addresses the issue of 'Scripture and Tradition,' concluding that while some differences exist, Evangelicals and Roman Catholics basically agree in the 'coherence of Scripture and tradition.' " The statement continues: "Tradition is not a second source of revelation alongside the Bible but must ever be corrected

---

[427] Glenny, 121-122.

[428] Ibid., 126.

[429] Johnson, *Preservation of the Bible*, cassette.

and informed by it, and Scripture itself is not understood in a vacuum apart from the historical existence and life of the community of faith."[430] When Fundamentalists use history to correct the Bible in the teaching of preservation, they are, then, very much in agreement with the Evangelicals and Catholics Together coalition.

In his 1998 encyclical *Fides et Ratio*, the Pope said,

> There are also signs of a resurgence of fideism, which fails to recognize the importance of rational knowledge and philosophical discourse for the understanding of faith. . . . One currently widespread symptom of this fideistic tendency is a "biblicism" which tends to make the reading and exegesis of Sacred Scripture the sole criterion of truth.[431]

The Pope argues against simply following the Bible (fideism) and advocates the use of reasoning in order to understand doctrine. But should not the Bible be the sole authority (II Timothy 3:16-17)? The Fundamentalists, however, with their appeal to history in order to understand the doctrine of preservation, are doing exactly what the Pope advocates! What strange bedfellows a departure from Scripture makes.

Criticizing Numbers

In the matter of I Samuel 13:5 the author was present in a class on the United Monarchy at Calvary Baptist Theological Seminary (1982-1983) when Professor Tuttle stated that thirty thousand chariots should perhaps be reduced by a factor of ten to three thousand. What is the difference between Tuttle's suggestion and how some approach the ages of hundreds of years for the Genesis patriarchs? In some people's estimation, the ages of the patriarchs do not make sense; therefore, they devise schemes to reduce these years to make them seem more credible. New Evangelical Roland K. Harrison writes:

> It would seem evident that while the numbers assigned to the ages of the patriarchs in Genesis had real meaning for those who were responsible for their preservation in the first instance, they cannot be employed in a purely

---

[430] "Evangelicals and Catholics Release Third Joint Statement," *Foundation*, Sept. – Oct. 2002, 33-34.

[431] Ibid., 34.

literal sense as a means of computing the length of the various generations mentioned in the text.[432]

Fundamentalists who criticize the largeness of some numbers sound just like New Evangelicals!

CONCLUSION

The ramifications of claiming that the Preserved Text numerical errors are (1) a questioning of Christ; (2) a questioning of verses; (3) a relinquishing of the battle for the Bible; (4) an opening of the door to criticism; (5) a treating of the Bible like any other ancient document; (6) a destroying of the foundation; (7) a destroying of faith; (8) a destroying of authority; (9) an exalting of human reasoning, supposition, and textual criticism; (10) a coming dangerously close to adding to or subtracting from the Bible; (11) a making it impossible to live by every Word of God; and (12) a getting closer to New Evangelicalism, Liberalism, and Catholicism. None of the ramifications are good. That Fundamentalists are involved in such things is shocking.

Instead of questioning Matthew 5:18 and other verses, Fundamentalists should receive, believe, and hear by faith the words of Matthew 5:18 as well as all other verses.

Instead of questioning many verses whereby Fundamentalists nurture a rejected-texts mindset, Fundamentalists should have a received-text mindset (John 17:8).

Instead of relinquishing the battle for the Bible, Fundamentalists should be at the front of the battle in earnestly contending "for the faith which was once delivered unto the saints" (Jude 3).

Instead of opening the door to criticism, Fundamentalists should shut the door to criticism. I Timothy 6:3-5 teaches that men who consent not to the Words of our Lord Jesus Christ (which words substantiate the absolute trustworthiness of all the words of the Old Testament) are men who dote about questions and strifes of words and that one ought to separate from them. May Fundamentalists heed the teaching of this passage and separate from the critics.

---

[432] Roland Kenneth Harrison, *Introduction to the Old Testament* (Grand Rapids: Eerdmans, 1969; reprint, Peabody, MA: Prince Press, 1999), 152 (page citations are to the reprint edition).

Chapter 6 — *Ramifications*

Instead of treating the Bible like any other ancient document by claiming that it has scribal errors, Fundamentalists need to receive the Word of God, "not as the word of men, but as it is in truth, the word of God" (I Thessalonians 2:13).

Instead of destroying the foundation by questioning the preserved texts; Fundamentalists need to uphold this foundation, for "if the foundations be destroyed, what can the righteous do?" (Psalm 11:3).

Instead of destroying faith, Fundamentalists need to promote faith in all the words of the Bible. In so doing, they would be following the example of Jesus Who came not to destroy the Old Testament (Matthew 5:17).

Instead of destroying the authority of the Old Testament by questioning the words of the Old Testament, Fundamentalists need to uphold the authority of the Old Testament. Fundamentalists should keep in mind the words of Isaiah 8:20: "To the law and to the testimony: if they speak not according to this word, it is because there is no light in them." The Words of God are the authority, not the words of the critics. When a Fundamentalist questions a number or word in the Old Testament text, he is not speaking "according to this word" and is thereby questioning the authority of "this word." When a Fundamentalists does this, he displays that he is walking in darkness. Let him come out of the darkness of doubt and criticism and, instead, walk in the light of God's authoritative words.

Instead of exalting human reasoning, supposition, and textual criticism which savour of the things of men; Fundamentalists ought to savour "the things that be of God" (Matthew 16:23).

Instead of coming close to adding to or subtracting from the Bible, Fundamentalists ought to make it clear that they will have nothing to do with such pursuits (Revelation 22:18-19).

Instead of removing words from the Bible thereby making it impossible for man to live by every word that proceedeth out of the mouth of God; Fundamentalists ought to be in harmony with Jesus Who says, "Man shall not live by bread alone, but by every word that proceedeth out of the mouth of God" (Matthew 4:4). And if the Fundamentalists are truly in harmony with Jesus, then let them repent and, therefore, stop taking words away from the preserved Old Testament text.

Instead of getting closer to New Evangelicalism, Liberalism, and Catholicism by (1) discrediting Chronicles and aiding the Liberal cause; (2) seemingly claiming that the Bible has moot points just like the New

Evangelicals; (3) holding to conceptual preservation as do New Evangelicals and Liberals; (4) placing faith in textual critics as also do the New Evangelicals and Liberals; (5) engaging in double-talk just like the New Evangelicals; (6) appealing to history as do the Liberals and Catholics; and (7) criticizing the numbers thereby sounding just like New Evangelicals—Fundamentalists need to come out from among them and be separate "and touch not the unclean thing" (II Corinthians 6:17).

Are Fundamentalists even aware of what they are doing when they discredit the preserved texts? On whose side are these Fundamentalists? If these Fundamentalists are truly for the Scriptures, then let them come out decidedly in favor of the Scriptures, instead of, as they are now doing, coming out decidedly in favor of questioning the Scriptures. It is sad, but true, some Fundamentalists are sounding more and more like Satan who said, "Yea, hath God said?" (Genesis 3:1). Instead, they should be sounding more like the Psalmist who said, "I esteem all *thy* precepts *concerning* all *things to be* right; *and* I hate every false way" (Psalm 119:128). And they should be sounding more like Jesus Who said, "Think not that I am come to destroy the law, or the prophets" (Matthew 5:17).

CHAPTER SEVEN:
APPARENT NUMERICAL CONTRADICTIONS IN
I SAMUEL

I SAMUEL 6:19

The Passage

I Samuel 6:19 says, "And he smote the men of Bethshemesh, because they had looked into the ark of the LORD, even he smote of the people fifty thousand and threescore and ten men: and the people lamented, because the LORD had smitten *many* of the people with a great slaughter."

The Apparent Problem

Although I Samuel 6:19 is not in apparent contradiction with any other passage in the Bible, the author includes it here because some Fundamentalists question *fifty thousand and threescore and ten*. As a student at Bob Jones University in 1977 – 1978, the author was told in an Old Testament Survey class that *fifty thousand and threescore and ten* could not be correct, and that the number should be much smaller. The same thing took place when the author later attended Calvary Baptist Theological Seminary.[433]

---

[433] For further details, see Chapter One.

Chapter 7　　　　　　　　　　　　　　　　　　　　　　　　　　　*I Samuel*

Henry Morris, in *The Defender's Study Bible*, says that *fifty thousand and threescore and ten* "may well represent a transmissional error."[434] At this point, Morris is in agreement with the Liberal Henry Preserved Smith who says, "The words are a late insertion."[435] It is a sad thing indeed when Fundamentalists find themselves in agreement with Liberals in giving an incorrect interpretation of a verse.

John Davis says, "It is doubtful that the expression 'fifty thousand' belongs in the text."[436] Blaikie writes, "It is the general opinion, however, that an error has slipped into the text. . . . Probably the threescore and ten, without the fifty thousand, is all that was originally in the text."[437] Apparently, none of these writers want to receive, believe, and hear this number and, instead, are willing to rely on conjecture and guesses.

One problem some raise is to suggest that Bethshemesh was a small village and, therefore, could not have had over fifty thousand people. Another problem some have with the number in I Samuel 6:19 involves the syntax of the Hebrew. Geisler and Howe write:

> The numerical designation in Hebrew usually follows a certain pattern in which the larger number is written first, then the smaller number. The normal manner to write such a number would be "fifty thousand men and seventy men." However, in this instance, the numbers appear backward. The text actually reads "seventy men fifty thousand men." In addition, numerical designations are almost always connected by the conjunction "and" so that the statement would read, "fifty thousand men and seventy men." Again this passage departs from the normal practice by omitting "and." These factors have led many to suspect that the text was inadvertently corrupted in transmission.[438]

---

[434] Henry Morris, 325.

[435] Henry Preserved Smith, *A Critical and Exegetical Commentary on the Books of Samuel* (Edinburgh: T & T Clark, 1899), 50. That Smith was a Liberal is evident from the fact that he "promised Charles A. Briggs that he would stand by him in his efforts to promote Biblical criticism in the church." Smith's address to this affect was "later published under the title *Biblical Scholarship and Inspiration*, [wherein he] denied the verbal inspiration of the Bible" (David O. Beale, *In Pursuit of Purity: American Fundamentalism Since 1850* (Greenville, SC: Unusual Publications, 1986), 147).

[436] Davis, 87.

[437] W .G. Blaikie, *The First Book of Samuel* (NY: A. C. Armstrong and Son, n.d.), 83.

[438] Geisler and Howe, 156. *The Interpreter's Bible* also objects to I Samuel 6:19 on grammatical grounds when it says, "**Because they looked into the ark of the LORD** is not

Chapter 7 *I Samuel*

The two problems that some see with I Samuel 6:19 involve the largeness of the number and the manner in which the verse presents the number.

Some Solutions

Several solutions are available for the problems that some see in I Samuel 6:19.

Receive the Number

Since *fifty thousand and threescore and ten* is in the Traditional Hebrew text, one should receive, believe, and hear it. This author rejects the "solution" which states, "The words '50,000 men' are wanting in Jos[ephus] (*Ant.* 6, 1-14) and in some Heb[rew] MSS. (Cod. Kenn. 84, 210, 418), and are" to be rejected.[439] The *New International Version* and the *English Standard Version* both eliminate *fifty thousand* from their translations. However, the author rejects the "solution" that rejects any of these words.

Receive the Syntax

The statement by Geisler and Howe wherein they claim that "Hebrew usually follows a certain pattern in which the larger number is written

---

a possible rendering of the Hebrew, which can mean only 'because they looked at the ark of the Lord': and there is nowhere else any indication that this was regarded as an offense. This fact, together with the repetition of the verb **he slew** and the fantastic numbers, makes the M.T. [Masoretic Text] thoroughly suspect" (George B. Caird, *I Samuel* in vol. 2 of *The Interpreter's Bible: The Holy Scriptures in the King James Version and Revised Standard Version with General Articles and Introduction, Exegesis, Exposition for Each Book of the Bible*, ed. George A. Buttrick (Nashville: Abingdon Press, 1953), 911-912). However, (1) the *King James Version* accurately translates the Hebrew; (2) looking into the ark is an offense (Numbers 4:18-20); (3) the verb *smote* is repeated twice in several other verses (Exodus 9:25; Joshua 7:5; 11:8; I Samuel 17:35; II Kings 15:16; and II Chronicles 28:5) and, therefore, should not be a problem here; and (4) the number is not fantastic, but is fully accurate. Such a statement in *The Interpreter's Bible* reveals its Liberal bias.

[439] David Erdmann, *The Books of Samuel in A Commentary on the Holy Scriptures: Critical, Doctrinal, and Homiletical, with Special Reference to Ministers and Students*, ed. John Peter Lange, trans. Philip Schaff (NY: Charles Scribner's Sons, 1877), 116. In the actual printing of this quote the words to be rejected are in brackets with a note from the translator, which states, "The words in brackets are not in the German—omitted probably by typographical error." It is rather ironic that while accusing the Bible of having a typographical error, they have one of their own. Oh, that they would see that they are indeed in error and that the preserved text is not.

first,"[440] implies that for the smaller number to come first is rare indeed. However, in looking at about 113 verses that have the word *score* as in *fourscore*, the author found twenty-one instances where a smaller number comes before a larger one (Exodus 7:7; 38:25; Numbers 1:27, 39; 2:4, 26; 3:43, 46, 50; 26:22, 25, 43; 31:33, 34, 37, 38, 39; Joshua 14:10; I Samuel 6:19; Nehemiah 7:72; and Esther 1:4). While it may be usual for the larger number to come before the smaller, it is certainly not rare for the smaller to come before the larger. Haley writes in a footnote,

> The Hebrew and Arabic allow a peculiar latitude in the expression of numbers. According to Nordheimer (*Hebrew Grammar*, i. 255), and Wright (*Arabic Grammar*, p. 211), both these languages permit one to write first the units, then the tens, hundreds and thousands, in their order; or he may reverse the method, writing the highest denomination first, and ending with the lowest.[441]

Also, Geisler and Howe state, "Numerical designations are almost always connected by the conjunction 'and' "[442] whereas I Samuel 6:19 does not use *and*. Again, the author found several examples where the Bible does not use *and* in numerical expressions: (1) between two numbers in a series of three (Numbers 31:37; I Kings 10:14; II Kings 19:35; I Chronicles 25:7; Nehemiah 7:18, 19, 26; 11:6, 18); (2) between four numbers in a series of five (Nehemiah 7:66); and (3) not at all in a series of five numbers (Ezra 2:64). Of particular note in this discussion are the parallel passages I Kings 10:14 with Hebrew word order, "six hundreds sixty and six" and II Chronicles 9:13 with Hebrew word order, "six hundreds and sixty and six." In this case, Chronicles uses an extra *and*. Ezra 2:64 which parallels Nehemiah 7:66 illustrates the same thing wherein Ezra has no *ands*, but Nehemiah uses one *and*. These examples illustrate that the syntax of I Samuel 6:19 is perfectly acceptable. The syntax, therefore, is not so abnormal and aberrant as some might think.

---

[440] Geisler and Howe, 156. Henry Preserved Smith states: "To the *seventy* men, the present text adds ungrammatically *fifty thousand men*—doubtless a gloss" (Henry Preserved Smith, 49). Geisler and Howe are in agreement with a Liberal! But this claim by Smith has no basis whatsoever, as shown above.

[441] Haley, 13-14. Numbers 31:39 is a verse that exhibits both patterns: larger before smaller and smaller before larger. The Hebrew word order is "30 thousand and 5 hundreds . . . one and 60."

[442] Geisler and Howe, 156.

Chapter 7 *I Samuel*

Understand the Population

Concerning the population of Bethshemesh several statements are in order. First, Bethshemesh was located "on the north-west slopes of the mountains of Judah, 14 miles west of Jerusalem."[443] It is conceivable, therefore, that when the ark arrived, those in Jerusalem and other places were notified and perhaps came to see the ark. When the Philistines captured the ark, it caused great sorrow (I Samuel 4:17-22). It is likely that the ark's return would cause a corresponding great interest (I Samuel 6:13) and that others would have come from the surrounding area to see the ark. Poole states: "All these were not the settled inhabitants of this place, but most of them such as did, and in all probability would, resort thither in great numbers upon so illustrious an occasion."[444]

Second, Bethshemesh was located near the Judean-Philistian border. Judea and Philistia were two hostile nations which had been engaged in a battle (I Samuel 4:1-11) seven months before this (I Samuel 6:1) wherein the Philistines killed 34,000 Israeli soldiers (I Samuel 4:10). It is conceivable that a number of soldiers were stationed in Bethshemesh to protect the interior of Judah and Jerusalem from another Philistine attack and such soldiers could have swelled the population of Bethshemesh.

Third, a combination of people from the surrounding area, soldiers, as well as the normal population of Bethshemesh could account for the 50,070 men.

Fourth, it is very possible that many men were living in Bethshemesh. About forty years after this incident, Joab reported that there were 500,000 men of Judah (II Samuel 24:9), not including women and children. Bethshemesh, a town in Judah, then, could have had a large population all by itself.

Any one of these explanations would suffice to explain this number of 50,070. The Bible does not present all the details about this event. However, the fact that the Bible says this was a *great slaughter* indicates that it was far more than just seventy men who were killed, for Scripture uses this very expression *great slaughter* in II Chronicles 28:5-6 of Pekah slaying 120,000 Judeans in one day.

---

[443] Easton, "Bethshemesh" in *Easton's Revised Bible Dictionary* in *Online Bible Millennium Edition* [CD-ROM] (Winterbourne, Ontario: Timnathserah, 2002).

[444] Matthew Poole, *A Commentary on the Holy Bible* (McLean, VA: MacDonald Publishing Company, n.d.), 1:528.

Allow for Two Possible Groups

The Hebrew text splits the number 50,070 into two groups: (1) seventy men; and (2) fifty thousand men. This provides for the possibility that instead of all 50,070 dying in Bethshemesh, two groups died in different places. Gill discusses this:

> Abarbinel is of opinion that only 70 men of Bethshemesh were slain, and that the other 50,000 were the Philistines that died on account of the ark while it was among them . . . and so this gives the sum of all that died on account of the ark, both while it was in the hands of the Philistines, and when returned to Bethshemesh, which is not an improbable sense.[445]

Many Philistines indeed died as a result of the ark being in their midst (I Samuel 5:6, 9-12).

No matter how one might explain this number, the 50,070 he should hear, that is, receive and believe this number.

I SAMUEL 13:1

The Passage

I Samuel 13:1 states: "Saul reigned one year; and when he had reigned two years over Israel."

The Apparent Problem

On the surface of it, no problem is apparent in this verse. Leon Wood, however, states a problem that many others see with this verse:

> I Samuel 13:1 . . . presents problems in its reading. Literally, it says, "A son of a year was Saul when he began to reign, and two years he reigned over Israel." The phrase "son of a year" is the regular Hebrew idiom for indicating a person's age. . . . But obviously Saul was more that one year old at his inauguration. . . . A number which gave Saul's age must at some time have been omitted by the copyist.[446]

---

[445] Gill, *Exposition of the Old & New Testaments*, 2:444.

[446] Leon J. Wood, *Israel's United Monarchy* (Grand Rapids: Baker, 1979), 122.

Word Biblical Commentary states that in the first part of I Samuel 13:1 "the number has dropped out."[447] Blaikie says, "There can be no doubt that something has been dropped out of the Hebrew text. . . . A figure seems to have dropped out after 'Saul was' and another after 'he reigned.' A blot of some kind may have effaced these figures in the original manuscript."[448] *The Defender's Study Bible* states, "The Hebrew text in this verse is defective, possibly because of some ancient copyist error."[449]

Central Baptist Theological Seminary also takes exception to this verse. In a book expressing the position of their faculty, W. Edward Glenny writes: "Apparently at least one of the numbers in this verse has been lost; it makes no sense as it reads."[450] At this point, Glenny is in agreement with Liberal Henry Preserved Smith who writes, "This verse as it stands . . . is meaningless."[451] Smith later writes: "It seems evident that a scribe, wishing to make his chronology complete, inserted the verse *without the numbers*, hoping to be able to supply these at a later date, which however he was unable to do."[452] Again, a Fundamentalist agrees with a Liberal in a wrong assessment of a Bible verse!

Additionally, the approach of Glenny, Wood and Blaikie places the Bible on the same level as other ancient literature. For instance, concerning a portion of the chronicles of the Chaldean Kings, Wiseman states, "The figure (38?) or object is now unfortunately lost."[453] Also, concerning the Assyrian Chronicle i 25 Grayson observes:

> The number of years which Tiglath-pileser III reigned . . . is missing. There are two possible explanations for the omission. The original tablet might have been broken at this point. . . . The other possibility . . . is that the original author of the chronicle did not know at the moment how many years Tiglath-pileser had ruled. He therefore left a blank space to be filled

---

[447] Ralph W. Klein, *1 Samuel*, vol. 10 of *Word Biblical Commentary*, ed. David A. Hubbard and Glenn W. Barker (Waco, TX: Word Books, Publishers, 1983), 122.

[448] Blaikie, 205,206.

[449] Henry Morris, 331.

[450] Glenny, "The Preservation of Scripture" in *The Bible Version Debate*, 85.

[451] Henry Preserved Smith, 91.

[452] Ibid., 92.

[453] D. J. Wiseman, *Chronicles of Chaldean Kings: (626-556 B.C.) in the British Museum* (London: The Trustees of the British Museum, 1961), 93.

in later when he had time to make the necessary calculation. He then forgot to do this. Buccellati . . . has collected other examples of such omissions of figures in Sumerian and Akkadian texts. He suggests this has also happened in I Samuel 13:1.[454]

Some treat some Bible passages as if they were just like the Assyrian or Babylonian Chronicles, but why would Fundamentalists treat the inspired, preserved Words of God in the same fashion as man-produced ancient literature? This is disconcerting to say the least.

Some Solutions

Several solutions are available for the problems some have with I Samuel 13:1.

Receive the Number

First, since Jesus states and promises that the Hebrew text is intact and will be preserved (Matthew 5:18), then one can have faith that no words are missing from I Samuel 13:1 despite what scholars might say. The King James translators have done a fine job in how they translated this verse from the preserved text. One should simply receive the Hebrew text and the accurate translation of that text.

Understand the Syntax

Second, while it is true that the syntax for *Saul reigned one year* usually expresses the age of the monarch, this is not always the case. For example, II Chronicles 22:2 says, "Forty and two years old was Ahaziah when he began to reign" whereas II Kings 8:26 says, "Two and twenty years old was Ahaziah when he began to reign." Both of these constructions are similar to the one in I Samuel 13:1, but if both are referring to the same time in Ahaziah's life, then it is obvious that both cannot be giving the physical age of Ahaziah. II Chronicles 22:2 is possibly presenting the age of the dynasty of which Ahaziah was a part or the age of

---

[454] A. Kirk Grayson, *Assyrian and Babylonian Chronicles* (Locust Valley, NY: J. J. Augustin, 1975; reprint, Winona Lake, IN: Eisenbraus, 2000), 72-73 (page citations are to the reprint edition). Grayson also writes: "One of the main problems encountered in reading the Synchronistic History is the number of errors in the preserved copies. Most of these are copyists' errors" (Grayson, 54). This is the same way many approach the preserved text of the Bible claiming that it too has scribal errors.

Chapter 7 *I Samuel*

his mother. Likewise, II Chronicles 36:9 says, "Jehoiachin was eight years old when he began to reign," whereas II Kings 24:8 says, "Jehoiachin was eighteen years old when he began to reign." Again, both of these constructions are similar to the one in I Samuel 13:1. The figure in II Chronicles 36:9 is possibly dating Jehoiachin's reign from the time of the Babylonian bondage. These examples demonstrate that the Bible possibly uses this type of syntactical construction of something other than the age of the monarch.[455] In the case of Saul, it expresses the age of his dynasty at that time, that is, one year. He was "the son of one year in his reigning."[456]

The Old Testament uses *son* metaphorically to express some type of relationship such as:

> The branch is a son with respect to the tree, Ps. lxxx. 15; . . . an arrow with respect to the bow or quiver, Job xli. 28; corn with respect to the threshingfloor, Isa. xxi. 10; a hill is the son of oil with respect to its fertility, Isa. v. 1; a wicked person guilty of a capital crime is a son of death, I Sam. xx. 31.[457]

The use of *son* in I Samuel 13:1 and possibly in II Chronicles 22:2 and 36:9 constitute a somewhat metaphorical use of the word which is in keeping with its use elsewhere.

Do Not Correct the Verse

Third, concerning the last part of this verse which Wood translates: "And two years he reigned over Israel" while linguistically allowable is not the only possibility. The translation of the King James, "And when he had reigned two years over Israel," is also allowable. Indeed, it is the correct translation because Acts 13:21 teaches that Saul reigned for a total of forty years, not just two years as Wood's translation suggests. Wood, in arguing for errors in I Samuel 13:1, introduces another error of his own in that his translation of I Samuel 13:1 contradicts Acts 13:21.

---

[455] The writer says, "Possibly" because there are explanations for these cases which state that in both cases the age of the monarch is presented, that is, that Ahaziah was anointed as king when 22 and then later at 42, and similarly for Jehoiachin. See discussion on these verses for more details.

[456] Poole, 1:542.

[457] William Wilson, *Wilson's Old Testament Word Studies* (Peabody, MA: Hendrickson Publishers, n.d.), 404. H. Haag presents a similar treatment on page 152 in volume II of *Theological Dictionary of the Old Testament*.

Chapter 7 — I Samuel

The *New American Standard Bible*, without any basis, translates: "And he reigned thirty-two years over Israel" and the *New International Version*, again with no basis, translates: "And he reigned over Israel forty-two years." Both of these translations also contradict Acts 13:21 wherein both of these translations say that Saul reigned for forty years. How could anyone take these kind of "answers" seriously?[458]

The *English Standard Version* reads, "Saul was . . . years old when he began to reign, and he reigned . . . and two years over Israel," thereby expressing it's belief that words are missing. But how can words be missing when Jesus promised that nothing is missing (Matthew 5:18)?

In contrast to those who think the Bible needs correction at this point, Sir Isaac Newton took this verse and the entire passage at face value when he wrote, "Saul was made King, that he might rescue Israel out of the hand of the Philistines, who oppressed them; and in the second year of his Reign [*sic*], the Philistines brought into the field against him thirty thousand chariots [see I Samuel 13:5]."[459] Isaac Newton, with all of his learning, did not try to correct the Bible in these places.

Nothing is wrong with I Samuel 13:1—let the reader receive it, believe it, and hear it.

I SAMUEL 13:5

The Passage

I Samuel 13:5 states: "And the Philistines gathered themselves together to fight with Israel, thirty thousand chariots, and six thousand

---

[458] Not only should a person not take the "answers" of the *New American Standard Bible* and the *New International Version* seriously, but also these "answers" illustrate the truth of Proverbs 30:6 which states: "Add thou not unto His words, lest He reprove thee, and thou be found a liar." The *New American Standard Bible* and the *New International Version* by adding to the Words of God in I Samuel 13:1 contradict Acts 13:21 and, therefore, are lying. It is interesting also to point out that Proverbs 30:5 states that "every word of God is pure"; but when editors of modern versions add to the pure Words of God, they make it impure.

[459] Isaac Newton, *The Chronology of Ancient Kingdoms Amended* (London: T. Cadell, 1770), 167. The author updated the spelling.

Chapter 7 *I Samuel*

horsemen, and people as the sand which is on the sea shore in multitude: and they came up, and pitched in Michmash, eastward from Bethaven."

The Apparent Problem

Again, if one simply takes this verse as it reads, he may not see a problem, but this does not stop some from seeing a problem. For example, the author was present in the course entitled "United Monarchy" at Calvary Baptist Theological Seminary when Professor Tuttle informed the class that *thirty thousand* could not be the correct. Henry Morris writes in *The Defender's Study Bible*, "The ancient Syriac translation, as well as some Septuagint and Arabic Bible manuscripts, read 'three thousand chariots.' This latter figure seems more correct."[460] The *New International Version* departs from the Masoretic Text and reads, "Three thousand chariots." Leon Wood opens the door to scribal error when he writes: "Some expositors believe the number 30,000 to be the result of a copyist's error, since so many chariots in the hill country of Michmash is hard to imagine."[461]

Archer states:

> Michmash overlooks a fairly extensive valley, and it is not inconceivable that 30,000 chariots could have been deployed in its vicinity. But the problem lies in the magnitude of the chariot force itself. Delitzsch (Keil and Delitzsch, *Samuel*, pp. 126-27) points out in his commentary on this verse that the listing of a mere 6000 horsemen in this Philistine army makes it almost conclusive that the actual number of chariots was considerably smaller. That is to say, everywhere else in the Old Testament where an army inclusive of both cavalry and chariotry comes on the scene, the number of the cavalry exceeds that of the chariots (cf. 2 Sam. 10:18; I Kings 10:26; 2 Chron. 12:3, etc.). Furthermore, such a large number of chariots in a single army has never been recorded in the annals of any ancient power, not even of the Egyptians, the Assyrians, the Chaldeans, or the Persians. It is most unlikely, therefore, that a third-rate little pentarchy like Philistia could have fielded the largest chariot force in all human history. . . . Much more likely, therefore, is the possibility that "3000" was the original number recorded in the earliest text of I Samuel 13:5 and that

---

[460] Henry Morris, 331.

[461] Wood, *Israel's United Monarchy*, 123.

somehow in the course of later textual transmission the notation for "3000" was miscopied as "30,000."[462]

But can Archer and others be certain that the number should be three thousand? Once they have opened the door to conjecture, how do they know when to stop? For instance, some think three thousand is still too large and adjust further down to three hundred. *The Pulpit Commentary* while mistakenly thinking that the writers used letters for numbers (see Chapter Three) states, "The numeral for 300, has been read with two dots, and so changed into 30,000."[463] *Word Biblical Commentary* states, "Even in its amended form, v 5 records an exceedingly large Philistine force of 3,000 chariots."[464] At this juncture, these commentaries are more in agreement with Liberal Henry Preserved Smith who writes that three thousand "is favoured by Bochart and others, but is still absurdly large. Egypt only mustered six hundred chariots, Ex. 14[7], and other notices show that this was the scale for large armies. But our author is prodigal of numbers."[465] How long will it be before Archer, Morris, Tuttle, and others succumb to further humanistic thinking and adjust this number downward even more?

Some Solutions

Several solutions are available for the problems that some see in I Samuel 13:5.

Receive the Number

While Archer admits that Michmash geographically could handle thirty thousand chariots,[466] he approaches I Samuel 13:5 from a humanistic and rationalistic position. Since no living human witnessed the event,

---

[462] Archer, 172-173.

[463] R. Payne Smith, *I Samuel* in vol. 4 of *The Pulpit Commentary*, 227.

[464] Klein, *1 Samuel*, vol. 10 of *Word Biblical Commentary*, 126.

[465] Henry Preserved Smith, 95.

[466] That Michmash could have supported 30,000 chariots has been denied by at least one teacher the author had in seminary and by several writers. However, what Archer admits in saying that Michmash overlooked an extensive valley and could have accommodated this many chariots is the case, therefore, there is no problem geographically with this number.

Chapter 7 *I Samuel*

one should receive, believe, and hear by faith the inspired and preserved record of the event. Even if human witnesses could contradict the account, one should still receive by faith God's preserved words. There is no problem with receiving *thirty thousand*.

But there is a problem with saying that the number is incorrect. If one were to approach Old Testament texts in the same fashion in which Archer approaches I Samuel 13:5, then how much of the Bible would survive? In suggesting that one reduce *thirty thousand* to a tenth of what is written, Archer is sounding much like those who will not receive the ages of the patriarchs of Genesis 5 and, therefore, try to reduce those numbers to a twelfth of what is written.[467] Furthermore, Archer's "solution" produces more problems than it solves for his suggestion flies in the face of the promises of Jesus concerning preservation (Matthew 5:18; Luke 16:17). Again, the "answer" of some scholars produces problems with other verses. And so, how could a person take Archer's "answer" seriously?

To bolster his claim that *thirty thousand* is incorrect, Archer states: "Everywhere else in the Old Testament where an army inclusive of both cavalry and chariotry comes on the scene, the number of the cavalry exceeds that of the chariots."[468] This, however, is an incorrect basis for not believing the verse. For instance, if one uses Archer's reasoning, he could argue in a similar fashion against the virgin birth by saying that everywhere else in the Bible where a birth of a child occurs, a father and mother were involved; therefore, a virgin birth is impossible. However, such reasoning is erroneous for a virgin birth did indeed take place and though the virgin birth goes contrary to the usual pattern, the believer receives it as fact. If the Bible mentions something that goes contrary to the usual pattern, then let the Bible student receive, believe, and hear it; instead of claiming the Bible is in error.

---

[467] In perusing various commentaries on Genesis 5:5, one can find the idea that the years are months; therefore, according to such faulty reckoning, Adam did not live for 930 years, but rather for 930 months or 77.5 years. This is nothing more than rampant unbelief. As Leupold points out, "The term 'year' knows of no such usage, and the suggestion must be treated as a mere surmise" (H. C. Leupold, *Exposition of Genesis* (Grand Rapids, MI: Baker Book House, 1978), 1:233-234). It seems also that reducing 30,000 to 3,000 is a mere surmise as well. Furthermore, while Archer supports the actual ages of the patriarchs (Archer, 77), simply receiving the Hebrew text for what it says about the patriarchs, he is not willing to do the same with the number in I Samuel 13:5.

[468] Archer, 172.

Chapter 7 — I Samuel

Receive the Size of the Army

Archer says, "Such a large number of chariots in a single army has never been recorded in the annals of any ancient power." But was this a single army? From the words *and people as the sand which is on the sea shore in multitude* in I Samuel 13:5, others beside the Philistines could have been involved in this battle.

Concerning the number of chariots, I Chronicles 19:7 states that Ammon hired thirty-two thousand chariots to fight David. In light of this, are thirty thousand chariots out of the question? No, and in light of the fact that Saul had earlier put together an army of 330,000 (I Samuel 11:8) and later that David would assemble an army of 1,570,000 (I Chronicles 21:5), the Philistines needed to be prepared. Furthermore, the Philistines had iron-making capability (I Samuel 13:19-20) and, therefore, the ability to make many chariots.

Allow for Possible Metonymy

Poole states:

> *Chariots* here may very well be put for the men that rode upon them, and fought out of them, by a figure called a *metonymy* of the subject for the adjunct, or the thing containing for the thing contained in it . . . the *basket* is put for the meat in it, Deut. xxviii. 5, 17; the *wilderness*, for the wild beasts of the wilderness, Psal. xxix. 8; the *nest*, for the birds in it, Deut. xxxii. 11; the *cup*, for the drink in it, Jer. xlix. 12; I Cor. x. 21. . . . a *horse* is put for a horse-load of wares laid upon it, I Kings x. 28; and *an ass of bread* is put for *an ass-load of bread*, . . . I Sam. xvi. 20, . . . *chariots* is manifestly put either for the horses belonging to them, or rather for the men that fought out of them; as 2 Sam. x. 18,[469] where it is said in the Hebrew that *David slew seven hundred chariots*; that is, *seven thousand men* which fought *in chariots*, as it is explained, I Chron. xix. 18; and I Kings xx. 21, where Ahab is said *to smite horses and chariots*; and I Chron. xviii. 4; Psal. lxxvi. 6, where *the chariot and horse* (i.e. the men that ride and fight in chariots, or upon horses) are said to be cast *into a dead sleep*; and Ezek. xxxix. 20, where it is said, *Ye shall be filled at my table with*

---

[469] II Samuel 10:18 says, "David slew *the men of* seven hundred chariots of the Syrians," but as the italics indicate, the translators supplied *the men of*. The verse literally states that David slew seven hundred chariots and the translators of the *Authorized Version* understanding that *chariots* is a metonymy have correctly inserted *the men of*.

horses and chariots, (i.e. with men belonging to the chariots; for surely the chariots of iron had been very improper food).[470]

In light of Poole's comments, it is possible that *chariots* denotes the men who fought out of them, so that *thirty thousand chariots* is possibly referring to thirty thousand men who fought out of the chariots. But whether *thirty thousand* is a metonymy or not, it is fully accurate and the Bible student should hear it.

I SAMUEL 16:10-11 AND I CHRONICLES 2:13-15

The Passages

I Samuel 16:10-11 states: "Again, Jesse made seven of his sons to pass before Samuel. And Samuel said unto Jesse, The LORD hath not chosen these. And Samuel said unto Jesse, Are here all *thy* children? And he said, There remaineth yet the youngest, and, behold, he keepeth the sheep. And Samuel said unto Jesse, Send and fetch him: for we will not sit down till he come hither."

I Chronicles 2:13-15 states: "And Jesse begat his firstborn Eliab, and Abinadab the second, and Shimma the third, Nethaneel the fourth, Raddai the fifth, Ozem the sixth, David the seventh."

The Apparent Problem

In I Samuel 16, Jesse presents David to Samuel after seven of his other sons indicating that David was Jesse's eighth son. However, I Chronicles 2:15 states that David is the seventh son of Jesse.

A Solution

It is possible that one of Jesse's sons died and that before his death, he had done nothing worthy of notice; therefore, by the time of the writing of I Chronicles, he is altogether forgotten. Archer makes an interesting and personal point:

---

[470] Poole, 1:543.

The writer of this article had an older brother who died quite young, which would bring up the count of the children to four. Yet after the death of that earlier son, the three surviving children always spoke of themselves as a family of three siblings. Perhaps a similar event happened in Jesse's family as well. The full number of his sons was eight, but only seven survived.[471]

It is good to see Archer hearing these numbers, but, oh, that he would hear the other numbers and influence others to do so as well.

I SAMUEL 18:27 AND II SAMUEL 3:14

The Passages

I Samuel 18:27 states, "Wherefore David arose and went, he and his men, and slew of the Philistines two hundred men; and David brought their foreskins, and they gave them in full tale to the king, that he might be the king's son in law. And Saul gave him Michal his daughter to wife."

II Samuel 3:14 says, "And David sent messengers to Ishbosheth Saul's son, saying, Deliver *me* my wife Michal, which I espoused to me for an hundred foreskins of the Philistines."

The Apparent Problem

In I Samuel 18:27 the Bible states that David slew two hundred men and brought their foreskins, that is, two hundred foreskins, to King Saul whereupon Saul gave Michal to him. On the other hand, in II Samuel 3:14 David says that he had espoused Michal for an hundred foreskins. The one verse seems to suggest that the dowry for Michal was two hundred foreskins, whereas the other verse suggests it was a hundred foreskins.

Haley includes I Samuel 18:27 in a list of verses wherein he thinks a copyist made an error.[472] And concerning I Samuel 18:27, *Word Biblical Commentary* states, "The MT [Masoretic Text] seems to exaggerate the

---

[471] Archer, 175.

[472] Haley, 382.

deed of David."[473] In other words, Haley and the *Word Biblical Commentary* say that one need not receive, believe, and hear *two hundred* in I Samuel 18:27. In so doing, both sound very much like the Liberal commentary, *The Interpreter's Bible* which says, "The killing of two hundred Philistines is an unnecessary and unoriginal exaggeration."[474] But how can this be an "unoriginal exaggeration," since it appears in the *it-is-written* Hebrew text? Since it is in the *it-is-written* text, it is original, and since it is original, it is not an exaggeration; but, instead, it is the truth. Oh, that men would not lean unto their own understanding, but, instead, would believe God.

A Solution

The giving of Michal to David was part of a plan on the part of Saul to have the Philistines kill David. I Samuel 18:25 states, "And Saul said, Thus shall ye say to David, The king desireth not any dowry, but an hundred foreskins of the Philistines, to be avenged of the king's enemies. But Saul thought to make David fall by the hand of the Philistines." Saul demanded one hundred foreskins for the dowry, but David delivered two hundred foreskins, which was twice the required amount. This must have irked Saul for he thought that David, in obtaining one hundred Philistine foreskins, the Philistines would kill him, but they did not. In fact, the Philistines did not kill him while he was obtaining twice as many foreskins, thereby giving them twice the opportunity. God surely was with David. No discrepancy is here. "Saul required 100 foreskins. David . . . delivered 200. But when he later referred back to the transaction, David stated the original price which was demanded by Saul."[475] Let the Bible student receive, believe, and hear these numbers.

---

[473] Klein, 190.

[474] George B. Caird, *I Samuel* in vol. 2 of *The Interpreter's Bible*, ed. George A. Buttrick (Nashville: Abingdon Press, 1953), 984. Concerning the Liberal nature of *The Interpreter's Bible*, Barber states that it contains "the latest in liberal scholarship" (Cyril J. Barber, *The Minister's Library* (Grand Rapids: Baker Book House, 1981), 46).

[475] Cloud, 46.

CHAPTER EIGHT:
APPARENT NUMERICAL CONTRADICTIONS IN II SAMUEL

II SAMUEL 2:8 AND I CHRONICLES 10:6

The Passages

II Samuel 2:8 states, "But Abner the son of Ner, captain of Saul's host, took Ishbosheth the son of Saul, and brought him over to Mahanaim."

I Chronicles 10:6 states, "So Saul died, and his three sons, and all his house died together."

The Apparent Problem

When Saul died so did his three sons as well as all his house (I Chronicles 10:6). However, if all Saul's house died, then how was Abner able to bring Ishbosheth, Saul's son, to Mahanaim after Saul's death (II Samuel 2:8)?

A Solution

I Samuel 14:49 states, "The sons of Saul were Jonathan, and Ishui, and Melchishua." I Chronicles 8:33 states, "Saul begat Jonathan, and Malchishua, and Abinadab, and Eshbaal." Ishui and Abinadab appear to be the same person with different names as is the case with Eshbaal and

Ishbosheth.[476] I Samuel 14:49 only mentions three of Saul's sons and perhaps it mentions these three because they are the three sons who died with Saul in battle. But Saul had more than three sons, for I Chronicles 8:33 indicates that he had four sons, and it was his fourth son, Ishbosheth, whom Abner took to Mahanaim after Saul's death. The Bible states that three of Saul's sons died when he died (I Chronicles 10:6), those sons being Jonathan, Ishui, and Malchishua. But Ishbosheth was not killed when Saul died.

However, I Chronicles 10:6 also states that when Saul died so did all his house. This raises this question: although Ishbosheth is not included in the phrase *his three sons*, yet would he not be included in the phrase *all his house*? The *Theological Dictionary of the Old Testament* concerning the word *house* says it

> includes the . . . father, . . . his wife . . ., his own and his adopted children . . ., his dependent relatives, his clients . . ., and his menservants and maidservants. . . . The household of Abraham was composed of Abraham, his wife Sarah, his concubine Hagar, his son Isaac and Ishmael, his dependent relative Lot and his family, his servants (including Eliezer of Damascus: Gen. 15:2), and his trained men (*chanikhav*, 14:14), who are described as . . . "born in his house."[477]

Such an understanding of *all his house* would mean that every dependent relative of Saul as well as others in his house died in the battle. But this is not what happened as Ishbosheth did not die nor did Saul's concubine, Rizpah (II Samuel 3:7; 21:11), nor did the two sons that Rizpah bore for Saul (II Samuel 21:8). In light of this, *all his house*, does not mean that every single member of Saul's house died with him, but instead means that all his house which was with him in battle died. I Samuel 31:6 supports such an understanding when it says, "So Saul died, and his three sons, and his armourbearer, and all his men, that same day together." This explains that *all his house* is not used in a broad sense, but is limited to *all his men*, that is, all that were with him in the battle. Since Ishbosheth did not die with Saul, then for some reason, he was not with Saul in the battle.

---

[476] Gill explains about Ishbosheth: "This man's name is Eshbaal in ICh 8:33; 9:39. Baal is the name of a shameful idol, and which was therefore sometimes called Bosheth, 'shame' " (Gill, *Exposition of the Old & New Testaments*, 2:570).

[477] Harry A. Hoffner, "בַּיִת" in *Theological Dictionary of the Old Testament*, 2:113-114.

Chapter 8 *II Samuel*

Geisler and Howe state:

> Ishbosheth was not encompassed by this statement [that is, *all his house*], since he was not part of Saul's house who had attended him or followed him to war. . . . Further, not all the grandchildren were killed, since Saul's son Jonathan had a handicapped son named Mephibosheth who also survived (2 Sam. 4:4). It is understandable that someone in his condition was not part of Saul's army and, therefore, did not die with Saul's other men in battle.[478]

II SAMUEL 3:14

See discussion under I Samuel 18:27.

II SAMUEL 6:23 AND II SAMUEL 21:8

The Passages

II Samuel 6:23 states, "Therefore Michal the daughter of Saul had no child unto the day of her death."

II Samuel 21:8 states, "But the king took the two sons of Rizpah the daughter of Aiah, whom she bare unto Saul, Armoni and Mephibosheth; and the five sons of Michal the daughter of Saul, whom she brought up for Adriel the son of Barzillai the Meholathite."

The Apparent Problem

II Samuel 6:23 states that Michal had no child unto the day of her death, whereas II Samuel 21:8 states that she had five sons.

The *New International Version* and the *English Revised Version* replace *Michal* with *Merab* in II Samuel 21:8. *The Expositor's Bible Commentary* says that Merab "is surely to be preferred to 'Michal' despite its weaker MS [manuscript] attestation."[479] Jamieson states, "Michal has by

---

[478] Geisler and Howe, 204.

[479] Ronald F. Youngblood, *1, 2 Samuel* in *The Expositor's Bible Commentary*, ed. Frank E. Gaebelein (Grand Rapids: Zondervan, 1992), 1057.

Chapter 8   II Samuel

an error been substituted in the text for Merab."[480] The *Word Biblical Commentary* states, "There is clearly some textual confusion . . . in 21:8. Thus either the wife's name is wrong or that of the husband."[481] Those who reject the Traditional Hebrew Text, which has *Michal* in II Samuel 21:8, are at the same time refusing to hear of "the five sons of Michal." Not only this, but also they sound a lot like the Liberal commentary, *The Interpreter's Bible* which states, "The name of Michal in the M. T. [Masoretic Text] is an obvious slip for Merab."[482]

Some Solutions

A couple of solutions are available for this apparent problem.

Michal, a Previous Wife of Adriel

Some suggest that Adriel married Michael who then gave birth to five sons before the statement in II Samuel 6:23, which was also before her marriage to David. Then after the incident in II Samuel 6, she was barren and bore David no children.[483] But was Michal previously married to Adriel? This does not appear likely since Saul gave Michal to David soon after giving Merab, his other daughter, to Adriel (I Samuel 18:17-27). As Saul's jealousy over David grew, David fled and Saul wrongfully took Michal and gave her to Phalti (I Samuel 25:44) from whom David reclaimed her (II Samuel 3:14-15). From these considerations, it does not at all appear likely that Michal was ever married to Adriel.

Michal, a Surrogate Mother for Merab

II Samuel 21:8 says, "And the five sons of Michal the daughter of Saul, whom she brought up for Adriel the son of Barzillai the Meho-

---

[480] Robert Jamieson, *II Samuel* in part 2, vol. 2 of *A Commentary Critical, Experimental, and Practical on the Old and New Testaments* (Grand Rapids: Eerdmans, 1984), 270.

[481] A. A. Anderson, *2 Samuel*, vol. 11 of *Word Biblical Commentary*, ed. David A. Hubbard and Glenn W. Barker (Dallas: Word Books, Publisher, 1989), 59.

[482] George B. Caird, *II Samuel* in vol. 2 of *The Interpreter's Bible*, 1159.

[483] Haley, 385. Haley writes, "Ewald and De Wette say, with the greatest probability, that *Michal*, in the first passage [II Samuel 21:8], is a copyist's mistake for *Merab*." Such an explanation is woefully lacking for it resorts to a correcting of the text, instead of a receiving of the text.

Chapter 8 — *II Samuel*

lathite." A careful reading of these words allows for the possibility that the five sons were not Michal's biological offspring but were sons she raised and to whom she became a mother figure. Merab, another one of Saul's daughters, married Adriel (I Samuel 18:19), but the sons born by Merab to Adriel were brought up by her sister Michal. Perhaps Merab was incapacitated in some way and since Michal could not have children she took her sister's sons and raised them as her own.

An Objection

Some may object to the above explanation because the verb *brought up*, in the last part of II Samuel 21:8, is the same as the verb in the first part of II Samuel 21:8 *bare*, both being Qal perfect third feminine singular verbs from יָלַד (*yalad*) Some contend that if יָלַד (*yalad*) literally means *bare* in the first usage, then it must literally mean *bare* in the second usage and should be translated as such. In fact, *The Pulpit Commentary* takes the *Authorized Version* to task at this point:

> **Whom she brought up for.** This is one of the many cases of untrustworthiness in the renderings of the Authorized Version. . . . The Hebrew says here "five sons of Michal, whom she bare to Adriel"; but Michal never bore a child, therefore something must be substituted which will save the Hebrew from this verbal inaccuracy, and Michal must be represented as having taken Merab's place (perhaps at her death), and foster-mother to her children.[484]

An Answer to the Objection

For a couple of reasons, this is an invalid criticism of the *Authorized Version*. First, יָלַד (*yalad*) can have both a literal and somewhat less literal meaning in the same context. For example, Ruth 4:15 says that Ruth bore a son. *Bore* is a Qal perfect third feminine singular verb with third masculine singular suffix from יָלַד (*yalad*). Then in Ruth 4:17 the neighbour women declare that a son is born to Naomi, Ruth's mother-in-law. *Born* is a Pual perfect third masculine singular verb from יָלַד (*yalad*) and is accompanied by לְ (*le*) before Naomi's name showing that she is the object of this verb. This same type of construction occurs nineteen times in the Hebrew Old Testament. In seventeen of those, the object of the

---

[484] R. Payne Smith, *II Samuel* in vol. 4 of *The Pulpit Commentary*, 513.

verb indicates the parentage of the child (Genesis 4:26; 6:1; 10:21, 25; 24:15; 35:26; 36:5; 41:50; 46:22, 27; Judges 18:29; II Samuel 3:2, 5; 21:20, 22; I Chronicles 1:19; Jeremiah 20:15). However, in Ruth 4:17 and in Isaiah 9:6, יָלַד (*yalad*) does not indicate the parentage of the child. Isaiah 9:6 says, "For unto us a child is born." This is not showing literal parentage, albeit it does show that Christ is of Israel. In Ruth 4:17, Obed was not Naomi's actual son, but was related to her. Likewise, in II Samuel 21:8, the five sons of Adriel were not Michal's actual sons, but were related to her. Just as Ruth 4:15, 17 allows for a literal and somewhat figurative usage of יָלַד (*yalad*) in close proximity to one another, so it is permissible that the same thing can occur in II Samuel 21:8.

Second, that יָלַד (*yalad*) can include the idea of bringing up, as the *Authorized Version* translators have translated it in II Samuel 21:8, is clear from Ruth 4:16 and Proverbs 23:24. Ruth 4:16 teaches that Naomi was the child's nurse, even before people said that a son was born to her (Ruth 4:17). In other words, she was engaging in activity that would help to bring up the child[485] and demonstrates that יָלַד (*yalad*) can include the idea of bringing up.

Proverbs 23:24 says, "The father of the righteous shall greatly rejoice: and he that begetteth a wise child shall have joy of him." A child is not wise at birth (Proverbs 22:15), but needs training so as to become wise (Proverbs 22:6). Therefore, *begetteth*, a Qal, active participle form of יָלַד (*yalad*), implies a bringing up of the child.

The translators of the *Authorized Version* in correctly understanding the background to II Samuel 21:8 have done a marvelous job in translating the verb with the words *brought up*. One should receive, believe, and hear *five* and *Michal*.

---

[485] Also, see Genesis 50:23 where the King James Translators translated the Pual form of יָלַד (*yalad*) brought *up*: "And Joseph saw Ephraim's children of the third generation: the children also of Machir the son of Manasseh were brought up upon Joseph's knees." Here they were quite literally brought up.

Chapter 8 — II Samuel

II SAMUEL 8:4 AND I CHRONICLES 18:4

The Passages

II Samuel 8:4 states, "And David took from him a thousand *chariots*, and seven hundred horsemen, and twenty thousand footmen: and David houghed all the chariot *horses*, but reserved of them *for* an hundred chariots."

I Chronicles 18:4 states, "And David took from him a thousand chariots, and seven thousand horsemen, and twenty thousand footmen: David also houghed all the chariot *horses*, but reserved of them an hundred chariots."

The Apparent Problem

II Samuel 8:4 speaks of David taking seven hundred horsemen from Hadadezer, the king of Zobah, whereas I Chronicles 18:4 says that he took seven thousand horsemen.

Concerning II Samuel 8:4 *The Defender's Study Bible* states, "I Chronicles 18:4 gives the number as 'seven thousand horsemen.' The apparent discrepancy is probably due to a copyist error., and most likely should be 'seven thousand'."[486] Central Baptist Theological Seminary also questions II Samuel 8:4 and will not hear, that is receive and believe, *seven hundred*.[487] Liberal Henry Preserved Smith states, "The original seems to have said that *David captured a thousand chariots and slew twenty thousand footmen*,"[488] that is, Smith wants to leave out the *seven*

---

[486] Henry Morris, 363.

[487] Glenny, 85.

[488] Henry Preserved Smith, 305. Smith also states: "The 7000 horses or horsemen are out of proportion to the chariots, so that probably the text is corrupt" (Smith, 307). If Smith is indicating that 7000 horsemen are out of proportion to 1000 chariots, he is wrong for Solomon had a similar ratio in having 12000 horsemen and 1400 chariots (II Chronicles 1:14). Smith further states: "It is surprising that if David took the foot soldiers prisoners we should not be told what he did with them, which is another reason for supposing the original text is lost" (Smith, 307). This is a very weak reason for claiming words are missing from the Bible and for ultimately rejecting the promises of Jesus to the contrary (Matthew 5:18; Luke 16:17). The fact is the Bible does not reveal all details (Deuteronomy 29:29); therefore, the silence of Scripture concerning what David did with the foot-

hundred horsemen. Both *The Defender's Study Bible* and Central Baptist Theological Seminary agree with Liberal Smith in wrongly questioning the *seven hundred horsemen* in II Samuel 8:4!

A Solution

Possibly the numberings of the horsemen involve two different sets of horsemen, that is, Samuel gives the number of horsemen captains (700), whereas Chronicles gives the total number of horsemen (7,000). That there may have been seven hundred captains over seven thousand horsemen, one captain over ten, is quite possible since Exodus 18:21 speaks of "rulers of tens" and Deuteronomy 1:15 speaks of "captains over tens" for the armies of Israel. Could the surrounding nations have divided their armies in a similar way? Likely they did, for when David, in a battle against the Syrians, slew the men of seven hundred chariots (II Samuel 10:18), this amounted to a total of seven thousand men (I Chronicles 19:18); therefore, each Syrian chariot had ten men. If one understands II Samuel 8:4 and I Chronicles 18:4 in this way with one captain over ten, then there is no contradiction. The Bible student should receive, believe, and hear both numbers.

II SAMUEL 8:13; I CHRONICLES 18:12; AND PSALM 60 (TITLE)

The Passages

II Samuel 8:13 states, "And David gat *him* a name when he returned from smiting of the Syrians in the valley of salt, *being* eighteen thousand *men*."

I Chronicles 18:12 states, "Moreover Abishai the son of Zeruiah slew of the Edomites in the valley of salt eighteen thousand."

Psalm 60 (title[489]) states, "To the chief Musician upon Shushaneduth, Michtam of David, to teach; when he strove with Aramnaharaim and with

---

men should not be a cause of alarm. These statements again reveal Smith's Liberal bias and the fallaciousness of his arguments.

[489] The author believes that the Psalm titles are part of the inspired Words of God, for (1) they are included in the Hebrew text and, in fact, are assigned their own verse number in the present printings of the Hebrew text; and (2) II Samuel 22:1, which no one dis-

Chapter 8   *II Samuel*

Aramzobah, when Joab returned, and smote of Edom in the valley of salt twelve thousand."

The Apparent Problems

If one understands these passages as referring to the same event then several problems surface. First, Samuel mentions David slaying, whereas Chronicles says Abishai, and Psalms says Joab. Second, Samuel says Syrians were slain, whereas Chronicles and Psalms say Edomites. Third, Samuel says, "Eighteen thousand men [18,000] men" were slain as does Chronicles, but Psalms says, "Twelve thousand [12,000]."

Haley lists these verses in a section wherein he supposes scribes made errors and, therefore, refuses to hear these numbers.[490]

Some Solutions

Several solutions are possible for these apparent discrepancies.

Different Accounts

One solution is to say that these three accounts are not at all parallel but speak of three different battles which all took place in the valley of salt.

Samuel and Chronicles, the Same Account

A second solution treats Samuel and Chronicles as parallel and Psalms as a separate battle.

Differences in Names

The differences in names, David in Samuel and Abishai in Chronicles, can be explained by realizing that Abishai was acting under David's command and, therefore, the credit for the battle can be equally ascribed to both. An example of a subordinate acting on behalf of a superior and

---

putes is part of the inspired Words of God, is the same as the title of Psalm 18, therefore, if II Samuel 22:1 is inspired, then so is the title to Psalm 18.

[490] Haley, 382.

the superior getting credit for the action occurs in the building of the Temple wherein the Bible says, "Solomon built the house and finished it" (I Kings 6:14). Solomon did not actually build, it was many workmen (I Kings 5:13-18); however, the Bible credits Solomon for the building of the temple, since he is the one who oversaw the project. Another example is in II Samuel 12:29 where the Bible credits David with the victory over Rabbah, whereas I Chronicles 20:1 credits the victory to Joab. David as king over Joab receives credit for the action of Joab, who was under David's command.

Differences in Slain

As far as the difference in people slain, Syrians and Edomites, Poole, commenting on II Samuel 8:13, says,

> *The Syrians*, or Edomites, as they are said to be, I Chron. xviii. 12. It is likely these two people were confederates, and that divers of the Syrians whom David had defeated in Syria [II Samuel 8:5-6] fled to Edom, and there joined with them against their common enemy, and made up together a very great army, (as the number of the men slain in it showeth) consisting of the veteran soldiers of both countries.[491]

Gill in the same vein offers this explanation:

> The Syrians and Edomites were confederates in this war; and that whereas the latter were auxiliaries to the former, the whole body of the army might be called Syrians, of which 22,000 were slain that were properly Syrians [II Samuel 8:5], and 18,000 Edomites, in all 40,000; which was a very great slaughter: or the sense is, that when he [David] had smitten the 22,000 Syrians [II Samuel 8:5], and was upon the return, he met with a body of Edomites, who came to the assistance of the Syrians, and he slew 18,000 of them.[492]

All Three Are the Same Account

A third solution treats all three as speaking of the same battle. Psalms explains that David "strove with Aramnaharaim and with Aramzobah, when Joab returned, and smote of Edom." Syria, Aramnaharaim,[493] and

---

[491] Poole, 1:602.

[492] Gill, *Exposition of the Old & New Testaments*, 2:598.

[493] *Aramnaharaim* is "the region between the rivers Euphrates and Tigris, i.e. *Mesopotamia*" ("Aramnaharaim" in *Cyclopedia*, ed. McClintock and Strong, 1:357). *Syria* is an

Chapter 8   *II Samuel*

Aramzobah[494] all refer to the same region of, or around Mesopotamia. While David battled the Syrians in the region of Mesopotamia (see II Samuel 8:5-6), Joab returned to deal with the Edomites which battle also involved Abishai, therefore, two battles were going on at once.

Differences in Names and Numbers

As for the difference in numbers, 18,000 and 12,000, Gill explains:

> Abishai first began the attack upon the Edomites, and slew six thousand of them; and then Joab fell upon them, and slew twelve thousand more, in all eighteen thousand; in 1Ch 18:12, this slaughter is ascribed to Abishai, because he began it, even the whole number; and in Ps 60:1[Hebrew], to Joab, the twelve thousand slain by him, who seconded Abishai; and the whole is here [II Samuel 8:13] attributed to David, because he was king, under whom Abishai and Joab served as generals.[495]

To review this third solution, according to II Samuel 8:5-6 David had battled the Syrians and others (Psalm 60:title) in the Mesopotamian region in the north. Before going to the north, David had dispatched Abishai to battle the Edomites in the valley of salt. Joab returns with David from the battle in the north and goes to assist Abishai. According to II Samuel 8:13, David also had gone to the valley of salt where he killed an additional 18,000 Syrians. Since the Syrians and Edomites were both in the valley of salt fighting against Israel, it seems that they were allies. David slew twenty-two thousand Syrians in the north (II Samuel 8:5), as well as another eighteen thousand Syrians in the valley of salt (II Samuel 8:13). Scripture credits David with slaying eighteen thousand Syrians in the valley of salt (II Samuel 8:13) because this was an extension of his campaign against the Syrians in the north. Furthermore, Abishai and Joab slew eighteen thousand Edomites in the valley of salt (I Chronicles 18:12). Concerning this last figure, Abishai killed six thousand and Joab twelve thousand (Psalm 60:title) all of which the Bible ascribes to Abishai as the one who started the battle (I Chronicles 18:12).

English translation of the Hebrew word אֲרָם (*'aram*) and "seems to have corresponded generally to the *Syria* . . . and *Mesopotamia* . . . of the Greeks and Romans" ("Aram" in *Cyclopedia*, ed. McClintock and Strong, 1:353).

[494] *Aramzobah* "extended from the Euphrates westward" ("Aramzobah" in *Cyclopedia*, ed. McClintock and Strong, 1:353).

[495] Gill, *Exposition of the Old & New Testaments*, II:598.

Chapter 8   *II Samuel*

Differences in Slain

As to the matter for why Samuel speaks of the Syrians and Chronicles of the Edomites, Eisemann writes:

> *Samuel* describes the campaign as having taken place against Aram [Syria] because the Edomites fought at the side of the Arameans [Syrians] in the Valley of Salt. It was thus part of the general Aramean campaign, although separate from the battles described in vs. 3-5 [of II Samuel 8]. (For this reason the casualty count for this battle [in II Samuel 18:13] is also given separately and is not included in the earlier count [of II Samuel 18:5].) *Psalms* and *Chronicles*, however, describe it as a separate battle against Edom, since it was really removed from the main theatre of operations and the Edomites were the primary opponents in this battle. . . . The two books [Samuel and Chronicles] are thus entirely consistent. *Samuel*, which ascribes the whole war to Aram, talks of the spoils of Aram; *Chronicles*, which sees it as a war against Edom, uses that description in v. 11 [I Chronicles 18:11].[496]

The Bible student should receive, believe, and hear *eighteen thousand* in II Samuel 8:13, *eighteen thousand* in I Chronicles 18:12, and *twelve thousand* in the title of Psalm 60.

II SAMUEL 10:18 AND I CHRONICLES 19:18

The Passages

II Samuel 10:18 states, "And the Syrians fled before Israel; and David slew *the men of* seven hundred chariots of the Syrians, and forty thousand horsemen, and smote Shobach the captain of their host, who died there."

I Chronicles 19:18 states, "But the Syrians fled before Israel; and David slew of the Syrians seven thousand *men which fought in* chariots, and forty thousand footmen, and killed Shophach the captain of the host."

---

[496] Moshe Eisemann, *I Chronicles / A New Translation with a Commentary Anthologized from Talmudic, Midrashic and Rabbinic Sources* (Brooklyn: Mesorah Publications, ltd., 1987), 259-260.

Chapter 8   *II Samuel*

The Apparent Problem

II Samuel 10:18 states, "David slew *the men of* seven hundred chariots," whereas I Chronicles 19:18 states, "David slew of the Syrians seven thousand men which fought in chariots."

The Defender's Study Bible will not hear, that is receive and believe, *seven hundred*, for it says about II Samuel 10:18, "The parallel account of the same battle between David and the Syrians in I Chronicles 19:18 says that 'David slew of the Syrians seven thousand men which fought in chariots.' The most likely explanation for this apparent discrepancy is a copyist's error."[497] In other words, *seven hundred* in II Samuel 10:18, according to *The Defender's Study Bible*, was not in the *autographa*. This is not much different from what Liberal Henry Preserved Smith states: "It is difficult to suppose that the clause *he slew seven hundred chariots* is original."[498] Fundamentalists need to agree with Jesus Who asserts the preservation of all the jots and tittles (Matthew 5:18), instead of agreeing with Liberals who continually question preservation.

A Solution

There is no problem here. Each chariot had ten men, so that David, in slaying the men of seven hundred chariots, slew seven thousand men. For further discussion, see the notes under I Samuel 13:5 and particularly the quote from Poole. Also see the discussion under II Samuel 8:4. Let the reader of Holy Scripture receive, believe, and hear these numbers.

II SAMUEL 14:27 AND II SAMUEL 18:18

The Passages

II Samuel 14:27 states, "And unto Absalom there were born three sons, and one daughter, whose name *was* Tamar: she was a woman of a fair countenance."

---

[497] Henry Morris, 365.

[498] Henry Preserved Smith, 316.

Chapter 8 — *II Samuel*

II Samuel 18:18 states, "Now Absalom in his lifetime had taken and reared up for himself a pillar, which *is* in the king's dale: for he said, I have no son to keep my name in remembrance: and he called the pillar after his own name: and it is called unto this day, Absalom's place."

The Apparent Problem

II Samuel 14:27 states that three sons were born to Absalom, but in II Samuel 18:18 Absalom says, "I have no son to keep my name in remembrance."

Some Solutions

A couple of solutions seem possible. First, it could be that Absalom's three sons died prior to his statement in II Samuel 18:18. Or, the solution could involve the words *to keep my name in remembrance* in which it is possible that if some of his sons were alive, he did not think them worthy "to keep up his name and honour."[499]

II SAMUEL 15:7 AND I KINGS 2:11

The Passages

II Samuel 15:7 states, "And it came to pass after forty years, that Absalom said unto the king, I pray thee, let me go and pay my vow, which I have vowed unto the LORD, in Hebron."

I Kings 2:11 states, "And the days that David reigned over Israel *were* forty years: seven years reigned he in Hebron, and thirty and three years reigned he in Jerusalem."

---

[499] Poole, 1:626. This second solution is well possible, since according to the discussion of the next apparent problem, Absalom was about 25 years old at the time of his death (see discussion including footnotes), which means that his children would not have been very old at the time he set up this pillar.

Chapter 8 — *II Samuel*

The Apparent Problem

Before stating the apparent problem, it is important to examine the context. II Samuel 15 speaks of Absalom stealing the hearts of the men of Israel. II Samuel 15:4-7 states,

> Absalom said *moreover*, Oh that I were made judge in the land, that every man which hath any suit or cause might come unto me, and I would do him justice! And it was *so*, that when any man came nigh *to him* to do him obeisance, he put forth his hand, and took him, and kissed him. And on this manner did Absalom to all Israel that came to the king for judgment: so Absalom stole the hearts of the men of Israel. And it came to pass after forty years, that Absalom said unto the king, I pray thee, let me go and pay my vow, which I have vowed unto the LORD, in Hebron.

If *forty years* refers to the length of time Absalom took to steal their hearts, then it would seem that Absalom was somewhat older than forty.[500] But such an understanding poses a problem. The problem is this: Absalom was born to David while David was king over Judah in Hebron (II Samuel 3:2-3). David reigned in Hebron for "seven years and six months" (II Samuel 2:11), and his entire reign was forty years (II Samuel 5:4). Since David's total reign was forty years and since Absalom was born during David's reign and since the event of II Samuel 15:7 occurs during David's reign, then Absalom had to be less than forty years old. For more about the chronology, see further.

The Defender's Study Bible refuses to hear *forty* as it says, "The number 'forty' here is apparently a copyist error."[501] Also Leon Wood writes, "The number given in II Sam. 15:7 is 'forty,' but this is impossible. . . . This must be a copyist's error and so is better read with the Syriac, Vulgate, Arabic, and others: 'four years'."[502] The *English Standard Version* for the beginning of II Samuel 15:7 reads, "And at the end of four years Absalom said to the king." Herein Wood the *English Standard Version* are in accord with Liberal Henry Preserved Smith who writes, "The most

---

[500] If the forty years refers to the length of time Absalom took to steal their hearts, then it is obvious that he did not get started as a baby, but as a man able to reason and to gain the people's confidence. If, for example, he started at twenty and if the forty years refer to the time it took him to win the men over, then this would mean that at this time Absalom would be sixty (20 + 40 = 60).

[501] Henry Morris, 371.

[502] Wood, 261.

obvious way out of the difficulty is to correct *forty* to *four*."[503] Smith, Wood, the *English Standard Version,* and *The Defender's Study Bible* refuse to receive, believe, and hear the Traditional Hebrew Text.

A Solution

After forty years does not refer to the length of time Absalom took to steal the hearts of the men of Israel. Nor does it refer to David's age. David began to reign at thirty (II Samuel 5:4) and since Absalom was born after David began to reign, then Absalom would have been at the most nine years old when David was forty. It is not likely that a ten-year-old boy would be able to steal the hearts of the men of Israel. Furthermore, Absalom had children (II Samuel 14:27), that is, more than one child which would be unlikely for a ten year old.

Some might think that *after forty years* refers to forty years into David's reign. If so, it would place the rebellion of Absalom at the end of David's reign since David reigned for forty years. However, this would not allow enough time for the events in II Samuel 16 and following to transpire.[504]

Floyd Jones states:

> The explanation is ascertained by deriving the context which is given in the sixth verse: "so Absalom stole the hearts of the men of Israel." That is, Absalom stole the hearts of the men of Israel from David and joined them to himself. When had David won over and bonded unto himself the hearts of the men of Israel? Forty years earlier when he slew the Philistine giant, Goliath, followed quickly by a succession of victories in the months that ensued (I Sam. 18:5, 16, 30). . . . Thus the "forty" years is not an error,[505] it is a major key in the chronology of David's life. . . . The Biblicist must exercise faith rather than doubt when he doesn't understand.[506]

---

[503] Henry Preserved Smith, 342.

[504] II Samuel 18 mentions Absalom's death, which was followed by (1) a mourning period and a procession bringing David back to Jerusalem (II Samuel 19); (2) the rebellion of Sheba, which David put down (II Samuel 20); (3) a three year famine, which David endured (II Samuel 21:1); (4) additional battles between David and the Philistines (II Samuel 21:15-22); and (5) more. From these considerations, Absalom's rebellion could not have occurred in the last year of David's reign.

[505] "Josephus, followed by Ewald, Hervey, and most critics, assumes there is a copyist's error in this case" (Haley, 393). "Barnes and Clarke and many other commentators claim the word 'forty' here is a clerical error and that it should read 'four.' Barnes

Chapter 8 — *II Samuel*

In other words, forty years after David had won the hearts of the men of Israel at the slaying of Goliath, Absalom stole the hearts of these men away from David. Bible students should receive, believe, and hear the number forty in this verse.

II SAMUEL 18:18

See discussion under II Samuel 14:27.

II SAMUEL 21:8

See discussion under II Samuel 6:23.

II SAMUEL 21:19

See discussion in Appendix C.

II SAMUEL 23:8 AND I CHRONICLES 11:11

The Passages

II Samuel 23:8 states, "These *be* the names of the mighty men whom David had: the Tachmonite that sat in the seat, chief among the captains; the same was Adino the Eznite: *he lift up his spear* against eight hundred, whom he slew at one time."

I Chronicles 11:11 states, "And this *is* the number of the mighty men whom David had; Jashobeam, an Hachmonite, the chief of the captains: he lifted up his spear against three hundred slain *by him* at one time."

---

calls it 'an obvious clerical error.' Adam Clarke says, 'There is no doubt that this reading is corrupt.' We do not believe the Authorized Version is in error. The weight of evidence, even from a strictly textual view, is overwhelmingly on the side of 'forty.' Clarke admits that the reading 'four' years 'is not supported by any Hebrew MS. yet discovered' " (Cloud, 55).

[506] Jones, 105. According to Jones, David was 58 at the time of Absalom's rebellion and Absalom about 25.

Chapter 8   *II Samuel*

The Apparent Problems

Some see a couple of problems here. First is the matter of the names: is it *Tachmonite* or *Hachmonite* and *Adino* or *Jashobeam*?

The second apparent problem is the matter of the numbers: is it *eight hundred* or *three hundred*? David Cloud observes:

> Many claim this is a contradiction caused by a copyist error. William Pettingill, for example, in *Bible Questions Answered*, says, "These are very obviously instances of copyists' errors." We fail to see that this is so obvious. To say that there is a copyist error is a mere conjecture. There is no evidence that the text is corrupt apart from the apparent contradiction. The textual evidence supports the translation as we have it in the KJV.[507]

Haley lists II Samuel 23:8 as a place where a scribal error has occurred in the number.[508] *The Defender's Study Bible* states, "The number in I Chronicles 11:11 probably represents a copyist's error."[509] Jamieson states, "The text is corrupt in this passage [II Samuel 23:8]; the number eight hundred should be three hundred."[510] Pettingill, Haley, *The Defender's Study Bible*, and Jamieson will not hear these numbers.

Some Solutions

A couple of solutions are available for the apparent problems in these verses.

Two Different Men

Perhaps Adino the Tachmonite and Jashobeam the Hachmonite are two different men and, therefore, the Bible presents two different exploits by two different men. That these might be different men is possible since the list in Samuel was written earlier than the one in Chronicles. In the intervening time, a change could have occurred where the man in Samuel, Adino, was replaced by Jashobeam in Chronicles.

---

[507] Cloud, 57.

[508] Haley, 383.

[509] Henry Morris, 382.

[510] Jamieson, *II Samuel* in part 2, vol. 2 of *A Commentary*, 284.

Chapter 8   *II Samuel*

The Same Man

If, however, both verses speak of the same man, then the difference in names and in numbers remains.

Differences in Names

Concerning the names, *Tachmonite* and *Hachmonite*, *The Brown-Driver-Briggs Hebrew and English Lexicon* indicates that *Tachmonite* of II Samuel 23:8 is the same as *an Hachmonite* of I Chronicles 11:11.[511] Indeed, these two words are very closely related in meaning. *Tachmonite* means "thou wilt make me wise"[512] and *Hachmonite* means "wise."[513]

Concerning *Jashobeam*, rather than being a formal name, it could be a descriptive title, for it "is a contraction of the two words יֹשֵׁב הָעָם ... *one who sits at the head of the people*, and [he] was called this . . . due to his wisdom."[514] *Jashobeam* means "*dweller* among the *people*, or *returner* to the *people*, otherwise, to whom *the people returns*,"[515] which harmonizes with the fact that he was wise; that is, because of his wisdom the people returned to him. If *Jashobeam* is a descriptive title rather than a formal name, then this would resolve the problem with *Jashobeam* and *Adino* such that *Adino* was his formal name.

But now this raises a question: how could he be both a Tachmonite and an Eznite as II Samuel 23:8 asserts? *The Pulpit Commentary* claims, "A man could not be a Tachmonite and an Eznite at the same time."[516] Such a statement reflects an unbelieving attitude in the preserved text. That a man was a Tachmonite and an Eznite at the same time II Samuel 23:8 attests, all one needs to do is simply to believe it. As explained earlier, *Tachmonite* refers to one having wisdom and may be another descriptive title rather than the name of a place and such an understanding

---

[511] Brown, *The Brown-Driver-Briggs Hebrew and English Lexicon*, 315.

[512] *Online Bible Hebrew Lexicon* in *Online Bible Millennial Edition* [CD-ROM], 08461.

[513] Ibid., 02453.

[514] Eisemann, 177,178.

[515] "Jashobeam" in *Cyclopedia*, ed. McClintock and Strong, 4:788.

[516] R. Payne Smith, 569.

Chapter 8 — *II Samuel*

would eliminate the objection posed by *The Pulpit Commentary*. Therefore, *Eznite* is a place and *Tachmonite* is a title.

Differences in Numbers

Now concerning the numbers, *eight hundred* and *three hundred*, these could be referring to two different encounters that Adino had or to two different ways of numbering the dead. Cloud writes:

> Samuel perhaps counts the entire number of soldiers slain by Adino during an entire day of battle; whereas Chronicles perhaps counts only the number of soldiers slain during the first part of that battle or only the number of chief men slain, etc. These possibilities are far more reasonable than to claim that God failed to preserve His Word and allowed mistakes to enter the text.[517]

Let the student of Holy Scripture receive, believe, and hear these accounts.

II SAMUEL 23:39

The Passage

II Samuel 23:39 states, "Uriah the Hittite: thirty and seven in all."

The Apparent Problem

II Samuel 23:39 is the last verse in a list discussing David's mighty men. A problem arises because the list only presents thirty-six names as opposed to thirty-seven. Those names are (1) Adino vs. 8; (2) Eleazar vs. 9; (3) Shammah vs. 11; (4) Abishai vs. 18; (5) Benaiah vs. 20; (6) Asahel vs. 24; (7) Elhanan vs. 24; (8) Shammah vs. 25; (9) Elika vs. 25; (10) Helez vs. 26; (11) Ira vs. 26; (12) Abiezer vs. 27; (13) Mebunnai vs. 27; (14) Zalmon vs. 28; (15) Maharai vs. 28; (16) Heleb vs. 29; (17) Ittai vs. 29; (18) Benaiah vs. 30; (19) Hiddai vs. 30; (20) Abialbon vs. 31; (21) Azmaveth vs. 31; (22) Eliahba vs. 32; (23) Jonathan vs. 32; (24) Shammah vs. 33; (25) Ahiam vs. 33; (26) Eliphelet vs. 34; (27) Eliam vs. 34; (28) Hezrai vs. 35; (29) Paarai vs. 35; (30) Igal vs. 36; (31) Bani vs. 36; (32)

---

[517] Cloud, 58.

Chapter 8   *II Samuel*

Zelek vs. 37; (33) Naharai vs. 37; (34) Ira vs. 38; (35) Gareb vs. 38; and (36) Uriah vs. 39.

Some Solutions

One solution is to include Joab in the list, since he was the general of the army. Including Joab would result in a total of thirty-seven: the thirty-six already listed plus Joab.

Another solution is to notice that in the second group of three worthies (vss. 18-23), where one might expect three names, the Bible mentions only two names, Abishai (vs. 18) and Benaiah (vs. 20), which leaves room for another person. Who is the other person? The other person may possibly be Joab, since he is first mentioned at this point (vs. 18, "And Abishai, the brother of Joab").

Whatever the solution, may the reader of Scripture hear the number of them.

II SAMUEL 24:9 AND I CHRONICLES 21:5

The Passages

II Samuel 24:9 states, "And Joab gave up the sum of the number of the people unto the king: and there were in Israel eight hundred thousand valiant men that drew the sword; and the men of Judah *were* five hundred thousand men."

I Chronicles 21:5 states, "And Joab gave the sum of the number of the people unto David. And all *they of* Israel were a thousand thousand and an hundred thousand men that drew sword: and Judah *was* four hundred threescore and ten thousand men that drew sword."

The Apparent Problems

These verses present a couple of apparent problems.

Chapter 8 *II Samuel*

Numbers

A couple of numbers seem to be in disagreement: (1) Samuel says, "Eight hundred thousand [800,000] men that drew sword," whereas Chronicles says, "A thousand thousand and an hundred thousand [1,100,000] men that drew sword"; and (2) Samuel says, "The men of Judah were five hundred thousand [500,000] men," whereas Chronicles says, "Judah was four hundred threescore and ten thousand [470,000] men."

Haley says of these verses: "There may be copyist's errors in one or both cases."[518] Herein Haley and a Liberal commentary agree, for *The Interpreter's Bible* states, "The numbers are handed down differently by the Chronicler . . . and cannot be trusted."[519] Why should not a person trust these numbers? Did not the Lord Jesus Christ put His stamp of approval on the entire Old Testament?

Largeness

Another problem, as far as some are concerned, is the largeness of the numbers. *The Expositor's Bible Commentary* states:

> A second problem relates to the hugeness of the numbers themselves. . . . Understanding them literally would "imply a population of at least six million in the small country of Palestine." . . . Most commentators, . . ., sense that the numbers are inordinately large when interpreted literally.[520]

Many refuse to hear these numbers.

Some Solutions

Each of the apparent problems have adequate solutions.

---

[518] Haley, 390.

[519] Caird, *II Samuel* in vol. 2 of *The Interpreter's Bible*, 1173. Henry Preserved Smith, another Liberal, says, "As in so many cases, the numbers are not to be relied upon" (Smith, 389).

[520] Youngblood, *1, 2 Samuel* in *The Expositor's Bible Commentary*, 1099. Youngblood is among those commentators who does not take this number literally as is J. Barton Payne (Payne, *1, 2 Chronicles* in *The Expositor's Bible Commentary*, 407).

Chapter 8   II Samuel

Numbers

Part of the solution to these apparent discrepancies in numbering involves a careful reading of the verses. Samuel specifically gives the number of valiant men in Israel who drew sword as eight hundred thousand. The key word here is *valiant*. On the other hand, Chronicles gives the number of men in Israel who drew sword as a thousand thousand and an hundred thousand, but not all of them are valiant men. Chronicles, then, gives all the men of Israel that drew sword, whereas Samuel gives only the men who were valiant. Also, Chronicles says, "All they of Israel," whereas Samuel does not indicate that it is giving "all they of Israel."

In regard to the numbering of Judah; Samuel says, "And the men of Judah were five hundred thousand men," whereas Chronicles says, "And Judah was four hundred threescore and ten thousand men that drew sword." The key words in this case are *that drew sword*. Chronicles gives the number of the men of Judah that drew sword, whereas Samuel with the bigger number for Judah does not limit its number to just those of Judah who drew sword and, therefore, includes more.

Largeness

As far as the largeness of these numbers, Eerdmann writes:

> There is no good reason to reject them as unhistorically *large*, since this fertile country was very thickly peopled. "We see this from the various places, whose ruins stand as near to one another, as villages in our more densely populated regions" (Arnold in *Herz[og]* XI. 23 sq.). Taking the military population as about one-fourth of the whole, Palestine (Israel) would have contained according to this census, a population of from five to six million souls, which is not too large a number.[521]

Davis writes:

> It has been estimated, however, that the boundaries given in II Samuel 24:2-12, with the exception of the Phoenician coast, would include an area of some 12,500 square miles. This being the case, there would be about 310 people per square mile which is not an unreasonable figure.[522]

The writers of *Hard Sayings of the Bible* state about these numbers:

---

[521] Erdmann, 606.

[522] Davis, 81.

Chapter 8 — *II Samuel*

> But what about the problem of such large numbers? If taken at face value, this would imply that Israel and Judah had a combined population of this time of something like three to six million people. However, all attempts to size down these numbers runs into the further problem of creating new dilemmas. For example, to say that the word for "thousand" . . . here means "tribal unit, contingent," . . . leaves us with pondering the question as to why it took three hundred days [II Samuel 24:8] to conduct a census of 1,570 outstanding military figures. Either someone was unusually slow in math, lazy, or the numbers are what they present themselves to be.[523]

The fact is the largeness of these numbers only presents a problem to those who do not want to hear them.

II SAMUEL 24:13 AND I CHRONICLES 21:11-12

The Passages

II Samuel 24:13 states, "So Gad came to David, and told him, and said unto him, Shall seven years of famine come unto thee in thy land? or wilt thou flee three months before thine enemies, while they pursue thee? or that there be three days' pestilence in thy land? now advise, and see what answer I shall return to him that sent me."

I Chronicles 21:11-12 states, "So Gad came to David, and said unto him, Thus saith the LORD, Choose thee either three years' famine; or three months to be destroyed before thy foes, while that the sword of thine enemies overtaketh *thee*; or else three days the sword of the LORD, even the pestilence, in the land, and the angel of the LORD destroying throughout all the coasts of Israel. Now therefore advise thyself what word I shall bring again to him that sent me."

The Apparent Problem

In Samuel, Gad speaks of seven years of famine; whereas, in Chronicles, he speaks of three years of famine.

---

[523] Kaiser, Jr., *Hard Sayings of the Bible*, 227.

Sir Robert Anderson believes that the differences are the result of "an error of copying."[524] Anderson's otherwise fine book is herein marred because he refuses to receive, believe, and hear these numbers.

The *English Standard Version*, rejecting the Traditional Hebrew Text, sides with the LXX in having the first half of II Samuel 24:13 read, "So Gad came to David and told him, and said to him, 'Shall three years of famine come to you in your land?' " Herein, the *English Standard Version* is in accord with the false interpretation of *A Catholic Commentary on Holy Scripture* which says, " 'Seven years': LXX and Chronicler's 'three years' are more in accord with the symmetrical 'three' in each punishment."[525]

Some Solutions

Both of the above passages deal with Gad coming to David after David ordered a census of Israel, which was a sin against the Lord (I Chronicles 21:3, 7, 8). God sent Gad to David to have David choose one of three punishments for his sin. With this in mind, a couple of solutions are available for this difficulty.

Reduction of Seven-Year Famine

A careful reading of the verses points to a significant difference in wording between the two passages and concludes that Gad came twice to David. In the first encounter as recorded by Samuel seven years of famine was offered as one of the choices, but in the second encounter as Chronicles records, it was reduced to three years of famine. Gleason Archer writes concerning this solution:

> Note that the wording here [in I Chronicles 21:11-12] is significantly different from that of 2 Samuel 24:13. . . . Rather than that simple question in 2 Samuel, we have it given here in I Chronicles as an alternative imperative.[526] . . . From this we may reasonably conclude that 2 Samuel records the first approach of Gad to David, in which the alternative prospect was

---

[524] Anderson, *The Bible and Modern Criticism*, 162.

[525] H. McKay, *1 & 2 Kings* in *A Catholic Commentary on Holy Scripture*, ed. Dom Bernard Orchard (NY: Thomas Nelson and Sons Ltd., 1953), 326.

[526] I Chronicles 21:11 uses a Piel, second, masculine, singular imperative for *choose* (קַבֵּל, *qabbel*), whereas II Samuel 24:13 uses a simple question.

Chapter 8   II Samuel

seven years; the Chronicles account gives us the second and final approach . . . to the king, in which the Lord (doubtless in response to David's earnest entreaty in private prayer) reduced the severity of that grim alternative to three years rather than an entire span of seven.[527]

Famine "in thy land"

II Samuel 24:13 says, "Shall seven years of famine come unto thee in thy land?," whereas I Chronicles 21:12 does not have *in thy land*. Herein is a key to another possible solution to this difficulty. Gad must have come to David twice and on one occasion spoke of seven years of famine coming in the land and in the other instance simply spoke of three years of famine. The reason Samuel mentions seven years of famine in the land is because only Samuel records the three years of a previous famine, which was God's judgment upon Israel for Saul's slaying of the Gibeonites (II Samuel 21:1). After the three year famine of II Samuel 21, another year would elapse before the crops would be ready to harvest again, and these years added to another three years of famine would make a total of seven years of famine in the land. That there was at least a year between the end of the three year famine concerning the Gibeonites and the announcement by Gad is evident from II Samuel 24:8, which teaches that the census, which took place after the Gibeonite famine, lasted for "nine months and twenty days." In addition to these nine months and twenty days, time must be added for the slaying, mourning, and burying of seven of Saul's sons (II Samuel 21:2-14), as well as another war with the Philistines (II Samuel 24:15-22). Poole, in explaining that David's sin of numbering the people was committed in the year after the three-year, Gibeonite famine, writes that the next year

> was in a manner a year of famine; either because it was the sabbatical year, wherein they might not sow or reap; or rather, because not being able to sow in the third year, because of the excessive drought, they were not capable of reaping this fourth year. And three years more being added to these four, make up the seven here mentioned. So the meaning of the words is this, As thou hast already had four years of famine, shall three years more come? And that it is said of these seven years, that they *shall come*, it is a synecdochical expression frequent in Scripture, because part of the years were yet to come; even as it is said of the Israelites, that they

---

[527] Archer, 189-190.

should *wander in the wilderness forty years*, Numb. xiv. 33, when part of that time was already spent.[528]

The solution to this apparent problem works out as follows: 3 years of famine of II Samuel 21:1 + 1 year to recover + 3 additional years of famine as a judgment for numbering the people according to I Chronicles 21:12 = 7 total years of famine in the land as mentioned in II Samuel 24:13.

Rejection of LXX

Concerning the apparent difficulty in these passages, several commentators seem to think that the LXX reading in II Samuel 24:13 of three years of famine is the correct reading.[529] For example, Joyce Baldwin comments on II Samuel 24:13, "The choice is *three years* (though the Hebrew has 'seven', the 'three' of 1 Ch. 21:12 and the LXX seems likely to be original)."[530] The problem with claiming the LXX reading is original for this verse or for any other verse, for that matter, is that the promise for preservation of the inspired words of the Old Testament only extends to the Hebrew alphabet and vowel points according to Matthew 5:18 (see detailed discussion in Chapter Two). Since the LXX is a Greek translation of the Hebrew Old Testament, the promise of Matthew 5:18 does not apply. Consequently, when commentators side with the LXX over the Traditional Hebrew Text they are abandoning God's promise of preservation and are relying on their own humanistic, naturalistic, and rationalistic judgment. The correct and true reading according to Matthew 5:18 is in the Traditional Hebrew Text and one should never abandon this text no matter what the difficulties. People should receive, believe, and hear the numbers in the Traditional Hebrew Text.

---

[528] Poole, 1:643. Another example of a synecdochical expression is in Daniel 7:17, which states that the four beasts are four kings, "which shall arise out of the earth." The first of these kings represents Babylon, which was already in existence, but Scripture says, "Shall" because more was yet to come. See Thomas M. Strouse, *But Daniel Purposed in His Heart: An Exegetical Commentary on Daniel* (Newington, CT: Emmanuel Baptist Theological Press, 2001), 112.

[529] This siding with the LXX over the Traditional Hebrew text is not only evident here, but in some of the previous apparent problems as well. In fact, some commentators routinely appeal to the LXX in an attempt to overthrow the reading in the Traditional Hebrew Text.

[530] Joyce G. Baldwin, *1 & 2 Samuel*, vol. 8, *Tyndale Old Testament Commentaries*, ed. D. J. Wiseman (Downers Grove, IL: Inter-Varsity Press, 1988), 296.

Chapter 8 — *II Samuel*

II SAMUEL 24:24 AND I CHRONICLES 21:25

The Passages

II Samuel 24:24 states, "And the king said unto Araunah, Nay; but I will surely buy *it* of thee at a price: neither will I offer burnt offerings unto the LORD my God of that which doth cost me nothing. So David bought the threshingfloor and the oxen for fifty shekels of silver."

I Chronicles 21:25 states, "So David gave to Ornan for the place six hundred shekels of gold by weight."

The Apparent Problems

Two problems present themselves in comparing the above verses. First, is the problem of the money that David paid: Samuel says, "Fifty shekels of silver," whereas Chronicles says, "Six hundred shekels of gold." And then is the problem of whom David paid. Samuel says that David paid Araunah, whereas Chronicles says Ornan.

In explaining the number of shekels, Haley gives three explanations of which the first is "that we have here a copyist's mistake, which could very easily happen."[531] Haley again advocates a non-hearing of these numbers.

Myers, in *The Anchor Bible*, after speaking of the whole account in I Chronicles 21 having "obvious legendary accretions and embellishments," assures his readers that "the nucleus of the story may be taken as historical."[532] Myers, either wittingly or unwittingly, has become the final arbiter of what part of the Bible is really from God, as opposed to what is not really from God. But should not one have his faith and confidence in Jesus Who assures everyone that everything in the Old Testament is correct?

---

[531] Haley, 390.

[532] Jacob M. Myers, *I Chronicles* in *The Anchor Bible*, ed. William Foxwell Albright and David Noel Freedman (Garden City, NY: Doubleday & Company, Inc., 1965), 147. What Myers espouses is a Liberal view and it comes as no surprise for he wrote the introduction and exegesis for Judges in the Liberal commentary, *The Interpreter's Bible* (*Joshua to II Samuel*, vol. 3, *The Interpreter's Bible*, x). Not only this, but *The Anchor Bible* is ecumenical for on page ii is this statement: "THE ANCHOR BIBLE is a project of international and interfaith scope: Protestant, Catholic, and Jewish scholars from many countries contribute individual volumes."

Chapter 8 — *II Samuel*

Some Solutions

Solutions are available for the apparent problems with these verses.

Differences in Numbers

First, concerning the different amounts that David paid, a careful reading of the two verses reveals that David paid fifty shekels of silver for the threshingfloor and the oxen (II Samuel 24:24), whereas he paid six hundred shekels of gold for the place (I Chronicles 21:25). The place was a bigger area, which included the threshingfloor. "A threshing floor is generally an area of modest dimensions, not usually broader than thirty or forty feet."[533] "The *place* as a whole would seem to refer to the entire area which later became the Temple—i.e., the entire Temple Mount."[534] Concerning *the place*, Archer says,

> Neither in the fifth century B.C., nor in any other period in ancient history, would a threshing floor have cost anything like six hundred gold shekels. Consequently we may safely conclude that Ornan possessed the entire area of Mount Moriah.
>
> About sixteen hundred feet long and on a commanding elevation, Mount Moriah was an extremely valuable piece of real estate, easily worth six hundred shekels of gold.[535]

Poole advances another possible answer concerning the difference in the amounts:

> There is a considerable difference in the phrase in these two places: here [II Samuel 24:24] he mentions for what David *bought* it, or what he was obliged to give for it; and in Chronicles what he actually *gave* for it, to wit, of his royal bounty, over and besides the full price of it.[536]

One should receive, believe, and hear these numbers.

---

[533] Archer, 190.

[534] Eisemann, 283.

[535] Archer, 190.

[536] Poole, 1:654.

Chapter 8　　　　　　　　　　　　　　　　　　　*II Samuel*

Differences in Names

Second, concerning the names, Araunah and Ornan, these could be two different names for the same person, for both are Jebusites (II Samuel 24:18; I Chronicles 21:18). Now, God commanded David to "rear an altar unto the LORD in the threshingfloor of Araunah the Jebusite" (II Samuel 24:18). In I Chronicles 21:18, God commanded David, for the same offering, to "set up an altar unto the LORD in the threshingfloor of Ornan the Jebusite." If Araunah and Ornan were two different men, then David would have reared up two different altars, but inasmuch as he raised up only one altar, it seems that Araunah and Ornan are the same person. In the Hebrew these two names are very close and it seems that Ornan (אָרְנָן) was a shortened form of Araunah (אֲרַוְנָה), just as Chet is a shortened form for Chester.

CHAPTER NINE:
APPARENT NUMERICAL CONTRADICTIONS IN I KINGS

Several of the apparent numerical contradictions from this point onward involve a harmonizing of the accounts of the kings of Israel with the kings of Judah. It is necessary, therefore, to set forth some chronological factors upon which to base the ensuing discussions.

CHRONOLOGICAL FACTORS

The chronological factors important in handling some of the apparent numerical discrepancies are type of calendar used, accession versus non-accession years, and tabulation of years.

Calendar

The first chronological factor involves calendars. Both kingdoms, Israel in the north and Judah in the south, used a Nisan (March/April) to Nisan calendar, except for the possible exception of the last king of Israel, Hoshea. It is beyond the scope of this book to delve into all the aspects concerning the use of calendars except to mention a few things. Thiele presents the case for Judah using a Tishri (September/October) to Tishri calendar while at the same time Israel was using a Nisan to Nisan calendar.[537] However, in the opinion of the author Thiele's arguments are suc-

---

[537] Thiele, 43-60.

cessfully countered by Jones' treatment.[538] Therefore, the author will not use the explanation of a supposed difference in calendar systems between the two kingdoms as a way to handle apparent problems. Concerning Hoshea, Jones writes:

> In harmonizing all of the data concerning his reign, the best synchronization with Judah favors Hoshea's having used the Tishri system. This he may have done either due to Assyrian influence or the desperate circumstances overhanging his kingdom as a result of the precarious Assyrian presence in the area, much of the northern kingdom having already been subjugated into captivity during Pekah's reign by Tiglath-pileser III (II Ki. 15:29; I Chr. 5:26; Isa. 9:1).[539]

Also because of Assyrian influence, Hoshea could have used an accession year. As Thiele points out: "In Assyria, Babylon, and Persia when a king first came to the throne, the year was usually called the king's *accession* year, but not till the first day of the first month of the next new year did the king begin reckoning events in his own first year."[540] The discussion at II Kings 15:30 gives further information about Hoshea. However, at this point a demonstration is in order. Hoshea started his reign in the twelfth year of Ahaz (II Kings 17:1). In the third year of Hoshea, Hezekiah started his reign (II Kings 18:1). The fourth year of Hezekiah "was the seventh year of Hoshea" (II Kings 18:9). And the captivity of Israel started "in the sixth year of Hezekiah, that *is* the ninth year of Hoshea" (II Kings 18:10). Using a Tishri to Tishri calendar for Hoshea and a Nisan to Nisan calendar for the Judean kings, Hoshea's time line would map as follows (ac = accession year; N = Nisan; T = Tishri):

II Kings 17:1	II Kings 18:1	II Kings 18:9	II Ki 18:10
Hoshea starts in 12th year of Ahaz	Hezekiah starts in 3rd year of Hoshea	Hezekiah's 4th = Hoshea's 7th	Hezekiah's 6th = Hoshea's 9th
↕	↕	↕	↕

Hoshea: T ac T 1st T 2nd T 3rd T 4th T 5th T 6th T 7th T 8th T 9th T
   ↕   ↕   ↕   ↕
Ahaz: N 12th N 13th N 14th N 15th N 16th
(Reigned 16 years **II Kings 16:2**)   ↕   ↕   ↕
Hezekiah: ac N 1st N 2nd N 3rd N 4th N 5th N 6th N

---

[538] Jones, 121-135.

[539] Ibid., 134.

[540] Thiele, 43.

Chapter 9 *1 Kings*

Using a Tishri to Tishri calendar system for Hoshea and a Nisan to Nisan calendar system for Ahaz and Hezekiah accommodates all the chronological data for the reigns involved.

Accession Versus Non-Accession

A second chronological factor concerns accession versus non-accession years. "In the accession-year system the year in which the king comes to the throne is called his accession year and for the purpose of counting his years of reign, his first official year is that which begins with the new year's day after his accession."[541] With the accession-year system, the accession year of the new king is the same as the last year of the out-going king. "In the non-accession-year system the year in which the ruler comes to the throne is counted as his first year regardless of how many days or months remain in that year, and his second year begins with the first new year's day (Tishri 1 or Nisan 1) after his accession."[542]

Judah usually used an accession-year system, whereas Israel typically used a non-accession-year system. One exception to the use of the non-accession-year system, as noted above, is Hoshea. This book notes other exceptions as it encounters them. While Judah typically used the accession-year system, not every king in Judah had an accession year. Finegan explains why some kings may not have had an accession year: "At what point is the reign considered to begin? This point most often coincides, no doubt, with the death of the preceding ruler, yet there may be an interval before the new king is selected, installed, or confirmed in office."[543] In light of this statement, it is conceivable that if a Judean king died a few weeks before Nisan 1 and the next king of Judah was delayed in coming to throne until or after Nisan 1, then he would not have an accession year.

Tabulation of Years

A third chronological factor concerns the tabulation of years. Scripture uses several principles in the tabulation of years. First, the length of

---

[541] Jack Finegan, *Handbook of Biblical Chronology*, rev. ed. (Peabody, MA: Hendrickson Publishers, 1998), 237.

[542] Ibid.

[543] Ibid., 77.

Chapter 9 — I Kings

the reign of a king does not include his accession year, but just his official years (see above under "Accession Versus Non-Accession").

Second, when the Bible uses a non-accession-year system, then the last year of a king is credited to him as well as to the new king resulting in that year being counted twice, once for the dead king and once for the new king. Jones states:

> In non-accession year dating, the *last* year of one king was the *first* official year of his successor even if he reigned but one day in that year. In this method, that year was counted *twice*; consequently, reigns so reckoned give one year more than the actual elapsed time. Hence with both sovereigns claiming the same year, it becomes necessary to subtract one year when computing the actual number of elapsed years. Conversely, accession reckoning gives official years equal to actual years.[544]

Third, the years of the kings of Judah and Israel are based upon the perspective from which the Bible presents them. For example, if Scripture tabulates the years of a Judean king from an Israelite perspective, then the accession year of the Judean king is the year in which he came to the throne, assuming that he had an accession year. In other words, an Israelite perspective views a Judean king's accession year as his first official year. On the other hand, if Scripture tabulates the years of a king of Israel from a Judean perspective, then the years of the king of Israel are marked according to the official years of the king of Judah. In other words, the Judean king's accession year is not used when tabulating the years of the Israelite king.

How can one tell if the Bible presents years from an Israelite perspective or from a Judean perspective? Scripture presents years from an Israelite perspective when it uses this formula: in the X year of the king of Israel. For example, "And in the twentieth year of Jeroboam king of Israel reigned Asa over Judah" (I Kings 15:9). In this case, Scripture presents the years from an Israelite perspective, namely that in the twentieth year of Jeroboam of Israel, Asa began his reign, which was Asa's accession year and not his first official year. The operative phrase is *of . . . king of Israel*. On the other hand, the Bible presents years from a Judean perspective when it uses the formula: in the X year of the king of Judah. For example, "In the twenty and sixth year of Asa king of Judah began Elah the son of Baasha to reign over Israel " (I Kings 16:8). In this case, Scripture presents the years from a Judean perspective, namely that in the

---

[544] Jones, 135.

Chapter 9 — *I Kings*

twenty-sixth official year of Asa of Judah, Elah begin to reign over Israel. The operative phrase in this case is *of . . . king of Judah*.

At this juncture, an example of how the Bible tabulates years, as well as an example of a king with no accession year is in order. Shortly after the start of Rehoboam's reign the northern tribes split from the kingdom and set up Jeroboam as their king (I Kings 12:1-20); therefore, Rehoboam's and Jeroboam's first years of reign both occurred in the same year. Rehoboam died after reigning for seventeen years (I Kings 14:21). And then "in the eighteenth year of king Jeroboam . . . reigned Abijam [Abijah] over Judah" (I Kings 15:1). From this Israelite perspective, it appears that Abijah did not have an accession year. If Abijah had an accession year, it would have occurred in the same year as Rehoboam's seventeenth year, which is the same as Jeroboam's seventeenth year. If this were so, then the Bible would have said, "Now in the seventeenth year of Jeroboam reigned Abijah over Judah." Why did Abijah not have an accession year? One cannot be certain, but, perhaps, Rehoboam died toward the end of the year and by the time Abijah became king, the new year had already started. After Abijah reigned for three years (I Kings 15:2), Asa replaced him and he began his reign in the twentieth year of Jeroboam (I Kings 15:9-10). In this case, Asa did have an accession year. If Asa did not have an accession year, then he would have come to the throne in Jeroboam's twenty-first year. A diagram might make these things a little clearer (ac = accession year).

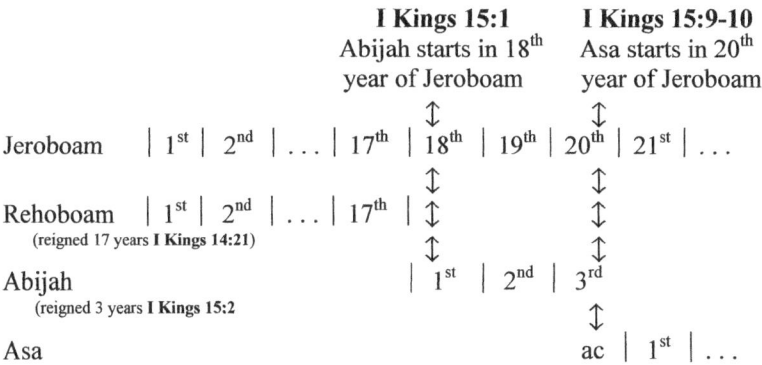

The above diagram illustrates that (1) Rehoboam started his reign in the same year as Jeroboam; (2) Rehoboam reigned for seventeen years; (3) Abijah then reigned for three years; and (4) Asa came to the throne in the twentieth year of Jeroboam, which year was Asa's accession year. In

Chapter 9 — I Kings

other words, the above diagram demonstrates that Abijah did not have an accession year, whereas Asa did.

Conclusion

The chronological factors of calendar, accession versus non-accession, and tabulation of years will assist the student in coming to grips with some of the apparent chronological difficulties between the kings. But even with these principles in hand, the student will have to invest much time in study, thought, and prayer. Matters such as apparent chronological problems are not easily answered in one or two sentences. Actually, to state the apparent problem in such cases is not always easy. If one does not understand the answers, then a suggestion is to read the answers again and even again. Also, one might try to diagram the situation on a piece of paper, in fact, if one can secure "Chart 5 Kings of the Divided Monarchy" by Floyd Jones, he may find that very helpful. The chart will serve as a road map; these answers will serve as a verbal explanation of what is on that map. If the student is still at a loss to figure out the answer, let him meditate further with the full assurance that based upon the promises of Scripture no real error is present at all.

I KINGS 2:11

See discussion under II Samuel 15:7.

I KINGS 4:26 AND II CHRONICLES 9:25

The Passages

I Kings 4:26 states, "And Solomon had forty thousand stalls of horses for his chariots, and twelve thousand horsemen."

II Chronicles 9:25 states, "And Solomon had four thousand stalls for horses and chariots, and twelve thousand horsemen; whom he bestowed in the chariot cities, and with the king at Jerusalem."

Chapter 9 — *I Kings*

The Apparent Problem

Kings states, "Solomon had forty thousand stalls," whereas Chronicles says, "Solomon had four thousand stalls."

The *Word Biblical Commentary* for II Chronicles 9:25 states, "The diversity and interrelatedness of the variants suggests a basic difficulty in the history of transmission, such that it is not possible to speak with confidence regarding the original text."[545] In other words, according to *Word Biblical Commentary* these verses have lost all authority; however, Jesus teaches otherwise (John 10:35).

Henry Morris, in *The Defender's Study Bible*, writes, "This number is given as 'four thousand stalls' in II Chronicles 9:25. This is best explained as a copyist error."[546] But how can this apparent problem be "best explained as a copyist error" when to accept such an explanation is not to receive, believe, and hear the promise of Jesus in Matthew 5:18? Leon Wood asserts, "The figure of 40,000 in I Kings 4:26 must be a scribal error in view of the figure of 4,000 in II Chron. 9:25 and the fact that 1,400 chariots [II Chronicles 1:14] suggests 4,000 horses, not 40,000."[547] Herein Wood and Morris are in agreement with a commentary done by The Order of St. Benedict when it incorrectly states: " 'Forty thousand stalls' may be a copyist's error for 'four thousand'."[548]

Concerning I Kings 4:26, Cogan, in *The Anchor Bible*, states:

> The inflated numbers employed here with reference to Solomon's horses and stalls, and later concerning the gold received as tribute (cf. 10:14), reflect a literary fashion similar to one employed in Assyrian royal inscriptions in which impossibly high numbers of booty and prisoners, as well as enemy dead, are recorded.[549]

---

[545] Raymond B. Dillard, *2 Chronicles*, vol. 15 of *Word Biblical Commentary*, ed. David A. Hubbard and Glenn W. Barker (Waco, TX: Word Books, Publisher, 1987), 74.

[546] Henry Morris, 391.

[547] Wood, 292.

[548] Jerome T. Walsh, *BERIT OLAM Studies in Hebrew Narrative & Poetry: I Kings*, ed. David W. Cotter (Collegeville, MN: The Liturgical Press, 1996), 88. That this commentary is connected with The Order of St. Benedict is evident from the copyright data on page ii, which states, "© 1996 by The Order of St. Benedict, Inc., Collegeville, Minnesota."

[549] Mordechai Cogan, *I Kings: A New Translation with Introduction and Commentary in The Anchor Bible* (NY: Doubleday & Company, Inc., 2000), 214.

In other words, Cogan regards the Bible as no better than other ancient records! While Cogan is wrong, yet his comment is insightful. When others treat *forty thousand* in I Kings 4:26 with suspicion, as does *Word Biblical Commentary, The Defender's Study Bible*, and Wood, are they not also treating this portion of the Bible like any other ancient literature? Are they not acting as if the preserved, inspired Words of the Living God are no better than Assyrian royal inscriptions?

David Cloud writes:

> Many commentators, because of the seeming discrepancy, claim there is a copyist's mistake here in Kings. . . . This is a rejection of the God-honored inspired Hebrew text for the sake of eliminating a SUPPOSED discrepancy. We reject this. To reject the Masoretic Hebrew text which was so diligently preserved by the Jews and which became the foundation of Bibles throughout the world until recent times, is to reject the preserved Word of God for novelties. If "some Septuagint" manuscripts are to be preferred above the Hebrew text (of which the Septuagint is a mere translation), there is no end to the novelties which can be introduced into the Old Testament. Since no one can PROVE that there is an error in the Hebrew text of I Kings 4:26, but can only ASSUME that there is a mistake, we refuse to accept the critic's judgment. We believe there is an answer for this apparent discrepancy just as there is for hundreds of others in the Bible.[550]

Amen, it is always best to hear, that is, to receive and to believe, what the preserved text says.

A Solution

A solution to this apparent problem relies on a careful reading of the verses. Kings speaks of "forty thousand stalls of horses for his chariots," whereas Chronicles speaks of "four thousand stalls for horses and chariots." In other words, Kings speaks of the number of horse stalls, the horses of which were used for Solomon's chariots, whereas Chronicles speaks of horse/chariot stalls. This understanding leads to the conclusion that either Solomon had two different facilities, one only having horse stalls and the other having horse/chariot stalls; or that each horse/chariot stall was further divided into ten horse stalls, therefore, 10 X 4,000 horse/chariot stalls = 40,000 horse stalls. That there were divisions of ten is something this book has demonstrated earlier (Exodus 18:21; Deuter-

---

[550] Cloud, 61.

Chapter 9 — *I Kings*

onomy 1:15; II Samuel 8:4 cf. with I Chronicles 18:4; II Samuel 10:18 cf. with I Chronicles 19:18).

Concerning Wood's contention that forty thousand horses would be too many for only one thousand four hundred chariots, Solomon had far more horses than he needed. Just as Solomon multiplied wives to himself (I Kings 11:3) contrary to God's command (Deuteronomy 17:17), so he sinned by multiplying horses to himself, which also violated God's command (Deuteronomy 17:16). That Solomon multiplied horses to himself is evident not only from I Kings 4:26 but also from other verses. Solomon was regularly given gifts of horses (I Kings 10:25); "gathered together chariots and horsemen" (I Kings 10:26); and "had horses brought out of Egypt" (I Kings 10:28), as well as "out of all lands" (II Chronicles 9:28). In light of this activity, it is not surprising that Solomon would have "forty thousand stalls of horses" (I Kings 4:26), just as the Bible declares. Let everyone receive, believe, and hear these numbers.

I KINGS 5:11 AND II CHRONICLES 2:10

The Passages

I Kings 5:11 states, "And Solomon gave Hiram twenty thousand measures of wheat *for* food to his household, and twenty measures of pure oil: thus gave Solomon to Hiram year by year."

II Chronicles 2:10 states, "And, behold, I will give to thy servants, the hewers that cut timber, twenty thousand measures of beaten wheat, and twenty thousand measures of barley, and twenty thousand baths of wine, and twenty thousand baths of oil."

The Apparent Problem

The Pulpit Commentary writes: "This passage [II Chronicles 2:10] is hard to reconcile with what is said in I Kings v. 11."[551]

The *English Standard Version*, abandoning the Hebrew and following the LXX, changes "twenty measures of pure oil" to "20,000 cors of beaten oil."

---

[551] P. C. Barker, *II Chronicles* in vol. 6 of *The Pulpit Commentary*, 21.

Chapter 9 *I Kings*

A Solution

The Pulpit Commentary further states: "This passage [II Chronicles 2:10] is hard to reconcile with what is said in I Kings v. 11; but meantime it is not certain that it needs to be reconciled with it. It is possible that the two passages are distinct."[552] And indeed this is the solution. While the passages sound similar, they are speaking of two different accountings. I Kings 5:11 refers to the payment to Hiram, whereas II Chronicles 2:10 refers to the payment to Hiram's servants.

I KINGS 5:15-16 AND II CHRONICLES 2:2, 17-18

The Passages

I Kings 5:15-16 states, "And Solomon had threescore and ten thousand that bare burdens, and fourscore thousand hewers in the mountains; beside the chief of Solomon's officers which *were* over the work, three thousand and three hundred, which ruled over the people that wrought in the work."

II Chronicles 2:2, 17-18 states, "And Solomon told out threescore and ten thousand men to bear burdens, and fourscore thousand to hew in the mountain, and three thousand and six hundred to oversee them." "And Solomon numbered all the strangers that *were* in the land of Israel, after the numbering wherewith David his father had numbered them; and they were found an hundred and fifty thousand and three thousand and six hundred. And he set threescore and ten thousand of them *to be* bearers of burdens, and fourscore thousand *to be* hewers in the mountain, and three thousand and six hundred overseers to set the people a work."

The Apparent Problem

While both Kings and Chronicles agree on the number of burden-bearers (70,000) and on the number of hewers (80,000); Kings lists three thousand and three hundred (3,300) "officers which were over the work," whereas Chronicles lists "three thousand and six hundred [3,600] overseers."

---

[552] Ibid.

Chapter 9 — *I Kings*

Jamieson states, "There is no way of reconciling these discrepancies, except by supposing there is an error in the numerical letters, which copyists were extremely liable to commit."[553] Such a suggestion by Jamieson puts him in the same camp with *A Catholic Commentary on Holy Scripture*, which states, "Kg [Kings] in MT [Masoretic Text] . . ., prob. through the accidental addition of one letter, has 3,300 overseers."[554] But this is not a Biblical way of reconciling the difficulty.

Some Solutions

One possible solution is that Kings speaks of "officers which were over the work . . . which ruled over the people that wrought in the work," whereas Chronicles speaks of "overseers to set the people a work." In other words, Kings and Chronicles count two different groups.

Another possibility is that both Kings and Chronicles are looking at the same group. The extra three hundred that Chronicles mentions were possibly a reserve. "So there were 3600 commissioned for the work, but only 3300 employed at one time; and therefore both computations may fairly stand together."[555] Indeed, the student of Scripture should receive, believe, and hear these numbers.

I KINGS 6:1 AND ACTS 13:18-20

The Passages

I Kings 6:1 states, "And it came to pass in the four hundred and eightieth year after the children of Israel were come out of the land of Egypt, in the fourth year of Solomon's reign over Israel, in the month Zif, which *is* the second month, that he began to build the house of the LORD."

---

[553] Robert Jamieson, *II Chronicles* in part 2, vol. 1, *A Commentary: Critical, Experimental, and Practical*, 524. This quote is in a comment on II Chronicles 8:10 wherein Jamieson links together I Kings 5:16; II Chronicles 2:18; and II Chronicles 8:10. For additional comments on these verses, see comments in this book on I Kings 9:23.

[554] E. F. Sutcliffe, *1 & 2 Paralipomenon* in *A Catholic Commentary on Holy Scripture*, 365.

[555] Poole, 1:661.

Chapter 9 *I Kings*

Acts 13:18-20 states, "And about the time of forty years suffered he their manners in the wilderness. And when he had destroyed seven nations in the land of Chanaan, he divided their land to them by lot. And after that he gave *unto them* judges about the space of four hundred and fifty years, until Samuel the prophet. And afterward they desired a king: and God gave unto them Saul the son of Cis, a man of the tribe of Benjamin, by the space of forty years."

The Apparent Problem

David Cloud presents a good statement of the apparent problem in these verses:

> There appears to be a discrepancy between the dates in these verses. I Kings 6:1 indicates that 480 years transpired from the exodus to the building of Solomon's temple. On the other hand, Acts 13:20 indicates the period of the judges alone lasted about 450 years. If we add to this the period of Israel's wandering in the wilderness (40 years), the period of Joshua (17 years), the period of Samuel and Saul (40 years), the reign of David (40 years), and the first 3 years of Solomon's reign, there would have been roughly 590 years from the Exodus to the building of Solomon's temple.[556]

In referring to *four hundred and fifty years* of Acts 13:20, Lange suggests, "The conjectural reading, three hundred and fifty, appears . . . preferable."[557] Lange is willing to rely on human conjecture instead of on the Christ-approved preserved Hebrew text.

In referring to I Kings 6:1, Haley says, "We may regard the 480 as a numerical error; or with Rawlinson, as 'an interpolation' of a comparatively recent date,"[558] that is, someone added it to the Bible. Farrah states: "In Kings vi. 1 we read 'in the 480th year after the children of Israel were come out of the land of Egypt.' This may possibly be a later gloss."[559] Both Haley and Farrah sound just like the Liberal commentary, *The Inter-*

---

[556] Cloud, 199.

[557] John Peter Lange, *The Book of Judges* in *A Commentary on the Holy Scriptures*, 13.

[558] Haley, 427.

[559] Frederick William Farrar, *The First Book of Kings* (Minneapolis: Klock & Klock, 1981), 150.

preter's Bible, which erroneously says, "The verse is a postexilic addition."[560]

Taking I Kings 6:1 literally poses a problem for some commentators because they reject an early date for the Exodus. *The Expositor's Bible Commentary* makes a good observation:

> If one is willing to accept Scripture as accurate and authoritative and yet is unwilling to accept the early date of the Exodus, then the figure 480 must be understood as an indefinite number indicating a time span of twelve generations, figuring forty years per generation as a literary device. Since in reality a generation might have been a little over twenty years, the real time span would have been much shorter than 480 years. But this is not at all a satisfactory view, since there is nothing in this verse or the context that would lead one to make such an assumption.[561]

In other words, it is not permissible for the Bible interpreter to take the four hundred eighty years figuratively, but he must interpret it literally. The author deliberately chose this quote from *The Expositor's Bible Commentary* because while this commentary defends the number in I Kings 6:1, it questions so many other numbers. Some walk by faith selectively, willing to believe some things, but not all things. The Lord, however, would have His people believe "all that the prophets have spoken" (Luke 24:25).[562]

Henry Morris makes a good statement about I Kings 6:1 in *The Defender's Study Bible*:

> Secular archaeologists dispute the Biblical chronology, as well as the events associated with it. The problems of correlating the events of the exodus and conquest with secular chronology have not yet been fully resolved, but the many uncertainties in secular dating methods certainly do not warrant confidence in them. We can be sure the Biblical record is fully reliable, and will eventually be fully validated.[563]

This is a tremendous statement by Morris.

---

[560] Norman H. Smith, *I Kings* in vol. 3 of *The Interpreter's Bible*, 55.

[561] R. D. Patterson and Herman J. Austel, *I and 2 Kings* in *The Expositor's Bible Commentary*, 62.

[562] I Kings is in the prophets' section of the Hebrew Bible.

[563] Henry Morris, 392. Morris shows the same dichotomy evident in others. The author hopes that those who manifest this dichotomy will decidedly side with Jesus on the text issue.

Chapter 9 — I Kings

Some Solutions

The Period of the Judges

One solution takes *about the space of four hundred and fifty years* in Acts 13:20 to refer to the period of the judges. This first solution has three different variations.

Judges from Moses to Samuel

Judges

The first variation understands *judges* in Acts 13:20 to refer to the time from Moses to Samuel. Acts 13:20 says, "Until Samuel" (ἕως Σαμουήλ). Does this include Samuel? Matthew 1:17 uses a similar expression: *to David* (ἕως Δαβίδ). Matthew 1:17 states: "So all the generations from Abraham to David are fourteen generations." In this case, Matthew lists David as the fourteenth generation in the first group of fourteen generations. In other words, *to David* (ἕως Δαβίδ) includes David. Likewise, *until Samuel* (ἕως Σαμουήλ) can include Samuel. A. T. Robertson states: "*Until Samuel the prophet* (*heōs Samouēl prophētou*). The *terminus ad quem.* He was the last of the judges and the first of the prophets who selected the first king (Saul) under God's guidance."[564] According to Robertson, Acts includes Samuel in the term *judges*. And indeed, he did function as a judge (I Samuel 7:6, 15-17). "Samuel judged Israel all the days of his life" (I Samuel 7:15). Samuel was the last of the judges and the first of the prophets; therefore, one can include him with the judges as well as with the prophets. *Until Samuel* includes Samuel.

The judges went up to and included Samuel. Samuel followed Eli (I Samuel 4:18), who followed the judges of the book of Judges (Judges 2:16-18). But are these all the judges? Consider this: God raised up Moses to deliver the children of Israel out of the hand of Egyptian bondage as "a ruler and a deliverer" (Acts 7:35-36; see also I Samuel 12:8); therefore, he functioned much as a judge. Furthermore, since Joshua replaced Moses and led the children of Israel out and brought them in (Numbers 27:15-23; Deuteronomy 31:23) and caused them to inherit the land (Deuteronomy 1:28; 3:28; 31:7), then Joshua also functioned as a

---

[564] Archibald. Thomas Robertson, *Word Pictures in the New Testament* (Nashville: Broadman Press, 1930), III:188-189.

Chapter 9 *I Kings*

judge. Based on the above analysis, *judges* can include those who ruled over Israel, or parts of Israel, from Moses to Samuel, inclusively.

If Moses is the first judge, and if his judgeship started at the Exodus when he led the children of Israel out of Egypt, then *about the space of four and fifty years* of Acts 13:20 starts at the Exodus. The time of the Exodus would be the same starting point as the 480 years of I Kings 6:1. If Samuel is the last judge, then *about the space of four and fifty years* ends at Samuel's death. The 480 years surpasses Samuel into Saul's remaining reign since he outlived Samuel, and then includes David's reign, and then further includes four years of Solomon's reign. Jones comments that "Samuel's life as a Judge overlaps Saul's reign until almost its end."[565] If Jones is correct, then Saul's reign extended about two years beyond Samuel's death (see last footnote for explanation). After Saul's death, David then reigned for forty years (II Samuel 5:4). Saul's remaining reign, David's reign, and four years of Solomon total forty-six years (2 + 40 + 4 = 46). Subtracting these years from the 480 year figure of I Kings 6:1 results in an amount of about 450 years (480 − 46 = 434 or about 450). *About* (ως) in *about the space of four hundred and fifty years* indicates a rough or rounded off figure, not an exact figure. Therefore, 434 years satisfies the *about the space of four hundred and fifty years* in Acts 13:20.

In David Cloud's statement of the apparent problem with I Kings 6:1 and Acts 13:18-20 (above), Cloud assumes that the wilderness wanderings

---

[565] Jones, 75. Jones arrives at this conclusion by comparing I Samuel 25:1 with I Samuel 27:7. I Samuel 25:1 speaks of Samuel's death at which time "David arose, and went down to the wilderness of Paran." The wilderness of Paran is just south of Judea and southeast of Philistia. "David heard in the wilderness that Nabal did shear his sheep" (I Samuel 25:4). The Bible does not indicate how long David had been in the wilderness before this encounter with Nabal; however, David and his men were with Nabal's shepherds for a period of time during the shearing of the sheep (I Samuel 25:16). Upon Nabal's refusal to provide food for David and his men, David plans to kill Nabal. Abigail intercepts David. On the next day, she informs Nabal of the plot on his life, the news of which causes him to die about ten days later (I Samuel 25:38). This incident with Nabal seems to have taken at least two or three months. After the incident with Nabal, the Ziphites inform Saul concerning David's whereabouts, leading Saul to pursue after David (I Samuel 26). This incident seems to have lasted at least several days. Because of Ziphite incident, David decides to dwell with the Philistines "and the time that David dwelt in the country of the Philistines was a full year and four months" (I Samuel 27:7). At the end of that full year and four months, Saul died in battle (I Samuel 28-31). The above examination of I Samuel 25-31 seems to indicate that the time in between Samuel's death and Saul's death was about two years; therefore, Saul's reign lasted about two years beyond Samuel's life.

and Saul's reign are separate and distinct from the about 450 years. However, the explanation set forth here understands the forty-year wilderness wanderings, as well as thirty-eight years of Saul's forty-year reign, to be included in *about the space of four hundred and fifty years*. The figures in I Kings 6:1 and Acts 13:20 are in agreement if *judges* refers to the time from Moses to Samuel inclusively.

After That

But a question arises concerning *after that* (μετὰ ταῦτα) in Acts 13:20: "And after that he gave *unto them* judges about the space of four hundred and fifty years." From a casual reading of Acts 13 *after that* seemingly refers to immediately after the events in Acts 13:19, namely, the destroying of seven nations in the land of Canaan and the dividing of the land by lot, which took place during the days of Joshua (Joshua 18:10; 23:4). However, the explanation set forth here understands *after that* to refer to the events after Acts 13:17, namely, God's choosing Israel, God's exalting them in Egypt, and God's bringing them out of Egypt. Can *after that* have such a sense? Normally, the Bible uses *after that* in a strict chronological fashion, that is, after one event another event happens, though there may be some time between the first event and the second event (Mark 16:12; Luke 5:27; 10:1; 12:4; 17:8; 18:4; John 3:22; 5:1, 14; 6:1; 7:1; 13:7; 21:1; Acts 7:7; 15:16; 18:1; Hebrews 4:8; I Peter 1:11; Revelation 1:19; 4:1; 7:1, 9; 9:12; 15:5; 18:1; 19:1; 20:3). For example, John 5:1 says, "After this (μετὰ ταῦτα) there was a feast of the Jews, and Jesus went up to Jerusalem." Possibly, from the end of John 4 to the beginning of John 5, some time had elapsed. *After that* does not necessarily indicate that something took place immediately after something else, but that the event occurred after something else chronologically.

Other Than Chronological?

If Acts 13:20 uses *after that* in a strict chronological sense, then the first solution fails. A couple of questions then arise: (1) can *after that* have a sense other than a strict chronological sense; and (2) if so, does the Bible ever use *after that* in such a way? The answer to the first question is yes. *After that* in the Greek is μετὰ ταῦτα. Ταῦτα is the neuter plural of οὗτος. Liddell and Scott state that οὗτος sometimes "indicates that which is not really nearest, but most important."[566] While they give no Biblical

---

[566] Henry George Liddell and Robert Scott, *A Greek-English Lexicon*, 9th ed., revised Henry Stuart Jones (Oxford: At the Clarendon Press, 1951), 2:1276.

example, yet the possibility exists for ταῦτα to refer to the most important item in a list, as opposed to the nearest; therefore, *after that* can have a sense other than a strict chronological sense. As this applies to Acts 13:20 and the list of events in verses 17 to 20, if the Exodus, wherein God brought Israel out of Egypt "with an high arm" (Acts 13:17), is the most important item in the list, then *after that* in Acts 13:20 could refer to after the Exodus, instead of after the events in verse 19. Consequently, *about the space of four hundred and fifty years* starts after the Exodus, instead of after the division of the land of Canaan.

Biblical?

An answer to the second question (does the Bible ever use *after that* in such a way?) comes from Leon Morris who, in comments on John 19, observes that μετὰ ταῦτα (after that) is not always used in a strict chronological sense. John 19 includes the account of Joseph requesting the body of Jesus wherein the chapter lists a sequence of events: (1) vs. 30 Jesus gives up the ghost; (2) vs. 31 the Jews beseech Pilate that the legs of the crucified be broken; (3) vs. 32 the soldiers break the legs of the thieves; and (4) vss. 33, 34 the soldiers do not break the legs of Jesus, but pierce His side in fulfillment of various prophecies (vss. 35-37). Then John 19:38 says, "And after this (μετὰ ταῦτα) Joseph of Arimathaea, being a disciple of Jesus, but secretly for fear of the Jews, besought Pilate that he might take away the body of Jesus: and Pilate gave *him* leave. He came therefore, and took the body of Jesus." Leon Morris comments on this usage of μετὰ ταῦτα:

> The expression does not appear to denote strict chronological sequence and accordingly does not necessarily place Joseph's approach to Pilate immediately after the incident with the spear. It may mean that Joseph went to Pilate as soon as Jesus' death appeared imminent, or perhaps had taken place.[567]

Here then is possible Biblical evidence that μετὰ ταῦτα does not always denote strict chronological sequence. Furthermore, Morris' understanding agrees with Liddell and Scott's statement that ταῦτα sometimes refers to what is most important, as opposed to what is nearest.

---

[567] Leon Morris, *The Gospel According to John* in *The New International Commentary of the New Testament*, ed. Ned B. Stonehouse, F. F. Bruce, and Gordon Fee (Grand Rapids: Eerdmans, 1995), 728.

Although Morris does not elaborate on why he thinks that μετὰ ταῦτα does not denote strict chronological sequence in John 19:38, yet a study of the parallel passages suggests a few reasons. Matthew 27:57-58 states, "When the even was come, there came a rich man of Arimathaea, named Joseph, who also himself was Jesus' disciple: he went to Pilate, and begged the body of Jesus. Then Pilate commanded the body to be delivered." The Jews had two evenings and used *even* ('οψίας) for both. The first evening went "from three to six o'clock, the second from six until night. Jesus died at three o'clock [Matthew 27:45-50], and the evening that Matthew has in mind is the first."[568] The death of Jesus and the start of the first evening occurred at about the same time at which time Joseph went to Pilate. Ryle states, "It is almost certain that he [Joseph] must have been near the cross at three o'clock, when our Lord gave up the ghost, or else how could he have known of His death, and had time to think of burying Him?"[569] It seems that Joseph went to Pilate soon after the death of Christ, shortly after three o'clock.

The Gospel of Mark adds a couple of important details. Mark 15:42-43 states, "And now when the even was come, because it was the preparation, that is, the day before the sabbath, Joseph of Arimathaea, an honourable counsellor, which also waited for the kingdom of God, came, and went in boldly unto Pilate, and craved the body of Jesus." Mark uses *now* (ἤδη) in the expression *and now when the even was come*. About ἤδη, Wuest says, "Omitted by Mt., but important, as indicating that the business Joseph had on hand—that of obtaining and using permission to take down and bury the body of Jesus—must be gone about without delay."[570] The reason he must hasten is that the even was now come, that is, the first even had already started. Joseph, then, had less than three hours before six o'clock and the start of the Sabbath (John 19:31) to go to Pilate, obtain Pilate's permission to take the body, take the body off the cross, wrap it in linen clothes with spices, and place it in the sepulchre (John 19:40-42).

Mark also mentions Pilate's amazement about Jesus already being dead (Mark 15:44-45). Herein Schilder writes:

---

[568] R. C. H. Lenski, *The Interpretation of St. Matthew's Gospel* (Minneapolis: Augsburg Publishing House, 1963), 1135-1136.

[569] J. C. Ryle, *Expository Thoughts on John* (Carlisle, PA: The Banner of Truth Trust, 1986), 3:382.

[570] Kenneth Wuest, *Mark in the Greek New Testament* (Grand Rapids: Eerdmans, 1975), 285-286.

Chapter 9 *I Kings*

> Very likely he [Joseph] applied to Pilate immediately, or at least very soon, after the Saviour died. For we read that Pilate was surprised to learn that Jesus died already. Hence the official request of the Jews to the effect that the victims be hurried to death by means of the crurifragium [John 19:31] had not yet been entered, or had been so recently granted that Pilate could not yet expect that it had been carried out. Or, if the request for the crurifragium had already been entered, we can be sure that the report had not yet come in.[571]

In other words, because of Mark 15:44-45, Schilder places Joseph's request for the body of Jesus either (1) before the request of the Jews for the legs to be broken; or (2) before the carrying out of the Jews' request; or (3) before the report had come in. The first two possibilities clearly place Joseph with Pilate before the piercing of Christ's side by the soldier (John 19:34). Concerning the third possibility, Mark states that Pilate, in Joseph's presence, needed confirmation of Jesus' death (Mark 15:44), which confirmation came from the spear being thrust into Jesus' side (John 19:34). Schilder writes:

> But when they [the soldiers] approach Jesus, they immediately see that He has already died. In His case the brutal instrument was no longer necessary. However, they had to have official evidence to show that He actually was dead; after all, it was just possible that a breath of life still stirred in Him. Hence, in order to put an end to all uncertainty, one of the soldiers takes a spear, and thrusts it into Jesus' side.[572]

Therefore, the third possibility also places Joseph with Pilate before the spear piercing. All of this lends support to Morris' contention that μετὰ ταῦτα in John 19:38 is not referring to strict chronological sequence. This is an interesting possibility; however, the author is aware that not all will accept it.[573] If, however, *after that* in Acts 13:20 refers to what is most

---

[571] K. Schilder, *Christ Crucified*, 3d ed. (Minneapolis: Klock & Klock, 1978), 553.

[572] Ibid., 547.

[573] One of the weaknesses with the above view is that the meaning assigned to μετὰ ταῦτα is not its usual meaning. Bible students, however, use a similar type of explanation in explaining Acts 2:38: "Then Peter said unto them, Repent, and be baptized every one of you in the name of Jesus Christ for (εἰς) the remission of sins, and ye shall receive the gift of the Holy Ghost." Usually, εἰς means *into* or *unto*, but here many Fundamentalists adopt the meaning *because of*. Support for such an interpretation comes from Matthew 12:41 and Philippians 4:16 where εἰς means *because of*. However, a response to understanding μετὰ ταῦτα in a way other than its usual meaning is that in Matthew 12:41 εἰς clearly means *because of* whereas in John 19:38 an alternate meaning for μετὰ ταῦτα is not as clear. H. A. W. Meyer retains the sense of strict chronological sequence for μετὰ ταῦτα in

Chapter 9 *I Kings*

important as opposed to what is nearest, then *about the space of four hundred and fifty years* could have started at the Exodus and be in complete harmony with I Kings 6:1.

Judges from Othniel to Eli

Matthew Henry gives another variation on *about the space of four and hundred and fifty years* referring to the judges:

> The government of the judges, from the death of Joshua to the death of Eli, was just *three hundred and thirty-nine years,* but it is said to be [ōs] as it were *four hundred and fifty years,* because the years of their servitude to the several nations that oppressed them, though really they were included in the years of the judges, are yet mentioned in the history as if they had been distinct from them. Now these, all put together, make *one hundred and eleven years,* which added to the *three hundred and thirty nine,* make them *four hundred and fifty;* as so many, though not really so many.[574]

A diagram of Henry's suggestion is as follows:

    8 years serving Chushanrishathaim (Judges 3:8);

    40 years of rest under Othniel (Judges 3:11);

    18 years serving Eglon (Judges 3:14);

    80 years of rest under Ehud (Judges 3:30);

    20 years of oppression under Sisera (Judges 4:1-3);

    40 years of rest under Deborah (Judges 5:31);

    7 years under Midian (Judges 6:1);

    40 years of rest under Gideon (Judges 8:28);

    3 years of Abimelech reigning (Judges 9:22);

    23 years of Tola (Judges 10:1-2);

John 19:38, believing that Joseph went to Pilate after the spear piercing; however, he fails to consider Matthew 27:57-58 and Mark 15:42-43, which seem to indicate that Joseph went to Pilate soon after Jesus expired (Heinrich August Wilhelm Meyer, *Critical and Exegetical Handbook to the Gospel of John,* trans. from the 5th German edition by William Urwick, ed. Frederick Crombie (Edinburgh: T & T Clark, 1874), 2:363-364).

[574] Matthew Henry, *Acts to Revelation* in vol. 6 of *Matthew Henry's Commentary,* 133.

Chapter 9 — I Kings

22 years under Jair (Judges 10:3);

18 years of vexing by the Philistines (Judges 10:8);

6 years of Jephthah (Judges 12:7);

7 years of Ibzan (Judges 12:8-9);

10 years of Elon (Judges 12:11);

8 years of Abdon (Judges 12:13-14);

40 years under Philistines (Judges 13:1);

20 years of Samson (Judges 15:20; 16:31); and

40 years of Eli (I Samuel 4:18).

If one were to total the sum of the servitudes and deliverances individually, he would arrive at 450 years, which though they overlapped,[575] were, according to Henry, as 450 consecutive years though not actually 450 years.

Henry's interpretation hinges on the meaning of *about the space of* (ὡς), which can mean "as if it were."[576] However, the author was unable to find a place where the Bible uses ὡς with numbers in the same sense as Henry poses. As the author examined 492 uses of ὡς in 433 verses he found that when the Bible uses ὡς with numerical quantities (Mark 5:13; 8:9; Luke 2:37; 8:42; John 1:39; 6:19; 11:18; 21:8; Acts 1:15; 5:7; 7:23; 13:18; 21:27; 25:14; 27:27; Revelation 8:1), it does not use ὡς in a com-

---

[575] The overlapping of these years is something that Henry admits in the above quote. Jones well demonstrates that these servitudes and deliverances overlapped (Jones, 73-98). One convincing evidence of the overlapping of these years is this: the sum of the years from the servitude under Chushanrishathaim to the start of Jephthah's judgeship is 319; however, Jephthah states that from the year before Israel entered Canaan to the start of his judgeship only 300 years had elapsed (Judges 11:26). The 300 years not only includes all the servitudes and judges up to Jephthah, but also all the events of the book of Joshua as well as those of Judges 1 and 2. Clearly, some overlapping of years occurred. Jack Moorman, who does not accept an overlapping of these years, suggests that Jephthah's calculation excluded some years when Israel did not have "possession of the eastern regions"; however, when Moorman excludes these years, he can only "come very close to the figure of 300 years" (Jack Moorman, *Bible Chronology: The Two Great Divides* (Collingswood, NJ: The Bible for Today, n.d.), 34). Moorman's calculations result in a period of 303 years, instead of 300 years; therefore, the author does not follow Moorman's line of reasoning.

[576] Zodhiates, 5613.

parative sense except in one place (II Peter 3:8), and in that one place the Bible explicitly states the comparison. II Peter 3:8 says, "But, beloved, be not ignorant of this one thing, that one day *is* with the Lord as (ὡς) a thousand years, and a thousand years as (ὡς) one day." Here the Bible uses ὡς twice to explicitly compare a day to a thousand years and a thousand years to a day. But there is a major difference between II Peter 3:8 and Acts 13:20. II Peter 3:8 explicitly states the comparison, that is, the two quantities it is comparing, *one day* and *a thousand years*, it clearly states. If, however, the Bible makes a comparison in Acts 13:20, it states only one quantity, that is, *four hundred and fifty years*. Acts 13:20 does not follow the same pattern as II Peter 3:8. In fact, when the Bible uses ὡς in a comparison, the two items it always states the two items it is comparing. For example, Acts 8:32, "He was led as (ὡς) a sheep to the slaughter"; Romans 9:27, "Though the number of the children of Israel be as (ὡς) the sand of the sea"; and I Thessalonians 5:2, "The day of the Lord so cometh as (ὡς) a thief in the night." If Acts 13:20 uses ὡς in a comparative sense, then one might expect the verse to say, "And after that he gave unto them judges for three hundred forty years which were as four hundred fifty years." But it does not say this; therefore, Henry's explanation of this apparent difficulty meets with a difficulty. David Cloud after quoting the above comment by Henry writes, "To our minds, this does not completely solve the problem, but it is the best attempt we have seen."[577]

Another problem with Henry's explanation is that it fails to include Samuel in its reckoning. Samuel should be included in the judges since he "judged Israel all the days of his life" (I Samuel 7:15). Despite these shortcomings, at least Henry attempted a God-honoring solution and the author commends him for that.

---

[577] Cloud, 200, no citation for the Henry quote. Earlier Cloud quotes Barnes: " 'There is reason to believe that that which is here mentioned was the common chronology of his [Paul's] time. It accords remarkably with that which is used by Josephus' " (Cloud, 200, no citation given for the Barnes quote). But Josephus' chronology was incorrect wherein he states that from the Exodus to Solomon was 592 years (Antiquities, VII, iii, 1), whereas I Kings 6:1 states that it was 480 years. To suggest that Paul may have followed the common and incorrect chronology of his time suggests that the inspired record of Acts transmits an error in chronology. This, however, is impossible since God's Word is truth (John 17:17).

Chapter 9 *I Kings*

Redemption Time

Jack Moorman presents a third variation of the first solution, a variation that *The Companion Bible* and *Dake's Bible* also present.[578] Moorman does not believe that the years of the judges and servitudes to various nations overlapped, therefore, he simply adds the years to total exactly 450 years thereby satisfying Acts 13:20.[579] But if the period of the judges is 450 years, then how does this reconcile with the 480 years of I Kings 6:1 which goes from the Exodus to Solomon's fourth year? According to Moorman, the actual number of years from the Exodus to Solomon's fourth year is 611 years,[580] but this conflicts with the Bible's statement that this time was only 480 years. To handle this difficulty Moorman suggests that the quantity 480 years in I Kings 6:1 is not actual time, but redemption time, wherein "the years out of fellowship are not counted."[581]

This author commends Moorman's desire not to tamper with the text, however, several problems arise from his solution. First, it is debatable whether exactly 450 years satisfies Acts 13:20 since Acts 13:20 states, "About four hundred and fifty years." The fact that Scripture uses *about* seemingly indicates that Acts 13:20 presents a rounded off figure, not an exact figure.[582] Second, Moorman's solution fails to include Samuel with the judges though "Samuel judged Israel all the days of his life" (I Samuel 7:15). Third, it seems that some overlapping between the servitudes and judgeships did occur as well as an overlap between Samuel and Saul (see previous discussion along with accompanying footnotes). Fourth, while Moorman states that "reading through Judges and I Samuel would never lead us to suspect that they [overlaps] exist,"[583] is not this same criticism true of his understanding of the 480 years? Who would suspect in reading I Kings 6:1 that Scripture uses "redemption time"? But further, the author begs to differ with Moorman's assessment that from reading through

---

[578] Jack Moorman, *Bible Chronology: The Two Great Divides* (Collingswood, NJ: The Bible for Today, n.d.), 26.

[579] Ibid., 29.

[580] Ibid., 26.

[581] Moorman, 40. See also pages 7-9.

[582] Interestingly, where Scripture does present an exact figure in Judges 11:26 of 300 years, Moorman allows for an amount which is "very close to the figure of 300 years" (Moorman, 34).

[583] Moorman, 39.

Chapter 9 — *I Kings*

Judges and I Samuel, one would never suspect that overlaps exists. Indeed, a careful reading of Judges 11:26 and I Samuel 25-31 reveals that there were overlaps (again, see previous discussion along with accompanying footnotes).

The Period before the Judges

A second solution understands *about the space of four hundred and fifty years* in Acts 13:20 to refer to the period before the judges with the judges starting in the book of Judges as opposed to including Moses and Joshua. Jones best presents this view. He understands *about the space of four hundred and fifty years* to refer to the 400 years of affliction (Acts 13:17; cf. Acts 7:6); the 40 years of wandering in the wilderness (Acts 13:18); and approximately "7 years of war until the actual distribution of the land (vs. 19 [of Acts 13]) totaling 447 years."[584] Acts 13:20, then,

> is a parenthetic remark summing the years from verse 17 up to the time of the division of the land after the defeat of the seven nations that dwelt in Canaan. This means that the twentieth verse is not telling us the duration of the period in which God gave Israel judges, rather it is telling us when they were given. Thus the first part of this verse is referring to the first part of the seventeenth, to the time when "the God of this people of Israel chose our fathers."[585]

Jones says that the above "interpretation is well substantiated by the literal reading in the Greek of verses 19 and 20 (cp. Acts 7:6): 'And having destroyed nations seven in [the] land of Canaan, he gave by lot to them their land. And after these things about years four hundred and fifty he gave judges until Samuel the prophet.'"[586] That is, *after these things* or *after that* in the *Authorized Version* refers to the events listed in verses 17 to 19, which events took *about years four hundred and fifty*, after which God gave judges to Israel. Jones also states:

---

[584] Jones, 77. The figure of 7 years for the conquering and distribution of the land is figured thusly: Caleb's age at Kadesh was 40 (Joshua 14:7); the number of years left to the wilderness wanderings at that point was 38 (Numbers 10:11-12; 13:17-20; 14:45; 21:12; Deuteronomy 2:14); therefore, Caleb's age at the time he crossed the Jordan River was 78. Caleb's age when the land was divided was 85 (Joshua 11:23; 14:10); therefore, it took 7 years to conquer and divide the land (85 − 78 = 7).

[585] Ibid.

[586] Ibid., 78.

Chapter 9 — *1 Kings*

Neither should the reader have undue concern over this forthright solution as though it were merely the desperate resolution of a single individual. Over a decade after making this determination, the author learned that in his annotations upon difficult texts, Sir Norton Knatchbull had reached similar conclusions as had Calmet and others.[587]

Adam Clarke writes on Acts 13:20:

> This is a most difficult passage, and has been termed by Scaliger, *Crux Chronologorum*. The apostle seems here to contradict the account in 1 Kings 6:1. . . .
>
> Sir Norton Knatchbull, in his annotations upon difficult texts, has considered the various solutions proposed by learned men of the difficulty before us; and concludes that the words of the apostle should not be understood as meaning how long God gave them judges, but when he gave them; and therefore proposes that the first words of this verse, και μετα ταυτα, ως ετεσι τετρακοσιοις και πεντηκοντα [and after that about years four hundred and fifty], should be referred to the words going before, Acts 13:17, that is, to the time when the God of the children of Israel chose their fathers.
>
> Now this time wherein God may properly be said to have chosen their fathers, about 450 years before he gave them judges, is to be computed from the birth of Isaac, in whom God may properly be said to have chosen their fathers; for God, who had chosen Abraham out of all the people of the earth, chose Isaac at this time out of the children of Abraham, in whose family the covenant was to rest. To make this computation evident, let us observe that from the birth of Isaac to the birth of Jacob are 60 years; from thence to their going into Egypt, 130; from thence to the exodus, 210; from thence to their entrance into Canaan, 40; from that to the division of the land (about which time it is probable they began to settle their government by judges) 7 years; which sums make 447: viz. $60 + 130 + 210 + 40 + 7 = 447$. And should this be reckoned from the year before the birth of Isaac, when God established his covenant between himself and Abraham, and all his seed after him, Genesis 17:19, at which time God properly chose their fathers, then there will be 448 years, which brings it to within two years of the 450, which is sufficiently exact to bring it within the apostle's ως, about, or nearly.[588]

This solution has much to commend it. First, it takes μετὰ ταῦτα in its usual sense of strict chronological sequence. Second, this solution

---

[587] Ibid.

[588] Adam Clarke, *John Through Acts* in *Clarke's Commentary* in *The Master Christian Library*, version 8 [CD-ROM] (Albany, Or: Ages Software, 1997), 595.

does not have to apply to ὡς a sense that does not fit the syntax of the verse. Third, it does not have to resort to expanding the term *judges* to include Moses and Joshua. Fourth, it retains the reading of the Received Text.[589] And fifth, it harmonizes I Kings 6:1 with *about the space of four hundred and fifty years* of Acts 13:20. *About the space of four hundred and fifty years* starts with the birth of Isaac and goes to the time of the division of the land. *The four hundred and eightieth year* of I Kings 6:1 starts with the Exodus and goes to the fourth year of Solomon. After presenting this solution, Jones states, "Thus all the principal difficulties long associated with this troublesome verse [Acts 13:20] have been removed so that it may be seen to perfectly harmonize with the 480 years of I Kings 6:1."[590] May students of the Bible receive, believe, and hear these numbers.

I KINGS 6:2, 17

The Passages

I Kings 6:2 states, "And the house which king Solomon built for the LORD, the length thereof *was* threescore cubits, and the breadth thereof twenty *cubits*, and the height thereof thirty cubits."

I Kings 6:17 states, "And the house, that *is*, the temple before it, was forty cubits *long*."

The Apparent Problem

I Kings 6:2 states that the length of the temple is sixty cubits, whereas I Kings 6:17 states that it is forty cubits.

---

[589] The Critical Text for Acts 13:20 differs from the Received Text. The Critical Text reads, "ὡς ἔτεσιν τετρακοσίοις καὶ πεντήκοντα. καὶ μετὰ ταῦτα ἔδωκεν κριτὰς ἕως Σαμουὴλ [τοῦ] προφήτουως," that is, "About years four hundred and fifty and after these things He gave judges until Samuel the prophet." Or, as the *New International Version* translates it: "All this took about 450 years. 'After this, God gave them judges until the time of Samuel the prophet.' " A point about the reading of the Critical Text is that the reading of the Textus Receptus is the more difficult reading, yet the editors of the Critical Text did not adopt it, contrary to one of their rules of textual criticism that the more difficult reading is the preferred.

[590] Jones, 78.

# Chapter 9	*I Kings*

A Solution

A solution to this problem is to notice that according to II Chronicles 3:4 the length of the porch of the temple was twenty cubits. Adding the twenty cubits of the porch to the forty cubits of I Kings 6:17, results in sixty cubits (20 cubits for the porch according to II Chronicles 3:4 + 40 cubits for the temple according to I Kings 6:17 = 60 cubits of I Kings 6:2).

I KINGS 7:15 AND II CHRONICLES 3:15

The Passages

I Kings 7:15 states, "For he cast two pillars of brass, of eighteen cubits high apiece: and a line of twelve cubits did compass either of them about."

II Chronicles 3:15 states, "Also he made before the house two pillars of thirty and five cubits high, and the chapter that *was* on the top of each of them *was* five cubits."

The Apparent Problem

The verses speak of the pillars, which Hiram set up in the porch (I Kings 7:21). Kings states that the two pillars were eighteen cubits high, whereas Chronicles states, "He made . . . two pillars of thirty and five cubits high."

J. Barton Payne says, "Their size, as stated in the present MT [Masoretic text], namely, 'thirty-five cubits long,' seems to be the result of a copyist's error."[591] Keil states, "The number 35 evidently arose from a confounding the numeral letters יח = 18 with לה = 35";[592] however, Chapter Three demonstrates that the writers of Scripture did not use letters

---

[591] J. Barton Payne, *1, 2 Chronicles* in *The Expositor's Bible Commentary*, 451.

[592] Keil, *Commentary on the First Book of Kings* in vol. 3 of *Commentary on the Old Testament*, 70. Edward Lewis Curtis and Albert Alonzo Madsen express this same view in *A Critical and Exegetical Commentary on the Books of Chronicles* in *The International Critical Commentary* (Edinburgh: T & T Clark, 1910), 328.

for numbers.[593] *The Pulpit Commentary* after discussing some other solutions states, "It is perhaps likelier that we have here simply a clerical error."[594] But could it be "simply a clerical error" especially in the light of Christ's promises to the contrary (Matthew 5:18; Luke 16:17; John 10:35)? *The Defender's Study Bible* states, "The apparent contradiction can be best attributed to a copyist error in the Chronicles reference."[595] The above sources are just not willing to hear these numbers. In fact, they are all in agreement with *A Catholic Commentary on Holy Scripture* which also refuses to hear the *thirty-five* of II Chronicles 3:15 when it comments on this verse, "They were 18 cubits high."[596]

A Solution

A careful reading of the verses results in a solution. Kings says the two pillars were eighteen cubits high apiece, that is, each pillar by itself was eighteen cubits high. Chronicles, however, does not use *apiece*; therefore, it is possible that Chronicles is looking at the combined height of the pillars as being thirty-five cubits. I Kings 7:15 states that the pillars were cast. Possibly, Hiram made one long mold of thirty-five cubits and then cut it in half to arrive at two pillars of eighteen cubits apiece. If the objection arises that half of thirty-five is not eighteen, but seventeen and a half; it is perfectly permissible to round to the nearest one's digit since the original figure of thirty-five is only accurate to the nearest one's digit itself. Or, as Gill states: "A half cubit in each may be allowed; either for the base or pedestal into which they were put; or the chapter at the top of them, into which they might so such a length."[597] The fact is Bible believers should receive, believe, and hear these numbers.

---

[593] Keil in rejecting the solution this book presents says, "According to Chronicles, they were thirty-five cubits long; which many expositors understand as signifying that the length of the two together was thirty-five cubits, so that each one was only 17 ½ cubits long, for which the full number 18 is substituted in out text. But this mode of reconciling the discrepancy is very improbable" (Keil, *Commentary on the First Book of Kings* in vol. 3 of *Commentary on the Old Testament*, 70). Is not the "solution" of Keil impossible in light of Jesus' words in Matthew 5:18?

[594] Barker, 35.

[595] Henry Morris, 394.

[596] Sutcliffe, *1 & 2 Paralipomenon in A Catholic Commentary on Holy Scripture*, 365.

[597] Gill, *Exposition of the Old & New Testaments*, 2:701.

Chapter 9 — *I Kings*

I KINGS 7:16 AND II KINGS 25:17

The Passages

I Kings 7:16 states, "And he made two chapiters *of* molten brass, to set upon the tops of the pillars: the height of the one chapiter *was* five cubits, and the height of the other chapiter *was* five cubits."

II Kings 25:17 states, "The height of the one pillar *was* eighteen cubits, and the chapiter upon it *was* brass: and the height of the chapiter three cubits; and the wreathen work, and pomegranates upon the chapiter round about, all of brass: and like unto these had the second pillar with wreathen work."

The Apparent Problem

I Kings 7:16 gives the height of the chapiter as five cubits, whereas II Kings 25:17 says it is three cubits.

Haley believes that this is the result of a scribal error.[598] Here are more numbers Haley refuses to hear.

Some Solutions

I Kings 7:16 possibly speaks of the height of the chapiter before it was placed atop the pillar, for it says, "To set upon the tops of the pillars." II Kings 25:17 speaks of the height of the chapiter after it was placed on top of the pillar, for it says, "The chapiter upon it." If this is correct, then the chapiter went over the top of the pillar a distance of two cubits so that only three cubits of the five cubit chapiter was above the original height of the pillar.

Gill offers another explanation:

> The height of the one chapiter was five cubits, and the height of the other chapiter was five cubits"; in 2Ki 25:17 they are said to be but three cubits high; but that is to be understood only of the ornamented part of them, the

---

[598] Haley, 382.

wreathen work and pomegranates on them, as there expressed; here [I Kings 7:16] it includes, with that, the part below unornamented.[599]

Despite what Haley says, the reader of the Bible should hear, that is, receive and believe these numbers.

I KINGS 7:20, 42; II CHRONICLES 4:13; AND JEREMIAH 52:23

The Passages

I Kings 7:20 states, "And the chapiters upon the two pillars *had pomegranates* also above, over against the belly which *was* by the network: and the pomegranates *were* two hundred in rows round about upon the other chapiter."

I Kings 7:42 states, "And four hundred pomegranates for the two networks, *even* two rows of pomegranates for one network, to cover the two bowls of the chapiters that were upon the pillars."

II Chronicles 4:13 states, "And four hundred pomegranates on the two wreaths; two rows of pomegranates on each wreath, to cover the two pommels of the chapiters which *were* upon the pillars."

Jeremiah 52:23 states, "And there were ninety and six pomegranates on a side; *and* all the pomegranates upon the network *were* an hundred round about."

The Apparent Problem

I Kings 7:20 speaks of two hundred pomegranates. I Kings 7:42 and Chronicles speak of four hundred pomegranates. Jeremiah also speaks of ninety and six pomegranates on a side with one hundred round about. It appears that the numbers are not in agreement.

The Pulpit Commentary states, "Some words have evidently dropped out of the Hebrew here. . . . The text, no doubt, originally stood 'two hundred in rows round about the one chapiter, and two hundred in rows

---

[599] Gill, *Exposition of the Old & New Testaments*, 2:701.

Chapter 9   *I Kings*

round about upon the other chapiter.' "[600] However, here is no need to resort to such a suggestion and thereby indirectly question Jesus' promise in Matthew 5:18.

A Solution

I Kings 7:42 says that the total number of pomegranates for both chapiters combined is four hundred. I Kings 7:42 also speaks of two networks, one for each chapiter, and that each network had two rows of pomegranates. In light of this, each network had two hundred pomegranates as I Kings 7:20 presents, and each row had one hundred pomegranates.

The one hundred pomegranates were arranged, according to Jeremiah, with ninety-six on a side. *On a side* in Jeremiah 52:23 is translated from רוּחָה (*rūchah*), which is from רוּחַ (*rūach*), which typically means breath, wind, or spirit.[601] In this case, רוּחָה (*rūchah*) has the directional ה (*h*) at the end of the word, giving it the meaning of windward or breath-ward with the idea that the pomegranates were strung up and suspended in the air. Jeremiah, then, speaks of ninety-six on a side or windward and a hundred in the network. In other words, ninety-six were suspended and the other four of the hundred were one each "at each corner."[602] "From the capital [chapiter] were suspended two strings of technical pomegranates, each string being strung with a hundred of them, four attached at the several quarters, leaving ninety-six in suspension."[603]

But since Jeremiah says, "All the pomegranates upon the network were an hundred" as opposed to two hundred, it could be that over time an entire row of pomegranates had been removed. That various people pillaged the temple from time to time prior to the time of Jeremiah 52 is evident from I Kings 14:26; 15:18; II Kings 12:18; 14:14; 16:8; 18:16. It is quite possible that at one of these times, or at some other time, someone

---

[600] J. Hammond, *The First Book of Kings* in vol. 5 of *The Pulpit Commentary*, 130.

[601] Brown, *A Hebrew and English Lexicon of the Old Testament*, 924-925.

[602] C. W. Edward Neagelsbach, *The Book of the Prophet Jeremiah* in *A Commentary on the Holy Scriptures*, ed. J. P. Lange (New York: Charles Scribner's Sons, 1914), 442.

[603] James A. Montgomery, *A Critical and Exegetical Commentary on The Book of Kings*, ed. Henry Snyder Gehman, in *The International Critical Commentary*, ed. S. R. Driver, A. Plummer, and C. A. Briggs (Edinburgh: T & T Clark, 1951), 171.

removed one of the strings of brass pomegranates from each pillar. Therefore, by Jeremiah's time only one row of one hundred pomegranates made up the entire network, instead of two rows as in Kings.

I KINGS 7:23

The Passage

I Kings 7:23 states, "And he made a molten sea, ten cubits from the one brim to the other: *it was* round all about, and his height *was* five cubits: and a line of thirty cubits did compass it round about."

The Apparent Problem

I Kings 7:23 verse speaks of the molten sea that Hiram made for the temple. II Chronicles 4:2 speaks of the same thing. A scientific problem arises concerning the value for the mathematical quantity π, an irrational number approximately equal to 3.1415926. According to the rules of Geometry, the circumference of a circle equals π times the diameter, that is, $C = \pi \cdot d$. From I Kings 7:23, however, some conclude that the circumference is thirty cubits and the diameter is ten cubits. Putting these values into the formula for circumference and solving for π gives a value for π of 3 instead of 3.1415926.

At this point, some allege that the Bible is in error. R. H. Mounce advocates a limited inerrancy, which is the belief that the Bible is without error in matters of faith, but is possibly erroneous in scientific or historical matters. He thinks that the molten sea is an example of error in the Bible. Mounce says, " 'It would be impossible for a *round* vessel to have a diameter of ten and a circumference of thirty.' "[604] *The Defender's Study Bible* says, "Critics who try to find scientific 'mistakes' in Scripture nearly always settle on this verse as one of their prime examples."[605] In

---

[604] Lindsell, 165, quoting Robert H. Mounce, "Clues to Understanding Biblical Accuracy" in *Eternity* (June 1966), 18.

[605] Henry Morris, 395. The note at this point goes on to answer the critics. It is commendable that *The Defender's Study Bible* defends the Bible here against the critics, but it is lamentable that it fails to defend the Bible against the critics in several other places.

Chapter 9 — *I Kings*

other words, many will not receive, believe, and hear the numbers in I Kings 7:23.

A Solution

A solution to the apparent problem involves a realization that the molten sea had a brim, which was an handbreadth thick (I Kings 7:26; II Chronicles 4:5). As Strouse states:

> Every school boy knows that the circumference of a circle equals the diameter times the constant *pi* (3.1416). Since the diameter of the molten sea was ten cubits, the circumference must really be 31.42 cubits, rather than 30 cubits. However, another factor must be considered, and that is the thickness of the brim, which was "an handbreadth" (v. 5 [of II Chronicles 4]). The apparent error is eliminated when one realizes that the writer gives the measurement for the outer diameter (10), and the measurement for the inner circumference (30), instead of the outer circumference (31.42).[606]

Let everyone receive, believe, and hear these numbers.

I KINGS 7:26 AND II CHRONICLES 4:5

The Passages

I Kings 7:26 states, "And it *was* an hand breadth thick, and the brim thereof was wrought like the brim of a cup, with flowers of lilies: it contained two thousand baths."

II Chronicles 4:5 states, "And the thickness of it *was* an handbreadth, and the brim of it like the work of the brim of a cup, with flowers of lilies; *and* it received and held three thousand baths."

The Apparent Problem

The verse in Kings speaks of the molten sea containing "two thousand baths," whereas Chronicles speaks of it holding "three thousand baths."

---

[606] Strouse, *The Lord God Hath Spoken*, 61.

Sara Japhet states, "The most plausible suggestion is still to regard one of the two numbers, probably the larger, as an error."[607] Concerning II Chronicles 4:5, *The Defender's Study Bible* states, "This could represent a copyist error."[608] Japhet and *The Defender's Study Bible* are in harmony with the wrong comments of *A Catholic Commentary on Holy Scripture*: "The divergence as to its capacity, here [that is, II Chronicles 4:5] 3,000 baths, in Kg [Kings] 2,000 is prob. to be explained by the accidental omission of 'three' in Kg."[609]

J. Barton Payne states, "One should consider the likelihood of accidental corruption by a later scribe."[610] The author has considered "the likelihood of accidental corruption" and rejects such "solutions" to the apparent problems of the Bible, especially in light of the promises of Jesus (Matthew 5:18; John 10:35). It is amazing how quickly commentators bring up the possibility of a scribal error whenever they encounter an apparent problem. This is an easy way out, but it is not at all the way to treat God's Words, which are "purified seven times" (Psalm 12:6).

Some Solutions

Kings might be looking at how much liquid the sea could hold, whereas Chronicles, which has the larger measure, is looking at dry measure, which would allow heaping and a considerable greater quantity for the sea to contain.

Or, another possible solution is "there were two sorts of baths, as of cubits, the one common, the other sacred."[611] "The *bath* is attested

---

[607] Sara Japhet, *I & II Chronicles: A Commentary* (Louisville: Westminster/John Knox Press, 1993), 565.

[608] Henry Morris, 490. Morris goes on to say, "Both statements could be true as they stand. That is, if the sea could receive 'three thousand baths' (a bath was about eighteen gallons), it could certainly contain two thousand" (Ibid.). While Morris offers this explanation which retains the integrity of the Masoretic Text, he still holds open the possibility of a scribal error at this point.

[609] Sutcliffe, *1 & 2 Paralipomenon* in *A Catholic Commentary on Holy Scripture*, 365.

[610] Payne, 453.

[611] Poole, 1:667.

archaeologically as varying locally from 18 to 45 litres."⁶¹² Therefore, it is possible that Scripture uses two different baths for the measurements, wherein Kings uses a bigger bath and Chronicles a smaller one.

Yet, another possible solution involves looking carefully at the words. Kings and Chronicles use different words to describe the amount in the sea. Kings says, "It contained two thousand baths," whereas Chronicles says, "It received and held three thousand baths." In the Hebrew, *contained* of I Kings 7:26 is exactly the same as *held* of II Chronicles 4:5, both being Hiphil imperfect third masculine singular verbs (יָכִיל , *yakil*). But Chronicles has the word *received*, which is a Hiphil participle from חָזַק (*chazaq*) and means "show strength or resolve, . . ., contain, . . ., keep hold of."⁶¹³ Poole says, "2 Chron. iv. 5 . . . speaks of what it could contain if it were filled to the brim, as it is implied in the Hebrew words, which differ from these [in I Kings 7:26], and properly sound thus, *strengthening itself*, (to wit, to receive and hold as much as it could, or being filled to its utmost capacity)."⁶¹⁴ In light of this, the account in Kings speaks of what the molten sea typically contained, whereas the account in Chronicles speaks of its maximum capacity. Furthermore, since the sea's use was "for the priests to wash in" (II Chronicles 4:6), then it is unlikely that it was filled to capacity. Not filling it to capacity would allow the level of water to rise when the priests washed.

Keil takes exception with the quantity of three thousand baths claiming that "the capacity of the vessel, from the dimensions given, could not exceed 2000 baths."⁶¹⁵ Not only does Keil fail to take into account the different standards in bath measurements as pointed out above, but, more importantly, he fails to hear the numbers that are in the preserved Hebrew text. Despite what the commentators say, the child of God should receive, believe, and hear these numbers.

---

⁶¹² Donald J. Wiseman, *I & 2 Kings: An Introduction & Commentary*, vol. 9, *The Tyndale Old Testament Commentaries*, ed. D. J. Wiseman (Downers Grove, IL: InterVarsity Press, 1993), 115.

⁶¹³ VanGemeren, ed., H2616 חָזַק.

⁶¹⁴ Poole, 1:667.

⁶¹⁵ Keil, *Commentary on the First Book of Kings* in vol. 3 of *Commentary on the Old Testament*, 75.

Chapter 9 — I Kings

I KINGS 7:42

See discussion under I Kings 7:20.

I KINGS 9:23 AND II CHRONICLES 8:10

The Passages

I Kings 9:23 states, "These *were* the chief of the officers that *were* over Solomon's work, five hundred and fifty, which bare rule over the people that wrought in the work."

II Chronicles 8:10 states, "And these *were* the chief of king Solomon's officers, *even* two hundred and fifty, that bare rule over the people."

The Apparent Problem

Kings says that there were five hundred and fifty chief of the officers, whereas Chronicles says there were only two hundred fifty.

Japhet writes, "The numerical discrepancy in the passage is probably due to textual corruption, in either one of the two texts."[616] Is this so? Not according to Jesus, for Jesus teaches there are no errors in the preserved Hebrew text (John 17:17).

Some Solutions

Perhaps Kings lists the officers "which bare rule over the people that wrought in the work," whereas Chronicles lists the officers "that bare rule over the people." In other words, there are two different groups of officers ruling over two different groups.

Another possibility is that the larger number in Kings is the total number of officers, including those who were in reserve, whereas Chronicles is the number that ruled at any one time.

---

[616] Japhet, 625.

Chapter 9 — *I Kings*

I KINGS 9:28 AND II CHRONICLES 8:18

The Passages

I Kings 9:28 states, "And they came to Ophir, and fetched from thence gold, four hundred and twenty talents, and brought *it* to king Solomon."

II Chronicles 8:18 states, "And Huram sent him by the hands of his servants ships, and servants that had knowledge of the sea; and they went with the servants of Solomon to Ophir, and took thence four hundred and fifty talents of gold, and brought *them* to king Solomon."

The Apparent Problem

Kings says that 420 talents of gold were brought from Ophir to Solomon, whereas Chronicles lists the amount as 450 talents.

J. Barton Payne writes, "First Kings 9:28 presents a variant reading of '420 talents,' probably due to a scribal confusion."[617] Jamieson writes, "The text in one of these passages is corrupt."[618] Keil states: "The difference between 420 and 450 may be accounted for from the substitution of the numeral letter נ (50) for כ (20)."[619] Among those who wrongly think a scribal error has occurred here is *A Catholic Commentary on Holy Scripture* which states: "The amount of gold obtained was 450 talents, MT [Masoretic Text], 400, Syr [Syriac], 420 Kg [Kings], MT, 120, Kg, LXX(B). The last figure is the most probable."[620] But is it the most probable? *The Anchor Bible*, presenting an ecumenical viewpoint, states:

> *Four hundred and twenty talents that they delivered to King Solomon.* Universally considered to be an exaggerated number, even larger in 2 Chr 8:18: "450"; LXX^B read "120" (favored by many as more reasonable).

---

[617] Payne, 468.

[618] Jamieson, *II Chronicles* in part 2, vol. 2 of *A Commentary*, 525.

[619] Keil, *Commentary on the First Book of Kings* in vol. 3 of *Commentary on the Old Testament*, 104.

[620] Sutcliffe, *1 & 2 Paralipomenon* in *A Catholic Commentary on Holy Scripture*, 366.

But the latter reading looks like an assimilation to the number that appears in I Kgs 9:14 and 10:10 and is not preferable.[621]

At this point *The Anchor Bible* ends its comment and leaves it up in the air as to what is the actual number.

All of these commentators refuse to hear a number and, in so doing, refuse to hear Jesus Who stated that the Hebrew text is correct (John 17:17). Once that text is rejected, it is interesting to see how varied the opinions are. Certainly to reject the preserved text is to abandon certainty and authority. Sadly, Conservatives and Fundamentalists are just one step from this uncertainty.

Some Solutions

One solution involves the possibility that there were two different voyages, albeit, with similar circumstances.

Another solution states, "In all there came to the king four hundred and fifty talents, whereof it seems that thirty talents were allowed by Solomon to Hiram and his men for the voyage, and so there were only four hundred and twenty that came clearly into the treasury."[622]

For those who want to retain the integrity of Scripture and have a mind to do so, there is a way to hear these numbers. And one ought to have a mind to do so especially if he listens to Jesus.

I KINGS 15:33; 16:6-8; AND II CHRONICLES 16:1

The Passages

I Kings 15:33 states, "In the third year of Asa king of Judah began Baasha the son of Ahijah to reign over all Israel in Tirzah, twenty and four years."

---

[621] Cogan, *1 Kings* in *The Anchor Bible*, 306-307. That *The Anchor Bible* is ecumenical is substantiated by a statement on page ii, which says, "THE ANCHOR BIBLE is a project of international and interfaith scope: Protestant, Catholic, and Jewish scholars from many countries contribute individual volumes."

[622] Poole, 1:677.

Chapter 9 — I Kings

I Kings 16:6-8 states, "So Baasha slept with his fathers, and was buried in Tirzah: and Elah his son reigned in his stead. And also by the hand of the prophet Jehu the son of Hanani came the word of the LORD against Baasha, and against his house, even for all the evil that he did in the sight of the LORD, in provoking him to anger with the work of his hands, in being like the house of Jeroboam; and because he killed him. In the twenty and sixth year of Asa king of Judah began Elah the son of Baasha to reign over Israel in Tirzah, two years."

II Chronicles 16:1 states, "In the six and thirtieth year of the reign of Asa Baasha king of Israel came up against Judah, and built Ramah, to the intent that he might let none go out or come in to Asa king of Judah."

The Apparent Problem

Baasha started his reign in the third year of Asa and reigned for twenty-four years (I Kings 15:33), and then he died in Asa's twenty-sixth[623] year (I Kings 16:8). But II Chronicles 16:1 states that Baasha attacked Asa in the thirty-sixth year of Asa. The verses seem to be in conflict.

Haley again advocates a copyist error.[624] *The Pulpit Commentary* states, "For **the six and thirtieth year**, read *six and twentieth*."[625] Keil also accuses the Bible of error: "The statement, 'In the thirty-sixth year of the reign of Asa, Baasha the king of Israel came up against Judah,' is inaccurate, or rather cannot possibly be correct."[626]

Floyd Jones, however, states:

> The individual's reaction upon his being made aware of such a circumstance as this depends solely upon his world view. . . . It does not depend upon the Scriptural statements themselves. The humanistic man centered world view will lead one to the immediate conclusion that an undeniable error exists between the accounts. Unfortunately, . . . many Christians—conservative fundamental evangelical Christians—concur. The true Bibli-

---

[623] There is no problem with Baasha dying in Asa's twenty-sixth year though he started in Asa's third year and reigned for twenty-four years. Baasha's first year was the same as Asa's third year and another twenty-three years added from this point would give Baasha twenty-four years of reign and still have him die in Asa's twenty-sixth year.

[624] Haley, 399.

[625] Barker, *II Chronicles*, 192.

[626] Keil, *The Second Book of the Chronicles* in vol. 3 of *Commentary on the Old Testament*, 623.

onservative fundamental evangelical Christians—concur. The true Biblicist, due to his world view, merely exercises faith in God's many promises to forever preserve His Word, knowing that somehow both statements must be accurate as well as trustworthy—and so they are.[627]

A Solution

A solution lies in determining the starting point of the thirty-six years in II Chronicles 16:1, which mentions "the six and thirtieth year of the reign of Asa." If the thirty-six years start at the division of the united monarchy, instead of when Asa actually first sat on the throne, then a solution is in hand. If such is the case, then Baasha attacked Judah in the thirty-sixth year of the kingdom of Judah, which thirty-sixth year of the kingdom of Judah was the sixteenth year of Asa[628] and the problem is removed.

But is this a proper way to understand II Chronicles 16:1? The word for *reign* (מַלְכוּת, *malkuth*) that II Chronicles 16:1 uses

> is often used even in the post-Exilic books to mean "kingdom" or "realm" . . . (e.g., 2 Chron. 1:1; 11:17; 20:30; Neh. 9:35; Esth. 1:14, etc.). . . . But it is without parallel [used] to refer to the kingdom of a nation as a whole and identify it thus with one particular king who comes later on in the ruling dynasty.[629]

While מַלְכוּת (*malkuth*) can mean kingdom or realm, it can also mean the reign of an individual king as in II Chronicles 15:10, which speaks of "the fifteenth year of the reign (מַלְכוּת, *malkuth*) of Asa." Poole addresses this issue:

> If it be objected that *the reign* or *kingdom of Asa* is otherwise understood of the time of Asa's personal reign, (as I may call it), [II Chronicles] chap. xv. 10; the answer is obvious that there are many instances in Scripture . . . where the same word or phrase is taken differently, and that in the very

---

[627] Jones, 144.

[628] Rehoboam reigned 17 years (II Chronicles 12:13); Ahijah 3 years (II Chronicles 13:2); then the 16th year of Asa is the 36th year of the kingdom (17 + 3 + 16 = 36).

[629] Archer, 225. While Archer makes the above observation, he, nonetheless, rejects it and favors an explanation of a scribal error. A question arises at this point: why would Archer abandon a solution that maintains the integrity of the preserved text in favor of one that questions its integrity? In light of what Jesus said in Matthew 5:18, one should accept a solution that upholds the integrity of the preserved Hebrew text.

same chapter and history. And particularly this variety is elsewhere used, both by sacred and profane writers, in the computation of the years of princes, which are sometimes reckoned from the beginning of their reign, and sometimes from other remarkable times and occurrences.[630]

As far as the Bible using the same word in different senses in close proximity to one another, see this book's discussion under II Samuel 6:23. As far as the Bible computing the years of kings in different ways, see (1) I Samuel 13:1; (2) II Kings 8:26 compared with II Chronicles 22:2; and (3) II Kings 24:8, 12 compared with II Chronicles 36:9. A different way of computing the years of kings answers an objection raised by Dillard in *Word Biblical Commentary*: "Of the hundreds of bits of data for the chronology of the divided monarchy, this would be the only occasion of dating from the schism."[631] While this is the only place where Chronicles dates chronology from the schism, yet, as the above verses attest, it is not the only place where Chronicles dates chronology from different starting points. Dillard's statement that "this would be the only occasion of dating from the schism" is incorrect, for Ezekiel 4:4 and 5 also date from the schism.[632]

Jones, commenting on the solution offered here, writes about another apparent problem that this interpretation solves:

---

[630] Poole, 1:836.

[631] Dillard, 124. Dillard raises a second objection to the years dating from the schism: "It ignores the plain statement of the text that these were the thirty-fifth and thirty-sixth years of Asa's reign" (Dillard, 124). The above discussion answers this objection. Dillard's third objection that "this reconstruction would also play havoc with the Chronicler's theological argument: the foot disease [II Chronicles 16:12] as retribution would come over twenty years after the offense" (Dillard, 124), seems to believe that the foot disease is a punishment for the sin of II Chronicles 16:1-10 that took place in the 36th year since the schism or the 16th year since the start of Asa's reign. But such a connection between the foot disease and the sin is not explicitly stated in the text; however, if there is a connection, then according to Dillard's understanding of the passage, the foot disease came 3 years after the offense. If the punishment came three years after the sin, then why could it not 23 years after? Is there a time limit on when sin is punished? Some sins were not punished until years later, for example, the sin of the Amalekites was not punished until several hundred years after the committing of the sin (I Samuel 15:2).

[632] For a further discussion of Ezekiel 4:4-5, consult the footnotes given under preliminary issues under a solution for II Kings 18:13.

Chapter 9 — I Kings

It completely eliminates the anomalous circumstance in which Baasha otherwise apparently waited 21 entire years before blocking the exodus of his citizens to Judah (II Chr. 14:1; 15:10, 19; and 16:1).[633]

An aftermath of Asa's startling victory over Zerah, the Ethiopian, and his enormous host was that many of the people of Israel deserted that kingdom for Asa and Judah . . . (II Chr. 15:9). Baasha would certainly have lost little time before taking the appropriate measures to insure his borders, thereby halting the southern flow out of Israel. Zerah's invasion took place in the 15th year of Asa (II Chr. 15:10, cp. 14:9) or the 35th year of the kingdom of Judah.[634]

I KINGS 16:8-10

The Passage

I Kings 16:8-10 states, "In the twenty and sixth year of Asa king of Judah began Elah the son of Baasha to reign over Israel in Tirzah, two years. And his servant Zimri, captain of half *his* chariots, conspired against him, as he was in Tirzah, drinking himself drunk in the house of Arza steward of *his* house in Tirzah. And Zimri went in and smote him, and killed him, in the twenty and seventh year of Asa king of Judah, and reigned in his stead."

The Apparent Problem

Since Elah started his reign in the twenty-sixth year of Asa and was killed in the twenty-seventh year of Asa, then some may think that the Bible should state his reign as only one year long (27 − 26 = 1), instead of two years.

---

[633] The anomalous circumstance that Jones speaks of is that some Israelites headed south into Judah in the 15th year of Asa (II Chronicles 15:9, 10); but Baasha did not react until the 36th year of Asa (II Chronicles 16:1). However, this anomalous circumstance disappears when one understands that the 15th year of the reign of Asa was the 15th year of his actual reign, whereas the 36th year of the reign of Asa was the 36th year of the kingdom of Judah which was the 16th year of Asa's actual reign. See discussion in the text.

[634] Jones, 144.

# Chapter 9	*I Kings*

A Solution

A solution is this: Elah's first year of reign occurred in the same year as Asa's twenty-sixth year so that in the year following, that is, the twenty-seventh of Asa, Elah's second year occurred. Elah reigned for part of two years, therefore, the Bible says that he reigned for two years. Elah reigned in Israel where a non-accession-year system was in use (see at beginning of this chapter "Chronological Factors"). Therefore, the Bible reckons the year wherein he came to the throne as his first official year and the next year as his second year.

I KINGS 16:15, 16, 23, 29

The Passages

I Kings 16:15-16 states, "In the twenty and seventh year of Asa king of Judah did Zimri reign seven days in Tirzah. And the people *were* encamped against Gibbethon, which *belonged* to the Philistines. And the people *that were* encamped heard say, Zimri hath conspired, and hath also slain the king: wherefore all Israel made Omri, the captain of the host, king over Israel that day in the camp."

I Kings 16:23 states, "In the thirty and first year of Asa king of Judah began Omri to reign over Israel, twelve years: six years reigned he in Tirzah."

I Kings 16:29 states, "And in the thirty and eighth year of Asa king of Judah began Ahab the son of Omri to reign over Israel: and Ahab the son of Omri reigned over Israel in Samaria twenty and two years."

The Apparent Problems

Two apparent problems are present here. The first problem involves the start of Omri's reign. I Kings 16:15-16 states that Zimri reigned for seven days in the twenty-seventh year of Asa and that after his brief reign Omri was made king, presumably also in the same year. But I Kings 16:23 states that Omri began to reign in the thirty-first year of Asa.

The second problem involves the end of Omri's reign. I Kings 16:23 states that Omri reigned for twelve years and that he began his reign in the thirty-first year of Asa. It would seem, therefore, that Omri's reign ended

Chapter 9 — *I Kings*

in the forty-second year of Asa.[635] But I Kings 16:29 says that Omri's son, Ahab, began to reign in the thirty-eighth year of Asa, presumably after Omri's death.

A Solution

A solution to both apparent problems lies in understanding that with the upheaval in Israel due to Zimri slaying the king, "the people of Israel divided into two parts: half of the people followed Tibni the son of Ginath, to make him king; and half followed Omri" (I Kings 16:21). But, then "the people that followed Omri prevailed against the people that followed Tibni the son of Ginath: so Tibni died, and Omri reigned" (I Kings 16:22). With these verses in mind, it becomes evident that the people were split as to whom they would follow as their king. Omri began his reign in the twenty-seventh year of Asa (I Kings 16:15-16) in competition with Tibni (I Kings 16:21). Omri finally won out and became the sole king in the thirty-first year of Asa (I Kings 16:23) and finished his reign of twelve total years (I Kings 16:23) in the thirty-eighth year of Asa (I Kings 16:29).[636]

I KINGS 16:29; 22:41, 51

The Passages

I Kings 16:29 states, "And in the thirty and eighth year of Asa king of Judah began Ahab the son of Omri to reign over Israel: and Ahab the son of Omri reigned over Israel in Samaria twenty and two years."

I Kings 22:41 states, "And Jehoshaphat the son of Asa began to reign over Judah in the fourth year of Ahab king of Israel."

---

[635] This conclusion follows because if Omri's first year was the same as Asa's thirty-first year, then adding another eleven years brings Omri to his twelfth year and Asa to his forty-second year.

[636] Omri's first year was the same as Asa's twenty-seventh and another eleven years added to this brings Omri to his twelfth and last year as well as to the thirty-eighth year of Asa (27 + 11 = 38).

Chapter 9 — *I Kings*

I Kings 22:51 states, "Ahaziah the son of Ahab began to reign over Israel in Samaria the seventeenth year of Jehoshaphat king of Judah, and reigned two years over Israel."

The Apparent Problem

Ahaziah, Ahab's son, began to reign in the seventeenth year of Jehoshaphat (I Kings 22:51); therefore, it seems that his father Ahab died in that same year. Since Jehoshaphat started his reign "in the fourth year of Ahab" (I Kings 22:41), which was his accession year (see "Chronological Factors" at the beginning of this chapter), then Jehoshaphat's first official year occurred in the next year or in the same year as Ahab's fifth year. Adding sixteen years to Jehoshaphat's first year and to Ahab's fifth year brings Jehoshaphat to his seventeenth year (1 + 16 = 17) and Ahab to his twenty-first year (5 + 16 = 21), which was the year in which Ahaziah started his reign. But herein is the problem: Ahab reigned for a total of twenty-two years (I Kings 16:29), that is, into Jehoshaphat's eighteenth year; therefore, why does not the Bible say that Ahaziah started his reign in the eighteenth year of Jehoshaphat?

Haley suggests that his readers not receive, believe, and hear these numbers: "Most probably the differences arose from a slight mistake in numeral letters."[637] A statement by Jones is applicable here:

> Anyone can "solve" a difficult chronological problem if he is free to resort to altering Scripture or declaring the problem passage as being corrupt, etc., as the need arises. Indeed, most of the many works examined during this study [i.e., during Jones' study for his book on OT chronology] are guilty of such unworthy practice, but it is neither necessary to address the perceived uncertainties nor allowable as God has promised to preserve His Word.[638]

A Solution

In the seventeenth year of Jehoshaphat, Ahaziah began to reign (I Kings 22:51), which seventeenth year occurred in the same year as Ahab's twenty-first year (see above). Ahaziah, therefore, began to reign in the same year as Ahab's twenty-first year. Since Ahab reigned for

---

[637] Haley, 396.

[638] Jones, 65.

twenty-two years (I Kings 16:29) and since Ahaziah came to the throne in the twenty-first year of Ahab, then it appears that Ahaziah had a co-reign with his father, Ahab, until Ahab's twenty-second and last year (I Kings 16:29). Therefore, Ahaziah came to the throne in the seventeenth year of Jehoshaphat, which was also the twenty-first year of Ahab, co-reigned with Ahab, and took over as sole monarch some time in the next year when Ahab died.

In making the suggestion of a co-reign, it is appropriate at this time to quote from Jones:

> It should be recalled that with regard to the problems inherent with the chronological computations of this period, chronologists have from the onset sought to reconcile the apparent discrepancies by assuming co-regencies (overlapping reigns), interregna [a period of no ruling king], or inaccuracies in the Biblical account. For the Biblicist, the latter is not an acceptable alternative. As for the first two, synchronization between the northern and southern Hebrew Kingdoms will be found impossible without them, yet their application to the distinct problems encountered is not dependent upon mere caprice. The harmonization of their data must be such that co-regencies and interregna be implemented only where there are clear indications in the text.[639]

Some object to the idea of a co-reign claiming that if the Bible does not explicitly say a co-reign occurred, then it is unreasonable to suggest one. However, just because Scripture does not explicitly state a co-reign, does not mean that one did not occur. Indeed, for years an attack against the book of Daniel was that Belshazzar was not the king of Babylon (see Daniel 5). However, archaeologists later discovered that Nabonidus, his father, had installed Belshazzar as co-regent. Scripture makes no reference to Nabonidus and to the fact that Belshazzar was co-regent. Just because Scripture does not explicitly mention a co-regency is not, therefore, conclusive evidence against a co-regency.

Several evidences point to Ahaziah having a co-reign with Ahab. First, a co-reign of one year fits the chronological data given in the Masoretic Text, which data is correct according to Jesus. Second, the section where the Bible presents Ahaziah's reign is a section that does not follow a chronological order of events after Ahab's death. I Kings 22:40 mentions Ahab's death and then the very next verse speaks of an event that happened in Ahab's lifetime. It is in this context that the Bible mentions Ahaziah's reign. In fact, the Bible mentions Ahaziah's reign after the

---

[639] Jones, 137.

statement of Jehoshaphat's death (I Kings 22:50), when his death was yet several years after that of Ahaziah. The point is this: the end of I Kings 22 is not following a chronological order. Therefore, it could allow for the reign of Ahaziah, which is mentioned after Ahab's death, to be partly or in whole a co-reign with his father. Some might raise on objection from I Kings 22:40, which says, "So Ahab slept with his fathers; and Ahaziah his son reigned in his stead." This seemingly indicates that Ahaziah reigned after Ahab died, but I Kings 22:40 could be simply indicating that Ahaziah took over solely as king after Ahab's death. Third, Ahab was planning war with Syria and as a precaution he may have set up his son as king in a co-reign (I Kings 22:2-40).

Let the man of God receive, believe, and hear these numbers; let him not reject them.

I KINGS 20:30

The Passage

I Kings 20:30 states, "But the rest fled to Aphek, into the city; and *there* a wall fell upon twenty and seven thousand of the men *that were* left. And Benhadad fled, and came into the city, into an inner chamber."

The Apparent Problem

On the surface of it, no problem is herein apparent, however, *The New Scofield Reference Bible* states, "The number is possibly a scribal error."[640] Donald Wiseman states, "The 'thousand' (*'elep̄*) might be revocalized without change of consonants to 'officer' (*'allûp̄*). . . . the number might represent twenty-seven officers killed."[641] In other words, some will not hear this number because it is too large! In so doing, Wiseman and *The New Scofield Reference Bible* find themselves in the same camp with *The Jerome Biblical Commentary*, a Catholic commentary, which

---

[640] C. I. Scofield, *The New Scofield Reference Bible* (NY: Oxford University Press, 1967), 419.

[641] Wiseman, *I & 2 Kings*, 178.

Chapter 9 — *I Kings*

fallaciously states, "The numbers are certainly exaggerated and are typical of popular stories."[642]

A Solution

A solution is simply to receive what is written: "A wall fell upon twenty and seven thousand of the men." Wiseman's suggestion that the vowels got mixed up is contrary to Jesus' promises in Matthew 5:18 and Luke 16:17 that not even one tittle will pass from the law. *The Jerome Biblical Commentary's* suggestion that the number is exaggerated denies the inerrancy of the Bible, whereas Jesus substantiates the inerrancy of the Old Testament in John 17:17. One should believe Jesus over the conjectures and bias of the scholars.

I KINGS 22:41, 51

See discussion under I Kings 16:29.

I KINGS 22:51 AND II KINGS 3:1

The Passages

I Kings 22:51 states, "Ahaziah the son of Ahab began to reign over Israel in Samaria the seventeenth year of Jehoshaphat king of Judah, and reigned two years over Israel."

II Kings 3:1 states, "Now Jehoram the son of Ahab began to reign over Israel in Samaria the eighteenth year of Jehoshaphat king of Judah, and reigned twelve years."

---

[642] Peter F. Ellis, *1-2 Kings* in *The Jerome Biblical Commentary*, ed. Raymond E. Brown (London: Prentice-Hall International, Inc., 1968), 196. That this commentary is a Catholic commentary is evident from the dedication to Pope Pius XII on page iii and from the *Imprimatur* from Lawrence Cardinal Shehan, Archbishop of Baltimore on page ii.

Chapter 9 — I Kings

The Apparent Problem

I Kings 22:51 states that Ahaziah of Israel began his reign in the seventeenth year of Jehoshaphat and reigned for two years. Since seventeen plus two is nineteen (17 + 2 = 19), it would seem that his reign ended in the nineteenth year of Jehoshaphat and that the next king, Jehoram of Israel, started his reign in the nineteenth year of Jehoshaphat according to the non-accession-year system (see "Chronological Factors" at the beginning of this chapter). But II Kings 3:1 says that Jehoram started his reign in the eighteenth year of Jehoshaphat.

A Solution

Ahaziah started his reign in the seventeenth year of Jehoshaphat so that Ahaziah's first year was in the same year as Jehoshaphat's seventeenth year. Ahaziah's second year started with Jehoshaphat's eighteenth year in which year Ahaziah died, but inasmuch as it was still Jehoshaphat's eighteenth year, then the Bible says that Jehoram started his reign in the eighteenth year of Jehoshaphat. Jones points out "that even a single day before or after 1 Nisan [the start of the Jewish year] is reckoned as one year."[643] Since Ahaziah started his reign during Jehoshaphat's seventeenth year and reigned for just a portion of Jehoshaphat's eighteenth year, it is not unusual for the Bible to state that Ahaziah reigned for two years. Jones quotes Beecher: " 'Regularly in the case of the earlier Kings of Israel, and occasionally in other cases, the broken year is counted to the following reign as well as to the previous reign (Israelite mode)'."[644] So, the last year of Ahaziah and the first year of Jehoram both occurred in the eighteenth year of Jehoshaphat.

---

[643] Jones, 137.

[644] Jones, 121, quoting Willis J. Beecher, "The Kings of Israel and Judah" in *American Presbyterian Review* (April 1880), n.p.

CHAPTER TEN:
APPARENT NUMERICAL CONTRADICTIONS IN II KINGS

II KINGS 1:17; 8:16

The Passages

II Kings 1:17 states, "So he died according to the word of the LORD which Elijah had spoken. And Jehoram reigned in his stead in the second year of Jehoram the son of Jehoshaphat king of Judah; because he had no son."

II Kings 8:16 states, "And in the fifth year of Joram the son of Ahab king of Israel, Jehoshaphat *being* then king of Judah, Jehoram the son of Jehoshaphat king of Judah began to reign."

The Apparent Problem

II Kings 1:17 states that Jehoram of Israel began his reign in the same year as the second year of Jehoram of Judah. II Kings 8:16, however, states that Jehoram of Judah began his reign in the same year as the fifth year of Jehoram (Joram) of Israel. In other words, "if 2 Kings 1:17 is correct, then Jehoram of Judah began his reign before Joram of Israel. But

Chapter 10 — *II Kings*

according to 2 Kings 8:16, Jehoram of Judah came to the throne in the fifth year of Joram of Israel"[645] and, therefore, after Joram of Israel.

Concerning II Kings 1:17, Jamieson writes, "The text is apparently corrupt."[646] But if one believes Jesus, then he knows the text is not corrupt. Whom will one believe, Jamieson or Jesus?

A Solution

The diagram below presents a solution to the apparent problem.

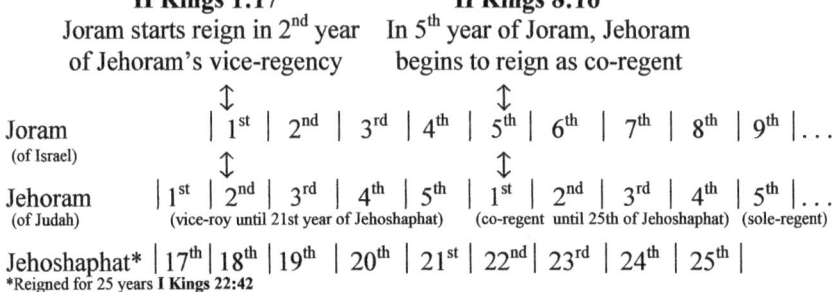

Haley refers to the same solution wherein "with Mr. Bullock, we may hold that Jehoram of Judah had two or three 'accessions': (1) when Jehoshaphat, on going to the battle of Ramoth-gilead, about the seventeenth year of his reign, intrusted [*sic*] the regency to Jehoram [I Kings 22]"; (2) when Jehoshaphat made Jehoram co-regent in his twenty-second year; and "(3) when in the twenty-fifth year, Jehoshaphat died."[647]

This is the first co-regency in the kingdom of Judah. The kingdom of Judah usually used the accession-year system. However, as diagrammed here, when a king went from a co-regency to a sole-regency, there was no accession year in between the two; instead, the monarch continued to reign and accumulate years with the years of his sole-reign being added to the sum of the years of his co-reign. In the case of Jehoram the four years

---

[645] Thiele, 36.

[646] Jamieson, *2 Kings* in part 2, vol. 1 of *A Commentary*, 372.

[647] Haley, 401.

Chapter 10 — II Kings

of co-reign plus four years of sole reign gives him a total of eight years (II Kings 8:17).

Note: the years during which the regency was entrusted to Jehoram did not count toward his total for his years reigned. The term for this period of time wherein the regency was entrusted to Jehoram from the seventeenth year through to the twenty-first year of Jehoshaphat is a viceroy or pro-rex. Jones points out:

> The distinction between the positions of viceroy and co-rex [a co-reign] is significant in that a viceroy does not possess the broader authority and powers of a co-regent. A further distinction which naturally follows is that years served in the capacity as co-regent are included along with the years served in the capacity of sole-rex in reckoning the total term of reign whereas the years passed as merely a viceroy (pro-rex) are not.[648]

Haley comes to the defense of these numbers and, therefore, receives, believes, and hears them; whereas in other cases he will not hear the numbers. This book documents this phenomena with other men and reveals how that a man at one time can walk by faith and then shortly thereafter walk by sight. It behooves Bible believers to consistently walk by faith and receive all that the Word of God says, even when they have difficulty explaining it.

II KINGS 3:1

See discussion under I Kings 22:51.

II KINGS 8:16

See discussion under II Kings 1:17.

---

[648] Jones, 147.

Chapter 10 — *II Kings*

II KINGS 8:25; 9:29

The Passages

II Kings 8:25 states, "In the twelfth year of Joram the son of Ahab king of Israel did Ahaziah the son of Jehoram king of Judah begin to reign."

II Kings 9:29 states, "And in the eleventh year of Joram the son of Ahab began Ahaziah to reign over Judah."

The Apparent Problem

II Kings 8:25 says King Ahaziah of Judah began to reign in the twelfth year of Joram of Israel, whereas II Kings 9:29 says he began to reign in the eleventh year of Joram of Israel.

A Solution

Ahaziah of Judah began his reign in the eleventh year of King Joram of Israel as viceroy (see discussion under II Kings 1:17) under his father, King Jehoram of Judah. In the twelfth year, he, then, took over as sole king and reigned as sole king for one year (II Kings 8:26). Therefore, both verses are right, with each looking at Ahaziah's reign from different starting points.

The above solution hinges on Ahaziah being viceroy with his father. That this may have been the case is bolstered by a couple of observations. First, when II Kings 8:25 states that Ahaziah begin to reign in the twelfth year of King Joram of Israel, it comes right after the announcement in the previous verse of the death of Jehoram the King of Judah and would indicate that this is when his sole reign began. Second, II Kings 8:26 states that Ahaziah's reign was one year, which was the one year of his sole reign. His viceroy year is not included in the sum of sole-reign years. Third, various enemies opposed King Jehoram of Judah (II Chronicles 21:16-17), and "the LORD smote him in his bowels with an incurable disease" (II Chronicles 21:18). In light of this, King Jehoram of Judah may have entrusted the regency to Ahaziah. Fourth, Athaliah, Ahaziah's mother may have promoted Ahaziah to the position of viceroy even though King Jehoram of Judah was still living (II Chronicles 22:2-3) so as to secure her son's position on the throne. And fifth, the explanation of

Chapter 10   *II Kings*

Ahaziah being viceroy for one year and then having a sole reign of one year satisfies the chronological data given in the preserved Hebrew text.

II KINGS 8:26 AND II CHRONICLES 22:2

The Passages

II Kings 8:26 states, "Two and twenty years old *was* Ahaziah when he began to reign; and he reigned one year in Jerusalem. And his mother's name was Athaliah, the daughter of Omri king of Israel."

II Chronicles 22:2 states, "Forty and two years old *was* Ahaziah when he began to reign, and he reigned one year in Jerusalem. His mother's name also *was* Athaliah the daughter of Omri."

The Apparent Problem

Kings says Ahaziah was twenty-two when he began to reign, whereas Chronicles says he was forty-two.

Many ascribe the problem to a scribal error. As this book documents in Chapter One, Bob Jones University states that the difference in numbers is the result of a scribal error. Leon Wood expresses the same view,[649] as does Haley,[650] Archer,[651] Payne,[652] *The Defender's Study Bible*,[653] Central Baptist Theological Seminary,[654] and others. *The Anchor Bible* states, "The chief LXX witnesses have '20,' while there is some minor support for '22,' which may be due to the influence of MT [Masoretic Text] of II Kings viii 26." *The Anchor Bible* then goes on to conjecture that "the MT of Chronicles may represent the conflation of two traditions and exhibits a striking example of the effort to preserve two divergent traditions. Originally the numbers were kept separate, e.g., 22 or

---

[649] Leon Wood, *A Survey of Israel's History* (Grand Rapids: Zondervan, 1979), 347.

[650] Haley, 398.

[651] Archer, 226.

[652] Payne, 508.

[653] Henry Morris, 507.

[654] Glenny, 85.

Chapter 10   *II Kings*

20, and only later added together."[655] The *English Standard Version* ignores the Hebrew text for II Chronicles 22:2 when it changes the number from *forty and two* to *twenty-two*, which is not at all honest with the text.[656] Instead of sticking with the Christ-approved Hebrew text, some rely on guesswork and conjecture. All of these will not receive, believe, and hear the numbers.

Floyd Jones writes:

> Ahaziah was 22, not 42 when he became sovereign of Judah. That this is the undeniable case may be seen in the simple fact that Jehoram, Ahaziah's father and predecessor, was 40 years old at the time of his death. This may be seen in that Jehoram was 32 when he ascended to the crown as co-regent with Jehoshaphat and ruled 8 years (32 + 8 = 40; II Ki. 8:16-17). Obviously a son cannot be 42 (unless adopted? II Chr. 22:9, but we think not) when his father is 40, thus 22 is the correct age for Ahaziah; but what of the number 42 as given in II Chronicles 22:2?
>
> For the non Biblicist, the solution is quite simple. The 42 is merely another scribal error where 42 was mistakenly written for 22. . . . the believing Biblicist would never have accepted such a solution as his frame of reference begins with a position of faith. Thus he reasons: "as both statements have been faithfully preserved by God to the 'jot and tittle,' how can both be true—for they must so be."[657]

Some Solutions

A couple of solutions are possible for the apparent problem.

Omri's Dynasty Age

The first solution lies in treating the Chronicles' account in a similar fashion as the thirty-fifth and thirty-sixth years of Asa. In that case the years were not referring to the time that Asa personally occupied the

---

[655] Jacob M. Myers, *II Chronicles* in *The Anchor Bible*, ed. William Foxwell Albright and David Noel Freedman (Garden City, NY: Doubleday & Company, Inc., 1965), 125. What Myers espouses is a Liberal view and comes as no surprise since he wrote the introduction and exegesis for Judges in the Liberal commentary, *The Interpreter's Bible* (*Joshua to II Samuel*, vol. 3, *The Interpreter's Bible*, x).

[656] There is not even a footnote to indicate the change, not that having a footnote would make it acceptable. Without a footnote, it seems to be a blatant disregard for the Preserved Hebrew Text.

[657] Jones, 145.

throne, but to the length of the Judean dynasty (see discussion under I Kings 15:33). Note: it was the author of Chronicles who referred to the length of the Judean dynasty during Asa's reign (II Chronicles 15:19; 16:1). Therefore, it should not come as a surprise that the same author would use a similar,[658] though not exactly the same,[659] technique again. With this in mind, Chronicles gives the age of the dynasty of Omri when Ahaziah came to the throne.

A couple of considerations demonstrate that Chronicles treats Ahaziah, King of Judah, as part of the dynasty of Omri, rather than as part of the dynasty of David. First, his mother, Athaliah, was Omri's grand daughter; therefore, Ahaziah was Omri's great grandson (II Kings 8:16-18, 24-26). Second, II Chronicles 22:3-4 emphasizes his connection with Ahab, Omri's son (I Kings 16:28): "He also walked in the ways of the house of Ahab . . .. Wherefore he did evil in the sight of he LORD like the house of Ahab." Third, II Kings 8:27 states that Ahaziah married into Ahab's house: "And he walked in the way of the house of Ahab, and did evil in the sight of the LORD, as did the house of Ahab: for he was the son in law of the house of Ahab." Fourth, Matthew 1:8 (a portion of the genealogy of Christ) does not list Ahaziah, Joash his son, and Amaziah his grandson because they were "judicially removed by the Holy Spirit in Matthew due to their relationship to Ahab's and Jezebel's wicked daughter Athaliah"[660] (see Exodus 20:5; Numbers 14:18; Psalm 109:13-15).

Two different methods of calculation, one erroneous and one correct, use the idea that *forty and two years* refer to the age of the dynasty of Omri. The first method, the erroneous one, uses six years for the reign of Omri. The second method uses twelve years for the reign of Omri.

---

[658] That the techniques are similar answers an objection by Japhet who writes: "As this is the only instance in Chronicles where chronological information of this kind deviates from source material, there seems to be no doubt that 'forty-two' is a textual error" (Japhet, 820). But Japhet seems to neglect the data about Asa, as well as the data about Jehoiachin wherein II Chronicles 36:9 differs from II Kings 24:8.

[659] That the techniques are not exactly the same is evident from the fact that II Chronicles 16:1 speaks of the reign of Asa, whereas in II Chronicles 22:2 the expression in the Hebrew is: "A son of forty and two years." When figuring, one must take into account this difference.

[660] Jones, 146.

Chapter 10　　　　　　　　　　　　　　　　　　　　*II Kings*

Using Six Years for Omri's Reign

Some arrive at an age of forty-two years for the dynasty of Omri by using a six-year reign for Omri, instead of twelve years. The Bible states, "In the thirty and first year of Asa of Judah began Omri to reign over Israel, twelve years: six years reigned he in Tirzah" (I Kings 16:23).[661] Those who use a six-year reign for Omri derive it from I Kings 16:23. They then add the twenty-two years of the next king, Ahab, the son of Omri (I Kings 16:29) To this, they add the two years of the king after Ahab, Ahaziah, Omri's grandson (I Kings 22:51). And then they add the twelve years of the king after Ahaziah of Israel, Joram, another grandson of Omri (II Kings 3:1). The calculation results in a total of forty-two years (6 + 22 + 2 + 12 = 42). It is important to note that this calculation uses twelve years for Joram of Israel. Not only did Joram's reign last for twelve years (II Kings 3:1), but it also was in the twelfth year of Joram of Israel that Ahaziah of Judah started his sole reign (II Kings 8:25).

Although the above calculation results in a total of forty-two years, it does not hold up under closer scrutiny for it fails to take into account a number of factors. First, it fails to take into account that one of Ahaziah of Israel's two years was as a co-reign with his father, Ahab (see discussion earlier in this book on I Kings 22:51). Therefore, Ahaziah of Israel's first year coincided with Ahab's last year, which means that Ahaziah of Israel had only one year of sole reign and should only count as one year instead of two.

Second, the above calculation fails to account for the non-accession year reckoning wherein "regularly in the case of the earlier Kings of Israel . . . the broken year is counted to the following reign as well as to the previous reign"[662] so that "part of one year may actually be counted twice— once for the outgoing king, once for the incoming king,"[663] which is known as non-accession year reckoning (see "Chronological Factors" at beginning of chapter on I Kings). Therefore, the year of Omri's death is not only reckoned as his last year, but also as the first year of Ahab so

> that year was counted *twice*; consequently, reigns so reckoned give one more year than the actual elapsed time. Hence with both sovereigns

---

[661] For further discussion on this verse see notes on I Kings 16:15-16, 23, 29 earlier in this book.

[662] Jones, 121.

[663] Cloud, 69.

Chapter 10 *II Kings*

claiming the same year, it becomes necessary to subtract one year when computing the actual number of elapsed years.[664]

Application of this factor results in the necessity of subtracting three years from the total, for there were three changes in the monarchy: one between Omri and Ahab; another between Ahab and Ahaziah; and a third between Ahaziah and Joram.

By taking into account Ahaziah's co-reign with Ahab, applying the non-accession year reckoning, and using six years for the reign of Omri; then there are thirty-eight years from Omri to the twelfth year of Jehoram, instead of forty-two. The calculation is as follows:

```
   6  years for Omri
  22  years for Ahab
   1  year for Ahaziah of Israel
+ 12  years for Joram
  41
 - 3  years due to non-accession year reckoning
  38  years from Omri to the end of Jehoram's reign
```

Using six years for the reign of Omri, fails to produce a forty-two year Omri dynasty.

Using Twelve Years for Omri's Reign

Method two for calculating the length of the Omri dynasty uses twelve years for Omri's reign and is built upon a number of observations. First, since Ahaziah of Judah first came to the throne as a viceroy in the eleventh year of Jehoram of Israel (II Kings 9:29),[665] then method two uses eleven years for Jehoram, instead of twelve. Second, method two uses the facts of Ahaziah's one-year co-reign with Ahab and the non-accession-year reckoning. Therefore, Ahaziah of Israel's reign counts as only one year, instead of two. Furthermore, one must subtract three years from the total to account for non-accession year reckoning. And third, since Chronicles only chronicles the Judean kings, then method two reckons the length of the Omri dynasty according to "Judaic reckoning"[666] which is a non-accession year reckoning (see "Chronological Factors" at

---

[664] Jones, 135.

[665] For more information, see discussion on II Kings 8:25 earlier in this book.

[666] Jones, 146.

Chapter 10 — II Kings

beginning of chapter on I Kings). Non-accession year reckoning does not count the first year. Another term for not counting the first year is non-inclusive reckoning. Therefore, the interpreter must subtract another year from the calculation. Here is the calculation:

```
  12  years for Omri
  22  years for Ahab
   1  year for Ahaziah of Israel
+ 11  years for Jehoram
  46  years
 - 3  years due to non-accession year reckoning
  43  years
  -1  year for Judaic or non-inclusive reckoning for length of dynasty
  42  years old
```

An alternative to utilizing Judaic reckoning is to recognize that *forty and two years old* in II Chronicles 22:2 is literally in the Hebrew *a son of forty and two years*. The earlier discussion of I Samuel 13:1 points out that while Scripture usually uses this expression of the age of the person, "yet it doth not always signify the age of the person";[667] therefore, the expression can refer to something else, such as the age of the dynasty. But, just as in figuring the age of an actual son wherein one would not count the first year, so here the Bible interpreter should not count the first year. For example, if a son were born on April 1, 2002, then he would not be reckoned one year old until April 1, 2003. Consequently, from April 1, 2002 to March 31, 2003, he is not considered one year old. April 1, 2002 to March 31, 2003 is his first year, but he is not one year old until April 1, 2003. In fact, during the entire length of his second year from April 1, 2003 to March 31, 2004, he is considered one year old. In such a case, one year must be subtracted from the second year in order to arrive at the correct age of the child; that is, the second year minus one year means the child is one year old $(2 - 1 = 1)$.

The writer of Chronicles by using *a son of forty and two years* is letting the reader know that the reader should not count the first year in order to arrive at the proper age of the dynasty. Hence, a dynasty that is in its forty-third year is actually forty-two years old. Verification that this is the correct understanding of *a son of* comes from I Samuel 13:1 where the Hebrew literally says, "A son of a year," which expression Scripture uses figuratively to refer to the length of Saul's reign to that point. The trans-

---

[667] Poole, 1:845.

Chapter 10   *II Kings*

lators of the *Authorized Version* understanding that the expression means that Saul was in his second year translate it, "Reigned one year." Note that *reigned* is in the past tense and means that the first year had already passed and that Saul was now in his second year and, therefore, a son of one year. The Omri dynasty was in its forty-third year and, therefore, was forty-two years old when Ahaziah of Judah took the throne in the eleventh year of Jehoram of Israel. A diagram of the entire period may be helpful.

Years old		*Year of Reign*				
0	[	1st				
1	]	2nd				
2	[	3rd				
3	]	4th				
4	[	5th				
5	]	6th	**Omri**, ruled for 12 years (I Kings 16:23)			
6	[	7th				
7	]	8th				
8	[	9th				
9	]	10th				
10	[	11th				
11	]	12th	1st	non-accession year		
12	[		2nd			
13	]		3rd			
14	[		4th			
15	]		5th			
16	[		6th			
17	]		7th			
18	[		8th			
19	]		9th			
20	[		10th			
21	]		11th			
22	[		12th	**Ahab**, reigned 22 years (I Kings 16:29)		
23	]		13th			
24	[		14th			
25	]		15th			
26	[		16th			
27	]		17th			
28	[		18th	**Ahaziah**, reigned 2 years (I Kings 22:51)		
29	]		19th	/ 1st year co-rex, 2nd year sole rex and non-accession year		
30	[		20th	/		
31	]		21st	1st		
32	[		22nd	2nd	1st	non-accession year
33	]				2nd	
34	[				3rd	

Chapter 10   *II Kings*

35	]		4th	
36	[		5th	
37	]		6th	**Joram**
38	[		7th	
39	]		8th	
40	[		9th	
41	]		10th	
42	[	**Ahaziah** of Judah (II Kings 9:29)	11th	

Ahaziah's Physical Age

The second solution considers both the *twenty and two years* and the *forty and two years* represent Ahaziah's physical age; that is, he was first made king when he was twenty-two (II Kings 8:26) and then made king again at forty-two (II Chronicles 22:2) at which time he actually reigned for one year. Support for this view comes from the case of Solomon, who was made king once (I Chronicles 23:1) and then later a second time (I Chronicles 29:22). The words, *made . . . king*, in I Chronicles 23:1 and I Chronicles 29:22 and the words, *when he began to reign*, in II Kings 8:26 and II Chronicles 22:2 all come from the same Hebrew root (מָלַךְ, *mālak*) and mean "to be or become king or queen, reign" when it is a Qal verb as it is in II Kings 8:26 and II Chronicles 22:2; or "to make one king or queen, cause to reign,"[668] when it is a Hiphil verb as it is I Chronicles 23:1 and 29:22. Therefore, it is possible that Ahaziah was made king earlier, but did not reign until later.

If *forty and two years* in II Chronicles 22:2 refers to Ahaziah's age, then twenty years prior, Ahaziah was twenty-two (42 – 20 = 22), which corresponds to the ninth year of Jehoshaphat[669] and may have been the

---

[668] *Online Bible Hebrew Lexicon*, 04427.

[669] To arrive at this calculation, one should consult the table presented with the discussion of II Kings 1:17. Jehoram had a four-year co-reign with Jehoshaphat and Jehoshaphat had a reign of 25 years. Since Jehoram reigned for 8 years (II Kings 8:17), then 4 of his 8 years were as a sole reign which years extended beyond the end of the reign of Jehoshaphat. It was in the 8th year of Jehoram, that is, 4 years after Jehoshaphat, when Ahaziah started his sole reign (see discussion above on II Kings 8:25). Counting back 20 years from 4 years beyond the end of Jehoshaphat's 25 year reign, takes the calculation back to Jehoshaphat's 9th year since 25 + 4 – 20 = 9.

time when Jehoshaphat "joined affinity with Ahab" (II Chronicles 18:1). Possibly at this time Jehoshaphat made Ahaziah king.

The Bible states that Ahaziah is the son of Jehoram (II Chronicles 22:1), the son-in-law of the house of Ahab (II Kings 8:27), and the son of Jehoshaphat (II Chronicles 22:9). But if II Chronicles 22:2 refers to Ahaziah's biological age, then Jehoram could not be Ahaziah's biological father;[670] therefore, Jehoram would have been his stepfather and Jehoshaphat would have been Ahaziah's actual father. If Jehoshaphat was Ahaziah's father, and since Athaliah was Ahaziah's mother (II Chronicles 22:2), then Jehoshaphat and Athaliah were married.

But if Jehoshaphat was Ahaziah's actual father and Jehoram was Ahaziah's step-father, then a problem arises. How did Jehoram become Ahaziah's step-father? Did he marry Athaliah? If Jehoram married Athaliah, and if Jehoshaphat had been her husband, then Jehoram, the son of Jehoshaphat (II Chronicles 21:1), married his father's wife, contrary to the injunction of Leviticus 18:8 and 20:11. The violation of the Levitical injunction could be the reason why Matthew's genealogy of Christ (Matthew 1:8) does not include Ahaziah, Joash (Ahaziah's son, II Kings 13:1), and Amaziah (Ahaziah's grandson, II Kings 14:13). The reader should also see Exodus 20:5; Numbers 14:18 and Psalm 109:13-15.

While the author has set forth the possibility that both the *twenty and two years* and the *forty and two years* represent Ahaziah's physical age as a possible solution, he must distance himself from one of the proofs proponents use for this view:

> Several years after this alliance [the one mentioned in II Chronicles 18:1] was forged, Ahab and Jehoshaphat engaged in a joint military venture against Syria (verse 2). Both kings went into battle (verse 28) and Ahab was killed (verses 33, 34). Prior to the battle the faithful prophet Micaiah is deported in chains to Amon where Joash is residing (I Kings 22:26). It is here, in this passage, we have a most revealing statement: Joash (the biological son of Ahaziah, 2 Chronicles 22:11) is called the "king's son"—indicating that Ahaziah was already a king! How could this possibly be??? If, as part of the affinity Jehoshaphat made with Ahab, Ahaziah

---

[670] See discussion under the statement of the problem. To summarize: Jehoram died at 40; therefore, he could not have a son aged 42.

was anointed king at this time, the pieces of the puzzle begin to fit together.[671]

In other words, the above proof combines I Kings 22:26 and II Chronicles 22:11 to say that the Joash of I Kings 22:26 is Ahaziah of Judah's biological son, but chronologically Joash could not have been Ahaziah's son. I Kings 22:26 occurs in the year of Ahab's death and, according to the above quote, would be the last year in which Joash of Judah could have been born. With that in mind, the chronological impossibility arises from the fact that after Ahab's death came the twelve year reign of Joram (II Kings 3:1). After Joram, Jehu reigned (II Kings 9:1-7, 24), and it was not until Jehu's seventh year that Joash took the throne of Judah (II Kings 12:1) at which time Joash was seven years old (II Chronicles 24:1). The fact that Joash was seven years old when he began to reign means that his birth took place just prior to the start of Jehu's reign and, therefore, in the last year of Joram's reign,[672] and not in the last year of Ahab's reign as the above quote demands. Therefore, the Joash of I Kings 22:26 is not Ahaziah of Judah's son. The question then arises, who is the Joash of I Kings 22:26? Since Ahab is speaking in I Kings 22:26, then it appears that the Joash of I Kings 22 was a son of Ahab.

Athaliah's Physical Age

Strouse offers another solution:

> It is often stated that the copyist made a mistake and ascribed to Ahaziah the incorrect age of 42, since he must have been 22, according to II Kings 8:17. However, the problem goes beyond the copies, since the Hebrew manuscripts read 22 and 42, respectively, and extends to the originals. In II Chr. 22:2, the Hebrew literally reads "a son of 42 years." It is possible that the 42 refers to Athaliah's age, since the Hebrew expression includes this possibility (cf. Psm. 127:4), and since Athaliah is stressed in this passage [that is, II Chronicles 22:2]. In other words, Ahaziah was 22 when he began to reign and to replace his father who died at 40 (II Chr. 21:20), and his mother, Athaliah, was 42.[673]

---

[671] Cloud, 71. See also Peter S. Ruckman, *The "Errors" in the King James Bible* (Pensacola: Bible Baptist Bookstore, 1999), 250.

[672] This conclusion is verified by the fact that when Jehu came to power he killed both Jehoram of Israel and Ahaziah of Judah (II Kings 9:24, 27) on the same day.

[673] Strouse, *The Lord God Hath Spoken*, 56-57.

Chapter 10 *II Kings*

The third solution appeals to Psalm 127:4: "As arrows are in the hand of a mighty man; so are children of the youth." The expression, *children of the youth*, in Hebrew is literally, "The sons of the youth," which refers to children born to a man in his youth. With this in mind, *a son of forty and two years* from II Chronicles 22:2 could be referring to Ahaziah's mother, thereby indicating that he was the son of someone who was forty-two years old.

Conclusion

At least three different solutions are available for the apparent contradiction between II Kings 8:26 and II Chronicles 22:2. Without further revelation, it is impossible to know which, if any of these, are the right solution. Though there is some ambiguity here, do not let anyone imagine that a real contradiction or error is present in these verses. The reader of Scripture ought to receive, believe, and hear these numbers.

II KINGS 9:29

See discussion under II Kings 8:25.

II KINGS 10:36; 12:1; 13:1

The Passages

II Kings 10:36 states, "And the time that Jehu reigned over Israel in Samaria *was* twenty and eight years."

II Kings 12:1 states, "In the seventh year of Jehu Jehoash [also Joash] began to reign; and forty years reigned he in Jerusalem. And his mother's name *was* Zibiah of Beersheba."

II Kings 13:1 states, "In the three and twentieth year of Joash [also Jehoash] the son of Ahaziah king of Judah Jehoahaz the son of Jehu began to reign over Israel in Samaria, *and reigned* seventeen years."

The Apparent Problem

In order to present the apparent problem with the above verses, one must be aware of a number of items. First, Joash of Judah came to the

Chapter 10   *II Kings*

throne in the seventh year of Jehu (II Kings 12:1), which would seem to be his accession year so that his first official year took place in Jehu's next or eighth year. Second, Jehu reigned for twenty-eight years (II Kings 10:36); therefore, in his eighth year he had twenty years left (28 – 8 = 20). Third, if the eighth year of Jehu is the same year as the first official year of Joash and with Jehu having twenty years left to his reign at that time, then it would seem that after Jehu's reigning for another twenty years it would be Joash's twenty-first year (1 + 20 = 21). Fourth, it would further seem that Jehu's last year, or the twenty-first year of Joash, would be the year wherein Jehu's successor, Jehoahaz would take over. But the Bible says that Jehoahaz did not come to the throne in the twenty-first year of the reign of Joash of Judah, but in the twenty-third year (II Kings 13:1).

Haley is quick to state that the apparent problem is the result of a scribal error.[674] Of all the books that the author has consulted, Haley is the only one who suggests a problem here. Even the otherwise ubiquitous Poole has missed this one. For Haley to state that there is an apparent problem, only to tell his readers that it is a scribal error is irresponsible. It would be better and more honoring to the Lord, not to say anything at all than to say there is a scribal error. The writer is certainly not advocating that one should ignore apparent problems. However, to be about the only one to bring an apparent problem to light and to then say that it is a scribal error is certainly not approaching the Old Testament in the same manner as Jesus Who said that He came not to destroy the law or the prophets (Matthew 5:17). On the contrary, the approach of Haley ministers questions rather than godly edifying (I Timothy 1:4).

A Solution

According to the statement of the apparent problem, the years are off by two for it would seem that Jehoahaz would have come to the throne in the twenty-first year of Joash, whereas the Bible states that it was the twenty-third year. Perhaps the statement of the problem makes some incorrect assumptions. As stated above, it would seem that in the seventh year of Jehu, Joash had his accession year so that his first official year was the next year, that is, the eighth year of Jehu.

---

[674] Haley, 400.

Chapter 10   *II Kings*

But if Joash had no accession year, then the first official year of Jehoash would have occurred in the seventh year of Jehu instead of in the eighth year and this would account for one of the two years difference. That Joash may not have had an accession year when he came to the throne is very possible in light of the fact that he took the throne after Athaliah was executed (II Kings 11:4-16). Athaliah was the illegitimate occupant of the throne and was justly executed under the authority of Jehoiada, the priest, who then put Joash on the throne in Athaliah's place. With Joash starting his reign without an accession year, it would indicate a direct break with the reign of wicked Athaliah. In the accession-year system (see "Chronological Factors" at the beginning of chapter on I Kings), the remainder of the year in which a monarch dies is accredited to the departed monarch. But Jehoiada, perhaps not wanting to acknowledge any legitimacy about Athaliah's reign, does not institute the practice of the accession year and has the remainder of the year be Joash's first official year.

With the understanding that Joash had no accession year, then Joash's first official year was Jehu's seventh, instead of the eighth. Since Jehu reigned for twenty-eight years (II Kings 10:36), then in his seventh year he had twenty-one years left ($28 - 7 = 21$). Since the seventh year of Jehu is the same as Joash's first year, assuming he had no accession year, and since at this point Jehu had twenty-one years left to reign, then Jehu ended his reign in the twenty-second year of Joash ($1 + 21 = 22$).

But this still leaves a problem. Taking into account the preceding explanation, it would now seem that Jehoahaz would come to the throne in the twenty-second year of Joash, whereas the Bible says that he came to the throne in the twenty-third year of Joash (II Kings 13:1). This can be solved by proposing a delay in the time between Jehu's death and when his son, Jehoahaz, got to the throne. Finegan states, "At what point is the reign considered to begin? This point most often coincides, no doubt, with the death of the preceding ruler, yet there may be an interval before the new king is selected, installed, or confirmed in office."[675] If Jehu died a little before Nisan 1, and there was a short delay in Jehoahaz coming to the throne, then he could have started his reign in the new year, which would also be the twenty-third year of Joash. The numbers have a story to tell and instead of following Haley who rejects them, the believer ought to receive, believe, and hear the numbers.

---

[675] Finegan, 77.

Chapter 10 *II Kings*

A diagram of the above solution is as follows:

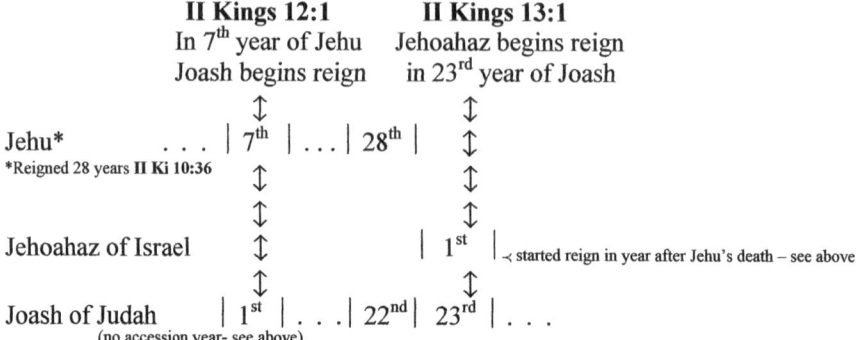

II KINGS 12:1

See discussion under II Kings 10:36.

II KINGS 13:1

See discussion under II Kings 10:36.

II KINGS 13:10; 14:1; AND II CHRONICLES 24:1

The Passages

II Kings 13:10 states, "In the thirty and seventh year of Joash king of Judah began Jehoash the son of Jehoahaz to reign over Israel in Samaria, *and reigned* sixteen years."

II Kings 14:1 states, "In the second year of Joash son of Jehoahaz king of Israel reigned Amaziah the son of Joash king of Judah."

II Chronicles 24:1 states, "Joash *was* seven years old when he began to reign, and he reigned forty years in Jerusalem. His mother's name also *was* Zibiah of Beersheba."

Chapter 10   *II Kings*

The Apparent Problem

Jehoash of Israel began his reign in the thirty-seventh year of Joash of Judah (II Kings 13:10) so that the first year of Jehoash of Israel is the same as the thirty-seventh year of Joash of Judah. Now inasmuch as Joash of Judah reigned for forty years (II Chronicles 24:1), then in his thirty-seventh year, he had three years left (40 − 37 = 3). Since the thirty-seventh year of Joash of Judah is the same as the first year of Jehoash of Israel, and since at this point, Joash of Judah had three years left, then Joash of Judah's last year would have been the same as Jehoash of Israel's fourth year (1 + 3 = 4). It would seem, then, that Amaziah, the son of Joash of Judah, would start his reign in the fourth year of Jehoash of Israel, if he had an accession year, as opposed to the second year (II Kings 14:1).

A Solution

A solution to this apparent problem starts with a comment from Poole upon II Kings 13:10,

> It may be gathered that Jehoahaz [of Israel] had two or three years before his death made his son Jehoash king with him [i.e., viceroy, see notes on II Kings 1:17]; which is very probable, because he was perpetually in the state of war [see II Kings 13:3], and consequently in danger of ultimate death, and because he was a man of valour, as is implied here, ver. 12, and declared [in] 2 Chron. xxv.[676]

How does the comment from Poole factor into a solution? Jehoahaz, the father of Jehoash of Israel started his reign in the twenty-third year of Joash of Judah and reigned for seventeen years (II Kings 13:1). This means that the first year of Jehoahaz and the twenty-third year of Joash of Judah both occurred in the same year and at this point Jehoahaz had sixteen years left to his seventeen year reign (17 − 1 = 16). Adding sixteen years to the twenty-third year of Joash of Judah brings Joash of Judah to his thirty-ninth year (23 + 16 = 39), which is the same as the last year of Jehoahaz's seventeen year reign. Now Jehoahaz of Israel made Jehoash viceroy in the thirty-seventh year of Joash of Judah (II Kings 13:10) for three years, that is, the thirty-seventh, thirty-eighth, and thirty-ninth years of Joash of Judah. Since Jehoahaz died in the thirty-ninth year of Joash of Judah and from the fact that Jehoash of Israel had been viceroy, then Je-

---

[676] Poole, 1:745.

Chapter 10 *II Kings*

hoash's first official year of sole reign started in the next year of Joash of Judah, that is, the fortieth year. Consequently, Jehoash of Israel's first year was the same as Joash of Judah's fortieth year.

But now a question arises. If Jehoash of Israel's first year of sole reign is the same as Joash of Judah's fortieth year in which year Joash of Judah died, then why does the Bible say that Amaziah of Judah came to the throne in the second year of Jehoash of Israel (II Kings 14:1), instead of the first year? Possibly, something may have delayed Amaziah starting his reign in the same year as the first year of Jehoash of Israel and forced him to wait until the second year of Jehoash of Israel. Just before Amaziah came to the throne several things happened in succession: (1) Jehoiada, the priest, died (II Chronicles 24:15); (2) Joash of Judah killed Jehoiada's son Zechariah (II Chronicles 24:21); (3) the host of Syria came against Joash of Judah (II Chronicles 24:23-24); (4) Joash of Judah had great diseases (II Chronicles 24:25); and (5) the people conspired against Joash of Judah and killed him (II Chronicles 24:25). It is possible that in light of all this turmoil, the start of Amaziah's rule was delayed into the second year of Jehoash of Israel. If Joash of Judah died late in his fortieth and last year, then the delay would only have to be a few days to move Amaziah's coronation into the next year. A diagram of the above solution is as follows:

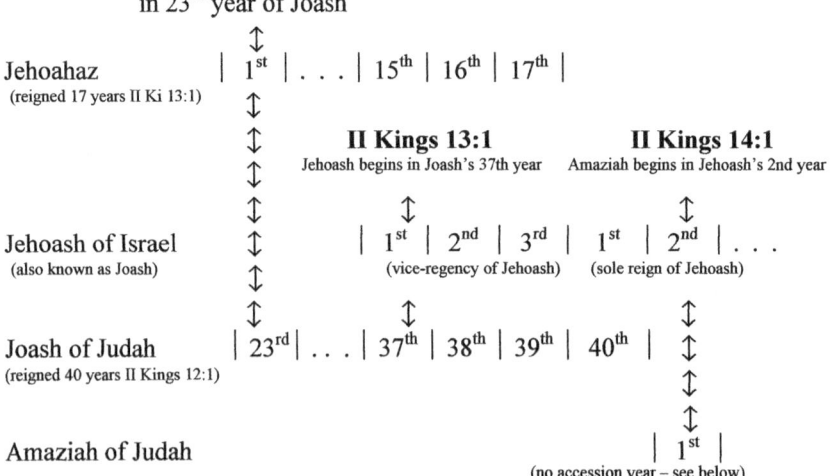

334

Chapter 10   *II Kings*

This is also another case where a king of Judah had no accession year. Abijah is one such king (see "Chronological Factors" in Chapter Nine) and Joash of Judah is another (see discussion under II Kings 10:36). When Amaziah came to the throne, it was the second year of Jehoash of Israel (II Kings 14:1) and since Jehoash of Israel reigned for sixteen years (II Kings 13:10), then at this point, he had fourteen years left (16 − 2 = 14). If Amaziah had no accession year, then his first official year was the same as Jehoash of Israel's second year at which point Jehoash of Israel had fourteen years left. When these fourteen years are added to Amaziah's first year it brings Amaziah to his fifteenth year (1 + 14 = 15), so that Amaziah's fifteenth year was the same as Jehoash of Israel's last year, which is the same year that Jehoash's son, Jeroboam, became king of Israel just as II Kings 14:23 states. In light of this, when Amaziah came to the throne he did not have an accession year, but started immediately with his first official year. The lack of an accession year in Amaziah's case could be a commentary on the reign of Joash whom the people slew (II Kings 12:20, also see notes under II Kings 10:36). A diagram is as follows:

```
                        II Kings 14:1                    II Kings 14:23
              Amaziah begins in Jehoash's 2nd year   Jeroboam begins in Amaziah's 15th year
                              ↕                                  ↕
Jehoash of Israel      | 1ˢᵗ | 2ⁿᵈ | . . . . . . . . . . | 16ᵗʰ |
Reigned 16 years II Kings 13:10     ↕                                  ↕
                              ↕         Jeroboam II of Israel    1ˢᵗ  | . . . .
                              ↕                                  ↕
Amaziah of Judah        | 1ˢᵗ | . . . . . . . . . . . | 15ᵗʰ |
  (no accession year)
```

II KINGS 14:1

See discussion under II Kings 13:10.

Chapter 10 *II Kings*

II KINGS 14:23; 15:1, 8; AND II CHRONICLES 25:1

The Passage

II Kings 14:23 states, "In the fifteenth year of Amaziah the son of Joash king of Judah Jeroboam the son of Joash king of Israel began to reign in Samaria, *and reigned* forty and one years."

II Kings 15:1 states, "In the twenty and seventh year of Jeroboam king of Israel began Azariah son of Amaziah king of Judah to reign."

II Kings 15:8 states, "In the thirty and eighth year of Azariah king of Judah did Zachariah the son of Jeroboam reign over Israel in Samaria six months."

II Chronicles 25:1 states, "Amaziah *was* twenty and five years old *when* he began to reign, and he reigned twenty and nine years in Jerusalem. And his mother's name was Jehoaddan of Jerusalem."

The Apparent Problems

Two apparent problems are present in the above verses.

Apparent Problem One

Before stating the first problem, it is necessary to present a number of items. The first item is this: in the fifteenth year of Amaziah of Judah, Jeroboam II started his reign in Israel (II Kings 14:23). Therefore, the first year of the reign of Jeroboam II and the fifteenth year of Amaziah occurred in the same year. The second item is this: Amaziah of Judah reigned for twenty-nine years (II Chronicles 25:1). Now since the first year of Jeroboam II and the fifteenth year of Amaziah occurred in same year and since, as of this time, Amaziah had fourteen more years left to his twenty-nine year reign (29 – 15 = 14), then the twenty-ninth and last year of Amaziah occurred in the same year as the fifteenth year of Jeroboam II (1st year of Jeroboam II + 14 more years left in Amaziah's reign = 15th year of Jeroboam II; see also II Kings 14:17 and II Chronicles 25:25). The third item is this: according to II Kings 15:1, Azariah, son of Amaziah, began his reign in the twenty-seventh year of Jeroboam II, but since his reign follows that of his father's, a problem arises. One would expect that since Amaziah's reign ended in the same year as the fifteenth year of Jeroboam II, that Amaziah's son, Azariah, would start his first year of

Chapter 10 *II Kings*

reign in the fifteenth year of Jeroboam II (according to accession-year reckoning, see "Chronological Factors" in Chapter Nine), instead of the twenty-seventh year as stated in II Kings 15:1.

Concerning this apparent problem Haley refers to "the best critics" who advocate a scribal error.[677] Haley finds himself in the company of Catholics when making such a suggestion for *A Catholic Commentary on Holy Scripture* states, "The chronology in chh 15 and 16 has been systematically glossed."[678] Jones writes:

> Once again, the Biblicist merely stands firm knowing that both Scriptures are true, and a reasonable way to reconcile them must exist. To reject this position denies and demeans God's promises to preserve His Word. Once this is done, it leaves open to the subjective whim of man the depraved notion that he has the right to select which Scripture should be accepted and which rejected. Such is an open ended argument and . . . the wrong path to follow.[679]

Apparent Problem Two

Since Azariah of Judah started his reign in the twenty-seventh year of Jeroboam II (II Kings 15:1), and since Zechariah, the son and successor of Jeroboam II, started his reign thirty-eight years later (see II Kings 15:8); then it would seem as if Jeroboam II's reign was about sixty-five years long (27 + 38 = 65). But the Bible states that Jeroboam II reigned for forty-one years (II Kings 14:23).

Some Solutions

Some Solutions to Apparent Problem One

A couple of solutions exist for apparent problem one. Apparent problem one is solved if Jeroboam II was viceroy (see discussion on II Kings 1:17) with his father, Jehoash of Israel, for twelve years. If this was the case, then the twenty-seven year figure of II Kings 15:1 takes into account the twelve years of being viceroy plus the fifteen years of sole reign (12 + 15 = 27). Therefore, Azariah came to the throne in the fifteenth

---

[677] Haley, 399.

[678] K. Smyth, *3 & 4 Kings* in *A Catholic Commentary on Holy Scripture*, 344.

[679] Jones, 149.

year of the sole reign of Jeroboam II and in the twenty-seventh year of the total combined reign of Jeroboam II. That Jeroboam II may have been viceroy with his father Jehoash of Israel is possible for a couple of reasons. First, Jeroboam II's father was going to war against Syria and may have felt the need to have a replacement on hand (II Kings 13:14-19). Second, Jeroboam II's father also faced the Moabites (II Kings 13:20) and again may have felt need to have a replacement on hand. However, a problem arises with this solution, which is that the solution must have the twelve years of a possible viceroy period added to the fifteen years of sole-reign to arrive at the twenty-seven year figure of II Kings 15:1. But doing so violates the practice of the years of viceroy not being added to the total length of reign (see discussion under II Kings 1:17).

In light of this, Jones offers another solution:

> When young Uzziah ascended the throne, he inherited a kingdom in dire circumstances from his father, Amaziah, who had not only been soundly defeated by Jehoash of Israel in open battle, but had been captured and brought back in shame to Jerusalem by that northern Monarch (II Ki. 14:8-14; II Chr. 25:17-24). Jehoash added to this humiliation by making an approximately two hundred yard breach in the wall of Jerusalem, plundering all the treasure in the Temple and Amaziah's house, and returned to Samaria with hostages thereby reducing Judah to vassalage, or at least nearly so, under the Kingdom of Israel. Thus the II Kings 15:1 passage could be understood to mean that in Jeroboam's 27th year an older maturing Uzziah finally succeeded in strengthening himself and his kingdom to the point in which he was able to break out from under the heavy hand of the northern kingdom (cp. II Chr. 26:15b) and from thence govern as indisputable sovereign.[680]

In other words, Uzziah came to the throne in the fifteenth year of Jeroboam II, but was not able to gain full control of the kingdom until the twenty-seventh year of Jeroboam II. Such an explanation avoids the problem of violating the usual practice wherein the years of being viceroy are not added with the total that the king reigned. Despite what "the best critics" say, may those who seek to honor the Lord receive, believe, and hear these numbers. A diagram of this second solution is as follows:

---

[680] Ibid.

Chapter 10 *II Kings*

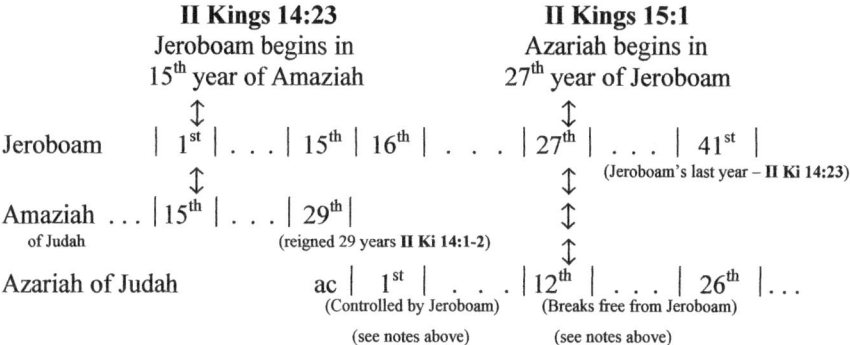

Some Solutions to Apparent Problem Two

A solution to the second apparent problem starts with the solution to the first apparent problem. Azariah of Judah did not start his reign in the twenty-seventh year of Jeroboam II, but broke free from Jeroboam's control in that year. The above diagram shows that Azariah of Judah started his first official year of reign in the same year as Jeroboam II's sixteenth year. This means that the first year of Azariah of Judah and the sixteenth year of Jeroboam II of Israel both occurred in the same year. Adding another thirty-seven years to this year brings Azariah to his thirty-eighth year (1 + 37 = 38), which is when Zechariah, the successor of Jeroboam, started his reign (II Kings 15:8). This still presents an apparent problem for it would seem as if Jeroboam II's reign was, therefore, about fifty-three years long (16 + 37 = 53), but the Bible states that Jeroboam II only reigned for forty-one years (II Kings 14:23), which would have ended in the same year as Azariah's twenty-sixth year, instead of his thirty-eighth year (see diagram above).

In the statement of this apparent problem, an assumption is made, which, if not valid, would provide the answer. The assumption made in the statement of the apparent problem is that Zachariah began his reign immediately after the death of Jeroboam II. However, if after Jeroboam II's forty-one years of sole reign (II Kings 14:23), an interregnum occurred from the twenty-sixth year to the thirty-eighth years of Azariah, then the apparent problem is solved. A period of about eleven and a half years without a king in Israel is possible since this was a very troublous period in Israel's history with assassinations and foreign intervention (II Kings 15:10-20). A diagram of this first solution is as follows:

Chapter 10 — II Kings

II Kings 15:8
Zachariah reigned 6 months
in Azariah's 38th year

Jeroboam ... | 15th | 16th | ... | 41st |

Zachariah of Israel →→→→→→→→→ |(interregnum) | 6 mos. |

Azariah of Judah | ac | 1st | ... | 26th | . . . | 38th | . .

Jones presents another possibility to this apparent problem:

> Of course, . . ., the term "interregnum" is not actually mentioned here by the Scripture although the data seems to require one.
>
> Again, though known to have occurred from time to time throughout the history of various empires, interregna are not generally palatable to the scholar's taste. This is all the more true here since the word does not appear with the account; hence most moderns are certain that an error of some kind must surely be present with regard to the data germane to Zachariah.
>
> For the Biblicist, no real problem is seen for throughout history, multiple assassinations of top leaders and interregna have often been signs that a regime was in its death throws [sic]. As Israel is undeniably at that threshold, resolving the issue by placing an interregnum between Jeroboam (II) and Zachariah is not only an acceptable resolution—it may well be historical fact. However, it is not the only Biblical possibility.[681]

Now, Jones points out the possibility that II Kings 15:8 simply says that in the thirty-eighth year of Azariah, Zachariah reigned for six months. In other words, II Kings 15:8 indicates that he reigned for sixth months of that year but does not state exactly when his reign started. Therefore, Zachariah possibly started his reign immediately after the death of Jeroboam, and this reign was terminated in the six month of the thirty-eighth year of Azariah. To substantiate this position, Jones states:

> The verses describing the time of enthronement of all the kings mentioned in the proximity of Zachariah's brief account include the single word "began" as in "began to reign" *but* not so with Zachariah (II Ki. 12:1; II Ki. 13:1, 10; II Ki. 14:1, cp. II Chr. 25:1; II Ki. 14:23; II Ki. 15:1; II Ki. 15:7, cp. verse 32; II Ki. 15:13, 17, 23, 27; II Ki. 16:1; II Ki. 17:1; II Ki. 18:1 etc.)! . . ..

---

[681] Jones, 150.

As can be seen, in stark contrast to all of the other monarchs listed in the above cited Scriptures there is no "began" associated with any of the verses concerning Zachariah's reign. Thus the justified conclusion may be reached that II Kings 15:8 is not speaking of the total length of his regime but rather is merely giving the data for establishing the *termination* of both his personal reign and that of the Jehuic dynasty (II Ki. 10:30), which had its prophetic duration fulfilled in Zachariah (II Ki. 15:12).[682]

A diagram of the above possibility is as follows:

II Kings 15:8
Zachariah's reign ends in the 6th month of Azariah's 38th year

Jeroboam . . . | 15th | 16th | . . . | 41st | $\updownarrow$

$\updownarrow$

Zachariah of Israel →→→→→→ | 1st | . . . | 12th | 6 mos. |

$\updownarrow$

Azariah of Judah | ac | 1st | . . . | 26th | . . . | 37th | 38th | . . .

Whatever may be the exact solution to this apparent problem, the child of God should receive, believe, and hear these numbers.

II KINGS 15:1, 8

See discussion under II Kings 14:23.

II KINGS 15:2, 27, 32

The Passages

II Kings 15:2 states, "Sixteen years old was he when he [Uzziah] began to reign, and he reigned two and fifty years in Jerusalem. And his mother's name *was* Jecholiah of Jerusalem."

II Kings 15:27 states, "In the two and fiftieth year of Azariah king of Judah Pekah the son of Remaliah began to reign over Israel in Samaria, *and reigned* twenty years."

---

[682] Ibid.

Chapter 10 — *II Kings*

II Kings 15:32 states, "In the second year of Pekah the son of Remaliah king of Israel began Jotham the son of Uzziah king of Judah to reign."

The Apparent Problems

Two apparent problems surface when examining these verses.

Apparent Problem One

The Bible states that Uzziah (also known as Azariah) reigned for fifty-two years (II Kings 15:2) and that in the fifty-second year of Uzziah, Pekah began to reign (II Kings 15:27). Therefore, one would expect, as viewed from Israel, that the son of Uzziah would have started his reign in the same year as the first year of Pekah (for more information see "Chronological Factors" at the beginning of Chapter Nine). But II Kings 15:32 states that it was in the second year of Pekah that Uzziah's son, Jotham began to reign.

Apparent Problem Two

II Kings 15:27 states that Pekah reigned for twenty years; however, "*twenty years* of reign is often considered impossible by comparison with Assyrian records."[683] Now concerning Assyrian records, "Marcus Dods in his book *The Bible: Its Origin and Nature* states, 'Professor Sayce, one of the most conservative living critics, tells us that "Assyrian inscriptions have shown that the chronology of the book of Kings is hopelessly wrong." ' "[684] Beegle, who wrote a book attacking Biblical infallibility, used this example of Pekah to argue "strongly that he has found the most positive proof of errancy in Scripture."[685] In other words, Beegle and others will not receive, believe, and hear this number.

---

[683] Donald J. Wiseman, *1 & 2 Kings*, 256.

[684] Lindsell, 171, quoting Marcus Dods, *The Bible: Its Origin and Nature* (1895), 146.

[685] Ibid., 172.

Chapter 10 — *II Kings*

Some Solutions

Solution to Apparent Problem One

Since Jotham was "over the house governing the people" for the last years of Uzziah (II Kings 15:5), he may have possibly acted as a viceroy (see notes on II Kings 1:17). But then the second year of Pekah was his first year as sole monarch. Also, being viceroy, he did not have a formal accession year, that is, the second year of Pekah and the first official year of Jotham took place in the same year. A diagram of this solution is as follows:

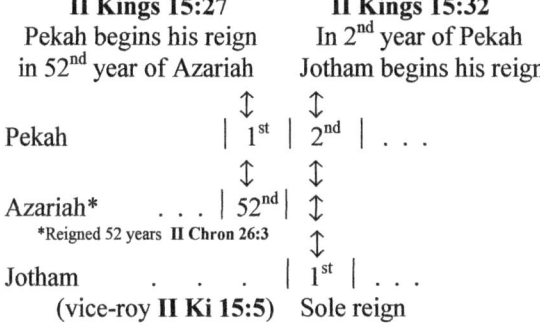

Solution to Apparent Problem Two

The answer to the second problem is to reject the Assyrian records whenever they contradict the Bible. In discussing the problems of relying upon Assyrian records, Jones writes:

> The Word of God is *its own commentary* and that it contains within itself all data necessary for its complete chronology. The secular-profane data may be examined along with the Scriptures, but it must not and will not be taken as judge. It is merely a witness. The Holy Scriptures—in context—are the only and final authority on the matter. Thus, where the secular fits, its witness has spoken the truth, where there is disparity—the witness has been misunderstood or has lied. This is the very opposite mind-set which we see in vogue before us today. Such imprudent men dare to place their intellects above the Word of the Living God and impiously sit in judgment over the Biblical account. This mind-set says in effect, if I cannot understand or ferret out the meaning of this verse of that statement from the Holy Writ, then the Scripture must be wrong. Far better and wiser would

Chapter 10 — II Kings

such be to humble one's intellect and education before Him "with whom we have to do" and admit to ignorance.[686]

Let the student of Holy Scripture make the Scripture his final authority and receive, believe, and hear all it has to say even when other documents contradict it.

II KINGS 15:8

See discussion under II Kings 14:23.

II KINGS 15:27

See discussion under II Kings 15:2.

II KINGS 15:30, 33

The Passages

II Kings 15:30 states, "And Hoshea the son of Elah made a conspiracy against Pekah the son of Remaliah, and smote him, and slew him, and reigned in his stead, in the twentieth year of Jotham the son of Uzziah."

II Kings 15:33 states, "Five and twenty years old was he when he began to reign, and he reigned sixteen years in Jerusalem. And his mother's name was Jerusha, the daughter of Zadok."

The Apparent Problem

II Kings 15:30 states that Hoshea killed Pekah and reigned in his stead in the twentieth year of Jotham, but II Kings 15:33 states that Jotham reigned for sixteen years.

Did Jotham reign for twenty years or sixteen years? *The Pulpit Commentary* "answers" this question: "This date [twentieth year of Jotham]

---

[686] Jones, 118. If one desires more information about the errors of the Assyrian records, as well as more about Pekah, he could consult Jones, 151-167, 177-186.

Chapter 10 — *II Kings*

stands in contradiction with ver. 33, where Jotham's entire reign is reckoned at sixteen years, and apparently must be a corrupt reading."[687] *The Pulpit Commentary* agrees with *The Anchor Bible*, an ecumenically based work, which wrongly states:

> This figure "twenty years," seems to be based on the assumption that Pekah ascended the throne in the fifty-second year of Azariah (v. 27) which was Azariah's last year (v. 2). Jotham, accordingly, began his reign in Pekah's first year and is credited with a parallel twenty-year reign (v. 27). But this calculation (by a late editor?) is historically in error.[688]

This can hardly be the answer.

A Solution

Both figures are correct. The sixteen-year figure presents the length of Jotham's sole reign. As for the twenty-year figure Poole writes:

> The meaning is, that he began his reign in the twentieth year after the beginning of Jotham's reign; or, which is the same thing, in the fourth year of Ahaz, son of Jotham, as appears from [II Kings] chap. xvi. 2. But the sacred writer, having not yet made mention of Ahaz, thought it more proper to number Hoshea's years by Jotham, of whom he had spoken, than by Ahaz. Besides, as Jotham did reign divers years in his father's life [Uzziah], so might Ahaz in Jotham's life, and Jotham might for diverse reasons (which it is needless here to inquire) resign up the administration of the kingdom wholly into Ahaz's hands some years before his death, and therefore might be said to reign but sixteen years, though he lived longer.[689]

At this point, a couple of explanations are in order. First, Poole mentions that Jotham's twentieth year is the same as Ahaz's fourth year. This is evident in that Jotham reigned for sixteen years solely (II Kings 15:33) and four years beyond this brings the total to his twentieth year as well as to Ahaz's fourth year (see diagram at the end of this discussion). Second, Poole mentions that Jotham reigned "divers years in his father's life." Jotham's father Uzziah became leprous and, therefore, "Jotham the king's

---

[687] G. Rawlinson, *II Kings* in vol. 5 of *The Pulpit Commentary*, 301.

[688] Mordehai Cogan and Hayim Tadmor, *II Kings: A New Translation with Introduction and Commentary* in *The Anchor Bible*, ed. William Foxwell Albright and David Noel Freedman (NY: Doubleday & Company, Inc., 1988), 181.

[689] Poole, 1:749.

Chapter 10 — *II Kings*

son *was* over the house, judging the people of the land" (II Kings 15:5; see also II Chronicles 26:23) as a viceroy (see discussion under II Kings 1:17). Third, Poole states that Ahaz might reign divers years in Jotham's life. Concerning such a possibility, Thiele writes:

> It is practically certain that Ahaz was raised to the throne . . . with the aid of a pro-Assyrian faction. . . . Assyria at this time was very active in the Mediterranean but was facing stiff resistance in many places. . . . Azariah [Jotham's father] is noted by Tiglath-Pileser as a leader in the resistance. Jotham no doubt was also an active agent in this resistance. Ahaz, however, proved himself to be a collaborationist and was put in power by those who favored conciliation.[690]

Support for Thiele's position that Ahaz collaborated with Assyria comes from II Kings 16:7-10.

Another issue arises. Since Jotham's first official year was the same as Pekah's second year (II Kings 15:32, see discussion on II Kings 15:2), and since Jotham reigned for sixteen years (II Kings 15:33); therefore, Jotham had fifteen years left to reign (16 − 1 = 15) and adding the fifteen years to Pekah's second year brings the total to Pekah's seventeenth year (2 + 15 = 17). In other words, Jotham's fifteenth year is the same as Pekah's seventeenth year. Since Pekah reigned for twenty years (II Kings 15:27), then in his seventeenth year he had three more years to reign (20 − 17 = 3). And since Pekah's seventeenth year is the same as Jotham's sixteenth year, and since at this point Pekah had three more years left to reign, then adding these three years to Jotham's sixteen years brings the calculation to Jotham's nineteenth year (16th year of Jotham + 3 more years of Pekah = 19th year of Jotham). In light of this, why does the Bible say that Hosea took over in the twentieth year of Jotham as opposed to the nineteenth year? The answer is that perhaps it was close to the end of the nineteenth year when Hoshea assassinated Pekah (II Kings 15:30) and then it took a few days to establish his government thereby taking him into the twentieth year of Jotham just as the Bible says. A diagram of the above explanation is as follows:

---

[690] Thiele, 133.

Chapter 10 — *II Kings*

II Kings 15:30
Hoshea reigns in Pekah's stead
in 20th year of Jotham

```
                                              ↕
Pekah  .. | 2ⁿᵈ | .. | 17ᵗʰ | 18ᵗʰ | 19ᵗʰ | 20ᵗʰ |  ↕
                                              ↕
Hoshea                              | 0* <  *see discussion on next passage
                                              ↕
Jotham    | 1ˢᵗ | .. | 16ᵗʰ | 17ᵗʰ | 18ᵗʰ | 19ᵗʰ | 20ᵗʰ |
   (Jotham's sole reign II Ki 15:33)

Ahaz                     ac  | 1ˢᵗ | 2ⁿᵈ | 3ʳᵈ | 4ᵗʰ | ...
```

II KINGS 15:30; 17:1

The Passages

II Kings 15:30 states, "And Hoshea the son of Elah made a conspiracy against Pekah the son of Remaliah, and smote him, and slew him, and reigned in his stead, in the twentieth year of Jotham the son of Uzziah."

II Kings 17:1 states, "In the twelfth year of Ahaz king of Judah began Hoshea the son of Elah to reign in Samaria over Israel nine years."

The Apparent Problem

II Kings 15:30 states that Hoshea started reigning in the twentieth year of Jotham, which corresponds to the fourth year of Ahaz (see discussion on II Kings 15:30, 33). But II Kings 17:1 states that Hoshea began to reign in the twelfth year of Ahaz.

Thiele says,

> When the editors of Kings were bringing that book into its final shape, they did not understand dual dating for Pekah. . . . In 2 Kings 17:1 the accession of Hoshea is placed in the twelfth year of Ahaz. That, however, is twelve years out of line with 2 Kings 15:30, where we are told that Hoshea

assassinated Pekah and then succeeded him as king in the twentieth year of Jotham.[691]

In thinking that an error is present in the Bible, Thiele is not willing to receive, believe, and hear these numbers. He speaks of "the editors of Kings," but whatever happened to inspiration? Clearly, Thiele holds to inspiration, but his quote makes it sounds as if Kings were more a research project by editors instead of the product of inspiration. Also, if Thiele regards these "editors" as the original writers of Kings who wrote inspired words, then what does such teaching do to the doctrine of inerrancy? It would seem that God inspired errors into the text! This is a fatal flaw in Thiele's presentation. Instead of accepting a theory about the editors of Kings, one should receive, believe, and hear what God says in His inspired and preserved Words.

A Solution

Possibly, when Hoshea assassinated Pekah in the fourth year of Ahaz, that is, the twentieth year of Jotham (II Kings 15:30); he took over the reign of Israel. But, perhaps, he was not able to retain the throne, was not recognized by the people, or did not independently rule until later. Therefore, he did not successfully control the throne until the twelfth year of Ahaz from which point he reigned for nine years (II Kings 17:1).

Several factors support the above view. First, when Pekah of Israel, along with Rezin of Syria, made war against Ahaz, Ahaz hired the Assyrians to defeat them (II Kings 16:5-9). The King of Assyria slew Rezin (II Kings 16:9); however, Hoshea slew Pekah (II Kings 15:30). Assyrian historical texts claim that the people "overthrew their king Pekah" at which time Tiglath-Pileser "placed Hoshea . . . as king over them."[692] While the Bible does mention that Hoshea slew Pekah (II Kings 15:30) in which, perhaps others assisted him; yet the Bible is silent about Tiglath-Pileser installing Hoshea as king. If it is true that Tiglath-Pileser made Hosea king, then Hoshea was a puppet of the Assyrians, and it may have taken him some time to throw off Assyrian control and reign independ-

---

[691] Thiele, 134. Thiele sounds a lot like Liberals who say, "The history of the last years of the kingdom of Israel was so confused that the Deuteronomic compiler, a hundred years later, was unable to secure any sort of consistency" (Norman H. Smith, *II Kings* in vol. 3 of *The Interpreter's Bible*, 271).

[692] James B. Pritchard, ed., *Ancient Near Eastern Texts Relating to the Old Testament*, 2d ed. (Princeton: Princeton University Press, 1955), 284.

Chapter 10 *II Kings*

ently over Israel. In fact, the Bible states that Hoshea brought a present year by year to the King of Assyria, however, Hoshea eventually stopped doing (II Kings 17:4). It could be at the point that he stopped sending gifts to the King of Assyria that he began to reign independently and did so until the Assyrians took him captive (see II Kings 17:4).

Second, the solution put forth here is similar to an earlier solution concerning Azariah or Uzziah (see discussion under II Kings 14:23) where Uzziah's reign started in the fifteenth year of Jeroboam II, as well as the twenty-seventh year, due to the outside foreign influence of Jeroboam II. And so here, Hoshea came to the throne in the fourth year of Ahaz, but, because of outside influence, he was not able to rule until the twelfth year of Ahaz. However, a difference between the case of Uzziah and this case with Hoshea is that the total years of Uzziah's reign include the period of outside control, whereas Hoshea's reign total does not include the years from the twentieth of Jotham to the twelfth of Ahaz, that is, eight years. Perhaps a reason for this difference in handling the reign totals is that the Assyrians or someone else (see below) had a stronger control over Israel in the time of Hoshea than Jeroboam's control over Judah in the days of Uzziah.

Third, Ahaz, king of Judah, is called "king of Israel" (II Kings 21:3; II Chronicles 28:19), which could possibly indicate that he was in control of Israel for a time. Perhaps with Ahaz's Assyrian connection he gained control of all Israel, but then in his twelfth year Hoshea was able to take Israel back so that he then became the king of Israel (II Kings 18:1, 9, 10). One weakness with the preceding statement is that while the Bible uses the expression *king of Israel* almost exclusively of the kings of the northern kingdom and of the kings of the united monarchy, one other time the Bible uses *king of Israel* of a king of Judah, specifically Jehoshaphat (II Chronicles 21:2). However, it could be that with Jehoshaphat's alliance with Ahab and the inter-marriage with Ahab's relatives (see discussion under II Kings 8:26), in a sense he was not only the king of Judah, but also of Israel. Jehoshaphat said to Ahab, the king of Israel, "I am as thou art" (I Kings 22:4; II Chronicles 18:3), and so Scripture may be indicating that, indeed, this was the case. In other words, Jehoshaphat had become so involved in compromise that he became the king of Israel, that is, just like Ahab. If the Bible uses *king of Israel* figuratively of Jehoshaphat, then it is possible that it also uses it in a figurative way of Ahaz. Be this as it may, the possibility still exists that the Bible uses *king of Israel* in a literal sense of Ahaz and that he was the acting king of Israel.

Let the Bible student receive, believe, and hear these numbers.

Chapter 10 — *II Kings*

II KINGS 15:32

See discussion under II Kings 15:2.

II KINGS 15:33

See discussion under II Kings 15:30, 33.

II KINGS 16:2; 18:2

The Passages

II Kings 16:2 states, "Twenty years old *was* Ahaz when he began to reign, and reigned sixteen years in Jerusalem, and did not *that which was* right in the sight of the LORD his God, like David his father."

II Kings 18:2 states, "Twenty and five years old was he [Hezekiah] when he began to reign; and he reigned twenty and nine years in Jerusalem. His mother's name also *was* Abi, the daughter of Zachariah."

The Apparent Problem

Since Ahaz was twenty years old when he started to reign, and since he reigned for sixteen years (II Kings 16:2), therefore it seems that he died at the age of thirty-six (20 + 16 = 36). Furthermore, since Hezekiah was twenty-five when he began to reign (II Kings 18:2), then it seems that Ahaz must have fathered Hezekiah at the young age of eleven (36 − 25 = 11).

Again, Haley states, "With many critics, we may assume a slight mistake in the numeral;"[693] however, such is not an acceptable solution to one who believes that God has perfectly preserved His Words (Psalm 12:6-7).

---

[693] Haley, 399. This is very much like the Liberal interpretation (see Norman H. Smith, *II Kings* in vol. 3 of *The Interpreter's Bible*, 272-273).

Chapter 10 — *II Kings*

The Solution

The solution is simply to take the Bible for what it says: namely, Ahaz fathered Hezekiah at eleven years old. This may seem very young to some, but it is not biologically impossible. Poole states: "There are some like instances mentioned by credible authors; which these very men will not deny, who are so ready to quarrel with the Holy Scriptures for such matters."[694] This solution should be "far more credible to any man of common prudence, than that these sacred books, whose Divine original hath been so fully evidenced both by God and men, are but the fictions and contrivances of a base impostor."[695] Forget what Haley and Liberals say: receive, believe, and hear these numbers.

II KINGS 17:1

See discussion under II Kings 15:30; 17:1.

II KINGS 18:2

See discussion under II Kings 16:2.

II KINGS 18:13

The Passage

II Kings 18:13 states, "Now in the fourteenth year of king Hezekiah did Sennacherib king of Assyria come up against all the fenced cities of Judah, and took them."

---

[694] Poole, 1:755.

[695] Ibid. While Poole makes an excellent statement, he does allow for scribal error in some of his solutions of the apparent discrepancies in the Bible as Appendix A documents. But, as far as the author has observed, in those difficulties upon which he writes he always gives one or more solutions that honor the teaching of preservation. He should have stuck with these answers, rather than admit the possibility of error in the preserved texts.

Chapter 10 — II Kings

The Apparent Problem

II Kings 18:13 is not in apparent contradiction with any other verse, but such a fact does not stop some from having a problem with it. Gleason Archer, after discussing what he believes to be copyist's errors and ways in which these errors occurred, says,

> The same was probably the case with the date of Sennacherib's invasion of Judah in 701 B.C. This is stated in 2 Kings 18:13 to have occurred in the "fourteenth" year of Hezekiah, which implies that Hezekiah must have begun his reign in 715. Yet the other six references to Hezekiah's chronology in 2 Kings make it clear that he was crowned as assistant king in 728 and became sole king in 725. Since Sennacherib did not become king in Assyria until 705 and the invasion occurred in the fourth year of his reign, the 701 date for the invasion is absolutely certain. Therefore we are to understand the "fourteen" in 2 Kings 18:13 as a miscopying of an original "twenty-four."[696]

Geisler and Howe say in the book *When Critics Ask*, "The claim that Sennacherib invaded Judah in the fourteenth year of Hezekiah is clearly a copyist error. Sennacherib actually invaded Judah in the twenty-fourth year of the reign of Hezekiah of Judah."[697] It is interesting that the title of this book, *When Critics Ask*, has been turned on its head so that the authors have actually become critics themselves.

E. J. Young writes:

> This simple and clear statement of Sennacherib's approach to the cities of Judah, however, is in reality a very difficult passage, and the difficulty is found in the numeral, "the fourteenth year." It is generally assumed that the campaign of the Assyrian king here mentioned occurred in the year 701 B.C., and if that were the case, then the accession of Hezekiah to the throne of Judah would have been in the year 715 B.C. Indeed, there are several scholars who believe that this is just what happened. Why may one not merely accept this year as the date of Hezekiah's accession? At first sight it would seem that there can be no objection to so doing, until it is noted that according to II Kings 18:1,2 Hezekiah began to reign in the third year of Hoshea king of Israel and reigned for twenty-nine years in Jerusalem. The northern kingdom, however, fell to Shalmanezer in 721 B.C. (II Kings 18:9 ff.) and so Hezekiah must have begun his reign six years before Samaria's downfall, i.e., in 727 B.C. If the statements of II

---

[696] Archer, 207.

[697] Geisler and Howe, 197.

Chapter 10 — *II Kings*

> Kings 18:1, 2 are correct, therefore, Hezekiah cannot have begun his reign in 715 B.C. ...
>
> Various attempts have been made to solve the difficulty raised by the mention of the fourteenth year of Hezekiah in II Kings 18:13 and Isaiah 36:1. No lengthy discussion can be attempted here, but there is one possible solution for this seeming error of chronology in the Scripture. Instead of reading "fourteenth" in the two passages adduced, one may simply read "twenty-fourth." ... If this is to be adopted, it would seem to clear up most of the difficulties involved.
>
> At the same time one must note that there is no manuscript evidence in its favor.[698]

Young's suggestion to change the preserved text would not "clear up most of the difficulties involved" but would, instead, produce many more difficulties.

Archer, Geisler and Howe, and Young are all in agreement with the Liberal commentary *The Interpreter's Bible*, which wrongly states: "The chronology is again at fault. The year was 701 B.C., the twenty-fourth year of Hezekiah's reign."[699]

The best course of action, however, is to hear this number. Jones states:

> The Hebrew language presents "fourteen" as "four (and) ten" ... which transliterates as "arba eser." The Hebrew for "twenty-four" is "four (and) twenty" ... transliterating into "arba esrim." Archer[700] is inaccurate when he understates that which would have been necessary to bring about the proposed scribal error. He basically said that all that would have been required was the "misreading of one letter," the miscopying of the "mem." However, as can be seen from the above, it would have required the copyist to have dropped out two letters—the "yod" and the "mem."
>
> Regardless, such is hardly in keeping with the testimony of Christ Jesus Who positively declared that neither jot nor tittle had been altered in the Hebrew Text during the nearly 1,500 years from Moses to His day (Mat. 5:18). Archer's proposed solution is certainly a far cry from this avowal of Christ's, yet it serves to demonstrate the attitude and place to which

---

[698] Edward J. Young, "Are the Scriptures Inerrant?" in *The Bible: The Living Word of Revelation*, ed. Merrill Tenney (Grand Rapids: Zondervan, 1968), 112, 113.

[699] Norman H. Smith, *II Kings* in vol. 3 of *The Interpreter's Bible*, 292.

[700] See Archer, *Encyclopedia of Bible Difficulties*, 211. Also, see Archer, *A Survey of Old Testament Introduction*, revised ed. (Chicago: Moody Press, 1974), 291, 292.

Chapter 10 — II Kings

most modern conservatism has plummeted. Simply stated, that posture has the mind set that when a problem is encountered which the intellect cannot readily solve, merely alter or reject the Scriptures.[701]

A Solution

In looking at a solution to the problems posed by those who will not simply receive II Kings 18:13, it is necessary to examine some preliminary issues first and then to take up the solution.

Preliminary Issues

First, the job of the Bible student is to take the Bible for what it says and to let the Bible correct him, and not he correct the Bible (II Timothy 3:16). Thiele, however, questions II Kings 17:1; 18:1, 9, and 10, which coordinate Hoshea's, reign with those of Ahaz and Hezekiah.[702] These verses did not fit with Thiele's explanations; therefore, he rejected them. Better, it is to reject the explanations and to receive the Scriptures.

Second, from Young's quote above, Young assumes that Hoshea's nine years of reign (II Kings 17:1) took place right after the reign of Pekah, but such is not necessarily the case (see discussion of II Kings 15:30 and 17:1).

Third, from Archer's quote above, Archer states that Hezekiah co-reigned with Ahaz. However, the discussion in this book on II Kings 15:30 and 17:1 shows that Hoshea did not start his nine-year reign immediately after Pekah's reign. Therefore, there is no need to resort to a co-reign of Hezekiah with Ahaz.

---

[701] Jones, 177.

[702] Thiele, 134,135. Others come up with the idea that it was not the original writers, who made an error here, but that it was the result of some later scribe who inserted this into the text. See Steinmann, Andrew E. "The Chronology of 2 Kings 15-18." *Journal of the Evangelical Theological Society* 30 (1987): 391-397. While such a suggestion removes a questioning of the inerrancy of the *autographa*, it raises other issues that are equally disturbing, one of which is that if some of the statements about Hezekiah's chronology are insertions, then how is one to know that other insertions have not occurred? Perhaps one does not like a certain doctrine, could he not claim that it was inserted by a later scribe who added it to the inspired words, and that he is, therefore, free to ignore it?

Chapter 10 *II Kings*

Fourth, some even advocate a co-reign of Jotham, Ahaz, and Uzziah and or a co-reign of Ahaz and Hezekiah[703] as a way to handle the supposed problems of II Kings 18:13. While it is commendable that those who advocate such a position are not willing to tamper with the Words of God and claim scribal error, yet these co-reigns are not necessary.[704]

---

[703] For example, see Leon Wood, *A Survey of Israel's History* (Grand Rapids: Zondervan, 1979), 352-357. Jotham acted as viceroy during the last years of Uzziah but did not have co-reign with him (see discussion on II Kings 15:2, 27, 32); therefore, his 16 years of reign were 16 years of sole reign.

[704] In the plan advocated by Wood (*A Survey of Israel's History*, 352-357), Jotham had no years of independent rule (353-354), Ahaz only 3 years (355), and Hezekiah 18 years (364), thereby giving a total of 21 years of sole rule for these three kings. The Bible states that Jotham reigned for 16 years (II Kings 15:33); Ahaz for 16 years (II Kings 16:2); and Hezekiah for 29 years (II Kings 18:2). If these are years of sole reign, then the total is 61 years, which is a difference of 40 years as compared to Wood's plan. Wood's plan results in an unprecedented three overlapping co-reigns (354) and proposes that four years of Hezekiah's chief rule not be included in the total years that he ruled (355), also contrary to usual practice: Wood presents 33 years of chief rule for Hezekiah, but the Bible only states 29 (II Kings 18:2).

But to remove 40 years from the amount of sole reign poses a problem with Ezekiel 4:4-5. In this passage God symbolically puts upon Ezekiel the years of the iniquity of Israel while Ezekiel lies on his side for 390 days with each day representing a year of Israel's sin, that is, 390 years. At the same time, Ezekiel depicts a siege against Jerusalem (Ezekiel 4:1-3, 7, 8), which is the punishment upon Israel for her 390 years of sin; therefore, while Ezekiel bears the iniquity of Israel, at the same time he depicts the punishment for that same sin. "Ezekiel, by his lying so long bound under the burden of Israel and Judah which was laid upon his side, is to show to the people how they are to be cast down by the siege of Jerusalem, and how, while lying on the ground, without the possibility of turning or rising, they are to bear the punishment of their sins" (Keil, *The Prophecies of Ezekiel* in vol. 9 of *Commentary on the Old Testament*, 42-43). Such an understanding of the passage upholds the main idea behind *bear the iniquity*, that is, to suffer punishment because of sin (Leviticus 5:1, 17; 7:18; 17:16; 19:8; 20:17, 19; Numbers 5:31; 14:34; 30:15; Ezekiel 14:10). Fairbairn states that *bear the iniquity* "frequently occurs in Scripture, and always in the sense of sustaining the punishment due to sin" (Patrick Fairbairn, *Commentary on Ezekiel* (Grand Rapids: Kregel, 1989), 58). Furthermore, such an understanding of Ezekiel 4:4-5 also places the 390 years before the fall of Jerusalem, instead of after its fall as does Feinberg (Charles Lee Feinberg, *The Prophet of Ezekiel: The Glory of the Lord* (Chicago: Moody, 1969), 33) and Alexander (Ralph H. Alexander, *Ezekiel* in vol. 6 of *The Expositor's Bible Commentary*, 769).

What is the duration of the 390 years? Since the siege is the punishment for the sin, then the 390 years goes to the start of the siege in 588 B.C., or, at the most, to the very end of the siege in 586 B.C. Also, since the passage speaks of both Israel and Judah (Ezekiel 4:6), then the starting point of the 390 years is either at the beginning of the northern kingdom of Israel or later. At the very beginning of the northern kingdom, Jeroboam, the first king of Israel, "drave Israel from following the LORD, and made them sin a great sin" (II

Chapter 10 — II Kings

Fifth, Archer states: "Since Sennacherib did not become king in Assyria until 705 and the invasion occurred in the fourth year of his reign, the 701 date for the invasion is absolutely certain."[705] Herein is a complete reliance upon Assyrian chronology. At times reliance upon Assyrian chronology is so great that where the Bible and Assyrian chronology disagree, some reject the God-preserved text of Scripture and in its place receive the man-produced chronologies of Assyria. What kind of confidence does such action show in the promises of Jesus (Matthew 5:18; Luke 16:17; John 10:35)? It is a serious problem when one will place a higher value upon Assyrian records and Assyrian scribes than in the

---

Kings 17:21), which seems to be the starting point for the 390 years and the ending is either 588 or 586 B.C. Either of these possibilities demand what Thiele deridingly refers to as "the so-called long systems of Hebrew chronology" (Thiele, 56). The "390 year declaration, taken in context, is most significant for it takes the date of the Schism . . . out of the hands of men and places it on a firm foundation" (Jones, 140). A 390 year period from the Schism to the fall of Jerusalem also removes the possibility of doing as Wood posits, wherein he removes 40 years from the sole reigns of various kings by suggesting several co-regencies. Thiele (Thiele, 79) and Wood (Wood, 423) give the span between the Schism to the fall of Jerusalem as only 345 years, contrary to the teaching of Ezekiel 4:5, which places it at 390 years or thereabouts. Hence, Wood's solution poses a difficulty with Ezekiel 4:5 and because of Ezekiel 4:5 the author will not set forth a solution for the fourteenth year of Hezekiah that involves a co-reign.

Block suggests an alternative view in stating that the 390 years starts with the moving of the Shekinah glory from the tabernacle to Solomon's temple in Solomon's 11th year and goes to 586 B.C. (Daniel I. Block, *The Book of Ezekiel Chapters 1-24* in *The New International Commentary on the Old Testament*, ed. R. K. Harrison and Robert L. Hubbard, Jr. (Grand Rapids: Eerdmans, 1997), 178). Block's suggestion results in a chronology somewhere between short and long. While Block does try to explain how the 390 years could start in the united monarchy, he fails to discuss how the sin of Israel started with the moving of the Shekinah glory. Inasmuch as the moving of the glory was an act of God (I Kings 8:10-11), how could this be the start of a sin?

For more information on the 390 years of Ezekiel 4:5 referring to the time from the division of the kingdom to the fall of Jerusalem, consult Jones, *Old Testament Chronology*, 24, 137-140; William Greenhill, *An Exposition of Ezekiel* (Carlisle, PA: The Banner of Truth Trust, n.d.), 129-131; Poole, *Matthew Poole's Commentary on the Holy Bible*, 2:673-674; Gill, *Exposition of the Old &New Testaments*, 6:20-21; A. R. Fausset, *Jeremiah – Malachi*, part 2 of vol.2 in *A Commentary Critical, Experimental, and Practical on the Old and New Testaments*, 213-214; *The Geneva Bible*, footnote on Ezekiel 4:4; John Calvin, *Commentaries on the First Twenty Chapters of the Prophet Ezekiel*, trans. Thomas Myers, in vol. 11 of *Calvin's Commentaries* (Grand Rapids, MI: Baker Books, 2005), 173-182; and Matthew Henry, *Isaiah to Malachi*, in vol. 4 of *Matthew Henry's Commentary*, 606-608.

[705] Archer, 207.

Chapter 10 *II Kings*

Words of God and in the Son of God (see discussion under II Kings 15:2, 27, 32). One should receive, believe, and hear the Scriptures over all else.

Solution

The solution hinges upon this: is the invasion of Judah mentioned in Assyrian records as having occurred in the third year of Sennacherib (702/701 B.C.) the same invasion that occurred in the fourteenth year of Hezekiah? Some assume the two events are the same,[706] but

> the result of this erroneous assumption is the production of a regnal chronology for the Hebrew Monarchs which neither harmonizes with the Biblical record nor secular history. . . . by so doing Thiele has created problems with the integrity of the Hebrew Text. Actually even Thiele's Assyrian date is not precise as the Assyrian records indicate that 705 BC is Sennacherib's accession year; thus his third is 702, but this is not the real issue here. The real problem is that the Scriptures have recorded the accounts of two Assyrian invasions; one being briefly described in II Kings 18:13-16 [also Isaiah 36:1] and the other from 18:17 to 19:37 (also in II Chr. 32:1-23; Isa. 36:2-37:38), but Thiele has combined them into a single event and then forced the Assyrian account and its date upon this composite.[707]

Edward Mack writing about some of the chronological difficulties in the Old Testament states:

> The chief difficulty is with the invasions of Sennacherib in Hezekiah's reign. The confusion is caused by the apparent dating of Sennacherib's famous and disastrous invasion of 701 in the 14th year of Hezekiah's reign (2 Kings 18:13). Various attempts [at] reconciliation have been made; one attempt has been to place the beginning of Hezekiah's reign in 715, which is out of the question entirely, as it disregards the exact terms in which the beginning of his reign is placed before the fall of Samaria (2 Kings 18:10). Another suggestion has been that "24th" be read instead of "14th"; but this is pure conjecture. There is a simple and satisfactory solution: in the chapters which contain the record (2 Kings 18 and Isaiah 36) it is evident that two invasions are described. Frequently in the Scriptures records are topical rather than chronological, and just so in this instance the topic is Sennacherib's menace of Judah, and the ultimate deliverance by Yahweh. The story includes two invasions: the first in the 14th year of Hezekiah (713) when Sennacherib led the armies of his father Sargon, the

---

[706] In addition to the writers already quoted, Thiele, 78, 175.

[707] Jones, 168.

Chapter 10 *II Kings*

end of which, so far as Jerusalem was concerned, was the payment of tribute by Hezekiah, as is accurately stated in 2 Kings 18:16. The second invasion, the description of which begins with the following verse (18:17), was the more serious, and is probably identified as that of 701,[708] when Sennacherib had become king. The necessary insertion of a paragraph indicator between 18:16 and 17 satisfies every demand for harmony.[709]

At this point a question arises. If the Assyrian invasion in the fourteenth year of Hezekiah occurred in 713 B.C., and if Sennacherib's accession year to the throne of Assyria did not take place until 705 B.C., then why does the Bible say that Sennacherib is king in the fourteenth year of Hezekiah (II Kings 18:13; Isaiah 36:1)? The answer is that "in the fourteenth year of Hezekiah's reign Sennacherib [was] co-regent (or viceroy) with his father Sargon";[710] therefore, both Sennacherib and Sargon were considered King of Assyria.

In the above-extended quote, Mack states that "in the Scriptures records are topical rather than chronological." For example, Revelation 20:6 speaks of the first resurrection, which resurrection has many aspects transpiring at various times (Christ, 2,000 years ago, Matthew 28:6; raptured saints, before the Tribulation, I Thessalonians 4:13-17; the two witnesses, at about the middle of the Tribulation, Revelation 11:11; Old Testament and tribulation saints, after the Tribulation, Revelation 20:6; and saints who die during the Millennial Kingdom). Another example of Scripture treating a subject topically rather than chronologically is in the book of Isaiah when Isaiah speaks of Babylon and mixes verses about a near-to-come judgment upon Babylon with verses about a far-off judgment (Isaiah 13 and 21). A third example of Scripture speaking topically and not chronologically is in Zechariah 12:10 where the Bible speaks of the Jews looking upon Him Whom they have pierced and mourning for Him. The looking upon Christ Whom the Jews pierced was fulfilled in John 19:33-37 at Christ's crucifixion, but the mourning for Him will not be until the end of the Tribulation. Other examples are in Isaiah 9:6; 61:1-2;

---

[708] As noted above this date is perhaps 702 B.C. But also, Jones (Jones, 167-177) puts forth reasons for why the second Assyrian invasion by Sennacherib was not the same as that recorded in the Assyrian records in the third year of Sennacherib. This information is not germane to the solution presented here, but is mentioned for those who desire to delve further into this.

[709] Edward Mack, "Chronology of the Old Testament" in *International Standard Bible Encyclopedia*, 2:953.

[710] Jones, 175.

Chapter 10 — II Kings

and Daniel 9:24-27. In light of the fact that Scripture at times deals with subjects topically rather than chronologically, it is possible that once the invasions of Assyria into Judah commenced in the fourteenth year of Hezekiah that Scripture continues with that theme and speaks of further invasions, without presenting all the chronological details.

Conclusion

One should receive, believe, and hear the fourteenth year in II Kings 18:13. There is no problem with the number.

II KINGS 22:3-4 AND II CHRONICLES 34:3-4

The Passages

II Kings 22:3-4 states, "And it came to pass in the eighteenth year of king Josiah, *that* the king sent Shaphan the son of Azaliah, the son of Meshullam, the scribe, to the house of the LORD, saying, Go up to Hilkiah the high priest, that he may sum the silver which is brought into the house of the LORD, which the keepers of the door have gathered of the people."

II Chronicles 34:3-4 states, "For in the eighth year of his [Josiah's] reign, while he was yet young, he began to seek after the God of David his father: and in the twelfth year he began to purge Judah and Jerusalem from the high places, and the groves, and the carved images, and the molten images. And they brake down the altars of Baalim in his presence; and the images, that *were* on high above them, he cut down; and the groves, and the carved images, and the molten images, he brake in pieces, and made dust *of them*, and strowed *it* upon the graves of them that had sacrificed unto them."

The Apparent Problem

Both of the passages speak of reforms that King Josiah undertook. Some suppose a problem in the passages for the one in Kings states that a reform took place in the eighteenth year of Josiah, whereas Chronicles states that a reform took place in the twelfth year.

Chapter 10 — *II Kings*

A Solution

Two different reforms are in view: one in the twelfth year and one later in the eighteenth year.

II KINGS 24:8 AND II CHRONICLES 36:9

The Passages

II Kings 24:8 states, "Jehoiachin *was* eighteen years old when he began to reign, and he reigned in Jerusalem three months. And his mother's name *was* Nehushta, the daughter of Elnathan of Jerusalem."

II Chronicles 36:9 states, "Jehoiachin *was* eight years old when he began to reign, and he reigned three months and ten days in Jerusalem: and he did *that which was* evil in the sight of the LORD."

The Apparent Problems

Two problems are apparent with the above verses. First, Kings states that Jehoiachin was eighteen years old when he began to reign, whereas Chronicles says he was eight years old. A second problem concerns the length of reign. Kings states that he reigned for three months, whereas Chronicles states that he reigned for three months and ten days.

This is another place wherein Central Baptist Theological Seminary claims a scribal error took place.[711] Sir Robert Anderson is also of the opinion that an error has occurred here.[712]

John C. Whitcomb, Jr. states: "He [Johoiachin] could hardly have been eight years at this time, for he had wives (II Kings 24:15). Therefore the number 'eight' in II Chron. 36:9 should read 'eighteen' as in II Kings 24:8."[713] Herein Whitcomb finds himself of the same mind as *The Inter-*

---

[711] Glenny, 85.

[712] Sir Robert Anderson, *The Bible and Modern Criticism*, 162.

[713] John C. Whitcomb, Jr., *Solomon to the Exile: Studies in Kings and Chronicles* (Grand Rapids: Baker, 1978), 147.

preter's Bible, a Liberal commentary, which incorrectly says of II Chronicles 36:9, "Read probably 'eighteen'."[714]

But Jones writes:

> As the two verses appear to contradict one another, this is commonly touted as a scribal error in the Hebrew Text. Surely in view of all the foregoing proofs and solutions which consistently have borne out the faithfulness and accuracy of the Holy Scriptures as well as the testimony of the manner in which we have seen the many mathematical chronological statements contained within that same Book perfectly fit together time and time again; by now, we "know" there is a Bible honoring solution.[715]

Indeed, one should receive, believe, and hear these numbers.

Some Solutions

Some Solutions to the First Apparent Problem

Eight years old in II Chronicles 36:9 in Hebrew is literally *a son of eight years old* (see discussion on II Kings 8:26). According to II Kings 24:12, the Babylonians took Jehoiachin captive in the eighth year of Nebuchadnezzar. Jehoiachin, therefore, was a son of eight years as measured by the reign of Nebuchadnezzar, although he was physically eighteen years old at this time.

Or possibly Jehoiachin was anointed king when he was eight and then again at eighteen. *The Communicator's Commentary* states: "Chronicles says he was eight years old, but that was probably his age at the time his father Jehoiakim designated him to be the next king."[716] That Jehoiachin may have been anointed or designated king at eight years old by his father, Jehoiakim, is bolstered by the fact that in the third year of Jehoiakim's reign (Daniel 1:1) Nebuchadnezzar besieged Jerusalem and took away captives. Jehoiakim, sensing that hostilities were on the increase, may have taken the precaution of anointing Jehoiachin king when Jehoiachin was eight, which would have been in the first official year of his reign and only two years prior to the event of Daniel 1:1. Since Jehoiakim

---

[714] W. A. L. Elmslie, *II Chronicles* in *The Interpreter's Bible*, 546.

[715] Jones, 201.

[716] Russell H. Dilday, *1, 2 Kings* in *The Communicator's Commentary*, ed. Lloyd J. Oglivie (Waco, TX: Word Books, 1987), 497.

Chapter 10   *II Kings*

reigned eleven years (II Chronicles 36:5), and since Jehoiachin started his reign at the age of eighteen (II Kings 24:8), which was right after the reign of Jehoiakim; then when Jehoiachin was eight, or ten years younger than eighteen, it was Jehoiakim's first year (11 − 10 = 1).

A third solution is that possibly Josiah anointed Jehoiachin to be king when Jehoiachin was eight years old, but Jehoiachin did not actually occupy the throne until he was eighteen.[717] This may seem in contradiction with the above solution, which states that Jehoiachin was eight years old in Jehoiakim's first year. While it is true that Jehoiachin was eight years old in Jehoiakim's first year, if, however, at this time he was almost nine, then nearly a year earlier he was still eight years old. Nearly a year earlier, Josiah was still on the throne; therefore, it is possible that for a portion of Josiah's last year, Jehoiachin was eight years old. Josiah reigned for thirty-one years (II Kings 22:1), after which came the three month reign of Jehoahaz (II Kings 23:31), and then the eleven year reign of Jehoiakim (II Kings 23:36). It is conceivable that the last bit of Josiah's thirty-first year, the three-month reign of Jehoahaz, and the accession year of Jehoiakim all took place in the same year. If this is correct, then it is quite conceivable that for a few days in Josiah's thirty-first year, Jehoiachin was eight years old and, therefore, could have been anointed by Josiah. Jones points out:

> Realizing that his sons were wicked, godly Josiah must have hoped that his grandson Jehoiachin (Jeconiah), though only eight year old at the time, would turn out better. As Josiah himself was but eight when he began to reign [II Kings 22:1], he would have few qualms in placing so young a child upon the throne of Judah.[718]

Also, toward the end of Josiah's reign, he was concerned about the Egyptians and may have realized that in going up against the Egyptians (II Kings 23:29), he might not return and, therefore, wanted to select his replacement beforehand. Jones points out that the only way that Josiah could anoint Jehoiachin as his replacement would have been for Josiah to adopt Jehoiachin as his son.[719] Evidence for an adoption is in Matthew 1:11 and II Chronicles 36:10. Matthew 1:11 states, "And Josias begat

---

[717] Jehoiachin did not occupy the throne immediately following Josiah's death because the people made Jehoahaz the next king (II Kings 23:30) and then Necho made Jehoiakim the next king after Jehoahaz (II Kings 23:3-4).

[718] Jones, 201-202.

[719] Ibid., 202.

Chapter 10 — *II Kings*

Jechonias [Jehoiachin] and his brethren, about the time they were carried away to Babylon." Concerning Matthew 1:11, Jones says,

> In a larger Biblical sense, it is permissible to speak of "begetting" descendents beyond the generation of one's own offspring, the context of this "begetting" would have occurred at the time of the adoption. The truth of this is clearly seen in that which follows: "and his brothers".
>
> Now this is indeed very strange, for the allusion is clearly to Josiah's sons and as such, are Jehoiachin's [that is, Jeconiah's] uncles and father – unless – unless he had been adopted. Then and only then could it be said that Josiah's sons are Jehoiachin's brothers![720]

Adding to Jones' understanding of Matthew 1:11 is II Chronicles 36:10, which states: "And when the year was expired, king Nebuchadnezzar sent, and brought him to Babylon, with the goodly vessels of the house of the LORD, and made Zedekiah his brother king over Judah and Jerusalem." The one whom Nebuchadnezzar brought to Babylon was Jehoiachin (II Chronicles 36:9); therefore II Chronicles 36:10 states that Zedekiah is Jehoiachin's brother. At this point Jones states:

> Again, how can Zedekiah be Jehoiachin's brother? Only by his [Jehoiachin's] being adopted to full sonship. However the people of the land did not abide by Josiah's decision, placing instead Josiah's twenty-three year old son Jehoahaz (not his eldest, II Ki. 23:36) on the throne (II Ki. 23:8).[721]

Whatever solution one accepts for this apparent problem, let him receive, believe, and hear the numbers.

Solution to the Second Apparent Problem

Jehoiachin reigned for three months which figure Kings gives, but from the death of his father to his actually occupying the throne was ten days, which amount Chronicles credits to the length of Jehoiachin's reign.

---

[720] Ibid.

[721] Ibid.

Chapter 10   *II Kings*

II KINGS 24:12 AND JEREMIAH 52:28

The Passages

II Kings 24:12 states, "And Jehoiachin the king of Judah went out to the king of Babylon, he, and his mother, and his servants, and his princes, and his officers: and the king of Babylon took him in the eighth year of his reign."

Jeremiah 52:28 states, "This is the people whom Nebuchadrezzar carried away captive: in the seventh year three thousand Jews and three and twenty."

The Apparent Problem

Kings states that Nebuchadnezzar took Jehoiachin captive in the eighth year of Nebuchadnezzar's reign, whereas Jeremiah speaks of it happening in the seventh year.

A Solution

"The Hebrews count the accession year of foreign monarchs as their first year reigning,"[722] whereas the Babylonians do not. "Thus Nebuchadnezzar's 7th year by Babylonian dating becomes his 8th year by Hebrew reckoning."[723] Jeremiah in his passage follows the Babylonian method of reckoning, whereas the writer of Kings follows the Hebrew method.

II KINGS 24:14 AND JEREMIAH 52:28-30

The Passages

II Kings 24:14 states, "And he carried away all Jerusalem, and all the princes, and all the mighty men of valour, *even* ten thousand captives, and

---

[722] Jones, 132.

[723] Ibid.

Chapter 10   *II Kings*

all the craftsmen and smiths: none remained, save the poorest sort of the people of the land."

Jeremiah 52:28-30 states, "This is the people whom Nebuchadrezzar carried away captive: in the seventh year three thousand Jews and three and twenty: in the eighteenth year of Nebuchadrezzar he carried away captive from Jerusalem eight hundred thirty and two persons: in the three and twentieth year of Nebuchadrezzar Nebuzaradan the captain of the guard carried away captive of the Jews seven hundred forty and five persons: all the persons *were* four thousand and six hundred."

The Apparent Problem

Kings states the number of captives as ten thousand (10,000), whereas Jeremiah gives a number of four thousand six hundred (4,600).

A Solution

Jeremiah speaks of Nebuchadnezzar carrying away captives in his seventh, eighteenth, and twenty-third years; whereas Kings, with the larger number, may include captives Nebuchadnezzar carried away at other times. That at least one other deportation took place is evident from Daniel 1:1, which says, "In the third year of the reign of Jehoiakim king of Judah came Nebuchadnezzar king of Babylon unto Jerusalem, and besieged it" at which time he brought "certain of the children of Israel, and of the king's seed, and of the princes" (Daniel 1:3) to Babylon. Since Daniel 2:1 speaks of the second year of Nebuchadnezzar's reign, and since Daniel 1 occurs chronologically before Daniel 2, then the deportation of Daniel 1 occurred in or before Nebuchadnezzar's second year and is not, therefore, included in Jeremiah's reckoning. The Kings' account, then, probably includes figures from all the deportations, whereas Jeremiah only gives the totals and the sum of three of the deportations.

II KINGS 25:8-9 AND JEREMIAH 52:12-13

The Passages

II Kings 25:8-9 states, "And in the fifth month, on the seventh *day* of the month, which is the nineteenth year of king Nebuchadnezzar king of Babylon, came Nebuzaradan, captain of the guard, a servant of the king of

Chapter 10 — *II Kings*

Babylon, unto Jerusalem: and he burnt the house of the LORD, and the king's house, and all the houses of Jerusalem, and every great *man's* house burnt he with fire."

Jeremiah 52:12-13 states, "Now in the fifth month, in the tenth *day* of the month, which *was* the nineteenth year of Nebuchadrezzar king of Babylon, came Nebuzaradan, captain of the guard, *which* served the king of Babylon, into Jerusalem, and burned the house of the LORD, and the king's house; and all the houses of Jerusalem, and all the houses of the great *men*, burned he with fire."

The Apparent Problem

Both passages seem to be speaking of the same event; however, Kings states that the event occurred on the seventh day of the month, whereas Jeremiah states that it took place on the tenth day of the month.

Haley suggests a scribal error is the reason for this difference.[724] Also, Keil makes the same suggestion,

> But since there are similar differences met with afterwards (vv. 17 and 19 [of II Kings 25]) in the statement of numbers, which can only be accounted for from the substitution of similar numeral letters, we must assume that there is a change of this kind here. Which of the two dates is the correct one it is impossible to determine.[725]

Again, Keil erroneously suggests that scribes used letters for numbers when such was not the case (see Chapter Three). Furthermore, according to Keil, it is impossible to determine which date is correct; therefore, the Words of God have no authority to decide the issue. However, based on Jesus' assessment of the Old Testament, both dates are correct.

Some Solutions

A couple of possible solutions exist for this apparent problem. First, Nebuzaradan "came to Jerusalem on the seventh day [II Kings 25:8], and burnt the temple on the tenth day [Jeremiah 52:12-13]."[726] Or, Kings

---

[724] Haley, 393.

[725] Keil, *Commentary on the Second Book of Kings* in vol. 3 of *Commentary on the Old Testament*, 363. For comments on II Kings 25:17, see comments on I Kings 7:26.

[726] Poole, 1:773.

Chapter 10 *II Kings*

speaks of Nebuzaradan's "departure from Riblah [II Kings 25:6; Jeremiah 52:9-10] towards Jerusalem, and Jeremiah speaks of his coming to Jerusalem, which was about three days' journey from Riblah."[727] These solutions are far better than to say that this is the result of a scribal error. Let the student of Scripture confidently receive, believe, and hear these numbers.

II KINGS 25:17

See discussion under I Kings 7:16.

II KINGS 25:19 AND JEREMIAH 52:25

The Passages

II Kings 25:19 states, "And out of the city he took an officer that was set over the men of war, and five men of them that were in the king's presence, which were found in the city, and the principal scribe of the host, which mustered the people of the land, and threescore men of the people of the land *that were* found in the city."

Jeremiah 52:25 states, "He took also out of the city an eunuch, which had the charge of the men of war; and seven men of them that were near the king's person, which were found in the city; and the principal scribe of the host, who mustered the people of the land; and threescore men of the people of the land, that were found in the midst of the city."

The Apparent Problem

Kings states that the captain of the guard (II Kings 25:18) took five men, whereas Jeremiah says that he took seven men.

Haley again places this in the category of a scribal error[728] and, therefore, will not hear these numbers.

---

[727] Ibid.

[728] Haley, 383.

Chapter 10 — II Kings

Some Solutions

One solution is this: perhaps "five were first taken, and two after them,"[729] making a total of seven.

Matthew Henry offers another solution when he writes that in II Kings 25:19

> it is said that there were five, here [Jeremiah 52:25] there were seven, of those that were *near the king,* which Dr. Lightfoot reconciles thus, that he took away seven of those that were near the king, but two of them were Jeremiah himself [Jeremiah 40:2-4] and Ebed-melech [Jeremiah 39:16-17], who were both discharged, as we have read before, so that there were only five of them put to death.[730]

Both of the above solutions are from sources that were available for some time before Haley wrote his book, yet he chose to go the way of scribal error. The solutions to many of these alleged problems are not new, but scholars refuse to walk in the old paths and, instead, accept the new teaching that the Bible is much like any other book. But those who love the Old Book need to walk in the old paths and receive, believe, and hear what this Book says.

II KINGS 25:27 AND JEREMIAH 52:31

The Passages

II Kings 25:27 states, "And it came to pass in the seven and thirtieth year of the captivity of Jehoiachin king of Judah, in the twelfth month, on the seven and twentieth *day* of the month, *that* Evilmerodach king of Babylon in the year that he began to reign did lift up the head of Jehoiachin king of Judah out of prison."

Jeremiah 52:31 states, "And it came to pass in the seven and thirtieth year of the captivity of Jehoiachin king of Judah, in the twelfth month, in the five and twentieth *day* of the month, *that* Evilmerodach king of

---

[729] Poole, 1:774.

[730] Matthew Henry, *Isaiah to Malachi* in vol. 4 of *Matthew Henry's Commentary,* 557.

Chapter 10 — II Kings

Babylon in the *first* year of his reign lifted up the head of Jehoiachin king of Judah, and brought him forth out of prison."

The Apparent Problem

Kings speaks of Evilmerodach lifting up Jehoiachin out of prison on the twenty-seventh day of the month, whereas Jeremiah speaks of this event occurring on the twenty-fifth day.

Once again, Haley suggests that this is the result of a copyist's error,[731] as does Keil,[732] but according to Jesus no error is present here (John 17:17). Whom will the reader believe?

A Solution

Gill states that the lifting up of the head of Jehoiachin out of prison "might have been determined and notified on the 25th, but not executed till the 27th; or it might be begun to be put in execution on the 25th, and not finished till the 27th."[733] A solution such Gill offers, honors the Scriptures and regards the Scriptures in the same way that Jesus regards them when He says, "Thy Word is truth" (John 17:17). May Bible believers believe Jesus. Instead of approaching the Bible as Haley does in claiming that the Bible contains scribal errors, let Bible believers approach the Bible with the view that the Bible is all truth and, therefore, let him receive, believe, and hear every part of it, including the numbers.

---

[731] Haley, 400.

[732] Keil, *Commentary on the Second Book of Kings* in vol. 3 of *Commentary on the Old Testament*, 367-368.

[733] Gill, *Exposition of the Old & New Testaments*, 5:697.

CHAPTER ELEVEN:
APPARENT NUMERICAL CONTRADICTIONS IN I CHRONICLES

I CHRONICLES 2:13-15

See discussion under I Samuel 16:10-11.

I CHRONICLES 2:22-23; JOSHUA 13:30; AND JUDGES 10:3-4

The Passages

I Chronicles 2:22-23 states, "And Segub begat Jair, who had three and twenty cities in the land of Gilead. And he took Geshur, and Aram, with the towns of Jair, from them, with Kenath, and the towns thereof, *even* threescore cities. All these *belonged to* the sons of Machir the father of Gilead."

Joshua 13:30 states, "And their coast was from Mahanaim, all Bashan, all the kingdom of Og king of Bashan, and all the towns of Jair, which *are* in Bashan, threescore cities."

Judges 10:3-4 states, "And after him arose Jair, a Gileadite, and judged Israel twenty and two years. And he had thirty sons that rode on thirty ass colts, and they had thirty cities, which are called Havothjair unto this day, which *are* in the land of Gilead."

Chapter 11 *I Chronicles*

The Apparent Problem

It seems that Jair had twenty-three cities (I Chronicles 2:22), sixty cites (I Chronicles 2:23 and Joshua 13:30), and thirty cites (Judges 10:3-4).

A Solution

A solution lies in a careful reading of the verses involved, for they are not all speaking of the same thing or of the same time. First, Judges 10:4 says, "They had thirty cites." *They* refers back to the sons of Jair who also had thirty ass colts. Judges 10:3 and 4 refer to Jair's sons, not to Jair. Second, I Chronicles 2:22-23 shows the development of Jair's holdings. In verse 22, the Bible states that he had twenty-three cites, and then verse 23 speaks of Jair taking more cities so that he had sixty cities altogether just as Joshua 13:30 states.

I CHRONICLES 3:10-13 AND MATTHEW 1:7-9

The Passages

I Chronicles 3:10-13 states, "And Solomon's son *was* Rehoboam, Abia his son, Asa his son, Jehoshaphat his son, Joram his son, Ahaziah his son, Joash his son, Amaziah his son, Azariah his son, Jotham his son, Ahaz his son, Hezekiah his son, Manasseh his son."

Matthew 1:7-9 states, "And Solomon begat Roboam; and Roboam begat Abia; and Abia begat Asa; and Asa begat Josaphat; and Josaphat begat Joram; and Joram begat Ozias; And Ozias begat Joatham; and Joatham begat Achaz; and Achaz begat Ezekias."

The Apparent Problem

Chronicles list six generations from Joram and Jotham (1. Joram; 2. Ahaziah; 3. Joash; 4. Amaziah; 5. Azariah (Uzziah); and 6. Jotham), whereas Matthew lists only three (1. Joram; 2. Ozias (Uzziah); and 3. Joatham).

Chapter 11 — I Chronicles

A Solution

A solution lies in noticing that Matthew does not include Ahaziah, Joash, and Amaziah. A possible reason for why Matthew does not include these three names is in the notes for II Kings 8:26.

I CHRONICLES 3:22

The Passage

I Chronicles 3:22 states, "And the sons of Shechaniah; Shemaiah: and the sons of Shemaiah; Hattush, and Igeal, and Bariah, and Neariah, and Shaphat, six."

The Apparent Problem

I Chronicles 3:22 lists five sons of Shemaiah and then concludes with the word *six*.

The Expositor's Bible Commentary says, "Since only five names now appear in the list of Shemiah's six sons, one must have fallen out,"[734] that is, one of the six names is now missing. Keil makes a similar observation in his commentary: "The number of the sons of Shechaniah is given as six, while only five names are mentioned . . . a name must have fallen out by mistake in transcribing."[735] But how can these assertions be true in the light of Jesus' promises in Matthew 5:18 and Luke 16:17?

Some Solutions

One solution is the possibility that one of Shemaiah's sons died in infancy and the Bible does not give his name, if he ever had a name, yet the Bible still remembers him in the total. Another solution is the likelihood that *six* includes Shemaiah with his five sons ($5 + 1 = 6$).[736] And this

---

[734] Payne, 339.

[735] Keil, *Commentary on the First Book of Chronicles* in vol. 4 of *Commentary on the Old Testament*, 425.

[736] Cloud, 76.

may be very likely since the verse starts out with "the sons of Shechaniah" so the six would represent one son and five grandsons.

I CHRONICLES 10:6

See discussion under II Samuel 2:8.

I CHRONICLES 11:11

See discussion under II Samuel 23:8.

I CHRONICLES 18:4

See discussion under II Samuel 8:4.

I CHRONICLES 18:12

See discussion under II Samuel 8:13.

I CHRONICLES 19:18

See discussion under II Samuel 10:18.

I CHRONICLES 21:5

See discussion under II Samuel 24:9.

I CHRONICLES 21:11-12

See discussion under II Samuel 24:13.

I CHRONICLES 21:25

See discussion under II Samuel 24:24.

Chapter 11 — *I Chronicles*

I CHRONICLES 22:14; 29:3-4

The Passages

I Chronicles 22:14 states, "Now, behold, in my trouble I have prepared for the house of the LORD an hundred thousand talents of gold, and a thousand thousand talents of silver; and of brass and iron without weight; for it is in abundance: timber also and stone have I prepared; and thou mayest add thereto."

I Chronicles 29:3-4 states, "Moreover, because I have set my affection to the house of my God, I have of mine own proper good, of gold and silver, *which* I have given to the house of my God, over and above all that I have prepared for the holy house, *even* three thousand talents of gold, of the gold of Ophir, and seven thousand talents of refined silver, to overlay the walls of the houses *withal*."

The Apparent Problem

In both of the passages, David speaks of what he has prepared for the temple. In I Chronicles 22:14, he speaks of having prepared "an hundred thousand [100,000] talents of gold, and a thousand thousand [1,000,000] talents of silver," whereas in I Chronicles 29:3-4, he speaks of having prepared "three thousand [3,000] talents of gold" and "seven thousand [7,000] talents of refined silver."

A Solution

Both of these passages could be talking about different amounts to be used for different purposes. The gold and silver of the I Chronicles 29:3-4 passage is "to overlay the walls of the houses," whereas the passage in I Chronicles 22:14 does not have that limitation.

In a note on I Chronicles 29:4 *The Defender's Study Bible* states: "I Chronicles 22:14 says that David gave a 'hundred thousand talents of gold' and a 'thousand thousand talents of silver' for the proposed temple. This could represent a copyist error, or more likely, two entirely separate gifts at two different times."[737] The author must ask this question, why

---

[737] Henry Morris, 485.

Chapter 11 *I Chronicles*

does *The Defender's Study Bible,* while stating that this is "more likely two separate gifts," even have to say that "this could represent a copyist error"? In suggesting a copyist error, *The Defender's Study Bible* ceases to defend the numbers. Morris' suggesting the presence of a copyist error is similar to what *A Catholic Commentary on Holy Scripture* does when it says, "No ancient reader would have thought of taking literally the amount of treasure here mentioned."[738] If *The Defender's Study Bible* wants to defend the Bible, then let it reject the suggestion of a copyist error and let it promote a receiving, believing, and hearing of the numbers.

---

[738] Sutcliffe, *1 & 2 Paralipomenon* in *A Catholic Commentary on Holy Scripture,* 363.

CHAPTER TWELVE:
APPARENT NUMERICAL CONTRADICTIONS IN II CHRONICLES

II CHRONICLES 2:2

See discussion under I Kings 5:15-16.

II CHRONICLES 2:10

See discussion under I Kings 5:11.

II CHRONICLES 2:17-18

See discussion under I Kings 5:15-16.

II CHRONICLES 3:4

The Passage

II Chronicles 3:4 states, "And the porch that was in the front *of the house*, the length *of it was* according to the breadth of the house, twenty cubits, and the height was an hundred and twenty: and he overlaid it within with pure gold."

Chapter 12 *II Chronicles*

The Apparent Problem

The porch height of one hundred twenty cubits poses a problem for some because it is so much higher than the temple itself, which was thirty cubits (I Kings 6:2, 17).

The Defender's Study Bible states: "This number should probably be 'twenty' cubits. It is likely that the 'hundred' was inadvertently added in transmission."[739] In other words, *The Defender's Study Bible* teaches its readers not to hear or defend this number and in doing so, finds itself in accord with a wrong Liberal interpretation as espoused by *The Interpreter's Bible*, which wrongly states, "**A hundred and twenty**: Read 'twenty.' The extra hundred cubits probably is a reader's annotation."[740]

The Solution

The solution: receive, believe, and hear what is written. It is as simple as that. Sir Isaac Newton did just this, for when writing of Solomon's temple he stated, "The Porch of the Temple was 120 cubits high."[741] This porch served not only as a porch but also as a steeple.

II CHRONICLES 3:15

See discussion under I Kings 7:15.

II CHRONICLES 4:2

See discussion under I Kings 7:23.

II CHRONICLES 4:5

See discussion under I Kings 7:26.

---

[739] Henry Morris, 489.

[740] Elmslie, 448.

[741] Newton, *The Chronology of Ancient Kingdoms Amended*, 341.

Chapter 12 — *II Chronicles*

II CHRONICLES 4:13

See discussion under I Kings 7:20.

II CHRONICLES 8:10

See discussion under I Kings 9:23.

II CHRONICLES 8:18

See discussion under I Kings 9:28.

II CHRONICLES 9:25

See discussion under I Kings 4:26.

II CHRONICLES 16:1

See discussion under I Kings 15:33.

II CHRONICLES 22:2

See discussion under II Kings 8:26.

II CHRONICLES 24:1

See discussion under II Kings 13:10.

II CHRONICLES 25:1

See discussion under II Kings 14:23.

II CHRONICLES 34:3-4

See discussion under II Kings 22:3-4.

Chapter 12

II CHRONICLES 36:9

See discussion under II Kings 24:8.

CHAPTER THIRTEEN:
SUMMARY AND CONCLUSION

SUMMARY

Chapter One documents the erroneous claim of many that one should not hear all the numbers of Scripture. What is alarming is that many Fundamentalists question some numbers in the Old Testament. Bob Jones University questions I Samuel 6:19 and II Chronicles 22:2. Central Baptist Theological Seminary questions I Samuel 13:1; II Samuel 8:4; II Chronicles 22:2; and 36:9. Calvary Baptist Theological Seminary questions I Samuel 6:19 and 13:5. *The Defender's Study Bible* questions I Samuel 6:19; 13:1, 5; II Samuel 8:4; 10:18; 15:7; I Kings 4:26; I Chronicles 11:11; 22:14; II Chronicles 3:4, 15; 4:5; and 22:2. Such an attitude, however, is contrary to that of the Apostle John who heard, that is, received and believed the largest number in all of the Bible, *two hundred thousand thousand* (Revelation 9:16). Where did John get the attitude that he should hear, receive, and believe the numbers of Scripture? John's Saviour, the Lord Jesus Christ, taught him that attitude.

Chapter Two, "Jesus Received the Old Testament," presents Jesus' attitude toward Scripture. Jesus has unique credentials and, therefore, one should believe Him on the text issue over all others. The Old Testament text of Jesus is a text in which the saints of old had the very words of the *autographa*, even though it was composed of copies of copies of the *autographa*. Jesus indicated that His Old Testament had the very words of the *autographa* by repeatedly (1) saying "it is written" of His Old Testament, indicating that the actual words of the Old Testament writers wrote were still in existence (Matthew 4:4, 7, 10; 11:10; 21:13; 26:24, 31; Mark 7:6; 9:12; 11:17; 14:21, 27; Luke 4:4, 8, 17-19; 7:27; 18:31; 19:46; 20:17;

Chapter 13 *Summary & Conclusion*

21:22; 22:37; 24:44, 46; John 6:31, 45; 8:17; 10:34; 12:14; and 15:25); (2) referring to Old Testament passages thereby demonstrating that the Old Testament is fully accurate and reliable (Matthew 6:29; 8:4; 9:13; 11:23; 12:3, 4, 5, 7, 40, 41, 42; 13:14, 15; 15:4, 8, 9; 17:11; 19:4, 5, 8, 18, 19; 21:16, 42; 22:32, 37, 39, 44; 23:35; 24:15, 37-39; Mark 1:44; 2:25, 26; 7:6, 7, 10; 9:12; 10:3-5, 6, 7, 8, 19; 12:10, 26, 29, 30, 31, 36; 13:14; Luke 4:17-19, 25-26, 27; 5:14; 6:3, 4; 10:12, 26-27; 11:29, 30, 31, 32, 49, 51; 12:27; 17:26-27, 28, 29, 32; 18:20; 20:37, 38, 42, 43; John 3:14; 6:32; 7:22; 12:38-41; and 19:28); (3) repeatedly referring to Old Testament numerical passages showing that the numbers are accurate and authoritative (Matthew 12:40; 18:16; 19:5, 6, 28; Mark 10:8; 12:29; Luke 4:25; 22:30; and John 8:17); (4) validating the Old Testament text in Matthew 5:17-18; 24:35; Mark 13:31; Luke 16:17; 21:33; 24:25; and John 10:35; 17:17; and (5) never once criticizing or correcting the Old Testament text of His day. In looking fairly at this evidence, Chapter Two concludes that the Traditional Hebrew Text is trustworthy, and that no one can legitimately say that it has error(s) without impugning the Person and character of the Lord Jesus Christ.

Chapter Three, "Receive the Old Testament Numbers," builds upon Chapter Two. Jesus' attitude toward the Old Testament gives the Bible student ample reason to hear, believe, and receive all the numbers of the Old Testament. Some, however, allege that scribes used the Hebrew alphabet or other notations as abbreviation systems for numbers, and that such systems are responsible for errors in the text. But such an allegation contradicts Jesus' assessment of the Old Testament. Chapter Three, therefore, demonstrates that an-abbreviated-system-for-numbers explanation for difficulties is completely without merit. Indeed, in the Preserved Hebrew Old Testament Text numbers are always written as words, not as symbols or abbreviations. The *it-is-written* words, even when giving numerical quantities are correct.

If the Traditional Hebrew Text is completely trustworthy, the natural question arises: "Why would God allow apparent contradictions?" It might seem that if God had wonderfully preserved the Old Testament text, then there would not be even the slightest difficulty. This is not the case, however, for it is abundantly clear that apparent contradictions exist, but why? Chapter Four presents fifteen possible reasons why God allows apparent contradictions to be part of the inspired and preserved record of His Words. These reasons are (1) to make an impression; (2) to promote study; (3) to provide meat on which to chew; (4) to humble the student; (5) to lead the student to pray to God; (6) to show God's mind; (7) to conceal God's mind; (8) to realize that some apparent contradictions arise

Chapter 13 — Summary & Conclusion

from the fact that the student that he is separated from the events that occurred; (9) to substantiate inspiration; (10) to define doctrine; (11) to complement accounts; (12) to test faith; (13) to remove chaff; (14) to confound unbelievers; and (15) to realize that some apparent contradictions come from the contradiction of sinners. God could have given the Bible with no apparent contradictions at all, and God could have limited the activity of sinners to point out so-called contradictions in the Bible, but He has not so chosen. The above reasons for why God might allow apparent contradictions manifest God's wisdom. Apparent contradictions aid the saved to grow in the Lord by means of humility, prayer, study, and faith, as well as in other areas. On the other hand, apparent contradictions cause several difficulties for the unsaved who are unwilling to believe the Bible. Indeed, the manner in which the Bible is written is, as it were, the savour of death unto death and the savour of life unto life (II Corinthians 2:16). For those who rightly divide the Word of Truth, the Bible is a precious fountain of life unto life.

A consideration of the reasons in Chapter Four points to the need to study further the subject of apparent contradictions. Since apparent contradictions exist in the preserved text, Bible scholars must know how to study them. Chapter Five presents thirteen ways on how to study properly the apparent contradictions of the Bible. The ways are that the student (1) must have salvation of Christ; (2) must have obedience to the Lord; (3) must accept the inspiration of the Bible; (4) must accept preservation of the Bible; (5) must not correct the Words of God; (6) must believe the Words of God; (7) must exercise humility before God; (8) must exercise prayer to God; (9) must exercise patience in God; (10) must utilize study of the Bible; (11) must understand the language of the Bible; (12) might ask a man of God; and (13) must accept word change by the Spirit of God.

Concerning the necessity for the student to accept the preservation of the Bible the writers of the New Testament repeatedly acknowledged that they had in their copy of the Bible the *it-is-written* Words of God, that is, that they had the very words of the *autographa*. Verses that demonstrate the New Testament writers belief that they had the very Words of God are Matthew 27:37; Mark 1:2; Luke 2:23; 3:4; 4:17; 23:38; John 2:17; 12:14, 16; 15:25; 19:19, 20; 20:31; Acts 1:20; 7:42; 13:29, 33; 15:15; 23:5; 24:14; Romans 1:17; 2:24; 3:4, 10; 4:17; 8:36; 9:13, 33; 10:15; 11:8, 26; 12:19; 14:11; 15:3, 9, 21; I Corinthians 1:19, 31; 2:9; 3:19; 4:6; 9:9; 10:7; 14:21; 15:45, 54; II Corinthians 4:13; 8:15; 9:9; Galatians 3:10, 13; 4:22, 27; Hebrews 10:7; I Peter 1:16; Revelation 1:3; 22:18, and 19. The preceding list clearly demonstrates that the writers of the New Testament, as well as others, use *it is written* to refer to all parts of the Old Testament as

Chapter 13 *Summary & Conclusion*

well as to the entire Old Testament (Acts 24:14; I Corinthians 4:6) demonstrating that these men had the same Bibliology as that of Jesus in that they believed that the words of the *autographa* were present in their day. Not only did they have this attitude toward the Old Testament Scriptures, but also toward the New Testament Scriptures (Matthew 27:37; Luke 23:38; John 19:19, 20; 20:31; and Revelation 1:3; 22:18-19).

Chapter Six, "Ramifications of Saying Preserved Text Has Numerical Errors," lists a dozen ramifications of claiming that errors are in the Masoretic Text. The ramifications of claiming that the Preserved Text numerical errors are (1) a questioning of Christ; (2) a questioning of verses; (3) a relinquishing of the battle for the Bible; (4) an opening of the door to criticism; (5) a treating of the Bible like any other ancient document; (6) a destroying of the foundation; (7) a destroying of faith; (8) a destroying of authority; (9) an exalting of human reasoning, supposition, and textual criticism; (10) a coming dangerously close to adding to or subtracting from the Bible; (11) a making it impossible to live by every Word of God; and (12) a getting closer to New Evangelicalism, Liberalism, and Catholicism. The Fundamentalist who claims that the Old Testament has numerical errors is in serious compromise, for he is very much in agreement with New Evangelicals, Liberals, and even Catholics.

Chapters Seven through Twelve apply the principles from Chapters One through Six to fifty-eight apparent numerical contradictions in the books of I and II Samuel, I and II Kings, and I and II Chronicles, as well as other books as needed. The passages that Chapters Six through Twelve cover are Joshua 13:30; Judges 10:3-4; I Samuel 6:19; 13:1, 5; 16:10-11; 18:27; II Samuel 2:8; 3:14; 6:23; 8:4, 13; 10:18; 14:27; 15:7; 18:18; 21:8; 23:8, 39; 24:9, 13, 24; I Kings 2:11; 4:26; 5:11, 15, 16; 6:1, 2, 17; 7:15, 16, 20, 23, 26, 42; 9:23; 15:33; 16:6-10, 15, 16, 23, 29; 20:30; 22:41, 51; II Kings 1:17; 3:1; 8:16, 25, 26; 9:29; 10:36; 12:1; 13:1, 10; 14:1, 23; 15:1, 2, 8, 27, 30, 32, 33; 16:2; 17:1; 18:2, 13; 22:3, 4; 24:8, 12, 14; 25:8, 9, 17, 19, 27; I Chronicles 2:13-15, 22, 23; 3:10-13, 22; 10:6; 11:11; 18:4, 12; 19:18; 21:5, 11, 12, 25; 22:14; 29:3, 4; II Chronicles 2:2, 10, 17, 18; 3:4, 15; 4:2, 5, 13; 8:10, 18; 9:25; 16:1; 22:2; 24:1; 25:1; 34:3, 4; 36:9; Psalm 60:(title); Jeremiah 52:12, 13, 23, 25, 28-30, 31; Matthew 1:7-9; and Acts 13:18-20. Plausible explanations exist for every one of the fifty-eight apparent contradictions. In each and every case the student of Scripture should do as John and hear, receive, and believe the numbers.

Chapter 13 *Summary & Conclusion*

CONCLUSION

Several conclusions are apparent from Jesus' teaching about the Old Testament. First, from Jesus' use of *it is written* and the general statements that Jesus makes concerning the Bible (Matthew 5:18; Luke 16:17; John 10:35; 17:17), it is clear that Jesus held to the perfect preservation not only of all the words, but of all the letters and of all the vowel points of the Hebrew Old Testament.

Second, *it is written* in Nehemiah's day, in David's day, and in the days of other Old Testament saints means that their copies of the Words of God had the words of the *autographa*. *It is written* in Jesus' day means that His copy also had the words of the *autographa*. Since there is only one *autographa*, then the *it-is-written* copies of Old Testament saints were the same as the *it-is-written* copy of Jesus: they all had the same words. The use of *it is written* directly connects the Old Testament of Jesus with the Old Testament of the saints of old, with each having the words of the *autographa*.

Third, since Jesus possessed an *it-is-written* copy of the Old Testament, and since Jesus' *it-is-written* copy had the words of the *autographa*, and since these words are the Words of God, and since the Word of God is truth (John 17:17); then Jesus possessed in His hands an infallible copy of the Hebrew Old Testament.

Fourth, from the fact that Jesus speaks of *jot* and *tittle* in Matthew 5:18 and *tittle* in Luke 16:17, which terms refer to the smallest Hebrew consonant and to the smallest Hebrew vowel point, then Jesus limited His teaching of perfect preservation and infallibility to the Hebrew and Aramaic of the Traditional Old Testament text. His promises in these verses do not extend to any other text. Albeit, if a translation of this perfectly preserved and infallible Hebrew Old Testament is accurate, then one can regard it as the Words of God in that language.

Fifth, if one follows the example of Jesus, then deciding which Old Testament text to use is a relatively easy matter. However, Paul's words apply here: "But I fear, lest by any means, as the serpent beguiled Eve through his subtilty, so your minds should be corrupted from the simplicity that is in Christ" (II Corinthians 11:3). Many have corrupted minds when it comes to this issue and make this issue far more complicated than it should be. The disciples never attempted to restore or recover the text, but simply received the text, just as Jesus did (John 17:8; Acts 2:41; 8:14; 11:1; 17:11; I Thessalonians 1:6; 2:13, James 1:21). The text that Jesus received was the Traditional Hebrew Old Testament passed down to Him by the Jews (Acts 7:38; Romans 3:2) and this is the text that believers today should receive as well – a text passed down to them by local churches (I Timothy 3:15), who equated the Ben Chayyim Masoretic Text with the Traditional Hebrew Text and made it the *Textus Receptus* of the Old Testament.

Sixth, since Jesus demonstrates such a high regard for the Hebrew Old Testament text, and since He rebuked His disciples for not believing it (Luke 24:25), and since He Himself promises that all of it would be preserved down to the smallest details (Matthew 5:18; Luke 16:17); then disputing the Traditional Masoretic Hebrew Old Testament text is questioning the truthfulness and ability of Jesus.

Seventh, Jesus never once criticizes the Old Testament, for He came not "to destroy the law, or the prophets" (Matthew 5:17). The Bible teacher should have this as his motto.

Eighth, from the fact that Jesus has impeccable credentials and since He received every word, letter, and vowel point of the Hebrew Old Testament; then those who question the Old Testament act as if they know more than Jesus! The Bible says, "Knowledge puffeth up" (I Corinthians 8:1). If one's knowledge puffs him up so much that He thinks that he knows more than Jesus, then he has the wrong kind of knowledge. Let him abandon such knowledge, and let him be instructed by Jesus to simply receive the preserved Words of God.

Ninth, "It must be said, however, that the question of our attitude to the Old Testament inevitably raises the question of our attitude towards the Lord Jesus Christ."[742] "The moment you begin to question the authority of the Old Testament, you are of necessity questioning the authority of the Son of God Himself, and you will find yourself in endless trouble and difficulty."[743]

Tenth, from the fact that Jesus rebuked His Own disciples for being slow of heart to believe all that the prophets spoke (Luke 24:25), then those "believers" who do not believe deserve a rebuke. "If God may not be trusted in the things He has revealed which do not relate to faith and life, how may He be trusted at all? How is one to decide what is a matter of faith and life and what is not?"[744] Jesus left no instruction on how to

---

[742] Lloyd-Jones, 1:187.

[743] Ibid., 1:188.

[744] Ibid., 85.

make such a distinction, for He teaches that one should hear, that is, receive and believe all of the Bible.

Eleventh, just as a person is saved by faith by putting his trust in the Lord Jesus Christ, so the believer should walk by faith and trust Christ on the text issue.

Twelfth, a Christian should follow Jesus' example. When a Fundamentalist says that an Old Testament passage has an error, he is not following the example of Jesus, but, rather, is following the example of Satan who says, "Yeah, hath God said?" (Genesis 3:1). This is very dangerous. The devil, in questioning God's Words, influenced Eve also to question God's Words, thereby bringing her down to the place where she no longer believed God. This was tragic for her. Likewise, Fundamentalists, who question the preserved text, persuade others also to question the Bible, thereby bringing them down to the place where they do not believe God, Who promises that He will preserve His Words. This, too, will be tragic for them.

From the example of Jesus it is clear what a person's attitude ought to be toward the Traditional Hebrew Text. However, there are Fundamentalists who claim that the Traditional Hebrew Text has numerical errors. The ramifications of suggesting that scribal errors exist in the preserved texts are many. None of the ramifications are good. That Fundamentalists are involved in such things is shocking.

Instead of questioning Matthew 5:18 and other verses, Fundamentalists should receive, believe, and hear by faith the words of Matthew 5:18 as well as all other verses.

Instead of questioning many verses whereby Fundamentalists nurture a rejected-texts mindset, Fundamentalists should have a received-text mindset (John 17:8).

Instead of relinquishing the battle for the Bible, Fundamentalists should be at the front of the battle in earnestly contending "for the faith which was once delivered unto the saints" (Jude 3).

Instead of opening the door to criticism, Fundamentalists should shut the door to criticism. I Timothy 6:3-5 teaches that men who consent not to the Words of our Lord Jesus Christ (which words substantiate the absolute trustworthiness of all the words of the Old Testament) are men who dote about questions and strifes of words and that one ought to separate from them. May Fundamentalists heed the teaching of this passage and separate from the critics.

Chapter 13 *Summary & Conclusion*

Instead of treating the Bible like any other ancient document by claiming that it has scribal errors, Fundamentalists need to receive the Word of God, "not as the word of men, but as it is in truth, the word of God" (I Thessalonians 2:13).

Instead of destroying the foundation by questioning the preserved texts; Fundamentalists need to uphold this foundation, for "if the foundations be destroyed, what can the righteous do?" (Psalm 11:3).

Instead of destroying faith, Fundamentalists need to promote faith in all the words of the Bible. In so doing, they would be following the example of Jesus Who came not to destroy the Old Testament (Matthew 5:17).

Instead of destroying the authority of the Old Testament by questioning the words of the Old Testament, Fundamentalists need to uphold the authority of the Old Testament. Fundamentalists should keep in mind the words of Isaiah 8:20: "To the law and to the testimony: if they speak not according to this word, it is because there is no light in them." The Words of God are the authority, not the words of the critics. When a Fundamentalist questions a number or word in the Old Testament text, he is not speaking "according to this word" and is thereby questioning the authority of "this word." When a Fundamentalists does this, he displays that he is walking in darkness. Let him come out of the darkness of doubt and criticism and, instead, walk in the light of God's authoritative words.

Instead of exalting human reasoning, supposition, and textual criticism which savour of the things of men; Fundamentalists ought to savour "the things that be of God" (Matthew 16:23).

Instead of coming close to adding to or subtracting from the Bible, Fundamentalists ought to make it clear that they will have nothing to do with such pursuits (Revelation 22:18-19).

Instead of removing words from the Bible thereby making it impossible for man to live by every word that proceedeth out of the mouth of God; Fundamentalists ought to be in harmony with Jesus Who says, "Man shall not live by bread alone, but by every word that proceedeth out of the mouth of God" (Matthew 4:4). And if the Fundamentalists are truly in harmony with Jesus, then let them repent and, therefore, stop taking words away from the preserved Old Testament text.

Instead of getting closer to New Evangelicalism, Liberalism, and Catholicism by (1) discrediting Chronicles and aiding the Liberal cause; (2) seemingly claiming that the Bible has moot points just like the New

Chapter 13   *Summary & Conclusion*

Evangelicals; (3) holding to conceptual preservation as do New Evangelicals and Liberals; (4) placing faith in textual critics as also do the New Evangelicals and Liberals; (5) engaging in double-talk just like the New Evangelicals; (6) appealing to history as do the Liberals and Catholics; and (7) criticizing the numbers thereby sounding just like New Evangelicals—Fundamentalists need to come out from among them and be separate "and touch not the unclean thing" (II Corinthians 6:17).

In providing solutions to fifty-eight apparent numeric contradictions and to several non-numeric apparent contradictions, this book demonstrates that there is no need to reject the Bibliology of Jesus and to adopt the claim that the Old Testament is in error. The fifty-eight alleged contradictions are not real contradictions at all. However, in showing that these problems are only apparent, a real problem has become very apparent. The problem is this: will Fundamentalists believe Jesus and His assessment of the Old Testament text and reject the critics' claims of error, or will they not? Instead of questioning the text of the Old Testament, Fundamentalists need to follow the example of the Apostle John who, when given the Revelation of Jesus Christ, heard the number of them (Revelation 9:16); that is, he received it and believed it. May Fundamentalists return to simply believing and receiving the Words of the Lord Jesus Christ and, therefore, hear the number of them, instead of questioning the number of them. By hearing the number of them, Fundamentalists will demonstrate faith in the Lord Jesus Christ and is not this what all Bible believers should do? The Psalmist said, "I esteem all *thy* precepts *concerning* all *things to be* right; *and* I hate every false way" (Psalm 119:128).

APPENDIX A: PRELIMINARIES

Appendix A presents (1) the methodology behind the work; (2) the delimitations of the work; and (3) the definition of terms in the work.

METHODOLOGY BEHIND THE WORK

The author desires to be objective in his research and conclusions. In obtaining a list of alleged numerical contradictions in I Samuel to II Chronicles, the author used an objective process of consulting various sources. From the internet, the author obtained lists of supposed contradictions from unbelievers on a number of web sites including the following: (1) http://www.islam.org.uk/ ie/ilm/dawah/0009.html "101 Clear Contradictions in the Bible" by Shabir Ally; (2) http://www.infidels.org/library/modern/jim_meritt/bible-contradictions.html "A List of Bible Contradictions"; and (3) http://www.ffrf.org/lfif/contra.html, which gives a list of alleged Bible contradictions. The author also culled alleged numerical contradictions from books on contradictions, as well as from Bible commentaries. From these sources, the author assembled a list of fifty-eight problem passages. Books on contradictions, as well as commentaries, do not discuss many of these passages, substantiating that the author is not deliberately avoiding problem passages.

Various writers take one of four approaches to alleged numerical contradictions in I Samuel to II Chronicles. First, the Liberal/New Evangelical view is that the problems show that the Old Testament *autographa* were fallible.[745] Second, the New Evangelical/Fundamentalist view is that the problems illustrate that the Masoretic Hebrew Old Testament text is

---

[745] Lindsell, 93-94, 113-114, 163-174.

fallible.[746] Third, the Peter Ruckman view is that through "advanced revelation" the *King James Bible* is able to correct the Masoretic Text.[747] Fourth, the Biblicist view, which agrees with Christ's assessment, is that the Traditional Text of the Old Testament is without error and, therefore, completely trustworthy.

An objective study of Christ's words in the Gospels demonstrates that this last view is the correct one. Chapter Two presents this study. The writer objectively sought to deduce Christ's view of the Old Testament by examining verses in which Jesus spoke directly about the Old Testament or used the Old Testament in His Own teaching. The author examined these verses according to sound principles of exegesis including, but not limited to, (1) word studies; (2) contextual studies; (3) grammatical relationships of the words used; (4) comparing Scripture with Scripture; (5) using a literal and consistent interpretation; and (6) prayer. In addition to applying these principles, the author consulted several commentaries and other writings dealing with the teaching of the Lord Jesus Christ.

Christ's assessment of the Old Testament assures that (1) the *autographa* were infallible (John 10:35; 17:17); (2) the Traditional Text preserves the words of the *autographa* (Matthew 5:18; Luke 16:17); and (3) the Traditional Hebrew Old Testament Text, therefore, is infallible and one should not correct it, but simply receive it (Luke 24:25). Christ's assessment of the Old Testament demonstrates that the Liberal/New Evangelical, the New Evangelical/Fundamentalist, and the Peter Ruckman views are improper ways to view the alleged numerical contradictions in the Old Testament.

In following Christ's view of the Old Testament, the author views the problem passages of the Old Testament not as real problems or contradictions, but only as apparent problems. The author, therefore, never questions the integrity of the preserved text of the Old Testament; instead, the author suggests various solutions to these apparent problems. In setting forth solutions the author has again sought for objectivity by applying several principles:

---

[746] W. Edward Glenny, "The Preservation of Scripture" in *The Bible Version Debate*, 84-85. Also see, W. Edward Glenny, "The Preservation of Scripture and the Version Debate" in *One Bible Only?*, 114-115. Many who write on alleged contradictions are in agreement with this view as they claim that scribal errors have marred the preserved text. See Chapter One for more information.

[747] Ruckman, 151-152, 278, 298, 317, 463.

Appendix A *Preliminaries*

1. Prayer (Psalm 119:18; James 1:5);

2. Word studies;

3. Grammatical studies;

4. Contextual studies;

5. Comparing Scripture with Scripture thereby seeking to support his solutions with other Biblical examples and, therefore, to avoid a private interpretation (II Peter 1:20);

6. Using a consistent and literal interpretation;

7. Consulting commentaries to examine various commentators' solutions;

8. Consulting books on Bible chronology, since some of the passages concern chronology;

9. Consulting writers on the subject of contradictions; and

10. Consulting various comments by those with other views so as to address their objections to answers which do not resort to the charge of scribal or other error(s).

In applying the above principles, the author sincerely believes he has achieved an objective and fair assessment of the issues involved with the apparent numeric contradictions in I Samuel to II Chronicles.

DELIMITATIONS OF THE WORK

Since the numbers in I Samuel to II Chronicles[748] have especially come under attack by both Liberals and Fundamentalists, this book will largely limit itself to a discussion of the apparent numerical discrepancies in those books.

Furthermore, this book receives the Traditional Text of the Old Testament and the Received Text of the New Testament as the texts that have the preserved words of the *autographa* and the *Authorized Version* as an accurate translation of these preserved texts into English. Consequently, this book will not claim that scribal errors exist in the preserved texts.

---

[748] Central Baptist Theological Seminary's book in a couple of paragraphs discusses "the problems in the Old Testament . . . [and] in the KJV." All the examples come from I Samuel to II Chronicles (W. Edward Glenny, "The Preservation of Scripture" in *The Bible Version Debate*, 84-85).

Appendix A *Preliminaries*

In light of the above statement, this book will not engage in textual criticism. However, the author may refer to readings other than those in the *Authorized Version* and its underlying original language texts in order to show the fallacy of those other readings.

Since this work discusses the numbers of Scripture, some may suppose that it will attempt to find hidden meanings in the numbers of the Bible; however, that is not at all its intent. While it is true that the number 666 is the number of a man (Revelation 13:18), and while it may be true that the number 7 is the number of perfection (Psalm 12:6; Revelation 1:4), yet these numbers, nonetheless, represent actual numerical quantities. Therefore, this book will treat the numbers of the Bible, as literal numerical quantities, instead of symbolic or figurative expressions.

DEFINITION OF TERMS IN THE WORK

Since this book deals with the exegesis of a number of Scripture passages, the author will define many terms as they appear. Several foundational terms, however, require definitions.

Apographa refers to the copies of the *autographa*.

Autographa refers to the actual inspired writings of those whom God used to write His Words. Many writers often use *autographa* and *originals* interchangeably, but in this book, *autographa* will be the word of choice.

Biblicist refers to one who believes that whatever the Bible says is true. A Biblicist is one who does not question the Bible, but makes the Bible, indeed all of the Bible, his rule for faith and practice. The author refers to himself as a Biblicist. While some use the terms *Fundamentalist* and *Biblicist* interchangeably, the author does not. In the opinion of the author, *Fundamentalist* is a more general term describing one who subscribes to a list of fundamental doctrines, whereas *Biblicist* is a more specific term describing one who subscribes to and defends the entire Bible. While all Biblicists are Fundamentalists, not all Fundamentalists are Biblicists.

Contradiction refers to a condition in which two or more statements made of the same event cannot possibly both be true at the same time. If one can explain apparently contradictory statements as being both true at the same time, then there is no real contradiction at all. The contention of this book is that no real contradictions of any type are in the Bible, only

Appendix A   *Preliminaries*

apparent ones which by one means or another the student of Scripture can reconcile. Specifically, the purpose of this book is to demonstrate that the alleged numerical contradictions of I Samuel through II Chronicles are not contradictions at all.

Fundamentalist[749] refers to one who holds to the fundamentals of the faith. These fundamentals usually include (1) the inspiration and inerrancy of the *autographa*; (2) the Trinity; (3) the deity of Christ; (4) the virgin birth of Christ; (5) the substitutionary atonement of Christ; (6) the bodily resurrection of Christ; (7) the ascension of Christ into heaven; (8) the second coming of Christ; (9) salvation by grace through faith in the finished work of Christ; (10) heaven; and (11) hell. In addition to holding to the fundamentals, a Fundamentalist is one who adheres to the principle of separation from error. It is the observation of the author that one can call himself a Fundamentalist without holding to baptism by immersion, eternal security, autonomy of the local church, pre-tribulation rapture, saved church membership, preservation of the Scriptures, as well as other important doctrines.

Inerrancy refers to the actuality of being without error.

Infallibility refers to the inability of having error.

> Although many use infallibility and inerrancy interchangeably, they have different meanings. Infallibility has to do with the inability to fall or to err. Inerrancy has to do with actuality of being without error. God is infallible and His Word is a product of infallibility; it is indeed inerrant since God does not have the ability to make errors.[750]

Inspiration refers to the process whereby God, that is, God the Father (II Timothy 3:16), God the Son (I Peter 1:11), and God the Holy Spirit (II

---

[749] Robert Lightner says of Fundamentalism that it is "the movement which was born in the early part of the twentieth century in opposition to and as a reaction against liberalism. It strongly reemphasizes the fundamentals of historic Christianity. In addition to other doctrines which were held to be basic and fundamental, the area of conflict centered around: (1) the inerrancy of Scripture; (2) the deity of Christ; (3) the virgin birth of Christ; (4) the substitutionary atonement of Christ; and (5) the physical resurrection and bodily return of Christ. The term was used to designate the defense of these fundamentals when it was first coined and this is the true meaning of it today" (Robert Lightner, *Neoevangelicalism Today* (Schaumburg, IL: Regular Baptist Press, 1979), 28-29). The definition in the main body of the text above is a more complete one and lists some of those "other doctrines" that Lightner does not list.

[750] Strouse, *The Lord God Hath Spoken*, 51-52.

Appendix A *Preliminaries*

Peter 1:21), moved in holy men to record accurately His Words so as to produce the Word of God.

Liberal refers to one who denies the fundamentals of the faith and, in particular, denies the miraculous, thereby seeking to explain away the miraculous in terms of naturalistic causes.

LXX refers to the Septuagint, a Greek translation of the Hebrew Old Testament.

New Evangelical refers to one who evinces a spirit of compromise with error, even to the point of fellowshipping with Liberals. George Dollar defines New Evangelicalism as

> an attitude or position which professes to adhere to the Fundamentals of the Faith but advocates a spirit of re-examination of the basic doctrines, an attitude of tolerance toward the Liberals and an entering into "dialogue" with them, and an emphasis on the love and mercy of God rather than on His holiness and righteousness.[751]

Preservation refers to the process by which God has insured that no words given by Him through the process of inspiration have been lost.

Preserved text(s), depending on the context, refers to (1) the Ben Chayyim Masoretic Text of the Old Testament; (2) the Received Text of the New Testament, that is, the 1598 edition of Beza, which the King James translators used; or (3) both.

Received Text refers to the 1598 edition of the *Textus Receptus* as prepared by Beza.

Textual Criticism refers to the naturalistic, humanistic, and rationalistic attempts allegedly to restore the words of the *autographa*.

Traditional text and *Traditional Hebrew Old Testament* refer to the Ben Chayyim Masoretic Text of the Old Testament.[752] The Ben Chayyim Masoretic Text of the Old Testament is also known as the Daniel Bomberg Hebrew edition of the Masoretic text.

---

[751] Dollar, 383.

[752] D. A. Waite, *Defending the King James Bible*, 27.

APPENDIX B: PREVIOUS STUDIES

Although no volume deals specifically and solely with the apparent numerical contradictions in the books from I Samuel to II Chronicles, yet a number of works bear on the subject. The author has divided these into works that deal with Bible difficulties, commentaries, and works that refer to Bible difficulties in passing.

WORKS TREATING BIBLE DIFFICULTIES

Haley

Perhaps the best known and still somewhat useful of the works dealing with Bible difficulties is *Alleged Discrepancies of the Bible* by John W. Haley. *The Minister's Library* says this work was "first printed nearly a century ago. In spite of recent advancements in archaeology, it remains a standard reference work in its field."[753] When Haley wrote his book, few works of this kind existed. Haley wrote: "I know of no work, ancient or modern, which covers the whole ground, treating the subject comprehensively yet concisely."[754] Indeed, Haley seems to cover just about every alleged discrepancy. The book has a nineteen page, triple-column index of Bible passages. Despite its comprehensive nature, its one major weakness is alleging scribal errors as a way to "solve" several discrepan-

---

[753] Cyril J. Barber, *The Minister's Library* (Grand Rapids: Baker, 1981), 61.

[754] Haley, vi.

cies. In fact, the author counted at least 115 verses wherein Haley suggests this "solution," which is conspicuously so in I Samuel to II Chronicles as pages 382 and 383 demonstrate in a section entitled "Concerning Numbers." Claiming scribal error is disconcerting to say the least.

Dehoff

It is appropriate at this point to mention *Alleged Bible Contradictions Explained* by George W. Dehoff. Dehoff's work is a reworking of Haley, for the flyleaf states, "Not since the monumental work of Haley in 1875 has such a work as this appeared. Here is all the best of the past brought up to date and much new material never before appearing in print."[755] Consequently, Dehoff's work follows a similar format as that of Haley and takes many comments directly from Haley, but it is far less thorough. However, in copying Haley, it suffers from the same weakness as Haley in also claiming that scribal errors are present in the preserved texts.[756]

Archer

Another book, which is also somewhat useful, is Archer's *Encyclopedia of Bible Difficulties*. While not as exhaustive as Haley's work, it nonetheless has a thirteen page, triple-column index of Bible passages. While Archer makes some wonderful statements concerning inspiration, some of which are quoted earlier; nonetheless, he claims scribal errors are in the preserved texts. He has a section entitled "The Role of Textual Criticism in Correcting Transmissional Errors,"[757] which starts at page 32 and continues to page 44. This section handles several passages in I Samuel to II Chronicles with the "explanation" that they are the result of scribal errors. Furthermore, Archer does not cover all the passages presented in this work. Among those not covered are I Samuel 18:27; II Samuel 2:8; 3:14; 6:23; 15:7; 21:8; 23:39; I Kings 2:11; 5:11, 15-16; 6:2, 17; 7:20, 26, 42; 16:15-16, 29; 22:41, 51; II Kings 10:36; 12:1; 13:1, 10; 14:1; 15:30, 33; 22:3-4; 24:12; 25:8-9, 17, 19, 27; I Chronicles 2:22-23; 3:22; 10:6; 18:12; and II Chronicles 2:2, 10, 17-18; 3:4, 15; 4:5, 13; 24:1; 34:3-4.

---

[755] DeHoff, front flyleaf.

[756] Ibid., 38-39.

[757] Archer, 32.

Appendix B   *Previous Studies*

Ruckman

Yet, another book treating Bible difficulties is a book by Peter S. Ruckman, *The "Errors" in the King James Bible*. Ruckman's book deals with over three hundred "problem" texts.[758] While never questioning the English text of the *King James Bible* and while providing a degree of insight on some of the apparent discrepancies of the Bible, it is limited in a couple of ways. First, many of its comments are very brief. Second, it does not cover all the passages that this book covers. Among those not covered by Ruckman are I Samuel 13:5; 18:27; II Samuel 3:14; 10:18; I Kings 6:1, 2, 17; 7:15, 23, 26; 15:33; 16:15-16, 23; 22:51; II Kings 8:25; 9:29; 10:36; 12:1; 13:1, 10; 14:23; 15:1, 2, 8, 27, 32; 16:2; 18:2, 9, 10, 13; 22:3-4; 24:12, 14; 25:8-9, 17, 19, 27; I Chronicles 2:22-23; 3:10-13, 22; 19:18; 22:14; 29:3-4; II Chronicles 3:4, 15; 4:5; 15:19; 24:1; and 34:3-4. Third, it promotes the English text over the Hebrew Traditional Text and the Greek Textus Receptus. Ruckman states:

> We shall deal with the English Text of the Protestant Reformation, and our references to Greek or Hebrew will only be made to enforce the authority of that text or to demonstrate the *superiority* of that text to Greek and Hebrew.[759]

> We candidly and publicly confess that the King James text of the Old Testament (*Authorized Version*) is far superior to Kittel's Hebrew text, DeRossi's Hebrew text, Kennicott's Hebrew text, or *any* Hebrew text that any of you are reading. We do not hesitate to state bluntly and openly that the King James text for the New Testament (*Authorized Version*) is superior to Erasmus' Greek text, Aland's Greek text, Metzger's Greek text, and any other that you are reading (or will read in the future).[760]

While Ruckman's attitude toward the *King James Version* results in his never questioning the King James text (something this book does not do either), it, however, promotes the English over the Hebrew and Greek of even the preserved texts. But it is upon those preserved texts that God's promise of preservation rests, not on an English translation of those preserved texts. For example, Matthew 5:18 speaks of not even a single jot or tittle passing from the law till all be fulfilled. *Jot* and *tittle* refer to the Hebrew language, not the English. Elevating the English above the He-

---

[758] Ruckman, 3.

[759] Ibid., xiv.

[760] Ibid., p xix, xx.

brew is not a practice the Bible supports.[761] Because Ruckman thinks that the English of the *King James Bible* is superior to the Hebrew and Greek of the preserved texts, his work does not deal extensively with Hebrew grammar and word studies as this work does on occasion.

Cloud

Perhaps the best book on apparent contradictions from a Biblicist standpoint is *Things Hard To Be Understood* by David W. Cloud. In the introduction of this book, Cloud very clearly states:

> WE DO NOT QUESTION THE BIBLE. In the process of researching this book, I have collected many volumes, both old and new, which address Bible difficulties. Many of these approach the Bible's difficulties from a naturalistic or partially naturalistic viewpoint. . . . There are many books on Bible difficulties which fall into this category, and they do not build confidence in God's Word. We believe the Bible is the inerrant, verbally-plenarily inspired Word of God. We do not doubt even one word of God's Holy Book, the Bible, and we would never question it. . . . WE DO NOT QUESTION THE AUTHORIZED VERSION OF THE BIBLE. We will go further, even, than saying that we do not question the Bible in general. We do not question the English Authorized Version of the Bible. Many of the books on Bible difficulties find solutions to alleged discrepancies by claiming scribal error and by attempting to correct the God-honored Received Text and English Authorized Version with modern critical opinions. We believe the King James Bible is an accurate translation of the preserved Word of God. We do not believe it needs to be corrected.[762]

The above statement is exactly the position of this book and it is a welcomed breath of fresh air to see a book like Cloud's. In fact, as far as the author knows, Cloud's book is the only one treating solely Bible difficulties which takes such a position. However, Cloud's book does not deal with all of the alleged numerical discrepancies in I Samuel to II Chronicles. Passages that Cloud does not handle are I Samuel 6:19; 13:1, 5; II Samuel 2:8; 23:39; I Kings 7:16, 23; 15:10, 33; 16:8, 15-16, 23, 28, 29; 22:41; 22:51; II Kings 1:17; 3:1; 8:16, 25; 9:29; 10:36; 12:1; 13:1, 10;

---

[761] Ruckman's position is not only unbiblical for the above-mentioned reason, but also it is illogical. The *King James Version* is a translation of the preserved texts of the Hebrew and Greek. Being a translation of those preserved texts, it can be at best only equal to them but certainly not superior to them.

[762] Cloud, 5.

Appendix B *Previous Studies*

14:1, 23; 15:1, 2, 8, 27, 32; 16:2; 18:1, 2, 9, 10, 13; 22:3-4; 24:12; 25:8-9, 17, 27; I Chronicles 3:10-13; 10:6; 22:14; 29:3-4; and II Chronicles 3:4; 16:1; 24:1; 25:1; 34:3-4. Furthermore, Cloud's treatment of the passages is less technical than this book's treatment since this book delves into grammar and Hebrew as necessary. Also, while Cloud deals with some introductory subjects such as the reasons for difficulties and how to interpret them, this book (1) goes into more detail on those subjects; (2) presents a thorough treatment of Christ's view of the Old Testament; and (3) gives the ramifications of claiming that scribal errors are in the preserved texts.

Other Older Works

Some older and not so thorough works are *Does the Bible Contradict Itself?*, *Bible Difficulties and Their Alleviate Interpretation*, and *Difficulties and Alleged Errors and Contradictions in the Bible*. The first work is only 134 pages long and allows for scribal errors in the preserved texts.[763] The second work discusses twenty-six difficult questions about the Old Testament such as "Was the World Made in Six Solar Days?"[764] The third work is only 125 pages in length and allows for scribal errors.[765] None of these works covers all the passages presented in this book.

Other Newer Works

Some more recent works are *When Critics Ask*, *Today's Handbook for Solving Bible Difficulties*, and *Hard Sayings of the Bible*. All three claim the preserved texts contain scribal errors in the numerical quantities.[766] O'Brien wrote *Today's Handbook for Solving Bible Difficulties* on more of a conversational level and is far less thorough than the other two.

---

[763] W. Arndt, *Does the Bible Contradict Itself?* (St. Louis: Concordia Publishing House, 1930), 9, 10, 47.

[764] Robert Stuart MacArthur, *Bible Difficulties and Their Alleviate Interpretation* (NY: E. B. Treat & Company, 1899), 11.

[765] R. A. Torrey, *Difficulties and Alleged Errors and Contradictions in the Bible* (Chicago: Moody Press, 1907), 18.

[766] Geisler and Howe, *When Critics Ask: A Popular Handbook on Bible Difficulties*, 24, 156, 159, 160, 171, 181, 194, 197, 199, 209, 562; David E. O'Brien, *Today's Handbook for Solving Bible Difficulties* (Minneapolis: Bethany House Publishers, 1990), 45-48; Kaiser, Jr., Davids, Bruce, and Brauch, *Hard Sayings of the Bible*, 51-54.

Appendix B *Previous Studies*

When Critics Ask includes in its 600 pages a twenty-four page, triple-column Scripture index. *Hard Sayings of the Bible* includes in its 800 pages a fifteen page, five-column Scripture index. Both of these works can be somewhat helpful in the studying of difficult passages but (1) suffer from the aforementioned problem of claiming the presence of scribal error in the preserved texts, (2) do not cover all of the passages dealing with alleged numerical discrepancies in I Samuel to II Chronicles,[767] and (3) neglect the role of the preservation of Scripture in properly understanding the apparent contradictions.

COMMENTARIES

Commentaries on the Whole Bible

Many commentaries claim scribal errors underlie the alleged numerical difficulties of the Bible.[768] A list of these works could be almost end-

---

[767] Of the two works, *When Critics Ask* seems to cover more of the apparent numerical discrepancies in I Samuel to II Chronicles but still does not cover all of them.

[768] Examples of such commentaries are (1) Albright, W. F. and David Noel Freedman, eds. *The Anchor Bible*. Garden City, NY: Doubleday and Co., 1970-; (2) Driver, S. R., Alfred Plummer, and Charles A. Briggs, eds. *International Critical Commentary*. NY: Charles Scribner's Sons, 1896-1937; (3) Jamieson, Robert, A. R. Fausset, and David Brown. *A Commentary, Critical, Experimental, and Practical on the Old and New Testaments*. Grand Rapids: Eerdmans, 1945; (4) Lange, John Peter, ed. *Commentary on the Holy Scriptures*. Grand Rapids: Zondervan, 1960; (5) Spence, H. D. M. and Joseph S. Exell, eds. *The Pulpit Commentary*. Grand Rapids: Eerdmans, 1963; (6) Hubbard, David A. and Glenn W. Barker, eds. *Word Biblical Commentary*. Waco, TX: Word Books, 1985; (7) Keil, C. F. and F. Delitzsch. *Commentary on the Old Testament*, 10 vols. Edinburgh: T. & T. Clark, 1866-91. Reprinted Peabody, MA: Hendrickson Publishers, 2001; (8) Wiseman, Donald J., ed. *Tyndale Old Testament Commentaries*. Grand Rapids: Eerdmans, 1968.; (9) Oglivie, Lloyd, John, ed. *The Communicator's Commentary*. Waco, TX: Word Books, 1982-; (10) Gaebelein, Frank E., ed. *The Expositor's Bible Commentary*. Grand Rapids: Zondervan, 1992; (11) Perowne, J. J. Stewart, ed. *Cambridge Bible for Schools and Colleges*. Cambridge: At the University Press, 1916; (12) Clarke, Adam. *Adam Clarke's Commentary*. Edited by Ralph Earle. Grand Rapids: Baker, 1967; (13) Buttrick, G. A., ed. *The Interpreter's Bible: The Holy Scriptures in the King James Version and Revised Standard Version with General Articles and Introduction, Exegesis, Exposition for Each Book of the Bible*. Nashville: Abingdon Press, 1953-1956; (14) Exell, Joseph S., ed. *The Biblical Illustrator*. Grand Rapids: Baker, n. d.; (15) Kelly, Balmer H. *The Layman's Bible Commentary*. Richmond, VA: John Knox Press, 1960; and (16) Wright, G. Ernest, John Bright, James Barr, and Peter Ackroyd, eds. *The Old Testament Library*. London: SCM Press Ltd., 1964. Mentioning these commentaries at this point is

Appendix B *Previous Studies*

less. More related to the concerns of this book are those commentaries that try to give plausible answers to the alleged numerical discrepancies of the Bible. Works dealing with the entire Bible, and at the same time giving answers to Bible difficulties, are John Gill's *An Exposition of the Old and New Testament*, Matthew Poole's *A Commentary on the Holy Bible*, and Matthew Henry's *Commentary on the Whole Bible*. While these works give answers to most of the alleged contradictions of the Bible, they nonetheless question the preserved text.

Henry

Concerning *fifty thousand and threescore and ten men* in I Samuel 6:19, Matthew Henry states:

> *He smote 50,070 men.* This account of the numbers smitten is expressed in a very unusual manner in the original, which, besides the improbability that there should be so many guilty and so many slain, occasions many learned men to question whether we take the matter aright.[769]

Although Henry opens the door to questioning the text at this point, later in his discussion he does give an answer that might help those who would not question the text. This is also true of the two other commentators, Poole and Gill.

Poole

Poole, commenting on *thirty thousand chariots* in I Samuel 13:5, says,

> *Thirty thousand chariots*: this number seems incredible to infidels; to whom it may be sufficient to reply, that it is far more rational to acknowledge a mistake in him that copied out the sacred text in such numeral or historical passages, wherein the doctrine of faith and good life is not directly concerned, than upon such a pretence to question the truth and divinity of the Holy Scriptures.[770]

---

not to say that these sets may not provide some help on some of the difficult passages, but it is to say that they are not nearly so helpful on the difficult passages as Gill, Henry, and Poole, which are discussed later.

[769] Henry, *Joshua to Esther* in vol. 2 of *Matthew Henry's Commentary*, 245.

[770] Poole, 1:543.

Appendix B *Previous Studies*

Although Poole opens the door to questioning the text, later in his treatment he supplies information that explains the number. Despite Poole's shortcomings,[771] his work is about the most helpful the author has found in dealing with Bible difficulties. If a person were looking for a single work to assist him in Bible difficulties this is it. The preface to Poole's work states:

> We have not willingly balked at any obvious difficulty, and have designed a just satisfaction to all our readers; and if any knot remain yet untied, we have told our readers what hath been most probably said for their satisfaction in the untying of it.[772]

This is mostly true. Of the fifty-eight apparent difficulties in Chapters Seven through Twelve of this book only ten are not covered by Poole,[773] however, of the forty-eight which Poole does cover, this work generally goes into more detail.

Gill

Gill also allows for the possibility of scribal error. Commenting on II Chronicles 22:2 (where Ahaziah's age is forty-two, whereas in II Kings 8:26 it is twenty-two), Gill says,

> Indeed it is more to the honour of the sacred Scriptures to acknowledge here and there a mistake in the copiers, especially in the historical books, where there is sometimes a strange difference of names and numbers, than to give in to wild and distorted interpretations of them, in order to reconcile them, where there is no danger with respect to any article of faith or manners.[774]

---

[771] In addition to I Samuel 13:5, Poole allows for the possibility of scribal error in II Samuel 15:7; 24:13; I Kings 4:26; II Kings 1:17; 24:8; I Chronicles 22:14; II Chronicles 22:2. But unlike some works, scribal error is not his only "answer" to the apparent numerical problems in these passages.

[772] Ibid., I, vii.

[773] The ten passages which Poole does not deal with cover the following verses: I Kings 7:23; 16:8-10, 15-16, 29; II Kings 10:36; 12:1; 13:1, 10; 14:1; 15:2, 27, 32; 18:13; 22:3-4; I Chronicles 2:22-23; 3:22; and II Chronicles 24:1; 34:3-4.

[774] Gill, *Exposition of the Old & New Testaments*, 3:73. The author believes that to say that the preserved text has errors is rather more to the dishonor of Scripture than to its honor. Rather than claim errors are in the preserved text or to resort "to wild and distorted interpretations," perhaps the better course is for the interpreter to leave the Scripture intact and to admit that he does not know the answer for the difficulty.

Appendix B — *Previous Studies*

During Gill's discussion of this difficulty, he offers better solutions than this one; nonetheless, he allows for possible error in the preserved Hebrew text.

Conclusion

While Henry, Poole, and Gill open the door to criticism of the preserved text, which is regrettable, their commentaries are different from most modern treatments, which either ignore the difficulty altogether, or simply say it is the result of a scribal error. All three of these men give answers that retain the words of the preserved text. This book, however, distinguishes itself from the works of Henry, Poole, and Gill in that it (1) does not suggest the presence of scribal errors in the preserved texts as a way to answer difficulties; (2) shows that it is very dangerous to suggest scribal errors and indeed is contrary to Christ; (3) demonstrates that it is very illogical and unbiblical to say that these supposed scribal errors only occurred in the matters of history; (4) demonstrates from grammatical usage that nothing is wrong with the wording of the preserved text of the Hebrew Old Testament in the difficult numerical passages in I Samuel to II Chronicles; and (5) corrects the common misconception among commentators that scribes used letters of the Hebrew alphabet in place of numbers.[775]

Commentaries on Individual Books

In addition to commentary sets on the entire Bible, various authors have written commentaries on individual books. Many of the commentaries written on the individual books of I Samuel to II Chronicles either do not cover the difficult passages or claim scribal errors as an "answer" to the difficult passages.[776] However, the author has come across two exceptions to this general trend.

---

[775] For example, Poole gives this as an answer to the difficulty between II Kings 8:26 and II Chronicles 22:2 where in the one verse the age of Ahaziah is twenty-two and in the other it is forty-two: "Some acknowledge an error in the transcribers of the present Hebrew copies, in which language the numeral letters for twenty-two and forty-two are so like, that they might easily be mistaken" (Poole, 1:845).

[776] Some examples are (1) Farrar, F. W. *The First Book of Kings*. Minneapolis: Klock & Klock, 1981; (2) Farrar, F. W. *The Second Book of Kings*. Minneapolis: Klock & Klock, 1981; (3) Driver, S. R. *Notes on the Hebrew Text and Typography of the Books of Samuel*. Oxford: At the Clarendon Press, 1913; (4) Japhet, Sara. *I & II Chronicles: A*

Appendix B *Previous Studies*

Eisemann

The first exception is commentaries on I and II Chronicles written by Moshe Eisemann: *I Chronicles / A New Translation with a Commentary Anthologized from Talmudic, Midrashic and Rabbinic Sources* and *II Chronicles / A New Translation with a Commentary Anthologized from Talmudic, Midrashic and Rabbinic Sources*. Both were published by Mesorah Publications in Brooklyn, NY in 1987 and 1992 respectively. These two volumes uphold the Hebrew text without question and seek to give an explanation to every difficulty. These volumes reflect Rabbinic teaching over the last two thousand years and are somewhat helpful in answering the difficulties of I and II Chronicles. As helpful as these commentaries are in handling difficulties, they do not, however, deal with the subject of the preservation of the text and the implications of saying errors are in the preserved text.

Slotki

Another exception to commentaries that question the Masoretic Text is one written by I. W. Slotki on the books of Chronicles.[777] The forward states: "The commentary is invariably based upon the received Hebrew text. When this presents difficulties, the most probable translation and

---

Commentary. Louisville, KY: Westminster/John Knox Press, 1993; (5) Whitcomb, Jr., John C. *Solomon to the Exile: Studies in Kings and Chronicles*. Grand Rapids: Baker, 1978; (6) Wood, Leon J. *Israel's United Monarchy*. Grand Rapids: Baker, 1979; (7) Walsh, Jerome T. *BERIT OLAM Studies in Hebrew Narrative & Poetry: I Kings*. Edited by David W. Cotter. Collegeville, MN: The Liturgical Press, 1996; (8) Hooker, Paul K. *First and Second Chronicles*. Louisville: Westminster John Know Press, 2001; and (9) Polzin, Robert. *Samuel and the Deuteronomist: A Literary Study of the Deuteronomic History, Part Two, I Samuel*. San Francisco: Harper & Row, Publishers, 1989.

[777] Slotki, I. W. *Chronicles: Hebrew Text & English Translation with an Introduction and Commentary* in *Soncino Books of the Bible*. Edited by A. Cohen. New York: The Soncino Press, 1985. The work on Chronicles is part of a 13 volume set on the Old Testament that was done "by Jewish scholars" and contains "the Hebrew text with an English translation, and an exposition based upon classical Jewish commentaries" (Barber, *The Minister's Library*, 82). The volume on Samuel in this set by Goldman, however, does question the Masoretic Text. For example, on I Samuel 13:1, Goldman writes, "We are forced to the conclusion that the complete numbers are wanting in the Hebrew text, not only, as in A.J., in the first clause, but in the second as well" (R. Goldman, *Samuel with Hebrew Text and English Translation* in *Soncino Books of the Bible*, ed. A. Cohen (London: The Soncino Press, 1951), 68).

Appendix B   *Previous Studies*

interpretation are suggested, without resort to textual emendation."[778] As commendable as this is, "the exposition is designed primarily for the ordinary Bible reader, rather than for the student,"[779] therefore, the comments are not overly technical or exegetical and do not lend themselves to an in-depth study. Also, the comments above regarding Eisemann's commentaries apply to Slotki's work as well.

WORKS REFERRING TO DIFFICULTIES IN PASSING

Several works deal with the alleged numerical discrepancies of the Bible simply in passing; that is, dealing with these discrepancies is not the major emphasis of the book, but serves merely to illustrate or prove that the Bible is reliable. All of these works are limited in that they do not cover all of the alleged numerical discrepancies in I Samuel to II Chronicles, but in passages on which they speak, they provide some help. These works fall into two categories: (1) general; and (2) chronological.

General Works

Four general works are by Collett,[780] Fuller,[781] Lindsell,[782] and Strouse.[783] In Collett's work, forty pages of a chapter on inspiration deal with various apparent contradictions wherein on page 116 Collett allows for the possibility of scribal errors. Fuller's work deals with twenty-eight apparent contradictions, none of which are numerical. Lindsell's book contains a chapter that discusses discrepancies of Scripture, three of which are numerical. And Strouse's tome, in the chapter on inerrancy, covers

---

[778] A. Cohen, "Foreword by the General Editor" in *Chronicles: Hebrew Text & English Translation with an Introduction and Commentary* in *Soncino Books of the Bible*, ed. A. Cohen. (New York: The Soncino Press, 1985), i.

[779] Ibid.

[780] Collett, Sidney. *All About the Bible: Its Origin—Its Language—Its Translation—Its Canon—Its Symbols—Its Inspiration—Its Alleged Errors and Contradictions—Its Plan—Its Science—Its Rivals*. Westwood, NJ: Fleming H. Revell Co., 1964.

[781] Fuller, Andrew. "Passages Apparently Contradictory" in vol. 1 of *The Complete Works of Andrew Fuller*. Harrisonburg, VA: Sprinkle Publications, 1988.

[782] Lindsell, Harold. *The Battle for the Bible*. Grand Rapids: Zondervan, 1977.

[783] Strouse, Thomas M. *The Lord God Hath Spoken: A Guide to Bibliology*. Newington: Emmanuel Theological Press, 2001.

Appendix B *Previous Studies*

twenty various discrepancies: three are apparent numerical discrepancies from Kings and Chronicles.

Chronological Works

Two chronological works are by Thiele and Jones. Since several of the difficulties in I Samuel to II Chronicles involve chronology, chronological works are helpful. Thiele's work, *The Mysterious Numbers of the Hebrew Kings*, limits itself to a discussion of the Hebrew kings. Jones' work, *Chronology of the Old Testament*, deals with the entire subject of Old Testament chronology and is, therefore, more extensive than Thiele's. But this is not the only difference. Thiele questions the accuracy of the preserved Hebrew text in the matter of Hezekiah's overlap with Hoshea (II Kings 18).[784] Jones, however, criticizes Thiele for his departure and unashamedly supports the preserved Hebrew text. Jones states in his preface:

> This dissertation addresses the conflict between the presuppositions and methodologies utilized by the modern school of Biblical chronology whose procedure rests on the Assyrian Eponym Canon, the royal inscriptions of the Assyrians and the Babylonians and the Ptolemaic Canon as being absolute and accurate as opposed to the traditional Biblically oriented school which regards the Holy Scripture as the factual source against which all other material must be weighed.
>
> The propositions advanced are: (1) There is academic justification that the chronology of the Biblical record can be fully substantiated with internal formulae . . . ; and (2) This internal structure has been preserved in a specific rendering of the Biblical record, namely, the Hebrew Masoretic Text and the Greek *Textus Receptus* (the only current English translation being the King James Bible). In support of these propositions, standard objections, i.e., "generation gaps," "scribal errors," etc. will be met with forthright solutions and alternatives based upon internal data, not by "emendations," "restorations" or "corrections" of the Text. . . .
>
> Moreover, Dr. Edwin R. Thiele, long recognized as their leading proponent in the field of Biblical Chronology, while claiming to have defended the reliability of the Hebrew Text will be shown to have again and again applied these mishandled Assyrian data in violation of the clear Hebrew

---

[784] Thiele, 134-138, 174-176.

Appendix B — *Previous Studies*

history. In so doing, he created problems with and greatly undermined the integrity of the Hebrew text. Dr. Thiele shall be refuted.[785]

While Jones' work takes the same approach to the Biblical text as does this book, his work is limited to chronology and does not concern itself with other apparent numerical discrepancies. Further, Jones does not set forth a detailed study on Jesus' view of the Old Testament, on why God might allow apparent contradictions, and on the ramifications of claiming scribal errors exist in the preserved texts.

CONCLUSION

Of the over forty works discussed in this section, none approaches the subject of apparent numerical discrepancies in the books of I Samuel to II Chronicles from the same perspective as this book. Most of the works claim scribal errors blight the preserved text. Only a few works take the same position on the text as this book and those works do not cover all the passages that this work covers. Nor do any of these works cover in the same detail as this book (1) Christ's view of the preservation of the Old Testament text;[786] (2) why God would allow apparent contradictions; (3) how to handle apparent contradictions; and (4) ramifications of claiming that scribal errors exist in the preserved texts.[787]

---

[785] Jones, iv.

[786] One book that touches upon the subject of Christ's view of the preservation of the Old Testament is Robert Lightner's *The Saviour and The Scriptures* (Grand Rapids: Baker, 1978), but Lightner wrote before the doctrine of preservation came under attack and, therefore, he does not present much about the subject. A similar book with a similar assessment is John W. Wenham's *Christ and the Bible* (London: Tyndale Press, 1972).

[787] The above statement is not meant to say that the various works do not touch upon these subjects, but it is to say that they do not deal with them in a detailed manner.

APPENDIX C: II SAMUEL 21:19

Soon after the first edition of *Those So-Called Errors*, the author received two inquiries concerning II Samuel 21:19 wherein both inquirers thought that the book would address the difficulties II Samuel 21:19. However, the author explained to the individuals that the book largely concerned numerical quantities and that as II Samuel 21:19 did not have numbers, the author did not include it. But a year after the publishing of *Those So-Called Errors*, the author did a paper on II Samuel 21:19 and presents much of that paper here. Many of the charges that conservative commentators level against the numbers of I Samuel to II Chronicles, they also level against II Samuel 21:19; therefore, it is appropriate to include an appendix answering these charges.

INTRODUCTION

II Samuel 21:19 states: "And there was again a battle in Gob with the Philistines, where Elhanan the son of Jaareoregim, a Bethlehemite, slew *the brother of* Goliath the Gittite, the staff of whose spear *was* like a weaver's beam." II Samuel 21:19 is in the midst of a passage (II Samuel 21:15-22) detailing encounters with various giants. I Chronicles 20:4-8 parallels II Samuel 21:18-22. Evidence for these passages being parallel is that (1) I Chronicles 20:4 and II Samuel 21:8 both speak of a battle with the Philistines in which Sibbechai the Hushathite slew Sippai[788]; (2) I

---

[788] In Samuel the name is Saph, but he may have had two names, as several in the Bible did (cf. John 1:42). Concerning, the difference in places Gob in II Samuel 21:18 and

Chronicles 20:5 and II Samuel 21:19 both speak of Elhanan[789] slaying the brother of Goliath the Gittite, whose spear staff was like a weaver's beam; (3) I Chronicles 20:6-7 and II Samuel 21:20-21 both speak of an event in Gath wherein Jonathan, the son of Shimea, David's brother, slew a giant with six fingers on each hand and six toes on each foot; and (4) I Chronicles 20:8 and II Samuel 21:22 both speak of the previous giants being born to the giant in Gath and that "they fell by the hand of David, and by the hand of his servants." While there are some differences in the passages (see footnotes for discussion), yet the overwhelming number of similarities leads to the conclusion that they are parallel passages.

The *King James Version* of II Samuel 21:19 seems plain enough, however, a great controversy looms over the italicized words *the brother of*. The fact that the translators italicized the words indicates that they have no exact equivalent in the Hebrew. The parallel verse, I Chronicles 20:5, states: "And there was war again with the Philistines; and Elhanan the son of Jair slew Lahmi the brother of Goliath the Gittite, whose spear staff *was* like a weaver's beam." I Chronicles 20:5 does not italicize *the brother of* and also provides the name of the brother (Lahmi). It seems that for II Samuel 21:19, the King James translators obtained *the brother of* from I Chronicles 20:5. In light of this, some claim that II Samuel 21:19 has words missing.

The Questioning of II Samuel 21:19

Among those who claim that II Samuel 21:19 is in error are Leon Wood, Gleason Archer, Norman Geisler, Thomas Howe, and Edward J. Young. Leon Wood states:

> The reading of I Chron. 20:5 is to be preferred over that of II Sam. 21:19. The latter omits "the brother of," making Goliath himself the victim of Elhanan. This conflicts with the earlier account of David's having slain Goliath. No doubt a copyist's error occurred in II Samuel.[790]

Gezer in I Chronicles 20:4, Poole states that "it seems *Gob* and *Gezer* were neighbouring places, and the battle fought in the confines of both" (Poole, I:637).

[789] Samuel says Elhanan is the son of Jaareoregim, whereas Chronicles says that he is the son of Jair. It seems that Jaareoregim is a fuller name and Jair a shorter. *Jaareoregim* literally means "forests of weaver" ("03296 יערי ארגים" in *Hebrew – Online Bible Lexicon* in *Online Bible Millennium Edition*). *Jair* means "forested" ("03265 יעור" in *Hebrew – Online Bible Lexicon*).

[790] Leon J. Wood, *Israel's United Monarchy* (Grand Rapids: Baker, 1979), 242.

Appendix C *II Samuel 21:19*

Gleason Archer declares that "the 2 Samuel 21 passage is a perfectly traceable corruption of the original wording, which fortunately has been correctly preserved in I Chronicles 20:5."[791] Geisler and Howe assert that "the passage in 2 Samuel 21:19 which reads, 'Elhanan the son of Jare-Oregim the Bethlehemite killed Goliath the Gittite, the shaft of whose spear was like a weaver's beam' (the italicized words *'the brother of'* are not in the Hebrew text), is obviously a copyist error."[792] Edward J. Young writes: "Careful examination will make it clear that II Sam. 21:19 and I Chr. 20:5 are closely related. In the course of transmission some copyist's errors have evidently crept in, particularly into I Sam. 21:19."[793] Young goes on to say that "some of the rough places in this section [that is, in II Samuel 21:19] may be due to the condition of the text."[794]

The Questioning of Samuel

The above observation by Young could be part of the reason why others have questioned the text of Samuel. Merrill Unger asserts "that the Hebrew text of Samuel is in a poorer state of preservation than any other part of the Old Testament" and, therefore, concludes that II Samuel 21:19 "has suffered corruption in the course of transmission."[795] Leon Wood, who questions II Samuel 21:19, states: "For some reason the text of I and II Samuel appears to have been more poorly preserved than that of I and II Kings, or of any of the other Old Testament books for that matter."[796] Could it be that Wood, as does Unger, would point to II Samuel 21:19 as evidence for his claim that the text of Samuel is poorly preserved? It seems likely. In any event, Wood's assessment of II Samuel 21:19 and the text of Samuel, no doubt, influenced Fundamentalism, for Wood was "professor of Old Testament at Grand Rapids Baptist Seminary from 1945 to 1976,"[797] and as of 1975 the then Fundamentalist group,[798] General As-

---

[791] Archer, 179.

[792] Geisler and Howe, 163.

[793] Edward J. Young, *An Introduction to the Old Testament* (Grand Rapids: Eerdmans, 1960), 197.

[794] Ibid., 198.

[795] Unger, 296.

[796] Wood, 15.

[797] Ibid., back flyleaf.

sociation of Regular Baptist Churches, recommended this school.[799] It is interesting that the purportedly Fundamentalist school, Central Baptist Theological Seminary, asserts in an endnote that "most notorious in the Masoretic tradition for its poorer quality is the book of Samuel."[800] Could they have based their assessment partly upon the statements of Young, Unger, and Wood? It is very likely.

The Preserving of Samuel and II Samuel 21:19

Despite what Archer, Young, Unger, Wood, Central Baptist Theological Seminary, Geisler, and Howe state about the text of Samuel and II Samuel 21:19 in particular, both the text of Samuel and II Samuel 21:19 are perfectly preserved and without error. The author can dogmatically make this claim based upon God's promises to preserve His Words. For instance, Psalm 12:6-7 states: "The words of the LORD *are* pure words: *as* silver tried in a furnace of earth, purified seven times. Thou shalt keep them, O LORD, thou shalt preserve them from this generation for ever." God's pure Words are perfectly preserved. Furthermore, Jesus affirmed: "For verily I say unto you, Till heaven and earth pass, one jot or one tittle shall in no wise pass from the law, till all be fulfilled" (Matthew 5:18). Clearly, according to Jesus, nothing has been lost from the text of Samuel or from II Samuel 21:19. To assert otherwise is to question God the Father and God the Son, and is to indirectly claim that they are misinformed, or, worse, lying. Such is the unenviable position in which some Fundamentalists find themselves. In contrast, the God-honoring position is to believe that II Samuel 21:19 is today as it was when it was first written under inspiration. The question then arises, why are the words *the brother of* not part of the Hebrew text of II Samuel 21:19? The answer to that question will form the basis for the rest of this appendix. Specifically, the author will examine four, non-scribal-error approaches to this question: (1) a typical use of *Goliath*; (2) a prepositional meaning of *with* for את (*'eth*), which occurs just before *Goliath*; (3) an elliptical view, wherein the translator must supply words to make the sense complete; and (4) a prepositional-elliptical view combining the prepositional and elliptical views.

---

[798] Dollar, 220.

[799] Ibid., 222.

[800] Beacham, "The Old Testament Text and English Versions" in *The Bible Version Debate: The Perspective of Central Baptist Theological Seminary*, 37.

Appendix C *II Samuel 21:19*

TYPICAL VIEW

If II Samuel 21:19 uses *Goliath* in a typical, rather than a literal or an historical sense, then the meaning is that *Goliath* in II Samuel is not referring to the historical Goliath of I Samuel 17, but is referring to someone who typifies Goliath. In other words, the Goliath of II Samuel would be a separate and distinct person from the Goliath of I Samuel, but would possess similar characteristics as the I Samuel Goliath.

Presentation of the Typical View

Eisemann explains this view:

> This Lachmi [Lahmi, the brother of Goliath (I Chronicles 20:5)] was as mighty a warrior as his brother Goliath, and that therefore his defeat had the same miraculous overtones – prompted them [the writers of Samuel] to immortalize the story of that combat in terms which would have been appropriate in describing David's victory over Goliath . . . . In this way people knew that reference was to the defeat of Lachmi at the hands of Elchanan [Elhanan] but at the same time they were made aware of just how miraculous an event this was.[801]

In this same way of thinking, Hertzberg states: "Perhaps even at this early stage the name 'Goliath' had come to designate a type."[802]

Poole writes that Elhanan

> slew . . . a *Goliath* (or another *Goliath*) . . . who may be here called *Goliath*, not only for his near relation to him, being his brother, but for his exact resemblance of him in feature, or in stature and strength, or in courage and military skill; as *John the Baptist* was called *Elias* for the like reason. Peradventure also, after the death of the first and famous Goliath the Gittite, I Sam. xvii., that name was either given to him by others, or taken by himself.[803]

Poole mentions John the Baptist. John the Baptist came in the spirit and power of Elias (Luke 1:17) and if the people had received John, then he would have been "Elias, which was for to come" (Matthew 11:14). In

---

[801] Eisemann, 273.

[802] Hans Wilhelm Hertzberg, *I & II Samuel: A Commentary* (Philadelphia: Westminster Press, 1964), 387.

[803] Poole, I:637.

speaking of John the Baptist, Jesus said, "That Elias is come already, and they knew him not" (Matthew 17:12). John was not the literal Elijah, but a typical Elijah, and had the people received him, he would have fulfilled Malachi's prophecy in Malachi 4:5. Therefore, the Bible, does at times, use names in a typical sense, as opposed to a literal or historical sense.

Another example of the Bible using names in a typical sense, instead of a literal or historical sense, is in the use of *Gog and Magog*. Both Ezekiel 38:2 and Revelation 20:8 refer to Gog and Magog. While both of these passages speak of future battles involving Gog and Magog, yet these passages have chronological, geographical, and corporeal differences. Concerning the chronological difference, Ezekiel 38 occurs during the tribulation[804]; whereas Revelation 20:8 occurs after the Millennial Kingdom as Revelation 20:7 makes clear. Concerning the geographical difference, Ezekiel speaks of Gog coming from the north (Ezekiel 38:14-15); whereas Revelation speaks of Gog and Magog coming from "the four quarters of the earth" (Revelation 20:8). And concerning the corporeal difference, Israel will take seven months to bury the dead bodies of Ezekiel (Ezekiel 39:1-12); whereas in Revelation, God will consume the bodies of the attackers with fire (Revelation 20:9). Clearly, these two passages are not using *Gog and Magog* in the same way. Concerning the use of *Gog and Magog* in Revelation, Walvoord states that possibly "the expression is used much as we use the term 'Waterloo' to express a disastrous battle, but one not related to the historic origination of the term."[805]

---

[804] Walvoord writes: "If Ezekiel 38-39 is studied carefully, it reveals a future invasion of the land of Israel by the armies of Russia and five other nations. Though sometimes confused with the battle of Armageddon, which will be a world conflict before the Second Coming, this war will be distinct, both in its objectives, its character, and its outcome. . . . As the prophecy was written 2,500 years ago, the question remains whether this has ever been fulfilled in the past. A search of history finds no such battle or outcome. Accordingly, as illustrated in countless other passages, prophecy that has not been fulfilled is subject to future fulfillment just as literally as the prophecies were fulfilled in the past. . . . The point of view adopted here places this war in the first half of the last seven years [of the tribulation], probably toward its close" (John F. Walvoord, *Every Prophecy of the Bible* (Colorado Springs: Chariot Victor Publishing, 1999), 190). Dwight Pentecost writes: "Twice a reference is made in chapter thirty-eight to a time element. It is said to take place 'in the latter years' (v. 8 [of Ezek 38]) and 'in the latter days' (v. 16 [of Ezek 38]). This has specific reference to the latter years and days of God's dealing with the nation Israel, which, since it is before the millennial age (ch. 40), must place it during God's dealing with Israel in the seventieth week of Daniel's prophecy" (J. Dwight Pentecost, *Things To Come* (Grand Rapids: Zondervan, 1958), 346).

[805] John F. Walvoord, *The Revelation of Jesus Christ: A Commentary* (Chicago: Moody, 1966), 303.

Appendix C   *II Samuel 21:19*

In other words, Revelation uses *Gog and Magog* in a typical sense, for clearly it is not referring to the same Gog and Magog of Ezekiel.

Weaknesses of the Typical View

Elias and *Gog and Magog* illustrate that the Bible does use proper names in a typical sense, but is II Samuel 21:19 using *Goliath* in a typical way? While understanding *Goliath* in II Samuel 21:19 in a typical sense would remove the apparent contradiction with I Samuel 17 and at the same time uphold the integrity of Scripture, it does, however, suffer from a couple of weaknesses.

Geographical Weakness

One weakness is that II Samuel 21:19 says, "Goliath the Gittite[806]," which gives a specific geographic location for this Goliath and would seem to indicate that the verse is using *Goliath* in a literal, rather than in a typical sense. Compare, for instance, the use of *Elias* or *Elijah*. The Bible calls the historical and literal Elijah *Elijah the Tishbite* (I Kings 17:1; 21:17, 28; II Kings 1:3, 8; 9:36); but when the Bible uses *Elias* of John the Baptist, it does not assign any specific geographic location. In other words, when the Bible uses *Elias* in a typical sense, it does not connect it to specific geographical data.

Compare also the discussion of *Gog and Magog*, Ezekiel, using it in a literal sense, connects specific geographical locations with it, such as Meshech and Tubal (Ezekiel 39:1); whereas when Revelation 20 uses *Gog and Magog* in a typical sense any geographical locations are very general ("the four quarters of the earth" (Revelation 20:8)). One answer to the geographic weakness of the typical view is to adopt Bullinger's nominal view: "Omit the italics [in II Samuel 21:19], and understand another giant of the same name as the Goliath of I Sam. 17."[807] If this is so, then Lahmi (I Chronicles 20:5), the brother of Goliath, also had Goliath's name. That men had more than one name is not unusual (for example, Matthew 4:18). Another answer to the geographical problem with the typical view comes from Slotki's titular view: "The mention of *Goliath* in the encounter with

---

[806] *Gittite* refers to "a native of the Philistine city of Gath" (M. G. Easton, "Gittite" in *Easton's Bible Dictionary* in *The Master Christian Library*, version 8 [CD-ROM] (Albany, OR: Ages Software, 1997), 450.

[807] E. W. Bullinger, *The Companion Bible* (Grand Rapids: Kregel, 1999), 439.

Appendix C   *II Samuel 21:19*

David the king, as well as in the contest which occurred when David was a young man, presents no difficulty if it is assumed that the word is not a proper name but a descriptive title like 'Pharaoh,' 'Rabshakeh,' 'Sultan'."[808] If Slotki is correct, then II Samuel 21:19 would be not be using *Goliath* in a truly typical sense, but more in the sense of a title indicating that the Goliath of II Samuel 21:19 was the current Goliath of Gath, having taken over for the dead Goliath of Gath.

Scriptural Weakness

While the nominal and titular suggestions may seem appealing, they partake of a second weakness with the typical view, which is that the parallel passage in I Chronicles 20:5 does not use a typical sense for *Goliath*, but, instead, uses a literal and historical sense, applying *Goliath* to one individual only, the Goliath of I Samuel 17. This presents a problem for the titular view, for Chronicles gives no indication that *Goliath* is a title for Lahmi. Also, Chronicles' historical and literal sense is a problem for the nominal view, for Chronicles clearly indicates that *Lahmi* and *Goliath* are two different names for two different people. Proponents of the typical view and its related titular and nominal views need to address these weaknesses. These are weaknesses that the *New American Standard Version*, *New International Version*, and *English Standard Version* share, for they omit the italics in II Samuel 21:19 and present the teaching that Elhanan slew Goliath, rather than the teaching that Elhanan slew the brother of Goliath.[809] In light of these weaknesses, it seems that a solution for the apparent difficulty between II Samuel 21 and I Samuel 17 lies in taking into account both II Samuel 21:19 and I Chronicles 20:5, instead of isolating one from the other. Such is the approach that the next three views present.

---

[808] I. W. Slotki, *Chronicles: Hebrew Text & English Translation with an Introduction and Commentary*, (NY: The Soncino Press, 1985), 113.

[809] *New American Standard Version* reads: "There was war with the Philistines again at Gob, and Elhanan the son of Jaare-oregim the Bethlehemite killed Goliath the Gittite, the shaft of whose spear was like a weaver's beam." *New International Version* reads: "In another battle with the Philistines at Gob, Elhanan son of Jaare-Oregim the Bethlehemite killed Goliath the Gittite, who had a spear with a shaft like the weaver's rod." *English Standard Version* reads: "And there was again war with the Philistines at Gob, and Elhanan the son of Jaare-oregim, the Bethlehemite, struck down Goliath the Gittite, the shaft of whose spear was like a weaver's beam."

Appendix C   *II Samuel 21:19*

PREPOSITIONAL VIEW

The Hebrew of II Samuel 21:19 places an אֵת (*'eth*) before *Goliath*. אֵת (*'eth*) can have either a prepositional or a particle use. The difficulty lies in the fact that the two uses "are sometimes confused.."[810] In light of this potential confusion it may be necessary for the interpreter to consider both uses in a particular verse in order to arrive at the correct meaning of the verse.[811] Such is the case with II Samuel 21:19.

Particle Use

As a particle, אֵת (*'eth*) can have a couple of grammatical uses: a nominative or an accusative use.

---

[810] Waltke and O'Connor, 177.

[811] Commentators provide several examples of their struggling to get at the exact meaning of אֵת (*'eth*) in various passages. Schroder on Ezekiel 31:4 states: "אֶת־ either: *with*, or taken accusatively: *what concerns*" (Wilhelm Julius Schroder, *The Book of the Prophet Ezekiel* in *A Commentary on the Holy Scriptures: Critical, Doctrinal, and Homiletical, with Special Reference to Ministers and Students*, ed. John peter Lange, trans. Philip Schaff (NY: Scribner, Armstrong & Co., 1876), 284.). On the same verse, Keil states: "The difficult words אֶת־נַהֲרֹתֶיהָ וגו are to be taken literally thus: as for its (the flood's) streams, it (the flood) was going round about its plantation, i.e., round about the plantation belonging to the flood or the place situated near it, where the cedar was planted. אֵת is not to be taken as a preposition, but as a sign of the accusative, and אֶת־נַהֲרֹתֶיהָ as an accusative used for the more precise definition of the manner in which the flood surrounded the plantation" (Keil, *Ezekiel* in *Commentary on the Old Testament*, IX:260).

Oswalt commenting on Isaiah 53:8 states: "If this is the case, then the *'et* prefixed to *dôr* cannot be taken as the direct object indicator, as it appears, but must be what Delitzsch calls an emphatic accusative of respect (so RSV 'as for')" (John N. Oswalt, *The Book of Isaiah Chapters 40-66* in *The New International Commentary on the Old Testament*, eds. R. K. Harrison and Robert L. Hubbard, Jr. (Grand Rapids: Eerdmans, 1998), 394). Alexander also refers to Isaiah 53:8 when he writes: "Neither of these objections lies against Ewald's modification of this same exposition, which makes אֵת a preposition, and continues the interrogation through the sentence—in (or among) his generation (*i. e.* his contemporaries), who considered that he was cut off from the land of the living?" (Joseph A. Alexander, *Commentary on Isaiah* (NY: Charles Scribner, 1867. Reprint, 2 vols. in 1, Grand Rapids: Kregel, 1992), II:300). Young also on Isaiah 53:8 states: "Differing interpretations of the following words have been given, but we may take the particle *'eth* as a preposition and render *with* or *among*" (Young, *The Book of Isaiah*, III:352).

The author realizes that some of these examples contradict one another; however, it is beyond the scope of this appendix to settle these points of interpretation. But the examples well illustrate the need for the interpreter to adequately account for אֵת (*'eth*).

Appendix C   *II Samuel 21:19*

Nominative Use

"The particle את is prefixed to nouns in the nominative function in both verbal and verbless clauses, usually in cases involving enumerations or appositions."[812] However, this syntax does not occur in II Samuel 21:19 as את (*'eth*) stands alone and, therefore, not prefixed to any noun.

Another nominative use is that "in verbal clauses את can mark the subject of transitive and intransitive active verbs and passive verbs," though "the use with transitives is extremely rare."[813] However, in II Samuel 21:19, while the main verb is *slew* (יַךְ (*yak*) from נָכָה (*nakah*)), which is a transitive verb, *Elhanan* is its clear subject[814], and since את (*'eth*) is not before *Elhanan*, then it is not serving as a marker of the subject.

Neither of the nominative, grammatical uses of את (*'eth*) apply to II Samuel 21:19.

Accusative Use

In its particle use, את (*'eth*) "is used most often to mark the *definite direct object* of a transitive verb."[815] In II Samuel 21:19 seems to follow the normal word order in a Hebrew verbal clause, which is "first the verb, then the subject (plus any modifiers), and finally the object (plus any modifiers),"[816] so that את (*'eth*) would seem to be the sign of the direct object. If it is the sign of the direct object, then II Samuel 21:19 is stating that Elhanan slew Goliath. But based upon contextual considerations this is an impossibility, for David slew Goliath the Gittite as I Samuel 17 re-

---

[812] Waltke and O'Connor, 182.

[813] Ibid.

[814] The fact that Elhanan is the subject of the verb *slew* rests upon several considerations: (1) it follows immediately after the verb and is, therefore, in the very position in which the subject of a Hebrew verb usually stands, for "the normal word order in a Hebrew verbal sentence is first the verb, then the subject" (Kelley, 87); (2) it has no particles or prepositions before it or prefixed to it to separate it from the verb; and (3) if it is not the subject of the verb, then it would be difficult to make sense out of the verse.

[815] Waltke and O'Connor, 179.

[816] Kelley, 87.

Appendix C *II Samuel 21:19*

lates. A further contextual consideration that eliminates the possibility of אֵת (*'eth*) being the sign of the accusative is that the parallel passage, I Chronicles 20:5, states that Elhanan "slew Lahmi the brother of Goliath the Gittite," instead of stating the he slew Goliath.

The elimination of the accusative use of אֵת (*'eth*) also rests upon a theological consideration involving the inspiration and preservation of the Words of the Bible. If אֵת (*'eth*) is the sign of the accusative, then this would have the affect of making II Samuel 21:19 to be in contradiction with I Samuel 17 and, therefore, would introduce an error into the Bible. Herein is a major problem with the way in which the *New American Standard Version*, the *New International Version*, and the *English Standard Version* translate II Samuel 21:19, for they state that Elhanan killed Goliath the Gittite, thereby introducing an error into the Bible. But since God gave pure words and promised to preserve those pure words (Psalm 12:6-7), then it is a theological impossibility that II Samuel 21:19 is in real contradiction with I Samuel 17.

Prepositional Use

The particle uses of אֵת (*'eth*) as either a sign of the nominative or as a sign of the accusative are not possible in II Samuel 21:19, which then leaves one use for אֵת (*'eth*) namely, the prepositional use. As a preposition אֵת (*'eth*) means (1) "with, together with, in the company or association of"; (2) "at, close to, beside, in the midst of"; (3) "with the help of, under the protection of"; (4) "provided with, in the possession of"; or (5) "to strive with someone, to fight with."[817] It is possible to eliminate meanings one, three, and five from consideration, since Elhanan did not slay together with Goliath (meaning one), for Goliath was already dead; and Elhanan did not slay with the help of Goliath (meaning three); nor did Elhanan slay to fight with Goliath (meaning five). This leaves meanings two (he slew close to Goliath) and four (he slew in the possession of Goliath). Meaning two conveys the idea of Elhanan slaying one who was close to or possibly related to Goliath. Meaning four conveys the idea of Elhanan slaying in the possession of Goliath, perhaps referring to one who was Goliath's heir or who had been under Goliath's influence, again pointing to the possibility of one related to Goliath. However, when one

---

[817] Horst Dietrich Preuss, "אֵת" in *Theological Dictionary of the Old Testament*, I:450.

Appendix C *II Samuel 21:19*

considers I Chronicles 20:5 it is no longer a possibility that Elhanan slew a relative of Goliath, but it is a certainty, for Chronicles clearly states that Elhanan slew the brother of Goliath. Poole states that Elhanan slew one "who was (which words are frequently understood in the Hebrew text) *with* (so *eth* [אֵת] is oft rendered, . . .) *Goliath the Gittite*, i. e. in his company, bred up with him to the war, and related to him as his brother."[818]

Based upon the above analysis of אֵת (*'eth*), the author concludes that II Samuel 21:19 uses אֵת (*'eth*) prepositionally, rather than as a grammatical particle. However, this still leaves one more issue to consider and that is this: why is it that II Samuel 21:19 does not have the words *the brother of* as does I Chronicles 20:5? The answer to this question leads to the third view to the problem posed by II Samuel 21:19.

ELLIPTICAL VIEW

While understanding אֵת (*'eth*) as a preposition provides considerable help in arriving at a solution for II Samuel 21:19, it does not completely solve all the difficulty. To completely solve the difficulty one must understand that the Biblical languages often make use of ellipsis.

General Use of Ellipsis in Scripture

Several writers make general observations about Scripture's use of ellipsis.

Moncrieff

Moncrieff in making a general observation about the Hebrew language states that "in many parts the language is very concise and even elliptical."[819] Further, he speaks of "those parts which are expressed in an abrupt, elliptical, proleptical style."[820] It is, therefore, the nature of Hebrew to be, at times, elliptical.

---

[818] Poole, I:637.

[819] John Moncrieff, *An Essay on the Antiquity and Utility of the Vowel-Points* (London: Whittaker, Treacher and Arnot, 1833), 24.

[820] Ibid., 73.

Appendix C *II Samuel 21:19*

Gill

Gill makes a similar observation when he writes: "The style of the Bible is generally short, concise, full of ellipsis and other figures, especially in the prophetic writings."[821] Gill's states that this is the case especially in prophetic writings. In light of this, it is interesting to note that II Samuel is part of the prophetic writings of the Hebrew Old Testament.

Poole

Concerning II Samuel 8:4 where the Bible says: "And David took from him a thousand *chariots*, and seven hundred horsemen, and twenty thousand footmen: and David houghed all the chariot *horses*, but reserved of them *for* an hundred chariots." Poole states: "*Chariots*; which word is fitly supplied out of I Chron. xviii. 4, such substantives being oft understood in the Hebrew language."[822]

Concerning II Samuel 5:8, which says: "And David said on that day, Whosoever getteth up to the gutter, and smiteth the Jebusites, and the lame and the blind, *that are* hated of David's soul, *he shall be chief and captain*. Wherefore they said, The blind and the lame shall not come into the house," Poole states: "*He shall be chief and captain*: these words are fitly supplied out of I Chron. xi. 6, where they are expressed; and they must needs be understood to make the sense complete. And such ellipses or defects of a part of the sentence are usual in promises, and oaths, and conditional offers, such as this was."[823] Poole observes that Scripture often makes use of ellipsis.

Genesis

The author's own research indicates that ellipsis is a frequent tool in the Bible. For instance, in the first five chapters of Genesis, the author has compiled a list of significant use of ellipsis.

> Genesis 1:9-10 – "And God said, Let the waters under the heaven be gathered together unto one place, and let the dry *land* appear: and it was so. And God called the dry *land* Earth; and the gathering together of the wa-

---

[821] John Gill, *A Dissertation concerning the Antiquity of Hebrew Language, LETTERS, VOWEL POINTS, and ACCENTS* (London: G. Keith, 1767), 70.

[822] Poole, I:602.

[823] Ibid., I:595.

ters called he Seas: and God saw that *it was* good." The context implies the use of *land*.

Genesis 1:16 – "And God made two great lights; the greater light to rule the day, and the lesser light to rule the night: *he made* the stars also." Here the translators supply *he made* from earlier in the verse.

Genesis 1:30 – "And to every beast of the earth, and to every fowl of the air, and to every thing that creepeth upon the earth, wherein *there is* life, *I have given* every green herb for meat: and it was so." The first part of this verse in the Hebrew is without a main verb, therefore, the necessity to supply *I have given*. The sign of the direct object (את *'eth*) before *every green herb* implies the main verb.

Genesis 2:19 – "And out of the ground the LORD God formed every beast of the field, and every fowl of the air; and brought *them* unto Adam to see what he would call them: and whatsoever Adam called every living creature, that *was* the name thereof." The context implies the use of *them*.

Genesis 4:20 – "And Adah bare Jabal: he was the father of such as dwell in tents, and *of such as have* cattle." The first half of the verse supplies and implies *of such as have* later in the verse.

Genesis 5:3 – "And Adam lived an hundred and thirty years, and begat *a son* in his own likeness, after his image; and called his name Seth." The context implies *a son*.

In this list are six examples of ellipsis, illustrating that substantives, verbs, objects, and pronouns are subject to ellipsis. These are six examples in just five chapters. If one were to simply pay attention while reading his *King James Bible*, he would become very aware that ellipsis is often present, especially when translating from Hebrew into English.

At this point, the author must issue a caution about ellipsis. It may seem to some that one could suppose ellipsis has occurred in just about any verse and then supply any number of words to suit his own objectives. However, to say that ellipsis is present in a verse requires evidence of some kind, one legitimately cannot merely conjecture that ellipsis has occurred. Further, the supplying of words for the ellipsis must also have substantial basis. For instance, in the above examples and in the examples which follow, the author and others give legitimate reasons for the supplied words. The following sections of this paper present evidence showing that II Samuel 21:19 has an ellipsis, and that the supplying of the words for the ellipsis rests upon a firm Biblical basis.

Appendix C *II Samuel 21:19*

Specific Use of Ellipsis in II Samuel 21:19

A couple of writers while mentioning that Scripture in general utilizes ellipsis, also comment on the use of ellipsis specifically in II Samuel 21:19.

Eisemann

Eisemann, commenting on the difficulty between I Chronicles 20:5 and II Samuel 21:19 states:

> A simply solution is suggested by *Ibn Janach* in ch. 25 of *Sefer HaRikmah*. In that chapter he demonstrates an idiosyncrasy of Scriptural writing which he calls חֶסְרוֹן, *missing* (*words*). This theory postulates that many verses in Scripture cannot be understood unless we assume that a word or two was intentionally omitted[824] and left to the reader to supply. . . . Among the many examples which he adduces is the verse in *Samuel* [II Samuel 21:19]. Based on *Chronicles*, he takes it for granted that Elchanan killed not Goliath but his brother, and he consequently sees a word 'missing' from the verse. The word אֲחִי, *brother of*, is to be understood before גָּלְיָת, *Goliath*. By this simple assumption the two verses agree with one another and have no bearing on the confrontation between David and Goliath.[825]

Poole

Poole writes on II Samuel 21:19: "*The brother of Goliath the Gittite*: the relative word *brother* is not in the Hebrew text, but is fitly supplied out of the parallel place, I Chron. xx. 5, where it is expressed. And such defects of relatives are not unusual in Scripture."[826] Poole gives several examples throughout the Bible of this very thing:

> Luke 6:16 says, "And Judas *the brother* of James, and Judas Iscariot, which also was the traitor." Here the genitive case implies *the brother*, for it implies a relationship between Judas and James, but the verse does not

---

[824] "Intentionally omitted" seems in this context to mean, not originally written, as the sentence before this states that he is demonstrating "an idiosyncrasy of Scriptural writing," which would imply at the time of inscripturation. Further, after this term, Eisemann places *missing* in quotes to indicate that nothing indeed is lost from the text of Scripture, but that Scripture never originally gave the words.

[825] Eisemann, 273.

[826] Poole, I:637.

Appendix C II Samuel 21:19

clearly state the relationship. Here the *King James Version* correctly inserts *the brother* for this was the relationship between them (Jude 1).

In Luke 3:23-38, the *King James Version* repeatedly supplies *the son*. Again the genitive case implies a relationship between these individuals. The Bible states the exact nature of the relationship in other verses and based on those other verses, the translators of the *King James Version* were justified in supplying *the son*.

Matthew 1:6 states: "And Jesse begat David the king; and David the king begat Solomon of her *that had been the wife* of Urias." In this case the feminine, genitive, singular article (τῆς) implies a relationship between *her* and *Urias*, which relationship the Old Testament states was a husband-wife relationship (II Samuel 11:3; 12:24).

Other examples of the genitive implying a relationship are in Matthew 4:21; 10:2, 3; Mark 15:47; 16:1; John 19:25; and Acts 1:13; 7:16.

Genesis 17:16 says, "And I will bless her, and give thee a son also of her: yea, I will bless her, and she shall be *a mother* of nations; kings of people shall be of her." The preposition *le* (meaning to[827]), which is attached to *nations*, implies *a mother* as does the end of the verse, which says, "Kings of people shall be of her."

Genesis 24:60 says, "And they blessed Rebekah, and said unto her, Thou *art* our sister, be thou *the mother* of thousands of millions, and let thy seed possess the gate of those which hate them." Again, the preposition *le*, which is attached to *thousands*, implies *the mother* as does the rest of the verse, which speaks of her seed.

1 Chronicles 7:15 says, "And Machir took to wife *the sister* of Huppim and Shuppim, whose sister's name *was* Maachah;) and the name of the second was Zelophehad: and Zelophehad had daughters." Again, the preposition *le*, which is attached to *Huppim*, implies *the sister*. Also, the context helps to decide this, for Huppim was the son of Aher (I Chronicles 7:12), therefore, Machir could not have taken Huppim as his wife, but he took one who was to or near Huppim, that is, his sister.

The last example from I Chronicles 7:15 is somewhat analogous to II Samuel 21:19 in a number of ways. First, the preposition *le* in I Chronicles 7:15 is in the sense of at or near (see footnote), which is a similar meaning for את (*'eth*) in II Samuel 21:19. Second, in both cases, a preposition before a proper noun indicates someone connected with that person,

---

[827] Waltke and O'Connor state that "the preposition *l* . . . marks location 'to, toward,' and 'at, near' " (Waltke and O'Connor, 183).

Appendix C   *II Samuel 21:19*

implying an ellipsis. Third, in both cases, the ellipsis must be supplied from the context. This example leads quite naturally to a discussion of the last view.

PREPOSITIONAL-ELLIPTICAL VIEW

The preposition-elliptical view combines both the prepositional and elliptical views.

II Samuel 21:19

The preposition אֵת (*'eth*) in II Samuel 21:19 teaches that Elhanan slew one who was close to or possibly related to Goliath (see discussion under Prepositional View), but since the verse does not clearly state who this one was, then it leaves some ambiguity and, therefore, seems to be a case of ellipsis. Concerning this ambiguity, Waltke and O'Connor observe: "One useful approach to the structural ambiguities associated with prepositions involves considering the perspective from which an action is viewed. Another approach involves *ellipsis*, the omission of part of a grammatical structure when that part can be recovered from the context."[828] They further state that "another source of structural ambiguity associated with prepositions can also be clarified by considering ellipsis."[829]

The above quotes from Waltke and O'Connor reveal a couple of things about Biblical Hebrew: (1) prepositions can have a certain degree of ambiguity, which is the status of the preposition אֵת (*'eth*) in II Samuel 21:19, simply indicating that Elhanan slew one close to Goliath, but not indicating exactly who; and (2) the context can alleviate the ambiguity and supply the words of the ellipsis, which is what the translator must do with II Samuel 21:19, supplying the words *the brother of* from I Chronicles 20:5.

---

[828] Waltke and O'Connor, 224.

[829] Ibid.

| Appendix C | II Samuel 21:19 |

Other Verses

Other places where אֵת (*'eth*) is in a similar construction as in II Samuel 21:19 and where the Bible uses it in a prepositional manner and with ellipsis are exceedingly rare. Indeed, the author after consulting over two thousand verses believes that he has found three examples, in addition to II Samuel 21:19. These examples are from Joshua 17:12 and Judges 1:19, 27. In these verses the Bible points the word as אֶת and attaches it to a following noun through the use of the *maqqeph*, which appears as a raised hyphen, but these differences have no affect on the possible uses for the particle/preposition that this appendix discussed earlier. Waltke and O'Connor state: "The particle אֵת/אֶת־ is homonymous with אֵת/אֶת־, the preposition 'with,' except with pronominal suffixes."[830] In other words, excepting when they have pronominal suffixes they sound the same and "are sometimes confused."[831] Since there are no pronominal suffixes attached to אֵת/אֶת־ in II Samuel 21:19, Joshua 17:12, and Judges 1:19, 27; then it can have the same functions as either particles or prepositions.

Joshua 17:12

In Joshua 17:12, the Bible states: "Yet the children of Manasseh could not drive out *the inhabitants of* those cities; but the Canaanites would dwell in that land." In this case, the Bible attaches אֶת־ to *cities*. The Manassites were unable to drive out these cities. But how does one drive out a city? Does he pick it up and move it out of the country? This is not what God desired, for they were to dwell in those cities (Deuteronomy 13:12), therefore, it was not the actual cities that they were unable to drive out, but it was those who inhabited those cites that they were unable to expel. Herein is an argument for אֶת־ being prepositional in nature, that is, the Manassites were unable to drive out ones who were with the cities. But the verse does not indicate who these ones were, therefore, this is also a case of ellipsis. Joshua 15:63 supplies the words for this ellipsis, for it states: "As for the Jebusites the inhabitants of Jerusalem, the children of Judah could not drive them out: but the Jebusites dwell with the children of Judah at Jerusalem unto this day." In Joshua 15:63, the Spirit of God, supplies the exact words (*the inhabitants of*) for the ellipsis in Joshua

---

[830] Waltke and O'Connor, 177.

[831] Ibid.

Appendix C   *II Samuel 21:19*

17:12. Is not this the Spirit of God's pattern with II Samuel 21:19, supplying the words for the ellipsis from the parallel verse in I Chronicles 20:5? Indeed, it is.

Judges 1:19

In Judges 1:19 the Bible states: "And the LORD was with Judah; and he drave out *the inhabitants of* the mountain; but could not drive out the inhabitants of the valley, because they had chariots of iron." This is similar to Joshua 17:12; however, in this case, the Bible attaches אֶת־ to *the mountain*. Because the Lord was with Judah, Judah was able to drive out something. Did Judah actually take a mountain and move it out of the region? In light of similar verses it does seem that they did so, but that they drove out those with the mountain, that is, this is prepositional use of אֶת־. Also, present here is an ellipsis, which the King James translators have supplied from other verses in this context where the Spirit of God gives the exact words *the inhabitants of* (Judges 1:30, 31, 32, 33).

Judges 1:27

In Judges 1:27 the Bible states: "Neither did Manasseh drive out *the inhabitants of* Bethshean and her towns, nor Taanach and her towns, nor the inhabitants of Dor and her towns, nor the inhabitants of Ibleam and her towns, nor the inhabitants of Megiddo and her towns: but the Canaanites would dwell in that land." Again, this is similar to the previous examples. Here the Bible attaches אֶת־ to *Bethshean*, and the author's comments made earlier apply here.

CONCLUSION

While many claim that II Samuel 21:19 contains a scribal error, the God-honoring student of the Bible will believe the promises of God concerning perfect preservation of all of His Words and, instead of claiming that II Samuel 21:19 has an error, he will search the Scriptures to better understand them. Studying II Samuel 21:19 with such an attitude produces some legitimate answers for the apparent difficulty presented by this verse, among which are a typical use for *Goliath*; a prepositional use of אֵת; the use of ellipsis; and a prepositional-elliptical construction.

The typical use of *Goliath* suffers from a geographical weakness, wherein II Samuel 21:19 speaks of Goliath the Gittite, indicating by this designation that it is referring to the same *Goliath* as I Samuel 17. Variations of the typical use of *Goliath* claim that Goliath is a title (titular view) or that it is the name of a second Goliath of Gath (nominal view); however, the typical, titular, and nominal views all suffer from a Scriptural weakness: namely that I Chronicles 20:5 explicitly states that it was Lahmi, whom Elhanan slew and that Lahmi and Goliath of Gath are two distinct people. In light of these considerations, the typical fails to adequately answer the difficulty in II Samuel 21:19.

The failure of the typical view leads to the prepositional view, which understands אֵת in II Samuel 21:19 as a preposition indicating that Elhanan slew one close to Goliath. But this view fails to answer who this one was.

This is where the elliptical view enters, for it states that Scripture often makes use of ellipsis and that the translator must look to the context or other verses to supply the words of the ellipsis. In this case, the parallel verse in I Chronicles 20:5 supplies the words of the ellipsis. Indeed, since Chronicles was written after Samuel, it seems that the Spirit of God was making sure that any obscurity in II Samuel 21:19 would be clearly resolved. This is not unusual as the Holy Spirit in the New Testament repeatedly clarifies prophetic verses of the Old Testament (cf. Matthew 2:15 and Hosea 11:1).

But inasmuch as prepositions are often ambiguous, which results in ellipsis and the need of supplying the words of the ellipsis, then this leads to the final and correct view: the prepositional-elliptical view. אֵת in II Samuel 21:19 as a preposition conveys a degree of ambiguity or ellipsis, the words of which the translator must supply from I Chronicles 20:5.

The King James translators demonstrating an acute knowledge of Hebrew's use of prepositions and ellipsis as well as a good grasp of the Bible itself have accurately translated II Samuel 21:19 by inserting the words *the brother of*. Modern translations such as the *New American Standard Version*, the *New International Version*, and the *English Standard Version* by eliminating the italicized words demonstrate an improper handling of the Hebrew text, which then leads them to introduce what appears to be a real contradiction in the Bible. What English Bible a person uses does matter. A person will not go wrong using the *King James Version*, which is an accurate translation of the Hebrew, Aramaic, and Greek into English. However, a person using one of the modern versions, which do not demonstrate a good handling of the original languages, may fall prey to doubt and confusion.

BIBLIOGRAPHY

The bibliography contains two sections: (1) Books; and (2) Articles, Sermons, and Videos. The Books section includes books on CD-ROM. The Articles, Sermons, and Videos section includes articles from periodicals, essays from books, sermons in books, and sermons on cassette.

BOOKS

Adams, Thomas. *A Commentary on the Second Epistle General of St. Peter*. Revised and corrected by James Sherman. Ligonier, PA: Soli Deo Gloria Publications, 1990.

Aland, Kurt, Matthew Black, Carlo M. Martini, Bruce M. Metzger, and Allen Wikgren, eds. *The Greek New Testament*, 3d ed. NY: American Bible Society, 1975.

Alexander, Joseph A. *Commentary on Isaiah*. 2 vols. NY: Charles Scribner, 1867. Reprint, 2 vols. in 1, Grand Rapids: Kregel, 1992.

_____. *Commentary on the Gospel of Mark*. Grand Rapids: Zondervan, n.d.

_____. *Commentary on the Acts of the Apostles*. 2 vols. in 1. Minneapolis: Klock & Klock, 1980.

Alexander, Ralph. *Ezekiel*. Chicago: The Moody Bible Institute, 1976.

Anderson, A. A. *2 Samuel*. Vol. 11, *Word Biblical Commentary*. Edited by David A. Hubbard and Glenn W. Barker. Dallas: Word Books, Publisher, 1989.

Anderson, Sir Robert. *The Bible and Modern Criticism: A Free and Popular Presentation of the Results of an Independent Study of the New Criticism as Set Forth in Representative Works*. London: Pickering & Inglis, n.d.

_____. *The Coming Prince* in *The Master Christian Library*, version 8. CD-ROM. Albany, OR: Ages Software, 1997.

Archer, Gleason L. *A Survey of Old Testament Introduction*, revised ed. Chicago: Moody Press, 1974.

_____. *Encyclopedia of Bible Difficulties*. Grand Rapids: Zondervan, 1982.

Arndt, W. *Does the Bible Contradict Itself?* St. Louis: Concordia Publishing House, 1930.

Arndt, William F. and F. Wilbur Gingrich. *A Greek-English Lexicon of the New Testament and Other Early Christian Literature: A translation and adaptation of the fourth revised and augmented edition of Walter Bauer's Griechisch-Deutsches Wörterbuch zu den Schriften des Neuen Testaments und der übrigen urchristlichen Literatur*, 2d ed. Chicago: University of Chicago, 1979.

Ashbrook, John E. *New Neutralism II*. Mentor, OH: Here I Stand Books, 1992.

Ashbrook, William E. *Evangelicalism the New Neutralism*. Columbus, OH: Calvary Bible Church, n.d.

Augustine. *Expositions – On the Book of Psalms*, vol. 8 of *The Nicene and Post-Nicene Fathers First Series*. Edited by Philip Schaff. Translated by A. Cleveland Coxe. Peabody, MA: Hendrickson Publishers, 1999.

_____. *On the Morals of the Catholic Church*, in vol. 4 of *The Nicene and Post-Nicene Fathers First Series*. Edited by Philip Schaff. Translated by Richard Stothert and Albert H. Newman. Peabody, MA: Hendrickson Publishers, 1999.

_____. *The Harmony of the Gospel*, in vol. 6 of *The Nicene and Post-Nicene Fathers First Series*. Edited and revised by Philip Schaff. Translated by William Findlay. Peabody, MA: Hendrickson Publishers, 1999.

Baldwin, Joyce G. *1 & 2 Samuel*. Vol. 8, *Tyndale Old Testament Commentaries*. Edited by D. J. Wiseman. Downers Grove, IL: Inter-Varsity Press, 1988.

_____. *Jonah* in *The Minor Prophets*, volume 2. Edited by Thomas Edward McComiskey. Grand Rapids: Baker, 2000.

Balz, Horst and Gerhard Schneider, eds. *Exegetical Dictionary of the New Testament*, 3 vols. Grand Rapids: Eerdmans, 1991.

Barber, Cyril J. *The Minister's Library.* Grand Rapids: Baker, 1981.

_____. *The Minister's Library Volume 2.* Chicago: Moody Press, 1987.

Barker, P. C. *I Chronicles* in *Chronicles*, vol. 6 of *The Pulpit Commentary.* Edited by H. D. M. Spence and Joseph S. Exell. Peabody, MA: Hendrikson Publishers, n.d.

_____. *II Chronicles* in *Chronicles*, vol. 6 of *The Pulpit Commentary.* Edited by H. D. M. Spence and Joseph S. Exell. Peabody, MA: Hendrikson Publishers, n.d.

Barnes, Albert. *Barnes' Notes*, 14 vols. Heritage Edition. London: Blackie & Son, 1847. Reprinted Grand Rapids, MI: Baker Book House, 2005.

Baxter, Richard. *The Saints' Everlasting Rest*, in vol. 3 of *The Practical Works of Richard Baxter.* Ligonier, PA: Soli Deo Gloria Publications, 1990.

Beacham, Roy E. and Kevin T. Bauder, eds. *One Bible Only? Examining Exclusive Claims for the King James Bible.* Grand Rapids: Kregel, 2001.

Beale, David O. *In Pursuit of Purity: American Fundamentalism Since 1850.* Greenville: Unusual Publications, 1986.

Beale, G. K. *The Book of Revelation: A Commentary on the Greek Text* in *The New International Greek Testament Commentary.* Edited by I. Howard Marshall and Donald A. Hagner. Grand Rapids: Eerdmans, 1999.

Beare, Francis Wright. *The Gospel according to Matthew.* San Francisco: Harper & Row, Publishers, 1981.

Bengel, John Albert. *New Testament Word Studies*, 2 vols. Trans. by Charlton T. Lewis and Marvin R. Vincent. Grand Rapids: Kregel, 1971.

Blaikie, W. G. *The First Book of Samuel.* NY: A. C. Armstrong and Son, n.d.

_____. *The Second Book of Samuel.* Minneapolis: Klock & Klock, 1978.

Blass, F. and A. Debrunner. *A Greek Grammar of the New Testament and Other Early Christian Literature: A Translation and Revision of the ninth-tenth German Edition incorporating supplementary notes of A. Debrunner, by Robert W. Funk.* Chicago: The University of Chicago Press, 1961.

Block, Daniel I. *The Book of Ezekiel Chapters 1-24* in *The New International Commentary on the Old Testament.* Edited by R. K. Harrison and Robert L. Hubbard, Jr. Grand Rapids: Eerdmans, 1997.

Boice, James Montgomery. *The Gospel of John*, 5 volumes. Grand Rapids: Baker, 1999.

Botterweck, G. Johannes, Helmer Ringgren, and Heinz-Josef Fabry, eds. *Theological Dictionary of the Old Testament: the Authorized and Unabridged Translation of Theologisches Wörterbuch Zum Alten Testament*, 11 vols. Translated by John T. Willis, David E. Green, and Douglas W. Stott. Grand Rapids: Eerdmans, 2000.

Bratcher, Robert G. *Old Testament Quotations in the New Testament*. NY: United Bible Societies, 1984.

Braun, Roddy. *1 Chronicles*. Vol. 14 of *Word Biblical Commentary*. Edited by David A. Hubbard and Glenn W. Barker. Waco, TX: Word Books, Publisher, 1986.

Broadus, John A. *Commentary on Matthew*. Grand Rapids: Kregel, 1990.

Bromiley, Geoffrey W. *Theological Dictionary of the New Testament*, abridged in one volume. Edited by Gerhard Kittel and Gerhard Friedrich. Translated by Geoffrey Bromiley. Grand Rapids: Eerdmans, 2000.

Brooks, Kenneth T. *Why Cumbereth It The Ground? An Examination of the origins and impact of American Christian Fundamentalism* (West Redding, CT: Danbury Baptist Press, 2008.

Brown, Colin, ed. *The New International Dictionary of the New Testament Theology: Translated, with additions and revisions, from the German Theologisches Begriffslexikno Zum Neuen Testament, edited by Lothar Coenen, Erich Beyreuther, and Hans Bietenhard*, 3 vols. Grand Rapids: Zondervan, 1979.

Brown, Francis, S. R. Driver, and Charles A. Briggs. *A Hebrew and English Lexicon of the Old Testament With an Appendix Containing the Biblical Aramaic: Based on the Lexicon of William Gesenuis as Translated by Edward Robinson*. Oxford: Clarendon Press, 1980.

Brown, Lesley, ed. *The New Shorter Oxford English Dictionary*, 2 vols. New York: Oxford University Press, 1993.

Brown, Raymond E., Joseph A. Fitzmyer, and Roland E. Murphy, ed. *The Jerome Biblical Commentary*. London: Prentice-Hall International, Inc., 1968.

Bruce, Frederick Fyvie. *Commentary on the Book of Acts* in *New International Commentary on the New Testament*. Grand Rapids: Eerdmans, 1954.

_____. *The Acts of the Apostles*. Grand Rapids: Eerdmans, 1965.

Bryce, Trevor. *The Kingdom of the Hittites*. Oxford: Clarendon Press, 1998.

Bullinger, E. W. *The Companion Bible*. Grand Rapids: Kregel, 1999.

Bunyan, John. *The Works of John Bunyan with an Introduction to each Treatise, Notes, and a Sketch of His Life, Times, and Contemporaries*, 3 vols. Edited by George Offor. Glasgow: W. G. Blaikie and Son, 1854. Reprinted Carlisle, PA: The Banner of Truth Trust, 1991.

Burnett, Stephen G. *From Christian Hebraism to Jewish Studies Johannes Buxtorf (1564-1629) and Hebrew Learning in the Seventeenth Century*. NY: E. J. Brill, 1996.

Bush, George. *Notes, Critical and Practical, on the Book of Exodus*. Minneapolis: Klock & Klock, 1981.

_____. *Notes, Critical and Practical, on the Book of Judges*. Minneapolis: Klock & Klock, 1981.

Buttrick, George A., ed. *The Interpreter's Bible: The Holy Scriptures in the King James Version and Revised Standard Version with General Articles and Introduction, Exegesis, Exposition for Each Book of the Bible*. Nashville: Abingdon Press, 1953-1956.

Caird, George B. "The First and Second Books of Samuel" in *The Interpreter's Bible*, vol. 2. Edited by George A. Buttrick. Nashville: Abingdon Press, 1953.

Calvin, John. *Calvin's Commentaries*, 22 vols. Grand Rapids, MI: Baker Books, 2005.

Chafer, Lewis Sperry and John F. Walvoord. *Major Bible Themes*. Grand Rapids: Zondervan, 1974.

Chafin, Kenneth L. *1, 2 Samuel* in *The Communicator's Commentary*. Edited by Lloyd J. Ogilvie. Dallas: Word Books, 1989.

Clarke, Adam. *Clarke's Commentary*, 8 vols., in *The Master Christian Library*, version 8. CD-ROM. Albany, OR: Ages Software, 1997.

Clearwaters, Richard V. *The Great Conservative Baptist Compromise*. Minneapolis: Central Seminary Press, n. d.

Cline, Eric H. *The Battles of Armageddon: Megiddo and the Jezreel Valley from the Bronze Age to the Nuclear Age*. Ann Arbor, MI: University of Michigan Press, 2000.

Cloud, David W. *Things Hard to be Understood: A Handbook of Biblical Difficulties*. Port Huron, MI: Way of Life Literature, 2001.

Cogan, Mordechai. *I Kings: A New Translation with Introduction and Commentary* in *The Anchor Bible*. NY: Doubleday & Company, Inc., 2000.

Cogan, Mordechai and Hayim Tadmor. *II Kings: A New Translation with Introduction and Commentary* in *The Anchor Bible*. NY: Doubleday & Company, Inc., 1988.

Cohn, Robert L. *BERIT OLAM Studies in Hebrew Narrative & Poetry: I Kings*. Edited by David W. Cotter. Collegeville, MN: The Liturgical Press, 1996.

Collett, Sidney. *All About the Bible: Its Origin—Its Language—Its Translation—Its Canon—Its Symbols—Its Inspiration—Its Alleged Errors and Contradictions—Its Plan—Its Science—Its Rivals.* Westwood, NJ: Fleming H. Revell, 1964.

Comfort, Philip Wesley, ed. *The Origin of the Bible*. Wheaton, IL: Tyndale House Publishers, Inc., 1992.

Craigie, Peter C. *The Book of Deuteronomy*. Grand Rapids: Eerdmans, 1981.

Crockett, William Day. *A Harmony of Samuel, Kings, and Chronicles*. Grand Rapids: Baker, 1997.

Cundall, Arthur E. and Leon Morris. *Judges & Ruth*, vol. 7 in *Tyndale Old Testament Commentaries*. Edited by D. J. Wiseman. Downers Grove, IL: Inter-Varsity Press, 1968.

Curtis, Edward Lewis and Albert Alonzo Madsen. *A Critical and Exegetical Commentary on The Books of Chronicles*. Edinburgh: T & T Clark, 1910.

Dana, H. E. and Julius R. Mantey. *A Manual Grammar of the Greek New Testament*. Toronto: MacMillan, 1957.

Davies, W. D. and Dale C. Allison. *A Critical and Exegetical Commentary on The Gospel According to Saint Matthew*, 3 vols., in *The International Critical Commentary on the Holy Scriptures of the Old and New Testaments*. Edited by J. A. Emerson, C. E. B. Cranfield, and G. N. Stanton. Edinburgh: T & T Clark, 1988.

Davis, John J. *Biblical Numerology: A Basic Study of the Use of Numbers in the Bible*. Grand Rapids: Baker, 1983.

_____. *Moses and the Gods of Egypt: Studies in the Book of Exodus*. Grand Rapids: Baker, 1981.

DeHoff, George W. *Alleged Bible Contradictions Explained.* Grand Rapids: Baker, 1951.

Derickson, Stanley L. *Derickson's Notes on Theology* in *The Master Christian Library*, version 8. CD-ROM. Albany, OR: Ages Software, 1997.

DeVries, Simon J. *1 Kings*, vol. 12 of *Word Biblical Commentary.* Edited by David A. Hubbard and Glenn W. Barker. Waco, TX: Word Books, Publisher, 1985.

Dickson, David. *A Commentary on the Psalms*, 2 vols. in 1. Carlisle, PA: The Banner of Truth Trust, 1995.

Dilday, Russell H. *1, 2 Kings* in *The Communicator's Commentary.* Edited by Lloyd J. Oglivie. Waco, TX: Word Books, 1987.

Dillard, Raymond B. *2 Chronicles*, vol. 15 of *Word Biblical Commentary.* Edited by David A. Hubbard and Glenn W. Barker. Waco, TX: Word Books, Publisher, 1987.

DiVietro, Kirk D. *Did Jesus and the Apostles Quote form the Septuagint (LXX).* Collingswood, NJ: Bible For Today, 1996.

Dollar, George W. *A History of Fundamentalism in America.* Greenville: Bob Jones University Press, 1973.

Driver, S. R. *Notes on the Hebrew Text and Typography of the Books of Samuel.* Oxford: At the Clarendon Press, 1913.

Dunnett, Walter M. *The Interpretation of Holy Scripture.* Nashville: Thomas Nelson, 1984.

Easton, M. G. *Easton's Bible Dictionary* in *The Master Christian Library*, version 8. CD-ROM. Albany, OR: Ages Software, 1996.

Edersheim, Alfred. *Bible History Old Testament.* Peabody, MA: Hendrickson Publishers, 1995.

_____. *The Life and Times of Jesus the Messiah*, 2 vols. New York: Longmans, Green, and Co., 1912.

Eisemann, Moshe. *I Chronicles / A New Translation with a Commentary Anthologized from Talmudic, Midrashic and Rabbinic Sources.* Brooklyn, NY: Mesorah Publications, ltd., 1987.

_____. *II Chronicles / A New Translation with a Commentary Anthologized from Talmudic, Midrashic and Rabbinic Sources*. Brooklyn, NY: Mesorah Publications, ltd., 1992.

Elliger, Karl and Wilhelm Rudolph, eds. *Biblia Hebraica Stuttgartensia*. Stuttgart: Deutsche Bibelstiftung, 1977.

Elmslie, W. A. L. *The First and Second Books of Chronicles* in *The Interpreter's Bible*. Edited by George A. Buttrick. Nashville: Abingdon Press, 1953.

Erdmann, David. *The Books of Samuel*. Translated, enlarged, and edited by C. H. Toy and John A. Broadus. In *A Commentary on the Holy Scriptures: Critical, Doctrinal, and Homiletical, with Special Reference to Ministers and Students*. Edited by John Peter Lange. Translated by Philip Schaff. NY: Charles Scribner's Sons, 1877.

Exell, Joseph S., ed. *The Biblical Illustrator*. Grand Rapids: Baker, n. d.

Falwell, Jerry, ed. *The Fundamentalist Phenomenon*. Garden City, NY: Doubleday, 1981.

Fairbairn, Patrick. *Commentary on Ezekiel*. Grand Rapids: Kregel, 1989.

Farrar, F. W. *The First Book of Kings*. Minneapolis: Klock & Klock, 1981.

_____. *The Second Book of Kings*. Minneapolis: Klock & Klock, 1981.

Fausset, A. R. *Fausset's Bible Dictionary* in *The Master Christian Library*, version 8. CD-ROM. Albany, OR: Ages Software, 1997.

_____. *The Book of the Prophet Isaiah* in *A Commentary Critical, Experimental, and Practical*, part 1 of vol. 2. Grand Rapids: Eerdmans, 1984.

Feinberg, Charles L. *Jeremiah: A Commentary*. Grand Rapids: Zondervan, 1982..

_____. *The Minor Prophets*. Chicago: Moody, 1982.

_____. *The Prophecy of Ezekiel*. Chicago: Moody, 1982.

Fenton, J. C. *The Gospel of St. Matthew* in *The Pelican Gospel Commentaries*. Edited by D. E. Nineham. Baltimore: Penguin Books, 1963.

Filson, Floyd V. *A Commentary on The Gospel According to St. Matthew* in *Harper's New Testament Commentaries*. Edited by Henry Chadwick. NY: Harper & Brothers, Publishers, 1960.

Finegan, Jack. *Handbook of Biblical Chronology*, rev. ed. Peabody, MA: Hendrickson Publishers, 1998.

Finney, Charles G. *Lectures to Professing Christians* in *The Master Christian Library*, version 8. CD-ROM. Albany, OR: Ages Software, 1997.

Fowler, Everett W. *A Christian Approach to the English Versions of the N.T.* Collingswood: The Bible for Today, 1971.

France, R. T. *The Gospel of Mark* in *The New International Greek Testament Commentary.* Edited by I. Howard Marshall and Donald A. Hagner. Grand Rapids: Eerdmans, 2002.

Friberg, Timothy and Barbara Friberg. *Analytical Greek New Testament.* Grand Rapids: Baker, 1981.

Fuller, David Otis, ed. *Counterfeit or Genuine Mark 16? John 8?* Grand Rapids: Grand Rapids International Publications, 1975.

_____. *True or False?* Grand Rapids: Grand Rapids International Publications, 1978.

_____. *Which Bible?* Grand Rapids: Grand Rapids International Publications, 1978.

Geisler, Norman and Thomas Howe. *When Critics Ask: A Popular Handbook on Bible Difficulties.* Wheaton: Victor Books, 1992.

Gill, John. *A Complete Body of Doctrinal and Practical Divinity: Or a System of Evangelical Truths Deduced from the Sacred Scriptures.* London: Mathews & Leigh, 1809. Reprinted Paris, Arkansas: The Baptist Standard Bearer, 1989.

_____. *A Dissertation Concerning the Antiquity of the Hebrew Language, Letters, Vowel-Points, and Accents.* London: G. Keith, 1767.

_____. *Exposition of the Old and New Testaments,* 9 vols. London: Mathews & Leigh, 1810. Reprinted Paris, Arkansas: The Baptist Standard Bearer, Inc., 1989.

Ginsburg, Christian D. *Jacob Ben Chajim Ibn Adonijah's Introduction to The Rabbinic Bible, Hebrew and English; with Explanatory Notes,* 2nd edition, in *The Library of Biblical Studies.* Edited by Harry M. Orlinsky. NY: KTAV Publishing House, Inc., 1968.

Girdlestone, Robert B. *Synonyms of the Old Testament: Their Bearing on Christian Doctrine,* 2d ed. Grand Rapids: Eerdmans, 1978.

Gloag, Paton J. *A Critical and Exegetical Commentary on the Acts of the Apostles*, 2 vols. Minneapolis: Klock & Klock, 1979.

Godet, Frederick Louis. *A Commentary on the Gospel of St. Luke*. New York: Funk & Wagnals, 1887.

_____. *Commentary on the Gospel of John*, 2 volumes. Grand Rapids: Zondervan, n.d.

Goldman, R. *Samuel with Hebrew Text and English Translation* in *Soncino Books of the Bible*. Edited by A. Cohen. London: The Soncino Press, 1951.

Gray, J. Comper. *The Acts of the Apostles and Romans*, vol. 3 of *The Biblical Museum: A Collection of Notes Explanatory, Homiletic, and Illustrative, on the Holy Scriptures, Especially Designed for the Use of Ministers, Bible Students, and Sunday School Teachers*. New York: Anson D. F. Randolph & Co., n.d.

Gray, James M. *The Concise Bible Commentary* in *The Master Christian Library*, version 8. CD-ROM. Albany, OR: Ages Software, 1999.

Grayson, A. Kirk. *Assyrian and Babylonian Chronicles*. Locust Valley, NY: J. J. Augustin, 1975. Reprint, Winona Lake, IN: Eisenbraus, 2000.

Green, Joel B. *The Gospel of Luke* in *The New International Commentary on the New Testament*. Edited by Ned B. Stonehouse, F. F. Bruce, and Gordon D. Fee. Grand Rapids: Eerdmans, 1997.

Greene, Oliver B. *Bible Prophecy*. Greenville, SC: The Gospel Hour, 1977.

_____. *The Acts of the Apostles*, 4 volumes. Greenville: The Gospel Hour, 1968.

_____. *The Gospel According to John*, 3 volumes. Greenville: The Gospel Hour, 1976.

_____. *The Second Coming of Jesus*. Greenville, SC: The Gospel Hour, 1975.

Greenhill, William. *An Exposition of Ezekiel*. Carlisle, PA: The Banner of Truth Trust, n.d.

Grisanti, Michael A., ed. *The Bible Version Debate: The Perspective of Central Baptist Theological Seminary*. Plymouth, MN: Central Baptist Theological Seminary, 1997.

Grogan, Geoffrey W. *Isaiah* in *The Expositor's Bible Commentary*, vol. 6. Edited by Frank E. Gaebelein. Grand Rapids: Zondervan, 1986.

Gundry, Robert H. *Matthew: A Commentary on His Literary and Theological Art.* Grand Rapids: Eerdmans, 1982.

Haley, John W. *Alleged Discrepancies.* Springdale, PA: Whitaker House, n. d.

Hammond, J. *I Kings* in *The Pulpit Commentary.* Edited by H. D. M. Spence and Joseph S. Exell. Peabody, MA: Hendrickson Publishers, n.d.

Hannah, Robert. *A Grammatical Aid to the Greek New Testament.* Grand Rapids: Baker, 1983.

Harrington, Daniel J. *The Gospel of Matthew*, vol. 1 in *Sacra Pagina Series.* Eidted by Daniel J. Harrington. Collegesville, MN: The Liturgical Press, 1991.

Harris, R. Laird, ed. *Theological Wordbook of the Old Testament*, 2 vols. Chicago: Moody, 1981.

Harrison, Roland Kenneth. *Introduction to the Old Testament.* Grand Rapids: Eerdmans Publishing Co., 1969. Reprint, Peabody, MA: Prince Press, 1999.

Hastings, James, ed. *A Dictionary of the Bible Dealing with Its Language, Literature, and Contents*, 4 vols. New York: Charles Scribner's Sons, 1898.

Hebrew Old Testament. London: Trinitarian Bible Society, 1998.

Hendriksen, William. *Exposition of the Gospel According to John.* Grand Rapids: Baker, 1979.

_____. *Exposition of the Gospel According to Luke.* Grand Rapids: Baker, 1981.

_____. *Exposition of the Gospel According to Mark.* Grand Rapids: Baker, 1982.

_____. *Exposition of the Gospel According to Matthew.* Grand Rapids: Baker, 1982.

_____. *Exposition of the Pastoral Epistles* in *Thessalonians, Timothy and Titus.* Grand Rapids: Baker, 1981.

Henry, Matthew. *Matthew Henry's Commentary*, 6 vols. Peabody, MA: Hendrickson Publishers, 1991.

Herzog, Chaim and Mordechai Gichon. *Battles of the Bible*. London: Greenhill Books, 1997.

Hertzberg, Hans Wilhelm. *I & II Samuel: A Commentary*. Philadelphia: Westminster Press, 1964.

Hiebert, D. Edmond. *Mark: A Portrait of the Servant*. Chicago: Moody, 1979.

_____. *Second Peter and Jude: An Expositional Commentary*. Greenville: Unusual Publications, 1989.

Hills, Edward F. *Believing Bible Study*, 2d ed. Des Moines: The Christian Research Press, 1977.

_____. *The King James Version Defended: A Space-Age Defense of the Historic Christian Faith*, 3d ed. Des Moines: The Christian Research Press, 1973.

Hindson, Edward E. and Woodrow Michael Kroll, eds. *The KJV Parallel Bible Commentary*. Nashville: Thomas Nelson Publishers, 1994.

Hobbs, T. R. *2 Kings*, vol. 13 of *Word Biblical Commentary*. Edited by David A. Hubbard and Glenn W. Barker. Waco, TX: Word Books, Publisher, 1985.

Hodge, Charles. *A Commentary on 1 & 2 Corinthians*. Carlisle, PA: Banner of Truth Trust, 1974.

Hodges, John C. and Mary E. Whitten. *Harbrace College Handbook 7th Edition*. New York: Harcourt Brace Jovanovich, Inc., 1972.

Hoehner, Harold W. *Chronological Aspects of the Life of Christ*. Grand Rapids: Zondervan, 1977.

Holladay, William L. *Jeremiah 2: A Commentary on the Book of the Prophet Jeremiah Chapters 26-52*. Edited by Paul D. Hanson. Minneapolis: Fortress Press, 1989.

Hooker, Paul K. *First and Second Chronicles*. Louisville: Westminster John Know Press, 2001.

Hutcheson, George. *An Exposition of John's Gospel*. Grand Rapids: Sovereign Grace Publishers, 1971.

Ifrah, Georges. *The Universal History of Numbers: From Prehistory to the Invention of the Computer*. NY: John Wiley and Sons, 2000.

Japhet, Sara. *I & II Chronicles: A Commentary*. Louisville, KY: Westminster/John Knox Press, 1993.

Johnson, Luke Timothy. *The Gospel of Luke*, vol. 3 in *Sacra Pagina Series*. Edited by Daniel J. Harrington. Collegesville, MN: The Liturgical Press, 1991.

Jones, Floyd Nolen. *Chronology of the Old Testament: A Return to the Basics*. The Woodlands, TX: KingsWord Press, 1999.

_____. *The Septuagint: A Critical Analysis*, 6th ed. The Woodlands, TX: KingsWord Press, 2000.

Josephus, Flavius. *The Works of Josephus*. Translated by William Whitson. Peabody, MA: Hendrickson Publishers, 1987.

Kaiser, Jr., Walter C., Peter H. Davids, F. F. Bruce, and Manfred T. Brauch. *Hard Sayings of the Bible*. Downers Grove, IL: InterVarsity Press, 1996.

Kautzsch, E., ed. *Gesenius' Hebrew Grammar*, 2d ed. Revised in accordance with the 29th ed. by A. E. Cowley. Oxford: Clarendon Press, 1982.

Keener, Craig S. *A Commentary on the Gospel of Matthew*. Grand Rapids: Eerdmans, 1999.

Keil, C. F. and F. Delitzsch. *Commentary on the Old Testament*, 10 vols. Edinburgh: T. & T. Clark, 1866-91. Reprint Peabody, MA: Hendrickson Publishers, 2001.

Kelley, Page H. *Biblical Hebrew: An Introductory Grammar*. Grand Rapids: Eerdmans, 1992.

Kelly, Balmer H. *The Layman's Bible Commentary*. Richmond, VA: John Knox Press, 1960.

Kennedy, D. James and Jerry Newcombe. *What if the Bible Had Never Been Written?* Nashville: Thomas Nelson, 1998.

Kent, Jr., Homer A. *Jerusalem to Rome: Studies in Acts*. Grand Rapids: Baker, 1972.

_____. *The Pastoral Epistles: Studies in I & II Timothy & Titus*. Chicago: Moody Press, 1979.

Kittel, Gerhard, and Gerhard Friedrich, eds. *Theological Dictionary of the New Testament.* Translated and edited by Geoffrey W. Bromiley, 10 vols. Grand Rapids: Eerdmans, 1993.

Klein, Ralph W. *1 Samuel*, vol. 10 of *Word Biblical Commentary.* Edited by David A. Hubbard and Glenn W. Barker. Waco, TX: Word Books, Publisher, 1983.

Knowling, R. J. *The Acts of the Apostles* in volume 2 of *The Expositor's Greek Testament.* Edited by W. Robertson Nicoll. Peabody, MA: Hendrickson Publishers, Inc., n.d.

Kulus, Chester. *One Tittle Shall in No Wise Pass: Destroying the Scholarly Myth that God Did Not Inspire the Vowels of the Old Testament.* Newington, CT: Emmanuel Theological Press, 2009.

Lambdin, Thomas O. *Introduction to Biblical Hebrew.* New York: Charles Scribner's Sons, 1971.

Lange, John Peter. *A Commentary of the Holy Scriptures: Exodus Leviticus.* Translated and edited by Philip Schaff. Grand Rapids: Zondervan, n. d.

_____. *A Commentary of the Holy Scriptures: John.* Translated and edited by Philip Schaff. Grand Rapids: Zondervan, n. d.

_____. *A Commentary of the Holy Scriptures: Joshua Judges Ruth.* Translated and edited by Philip Schaff. Grand Rapids: Zondervan, n. d.

_____. *The Gospel According to Matthew* in *A Commentary on the Holy Scriptures: Critical, Doctrinal, and Homiletical, with Special Reference to Ministers and Students.* Translated and edited by Philip Schaff. New York: Charles Scribner & Co., 1868.

_____. *The Life of the Lord Jesus Christ: A Complete Critical Examination of the Origin, Contents and Connection of the Gospels*, 4 vols. Edited by Marcus Dods. Grand Rapids: Zondervan, 1958.

Lechler, Gotthard Victor. *The Acts of the Apostles: An Exegetical and Doctrinal Commentary.* Translated from the 2d German edition by Charles F. Schaeffer. In *A Commentary on the Holy Scriptures: Critical, Doctrinal, and Homiletical, with Special Reference to Ministers and Students.* Edited by John P. Lange. Translated by Philip Schaff. New York: Charles Scribner, & Co., 1866.

Lenski, R. C. H. *The Interpretation of St. John's Gospel.* Minneapolis: Augsburg Publishing House, 1963.

_____. *The Interpretation of St. John's Revelation.* Minneapolis: Augsburg Publishing House, 1963.

_____. *The Interpretation of St. Luke's Gospel.* Minneapolis: Augsburg Publishing House, 1963.

_____. *The Interpretation of St. Mark's Gospel.* Minneapolis: Augsburg Publishing House, 1963.

_____. *The Interpretation of St. Matthew's Gospel.* Minneapolis: Augsburg Publishing House, 1963.

_____. *The Interpretation of St. Paul's Epistles to the Colossians, to the Thessalonians, to Timothy, to Titus, and to Philemon.* Minneapolis: Augsburg Publishing House, 1964.

_____. *The Interpretation of the Acts of the Apostles.* Minneapolis: Augsburg Publishing House, 1963.

_____. *The Interpretation of the Epistle to the Hebrews and the Epistle of James.* Minneapolis: Augsburg Publishing House, 1966.

Let God Be True. Brooklyn, NY: Watchtower Bible and Tract Society, 1946.

Letis, Theodore P. *A New Hearing for the Authorized Version.* Philadelphia: The Institute for Renaissance and Reformation Biblical Studies, 1978.

Leupold, H. C. *Exposition of Genesis*, 2 volumes. Grand Rapids, MI: Baker Book House, 1978.

Liddell, Henry George and Robert Scott. *A Greek-English Lexicon*, 9th ed., 2 volumes. Revised by Henry Stuart Jones. Oxford: The University Press, 1951.

Lightner, Robert P. *Neoevangelicalism Today.* Schaumburg, IL: Regular Baptist Press, 1979.

_____. *The Saviour and The Scriptures.* Grand Rapids: Baker, 1978.

Lillie, John. *Lectures on the First and Second Epistles of Peter.* Minneapolis: Klock & Klock, 1978.

Lindsell, Harold. *The Battle for the Bible.* Grand Rapids: Zondervan, 1977.

Lockyer, Herbert. *All the Doctrines of the Bible.* Grand Rapids: Zondervan, 1964.

_____. *All the Men of the Bible.* Grand Rapids: Zondervan, 1958.

_____. *All the Messianic Prophecies of the Bible*. Grand Rapids: Zondervan, 1973.

Luz, Ulrich. *Matthew 1-7: A Commentary*. Translated by Wilhelm C. Linss. Augsburg, MN: Augsburg Fortress, 1985.

MacArthur, Robert Stuart. *Bible Difficulties and Their Alleviate Interpretation*. NY: E. B. Treat & Company, 1899.

Machen, J. Gresham. *Christianity & Liberalism*. Grand Rapids: Eerdmans, 1987.

_____. *New Testament Greek for Beginners*. Toronto: MacMillan, 1951.

Mahan, Milo. *Palmoni; or, the Numerals of Scripture a Proof of Inspiration*. New York: D. Appleton and Company, 1863.

Martin, Alfred. *Isaiah "The Salvation of Jehovah."* Chicago: Moody, 1982.

Marshall, I. Howard. *The Gospel of Luke: A Commentary on the Greek Text* in *The New International Greek Testament Commentary*. Edited by I. Howard Marshall and W. Ward Gasque. Grand Rapids: Eerdmans, 1978.

McKane, William. *A Critical and Exegetical Commentary on Jeremiah*, 2 vols., in *The International Critical Commentary on the Holy Scriptures of the Old and New Testaments*. Edited by J. A. Emerton, C. E. B. Cranfield, and G. N. Stanton. Edinburgh: T & T Clark, 1996.

McCarter, Jr., P. Kyle. *I Samuel: A New Translation with Introduction, Notes and Commentary* in *The Anchor Bible*. NY: Doubleday & Company, Inc., 1980.

_____. *II Samuel: A New Translation with Introduction, Notes and Commentary* in *The Anchor Bible*. NY: Doubleday & Company, Inc., 1986.

McClintock, John and James Strong, eds. *Cyclopedia of Biblical, Theological, and Ecclesiastical Literature*, 12 volumes. New York: Harper & Brothers, 1891.

McComiskey, Thomas Edward, ed. *The Minor Prophets*, 3 volumes. Grand Rapids: Baker, 2000.

Meyer, Heinrich August Wilhelm. *Critical and Exegetical Handbook to the Acts of the Apostles*, 2nd ed. Translated from the 4th German edition by Paton J. Gloag. Revised and edited by William P. Dickson. NY: Funk & Wagnalls, Publishers, 1889.

_____. *Critical and Exegetical Handbook to the Gospel of John*, 2 volumes. Translated from the 5th German edition by William Urwick. Revised and edited by Frederick Crombie. Edinburgh: T & T Clark, 1874.

_____. *Critical and Exegetical Handbook to the Gospels of Mark and Luke*, 2 volumes. Translated from the 5th German edition by Robert Ernest Wallis. Revised and edited by Frederick Crombie. Edinburgh: T & T Clark, 1880.

_____. *Critical and Exegetical Handbook to the Gospel of Matthew*, 2 volumes. Translated from the 6th German edition by Peter Christie. Revised and edited by Frederick Crombie. Edinburgh: T & T Clark, 1894.

Miller, Edward. *A Guide to the Textual Criticism of the New Testament*. Collingswood: The Dean Burgon Society, 1979.

Moll. *The Psalter* in *A Commentary on the Holy Scriptures: Critical, Doctrinal, and Homiletical, with Special Reference to Ministers and Students*. Edited by John Peter Lange. Translated by Philip Schaff. Grand Rapids: Zondervan, n. d.

Moncrieff, John. *An Essay on the Antiquity and Utility of the Vowel-Points*. London: Whittaker, Treacher and Arnot, 1833.

Montgomery, James A. *A Critical and Exegetical Commentary on the Books of Kings*. Edited by Henry Snyder Gehman. In *The International Critical Commentary*. Edited by S. R. Driver, A. Plummer, and C. A. Briggs. Edinburgh: T & T Clark, 1986.

Moorman, Jack. *Bible Chronology: The Two Great Divides*. Collingswood, NJ: Bible For Today, n.d.

Morris, Henry M. *The Biblical Basis for Modern Science*. Grand Rapids: Baker, 1987.

_____. *The Defender's Study Bible*. Iowa Falls: World Publishing, 1995.

_____. *The Revelation Record: A Scientific and Devotional Commentary on the Book of Revelation*. San Diego: Creation-Life Publishers, 1983.

Morris, Leon. *The Gospel According to John*, revised edition, in *The New International Commentary on the New Testament*. Edited by Ned B. Stonehouse, F. F. Bruce, and Gordon D. Fee. Grand Rapids: Eerdmans, 1995.

Morris, William, ed. *The American Heritage Dictionary of the English Language*. Boston: Houghton Mifflin, 1982.

Mounce, William. *Basics of Biblical Greek Grammar*. Grand Rapids: Zondervan, 1993.

Murphy, James G. *A Critical and Exegetical Commentary on the Book of Exodus*. Minneapolis: Klock & Klock, 1979.

Myers, Jacob M. *I Chronicles* in *The Anchor Bible*. Garden City, NY: Doubleday & Company, Inc., 1965.

_____. *II Chronicles* in *The Anchor Bible*. Garden City, NY: Doubleday & Company, Inc., 1965.

Neagelsbach, C.W. Edward. *Isaiah* in *A Commentary on the Holy Scriptures: Critical, Doctrinal, and Homiletical, with Special Reference to Ministers and Students*. Edited by John Peter Lange. Translated by Philip Schaff. Grand Rapids: Zondervan, n. d.

_____. *The Book of the Prophet Jeremiah* in *A Commentary on the Holy Scriptures: Critical, Doctrinal, and Homiletical, with Special Reference to Ministers and Students*. Edited by John Peter Lange. Translated by Philip Schaff. New York: Charles Scribner's Sons, 1914.

Nelson's Complete Book of Bible Maps & Charts. Nashville: Thomas Nelson Publishers, 1996.

Newton, Isaac. *The Chronology of Ancient Kingdoms Amended*. London: T. Cadell, 1770.

Oakeshott, R. Ewart. *The Archaeology of Weapons*. Mineola, NY: Dover Publications, Inc., 1996.

O'Brien, David E. *Today's Handbook for Solving Bible Difficulties*. Minneapolis: Bethany House Publishers, 1990.

Online Bible Millennium Edition. CD-ROM. Winterbourne, Ontario: Timnathserah Inc., 2002.

Orchard, Dom Bernard, ed. *A Catholic Commentary on Holy Scripture*. NY: Thomas Nelson and Sons Ltd., 1953.

Oswalt, John N. *The Book of Isaiah Chapters 1-39* in *The New International Commentary on the Old Testament*. Edited by R. K. Harrison and Robert L. Hubbard, Jr. Grand Rapids: Eerdmans, 1986.

_____. *The Book of Isaiah Chapters 40-66* in *The New International Commentary on the Old Testament*. Edited by R. K. Harrison and Robert L. Hubbard, Jr. Grand Rapids: Eerdmans, 1998.

Owen, John. *The Works of John Owen*, 23 volumes. Edited by William H. Goold. CD-ROM. Albany, OR: Ages Software, 2000.

Owen, John Joseph. *Analytical Key to the Old Testament*, 4 vols. Grand Rapids: Baker, 2000.

Paisley, Ian R. K. *My Plea for the Old Sword.* Greenville, SC: Ambassador, 1997.

Patte, Daniel. *The Gospel According to Matthew: A Structural Commentary on Matthew; Faith.* Philadelphia: Fortress, 1973.

Pentecost, J. Dwight. *The Words & Works of Jesus Christ.* Grand Rapids: Zondervan, 1981.

_____. *Things to Come.* Grand Rapids: Zondervan, 1977.

Perowne, J. J. Stewart, ed. *Cambridge Bible for Schools and Colleges.* Cambridge: At the University Press, 1916.

Pickering, Ernest. *Biblical Separation: The Struggle for a Pure Church.* Schaumburg, IL: Regular Baptist Press, 1979.

Pink, Arthur. *The Divine Inspiration of the Bible* in *The Master Christian Library*, version 8. CD-ROM. Albany, OR: Ages Software, 1997.

Plummer, Alfred. *A Critical and Exegetical Commentary on the Gospel according to St. Luke.* Edinburgh: T & T Clark, 1913.

_____. *An Exegetical Commentary on the Gospel according to St. Matthew.* Grand Rapids: Eerdmans, 1956.

Polzin, Robert. *Samuel and the Deuteronomist: A Literary Study of the Deuteronomic History, Part Two, 1 Samuel.* San Francisco: Harper & Row, Publishers, 1989.

Poole, Matthew. *A Commentary on the Holy Bible*, 3 vols. McLean, VA: Macdonald Publishing Co., n. d.

Pritchard, James B. *Ancient Near Eastern Texts Relating to the Old Testament.* Princeton, NJ: Princeton University Press, 1955.

Quebedeaux, Richard. *The Worldly Evangelicals.* San Francisco: Harper & Row, Publishers, 1978.

Rackham, Richard Belward. *The Acts of the Apostles.* Grand Rapids: Baker, 1964.

Ramsay, George Gilbert. *The Annals of Tactitus: Books I.—VI. An English Translation.* London: John Murray, 1904.

Raper, Christopher B. *Gegraptai, "It Is Written": Significance to the Doctrine of Text Preservation.* Pensacola, FL: Pensacola Theological Seminary, 2001.

Rawlinson, G. *II Kings* in *The Pulpit Commentary.* Edited by H. D. M. Spence and Joseph S. Exell. Peabody, MA: Hendrickson Publishers, n.d.

Redford, Donald B. *Egypt, Canaan, and Israel in Ancient Times.* Princeton: Princeton University Press, 1992.

Roberts, Alexander and James Donaldson, eds. *The Ante-Nicene Fathers: The Writings of the Fathers down to A. D. 325*, 10 vols. Revised by A. Cleveland Coxe. Peabody, MA: Hendrickson Publishers, 2004.

Robertson, A. T. *A Grammar of the Greek New Testament in the Light of Historical Research.* Nashville: Broadman Press, 1934.

Rogers, Richard. *A Commentary on Judges: Facsimile of 1615 Edition.* Carlisle, PA: Banner of Truth Trust, 1983.

Ruckman, Peter S. *The "Errors" in the King James Bible.* Pensacola, FL: Bible Baptist Bookstore, 1999.

Ryle, J. C. *Expository Thoughts on John*, 3 volumes. Carlisle, PA: The Banner of Truth Trust, 1986.

_____. *Expository Thoughts on Luke*, 2 volumes. Carlisle, PA: The Banner of Truth Trust, 1986.

_____. *Expository Thoughts on Mark.* Carlisle, PA: The Banner of Truth Trust, 1986.

_____. *Expository Thoughts on Matthew.* Carlisle, PA: The Banner of Truth Trust, 1986.

Schilder, K. *Christ Crucified*, 3d ed. Translated by Henry Zylstra. Minneapolis: Klock & Klock, 1978.

Schweizer, Eduard. *The Good News According to Matthew.* Trans. by David E. Green. Atlanta: John Knox Press, 1975.

Scofield, C. I., ed. *The Scofield Study Bible*. New York: Oxford University Press, 1945.

_____. *The New Scofield Reference Bible*. New York: Oxford University Press, 1967.

Scott, Thomas. *The Holy Bible Containing the Old and New Testaments, with Original Notes, Practical Observations and Copious References*, 6 volumes. New York: Whiting and Watson, 1812.

Schroder, Wilhelm Julius. *The Book of the Prophet Ezekiel* in *A Commentary on the Holy Scriptures: Critical, Doctrinal, and Homiletical, with Special Reference to Ministers and Students*. Edited by John Peter Lange. Translated by Philip Schaff. New York: Scribner, Armstrong & Co., 1876.

Scrivener, Frederick H. A. *Scrivener's Annotated Greek New Testament: Being the Exact Greek Textus Receptus the Underlies the King James Bible*. Collingswood, NJ: Dean Burgon Society Press, 1999.

Scroggie, W. Graham. *A Guide to the Gospels*. Old Tappan, NJ: Fleming H. Revell Company, n.d.

Seiss, J. A. *The Apocalypse Lectures on the Book of Revelation*. Grand Rapids: Zondervan, n. d.

Senior, Donald. *Matthew* in *Abingdon New Testament Commentaries*. Edited by Victor Paul Furnish. Nashville: Abingdon Press, 1998.

Shedd, William G. T. *Dogmatic Theology*, vol. 1. Minneapolis: Klock & Klock, 1979.

Shenkel, James Donald. *Chronology and Recensional Development in the Greek Text of Kings*. Cambridge, MA: Harvard University Press, 1968.

Shepard, W. E. *Wrested Scriptures Made Plain* in *The Master Christian Library*, version 8. CD-ROM. Albany, OR: Ages Software, 1997.

Showers, Renald. *Maranatha Our Lord, Come!* Bellmar, NJ: The Friends of Israel Gospel Ministry, 1995.

Slotki, I. W. *Chronicles: Hebrew Text & English Translation with an Introduction and Commentary*. NY: The Soncino Press, 1985.

Smith, Henry Preserved. *A Critical and Exegetical Commentary on the Books of Samuel*. Edinburgh: T & T Clark, 1899.

Smith, Norman H. *The First and Second Books of Kings* in *The Interpreter's Bible*. Edited by George A. Buttrick. Nashville: Abingdon Press, 1953.

Smith, R. Payne. *I Samuel* in *The Pulpit Commentary*, vol. 4. Edited by H. D. M. Spence and Joseph S. Exell. Peabody, MA: Hendrikson Publishers, n.d.

_____. *II Samuel* in *The Pulpit Commentary*, vol. 4. Edited by H. D. M. Spence and Joseph S. Exell. Peabody, MA: Hendrikson Publishers, n.d.

Sorenson, David H. *Touch Not The Unclean Thing: The Text Issue and Separation*. Duluth, MN: Northstar Baptist Ministries, 2001.

Spence, H. D. M. and Joseph S. Exell, eds. *The Pulpit Commentary*, 23 vols. Peabody, MA: Hendrickson Publishers, n.d.

Spurgeon, Charles H. *Commenting & Commentaries: A Reference Guide to Book Buying for Pastors, Students, and Christian Workers*. Grand Rapids: Baker, 1981.

_____. *The Greatest Fight in the World* in *The Charles H. Spurgeon Library*, version 2. CD-ROM. Albany, OR: Ages Software, 1998.

_____. *The Metropolitan Tabernacle Pulpit*, 63 vols. Pasadena, TX: Pilgrim Publications, 1969.

_____. *The Treasury of David containing an Original Exposition of the Book of Psalms; a Collections of Illustrative Extracts from the Whole Range of Literature; a Series of Homiletical Hints upon Almost Every verse; and Lists of Writers upon Each Psalm*, 3 vols. Peabody, MA: Hendrickson Publishers, n.d.

Stanton, Graham N. *A Gospel for a New People: Studies in Matthew*. Louisville, KY: Westminster/John Knox Press, 1992.

Stein, Robert H. *The Synoptic Problem: An Introduction*. Grand Rapids: Baker, 1988.

Streeter, Lloyd L. *Seventy-five Problems with Central Baptist Seminary's Book The Bible Version Debate*. Kearney, NE: Morris Publishing, 2001.

Strong, Augustus H. *Systematic Theology*. Valley Forge: Judson Press, 1976.

Strouse, Thomas M. *A Critique of D. A. Carson's The King James Version Debate*. Watertown: Maranatha Baptist Bible College, 1980.

_____. *But Daniel Purposed in His Heart: an Exegetical Commentary on Daniel.* Newington, CT: Emmanuel Baptist Theological Press, 2001.

_____. *But God Meant It Unto Good: An Exegetical Commentary on Genesis*. Virginia Beach: Tabernacle Baptist Theological Press, 1999.

_____. *"But Jonah . . ."*: *An Exegesis of the Book of Jonah*. Newington, CT: Emmanuel Baptist Theological Press, 2002.

_____. *"But My Words Shall Not Pass Away": The Biblical Defense of the Doctrine of the Preservation of Scripture*. Newington, CT: Emmanuel Baptist Theological Press, 2001.

_____. *I Will Build My Church: The Doctrine and History of Baptists*. Newington, CT: Emmanuel Baptist Theological Press, 2001.

_____. *Sound Doctrine: The Theology of I and II Timothy*. Newington, CT: Emmanuel Baptist Theological Press, 2001.

_____. *The Lord God Hath Spoken: A Guide to Bibliology*. Newington: Emmanuel Theological Press, 2001.

Strouse, Thomas M. and Jeffrey Khoo. *Reviews of the book From the Mind of God to the Mind of Man*. Pensacola: Pensacola Theological Seminary, 2001.

Tatford, Frederick A. *The Revelation*. Minneapolis: Klock & Klock, 1985.

Tenney, Merrill C., ed. *The Bible – The Living Word of Revelation*. Grand Rapids: Zondervan, 1968.

_____, ed. *The Zondervan Pictorial Encyclopedia of the Bible*, 5 vols. Grand Rapids: Zondervan, 1976.

Thayer, Joseph H. *A Greek-English Lexicon of the New Testament*. Grand Rapids: Baker, 1977.

The Holy Bible: English Standard Version. Wheaton, IL: Good News Publishers, 2002.

The Holy Scriptures of the Old Testament Hebrew and English. London: The British & Foreign Bible Society, n. d.

Theissen, Henry Clarence. *Introductory Lectures in Systematic Theology*. Grand Rapids: Eerdmans, 1976.

The Parallel Bible Hebrew-English Old Testament with the Biblia Hebraica Leningradensia and the King James Version. Peabody, MA: Hendrickson Publishers, 2003.

Thiele, Edwin R. *The Mysterious Numbers of the Hebrew Kings*. Grand Rapids: Kregel, 1994.

Thomas, D. Winton, ed.. *Documents from Old Testament Times*. NY: Thomas Nelson and Sons Ltd., 1958.

Thomas, Robert L. *Revelation 1-7: An Exegetical Commentary*. Edited by Kenneth Barker. Chicago: Moody, 1992.

_____. *Revelation 8-22: An Exegetical Commentary*. Edited by Kenneth Barker. Chicago: Moody, 1995.

Thompson, Frank Charles. *The Thompson Chain-Reference Bible*, fifth ed. Indianapolis: B.B. Kirkbride Bible Co., 2000.

Thompson, J. A. *Deuteronomy*. Downers Grove, IL: Inter-Varsity Press, 1974.

_____. *The Book of Jeremiah* in *The New International Commentary on the Old Testament*. Edited by R. K. Harrison. Grand Rapids, Eerdmans, 1982.

Tillich, Paul. *Systematic Theology*, combined volume. Digswell Place, England: James Nisbet & CO LTD, 1968.

Torrey, R. A. *Difficulties and Alleged Errors and Contradictions in the Bible*. Chicago: Moody Press, 1907.

Torrey, R. A., A. C. Dixon, et al., eds. *The Fundamentals – A Testimony to the Truth*, 4 vols. in *The Master Christian Library*, version 8. CD-ROM. Rio, WI: Ages Software, 2000.

Trench, Richard C. *Synonyms of the New Testament*, 9th ed. Grand Rapids: Eerdmans, 1980.

Tuttle, Jeffrey. "United Monarchy #623 Syllabus." Lansdale, PA: Calvary Baptist Theological Seminary, 1982.

Unger, Merrill F. *Introductory Guide to the Old Testament*. Grand Rapids: Zondervan, 1979.

Van Doren, W. H. *Gospel of John*. Grand Rapids: Kregel, 1981.

VanGemeren, Willem A., ed. *New International Dictionary of Old Testament Theology and Exegesis*, version 2.8. CD-ROM. Grand Rapids: Zondervan Reference Software, 2001.

Vanhetloo, Warren. "Hebrew Syntax 202 Syllabus." Lansdale, PA: Calvary Baptist School of Theology, 1980.

Van Oosterzee, J. J. *The Gospel According to Luke* in *A Commentary on the Holy Scriptures: Critical, Doctrinal, and Homiletical, with Special Reference to Ministers and Students.* Edited by John Peter Lange. Translated by Philip Schaff. Grand Rapids: Zondervan, n. d.

_____. *The Two Epistles of Paul to Timothy* in *A Commentary on the Holy Scriptures: Critical, Doctrinal, and Homiletical, with Special Reference to Ministers and Students.* Edited by John Peter Lange. Translated by Philip Schaff. New York: Charles Scribner & Co., 1868.

Vine, W. E., Merrill F. Unger, and William White, Jr., eds. *Vine's Expository Dictionary of Biblical Words.* Nashville: Nelson, 1985.

Waite, D. A. *Defending the King James Version.* Collingswood, NJ: The Bible for Today Press, 1992.

_____. *Dr. Stewart Custer Answered on the T. R. & K. J. V.* Collingswood, NJ: The Bible for Today, 1985.

Wallace, Daniel B. *The Basics of New Testament Syntax.* Grand Rapids: Zondervan, 2000.

Walsh, Jerome T. *BERIT OLAM Studies in Hebrew Narrative & Poetry: I Kings.* Edited by David W. Cotter. Collegeville, MN: The Liturgical Press, 1996.

Waltke, Bruce K. and M. O'Connor. *An Introduction to Biblical Hebrew Syntax.* Winona Lake, IN: Eisenbraus, 1990.

Walvoord, John F. *Daniel: The Key to Prophetic Revelation.* Chicago: Moody, 1977.

_____. *Every Prophecy of the Bible.* Colorado Springs: Chariot Victor Publishing, 1999.

_____. *The Revelation of Jesus Christ.* Chicago: Moody, 1979.

Walton, John H. *Chronological and Background Charts of the Old Testament.* Grand Rapids: Zondervan, 1994.

Wenham, John W. *Christ and the Bible.* London: Tyndale Press, 1972.

Whitcomb, Jr., John C. *Solomon to the Exile: Studies in Kings and Chronicles.* Grand Rapids: Baker, 1978.

White, Andrew D. *History of Warfare of Science with Theology in Christendom*, 2 vols. in *The Master Christian Library*, version 8. CD-ROM. Albany, OR: Ages Software, 1997.

White, James R. *The King James Only Controversy: Can You Trust the Modern Versions?* Minneapolis: Bethany House Publishers, 1995.

Williams, James B., ed. *From the Mind of God to the Mind of Man: A Layman's Guide to How We Got Out Bible*, 3d ed. Greenville, SC: Ambassador-Emerald International, 1999.

_____. *God's Word in Our Hands The Bible Preserved for Us*. Greenville, S.C.: Ambassador Emerald International, 2003.

Willoughby, C. Allen. *A Critical and Exegetical Commentary on The Gospel According to Saint Matthew*, 3rd ed., in *The International Critical Commentary on the Holy Scriptures of the Old and New Testaments*. Edited by Samuel Rolles Driver, Alfred Plummer, and Charles Augustus Briggs. Edinburgh: T & T Clark, 1985.

Wilson, William. *Wilson's Old Testament Word Studies*. Peabody, MA: Hendrickson Publishers, n.d.

Wiseman, D. J. *1 & 2 Kings: An Introduction & Commentary*, vol. 9, *The Tyndale Old Testament Commentaries*. Edited by D. J. Wiseman. Downers Grove, IL: InterVarsity Press, 1993.

_____. *Chronicles of Chaldean Kings*. London: The Trustees of the British Museum, 1961.

Wolf, Herbert M. *Interpreting Isaiah*. Grand Rapids: Zondervan, 1985.

Wood, Leon J. *A Commentary on Daniel*. Grand Rapids: Zondervan, 1979.

_____. *A Survey of Israel's History*. Grand Rapids: Zondervan, 1979.

_____. *Distressing Days of the Judges*. Grand Rapids: Zondervan, 1975.

_____. *Israel's United Monarchy*. Grand Rapids: Baker, 1979.

Wright, G. Ernest, John Bright, James Barr, and Peter Ackroyd, eds. *The Old Testament Library*. London: SCM Press Ltd., 1964.

Wuest, Kenneth S. *Wuest's Word Studies from the Greek New Testament*, 3 vols. Grand Rapids: Eerdmans, 1975.

Yates, Kyle M. *The Essentials of Biblical Hebrew*. Revised by John Joseph Owen. New York: Harper & Row, 1954.

Yeager, Randolph O. *Matthew 1-7* in *The Renaissance New Testament*. Gretna, LA: Pelican Publishing Co., 1986.

Young, Edward J. *The Book of Isaiah*, 3 vols. Grand Rapids: Eerdmans, 1978.

_____. *An Introduction to the Old Testament*. Grand Rapids: Eerdmans, 1960.

Youngblood, Ronald F. *1, 2 Samuel* in *The Expositor's Bible Commentary*. Edited by Frank E. Gaebelein. Grand Rapids: Zondervan, 1992.

Zockler, Otto. *The Book of the Prophet Daniel* in *A Commentary on the Holy Scriptures: Critical, Doctrinal, and Homiletical, with Special Reference to Ministers and Students*. Edited by John Peter Lange. Translated by Philip Schaff. New York: Scribner, Armstrong & Co., 1876.

_____. *The First and Second Book of Chronicles* in *A Commentary on the Holy Scriptures: Critical, Doctrinal, and Homiletical, with Special Reference to Ministers and Students*. Edited by John Peter Lange. Translated by Philip Schaff. Grand Rapids: Zondervan, n. d.

Zodhiates, Spiros. *The Complete Word Study Bible & Reference CD*. CD-ROM. Chattanooga, TN: AMG Publishers, 1997.

ARTICLES, SERMONS, AND VIDEOS

Aland, Kurt. "The Text of the Church?" *Trinity Journal* 8 (1987): 131-144.

Anderson, Debra E. "A Brief History of the Hebrew Bible." London: Trinitarian Bible Society, n.d. Article on-line. Available from http:\www. trinitarianbiblesociety.org. Internet.

Anderson, Robert. "Christ and Criticism" in *The Fundamentals – A Testimony to the Truth*, vol. 1. Edited by R. A. Torrey, A. C. Dixon, et. al. In *The Master Christian Library*, version 8. CD-ROM. Rio, WI: Ages Software, 2000.

Ashbrook, John E. "The History of the Textus Receptus" in *From the Mind of God to the Mind of Man: A Layman's Guide to How We Got Out Bible*, 3d ed. Edited by James B. Williams. Greenville, SC: Ambassador-Emerald International, 1999.

Barrick, William D. "Ancient Manuscripts and Biblical Exposition." *Master's Seminary Journal* 9 (1998): 25-38.

Basinger, David. "Biblical Paradox: Does Revelation Challenge Logic?" *Journal of the Evangelical Theological Society* 30 (1987): 205-213.

Bauder, Kevin T. "An Appeal to Scripture" in *One Bible Only? Examining Exclusive Claims for the King James Bible*. Edited by Roy E. Beacham and Kevin T. Bauder. Grand Rapids: Kregel, 2001.

Beacham, Roy E. "The Old Testament Text and English Versions" in *The Bible Version Debate: The Perspective of Central Baptist Theological Seminary*. Edited by Michael A. Grisanti. Plymouth, MN: Central Baptist Theological Seminary, 1997.

Beckwith, R. T. "The Canon of the Old Testament" in *The Origin of the Bible*. Edited by Philip Wesley Comfort. Wheaton, IL: Tyndale House Publishers, Inc., 1992.

Beecher, Willis J. "Chronicles, Books of" in *International Standard Bible Encyclopedia*, vol. 1. Edited by James Orr. Grand Rapids, MI: Wm. B. Eerdmans Publishing Co., 1939.

Bettex, F. "The Bible and Modern Criticism" in *The Fundamentals – A Testimony to the Truth*, vol. 1. Edited by R. A. Torrey, A. C. Dixon, et. al. In *The Master Christian Library*, version 8. CD-ROM. Rio, WI: Ages Software, 2000.

Borland, James A. "The Preservation of the New Testament Text: A Common Sense Approach." *Master's Seminary Journal* 10 (1999): 41-51.

Brake, Donald L. "The Preservation of the Scriptures" in *Counterfeit or Genuine Mark 16? John 8?* Edited by David Otis Fuller. Grand Rapids: Grand Rapids International Publications, 1975.

Brown, Francis. "Chronicles, I. and II." in *A Dictionary of the Bible Dealing with Its Language, Literature, and Contents*, volume 1. Edited by James Hastings. New York: Charles Scribner's Sons, 1898.

Brown, Harold O. J. "The Inerrancy and Infallibility of the Bible" in *The Origin of the Bible*. Edited by Philip Wesley Comfort. Wheaton, IL: Tyndale House Publishers, Inc., 1992.

Bruce, F. F. "The Bible" in *The Origin of the Bible*. Edited by Philip Wesley Comfort. Wheaton, IL: Tyndale House Publishers, Inc., 1992.

Caven, William. "The Testimony of Christ to the Old Testament" in *The Fundamentals – A Testimony to the Truth*, vol. 1. Edited by R. A. Torrey, A. C. Dixon, et. al. In *The Master Christian Library*, version 8. CD-ROM. Rio, WI: Ages Software, 2000.

Chafer, Lewis Sperry. "Part 1: Introduction to Bibliology." *Bibliotheca Sacra* 94 (1937): 132-152.

Chrysostom, John. "Homily on the Paralytic Let Down Through the Roof" in *The Life and Work of St. Chrysostom* in *The Nicene and Post-Nicene Fathers First Series*, vol. 9. Edited by Philip Schaff. Peabody, MA: Hendrickson Publishers, 1994.

Combs, William. "The Preservation of Scripture." *Detroit Baptist Seminary Journal* 5 (Fall 2000): 3-44.

Coray, Henry W. "The Incomparable Wilson the Man Who Mastered Forty-five Languages and Dialects" in *Which Bible?* Edited by David Otis Fuller. Grand Rapids: Grand Rapids International Publications, 1978.

Curtis, E. L. "Chronology of the Old Testament" in *A Dictionary of the Bible Dealing with Its Language, Literature, and Contents*, Volume 1. Edited by James Hastings. New York: Charles Scribner's Sons, 1898.

Eichhorst, William R. "The Issue of Biblical Inerrancy in Definition and Defense." *Grace Journal* 10 (1969): 3-17.

"Evangelicals and Catholics Release Third Joint Statement." *Foundation*, Sept. - Oct. 2002, pp. 33-35.

Fausset, A. R. "Chronicles, 1 & 2" in *Fausset's Bible Dictionary*, vol. 1 in *The Master Christian Library*, version 8. CD-ROM. Albany, OR: Ages Software, 2000.

_____. "Chronology" in *Fausset's Bible Dictionary*, vol. 1 in *The Master Christian Library*, version 8. CD-ROM. Albany, OR: Ages Software, 2000.

_____. "Gospels" in *Fausset's Bible Dictionary*, vol. 2 in *The Master Christian Library*, version 8. CD-ROM. Albany, OR: Ages Software, 2000.

_____. "Kings, Books Of" in *Fausset's Bible Dictionary*, vol. 6 in *The Master Christian Library*, version 8. CD-ROM. Albany, OR: Ages Software, 2000.

Fuller, Andrew. "Passages Apparently Contradictory" in *The Complete Works of Andrew Fuller*, vol. 1. Harrisonburg, VA: Sprinkle Publications, 1988.

Fundamentalism and the Word of God. Allen Park, MI: Coalition for the Defense of the Scriptures, 1998. Videocassette.

Gephart, Keith. "Are Copies Reliable?" in *God's Word in Our Hands The Bible Preserved for Us*. Edited by James B. Williams. Greenville, S.C.: Ambassador Emerald International, 2003.

Gerstner, John H. "An Outline of the Apologetics of Jonathan Edwards. Part IV: The Proof of God's Special Revelation, The Bible—Continued," *Bibliotheca Sacra* 133 (1976): 291-298.

Glenny, W. Edward. "The Preservation of Scripture" in *The Bible Version Debate: The Perspective of Central Baptist Theological Seminary*. Edited by Michael A. Grisanti. Plymouth, MN: Central Baptist Theological Seminary, 1997.

Goldberg, J. "Two Assyrian Campaigns against Hezekiah and Later Eighth Century Biblical Chronology," *Biblica* 80 (1999): 360-390.

Gray, James M. "The Inspiration of the Bible – Definition, Extent and Proof" in *The Fundamentals – A Testimony to the Truth*, vol. 2. Edited by R. A. Torrey, A. C. Dixon, et. al. In *The Master Christian Library*, version 8. CD-ROM. Rio, WI: Ages Software, 2000.

Hague, Dyson. "The History of the Higher Criticism" in *The Fundamentals – A Testimony to the Truth*, vol. 1. Edited by R. A. Torrey, A. C. Dixon, et. al. In *The Master Christian Library*, version 8. CD-ROM. Rio, WI: Ages Software, 2000.

Harris, R. Laird. "The Problem of Communication" in *The Bible – The Living Word of Revelation*. Edited by Merrill C. Tenney. Grand Rapids: Zondervan, 1968.

Henry, Carl F. H. "The Authority of the Bible" in *The Origin of the Bible*. Edited by Philip Wesley Comfort. Wheaton, IL: Tyndale House Publishers, Inc., 1992.

Johnson, Dell. *PCC's Response to Coalition Critics*. Pensacola: Pensacola Christian College, 1999. Videocassette.

_____. *Preservation of the Bible: A Bible Foundational Doctrine*. Pensacola: Pensacola Christian College, March 7, 2002. Cassette.

_____. *The Bible . . . Preserved from Satan's Attack*. Pensacola: Pensacola Christian College, 1996. Videocassette.

Johnson, Dell, J. Michael Bates, and Theodore Letis. *The Bible . . . The Text Is the Issue*. Pensacola: Pensacola Christian College, 1997. Videocassette.

Johnson, Dell and Theodore Letis. *The Leaven in Fundamentalism*. Pensacola: Pensacola Christian College, 1998. Videocassette.

Johnson, Franklin. "Fallacies of the Higher Criticism" in *The Fundamentals – A Testimony to the Truth*, vol. 1. Edited by R. A. Torrey, A. C. Dixon, et. al. In *The Master Christian Library*, version 8. CD-ROM. Rio, WI: Ages Software, 2000.

Jordan, E. Robert. "A Critique on The Fundamentalist Phenomenon. Edited by Jerry Falwell. New Evangelicalism Restated." Lansdale, PA: Calvary Baptist Church, n.d.

Kantzer, Kenneth S. "Neo-Orthodoxy and the Inspiration of Scripture." *Bibliotheca Sacra* 116 (1959): 15-30.

Konig, E. "Number" in *A Dictionary of the Bible Dealing with Its Language, Literature, and Contents*, volume 3. Edited by James Hastings. New York: Charles Scribner's Sons, 1900.

Kutilek, Douglas K. "The Background and Origin of the Version Debate" in *One Bible Only? Examining Exclusive Claims for the King James Bible*. Edited by Roy E. Beacham and Kevin T. Bauder. Grand Rapids: Kregel, 2001.

Kyle, M. G. "The Recent Testimony of Archaeology to the Scriptures" in *The Fundamentals – A Testimony to the Truth*, vol. 1. Edited by R. A. Torrey, A. C. Dixon, et. al. In *The Master Christian Library*, version 8. CD-ROM. Rio, WI: Ages Software, 2000.

Lloyd-Jones, Martin. "Christ and the Old Testament" in *Studies in the Sermon on the Mount*, volume 1. Grand Rapids: Eerdmans, 1989.

_____. "Christ Fulfilling the Law and the Prophets" in *Studies in the Sermon on the Mount*, volume 1. Grand Rapids: Eerdmans, 1989.

Mack, Edward. "Chronology of the Old Testament" in *International Standard Bible Encyclopedia* in *International Standard Bible Encyclopedia*, vol. 2. Edited by James Orr. Grand Rapids, MI: Wm. B. Eerdmans Publishing Co., 1939.

McClain, Alva J. "What Is 'The Law'." *Bibliotheca Sacra* 110 (1953): 333-341.

McClintock, John and James Strong, eds.. "Chronicles" in *Cyclopedia of Biblical, Theological, and Ecclesiastical Literature*, vol. 2. New York: Harper & Brothers, 1883.

_____. "Criticism, Biblical" in *Cyclopedia of Biblical, Theological, and Ecclesiastical Literature*, vol. 2. New York: Harper & Brothers, 1883.

_____. "Deuteronomy" in *Cyclopedia of Biblical, Theological, and Ecclesiastical Literature*, vol. 2. New York: Harper & Brothers, 1883.

_____. "Exodus" in *Cyclopedia of Biblical, Theological, and Ecclesiastical Literature*, vol. 3. New York: Harper & Brothers, 1883.

_____. "Unbelief" in *Cyclopedia of Biblical, Theological, and Ecclesiastical Literature*, vol. 10. New York: Harper & Brothers, 1891.

_____. "Vowel Points" in *Cyclopedia of Biblical, Theological, and Ecclesiastical Literature*, vol. 10. New York: Harper & Brothers, 1891.

Merrill, Eugene H. "Paul's Use of 'About 450 Years' in Acts 13:20." *Bibliotheca Sacra* 138 (1981): 246-258.

Mimcy, John. "Preservation of the Copies" in *God's Word in Our Hands The Bible Preserved for Us*. Edited by James B. Williams. Greenville, S.C.: Ambassador Emerald International, 2003.

Minnick, Mark. "Let's Meet the Manuscripts" in *From the Mind of God to the Mind of Man: A Layman's Guide to How We Got Out Bible*, 3d ed. Edited by James B. Williams. Greenville, SC: Ambassador-Emerald International, 1999.

Mutsch, Greg. *Approaches to the Text Issue: Faith, Scientific, or Extremist* in *PCC's Response to Coalition Critics*. Pensacola: Pensacola Christian College, 1999. Videocassette.

Murphy, James G. "Introduction the Bible" in *A Commentary on the Book of Genesis* in vol. 1 of *Barnes' Notes*. Heritage Edition. London: Blaikie & Son, 1847. Reprinted Grand Rapids, MI: Baker Book House, 2005.

Norton, Mark R. "Texts and Manuscripts of the Old Testament" in *The Origin of the Bible*. Edited by Philip Wesley Comfort. Wheaton, IL: Tyndale House Publishers, Inc., 1992.

Orr, James. "Holy Scripture and Modern Negations" in *The Fundamentals – A Testimony to the Truth*, vol. 1. Edited by R. A. Torrey, A. C. Dixon, et. al. In *The Master Christian Library*, version 8. CD-ROM. Rio, WI: Ages Software, 2000.

_____. "Light to the friend, darkness to the foe" in *Exodus* in vol. 1 of *The Pulpit Commentary*. Peabody, MA: Hendrickson Publishers, n.d.

_____. "Science and Christian Faith" in *The Fundamentals – A Testimony to the Truth*, vol. 1. Edited by R. A. Torrey, A. C. Dixon, et. al. In *The Master Christian Library*, version 8. CD-ROM. Rio, WI: Ages Software, 2000.

_____. "The Early Narratives of Genesis" in *The Fundamentals – A Testimony to the Truth*, vol. 1. Edited by R. A. Torrey, A. C. Dixon, et. al. In *The Master Christian Library*, version 8. CD-ROM. Rio, WI: Ages Software, 2000.

Owen, John. "Of the Divine Original of the Scriptures" in *The Works of John Owen*, vol. 16. Edited by William H. Goold. London: Johnstone & Hunter, 1853. Reprinted Carlisle, PA: The Banner of Truth Trust, 1968.

_____. "Integrity and Purity of the Hebrew and Greek Text of the Scripture" in *The Works of John Owen*, vol. 16. Edited by William H. Goold. London: Johnstone & Hunter, 1853. Reprinted Carlisle, PA: The Banner of Truth Trust, 1968.

_____. "Causes, Ways, and Means of Understanding the Mind of God" in *The Works of John Owen*, vol. 4. Edited by William H. Goold. London: Johnstone & Hunter, 1853. Reprinted Carlisle, PA: The Banner of Truth Trust, 1968.

_____. "The Reason of Faith" in *The Works of John Owen*, vol. 4. Edited by William H. Goold. London: Johnstone & Hunter, 1853. Reprinted Carlisle, PA: The Banner of Truth Trust, 1968.

Payne, J. B. "Chronology of the Old Testament" in *The Zondervan Pictorial Encyclopedia of the Bible*, volume 1. Edited by Merrill C. Tenney. Grand Rapids: Zondervan, 1976.

_____. "The Relationship of the Reign of Ahaz to the Accession of Hezekiah." *Bibliotheca Sacra* 126 (1969): 40-52.

Pierson, Arthur T. "The Testimony of the Organic Unity of the Bible to its Inspiration" in *The Fundamentals – A Testimony to the Truth*, vol. 2. Edited by R. A. Torrey, A. C. Dixon, et. al. In *The Master Christian Library*, version 8. CD-ROM. Rio, WI: Ages Software, 2000.

Porcher, Jr., Joel P. "Psalm 12:6-7 Grammatical Study of the Hebrew Text and the Rendering of the Authorized Version in English." Pensacola, FL: Pensacola Theological Seminary, 2001.

Reeve, J. J. "My Personal Experience with the Higher Criticism" in *The Fundamentals – A Testimony to the Truth*, vol. 1. Edited by R. A. Torrey, A. C. Dixon, et. al. In *The Master Christian Library*, version 8. CD-ROM. Rio, WI: Ages Software, 2000.

Ryken, Leland. "The Bible as Literature" in *The Origin of the Bible*. Edited by Philip Wesley Comfort. Wheaton, IL: Tyndale House Publishers, Inc., 1992.

Schaff, Philip. "The Influence of St. Augustin upon Posterity and His Relation to Catholiciism and Protestantism" in "Prolegomena: St. Augustine's Life and Work" in *The Nicene and Post-Nicene Fathers First Series*, vol. 1. Edited by Philip Schaff. Peabody, MA: Hendrickson Publishers, 1999.

Schultz, S. J. "Chronicles, Books of" in *The Zondervan Pictorial Encyclopedia of the Bible*, volume 1. Edited by Merrill C. Tenney. Grand Rapids: Zondervan, 1976.

Shaylor, Randolph. "Our Final Authority" in *From the Mind of God to the Mind of Man: A Layman's Guide to How We Got Out Bible*, 3d ed. Edited by James B. Williams. Greenville, SC: Ambassador-Emerald International, 1999.

Shealy, Brian A. "Redrawing the Line Between Hermeneutics and Application." *Master's Seminary Journal* 8 (1997): 83-106.

Smallman, William H. "Printed Greek Texts" in *From the Mind of God to the Mind of Man: A Layman's Guide to How We Got Out Bible*, 3d ed. Edited by James B. Williams. Greenville, SC: Ambassador-Emerald International, 1999.

Spurgeon, Charles H. "A Loving Entreaty" in *The Metropolitan Tabernacle Pulpit*, vol. 29. Pasadena, TX: Pilgrim Publications, 1969.

_____. "Mongrel Religion" in *The Metropolitan Tabernacle Pulpit*, vol. 27. Pasadena, TX: Pilgrim Publications, 1969.

_____. "The Hairs of Your Head" in *The Metropolitan Tabernacle Pulpit*, vol. 34. Pasadena, TX: Pilgrim Publications, 1969.

_____. "The Hexapla of Mystery" in *The Metropolitan Tabernacle Pulpit*, vol. 18. Pasadena, TX: Pilgrim Publications, 1969.

_____. "The Key-Note of a Choice Sonnet" in *The Metropolitan Tabernacle Pulpit*, vol. 26 in *The Charles H. Spurgeon Library*, version 2. CD-ROM. Albany, OR: Ages Software, 1997.

_____. "The Resurrection Credible" in *The Metropolitan Tabernacle Pulpit*, vol. 28. Pasadena, TX: Pilgrim Publications, 1969.

_____. "What God Cannot Do!" in *The Metropolitan Tabernacle Pulpit*, vol. 10. Pasadena, TX: Pilgrim Publications, 1969.

Steinmann, Andrew E. "The Chronology of 2 Kings 15-18." *Journal of the Evangelical Theological Society* 30 (1987): 391-397.

Stigers, Harold G. "Preservation: The Corollary of Inspiration." *Journal of the Evangelical Theological Society* 22 (1979): 217-222.

_____. "The Interphased Chronology of Jotham, Ahaz, Hezekiah, and Hoshea." *Journal of the Evangelical Theological Society* 9 (1966): 81-91.

Strouse, Thomas M. "Article Review: A review of Combs, William W. 'The Preservation of Scripture.' " Newington, CT: Emmanuel Baptist Theological Seminary, 2001.

_____. "Psalm 12:6-7 and the Permanent Preservation of God's Words." Newington, CT: Emmanuel Baptist Theological Seminary, 2001.

_____. "Strouse's Law of the Tendency for Hebrew Pronouns to Masculinize their corresponding Feminine Antecedents." Newington, CT: Emmanuel Baptist Theological Seminary, 2006.

_____. "The Lord Jesus Christ and 'Scribal Errors'." Newington, CT: Emmanuel Baptist Theological Seminary, 2002.

_____. "The Lord Jesus Christ and the Received Bible John 17:8." Newington, CT: Emmanuel Baptist Theological Seminary, 2002.

_____. "The Translation Model Predicted By Scripture." Newington, CT: Emmanuel Baptist Theological Seminary, 2000.

The Committee on the Bible's Text and Translation. "The Changing King James Version" in *From the Mind of God to the Mind of Man: A Layman's Guide to How We Got Out Bible*, 3d ed. Edited by James B. Williams. Greenville, SC: Ambassador-Emerald International, 1999.

Thomas, W. H. Griffith. "Old Testament Criticism and New Testament Christianity" in *The Fundamentals – A Testimony to the Truth*, vol. 1. Edited by R. A. Torrey, A. C. Dixon, et. al. In *The Master Christian Library*, version 8. CD-ROM. Rio, WI: Ages Software, 2000.

Thompson, Clive A. "Certain Bible Difficulties." *Bibliotheca Sacra* 96 (1939): 459-478.

Tuck, R. "God in revelation the same as God in nature" in *The Book of* Psalms, vol. 2 in *The Pulpit Commentary*, vol. 8. Peabody, MA: Hendrickson Publishers, n.d.

Van Pelt, J. R. "Discrepancies, Biblical" in *The International Standard Bible Encyclopedia*, vol. 2. Edited by James Orr. Grand Rapids, MI: Wm. B. Eerdmans, 1939.

Wallace, Daniel B. "Inspiration, Preservation, and New Testament Textual Criticism." *Grace Theological Journal* 12 (1991): 21-50.

_____. "The Majority Text and the Original Text Are They Identical?" *Bibliotheca Sacra* 148 (1991): 151-169.

_____. "The Majority Text Theory: History, Methods and Critique." *Journal of the Evangelical Theological Society* 37 (1994): 185-215.

Walvoord, John F. "Contemporary Problems in Biblical Interpretation. Part 1: Is the Bible the Inspired Word of God?" *Bibliotheca Sacra* 116 (1959): 3-14.

_____. "The Pragmatic Confirmation of Scriptural Authority" in *The Bible – The Living Word of Revelation*. Edited by Merrill C. Tenney. Grand Rapids: Zondervan, 1968.

Watts, Malcolm H. "The Lord Gave the Word: A Study in the History of the Biblical Text." London: Trinitarian Bible Society, 1998. Article on-line. Available from http:\www.triniarianbiblesociety.org. Internet.

Wesley, John. "A Compendium of Logic" in *Wesley's Works*, vol. 14 in *The Master Christian Library*, version 8. CD-ROM. Albany, OR: Ages Software, 1997.

White, H. A. "Chariot" in *A Dictionary of the Bible Dealing with Its Language, Literature, and Contents*, Volume 1. Edited by James Hastings. New York: Charles Scribner's Sons, 1898.

Wilson, Robert Dick. "Is the Higher Criticism Scholarly?" in *Which Bible?* Edited by David Otis Fuller. Grand Rapids: Grand Rapids International Publications, 1978.

Woudstra, Marten H. "The Inspiration of the Old Testament" in *The Bible – The Living Word of Revelation*. Edited by Merrill C. Tenney. Grand Rapids: Zondervan, 1968.

Wright, George Frederick. "The Testimony of the Monuments to the Truth of the Scriptures" in *The Fundamentals – A Testimony to the Truth*, vol. 1. Edited by R. A. Torrey, A. C. Dixon, et. al. In *The Master Christian Library*, version 8. CD-ROM. Rio, WI: Ages Software, 2000.

Yamauchi, Edwin M. "Archaeological Backgrounds of the Exilic and Postexilic Era. Part I: The Archaeological Background of Daniel." *Bibliotheca Sacra* 137 (1980): 3-16.

Young, Edward J. "Are the Scriptures Inerrant?" in *The Bible – The Living Word of Revelation*. Edited by Merrill C. Tenney. Grand Rapids: Zondervan, 1968.

SCRIPTURE INDEX

GENESIS

1:5 182
1:8 182
1:9-10 423
1:13 182
1:16 424
1:19 182
1:23 182
1:27 .... 34, 36, 140
1:30 424
1:31 .... 160, 182
2:7 130
2:19 424
2:24 .... 17, 34, 36, 41
3:1 .... 5, 88, 108, 160, 178, 216, 387
3:4 164
3:15 33
4:8 168
4:8-9 .... 34, 35, 36
4:20 424
4:26 240
5 229
5:3 424
5:5 229

6-9 .... 34, 35, 36
6:1 240
6:6 160
10:21 240
10:25 240
12:13 164
12:19 161
14 154
14:14 236
15:2 236
15:5 42
15:6 42
16 130
16:1 42
17:5 129
17:16 426
17:19 289
19 .... 33, 35, 36
19:21 42
19:25 42
19:26 .... 35, 36
19:29 42
20:1-13 164
20:2 161
21 130
22:16 56
22:18 131

24:15 240
24:60 426
26:7 161
32:1 140
35:26 240
36:5 240
41:50 240
46:22 240
46:27 240
49:10 .... 32, 55
49:28 41
50:23 240

EXODUS

3:4 90
3:6 .... 17, 34, 35, 36, 38, 39
3:14 .... 38, 136
3:15 38
3:16 38
4:22 56
4:31 158
5:19-23 158
6:9 158
7:1 72

7:7 220	18:8 327	25:9 185
9:25 219	19:2 64	26:22 220
13:2 129	19:8 355	26:25 220
14:7 228	19:12 62	26:43 220
14:13 43	19:18 .... 34, 35, 63	27:15-23 278
16 36	20:8 140	28:9 33
16:18 130	20:9 34	30:15 355
18:21 .... 242, 272	20:11 327	31:33-34 220
20:5 .... 321, 327	20:17 355	31:37 220
20:8-11 182	20:19 355	31:38 220
20:10 140	20:26 64	31:39 220
20:12 34	22:31 140	33:2 18
20:12-16 ..... 34, 35	24:20 63	
20:13 62	26:3 140	**DEUTERONOMY**
20:14 62	26:33 140	
21 136		1:15 .... 242, 273
21:17 34	**NUMBERS**	1:28 278
21:24 63		2:14 288
21:29 136	1:27 220	3:28 278
21:36 136	1:39 220	5:16 34
22:38 129	2:4 220	5:16-20 ..... 34, 35
23:19 .... 55, 56	2:16 96	5:17 62
24:4 .... 18, 19, 41, 56,	2:26 220	5:18 62
57, 74, 90, 114	3:43 220	6:4 .... 35, 41, 114
24:7 157	3:46 220	6:5 .... 34, 35
28:21 41	3:50 220	6:6-9 .... 21, 90
32:6 130	4:18-20 219	6:13 30
32:19 .... 19, 74	5:31 355	6:16 30
34:1 .... 18, 19	10:11-12 ... 288	6:17 141
34:6 142	11:18-23 ... 156	6:20 141
34:27 .... 18, 56	11:19-23 ... 43	8:3 .... 30, 85
38:25 220	11:20-23 ... 70	10:12 .... 34, 35
38:26 11	11:21-22 ... 118	11:20 .... 21, 90
39:14 41	11:21-23 ... 71	13:12 428
	11:23 119	17:6 .... 31, 41
LEVITICUS	13:17-20 ... 288	17:16 273
	14:13 43	17:17 273
5:1 355	14:18 .... 321, 327	17:18 .... 20, 21, 90
5:17 355	14:33 261	17:18-19 .... 21, 22
7:18 355	14:34 355	17:19 157
11:44 131	14:45 288	18:13 64
12:3 36	15:39 140	19:15 .... 31, 41
13:29 140	20:9 34	19:21 63
14 .... 33, 34, 35	21:8-9 36	21:23 130
17:16 355	21:12 288	23:23 63

24:1 .... 34, 62
24:16 24
25:4 130
27:1-3 .... 21, 90
27:8 .... 21, 90
27:26 130
28:5 230
28:17 230
29:4 129
29:29 .... 112, 241
31:1-19 .... 21, 90
31:7 278
31:9 18
31:11 157
31:23 278
31:24 .... 18, 57
31:25-26 ..... 18, 25
32:18 53
32:35 130
33:11 230

JOSHUA

1:7 139
1:8 .... 24, 26, 157
2:4 164
3:12 41
4:8 41
5:13-15 32
7:5 219
8:30-32 ...... 21, 90
8:31 .... 23, 24, 26
8:34 .... 24, 26
8:34-35 157
11:8 219
11:23 288
13:30 .... 371-372, 384
14:7 288
14:10 .... 220, 288
17:12 .... 428, 429
18:10 280
21:36-37 83
23:4 280
23:6 .... 23, 24, 26
24:26 18

JUDGES

1 285
1:19 .... 428, 429
1:27 .... 428, 429
1:30 429
1:31 429
1:32 429
1:33 429
2 285
2:16-18 278
3:8 284
3:11 284
3:14 284
3:30 284
4:1-3 284
5:31 284
6:1 284
8:28 284
9:22 284
10:1-2 284
10:3 285
10:3-4 .... 371-372, 384
10:4 372
10:8 285
11:26 .... 285, 287, 288
12:7 285
12:8-9 285
12:11 285
12:13-14 ... 285
13:1 285
15:16 48
15:20 285
15:63 428
16:31 285
18:29 240
21:21 140

RUTH

4:15 .... 239, 240
4:16 240
4:17 240

I SAMUEL

4:1-11 221
4:10 221
4:17-22 221
4:18 .... 278, 285
5:6 222
5:9-12 222
6:1 221
6:13 221
6:19 .... 5, 7, 8, 9, 13, 177, 203, 204, 217-221, 381, 384, 400, 403
7:6 278
7:15 .... 278, 286, 287
7:15-17 278
9:9 112
10:25 .... 18, 25
11:8 230
12:8 278
13:1 .... 6, 8, 9, 13, 32, 177, 182, 186, 201, 204, 222-226, 305, 324, 381, 384, 400, 406
13:5 .... 7, 8, 13, 177, 182, 186, 203, 213, 226, 226-231, 247, 381, 384, 39, 400, 403, 404
13:19-20 230
14:49 .... 235, 236
15:2 305
16 231
16:10-11 .... 231-232, 371, 384
16:20 230
17 .... 415, 417, 418, 420, 421, 430
17:35 219
18:5 250
18:16 250
18:17-27 238

18:19.........239
18:25.........233
18:27.........232-233, 237, 384, 398, 399
18:30.........250
20:3............22
20:31.........22, 225
21:1-7........33, 34, 35
22:7-13......22
23:19.........162
23:26-27....22
24:6............162
25:1............279
25:4............279
25:16.........279
25:38.........279
25:44.........238
25-31.........278, 288
26..............279
26:1............162
26:9............22, 162
27:7............279
28-31.........279

II SAMUEL

1:14............72
2:8.............235-237, 374, 384, 398, 400
2:11............249
3:2..............240
3:2-3...........249
3:5..............240
3:7..............236
3:14............232-233, 237, 384, 398, 399
3:14-15......238
4:4..............237
5:4..............249, 250, 279
5:8..............423
6.................238
6:23............237-240, 251, 305, 384, 398
8:3-5..........246
8:4..............6, 8, 9, 177, 204, 241-242, 247, 273, 374, 381, 384, 423
8:5..............244, 245
8:5-6..........244, 245
8:13...........242-246, 374, 384
10:18.........8, 9, 177, 204, 227, 230, 242, 246-247, 273, 374, 381, 384, 399
11:3............426
12:24.........426
12:29.........244
14:27.........247-248, 250, 251, 384
15:4-7........249
15:7............8, 177, 204, 248-251, 270, 381, 384, 398, 404
16...............250
18...............250
18:5............246
18:18.........247-248, 251, 384
19...............250
20...............250
21................260, 413, 418
21:1............242, 243, 250, 260, 261
21:2-14......260
21:8............236, 237-240, 251, 384, 398, 411
21:11..........236
21:15-22....250, 411
21:18..........411
21:18-22....411
21:19..........vii, 4, 251, 411-430
21:20..........240
21:20-21....412
21:22..........240, 412
22................82
22:1............242, 243
22:26-27....60
23:2............123
23:8............203, 251-254, 374, 384
23:9............254
23:11..........254
23:18..........254, 255
23:18-23....255
23:20..........254, 255
23:24..........254
23:25..........254
23:26..........254
23:27..........254
23:28..........254
23:29..........254
23:30..........254
23:31..........254
23:32..........254
23:33..........254
23:34..........254
23:35..........254
23:36..........254
23:37..........255
23:38..........255
23:39..........177, 254-255, 384, 398, 400
24:2-12......257
24:8............258, 260
24:9............221, 255-258, 374, 384
24:13..........108, 204, 258-261, 374, 384, 404
24:15-22....260
24:18..........264
24:24..........262-264, 374, 384

I KINGS

2:3 ....22, 23, 90
2:11 ....248-251, 270, 384, 398
4:26............8, 177, 186, 204, 270-273, 379, 381, 384, 404
5:11 ....273-274, 377, 384, 398
5:13-18......244
5:15-16......274-275, 377, 384, 398
5:16...........275
6:1 ....275-290, 384, 399
6:2.............290-291, 378, 384, 398, 399
6:12...........140
6:14...........244
6:17...........290-291, 378, 384, 398, 399
7:15 ....203, 291-292, 378, 384, 399
7:16...........293-294, 367, 384, 400
7:20...........294-296, 300, 379, 384, 398
7:21...........291
7:23 ....296-297, 384, 399, 400, 404
7:26 ....203, 297-299, 366, 378, 384, 398, 399
7:42...........294-296, 300, 384, 398
8:10-11......356
9:14...........302
9:23...........275, 300, 379, 384
9:28...........94, 301-302, 379
10 ....33, 35, 37
10:1-13......34, 35, 37
10:10.........302
10:14.........220, 271
10:25 273
10:26 ....227, 273
10:28 ....230, 273
11:3 273
12:1-20 269
14:21 269
14:26 295
15:1 269
15:2 269
15:9 268
15:9-10 269
15:10 400
15:18 295
15:33 ....302-306, 321, 379, 384, 399, 400
16:6-10 384
16:6-8 302-306
16:8 ....268, 400
16:8-10 .....306-307, 404
16:15-16 ...307-308, 322, 384, 398, 399, 400, 404
16:21 308
16:22 308
16:23 ....307-308, 322, 325, 384, 399, 400
16:28 ....321, 400
16:29 ....307-311, 312, 322, 325, 384, 398, 400, 404
17:1 ....45, 417
17:4 55
17:8-24 .....35, 37
18:1 ....35, 41, 45
18:31 41
18:45 ....35, 41, 45
20:21 230
20:30 ....9, 177, 311-312, 384
21:17 417
21:28 417
22….........311, 316, 328
22:2-40......311
22:4...........349
22:26.........328
22:40.........310, 311
22:41.........308-311, 312, 384, 398, 400
22:42.........316
22:50.........311
22:51.........308-313, 317, 322, 325, 384, 398, 399, 400

II KINGS

1:3 417
1:8 417
1:17...........315-318, 326, 333, 337, 338, 343, 346, 384, 400, 404
3:1..............312-313, 317, 322, 327, 328, 384, 400
5 ....35, 37
6:25...........119
7 119
7:1..............119
7:1-2..........43
7:2..............119
7:17............119
7:17-20......43
8:16...........315-317, 384, 400
8:16-17......320
8:16-18......321
8:17............317, 326, 328
8:24-26......321
8:25...........318-319, 322, 323, 326, 329, 384, 399, 400
8:26...........5, 180, 203, 204, 224, 305, 318, 319-329, 349, 373, 379, 384, 404
8:27...........321, 327

9:1-7..........328
9:24..........328
9:27..........328
9:29..........318-319, 323, 326, 329, 384, 399, 400
9:36..........417
10:30..........341
10:36..........329-332, 335, 384, 398, 399, 400, 404
11:4-16......331
11:9-12......21, 90
11:12..........20
12:1..........328-332, 340, 384, 398, 399, 400, 404
12:18..........295
12:20..........335
13:1..........329-334, 340, 384, 398, 399, 400, 404
13:3..........333
13:10..........332-335, 340, 379, 384, 398, 399, 400, 404
13:12..........333
13:14-19....338
13:20..........338
14:1..........332-335, 340, 384, 398, 401, 404
14:1-2..........339
14:6..........23, 24
14:8-14......338
14:13..........327
14:14..........295
14:17..........336
14:23..........335-341, 349, 379, 384, 399, 401
15..............337
15:1..........336-341, 384, 399, 401
15:2..........341-344, 346, 350, 355, 357, 384, 399, 401, 404
15:5..........343, 346

15:7..........340
15:8..........336-341, 344, 384, 399, 401
15:10-20...339
15:12..........341
15:13..........340
15:16..........219
15:17..........340
15:23..........340
15:27..........340-344, 346, 355, 357, 384, 399, 401, 404
15:29..........266
15:30..........266, 344-349, 350, 351, 354, 384, 398
15:32..........340-344, 346, 350, 355, 357, 384, 399, 401, 404
15:33..........344-347, 350, 355, 384, 398
16..............337
16:1..........340
16:2..........266, 345, 350-351, 355, 384, 399, 401
16:5-9........348
16:7-10......346
16:8..........295
16:9..........348
17:1..........266, 340, 347-349, 351, 354, 384
17:4..........349
17:21..........356
17:41..........115
18..............357, 408
18:1..........182, 266, 340, 349, 354, 401
18:1-2........353
18:1-10.....182
18:2..........350-351, 355, 384, 399, 401
18:9..........182, 266, 349, 354, 399, 401
18:9ff..........352

18:10..........182, 266, 349, 354, 357, 399, 401
18:13..........44, 75, 98, 171, 204, 305, 351-359, 384, 399, 401, 404
18:13-16....357
18:13-20:19...82
18:16..........295, 358
18:17..........358
18:17-19:37..357
19:35..........220
21:3..........349
22:1..........362
22:3-4..........359-360, 362, 379, 384, 398, 399, 401, 404
23:2..........157
23:8..........363
23:29..........362
23:30..........362
23:31..........362
23:36..........362, 363
24:8..........93, 117, 149, 152, 203, 204, 225, 305, 321, 360-363, 380, 384, 404
24:12..........305, 361, 364, 384, 398, 399, 401
24:14..........364-365, 384, 399
24:15..........360
24:18-25:30...82
25:6..........367
25:8..........366
25:8-9..........365-367, 384, 398, 399, 401
25:17..........293-294, 366, 367, 384, 398, 399, 401
25:18..........367
25:19..........366, 367-368, 384, 398, 399

25:27.........368-369, 384, 398, 399, 401

I CHRONICLES

1:19...........240
2:13-15......231-232, 371, 384
2:15...........231
2:22...........372
2:22-23......371-372, 384, 398, 399, 404
2:55...........21
3:10-13......372-373, 384, 399, 401
3:22...........373-374, 384, 398, 399, 404
5:26...........266
7:12............426
7:15...........426
8:33............235, 236
9:14............25
9:39...........236
10:6...........235-237, 374, 384, 398, 401
11:6...........423
11:11.........8, 9, 177, 203, 251-254, 374, 381, 384
16:23-33....82
16:34-36....82
16:40.........24
17:11-12....33
18:4...........230, 241-242, 273, 374, 384, 423
18:11.........246
18:12.........242-246, 374, 384, 398
19:7...........230
19:18.........230, 242, 246-247, 273, 374, 384, 399
20:1...........244
20:4...........411, 412
20:4-8........411

20:5 ....412, 413, 415, 417, 418, 421, 422, 425, 427, 429, 430
20:6-7 412
20:8 412
21...............262
21:3 259
21:5 ....9, 230, 255-258, 374, 384
21:7 259
21:8 259
21:11 259
21:11-12 ... 108, 258-261, 374, 384
21:12 ....259, 261
21:18 264
21:25 ....262-264, 384
22:14 ....8, 177, 203, 375-376, 381, 384, 399, 401, 404
23:1 326
25:7 220
29:3-4 ....375-376, 384, 399, 401
29:4 375
29:10 114
29:22 326
29:29 ....24, 26

II CHRONICLES

1:1 304
1:14 ....241, 271
2:2 ....9, 274-275, 377, 384, 398
2:10 ....273-274, 377, 384, 398
2:17-18 .....9, 274-275, 377, 384, 398
2:18 275
3:4 ....8, 9, 177, 203, 204, 291, 377-378, 381, 384, 398, 399, 401

3:15............8, 177, 203, 291-292, 378, 381, 384, 398, 399
4:2..............296, 378, 384
4:5..............8, 203, 297-299, 378, 381, 384, 398, 399
4:6..............299
4:13............294-296, 379, 384, 398
8:10............275, 300, 379, 384
8:18............9, 94, 301-302, 379, 384
9.................33, 35, 37
9:1-12.........34, 35, 37
9:13............220
9:25...........270-273, 379, 384
9:28............273
11:17.........304
12:3............227
12:13.........304
13:2............304
14:1............306
14:9............306
15:9............306
15:10.........304, 306
15:19.........306, 321, 399
16:1............302-306, 321, 379, 384, 401
16:1-10......305
16:12.........305
18:1............327
18:2............327
18:3............349
18:28.........327
18:33-34....327
19:6............72
20:30.........304
21:1............327
21:2............349
21:16-17....318
21:18.........318

21:20.........328
22:1...........327, 349
22:2............5, 6, 7, 8, 9,
   177, 180, 203, 224,
   225, 305, 319-329,
   379, 381, 384, 404,
   405
22:2-3.........318
22:3-4.........321
22:9...........320, 327
22:11.........327, 328
23:9-11......21, 90
23:11.........20
23:18.........23, 24
24:1...........328, 332-335,
   379, 384, 398, 399,
   401, 404
24:15.........334
24:20.........168
24:20-21....34, 35, 36
24:21.........334
24:23-24....334
24:25.........334
25...............333
25:1...........336-341, 379,
   384, 401
25:4...........24
25:17-24....338
25:25.........336
26:3...........343
26:15.........338
26:23.........346
28:5...........219
28:5-6........221
28:19.........349
30:5...........23, 24
30:18.........23, 24
31:3...........24
32:1-23......357
32:32.........24, 26
33:19.........24, 26
34:3-4........359-360, 379,
   384, 398, 399, 401,
   404
34:14.........18
34:30.........157

35:26 24
36:5 362
36:9 ....7, 9, 93,
   117, 149, 152, 177,
   203, 225, 305, 321,
   360-363, 380, 381,
   384
36:10 ....362, 363
36:15-16 ...35
36:17-19 ...25

EZRA

2.................95
2:64 ....11, 220
3:2 ....23, 24, 25
3:4 ....23, 24, 25
6:17 41
7:6 ....21, 90
7:11 ....21, 90

NEHEMIAH

7..................95
7:18-19 220
7:26 220
7:66 ....11, 220
7:68 83
7:71-72 11
7:72 220
8:3 157
8:1-8 90
8:14 24
8:14-15 .....22, 24, 25,
   90
8:15 23
8:18 157
9:3 157
9:13 143
9:35 304
10:34-36 ...24, 25
11:6 220
11:18 220
12:23 ....24, 25
13:1 ....24, 25

ESTHER

1:4.............220
1:7.............11
1:14...........304

JOB

5:13...........130
19:25.........33
19:25-26....38
24:12.........55
25:3...........64
37:23.........55
41:28.........225

PSALMS

1..................22
1:2..............22, 157
2..................32
2:7..............129
2:9..............55
8:2..............34
11:3............215, 388
12................138
12:1-4.........137
12:2............137
12:5...........136, 137,
   138, 140
12:5-6........137
12:6............117, 138,
   139, 141, 298, 394
12:6-7.........2, 20, 24, 26,
   61, 64, 82, 101, 135-
   141, 145, 350, 414,
   421
12:6-8........137
12:7...........vii, 20, 90,
   136, 137, 138, 139,
   141
14...............82
14:1-3........129
17:15.........60
18..............82, 243

18:25-26....60	82:6 ....31, 59, 72, 73, 75, 76, 133	119:160.....78, 90, 142-143, 145, 153
18:49.........130	86:15 142	119:167.....139
19:7............123, 149	93:5 56	127:4.........328, 329
19:7-11......89	96...............82	138:2.........40, 73
19:9............143	100:5 ....90, 142-143, 145	146:6.........142
19:10.........143	106:1 82	
22...............32	106:47 82	**PROVERBS**
24:2............142	106:48 82	
24:3-4........61	108:2-6 82	12:19.........55
25:14..........153	108:7-14 ...82	16:25.........199
27:14..........154	109:13-15 .321, 327	20:22.........154
29:8............230	110:1 ....34, 35	22:6............240
34...............166	110:4 59	22:15.........240
34:12-16....61	111:7 56	23:24.........240
34:20.........166	112:9 130	25:1............21, 90
35:19.........31, 59, 129	116:10 130	25:2............112
37:11.........60	118:22 ......16, 31, 34, 35	29:14.........55
37:34.........154	119............22, 142, 157	30:5............226
40 167	119:4-6 .....62, 64	30:6............226
40:6............167	119:12 153	
40:7............130	119:18 ......153, 393	**ECCLESIASTES**
40:14-18....82	119:19 22	
41:9............30	119:23 22	5:4..............4, 63
44:21.........105	119:27 153	12:10.........24, 26
44:22.........129	119:33 153	12:12.........156
51:1-3........129	119:43 143	
51:4............129	119:66 153	**ISAIAH**
52 82	119:87 22	
57:8-12......82	119:89 ......61, 64	2:2-4..........82
60:Title 242-246, 384	119:97-99 .22	5:1..............225
60:1............245	119:99-100..150	6:9-10........34, 37
60:7-14......82	119:97-104..157	7:14............168
66:18.........125	119:105.....122	8:14............129
68:18.........33	119:111.....139	8:20............215, 388
69:4............31, 59, 129	119:128.....5, 216, 389, 488	9:1..............266
69:9............129, 130	119:129.....139	9:6..............16, 240, 358
69:21.........36	119:142.....143	11...............66
69:26.........129	119:151.....143	11:2............16
70 82	119:152.....61, 64, 90, 139, 141-142, 145, 153	13...............358
73:1............60		19:10.........55
76:6............230		20:1............154
76:11.........63		21...............358
78:5............140		21:10.........225
78:24-25....31		21:13.........55
80:15.........225		

25:8 130
26:19 38
28:11-12 ....59, 130
28:16 ....72, 129
29:10 129
29:13 ....30, 34, 37
29:14 130
30:8 ....21, 143-144, 145
30:9ff 143
34:16 ....21, 158
35:10 171
36 357
36-39 ....26, 82
36:1 ....44, 75, 98, 171, 184, 353, 357, 358
36:2-37:38 ..357
40:3 ....30, 128, 129
40:8 ....62, 64, 90, 144, 145
43:25 102
43:26 102
44:4 130
45:6 114
45:21 114
45:23 130
52:5 129
52:7 129
52:15 130
53 32
53:1 37
53:4-9 30
53:8 419
53:12 31
54:13 31
55:8-9 110
56:7 ....30, 31
57:15 59
59:20 130
61:1-2 ....30, 35, 129, 358
61:2-3 60
65:13 60
65:17 ....66, 69
66:1 63

66:2 59
66:5 61
66:22 66

JEREMIAH

8:8 ....21, 90
8:13 55
9:23-24 130
15:19 55
17:5 201
20:15 240
23:5-6 32
25:11 ....43, 109
25:24 55
28:1-4 ....43, 109
28:10-17 ...43, 109
28:15 109
28:16 109
30 20
30:2 ....19, 20, 56, 74
31 20
31:34 31
36 ....19, 74
36:1-4 ....21, 56, 90
36:6 157
36:23 74
36:27-28 ...19
36:32 ....21, 90
39:16-17 ...368
40:2-4 368
44:28 138
45:1 ....21, 90
48:4 55
49:12 230
50:38 55
51:60 ....24, 26
52 ....82, 295
52:9-10 367
52:12-13 ...365-367, 384
52:23 ....294-296, 384
52:25 ....367-368, 384

52:28 364
52:28-30 ....364-365, 384
52:31 ....368-369, 384

EZEKIEL

4:1-3 355
4:4 356
4:4-5 ....305, 355-356
4:5 356
4:6 355
4:7-8 355
5:6 140
13:7 201
14:10 355
18:19 140
31:4 419
36:20 129
36:23 129
37:16-17 158
37:18-22 158
37:24 140
38 416
38-39 416
38:2 416
38:8 416
38:14-15 416
38:16 416
39:1 417
39:1-12 416
39:20 230
40 416
47:13 41

DANIEL

1 365
1:1 ....361, 365
1:3 365
2 365
2:1 365
2:44 59

5 310
7:17 261
9:2 .... 25, 109
9:11 .... 23, 24
9:13 .... 22, 23, 24, 25, 90
9:22 109
9:24-27 ...... 106, 359
9:26-27 30
9:27 .... 34, 35, 37, 55
10:21 .... 73, 142
12:1 24
12:2 38
12:11 .... 34, 35, 37

HOSEA

6:6 .... 33, 49
11:1 .... 166, 430
13:7 55
14:9 124

AMOS

5:25-26 129
9:11-12 129

OBADIAH

15 33

JONAH

1:17 .... 34, 35, 37, 41, 45
3:4 42
3:5-10 .... 34, 35, 37
4:11 .... 11, 42

MICAH

4:1-3 82
4:1-4 31
5:2 16
6:9 55

HABAKKUK

2:4 129

ZEPHANIAH

3:8 55

ZECHARIAH

9:9 .... 31, 129
12:10 .... 166, 358
13:7 30

MALACHI

2:3 55
3:1 .... 30, 33, 128
3:1-2 129
4:5 416
4:5-6 34

MATTHEW

1:6 426
1:7-9 .... 372-373, 384
1:8 .... 321, 327
1:11 .... 362, 363
1:17 278
1:20-23 110
2:15 .... 166, 430
4:4 .... 22, 28, 30, 47, 56, 79, 82, 85, 90, 132-133, 146, 148, 178, 201, 208, 215, 381, 388
4:7 .... 28, 30, 381
4:10 .... 30, 381
4:18 417
4:21 426
5 59
5:1 51
5:3 .... 59, 102
5:3-5 103
5:4 .... 59, 102
5:5 60
5:6 60
5:7 60
5:8 60
5:9 61
5:10-12 61
5:17 .... 48, 49, 65, 88, 91, 215, 216, 330, 384, 388
5:17-18 ...... 48-67, 88, 179, 382, 386
5:17-19 65
5:18 .... vii, 15, 23, 24, 50, 51, 52, 53, 54, 56, 57, 59, 61, 64, 65, 66, 68, 69, 70, 83, 85, 86, 87, 88, 90, 93, 95, 101, 126, 131, 135, 144, 145, 147, 168, 172, 174, 175, 176, 177, 183, 184, 202, 205, 208, 211, 214, 224, 226, 229, 241, 247, 261, 271, 292, 295, 298, 304, 312, 353, 356, 373, 385, 386, 387, 392, 399, 414
5:19 .... 55, 62, 64, 65
5:21 62
5:21-48 80
5:22 50
5:27 62
5:28 50
5:31 62
5:32 .... 50, 107
5:33 62
5:34 50
5:34-35 63
5:36 54
5:38 63
5:39 50
5:43 63
5:44 50

5:45 64
5:48 64
6:29 ....33, 37, 382
7:6 122
7:12 ....49, 168
7:28-29......51
8:4 ....33, 382
9:13 ....33, 49, 382
10:2 426
10:3 426
10:25 17
10:39 102
11:10 ....30, 381
11:13 ....49, 168
11:14 415
11:23 ....33, 36, 382
12:1-13......80
12:3-4.......33
12:3 ....158, 382
12:4 382
12:5 ....33, 59, 158, 382
12:7 ....33, 49, 382
12:8 49
12:18 16
12:40 ....17, 34, 37, 41, 45, 382
12:41 ....34, 37, 283, 382
12:42 ....34, 37, 382
13:13 122
13:14-15....34, 37, 382
13:21 121
14:21 160
15:1-9........80
15:4 ....34, 382
15:8-9........34, 382
15:38 160
16:16-17....43
16:21-22....43, 188
16:21-23....70, 71, 156, 176
16:23 ....43, 188, 215, 388
17:11 ....34, 382
17:12 416

18:16 ....41, 382
19:4 ....34, 36, 158, 382
19:4-5 ....36, 73
19:4-6 205
19:5 ....17, 34, 45, 382
19:5-6 ....41, 382
19:8 ....34, 382
19:18-19 ...34, 382
19:28 ....67, 382
19:30 103
20:1 164
20:16 103
21:13 ....30, 381
21:16 ....34, 158, 382
21:25-27 ...200
21:42 ....16, 34, 158, 382
22.............38
22:23-32 ...16
22:23-33 ...80
22:31 ....39, 56, 158
22:32 ....17, 34, 38, 39, 382
22:34 83
22:36 59
22:37 ....34, 382
22:39 ....34, 382
22:40 49
22:41 168
22:43-44 ...76
22:44 ....34, 382
23:35 ....34, 36, 382
24:15 ....34, 37, 382
24:35 ....15, 48, 56, 58, 67-68, 90, 93, 144, 145, 177, 382
24:37-39 ...34, 36, 205, 382
24:38-39 ...17
25:21 156
26:24 ....30, 381
26:31 ....30, 381
27:5 116
27:7 116

27:7-8........115
27:37 ....113, 128, 131, 159, 384
27:45-50....282
27:57-58....282, 284
28:6 358
28:19-20....83
28:20 ....90, 136

MARK

1:2 ....28, 128, 383
1:44 ....34, 382
2:25 158
2:25-26......34, 382
2:28 49
5:13 285
6:12 280
7:6 ....30, 381
7:6-7...........34, 382
7:9 212
7:10 ....34, 382
7:13 77
7:18-19......49
8:9 285
9:12 ....30, 34, 381, 382
9:35 103
10:2-9........36
10:3-5........34, 382
10:6 ....34, 382
10:7-8........34, 382
10:8 ....41, 45, 382
10:19 ....35, 382
10:31 103
11:12-13....113
11:17 ....30, 381
12:10 ....72, 158, 382
12:10-11....35
12:26 ....35, 36, 158, 382
12:29 ....35, 41, 45, 46, 382
12:30 ....35, 382
12:31 ....35, 382

12:35-37....16
12:36.........35, 123, 382
13:14.........35, 382
13:31.........15, 48, 58, 67-69, 144, 145, 382
14:21.........30, 381
14:27.........30, 381
15:26.........113, 159
15:28.........72
15:42-43....282, 284
15:44.........283
15:44-45....282, 283
15:47.........426
16:1...........426
16:9-20......178
16:12.........280

LUKE

1:17...........415
2:22...........59
2:23...........59, 129, 383
2:24...........59
2:27...........59
2:37...........285
2:39...........59
2:46-47......16
3:4.............129, 383
3:23-38......426
4:4.............30, 85, 381
4:8.............30, 381
4:17...........27, 129, 383
4:17-19......30, 35, 381, 382
4:21...........72
4:25...........41, 44, 45, 382
4:25-26......35, 37, 382
4:27...........35, 37, 382
5:14...........35, 382
5:27...........280
6:3.............158
6:3-4..........35, 382
6:5.............49
6:16...........425

6:46...........91
7:27...........30, 381
8:42...........285
9:55...........80
10:1...........280
10:12.........35, 382
10:26.........30
10:26-27...35, 382
11:29-30...35, 382
11:31........16, 35, 382
11:32.........35, 382
11:38-42...80
11:49.........35, 382
11:51.........35, 36, 168, 382
12:1...........11
12:4...........280
12:7...........40
12:27.........35, 382
13:30.........103
16:10.........53, 147
16:16.........49
16:17.........15, 23, 48, 52, 69-70, 83, 85, 86, 87, 90, 93, 126, 144, 145, 147, 168, 172, 173, 179, 229, 241, 292, 312, 356, 373, 382, 385, 386, 392
16:19-31...80
17:8...........280
17:26-27...35, 36, 382
17:28-29...35, 36, 382
17:32.........35, 36, 382
18:4...........280
18:20.........35, 382
18:9-14.....80
18:31.........27, 30-31, 381
19:46.........31, 381
20:17.........27, 31, 381
20:37-38...35, 382
20:42-43...35, 382
21:22.........27, 31-32, 382

21:33.........15, 48, 58, 67-69, 144, 382
22:30.........41, 382
22:37.........27, 31, 382
23:38.........113, 129, 131, 159, 169, 384
24:20-21....70
24:24.........168
24:25.........15, 48, 56, 70-72, 88, 87, 91, 127, 277, 382, 386, 392
24:25-27....32
24:27.........31, 32
24:44.........27, 31-32, 49, 88, 89, 168, 382
24:44-46....32
24:46.........31, 382

JOHN

1:1.............16, 78
1:1-3..........37
1:9.............16
1:12...........125, 195
1:17...........59
1:23...........56
1:39...........285
1:42...........411
1:45...........59
2:17...........129, 383
2:22...........72
2:24...........16
3:6.............123, 125
3:12...........147, 189
3:14...........36, 382
3:22...........280
4................280
5................280
5:1.............280
5:2.............169
5:4.............178
5:14...........280
5:27...........16
5:39...........31, 49, 158

6 .... 120, 121
6:1 280
6:19 285
6:31 .... 27, 31, 382
6:32 .... 36, 382
6:37 58
6:45 .... 27, 31, 382
6:49 17
6:51 120
6:52 120
6:53 121
6:53-58 121
6:60 121
6:66 121
7:1 280
7:17 .... 122, 126
7:19-23 80
7:22 .... 36, 382
7:23 59
7:38 72
7:42 72
7:52-8:12 ... 178
8:5 59
8:12 16
8:17 .... 31, 41, 59, 382
8:47 178
8:58 16
10:7 16
10:11 16
10:27 178
10:34 .... 27, 31, 59, 72, 73, 76, 88, 382
10:34-35 88
10:35 .... 15, 20, 23, 48, 56, 72-76, 77, 79, 85, 88, 90, 93, 126, 133, 145, 172, 179, 184, 211, 271, 292, 298, 356, 385, 392
11:18 285
12:14 .... 27, 31, 129, 382, 383
12:16 .... 129, 383
12:34 59
12:38 56

12:38-41 ... 37, 382
12:48 .... 69, 178, 179
13:7 280
13:18 72
14:6 16
14:26 77
15:25 .... 27, 31, 59, 129, 382, 383
16:13 .... 77, 166, 169
17:8 .... 23, 57, 87, 90, 101, 117, 127, 178, 179, 191, 214, 385, 387
17:12 72
17:17 .... 2, 15, 48, 56, 75, 76-78, 79, 85, 86, 89, 93, 117, 126, 145, 147, 148, 157, 172, 179, 184, 208, 209, 286, 300, 302, 312, 369, 385, 392
18:37 16
19 281
19:13 169
19:17 169
19:19 .... 113, 159
19:19-20 ... 129, 131, 384
19:24 72
19:25 426
19:28 .... 36, 72, 382
19:30 .... 29, 281
19:31 .... 281, 282, 283
19:32 281
19:33-34 ... 281
19:33-37 ... 358
19:34 283
19:35-37 ... 281
19:36-37 ... 72, 166
19:38 .... 281, 282, 283, 284
19:40-42 ... 282
20:9 72

20:31 .... 129, 131, 384
21:1 280
21:8 285
21:25 112

ACTS

1:7 112
1:13 426
1:15 285
1:16 .... 72, 123
1:18 115
1:19 116
1:20 .... 129, 383
2:11 90
2:14-36 134
2:16-21 134
2:25-28 134
2:34-35 134
2:28 283
2:41 .... 87, 90, 178, 191, 385
2:41-42 163
3:12-26 134
3:14 16
3:18 134
3:19 vi
3:21-24 134
3:22 56
4:8-12 134
4:11 134
4:12 v
4:13 114
4:25 22
5:3-4 114
5:7 285
6:13 59
7:6 288
7:7 280
7:16 426
7:23 285
7:35-36 278
7:38 .... 74, 81, 87, 90, 101, 136, 386

7:42 .... 129, 383
7:48-49 56
7:53 59
8:14 .... 87, 90, 178, 191, 385
8:26-35 165
8:32 .... 72, 286
8:32-34 56
8:35 72
8:37 178
10:34-43 134
10:43 .... 32, 134
11:1 .... 87, 90, 178, 191, 386
11:28 13
13 280
13:17 .... 280, 281, 288, 289
13:17-19 288
13:17-20 281
13:18 .... 285, 288
13:18-20 .... 275-290, 384
13:19 .... 280, 281, 288
13:20 .... 276, 278, 279, 280, 281, 283, 286, 287, 288, 289, 290
13:21 .... 225, 226
13:29 .... 129, 383
13:33 .... 129, 383
13:39 59
15:5 59
15:7-11 134
15:15 .... 129, 383
15:16 280
17:6 163
17:11 .... 87, 90, 158, 178, 191, 386
18:1 280
18:13 59
21:20 .... 11, 59
21:27 285
21:40 169
22:2 169
23:3 59
23:5 .... 129, 383

24:14 .... 129, 384
25:14 285
26:14 169
27:27 285
28:33 59
28:25 .... 56, 123

ROMANS

1:2 73
1:17 .... 129, 383
2:12 59
2:13 59
2:15 59
2:18 59
2:20 59
2:23 59
2:24 .... 129, 383
2:25 59
2:26 59
2:27 59
3:2 .... 74, 81, 83, 87, 90, 101, 127, 136, 386
3:4 .... 120, 129, 383
3:10 .... 27, 129, 383
3:19 59
3:20 59
3:23 v
4:3 72
4:15 59
4:17 .... 22, 90, 129, 383
4:23-24 ..... 40, 90
5:9 v
6:23 v
7:1 59
7:5 59
7:14 59
8:3 59
8:9 .... 123, 125
8:36 .... 129, 383
9:13 .... 129, 383
9:17 .... 72, 73
9:27 286

9:29 56
9:33 .... 129, 383
10:8 178
10:11 72
10:13 vi
10:15 .... 129, 383
10:17 190
11:2 72
11:8 .... 129, 383
11:26 .... 130, 383
11:33 111
11:33-34 112
12:19 .... 56, 130, 383
14:11 .... 56, 130, 383
15:3 .... 130, 383
15:4 .... 40, 90
15:9 .... 130, 383
15:21 .... 130, 383

I CORINTHIANS

1:19 .... 130, 383
1:31 .... 130, 383
2:5 199
2:9 .... 130, 383
2:12-13 ...... 161, 199
2:14 123
3:1-2 126
3:19 .... 130, 383
4:6 .... 130, 131, 384
5:6 .... 9, 181, 185, 204
7:10 107
8:1 .... 87, 386
9:8 59
9:9 .... 23, 59, 130, 383
9:9-10 .... 40, 90
9:10 56
10:6 .... 40, 90
10:7 .... 130, 383
10:8 185
10:11 .... 40, 90
10:21 230
14:21 .... 59, 130, 383

483

15 134
15:45 .... 130, 383
15:54 .... 130, 383
15:56 59

II CORINTHIANS

2:16 .... 124, 383
2:17 .... 74, 90, 135
3:2-3 164
4:2 .... 74, 90, 210
4:13 .... 130, 383
5:7 .... 47, 199
6:17 .... 216, 389
8:15 .... 130, 383
9:9 .... 130, 383
11:3 .... 87, 385

GALATIANS

2:19 59
3:8 72
3:10 .... 130, 383
3:13 .... 59, 130, 383
3:16 .... 131, 146
3:17 59
3:21 59
3:22 72
3:23 59
3:24 59
4 164
4:4 59
4:21 59
4:22 .... 130, 383
4:27 .... 130, 383
4:30 72

EPHESIANS

1:22 16
2:8 vi
2:9 .... vi, 114
2:15 59
4:11-12 165
4:11-14 163

5:11 204

PHILIPPIANS

4:16 283

COLOSSIANS

1:18 16
2:3 16
2:16-17 ...... 32, 49

I THESS.

1:6 .... 87, 90, 178, 191, 385
2:13 .... iii, 87, 90, 100, 124, 127, 178, 188, 191, 215, 385, 388
4:13-17 358
5:2 286
5:27 158

II THESS.

2:1-2 74
2:2 95
2:5 95

I TIMOTHY

1:4 .... 2, 8, 330
1:8 59
1:9 59
3:2 165
3:15 .... 82, 84, 87, 90, 101, 127, 133, 386
3:16 .... 16, 110, 114
4:6 178
4:7 107
4:13 157
5:18 72
6:3-5 .... 214, 387

6:20 149

II TIMOTHY

2:2 .... 163, 165
2:15 .... 104, 105, 108, 156
3:15 .... 128, 134
3:15-17 211
3:16 .... 46, 47, 72, 101, 126, 128, 133, 146, 149, 354, 395
3:16-17 ...... 40, 56, 90, 128, 134, 213
4:1-4 163
4:2 134
4:13 162

PHILEMON

19 114

HEBREWS

2:16 32
3:7 56
4:8 280
5:12-14 106
7:5 59
7:12 59
7:19 59
7:26 16
7:28 59
9:22 59
10:1 .... 32, 49, 59
10:5-6 167
10:7 .... 130, 383
10:10-14 29
10:25 163
10:38 183
11:3 183
11:6 117
12:2 16
12:22 11
13:13 180

JAMES

1:5 ....109, 154, 393
1:6 164
1:21 ....89, 90, 178, 191, 385
2:8 72
2:18 114
2:23 72
3:6 164
4:5 72
5:12 210
5:17 45

I PETER

1:10-11 ......67, 105-106, 108, 112
1:11 ....16, 123, 280, 395
1:16 ....131, 383
1:20 72
1:23 74
1:23-25 ......101, 133-135, 145
1:25 ....134, 144
2:6 72
2:8 126
5:4 16
5:5 153

II PETER

1:19 56
1:20 ....73, 393
1:20-21 123
1:21 ....166, 396
2:4 12
3:2 56
3:3-7 51
3:4 51
3:8 286
3:9 122
3:15-16 ......74, 110
3:18 126

I JOHN

5:7 ....1, 103, 110, 115, 178
5:8 103
5:13 89

JUDE

3 ....83, 90, 136, 178, 180, 196, 214, 387
6 12
14 11

REVELATION

1:1 ....12, 13
1:2 13
1:3 ....131, 384
1:4 394
1:8 16
1:19 280
3:8 ....83, 90, 136
3:10 ....83, 90
3:14 ....16, 80
4:1 280
5:11 11
7:1 280
7:9 280
8:1 285
9:11 169
9:12 280
9:13-15 10
9:14-15 12
9:15-18 10
9:16 ....1, 2, 6, 9, 10, 11, 12, 91, 381, 389
9:17 12
11:11 358
13:8 24
13:18 ....1, 394
15:5 280
16:16 169
17:8 24
18:1 280
19:1 280
19:16 16
20 417
20:3 280
20:6 358
20:8 ....416, 417
20:9 416
20:14-15 v
22:16 32
22:18 131
22:18-19 ....131, 134, 201, 215, 384, 388
22:19 131

BIOGRAPHICAL SKETCH

Dr. Chester W. Kulus received Christ in 1975 after graduating from Tilton School in Tilton, New Hampshire. In response to an invitation from one of the school's janitors, he attended "The Burning Hell," a film put on by Calvary Independent Baptist Church, which was renting the school's chapel. At the invitation, Dr. Kulus responded and received Jesus Christ as his personal Savior. The following year he attended Worcester Polytechnic Institute and, while being an active witness for Christ, answered the call to enter the ministry. In the fall of 1976, he transferred to Bob Jones University and graduated in 1979 with a B. A. in Pastoral Studies. During his time at college, he married Miss Nancy Dowie who had also received Christ through the same ministry in Tilton.

After college, Dr. Kulus desired more training and, at that time, made an unpopular decision with his alma mater to attend Calvary Baptist Theological Seminary in Lansdale, PA. He received his Master of Divinity degree in 1982 and started work on a Master of Theology degree the following year. In 1983, through God's leading, and under the direction of Pastor G. Richard Anderson, Dr. Kulus started Calvary Independent Baptist Church in a storefront on Main Street in Enfield, NH, an area where there was no Independent Baptist Church. In 1998, through God's grace, the church purchased a piece of land in Lebanon and built a new building just off exit 17 of Interstate-89 and is still there today.

In 2001, Dr. Kulus started taking video-courses with Emmanuel Baptist Theological Seminary in Newington, CT. By 2003, he had finished his Doctor of Ministry work and graduated in May of the same year. In the summer of 2003, he published his first book, *Those So-Called Errors: Debunking the Liberal, New Evangelical, and Fundamentalist Myth that*

You Should Not Hear, Receive, and Believe All the Numbers of Scripture. After publishing his first book, Dr. Kulus began study toward a Doctor of Theology degree with Emmanuel Baptist Theological Seminary, which he finished in 2006.

In April of 2007 with the passing of Dr. Anderson, the pastor of Calvary Independent Baptist Churches of Plymouth and Tilton, NH, Dr. Kulus became the interim-pastor of those churches as well as the principal of Calvary Christian School, a ministry of the church in Plymouth. In January of 2008, Dr. Kulus, in addition to pastoring the Calvary Independent Baptist Church of Lebanon, became the pastor of the Calvary Independent Baptist Churches of Plymouth and Tilton. The Lord has blessed in great ways and Dr. Kulus thanks the Lord for His strength and wisdom and the opportunity to serve such a wonderful Saviour.

In 2009, Dr. Kulus published his second book, *One Tittle Shall in No Wise Pass: Destroying the Scholarly Myth that God Did Not Inspire the Vowels of the Old Testament.* It is Dr. Kulus' desire that his books will encourage people to have full confidence in all that God has said. The Psalmist said in Psalm 119:128, "Therefore I esteem all *thy* precepts *concerning* all *things to be* right, *and* I hate every false way."

www.ingramcontent.com/pod-product-compliance
Lightning Source LLC
Chambersburg PA
CBHW071618230426
43669CB00012B/1981